THE PSALMS

Books by
W. O. E. OESTERLEY, D.D.

Ancient Hebrew Poems.

An Introduction to the Books of the Apocrypha.

Readings from the Apocrypha.

The Wisdom of Ben Sira (Ecclesiasticus).

The Wisdom of Egypt and the Old Testament. In the light of the newly discovered Teaching of Amem-em-Ope.

The Sayings of the Jewish Fathers. (Pirke Aboth.)

Tractate Shabbath. (Mishnah.)

The Psalms, Book III. Hebrew Text (lxxiii–lxxxix)

The Psalms, Book IV. Hebrew Text (xc–cvi).

WITH
G. H. BOX, D.D.

A Short Survey of the Literature of Rabbinical and Mediæval Judaism.

WITH
T. H. ROBINSON, D.D.

Hebrew Religion. Its Origin and Development.

An Introduction to the Books of the Old Testament.

BY
T. H. ROBINSON, D.D.

The Book of Amos. Hebrew Text.

THE PSALMS

TRANSLATED
WITH TEXT-CRITICAL AND
EXEGETICAL NOTES

by

W. O. E. OESTERLEY
D.D., Litt.D.

LONDON
S · P · C · K
1962

First published in 1939
by S.P.C.K.
Holy Trinity Church, Marylebone Road, London, N.W.1
Reprinted 1953, 1955, 1959, 1962

Printed in Great Britain by Offset Lithography by
Billing and Sons Ltd., Guildford and London

CONTENTS

PREFATORY NOTE

IT had been my hope that the following work might have been done in collaboration with my dear friend Dr. Theodore Robinson; but exacting duties in other directions prevented this. I am, however, indebted to him for having contributed twenty-two of the psalms to the Commentary, and four chapters in the Introduction, for which I express my sincere thanks.*

In dealing with the individual psalms in the Commentary the following procedure has been adopted : first an introductory section giving a short account of the nature and contents of the psalm. Then comes the translation; in this the endeavour is made to keep as closely as possible to the Hebrew, and to reproduce the metrical structure of the original. It is fully realized that the English rendering does not, at times, run smoothly; this is to be regretted, but in some cases it is extremely difficult to give a pleasing translation without paraphrasing. The text-critical notes which follow are, of course, meant for the Hebrew student. Indebtedness to various scholars is indicated when called for. Textual emendation is confessedly a difficult, and often controversial, task; but in a great number of cases it is unavoidable. The endeavour is here made to suggest emendations only where absolutely demanded. The exegetical notes which are then given are as brief as possible; but it is hoped that all essential matters have received attention. Divergent views are only incidentally mentioned, for to discuss these in every case would take up far too much space. The verse-numbering in these notes is that of the English Bible, but where that of the Hebrew Bible differs it is indicated. Finally, there is a short section on the religious teaching of the psalm in question. Here the object is merely to lay stress on the special religious theme, or themes, of the psalm, not to elaborate them, which would be inappropriate in a Commentary. In some cases this section is omitted in order to avoid unnecessary repetition.

The Commentary is written primarily for non-Hebraists; but the student of Hebrew may, it is hoped, find some help in the text-critical notes.

I must express my sincere thanks to Prof. S. H. Hooke for a number of valuable suggestions.

W. O. E. OESTERLEY.

---

* Pss. 55-60, 68, 73-84, 86, 88, 90 ; and Chaps. I, II, IV, V.

ABBREVIATIONS

G   = Septuagint.

GK   = Gesenius' *Hebrew Grammar*, ed. Kautzsch (Engl. transl. by Cowley, 1910).

MT   = Masoretic Text.

RV   = Revised Version.

S   = Syriac Version (Peshitta).

T   = Targum.

V   = Vulgate.

ZAW   = *Zeitschrift für die alttestamentliche Wissenschaft.*

SELECTED BIBLIOGRAPHY

BAETHGEN, *Die Psalmen* (1904).

BARNES, *The Psalms* (1931).

BERTHOLET, in Kautzsch, *Die Heilige Schrift des Alten Testaments*, II, pp. 113-276 (1923).

BRIGGS, *A Critical and Exegetical Commentary on the Book of Psalms* (1906-1907).

BUDDE, *Die schönsten Psalmen* (1915).

BUTTENWIESER, *The Psalms* (1938).

CALÈS, *Le livre des Psaumes* (1936).

CHEYNE, *The Book of Psalms* (1888).

—— *Origin of the Psalter* (1891).

—— *The Book of Psalms* (1904).

DUHM, *Die Psalmen* (1922).

EHRLICH, *Die Psalmen* (1905).

EWALD, *Dichter des alten Bundes* (1866).

GRAETZ, *Kritischer Kommentar zu den Psalmen* (1882, 1883).

GUNKEL, *Die Psalmen* (1926).

—— -BEGRICH, *Einleitung in die Psalmen* (1933).

HERKENNE, *Das Buch der Psalmen* (1936).

KEET, *A Liturgical Study of the Psalter* (1928).

KITTEL, *Die Psalmen* (1929).

MOWINCKEL, *Psalmenstudien* (1921-1924)

OESTERLEY, *The Psalms, Bk. III* (73-89), *Hebrew Text with notes* (1933).

—— *The Psalms, Bk. IV* (90-106), *Hebrew Text with notes* (1936).

——*A Fresh Approach to the Psalms* (1937).

PERLES, *Analekten zur Textkritik des alten Testaments* (1895, 1922).

PEROWNE, *The Psalms* (1864).

PETERS, *Das Buch der Psalmen* (1930).

SCHLÖGL, *Die Psalmen hebräisch und deutsch* (1911).

SCHMIDT, HANS, *Die Psalmen* (1934).

SIMPSON, ed., *The Psalmists* (1926).

SNAITH, *Studies in the Psalter* (1934).

WELLHAUSEN, *The Book of Psalms* (1898).

WUTZ, *Die Psalmen textkritisch untersucht* (1925).

—— *Systematische Wege von der Septuaginta zum Hebräischen Urtext*, Erster Teil, pp. 965 ff. (1937).

CHAPTER I

THE ORIGIN AND GROWTH OF THE PSALTER

IN the opening essay of *The Psalmists* (1933), the late Hugo Gressmann noted and deplored the fact that no one has yet attempted to write a history of Hebrew psalmody. He had apparently overlooked the work of Cheyne, written during the best period of that great, but eccentric, scholar. *The Origin of the Psalter* (1891) is an attempt to discover from the psalms themselves, how the book reached its present form, and the periods to which individual psalms and groups of psalms may be ascribed. Cheyne started from the latest date and worked backwards, and was strongly under the influence of a Maccabæan theory, but his work was, in many ways, of permanent value, and he did, at least, recognize that the Psalter had a long history.

It may be doubted whether we can profitably discuss the earlier stages of development in this field. Poetry and religion have always gone hand in hand. The spiritual exaltation with which man approaches the object of his worship, even on the lowest levels, tends to find expression in ordered and symmetrical language. The deeper *strata* of personality, from which alone true poetry can spring, are those to which the divine makes its appeal, and in which the divine most readily and surely finds its response. The earliest forms of ritual which we know give rise to poetry, or to something closely akin to poetry (the sacred dance, for example),[1] and some of the earliest poetry known to us, *e.g.*, the great Mesopotamian epics, had a definite place in the *cultus*.

We may, then, take it for granted that from the beginning Israelite ritual involved the use of sacred poems. It is even possible that really primitive snatches and fragments have survived and have been incorporated in the psalms as we now have them, though it is no longer possible even to attempt their identification. But we do, from time to time, meet with phrases and metaphors which carry us back to a much older stage in the religious thought of Israel than that to which the Psalter has been adapted.

It seems probable, then, that the Psalter was compiled for use in the *cultus*, and was intended to supply what was necessary for every form of worship (see further pp. 5 ff.). But men's ideas change as time passes. Their theological conceptions develop, and the forms of the

---

[1] Cp., *e.g.*, Oesterley, *The Sacred Dance* (1923).

cultus are modified. The final compilation of the Psalter undoubtedly comes from an age when the religion of Israel was fundamentally, and even aggressively, monotheistic. But there survive phrases which imply a polytheistic outlook; while Yahweh is the supreme God, and the only God to receive the highest honours, others are admitted as valid deities, though of lower rank and inferior quality. The position recalls the "kathenotheism" which appears in so many of the hymns of the Rigveda. In a few instances we have a rejection of sacrifice which would have been inconceivable except at a late stage of religious development, and even the belief in a true immortality may be found in one or two psalm-passages.

Many of the psalms themselves, then, have had a long history, in the course of which they have been modified to meet the changing needs of the *cultus* and of the national outlook on religion. No one supposes that such forms of ritual as the enthronement festival or the mimic wedding and death of the God at each New Year still survived when our Psalter was compiled, yet it seems undeniable that some of our psalms, in their original form, were related to these ceremonial occasions. We may even go so far as to suggest that some of the psalms once formed portions of great dramatic epics, such as those which are familiar to us from the *cultus* of Babylon and Ugarit. But it is only a knowledge of other religions which makes such a conjecture possible; the psalms themselves have been so altered as to fit them for a purer and simpler ritual.

A history of Hebrew psalmody along these lines, however, can never take us very far. We are on much surer ground when we observe that there must have been collections of psalms existing independently before the formation of our present book, and that these have been extensively used by the compilers. For the identification of these smaller and older books we have to rely on *criteria* of two kinds : (a) the evidence to be gathered from the text, (b) the titles prefixed to a large number of the poems in the book.

(a) The Psalter is now divided into five books, probably in imitation of the "five-fifths" of the Law: I, 1–41; II, 42–72; III, 73–89; IV, 90–106; V, 107–150. But it is clear that this division is late; there seems to be no ground, for instance, for drawing a line between Pss. 106 and 107. But we do find in Pss. 42–89 (Bks. II and III) one striking peculiarity. Except for the last six, they show a definite attempt to avoid the divine name *Yahweh*, the word *Elohim* being substituted, even where the God of Israel is in view. Thus we have in Ps. 43[4] "O God, my God", in 51[14] "O God, God of my salvation", in 63[1] "O God, thou art my God", where a proper name would have been more suitable than the general term, at least in the vocative. Further, we have parallels in different parts of the Psalter. Thus Pss. 14 and 53 are almost identical, but 14[2] has *Yahweh* where 53[2]

has God (*Elohim*).   So also in $14^4 (= 53^5)$, 14^6 (cf. 53^6), 14^7 ($=53^7$);
the name Yahweh does not occur in Ps. 53 at all.   On the other hand,
Ps. 108, which is a combination of Pss. 57^{7-11} and 60^{6-11}, does not use
the name Yahweh, a fact which must be taken into account in another
connexion.   It seems clear that Pss. 42–83 once formed an independent
collection which has been transferred bodily to our present Psalter.

Further, we have in certain cases psalms which are grouped together
by their subject-matter.   Here we may mention the " Enthronement "
psalms (on which see pp. 6 f.), the " Hallelujah " psalms (Pss. 111–114,
116–118, 135, 136, 146–150), which are among the latest in the Psalter,
and the " Songs of Ascents " (Pss. 120–134) sung by pilgrims as they
ascended Mount Zion for the great annual festivals.   It is at least
probable that these originally formed small collections, from which they
have been transferred to the larger book; it will be noted that psalms
of each type tend to stand together even in our present book.

(*b*) The titles of the psalms are discussed elsewhere; it is sufficient
here to observe their bearing on the question of earlier collections.   It
has been supposed (*e.g.*, by Briggs) that a number of the words in the
titles indicated earlier collections, *e.g.*, " Miktam ", " Of the Choir-
master ", " Maskîl ", " Mizmôr ", but in these cases it would appear
ᵗhat the evidence hardly justifies the conclusion, since these psalms are
scattered throughout the book.   But we do find that psalms whose
titles include certain personal names tend to come together, and these
may well have been taken from earlier collections.   Thus nearly all the
psalms in Bk. I (the exceptions are Pss. 1, 2, 33; 10 is a part of the
same psalm as 9) include the term " David's " in the heading.   It is
difficult not to believe that these once formed a separate collection.

Again, at the close of Ps. 72 we have the remark: " The prayers of
David, the son of Jesse, are ended ".   The title ascribes Ps. 72 itself to
Solomon, and Pss. 51–65, 68–70 bear the name of David at the head.
Here, again, the facts suggest that we have a second Davidic collection,
which included the word " prayer " in its general title.   The other
Davidic psalms are sporadic (86, 101, 103, 108–110, 122, 124, 131, 133,
138–145); some of these are included in the " Songs of Ascents " and
others in the " Hallelujah " psalms.   There is no reason why a psalm
should not have appeared in more than one collection; in fact, the evidence
shows that this almost certainly happened, but, except possibly in the
case of the last group of eight psalms, it seems more probable that the
name of David was added at a later time.   Both parts of Ps. 108, of
course, are taken from poems which already had the name of David at
their head.

Two other names must be considered.   The first of these is " Of
the sons of Qorah ", the reference being, apparently, to the guild of
temple-singers mentioned in 1 Chron. $9^{19, 31}$, 12^6.   There are eleven

of these, falling into two groups : Pss. 42–49 and 84, 85, 87, 88—it is easy to suppose that Ps. 86 was inserted between Pss. 85 and 87 by the final compiler. Here, again, we feel justified in assuming an earlier collection, which may once have contained many more psalms than those which have come down to us.

The same remark may apply to the other collection, that of " Asaph " ; whether the name be understood as referring to the individual mentioned in 1 Chron. 16[5] and elsewhere, or whether it stands for " the sons of Asaph ", a guild of singers alluded to in 2 Chron. 29[13], etc., is not a matter of importance. Eleven of these stand together (Pss. 73–83), and a twelfth appears in Ps. 50. Again, we may well understand that a single transposition may have been made by the final compiler of the Psalter, and we may conclude that these twelve also were taken from a separate collection.

While, then, the evidence is somewhat scanty, it is sufficient to justify us in the belief that our present Psalter was compiled from earlier collections. The earliest may well have been the first Davidic group, now practically forming Bk. I. The second large collection, which we may call " Elohistic ", had as its main sources three such collections, one bearing the name of the " Sons of Qorah ", one that of " Asaph ", and one the title " The Prayers of David ". The third main group was brought together after the completion of the second, as the evidence of Ps. 108 shows, and included the " Songs of Ascents ", the " Hallelujah " psalms, and, possibly, a section from a third Davidic collection. We have every reason to be thankful for the care and spiritual insight of the men who preserved for us these specimens of the sacred poetry of Israel.

CHAPTER II

THE CLASSIFICATION OF THE PSALMS

THE higher criticism of the Psalter has undergone a complete revolution in the last quarter of a century. The older effort was concentrated on authorship, and sought to know the circumstances which gave rise to each particular psalm. This tendency is reflected in the titles of many of our psalms, whose bearing is discussed elsewhere. Over a century ago it became clear that this method of approach could yield no reliable conclusions, and it was gradually abandoned, though even to-day a number of commentators still identify some of the psalms as the work of David. But the identity of the author was felt to be subordinate to the age which produced the poem, and from the time of Ewald onwards it has been customary to assign individual psalms to various periods in the history of Israel.

The newer criticism, while not oblivious of the possibility of suggesting a rough date for many of the psalms, has concentrated on their function—that is, on the part they were designed to play in the life of Israel. Naturally, they were designed for worship, and that meant for worship in the temple. The use of religious poetry for private meditation and prayer is a comparatively modern phenomenon, and we may take it for granted that, with few exceptions, the psalms were designed for use in one form or other of the *cultus*. It should, however, be pointed out that the use of psalms by an individual is not excluded; on the contrary, a good deal of the ritual was private, though performed in the temple. A vow was made by an individual, and he spoke in his own name, and in that of no other, when he went through the various forms of service which were connected with the fulfilment of his promise. There seems to have been no general or communal act of worship in the presentation of tithes; each man brought his own basket of produce, as was convenient for himself, and offered it as a personal gift. A great deal of judicial work was done in the temple, which was the supreme court of appeal in all cases. We may be certain that litigants, in stating their case and in receiving judgement, had prescribed forms of words to repeat, and each case implied a ritual and ceremonial procedure. Some of the psalms look like oaths of purgation, and our evidence shows us that an oath of this kind was often employed to settle a dispute. It is true that national psalms, designed for use by a representative of the whole people in time of crisis, might use the first person singular. The

5   B

concept of corporate personality made this possible, indeed, almost inevitable. But we can generally see fairly well whether the worshipper is speaking for himself alone, or whether his " I " is the whole group which he, for the time, represents.

The leading exponent of the newer method in psalm-criticism is Gunkel, though others, notably Gressmann, Mowinckel, and Hans Schmidt, have made important contributions. It will be well to sketch here in outline the position as the first-named scholar states it. He finds the following " types " or " classes " (*Gattungen*) :

    1. Hymns, or songs of praise ; a special class is formed by the " Enthronement " psalms.
    2. Laments of the community.
    3. Royal psalms.
    4. Laments of the individual.
    5. Thanksgiving of the individual.

To these larger groups several smaller classes have to be added :

    6. Blessings and curses.
    7. Pilgrim psalms.
    8. Thanksgiving of the Israelite nation.
    9. Legends.
    10. Psalms dealing with the Law.
    11. Prophetic psalms.
    12. Wisdom psalms.

A number of psalms are " mixed " in type, and may be assigned to more than one class. Sometimes a single psalm contains a veritable " liturgy " in which several classes alternate with one another.

Every " class " has its own special forms, with a characteristic introduction and conclusion. Thus the Hymns always begin with an introduction in which the singer says that he is about to praise Yahweh, or calls on others to do so. Then follows the reason ; sometimes it is because of the mighty deeds that have been wrought in the past, through creation or history, and sometimes it is because of some more recent event. Among many others, Pss. 113, 117, and 135 are cited as examples. Ps. 103 is another which many serve as typical of this class ; here the psalmist addresses his own " soul ", and calls for a blessing on Yahweh. The reasons are given first in a series of sentences introduced by a participle with the article, equivalent to a relative clause. Further statements as to Yahweh's great and loving acts follow, and the psalm closes with a repetition of the call to praise, though this time the address is much wider, and includes angels as well as men.

" Enthronement " psalms, which, as we have seen, Gunkel regards as a special class of Hymns, are characterized by the opening formula

"Yahweh is King!" (or "Yahweh is become King!"). To this group belong such psalms as 93, 97, and 99. They suggest a ceremonial procession, following on the great acts of enthronement, anointing, and coronation, and may include elements derived from the ritual pattern already mentioned. Gunkel himself regarded these psalms as being eschatological, a view which is discussed elsewhere (see pp. 51 f.).

"Laments of the Community" were especially adapted for use in the ritual of fast-days. Typical of this class are Pss. 44, 74, and 80. They begin with a plea for a hearing, or with bewildered wonder as to why calamity has fallen on the people. Sometimes, as in Ps. 44, this is omitted, and the psalmist passes directly to a recollection of the great deeds done by Yahweh in the past, a normal element in such a psalm. There is, naturally, some description of the calamity which has led to the great day of humiliation and prayer. Its terms are usually vague, since it has to be employed on a variety of occasions, a fact which creates serious problems for commentators who still wish to assign a specific event to every psalm. Sometimes, it is true, the references are sufficiently detailed to make reasonable conjecture possible, but even then there is usually room for more than one explanation. As a rule, such psalms end, or at least include, an expression of confidence in the saving power of Yahweh and of the conviction that the prayer will be answered as the worshipper desires.

"Royal" psalms are not to be confused with the "Enthronement" psalms. The latter are hymns which celebrate the reign of Yahweh; the former are prayers for the prosperity of an earthly monarch. The class includes such pieces as Pss. 18, 45, 72, and 110. It must be remembered that, to the mind of the Ancient East, the king was more than an individual: he was an epitome of the nation, and the prosperity of the whole community was in some way bound up with his success. So, in spite of the natural Israelite insistence on the humanity of the king, and on his essential equality with his subjects in the sight of God, the great events of his life were a matter of concern for the whole people, and might demand a special ritual. The occasions for which these psalms were employed may have varied; some appear to have been used at his coronation, others may have formed part of a special service performed on his birthday, one (Ps. 45) was designed for the royal marriage, while protection and success in battle are natural objects of prayer. Their tone is generally that of petition for the king's safety or for divine guidance in the duties of his government.

The "Laments of the Individual" form a fairly large class, and were probably adapted to a number of different occasions. Some of them imply that the worshipper is standing by the altar, and is about to offer a sacrifice which, he hopes, will induce Yahweh to deliver him from his troubles. Psalms of this class not infrequently include a small liturgy, in the course of which a divine oracle is given, promising to the worshipper the satisfaction of his need, and enabling him to close with thanksgiving for the coming benefit.   The words of the oracle sometimes have to be assumed, but the happy ending shows that they were used in the actual ritual.   Illustrations may be seen in Pss. 7 and 56 ; Ps. 20 may be the latter part of such a psalm, giving only the divine oracle and the final expression of confidence.   To this class belong also some of the so-called " penitential psalms ".

The occasions for these psalms were varied.   A large proportion, however, clearly imply that the singer is the object of attack from personal enemies, and, as Hans Schmidt has shown, some may have been prescribed for use in judicial process, in protest against false accusation and in assertion of innocence.   Ps. 26 is a good illustration of this class, while in Ps. 142 the singer is actually in prison (cf. *v.* 7).

Gunkel includes about a dozen of the pieces in the Psalter under the head of " Thanksgiving of the Individual ".   Here, more clearly than anywhere else, a place can be found in the ritual, for such psalms are particularly adapted to the ritual for the thank-offering or for the fulfilment of a vow.   Yet they tend to overlap other classes, and Gunkel himself includes Ps. 18, which has already been classed as a " Royal " psalm.   Others mentioned by him are Pss. 30, 32, 41, and 138.   They naturally recount the special occasion which has called for thanksgiving, and are sometimes so to be read as to allow an interval for the actual presentation of a sacrifice on the altar.

We need not follow Gunkel further into his account of the smaller groups.   Enough has been said to indicate the main lines on which the newer criticism is proceeding.   It is still in its infancy, and the fact that it finds comparatively little mention in the following pages is not due to neglect of its importance, but rather to the feeling that it must be still further developed and more securely based before it can be accepted as finally valid.   Its great weakness, as Gunkel himself states it, lies in the somewhat rigid *formulæ* which it presupposes.   Psalms are not always as easy to classify as the theory appears to imply ; Gunkel includes Ps. 23 among the " Psalms of Confidence ", though he admits that it is not characteristic of its class.   The " Psalms of Confidence " are a minor subdivision of the " Laments of the Individual ", and any classification which brings Ps. 23, however remotely, under that head, needs some revision.   But it must be freely admitted that the door has been opened on to a new line of study, and we may well hope that the years will bring us fresh light, not only on the Psalter itself, but also on the whole religious life of those for whose needs it was compiled.

CHAPTER III

THE TITLES OF THE PSALMS

ALTHOUGH the titles occurring at the head of most of the psalms formed no part of the text in its original form, some consideration of them is demanded, since there is reason to believe that in a number of cases, so far as the musical accompaniment was concerned, they reflect traditional usage. In this connexion we may refer to what is said under Ps. 150, where it will be seen that musical instruments mentioned in various psalms were of great antiquity, since the identical names occur on monuments dating back to the third millennium. Another reason for discussing these titles is that many of them indicate the collection to which the psalm in question belonged before being incorporated in the Psalter in its present form, a subject which is not without interest (see further p. 3).

It is only to be expected that differences of opinion should exist as to the meaning of some of the titles; to some of these we shall refer; but an exhaustive discussion of all the different views does not seem to be called for. It must be recognized that in some cases the meaning of a title is uncertain.

For facility of reference we shall take the psalms in the order in which they now stand. First, however, it is necessary to say a brief word about the title of the Psalter as a whole. In the Hebrew Bible the title is *Tehillim*, in a contracted form *Tillim*, and *Sepher* (" Book ") *Tillim* (Aramaic *Tillin* [1]). The word comes from the root *HLL*, " to praise "; it therefore means " Praises " or " Hymns ". This title is not an appropriate one, for a large number of the psalms are not hymns of praise. Judging from the note added at the conclusion of Ps. 72, " The Prayers of David, the son of Jesse, are ended ", it would seem that at one time this part of the Psalter had the general title *Tephillôth*, " Prayers "; but if so, it was equally inappropriate, for not many of these psalms are in the nature of prayers, and one only, the seventeenth, is called " A Prayer ". In the Septuagint the title differs slighty in the MSS, usually Βίβλος Ψαλμῶν or Ψαλμοί (" Book of Psalms ", or " Psalms ") occur, but in Cod. A. it is Ψαλτήριον, which means a " stringed instrument " (cp. " psaltery " in Ps. 33[2], 144[9] and elsewhere), and then a " song " sung to the accompaniment of a stringed instrument, or instruments. The title Ψαλμοί is the plural of a word

---

[1] E. G. Hirsch, in the *Jewish Encycl.*, x, 241 *b*.

9

corresponding to the Hebrew *mizmôr*, on which see below.   The Syriac and Latin Versions follow the Septuagint.

We shall now take the psalms in order and discuss the titles as they occur.

Ps. 1 : this, together with thirty-three other psalms, has no title ; they are known as " Orphan " psalms ; the term is Talmudic (*Abodah Zara* 24 *b*).

Ps. 2 : " *Orphan.* "

Ps. 3 : *A Psalm.   David's.   When he fled from the face of Absalom, his son.*

First, as to the term *Mizmôr*, " psalm ", which occurs in the titles of fifty-seven psalms.   It comes from the root *ZMR*, meaning to " pluck ", *i.e.*, taking hold of the strings of an instrument with the fingers, and thus implies that the psalms in question were sung to the accompaniment of a stringed instrument, or instruments.   *David's* raises the question as to how we are to understand the prefix *lamed* (*Lᵉ*) which occurs so frequently, in different connexions, in the titles.   It is the Hebrew preposition meaning " to ", " belonging to ", " of ", " for " ; it has also other shades of meaning according to the context.   The traditional explanation is that this *Lᵉ* denotes authorship, hence the expression *lamed auctoris*.   This cannot, however, always be its meaning because it occurs, *e.g.*, in connexion with " the sons of Qorah ".   Briggs denies that it refers to authorship ; he says : " The earliest collection of psalms for use in the synagogue was made under the name of David, the traditional father of religious poetry and of the temple worship.   The later editors left this name in the titles, with the preposition *Lᵉ* attached, to indicate that these psalms belonged to that collection."   There may be something in this.   In any case, it is difficult to understand why the name of David became attached to some quite late psalms.   It occurs in the titles of seventy-three psalms ; and in the Septuagint in fourteen others.   In our rendering we have put " David's " in the titles in question, for we realize the difficulty of coming to a definite conclusion on the matter ; and this can be taken either in the sense of Davidic authorship, or in that of belonging to the Davidic collection.   The remainder of the title under consideration, referring to an episode in the life of David (see 2 Sam. 15), is due to an editor who believed to discern in the psalm a reference to this, see especially *v.* 6, or who felt that it might appropriately have been composed, or used, by David on this occasion.

Ps. 4 : *For the Precentor : With stringed instruments.   A Psalm. David's.*

The term " For the Precentor " (*Lamnazeaḥ*), which occurs here for the first time (it appears fifty-five times in the titles), is again one which is differently interpreted.   It comes from the root meaning lit. " to shine ", and from the form of the verb which implies intensity; as the word is a participle, it must refer to an individual, thus, one who shines, *i.e.*, who is pre-eminent, and therefore occupying a leading position. This is supported by the use of the verb in 1 Chron. 15²¹, where it means "leading" the stringed instruments in the liturgical service of song. In most of the titles in which the term occurs musical directions of some kind are added, so that the rendering "Precentor" seems justified. At the same time, it must be recognized that the term was not so understood by the ancient translators. Briggs thinks that there was "a Psalter collected under the name of the Director, or choir-master", and that the psalms with this title "were taken from a Psalter bearing the Director's name ". There is, however, nothing to show that such a Psalter ever existed. Another view is put forward by Haupt, and tentatively followed by Gunkel; by a change in the vowel-points he reads the word as *Laminzah*, which would mean "in regard to the musical rendering ". There is a great deal in this view; the difficulty in regard to it, however, is that the use of the term is, relatively, so restricted; it does not occur in the great majority of the titles. This difficulty applies also, of course, to the rendering " For the Precentor ", excepting that, as we have seen, there is more support for this. Once more, Mowinckel, taking the word in its literal sense, explains it as a liturgical abbreviation of the expression " to cause the face of Yahweh to shine ", an antique anthropomorphic expression meaning to induce him to be favourably disposed (cp. Exod. 32¹¹); so that, according to this interpretation, the psalm was to be a means of propitiating God by sacred song and instrumental music. Its comparative rarity tells more against this view than against the others mentioned; if some psalms were a means of propitiation, why not all ? But apart from this, the verb is never used in this sense either in Biblical or later Hebrew. We have drawn attention to these views both because of their interest, and because they are accepted, respectively, by different scholars; but we have retained the rendering " For the Precentor " (*i.e.*, instructions for the Precentor) as open to the least objection, and as having definite Biblical support in its favour. In the title under consideration there is, further, the instruction "with stringed instruments " (*bin'ginôth*), meaning that the singing of the psalm is to be accompanied by these (for details see under Ps. 150); the direction occurs in six other titles.

Ps. 5: For the Precentor. To the Neḥilôth. A Psalm. David's.

What is meant by " To the Neḥilôth " is a problem difficult of solution, if indeed it can be solved. It has been interpreted as meaning " to (the accompaniment) of Flutes "; this interpretation is justified in so far that we know from Isa. 30²⁹ that the flute was used in liturgical worship (see also 1 Kgs. 1⁴⁰); a usage occurring among other Semites too (see under Ps. 150). On the other hand, although the word in the title looks as though it were derived from the root meaning " to pipe ", the noun *nehilah* does not occur elsewhere in the Bible ; the ordinary word for " flute " is *halîl* (lit. " reed-pipe ") ; so that if flutes were meant in the title, the word ought to be *Bahălilîm*. The interpretation mentioned above can, therefore, hardly be correct. In the Septuagint the term is rendered ὑπὲρ τῆς κληρονομούσης, and Jerome renders this *pro hereditatibus* ; they, therefore, read N*halôth* ; the meaning would then be : " To (the tune of) the Inheritances ", *i.e.*, the psalm was to be sung to the melody of the well-known song, based (if the supposition is not too fanciful) on Isa. 49[8], which ends with : " to make (them) inherit the desolate heritages " (*l*hanhîl n*halôth šomēmôth*). There are other cases, to which reference will be made, of psalms being sung to the tunes of well-known songs.

Ps. 6 : *For the Precentor : With stringed instruments. On the eighth. A Psalm. David's.*

The only term which demands consideration here is : " On the eighth " ('*al-haššinîth*, or " According to the eighth "). The rendering " On the octave " ignores the fact that the Hebrews had no eight-toned scale. All authorities are agreed that the ancient music of the Hebrews was similar in style to that of the *primitive* type of Arab music, which may still be heard in parts of Arabia ; in this, quarter-tones as well as semitones are recognized ; it follows that they have no octave consisting of eight tones and thirteen semitones ; and this must be presumed of ancient Hebrew music. There can, then, be no doubt that this term cannot mean " On the octave ", *i.e.*, that the musical instruments (cp. 1 Chron. 15[21]) were to be played, or that the male voices were to sing, an octave lower, as has been maintained. Hence some commentators explain the term as the eighth (psalm) of a collection, meaning, presumably, that the psalm was to be sung to the tune of that of the eighth in the collection. This is ingenious, but not very convincing ; for one might reasonably expect references to the number of various other psalms in other collections in such a large body of psalms as those contained in the Psalter. The term occurs in the title of Ps. 12 ; but nowhere else is there any reference to a number in the titles. What is meant by the term remains an enigma ; the Septuagint merely reproduces the Hebrew. See further on the title of Ps. 46.

Ps. 7 : *Šiggaiôn. David's, which he sang to Yahweh because of the words of Kush the Benjamite.*

The term *Šiggaiôn* is traditionally interpreted as a noun derived from the root meaning " to go astray ", or " to meander " (*ŠGH*) ; the psalm being thus described as of a wild character, dithyrambic. The contents of the psalm do not, however, bear this out. It can hardly be doubted that the word is a corruption, perhaps of *Higgaiôn* (see below) ; the Septuagint evidently read *Mizmôr*. In the title of the psalm in

Hab. 3, where the plural of the word occurs (*Šigiônôth*), the Septuagint again read *Mizmôr* (cp. *Psalms of Solomon* 15[1]). The episode in the life of David referred to in the title is difficult to identify ; if, with the Versions, we read " Kushite ", the reference may be to 2 Sam. 18[31–33] ; but the Kushite there is not a Benjamite ; possibly he was mistakenly identified with the " Benjamite " of 2 Sam. 16[11].

Ps. 8 : *For the Precentor. On the Gittîth. A Psalm. David's.*

" *On the Gittîth* " is sometimes held to refer to some musical instrument which took its name from Gath, the Philistine city. In the Targum this is the explanation, and is suggested by the fact that the form " Gittîth " is equivalent to " Gath-like ". There is, however, no reason to suppose that the Israelites ever borrowed an instrument from the Philistines. A far more likely explanation is that suggested by the Septuagint rendering, " For the wine-presses " ; for the Hebrew word for " wine-press " is *gath*, and if, following the Septuagint, we read the plural *Gittôth* for *Gittîth*, the term would mean that the psalm is described as one that was sung to the melody of a vintage-song, sung when the grapes were trodden out. The joyous character of the psalm bears this out, and it is worth noting that the same term occurs in the titles of Pss. 81, 84, the former of which was one of the proper psalms for the Feast of Tabernacles, the autumn feast, the time of the vintage. In the *Midrash* on the *Psalms*, moreover, in dealing with this title reference is made to Joel 3[13] (Hebr. 4[13]), where it is said : " Put ye in the sickle, for the vintage is ripe ; come, tread ye, for the wine-press (*gath*) is full, the fats overflow ". Gunkel explains the term as in reference to a " Gathite " mode ; but there is no evidence to show that the Israelites adopted a Philistine mode of singing (if there was one ?) in their temple-worship.

Ps. 9 : *For the Precentor. 'Almûth labbēn. A Psalm. David's.*

The words '*Almûth labbēn*, "According to (the melody of) ' Die for the son ' (or ' The Death of the son ')," may mean that this was the title of a song to the melody of which the psalm was to be sung. It is possible, however, that we have here a word which has suffered corruption, and that we should read '*Al-'alamôth*, on which see the title to Ps. 46. The Versions give no help. At the end of *v.* 16 of the psalm the term *Higgaion* occurs ; it comes from the root (*HGH*) meaning " to muse ", or " meditate " ; but, judging from its use in Ps. 92[3], it must refer to music in connexion with a stringed instrument. Here, therefore, it probably means that the musical accompaniment is to be played by stringed instruments, lyres or harps.

Pss. 10–15 : Terms already dealt with.

Ps. 16 : *Miktam. David's.*

The term *Miktam* occurs also in the titles of Pss. 56–60. Its meaning is uncertain. In Rabbinical writings it is connected with the word

Kethem, " gold ", and is explained as " a golden piece ", beautiful and valuable. Another word with which it might be connected is *Katham,* something " hidden " ; in this case the term would mean that the psalm was of hidden import, not understood by all. It may well be, however, that Mowinckel has hit upon the true meaning ; he connects the term with the Assyrian *Katamu* " to cover ", *i.e.,* to cover sin ; so that *Miktam* would be employed in reference to a psalm which dealt with the subject of covering, or atoning for, sin, or uncleanness, or else sickness, the result of sin ; it might even have been held that the saying or singing of the psalm was of atoning efficacy.

Ps. 17: *A Prayer. David's.*

The contents of this psalm show the appropriateness of its being called a *Tephillah,* " prayer ". Only one other psalm (86) is so called ; and the word occurs in the titles of 90, 102, 142 ; see also the note appended at the end of 72, " The prayers of David, the son of Jesse, are ended ".

Ps. 18: *For the Precentor : David's, the servant of Yahweh ; who spake unto Yahweh the words of this song in the day that Yahweh delivered him from the grasp of all his enemies and from the hand of Saul ; and he said.*

The reference here is to 2 Sam. 7$^{13-16}$

The content of this psalm shows that, at any rate in its present form, Davidic authorship is out of the question ; for details see the Commentary.

The only term to be considered here is *Širah* " song " ; it occurs nowhere else in the titles ; but its commoner form *Šir* is often used. We shall deal with it under Ps. 30. The rest of the title, with slight variations, is as in 2 Sam. 22^{1}, where Ps. 18 appears again.

Pss. 19–21 : Terms already dealt with.

Ps. 22: *For the Precentor : According to " The Hind of the Dawn ". A Psalm. David's.*

Here we have, in all probability, the name of a well-known song to the tune of which this psalm was to be sung.

Pss. 23–29 : Terms already dealt with.

Ps. 30: *A Psalm. A Song for the Dedication of the House. David's.*

The term *Šir,* " song ", occurs here for the first time in the titles. It is the most ancient word employed in reference to a poem, whether sacred or secular. As a rule, in the titles, it stands alone, like *Mizmôr* (in twelve titles) ; here, as in Pss. 45, 120–134, it is connected with some word, defining its nature more definitely. The mention of the " Dedication of the House ", *i.e.,* the temple, cannot, of course, refer to any episode in the life of David. The obvious inference, at first sight, is that the words refer to the re-dedication of the temple by Judas Maccabæus after its desecration by Antiochus Epiphanes (see 1 Macc.

4$^{52-59}$); that the psalm may have been used on this occasion is likely enough, and this was probably the reason why the words were added in the title; but that the psalm itself is Maccabæan is, of course, out of the question.

Ps. 31. Terms already dealt with.

Ps. 32. *David's. Maskîl.*

As the root from which the term " Maskîl " comes has a variety of meanings, according to the context, it is natural that it should be differently explained, especially as the contents of the psalms which have the term in their titles (thirteen) are of various character. Following the Septuagint rendering, the term is perhaps best understood as " instruction ", the psalms in question being of an instructive kind. This, to be sure, would apply to many another psalm which is not called a " Maskîl "; the term would, therefore, seem to have been employed somewhat arbitrarily.

Ps. 33 : " *Orphan* ".

Ps. 34 : *David's ; when he changed his behaviour before Abimelech, and he drove him away, and he went.*

This reference to the episode in the life of David is from 1 Sam. 21$^{10-15}$, though the Philistine king there mentioned is Achish. There is nothing in the psalm which points to this occasion. Like the references to David in some of the other titles, it is due to the imagination of some editor.

Ps. 35 : Term already dealt with.

Ps. 36 : *For the Precentor : David's, the servant of Yahweh.*

For this designation of David see 1 Sam. 23$^{10, 11}$. The title was probably suggested by *v.* 10.

Ps. 37 : Term already dealt with.

Ps. 38 : *Mizmôr. David's. To bring to remembrance (l'hazkîr).*

The term *l'hazkîr* is probably a corruption of *l'azkarah* (Lev. 24^7); this was the " memorial offering ", used in connexion with the *Minḥah*, " meal offering " (see Lev. 2$^{1-3}$). Its mention in the title will, therefore, mean that this psalm was sung while the " memorial offering " was being burned. The term occurs again in the title of Ps. 70.

Ps. 39 : *For the Precentor : Jeduthun's. A Psalm. David's.*

" Jeduthun ", or " Jedîthun ", according to the Versions, was the name of a founder of a guild of temple-singers, but the name is also applied to the guild itself (1 Chron. 16^{41}, and 1 Chron. 25$^{1, 3}$, and elsewhere). The name in the title probably refers to the mode of singing adopted by this guild, and that the psalm was to be sung after this mode.

Pss. 40, 41 : Terms already dealt with.

Ps. 42 : *For the Precentor : Maskil. Belonging to the sons of Qorah.*

The " Sons of Qorah " were a guild of temple-singers, Levites

(1 Chron. 9¹⁹, ³¹, 12⁶). The psalms which have " Of ", or " Belonging to, the Sons of Qorah ", twelve in number, were presumably taken from a collection in possession of this guild.

Pss. 43, 44 : Terms already dealt with.

Ps. 45 : *For the Precentor : To " Lilies ".   Belonging to the Sons of Qorah.   Maskil.   A Song of Loves.*

" Šošannim ", usually translated " Lilies ", means, properly speaking, " Anemones ". The reference is again to the name of some favourite song, to the tune of which this psalm was to be sung. " A Song of Loves " is a very appropriate name for the psalm, as its contents show. In the *Song of Songs* anemones are often referred to in connexion with a lover. See further the titles to Pss. 60, 80.

Ps. 46 : *For the Precentor : Belonging to the Sons of Qorah.   According to ʻAlamôth.   A Song.*

" ʻAlamôth " means " young women "; in 1 Chron. 15¹⁷⁻²¹ we read that among the singers and players appointed by the Levites were some who played " with harps (*nebel*) set to ʻAlamôth ", and others who played " with lyres (*kinnôr*) set to the *šemînîth*, to lead ". Some commentators explain these, respectively, as in reference to women's voices, and to men's voices, an octave lower ; or else, since women took no part in the service of song, to men's falsetto voices. Against this it must be urged that, as we have already seen, the Hebrews had no eight-toned scale ; and if falsetto voices were meant, the comparison would not be to women's voices, but to boys' voices. Moreover, the expressions in question are used in connexion with harps and lyres, therefore with instrumental, not vocal, music. As the *kinnôr* was the smaller of these two stringed instruments, the term " *šemînîth* " might conceivably refer to its eight strings ; Josephus says that the larger *nebel* had twelve strings (*Antiq.* vii. 306) ; but this does not explain the term " ʻAlamôth ", which, we must confess, we do not understand.

Pss. 47–49 : Terms already dealt with.

Ps. 50 : *A Psalm.   Asaph's.*

In 1 Chron. 6²⁴ ⁽³⁹⁾, Asaph is mentioned as one of the leaders of the Levitical choir (cp. 1 Chron. 15¹⁷, 2 Chron. 29³⁰, where he is spoken of as a " seer "). As " the Sons of Asaph " formed one of the guilds of temple-singers, the question is whether " Asaph's " here, and in the titles of Pss. 73–83, is an abbreviation for " the Sons of Asaph ", who possessed a collection of psalms, or whether he was personally the author of this psalm ; as Asaph was a " seer ", it is quite possible that the latter was the case.

Ps. 51 : *For the Precentor : A Psalm.   David's ; when the prophet Nathan came unto him after he had gone in unto Bath-sheba.*

For the reference here to the episode in the life of David, see

2 Sam. 11, 12 ; the penitential content of the psalm suggested the title to some editor, for Davidic authorship is out of the question (see the intr. section to this psalm in the Commentary).

Ps. 52 : Terms already dealt with.

Ps. 53 : *For the Precentor : 'Al-Maḥalath. Maskil. David's.*

The meaning of " 'Al-Mahalath " is very uncertain ; the word may come from a root meaning " sickness " ; hence some commentators think that the psalm was meant to be sung during sickness ; or that it was the title of a song, to the tune of which the psalm was to be sung ; or, reading " 'Al-Mahalatîth ", that it was to be sung to the mode of Maḥalath, the wife of Esau (Gen. 28⁹) ; or else, reading " 'Al-Meho-latîth ", in reference to the city of Abel-Meholah (Judg. 7²², 1 Sam. 18¹⁹). With the exception of the first, none of these strike us as likely to be the true meaning (see the title to Ps. 88). Perhaps the Septuagint is to be followed, where it is written Maeleth, and taken to be a proper name, conceivably a corruption of Maḥli or Maḥali, one of the Levites " who did the work for the service of the house of Yahweh " (1 Chron. 23²³, ²⁴).

Pss. 54, 55 : Terms already dealt with.

Ps. 56 : *For the Precentor : To " The Dove of the far-off terebinths." David's. Miktam. When the Philistines took him in Gath.*

Here we have again the title of a well-known song : " The Dove of the far-off terebinths ", to the tune of which the psalm was to be sung. The reference to David in Gath is inexact, for neither in 1 Sam. 21¹⁰, ¹¹, nor in 27¹⁻⁴, is he taken by the Philistines ; he went to Gath of his own free will.

Ps. 57 : *For the Precentor : To " Destroy it not ". David's Miktam. When he fled from the face of Saul into the cave.*

" 'Al-tashheth ", meaning " Destroy it not ", was evidently taken from the opening of a popular vintage-song, to the tune of which the psalm was to be sung (so, too, in the titles of Pss. 58, 59, 75). The song is quoted in Isa. 65⁸ : ". . . As the new wine is found in the cluster, and one saith, ' Destroy it not, for a blessing is in it ' . . ." For the reference to David see either 1 Sam. 22¹, the cave of Adullam, or 24¹ᵃ, the cave of Engedi.

Ps. 58 : Terms already dealt with.

Ps. 59 : The terms are as in the title of Ps. 57 ; they are followed by : *When Saul sent, and they watched the house to kill him.*

The reference is to 1 Sam. 19¹¹.

Ps. 60 : *For the Precentor : To " The Lily of Witness ". Miktam. David's. To teach. When he strove with 'Aram-naharaim and with 'Aram-Zobah ; and Joab returned and slew Edom in the Valley of Salt, twelve thousand men.*

Šušan 'Edûth. " The Lily [better Anemone] of Witness " is

probably the name of the song referred to in the titles of Pss. 45, 69, 80. " To teach " (cp. 2 Sam. 1[18]) suggests that the psalm was taught to young warriors, as it is of a distinctly war-like character.   For the rest of the title see 2 Sam. 8[3 ff., 13–14].

Pss. 61, 62 : Terms already dealt with.

Ps. 63 : *A Psalm.   David's.   When he was in the wilderness of Judah.*

For the reference to the episode in the life of David, see 1 Sam. 24[4], since Engedi was in the south of Judah ; the phrase " the wilderness of Judah " occurs elsewhere only in Judg. 1[16].

Pss. 64–70 : Terms already dealt with.

Ps. 71 : " *Orphan* ".

Ps. 72 : *Solomon's.*

The contents of this psalm fully account for its ascription to Solomon ; but that he was the writer is out of the question ; see the exegetical notes to the psalm in the Commentary.

Pss. 73–87 : Terms already dealt with.

Ps. 88 : *A Song.   A Psalm.   Belonging to the Sons of Qorah.   For the Precentor : 'Al-Maḥalath, Lᵉ'annôth.   Maskil of Heman the Ezrahite.*

It is evident that at least two titles have become mixed up together here.   Probably the original title began with " For the Precentor ". For " 'Al-Maḥalath " see the title of Ps. 53.   Very uncertain as the meaning of this is, the contents of this psalm support the meaning " For sickness ", *i.e.*, a psalm to be sung by one suffering sickness.   The word " Lᵉ'annôth " means " to afflict ", and is probably to be connected with the preceding.   Heman (he is not called " the Ezrahite " elsewhere) was the name of one of David's singers (1 Chron. 15[17, 19], 25[5]), and also that of one of Solomon's wise men (1 Kgs. 4[31], Hebr. 5[11]) ; he is mentioned together with Ethan the Ezrahite, who was likewise a wise man and a singer ; but there may well have been two Hemans and two Ethans.

Ps. 89 : *Maskil of Ethan the Ezrathite.*

See the foregoing.

Ps. 90 : *A Prayer of Moses, the man of God.*

Of this title it can only be said that it illustrates the unreliability of the titles when they deal with authorship.   It is different when musical directions are in question.

Ps. 91 : " *Orphan* ".

Ps. 92 : *A Psalm.   A Song for the Sabbath Day.*

The title does not necessarily mean that the psalm was originally composed for singing on the Sabbath, but rather that it was chosen for this day.   It has been used as one of the special psalms for the Sabbath by the Jewish Church up to the present day.

Pss. 93–97 : " *Orphan* ".

Ps. 98 : Term already dealt with.

Ps. 99 : " *Orphan* ".

Ps. 100 : *Mizmôr. For thanksgiving.*

This title indicates that the psalm was sung during the offering of the " Tôdah " (" Thanksgiving "), which belonged to the type of sacrifices known as the " Peace offerings " (*Šelamîm*), see Lev. 7^{11-15}, Am. 4^5.

Ps. 101 : Terms already dealt wi th.

Ps. 102 : *A Prayer for an afflicted one when he becometh faint, and poureth out his complaint before Yahweh.*

This title explains itself, and the contents of the psalm show its appropriateness.

Ps. 103 : Term already dealt with.

Pss. 104, 105 : " *Orphan* ".

Ps. 106 : The " Hallelujah " which stands as a title to this psalm has been repeated from the conclusion of the previous psalm ; it is omitted by a number of MSS. The psalm is an " Orphan " one.

Ps. 107 : " *Orphan* ".

Pss. 108–110 : Terms already dealt with.

Pss. 111–113 : In these psalms " Hallelujah " stands as a title.

Pss. 114–119 : " *Orphan* ".

Pss. 120–134 : " Songs of Ascents "; Pss. 122, 124, 131, 133 add " David's ", omitted, however, by some MSS; Ps. 127 adds " Solomon's ". For a discussion on what is meant by this term, see the introductory section to Ps. 120 in the Commentary.

Ps. 135 : " Hallelujah " again stands as the title.

Pss. 136, 137 : " *Orphan* ".

Pss. 138–141 : Terms already dealt with.

Ps. 142 : *Maskil. David's, when he was in the cave. A Prayer.*

See the title to Ps. 57. The title was probably suggested by what is said in *v.* 7, " Bring my soul out of prison ".

Pss. 143, 144 : Terms already dealt with.

Ps. 145 : *Praise. David's.*

This is the only occurrence in the titles of the term " T'hillah ", meaning " Praise ". The contents of the psalm show it to be very fitting. The addition of " David's " illustrates the haphazard way in which the name has been made use of in the titles.

Pss. 146–150 : All these psalms have the heading " Hallelujah "; in most cases it is in the nature of a title, but in Ps. 147 it belongs to the text itself.

CHAPTER IV

THE FORMS OF HEBREW POETRY [1]

FOR many centuries it was believed that there was no distinction to be made in form between Hebrew prose and Hebrew poetry. The language itself, owing to the great strength of its accentuation, is so wonderfully musical that even its prose has a poetic quality and ring. In the early Christian centuries, it is true, some scholars (*e.g.*, Philo and Josephus among Jews, and Origen and Jerome among Christians) claimed that metres similar to those of Greek poetry were used in Hebrew, but their statements are usually attributed to a desire to glorify the Scriptures from every point of view. Origen, indeed, apparently had some idea of the true nature of Hebrew poetic form, but he does not seem to have applied his theories regularly, and was not followed. It was only in the eighteenth century that the world of Hebrew scholarship first had any light on the subject.

The pioneer in this work was Robert Lowth, whose lectures on Hebrew poetry were published in 1753 under the title *De Sacra Poesi Hebræorum Prælectiones Academicæ.* He observed that every line of Hebrew poetry is divided into at least two parts, of which the second frequently repeats the thought of the first. This he called *parallelism of verse-members*; for the mind of the writer, instead of proceeding in a continuous line, as a prose-author would do, goes back, and moves along a line parallel to its former course. Lowth distinguished between three types of parallelism:

(*a*) *Synonymous,* in which the same thought is repeated with some exactness, *e.g.*, Ps. 83[14]:

> *As when fire kindleth in the forest,*
> *as when flame blazeth on the hills.*

(*b*) *Antithetic,* involving a contrast, and sometimes expressing the same idea first positively and then negatively, *e.g.*, Ps. 90[6]:

> *At morn it doth blossom and burgeon,*
> *at eve it doth droop and wither.*

or Prov. 27[6]:

> *Faithful are the wounds of a friend,*
> *but deceitful the kisses of an enemy.*

(*c*) *Synthetic,* where the sense runs on continuously, *e.g.*, Ps. 2[6]:

> *And I have anointed my king*
> *on Zion, my holy hill.*

---

[1] The rendering of some of the quotations given in this chapter differs from that appearing in the Commentary, but the *sense* is mostly the same.—T. H. R.

It is, we may at once remark, generally recognized that this last type is not true parallelism in thought, though each member of the line has the same number of significant words in Hebrew. A much better name for this type of line is that used by Gray, *formal parallelism*.

It is very seldom that two members of a line correspond exactly, and there are numerous modifications which deserve even more attention than they have yet received. Lowth fully recognized the facts, and did something to classify variations. His fundamental principles have never been challenged (though they have sometimes been neglected), and still remain the basis of all sound study of Hebrew poetic form.

For a century and a half little advance was made on Lowth. C. A. Briggs, in his commentary on the *Psalms* (1907), cites three more types of parallelism, identified by earlier scholars:

(*d*) *Emblematic*, e.g., Ps. 103[13]:

> *Like as a father pitieth his children,*
> *so Yahweh pitieth them that fear him.*

(*e*) *Stair-like*, where a part of a member is repeated, and made the starting-point for fresh progress, *e.g.*, Ps. 29[5]:

> *The voice of Yahweh breaketh the cedars,*
> *Yahweh breaketh the cedars of Lebanon.*

(*f*) *Introverted*, which involves a series of lines in which the parallelism is chiastic, the first and last being parallel, and the intervening lines corresponding with one another. Briggs cites, among other passages, Ps. 6[9-11]:

> *Depart, ye workers of trouble, from me;*
> *For he hath heard the voice of my weeping,*
> *Yahweh hath heard my supplication,*
> *Yahweh accepteth my prayer.*
> *They will turn back, they will be put to shame in a moment.*

But the first real advance was made by Gray, in his *Forms of Hebrew Poetry* (1915). He distinguished two broad classes of parallelism: (*a*) complete, in which every word in one member was balanced by a word in the corresponding member; (*b*) incomplete. The latter class, again, might have two forms. There might be in the second member an additional word " compensating " for the omission of a word in the first member, or the second member might be left without any compensation. We might have schemes like

> a.   b.   c.
> a'.   b'.   c'.   (complete parallelism,
>   cf. Ps. 83[14], cited above).
> a.   b.   c.
> a'.   b'.   d.   E.g., Ps. 75[6]:

> *For not from east nor from west*
> *Nor from wilderness*   *cometh uplifting.*

c

A very common type of incomplete parallelism with compensation is the form

a. b.   c.
  b'. c'. d.   E.g., Ps. 59[16] :

> *But I will sing of thy might,*
> *exult loudly in thy love at morn.*

Often in parallelism of this kind two terms in one member correspond to one term in the other: again more than one form may appear. We may have the scheme

a. b. c.
a'. b' + d.   E.g., Ps. 57[4] :

> *Their teeth are lance and arrows,*
> *their tongue a sharp sword.*

Another common form is

a. b.   c.
  b'. c' + d.   E.g., Ps. 90[8] :

> *Thou hast set our iniquities before thee,*
> *our secret sins in the light of thy face.*

Sometimes only one term in the first member is represented in the second, and there are two new terms giving a form

a. b. c.
  c'. d. e.   E.g., Ps. 81[10] :

> *I am Yahweh thy God,*
> *that brought thee up from the land of Egypt.*

But the different types of incomplete parallelism with compensation are too numerous for detailed description, and not a little of the formal beauty of Hebrew poetry depends on the variety shown in its use. We should, however, note that there are many cases in which each member has only two terms, and that here, too, similar principles apply. Thus we may have complete parallelism, with a scheme

a. b.
a'. b'.   E.g., Ps. 29[4] :

> *The voice of the Lord in strength,*
> *the voice of the Lord in splendour.*

Much commoner is

a. b.
a'.   c.   E.g., Ps. 23[4] :

> *Thy rod and thy staff,*
> *they   comfort me.*

But in the Psalter lines of two-term members are much more often

continuous in sense, giving what Lowth called synthetic parallelism.
To this point we shall return later.

Incomplete parallelism without compensation normally results in
two verse-members of uneven length.   In these cases the second, which
is usually the shorter, is often a kind of echo of the first.   We may
thus have a scheme

$$a. \quad b. \quad c.$$
$$a'. \quad b'. \qquad \textit{E.g., Ps. } 57^9:$$

I will praise thee among the peoples, O Lord,
hymn thee among the nations.

Or (a common type)

$$a. \quad b. \quad c.$$
$$b'. \quad c'. \qquad \textit{E.g., Ps. } 57^{10}$$

For great unto the heavens is thy love,
and unto the skies thy truth.

As an illustration of the form

$$a. \quad b. \quad c.$$
$$a'. \qquad c'. \quad \text{we may take Ps. } 84^4:$$

Yea, the sparrow hath found a house,
and the swallow   her nest.

Naturally the possibilities of variation are less numerous than they
are in the longer lines, but, nevertheless, they have a fairly wide range.

So far we have been considering the parallelism of the members
within a line.   But we also frequently have parallelism which involves
two or more whole consecutive lines.   This we may distinguish as
external parallelism.   It is not common with the longer lines, and
where it occurs in these it generally appears as a repetition of the general
sense without exact correspondence of terms.   But an example may
be seen in Ps. 59^{1-2}:

Deliver me from my foes, O my God ;   *from them that exalt themselves against*
                                          me protect me ;
Deliver me from workers of iniquity ;   *and from men of blood save me.*

Here we have an almost exact correspondence between the two complete
lines, and we note that there is also internal parallelism, incomplete
with compensation in the first line, but complete in the second.   Sometimes two lines are linked by parallelism between the second member
of the first and the first member of the second, *e.g.*, in Ps. 78^8 we have :

And not become as their fathers,   *a generation perverse and defiant,*
A generation that set not its heart,   *whose spirit was not faithful with God.*

This gives us a " stair-like " parallelism.   But most commonly external
parallelism is loose in the longer lines, and is merely a repetition of
the same general idea.   In the shorter lines, however, it is **much more**

frequent and exact, and in lines with two-term members it is usual, though not invariable. We may have the form which appears in Ps. 79[9] :

Help us, O God of our salvation,	*for thy glorious name's sake.*
And deliver us and atone for our sins,	*for thy name's sake.*

Here the internal parallelism (if we may so describe it at all) is " synthetic ", while the external parallelism is clearly marked, though not exactly complete. In lines with two-term members, as has already been pointed out, this type of parallelism becomes normal. Thus we have almost exact correspondence between two successive lines in Ps. 74[15] :

Thou didst rend open	*fountain and wadi,*
Thou didst dry up	*rivers of yore.*

Such an arrangement has the appearance of four-member lines, but the parallelism in other parts of the poem shows that this interpretation of the phenomena is hardly justified, *e.g.*, the line following those just quoted runs :

> *Thine is the day,   yea, thine the night ;*

where the internal complete parallelism is obvious. A good instance of incomplete external parallelism, giving the " stair-like " arrangement, is to be seen in Ps. 29[1-2] :

Give to Yahweh,	*ye sons of gods,*
Give to Yahweh	*glory and strength,*
Give to Yahweh	*the glory of his name.*

We might represent this by the formula :

> *a. b. c. d.*
>
> *a. b.   e. f.*
>
> *a. b.   e.   g.*

It must be admitted that what has been said is but a superficial sketch of the subject. But the more we study the different forms and types that parallelism may take in Hebrew poetry, the more we are impressed by its variety and flexibility. The illustrations given above have all been taken from the Psalter ; had we included references to other poetical works—*Job, Lamentations*, and the prophets in particular—we should have found our range increased and our conclusions reinforced. There is something to be said for the view that parallelism in thought is the basis of all forms of poetry, developing only later into that parallelism in sound which is now recognized as its most prominent characteristic. But a discussion of this aspect would take us too far afield, and we must be content to draw certain conclusions which, though sometimes neglected, seem to the present writer to be inevitable corollaries of the principle of parallelism.

The first of these is that the rhythm of Hebrew poetry is essentially a rhythm of sense, and not of sound. It is the logical terms which balance one another, not the number, length, or stress of the syllables. Numerous attempts have been made to establish systems of Hebrew rhythm on a phonetic basis, and in dealing with a language like Hebrew this is only natural. But it must never be forgotten that the phonetic element is always secondary and the logical element primary. An exposition of the nature of Hebrew poetic form which concentrates on the former is foredoomed to failure, and it must be admitted that a great deal of time and strength has been spent by scholars in a futile quest. The analysis of the metrical unit carried out by men like Sievers (to take a conspicuous example) is of value in determining the musical character and qualities of the Hebrew language in general, but has little specific bearing on its prosody. We use terms like " accent ", " beat ", " stress ", because we have no other convenient phraseology, but we must not forget the basic principle that the sound is but the expression of the thought, and that in Hebrew poetry it is the latter, and not the former, which creates and dominates the form. The strength of the accent in Hebrew naturally tends to link meaning and sound, summing up the whole content of an idea, as it does, in a heavily accented syllable at or near the end of the sound-group. The enumeration of significant terms will almost certainly coincide with that of the most strongly accented syllables, but it was the former, and not the latter, which determined the poetic structure.

From what has been said, it follows that the metrical unit and the logical unit must always coincide. The logical unit itself may be somewhat complex, and may embrace more than one " word ". Two nouns standing in the construct relation may be regarded as a single entity by the poet, especially if the two form a familiar phrase. The word " all ", for example, is rarely independent unless its meaning be reinforced with a conjunction; in Ps. 56[1] " every day " is a single concept and forms a single unit. The relative pronoun standing alone is seldom if ever treated as a metrical unit, though with a preposition it may attain independent status, and the same remark may be made of the shorter prepositions, though the longer forms, which still show clearly their nominal character, are more likely to stand alone, and a preposition with a pronominal suffix is nearly always a significant unit. If a negative counts in the verse-enumeration, it is because the poet laid an overwhelming stress upon it, e.g., in Isa. 1[3]:

The ox knoweth his owner,   and the ass his master's crib ;
Israel doth NOT know ;   my people doth NOT consider.

On the other hand, a single " word " may sometimes (though not often) have the metrical value of two units, if it be sufficiently charged with meaning. On the rare occasions when this phenomenon occurs, the word is generally in the plural and has a suffix, a prefix, or both. Thus in Ps. 59[1] we have the term " from those that exalt themselves against me ", which is a single word in Hebrew, but is clearly capable of bearing the weight of more than one sense-unit. It is, however, to be noted that such two-unit words never form whole verse-members by themselves ; they are found only as supplying two terms in three-term verse-members.

When we pass from the single thought-unit to the larger verse-unit into which the thought-units are combined, we must observe the same principle that it is the logical element which dominates the whole. The verse-member and the full line alike have a logical basis, and each is a group of significant terms, with breaks in the rhythm corresponding to the breaks in the thought. As we have seen, every line consists of at least two members, with a greater or lesser pause between them ; the name *cæsura* is commonly used to indicate this pause. Now, we cannot have, in Hebrew verse, a greater pause, or a stronger *cæsura*, within a verse-member than that which separates the verse-members of a line from one another. It may sometimes seem to us, on a superficial reading, that this rule is violated, but a closer examination of the facts and a fuller understanding of the poet's mental processes will show us that the first impression has been misleading. Such a line as Ps. 103[6],

Yahweh worketh righteousness and judgement for all the oppressed,

may look at first sight as if " righteousness " and " judgement " were more closely connected than " worketh " and " righteousness " on the one hand, and " judgement " and " for all the oppressed " on the other. But as soon as we realize that the poet naturally thought in parallels, we see that the words " and judgement for all that are oppressed " take up and carry on the thought of " righteousness ". In other words, the true arrangement is :

Yahweh worketh righteousness,
              and judgement for all the oppressed,

and we have a case of incomplete parallelism with compensation, with the formula :

$$a. \quad b. \quad c.$$
$$c'. \quad d. \quad e.$$

The Hebrew habit of making a pause before launching out on some emphatic expression will account for, and is illustrated by, a number of cases in which we should be inclined to put a *cæsura* in a place where it would not naturally fit the verse-scheme (see below on the 2 : 3 form). In fact, there are very few combinations of words which prohibit a division between them ; perhaps the only type of connexion in which we can be certain that no pause can be made is when two nouns stand in the construct relation, or (really a special case of this combination) when a preposition immediately precedes a noun.

It follows that in Hebrew poetry there can be no such thing as *enjambement.* While the thought and the syntax may run on from one line to the next, or from one verse-member to the next (as in " synthetic parallelism "), each unit has a certain self-consistency and independence of its neighbours. We may take such a series of lines as that which occurs in the Psalm just quoted, Ps. 103$^{2\,\text{a.}}$:

> *Bless Yahweh, O my soul,*
>   *and forget not all his benefits ;*
> *Who forgiveth all thine iniquities,*
>   *who healeth all thy diseases ;*
> *Who redeemeth thy life from the Pit,*
>   *who crowneth thee with love and tenderness. . . .*

Here the thought is in a sense continuous, and, syntactically, all the relative clauses in the second and third lines (in Hebrew they are all participles with the definite article) are dependent on the pronoun at the end of *v.* 2. But not only each separate line, but each separate verse-member, is self-contained, with a clear break in thought separating it both from what precedes and from what follows. Such an arrangement as Tennyson's :

> " Let knowledge grow from more to more,
>   But more of reverence in us dwell,
>   That mind and soul, according well,
> May make one music as before,
>
> But vaster. We are fools and slight
>   And mock thee when we do not fear . . . "

is utterly inconceivable in classical Hebrew poetry.

A further result of the principle of parallelism is that there can be no such thing as an isolated verse-member.[1] The very idea of parallelism connotes at least two members ; a single " parallel " line is as impossible in Hebrew metrics as it would be in mathematics. Some commentators (Briggs is an outstanding example) are in the habit of treating a three-term member as an independent unit. But even where a group of lines contains an odd number of verse-members, it will usually be found that in one or more places three members are best taken together. There can be no objection to a three-member unit on the score of parallelism, and this arrangement does at times occur regularly, *e.g.,* in Ps. 77$^{16-19}$.

---

[1] It is only right to say at this point that Dr. Oesterley believes that a two-term member can exist as an independent line. It is true that Dussaud (*Les Découvertes de Ras Shamra et l'Ancien Testament,* pp. 66f. [1937]), and Schaeffer (*The Cuneiform Texts of Ras Shamra-Ugarit,* p. 58 [1939]), maintain that two-beat members occur in the Ras Shamra poems, though not often. After most careful consideration, however, I feel that the facts are capable of other explanations, and are not really at variance with the principle of parallelism.—T. H. R.

We may now proceed to consider the different types of line which are found in Hebrew poetry—in other words, the recognizable metres. It is usual to " scan " Hebrew poetry by enumerating the significant terms of each verse-member. The smallest combination of terms is, of course, a pair, and the simplest metre is the 2 : 2, *i.e.*, one in which each verse-member contains two terms. The lines cited above from Ps. 74[15] belong to this class. But it is very rare as the only metre used in a Hebrew poem; it is comparatively seldom even the dominant rhythm. Examples, however, may be found in Pss. 29, 74. It is not uncommon in the prophetic books; a fine example occurs in the stirring account of the sack of Nineveh, Nah. 3[1-3]. In this passage the parallelism is mainly internal, but as a rule, especially in the Psalter, the parallelism is external, and some scholars would even scan the metre as 4 : 4. The occasional appearance of a genuine 2 : 2, however, makes the assumption of a longer verse-member improbable.

Much more common than the 2 : 2 is a form in which one member, usually the first, is expanded by the addition of an extra term, giving either 3 : 2 or (more rarely) 2 : 3. This metre was noticed by Budde in *Lamentations*, and has therefore received the name of *Qinah*, or Dirge metre. The parallelism is often internal, being incomplete without compensation; it is, however, sometimes external, and there are scholars who feel a difference between the two types. The divergence, however, does not seem to be great enough to justify us in regarding the two as being essentially different metres. The 2 : 3 is in a different position, and it is often held that its appearance is due either to textual corruption or to misunderstanding of the spirit manifested in the verse. The Hebrew mind was prone to emphasize a word, or even a syllable, by dwelling on that which preceded it, and even making a slight pause. This tendency is manifest even in the basic phonetic principles of the language, where a long vowel in an open syllable naturally precedes the heavily stressed tone-syllable. The mind is kept, as it were, in suspense, and the effect of what follows is thereby greatly heightened. So in Ps. 42[4] it may well be that the poet meant us to read :

> " Should I recall this, then I would pour out—
>   my (very) self upon me ! "

There are, however, lines which can be nothing but 2 : 3. Thus in Ps. 76[5b] we have :

> *Nor find   any men of valour their hands,*

where the words " any men of valour ", being connected by the construct relation, cannot admit of any division between them. Again, Ps. 79[13] runs :

> *We will praise thee for ever   to all generations will we tell thy praise,*

and the term " to all generations " is almost certainly a balance to " for ever " in the first verse-member.[1]

There is some close and intimate connexion between the 2 : 2 and the 3 : 2 (2 : 3). It is seldom that we find any poem in which either occurs alone. Usually the majority of the lines are 3 : 2, with a small number of 2 : 2 and an occasional 2 : 3. Thus Ps. 23 is 3 : 2 except in *v.* 4, which consists of three 2 : 2 lines, and here it is noticeable that the quicker rhythm may indicate a heightening of the emotional tension. In Ps. 55 we have approximately thirty 3 : 2 lines, and not more than six in 2 : 2. Ps. 84 contains nineteen lines, of which fifteen are 3 : 2, three 2 : 2, and one (the last) 2 : 3. Even in *Lamentations* a fair proportion of 2 : 2 lines appears, and we may safely say that the variation was felt to be no irregularity by the Hebrew poet.

Another mode of expansion was by a process of triplication. This might take three forms. The simplest method was to add a term to each member, producing 3 : 3. This is by far the commonest metre in the *Psalms*, and the whole of the poem of Job is written in it. Its parallelism is usually internal, and, as we have already seen, it is capable of a very wide range of variety.

The second method is the addition of a whole two-term verse-member, yielding a 2 : 2 : 2. This is far from common in the *Psalms*, though it is not infrequent in the prophets, and occasionally appears even in *Job*. Occasionally all three members seem to stand apart, and the two *cæsuras* are of equal value. In this case we may have a threefold internal parallelism as, for instance, in Ps. 59[6] :

> *They come back at even,   they growl as dogs,   and go about the city.*

More often, however, one of the *cæsuras* is weaker than the other, though both are always there ; the line may look rather like 4 : 2 or 2 : 4. Thus in Ps. 73[18] we have a line in which the third member is parallel to the first two taken together :

> *Surely in slippery places   thou settest them,*
> *in beguiling thou bringest them down.*

On the other hand, in Ps. 75[7] we have :

> *For God is Judge,   one he bringeth low,   and one he lifteth up.*

where the three members are quite distinct, but the second is more closely allied through parallelism to the third than to the first.

The 2 : 2 : 2 is rarely if ever found alone. There are a few passages in the prophets in which it is the only form, but these are always very short, and are almost certainly no more than fragments. Three consecutive 2 : 2 : 2 lines occur in Ps. 68[7-8], but here again we are dealing

---

[1] For full discussion of this point see Gray, *Forms of Hebrew Poetry*, pp. 176 ff.

with a mosaic of short extracts. The metre is normally an occasional variation in the midst of 3 : 3 lines. Of the twenty complete lines composing what is left of Ps. 59, three are 2 : 2 : 2, and two of the three are identical. Of the ten lines in Ps. 75$^{2-10}$, nine are 3 : 3 and one is 2 : 2 : 2. Ps. 88 (twenty lines) contains one 2 : 2 : 2. Though a " regular " variant to the 3 : 3 (the prophetic evidence is much stronger than that of the Psalter), it is much less frequent than the 2 : 2 interchanging with the 3 : 2.

Finally we may have a triplication even of the 3 : 3, a third and similar member being added. In lines of this type the three parts may be equally connected, all being parallel to one another. Thus Ps. 60^8 runs :

Moab is my wash-pot ;   over Edom will I cast my shoe ;   over Philistia I raise a shout.

In Ps. 79^2, however, we have a line in which the third member is really parallel to the first two taken together :

They have given the carcases of thy servants   as food to the birds of the heavens,
the flesh of thy saints to the beasts of the field.

The 3 : 3 : 3 occurs as an occasional variant to the 3 : 3, being a little more frequent than the 2 : 2 : 2. There are, however, from time to time, longer consecutive sections, and even whole poems, written in this metre. It runs all through Ps. 77$^{16-19}$, which, on grounds independent of metre, seems to be taken from another source than that of the earlier verses of the psalm. Ps. 93 is a particularly fine example, owing to the striking effect of the " stair-like " internal parallelism, which brings each line to a climax.

We have thus two main types of metre : a 3 : 2 varied by 2 : 3 and 2 : 2, and a 3 : 3 varied by 2 : 2 : 2 and 3 : 3 : 3. A third is found, though it is rare. This is a line in which there are seven terms, usually arranged as 4 : 3, though occasionally as 3 : 4. It nearly always happens that the four-term member is capable of still further subdivision into 2 : 2. The best illustration in the Hebrew Bible is the great chaos-vision in Jer. 4$^{23-26}$, but it is found in a few psalms, e.g., in Ps. 58, and frequently occurs in isolated lines in *Proverbs*. A glance at the parallelism shows that it really is a three-member line. Thus in Jer. 4^{23} we have :

I beheld the earth,   and lo ! chaos ;   and the heavens, and light had they none.

Here, while the first two members are quite distinct, the third is parallel to the two taken together. The first two members are even closer in Ps. 58^6 :

O God, crush   their teeth in their mouth,   the fangs of the young lion uproot;

but in Ps. 58^3 :

Estranged are the wicked,   from the womb do they err,   from birth they speak falsehood, we have three members which are co-ordinately parallel, though the third member is longer than either of the others.

One other feature of Hebrew poetry requires mention. It happens from time to time that a word at the beginning of a line stands by itself, remaining outside the metrical scheme and forming an *anacrusis*. Again we meet with the Hebrew tendency to use a pause for emphasis. Only a few words are found in this position, and they are mostly inter-jections, vocatives, and pronouns, though sometimes a word of saying takes this place. An illustration is to be found in Ps. 55[6], where the insertion of " And I said " between two lines tends to bring out into strong relief the force of the words which follow—so in Ps. 73[11], 83[5]. An emphatic pronoun appears in Ps. 77[14] and 88[13], and a vocative in Ps. 88[1], 90[1]. The " Wherefore ? " of Ps. 88[14] and the " How long ! " of Ps. 79[5] are interjections rather than interrogatives, and " Therefore " in Ps. 78[21] serves to bring out strongly the consequences of Israel's unbelief as described in the preceding verses.

There is one question relating to metre on which the opinion of Old Testament scholars is still sharply divided. There are, on the one hand, those who hold that the same metre always persisted throughout a poem, and that any irregularity must be due to textual corruption. On the other hand, many believe that a poet might intro-duce more than one metre, or might even mix them indiscriminately. A discussion of this point would take far too much space ; suffice it to say that the present writer is inclined to the former of the two views mentioned, and holds that the metre of each poem was normally " regular ". Earlier students of metre were apt to be very rigid ; but a large number of " irregularities " disappear when it is realized that certain variations—2 : 2 with 3 : 2 and 2 : 2 : 2 with 3 : 3—are " regu-lar ", just as the dactyl and the spondee both occur in the classical hexameter. Other variations—3 : 3 with 3 : 2 and vice versa—seem to be due to later modification of the text. Where we have parallel passages in the Old Testament, we can sometimes see that one form is " regular ", while the other is not, and the evidence of the Septuagint (more in some books than in others) points in the same direction. We know that our texts have suffered in course of transmission, and it is hoped that the small number of conjectural emendations made *metri gratia* in the following pages will not appear to be excessive.

There still remains an aspect of Hebrew poetic form on which we must briefly touch. We have glanced at the smallest unit, the sig-nificant term, at the combination of terms into verse-members, and the linking of verse-members to form single lines. Can we discover a still larger unit, corresponding to the stanza in modern poetry ? The analogy of many other kinds of liturgical poetry suggests that we can, and since the beginning of the last century it has been customary to

speak of the " strophes " of a Hebrew poem. The term is less suitable
than " stanza ", for the sections of poetry indicated by it are more
closely allied to the " verses " of a modern hymn than to the divisions
of a Greek chorus, but the word has become so familiar that it may be
retained.

Strophic theory owes its origin to an article by Kösters which
appeared in the *Theologische Studien und Kritiken* for 1831. It was
extremely simple, and was based on the number of verses which went
to make up the strophe. From this point of view, there are two broad
classes of poems : (*a*) those which have similar strophes, *i.e.*, those in
which all the strophes contain the same number of lines, though
sometimes an " interpolated " verse occurs between two strophes ;
(*b*) those which have dissimilar strophes. The latter, again, may be
still further classified into (i) poems with parallel strophes, in which
groups of the same length are repeated or alternate regularly, (ii) antistrophic poems, where a series of dissimilar strophes is repeated ;
(*c*) climactic poems, in which each strophe is regularly longer than its
predecessor ; (*d*) dithyrambic poems, in which the arrangement is
completely free. Three criteria may be used in determining the limits
of the strophes within a poem : (*a*) a " refrain ", which may occur at
the beginning, at the end, or in the middle of a strophe ; (*b*) a break in
the sense ; (*c*) the presence of *Selah* at the end of a strophe.

A few illustrations may be cited from those given by Kösters.
Ps. 2 has four similar strophes of three verses each. Ps. 110 contains
two three-verse strophes with an interpolated verse between them.
Ps. 46 has three three-verse strophes, each closed with *Selah*, and there
is a refrain at the end of the second and third strophes. Ps. 45 is
antistrophic, being of the following form : 1 : 1 : 3 : 3 : 1 : 3 : 3 : 1 : 1.
Ps. 27 has four strophes arranged in parallels : 3 : 3 : 4 : 4.

Kösters' views have been widely accepted, with some slight modification. Instead of the Masoretic verse, the actual poetic line has
been regarded as the unit to be counted in estimating the length of a
strophe, an improvement first suggested by Merx in 1857. There
has been a tendency to insist that all the strophes of any particular
poem must be of the same length, and, indeed, it would seem that this
is almost necessary if the strophe is to have any real meaning as an
element in poetic form. Certainly Kösters' last type consists simply
of poems in which there is no systematic grouping of verses or lines,
though, naturally, the whole may be divided into paragraphs, and we
might as well reduce *Paradise Lost* to stanza form. The rigid application of strophic theory, as it may be seen, for instance, in the work of
Briggs, inevitably results in some very drastic surgery. No doubt our
texts have suffered corruption as they have been handed down, but we
are suspicious of a principle which requires the rejection of so large

a number of lines as this does. The divisions, too, are at times some-what arbitrary, and it may be doubted whether we can say that all Hebrew poems were originally intended to be strophic in form. Where we have a refrain, as in Pss. 42–43, we may be reasonably certain that the sections were originally intended to balance one another. Alpha-betic poems like Ps. 119 are clearly capable of such an arrangement, though in one instance, Lam. 3, the sense-divisions do not always correspond to the alphabetic structure. There are psalms—e.g., Ps. 77—in which it seems possible that *Selah* marked the end of each division, and that these divisions were once of uniform length. On the other hand, none of these criteria can be said to indicate proper strophic division in every psalm in which it appears, and we shall do well to find a strophic structure only in a limited number, where it is fairly obvious. The theory is of value in some instances, but it may easily be pressed too far.

CHAPTER V

FROM one point of view the text of the Psalter presents us with problems which hardly arise in dealing with other books of the Old Testament. It is generally admitted that many of the psalms have a fairly long history behind them. Some of them may have been, and probably were, comparatively ancient, but each period in the history of Israel's religion has modified and adapted them to suit its own needs or its own special point of view. The recovery of the original form is practically impossible, for every attempt is necessarily exposed to a high degree of subjectivity. There are instances, it is true, in which the alterations are sufficiently obvious to enable us to say with some certainty what the earlier text was, but this seldom carries us far. In Pss. 42–83, for example, we have a whole collection of psalms in which the word *Elohim* (= God; a general term) has been substituted for the personal name of the God of Israel, *Yahweh*. Even here, it seems, copyists have occasionally gone back to the original reading, though they have left the modified text in the great majority of cases. Are we, then, to restore " Yahweh " wherever it seems desirable in this group ? That is the method adopted by many commentators, and there is much to be said for it. In the following pages, however, the text has, generally, been retained in this matter, as it has come down to us, on the ground that this is but one of numerous changes that have taken place during the history of individual psalms, and, since there is practical unanimity among our witnesses (the change was made before the book was translated into Greek, and, indeed, before the Psalter reached its present form), it has been felt that the right course to pursue has been to try to maintain the text as it stood when the final compilation of the book was effected. An exception has been made in those cases where we have two versions of the same psalm in our present book, *e.g.*, in treating of Pss. 14 and 53. Here we have evidence which we can regard as sufficiently reliable to enable us to say with some assurance what the common text was in certain passages. For the rest it has been necessary to depend on the normal methods of textual criticism.

As in other books of the Old Testament, the Masoretic text, which is the official Hebrew text handed down through ancient Palestinian tradition, presents us with very few variations. Differences as between Hebrew MSS. seldom go beyond minor details in pointing, and are generally due to the grammatical theories of the scribes, the inclusion or omission of the letters *Waw* and *Yodh* where they have been inserted to indicate long vowels, and the " accents ". The widest differences are probably those to be noted in a MS. now in the library of Trinity College, Cambridge, known as GI, but even here the variations in the consonantal text are almost confined to letters easily confused in the square script, such as *Beth* and *Kaph* or *He* and *Ḥeth*. Where it is probable that the text is corrupt, we have to rely on other evidence and other methods for correcting it.

We are thus compelled to turn to the ancient Versions. Among these the old Greek Version, known as the Septuagint, stands pre-eminent. It was made in Egypt, and, as quotations in the New Testament and contemporary literature show, was well established by the beginning of the Christian era (it may be remarked that Philo's citations sometimes exhibit verbal differences from the received Greek text, but nowhere suggest an independent translation ; the modifications belong rather to the sphere of Septuagint criticism). Here we have a text which, in places, differs considerably from that of the Palestinian tradition, though we are sometimes inclined to suspect that the translators were ignorant of the meaning of a Hebrew word and simply guessed it. Next to the Masoretic text itself, however, the Septuagint remains the most valuable witness we have, and it has frequently been used in the following pages for the restoration of doubtful passages. In this connexion it may be as well to point out that in a very large number of cases where there is disagreement between the two, the Masoretic text has been preferred. There are three other well-known Greek versions : those of Aquila, Symmachus, and Theodotion. Of these, in so far as they have survived, that of Aquila is the most useful, since it is a slavishly literal rendering of the Hebrew text which the translator had before him. That text differed but little from the traditional Hebrew form, though occasionally it offers us an interesting variation.

Next in age and importance to the Septuagint comes the Syriac Version, commonly called the Peshitta. Its origin is obscure ; we are not even certain whether it is Jewish or Christian. While certain crucial passages are interpreted in a Christian sense (*e.g.*, Isa. 7¹⁴), we have to allow for the possibility of deliberate Christian modification. In the particular instance cited, the rendering might have been defended on the ground that it corresponded to that of the Septuagint, which was certainly pre-Christian. The Syriac Version of the Psalter was made from the Palestinian Hebrew text, and stands much nearer to it than does the Septuagint. There are, however, clear indications which show that the translators were aware of the Greek Version and were, to some extent, influenced by it. A striking instance is the rendering of the familiar *Selah*, for which the Syriac has a transliteration of the Greek *Diapsalma*. It is comparatively seldom that this Version offers an independent reading which may be accepted as original.

The only other Version which needs to be considered is the Vulgate. The first translation into Latin was made from the Septuagint, and is valuable as evidence for the text of that Version, but it is not a direct witness to the Hebrew text. The wide differences between the current Old Testament and the Hebrew text led Jerome to undertake a completely new revision of the whole. This is the version which has become the official Bible of the Roman Catholic Church. The fourth-century text attested by this Vulgate differed only slightly from the Hebrew as it has come down to us; occasional variations may be detected by comparing the Prayer-Book Version of the *Psalms* with that of the Authorized Version, *e.g.*, the two readings in Ps. 19[4]: " Their sound is gone out " (P.B.V.) and " Their line is gone out " (A.V.) imply a difference of one consonant in the Hebrew text. It is, however, comparatively seldom that a reading peculiar to the Vulgate commends itself as being original against the weight of all other authorities.

When, however, all available help has been received from the Versions, there remain countless passages in which the reader of the Hebrew text feels that it cannot be as the psalmist wrote it. Sometimes there is direct violation of a basic rule of grammar; sometimes the words make no sense whatever (in some of these cases, it may be remarked, the English Versions tacitly alter the text). Here we may admit that if our knowledge of Hebrew were more extensive than it is, it might be possible to discover a meaning for the text as it stands, and a good deal has been done in recent years by the use of comparative philology to elucidate passages hitherto regarded as unintelligible. But this expedient also carries us only a short distance, and in a very large number of places we are forced to guess at what the original text was. A few of these guesses commend themselves at once, and will receive general acceptance, but in the great majority of the passages where the text has been emended in the following pages it is frankly admitted that we cannot be at all certain that the text translated is what the psalmist wrote. We can only say that, in the judgement of the best Hebrew scholarship available, the words adopted are grammatical and intelligible, and may well have been those which the writer actually used. Conjectural emendation is inevitable; to use a phrase employed by one of our great scholars, it is at least as defensible as " conjectural translation ". We can only hope that we have been rightly guided in our choice of the text, and that the readings adopted in this commentary will at least help to bring home the message of the psalmists.

CHAPTER VI

THE PSALMS AND THE LITERATURES OF THE ANCIENT EAST

THE religious literature of the Ancient East, of which a large amount of material has come down to us, consists of mythological epics, festal odes, songs of praise, hymns of thanksgiving, penitential psalms, prayers, and didactic poems. That similar compositions appear in the *Psalms*, showing numerous points of contact in thought, as well as verbal parallels, with the writings of other ancient peoples, amply justifies the contention that the Hebrew psalms must be regarded as part of a world-literature. That in numerous instances the Hebrew psalmists were indebted to extraneous influences in composing their psalms is, therefore, highly probable; but in such cases adaptation rather than imitation was their guiding principle. For numerous as borrowed thoughts and parallels are, what appears as the most striking phenomenon in comparing the different bodies of literature is the manifest superiority of the Hebrew psalms as religious compositions. So much so that, while fully recognizing Hebrew psalmody as part of a world-literature, it must nevertheless be regarded as *sui generis*. This is not to deny the great beauty and the many indications of deep religious feeling expressed in Babylonian and Egyptian hymns; but what must be insisted on is that the Hebrew psalms, regarded from the purely religious point of view, stand on a different, and incomparably higher, level. At the same time, it is in no sense derogatory to these to say that the type of devotional literature of which the Biblical psalms are the supreme example, was not the exclusive possession of any one nation of antiquity; but that the innate urge of expressing the relationship felt by men between them and supernatural powers, impelled many devout spirits of various nationality to put their feelings into the concrete form of religious poems.

We shall now give some illustrations from the religious literatures of Babylonia and Egypt in order to show in how many respects there is a similarity of *genus* between these and Hebrew psalmody.

For the illustrations to be offered we are indebted to the following authors :—

Bertholet,   *Religionsgeschichtliches Lesebuch* (1908).
Erman,   *Die Literatur der Ägypter* (1923).
   „   *Die Religion der Ägypter* (1934).
Gressmann, *Altorientalische Texte Zum Alten Testament* (1926).
Gunkel,   *Ausgewählte Psalmen* (1904).

Jastrow,   *Die Religion Babyloniens und Assyriens* (1905, 1912).
Jeremias,   *Handbuch des altorientalischen Geisteskultur* (1929).
  „   *Das Alte Testament im Lichte des alten Orients*
            (1930).
Meissner,   *Babylonien und Assyrien* (1920, 1925).
Winckler,   *Keilinschriftliches Textbuch zum Alten Testament*
            (1909).
Zimmern,   *Babylonische Hymnen und Gebete* ("Der alte
            Orient," 1905–1911).

In order to avoid giving a large number of footnotes, we shall not
indicate the references to the various quotations taken from these
works.

It may be pointed out, first, that in outward form, *i.e.*, the *cæsura*
making a pause between the two halves of a line, the Hebrew psalms
are similar to Babylonian and Egyptian poetical form,[1] and this is also
true as regards metrical beats. Thus, to quote a few lines from a
Babylonian psalm :

Every day pay homage	unto thy god,
With sacrifice, prayer,	and incense, due.
Unto thy god	be thine heart's inclination,
That is the thing	which is due to the deity.
Supplication, entreaty,	with thy face to the ground,
Bring before him at morn ;	then mighty will be thy strength,
And with great abundance	will be thy pleading with the god.

The last line means that the petitioner's prayer will be abundantly
answered. Not that this metrical form occurs always ; there are
plenty of poems in which it is entirely absent ; but the fact that it is,
nevertheless, often found is interesting in view of Hebrew usage. In
Egyptian poems the same holds good ; *e.g.*, in a harvest-song we have
what certainly reads like the divided line :

Thresh for yourselves,	thresh for yourselves, ye oxen !
Thresh for yourselves,	thresh for yourselves !
The straw is for fodder,	the corn for your masters ;
Be not weary,	(the air) is cool.

So far as metrical beats are concerned, there seems to be some uncertainty ; but Erman believes that their presence must be postulated in
many cases. He also mentions the frequent occurrence of the repetition
of the same thought in each half of a line ; *e.g.* :

Then spake these friends of the king,	and they answered before their god ;

the same thing occurs in Babylonian hymns ; thus, in a hymn in
honour of the goddess of healing, Ninkarrag, it is said :

Ninkarrag, the daughter of Anu,	will I praise !
Out of her house of joy,	out of her chamber, hath she gone forth.

---

[1] The Ras Shamra poetry also shows normally the parallelism so characteristic
of Hebrew poetry.

In the Hebrew psalms this often occurs. So much, then, for the outward form of ancient poems.

To come now to some of the Babylonian and Egyptian hymns and psalms in which we find points of thought-contact with the Hebrew psalms. As an illustration of the mythological ode, we may give a quotation from the Babylonian Creation-myth (Fourth Tablet), which lies at the back of such passages as Ps. 74^{13-15}, 89^{9-14}, 104^{6-9}—namely, the conflict between Marduk and Tiamat; the Hebrew psalmist has taken the *rôle* of the hero-god Marduk, and applied it to Yahweh:

Then did stand forth,	Tiamat and Marduk, the wise one of the gods,
They arose for the battle	drawing near for the fray.
The lord spread forth	his net, he caught her therein,
The blast behind him	he let loose before her;
Then Tiamat opened her mouth	that she might engulph him,
He caused the blast to gush into her,	so that she could not close her lips;
The raging gusts	then filled her belly,
Her heart was o'erwhelmed,	her mouth she opened wide,
He thrust in his lance,	split open her belly,
Cut into her inside,	tore her heart in twain.
When he had overcome her,	he destroyed her life;
Her carcase he threw down,	upon it he stood.

Then, after the description of how he vanquished all those who had sided with Tiamat, it continues:

Thereupon the lord rested,	surveying her corpse,
To divide the bulk,	to perform a device.
He rent her like a shell,[1]	into two parts;
One half of her he placed,	and covered heaven's roof therewith,
He drew a bolt,	and stationed watchers,
Not to let her waters issue forth	did he give them charge.
He traversed the heavens,	he surveyed the spaces,
He placed over against them [2] Apsu,[3]	Nudimmud's [4] dwelling-place.

In spite of this somewhat involved description, the central point will be recognized—viz., the primeval combat between Marduk and Tiamat, representing the victory of the god over the powers of evil. This is what is borrowed, and adapted to Yahweh in a number of Old Testament passages, among them several psalms.

Our next illustration is an Egyptian hymn of praise in honour of the Sun-god, Amon-Re, the highest among all the gods; it belongs to the middle of the fifteenth century B.C. As will be seen, there are various instances in it of thoughts and expressions which find a parallel in verses of some of the Hebrew psalms. There is no question here of borrowing; but such parallels illustrate the existence of similarity of mental outlook on the part of religious poets, expressed in their poems. This hymn of praise has, like some of the Hebrew psalms, a somewhat lengthy title; it runs: "Praise of Amon-Re, the Bull of

---

[1] According to some authorities " gazelle ".
[2] *I.e.*, the heavens.   [3] The Deep.
[4] Ea, one of the great gods, and father of Marduk.

Heliopolis, chief of all the gods, of the good god, the loved one, who giveth life to all that liveth, and to every healthy herd ". The hymn then follows :

> Praise to thee, Amon-Re, thou lord of Karnak, thou chief one of Thebes !
> Thou Bull of its mother, who art supreme on his field ! [1]
> Thou that proceedest o'er wide spaces, thou chief one of Upper Egypt, lord of Matoiland, and lord of Punt.
> Thou, greatest in heaven (cp. Ps. 89[6]), most ancient on earth; thou, lord of all that is, that abidest in all things. [2]
> The only one of his kind among the gods (cp. Ps. 86[8], 96[4], 135[5]), the stately Bull [3] of the thrice-three gods, [4] the lord of all gods.
> Lord of truth (cp. Ps. 31[6]), father of the gods, who made men, and created the beasts (cp. Ps. 33[6], 65[9-13], 148[3-10]).
> Lord of all that is, who bringeth forth fruit-trees, who formeth the herbs, who nourisheth the cattle (cp. Ps. 104[14]).
> The beautiful figure, formed by Ptah [5]; the comely youth, honoured by the gods.
> Who made those above and those beneath [6]; who giveth light to the two lands,[7]
> Who rideth, exulting, across the skies (cp. Ps. 19[6]), the king of Upper and Lower Egypt, Re, the justified one ; [8]
> The chief of the two lands, the mighty one, the lord of power ; the most exalted who formed the whole land.
> More excellent in nature than any god, whose beauty the gods proclaim ; he is glorified in his temple, and crowned in the flame-sanctuary (cp. Ps. 11[4], 134[2]); [9]
> Whose sweet odour the gods love, when he cometh from Punt [10] ; rich in perfume when he cometh down from Matoiland, with his lovely countenance from the land of the god.[11]
> The gods crouch close at his feet when in his majesty they acknowledge him as their lord, the terrible and fearsome one, of glorious nature, mighty in appearance, nourished by offerings, and giver of food.
> Praise to thee, who didst create the gods, who didst raise the heavens on high, and didst stretch forth the earth.

For another illustration of a hymn of praise to the Sun-god, see under Ps. 104.

In the Psalter there are about twenty psalms of thanksgiving ; in the following one of similar character, sung to Amon, it will be seen that thoughts and expressions occur which have their parallel in some of the Hebrew psalms of thanksgiving :

In Praise of Amon.

> I sing hymns of praise to his name (cp. Ps. 30[4], 34[2], 116[4]),
> I praise him, as high as the heaven, as wide as the earth (cp. Ps. 57[5, 11]),
> I will tell of his power to him that goeth up and him that goeth down.[12]

---

[1] " The sun is the husband of the goddess of heaven, and as the sun of each day he is also her son. Just as the bull is supreme in the field in which he grazes, so is the sun supreme in the heavens (his field), since he is the greatest of the constellations " (Erman).
[2] *I.e.*, the sun penetrates everywhere.
[3] Synonym for " leader " (Erman).
[4] The divine triad, father, mother, and child, often appearing in early Egyptian religion.
[5] The artist among the gods who constructed the figure of Amon.
[6] *I.e.*, the stars (gods) above, and men beneath.
[7] *I.e.*, Upper and Lower Egypt.
[8] Re once reigned as king on earth, his excellence is justified by his having become a god.
[9] The reference is to the two sanctuaries in the ancient capitals of Upper and Lower Egypt (Erman).
[10] The coast-land of the present Abyssinia and Somaliland, whence incense was brought.
[11] *I.e.*, where the sun rises, the east.
[12] The reference is to those who passed his temple in sailing up and down the Nile.

Take heed before him ! Tell of it to son and daughter, to great and small ;
Tell of it from generation to generation, even to the generations not yet born
(cp. Ps. 22[30, 31]) ;
Tell of it to the fish in the water, and to the birds of the air ;
Tell of it to him that knoweth, and to him that knoweth not.
Take heed before him !
Thou, Amon, art lord of the silent one, that comest at the voice of the poor (cp.
Ps. 34[6], 40[17]) ;
When I cried unto thee in my trouble, thou didst come to deliver me (cp. Ps. 66[17 19]),
to give breath to the feeble, to save me, a prisoner (cp. Ps. 142[7]) ;
Thou art he, Amon-Re of Thebes, who deliverest him that is in the underworld
(cp. Ps. 30[3], 116[3, 4, 9]) ;
When one crieth unto thee thou dost come from afar (cp. Ps. 119[169]).

In this hymn the thanksgiving is implicit, the god's mercies
being acknowledged.

Our next illustration is a Babylonian penitential psalm :

O warrior Marduk, whose wrath is a storm-flood (cp. Ps. 21[9]),
Whose forgiveness is that of a merciful father (cp. Ps. 103[13]),
My cry unheeded, hath cast me down,
My entreaty unanswered, hath oppressed me sore ;
My strength is torn from mine heart,
I am bowed down like an aged man.
O mighty lord, Marduk, the merciful,
Who among all men that are living
Is there that discerneth my state ?
Who is not wanting, who hath not sinned ? (cp. Ps. 69[5]).
Who apprehendeth the way of a god ? (cp. Ps. 139[6]).
Let me give praise that I err not in godlessness,
Let me be present in the place of life (*i.e.*, the sanctuary, cp. Ps. 27[4]).[1]

Finally, a few isolated passages which offer some interesting parallels ;
they are taken from both Babylonian and Egyptian hymns, but it will
not be necessary to indicate these, as our object is simply to illustrate
some points of general similarity in the religious literatures of the
Ancient East.

In Ps. 2[11] we have given reasons in the Commentary for emending
the text so as to read : *Serve Yahweh in fear, and with trembling kiss
his feet* ; as a synonym for submission, whether to a conqueror or to a
god, to " kiss the feet " is a frequent phrase in ancient inscriptions and
hymns ; thus, it is said in a Babylonian hymn to Marduk that Ea
" hath commanded the kissing of thy feet, and hath ordained submission
unto thee ".

Again, in Ps. 18[37-40] it is told how by the help of Yahweh enemies
are overcome :

I pursued mine enemies and overtook them,   and turned not till they were consumed . . .
Thou didst gird me with strength for the battle,   thou didst bow down beneath me those
that rose up against me.

With the same trust in divine help the Egyptian king, Ramses II,
in a hymn to the god Amon, says, on finding himself in straits during
a battle against the Hittites :

---

[1] Further interesting illustrations of such penitential hymns are given also by
Witzel, *Tammuz Liturgie und Verwandtes* (1935).

But I cry, and perceive that better for me is Amon than millions of foot-soldiers, and hundreds of thousands of charioteers . . . the striving of many men is nought; Amon is better than they.

In Ps. 66[11] the metaphor of a " net " is used to denote the entanglement in which Yahweh involved his people in order to test them; the same metaphor is used of Yahweh punishing the people (Ezek. 12[13]). Similarly, it is told of the Babylonian god Bel that he casts his net: " O father Bel, thou dost cast the net, and that net becometh a hostile net."

We may consider next some interesting parallels regarding the person of the king. Ps. 72 is a psalm sung on the occasion of the enthronement of a king; it is too long to quote, but it may be pointed out that his advent is hailed with delight, for he will have a care for the poor and needy (vv. 4, 12, 13), and will save them from oppression and violence (v. 14), all kings shall fall down before him, and all nations shall serve him (v. 11), and his name shall endure for ever (v. 17); all is ascribed to the wondrous things that Yahweh accomplishes (v. 18). It will be seen that similar words are said in a hymn in honour of Ramses IV, on his enthronement:

A glorious day ! Heaven and earth rejoice, for thou art the great ruler of Egypt.
They that fled have returned to their cities, and they who had hidden have come back again.
They that hungered are satisfied and joyful, they that were thirsty drink their fill.
They that were naked are clothed in fine linen, and they that were filthy have white garments.
They that were in prison are set at liberty, and they that were bound are full of joy . . .
The maidens rejoice and sing exultingly; they are adorned, and say . . . O thou ruler, thou endurest for ever . . .
All the nations say to him : Glorious is the king on Amon's throne, who hath sent him forth, the protector of the king, who leadeth all peoples to him.

Finally, two or three miscellaneous parallels. With the conception of the thunder being the voice of Yahweh (Ps. 29) we may compare the following from a hymn to the Babylonian god Adad-Ramman (the storm-god):

At thy thunder doth shake   the great mountain, father Enlil,[1]
At thy roaring doth tremble   the great mother Ninlil.[2]

Again, there is a close parallel between Ps. 42[4]: *My tears have been my meat day and night*, and the plaint in a Babylonian hymn : " Food I ate not, weeping was my bread; water I drank not, tears were my drink "; and in another penitential psalm of similar character: " Weeping and tears cease not, with my sighs am I daily sated ". Finally, in Ps. 34[13] it is said:

Keep thy tongue from evil, and thy lips from speaking guile ;

---

[1] The god of the earth ; it means that the earth shakes.
[2] The spouse of Enlil, also representing the earth.

with which we have a parallel in a Babylonian text:

Slander not, speak sweetly,   Say nought that is evil, utter that which is good.

These illustrations could be greatly multiplied, but it is hoped that it has been sufficiently shown how much common ground there is between Hebrew psalmody and the devotional literature of other peoples; thus justifying the contention that the Hebrew psalms, great as is their superiority over all others, must nevertheless be recognized as belonging to a world-literature.

CHAPTER VII

THE KINGSHIP OF YAHWEH

SOME consideration of this subject is demanded, because in a certain number of psalms there are indications of their having been sung in celebration of the " Enthronement of Yahweh ". That this was a ceremony of great significance there can be no shadow of doubt. At the same time, it must be insisted on that to speak of the " Festival of the Enthronement of Yahweh " as though it constituted in itself a festival, is a mistake; for there was certainly no festival of this name known to the Israelites. A significant fact in this connexion should be noted: in the early accounts of the celebration of the New Year Festival in the Synagogue mention is made of a number of thoughts and expressions which occur in the " Enthronement " psalms, viz. the Kingship of Yahweh, his Kingdom over all the world, Yahweh as Judge, the holiness of his name, the " shout ", and the shôphar-blast; but there is not a hint of the Enthronement ceremony.[1] If there had ever been a Festival of the Enthronement, a reference to it of some kind would surely have been forthcoming. The Enthronement of Yahweh was the initial ceremony, though one of central importance, performed at one of the great feasts. Which of these feasts it was at which this ceremony took place, what the origin of that feast was, its significance and purpose, are matters which will be discussed as we proceed.

Opinions differ markedly as to the number of psalms in which this ceremony is referred to; some scholars believe they can see references to it in a large number of psalms [2]; we submit, however, that when once it is recognized that the Enthronement of Yahweh did not constitute a festival in itself, but was only the initial ceremony of one of the feasts, the number of psalms which refer to the ceremony is reduced to those which make actual mention of it; these are the psalms in which the phrase " Yahweh is become King " occurs.

We shall begin our discussion by quoting all the passages in the psalms which refer to the Kingship of Yahweh. They are of three classes: (1) those in which Yahweh is spoken of as ' " King "; (2) those

[1] Elbogen, Der jüdische Gottesdienst . . ., pp. 140–149 (1913).
[2] We have made a study of Mowinckel, Psalmenstudien, II. Das Thronbesteigungsfest Jahwäs . . . (1922), and of Hans Schmidt, Die Thronfahrt Jahves (1927), and must confess that their arguments entirely fail to convince us; the large number of psalms they quote, especially the former, as referring to the " Festival of Yahweh's Enthronement " refer to the feast of which this was only one element.

in which the "throne" of Yahweh is referred to; and (3) those in which the phrase "Yahweh is become King" occurs.

(1) THE TITLE OF "KING" APPLIED TO YAHWEH:

5^2. Hearken unto the voice of my cry, my King and my God.

10^{16}. Yahweh is King for ever and ever.

24^{7-10}. . . . Who is the King of glory? Yahweh, strong and mighty . . .

29^{10}. Yahweh sitteth as King for ever.

48^2. . . . mount Zion, the city of the great King.

74^{12}. God is my King from of old; some commentators, probably rightly, would read Thou, Yahweh, art my King from of old.

84^3. . . . Yahweh Zebaoth, my King and my God.

95^3. For Yahweh is a great God, and a great King above all gods.

98^6. Make a joyful noise before the King; "Yahweh" is probably a later addition as it overloads the half-line.

149^2. Let the children of Zion be joyful in their King.

In 9^7, cp. 29^{10}, the title is, no doubt, implied. In 20^9 the title is not applied to Yahweh, but is in reference to the earthly king. It occurs also in 47^2, but this comes also under our third class of passages. It may be added that the title of "King" is applied to Yahweh in Isa. 44^6, Mic. 2^{13}, Zeph. 3^{15}.

(2) REFERENCES TO THE THRONE OF YAHWEH:

9^4. Thou satest on thy throne judging righteously.

9^7. He hath set up his throne for judgement.

11^4. Yahweh, in heaven is his throne.

47^8. . . . he sitteth upon his holy throne.

89^{14}. Righteousness and justice are the stay of thy throne.

93^2. Established is his throne from of old.

97^2. Righteousness and justice are the foundation of his throne.

103^{19}. Yahweh in the heavens hath established his throne.

Outside the Psalter the mention of Yahweh's throne occurs in 1 Kgs. 22^{19}, 2 Chron. 18^{18}, Isa. 6^1, 66^1, Jer. 14^{21}, 17^{12}, Lam. 5^{19}, Ezek. 1^{26}, 10^1, 43^7.

(3) PASSAGES IN WHICH THE PHRASE "YAHWEH IS BECOME KING" OCCURS:

$47^{7,8}$. in both verses we should probably read "Yahweh" for "God": Yahweh is become King of all the earth; Yahweh is become King over the nations.

93^1. Yahweh is become King apparelled in majesty.

96^{10}. Declare among the nations, Yahweh is become King.

97^1. Yahweh is become King, let the earth rejoice.

99^1. Yahweh is become King, let the peoples tremble.

The phrase occurs also in Isa. 24^{23}; in Mic. 4^7 the text is uncertain. When we come to inquire, What is the significance of speaking of Yahweh as "King", and of the phrase "Yahweh is become King"? we enter upon a very controversial subject. According to some authorities, among whom Gunkel [1] is an outstanding figure, the expression "Yahweh is become King" is an adaptation of the saluta-

[1] Einleitung in die Psalmen, pp. 95 ff. (1933).

tion addressed to the newly made temporal king, to a spiritual use. In 2 Sam. 15[10], for example, it is said : " But Absalom sent spies throughout all the tribes of Israel, saying, As soon as ye hear the sound of the ram's-horn (*šôphar*) then shall ye say, Absalom is become king in Hebron ". It must, however, be observed that as a technical expression, addressed to a newly made king, ". . . is become king ", does not occur elsewhere ; if it were the usual mode of recognition, we should expect to find it more frequently expressed.

On the other hand, as Gunkel clearly shows, the *ceremonial* observed at the enthronement of the king has a number of parallels in the psalms referred to ; two especially outstanding ceremonies are described : the anointing by a priest with the placing of the crown on the king's head, followed by a solemn procession up the hill of Zion, and the formal sitting on the throne (1 Kgs. 1[34, 38 ff.], 2 Kgs. 11[12 ff.], 1 Chron. 29[23]).

In celebration of such a highly important event it would have been the obvious duty of the court poets to compose poems proper to the occasion, just as we have in Ps. 45 a poem written in honour of a royal marriage. But none such have come down to us. Gunkel, however, maintains that they must have existed, and that the so-called Enthronement psalms (*i.e.*, those mentioned above) were the sacred counterpart of such secular songs. But, as he points out—and this is the point of main importance—in adapting these secular songs, the psalmists brought into their sacred compositions eschatological elements (see below). Here some questions necessarily suggest themselves : Why was the title " King " applied to Yahweh ? How are we to understand the phrase, " Yahweh is become King " ? What was the point and object of his Enthronement at the feast at which it was celebrated ? Why did the psalmists embody eschatological material in the psalms in question ?

In seeking to give answers to these questions we shall have to travel over a somewhat wide field, and the answers cannot always be kept distinct from one another, for the subjects to be dealt with do not admit of being separated off into different compartments.

It is common knowledge, and needs no emphasis, that the Israelites, in every stage of their history, were subject to extraneous influences, religious, cultural, and others ; these influences were the more likely to have been effective in that they were exercised by peoples of greater antiquity and higher culture than the Israelites. In answer to our first question, Why was the title " King " applied to Yahweh ? it must be replied that there was, so far as Israel was concerned, no justifiable reason for this ; to apply a human title to their God, who was so immeasurably above men in every conceivable way, was alien to their religious sense. But owing to the force of extraneous influence, exercised by their powerful neighbours, they fell into the use ; though it occurs but rarely until later times, when it had acquired a special, an eschatological, meaning. The idea of a god as king is found among the Babylonians and the Egyptians. In the Babylonian Creation Epic known as *Enuma eliš*, from the opening words, " When above ", it is told of how the gods, in their gratitude to Marduk for having overcome the monster Tiamat, " rejoiced, and rendered him homage (saying), Marduk is become king ".[1]   In another text it is said that the Kingdom, *i.e.*, the idea of royalty, came down from heaven.[2] Again, in Egyptian religion the god Horus was the king who first ruled over all men. The sign of the falcon stands both for " god " and " king ".[3] Other illustrations could be given. We submit, therefore, that whatever significance may have become attached to the title in later Jewish thought, in origin it was due to extraneous influence.

The answer to our next question, How are we to understand the phrase " Yahweh is become King " ? is far more complicated. We must preface our remarks by asserting that the title of " King " applied to Yahweh has not *necessarily* any connexion with the technical phrase " Yahweh is become King ", and all that it implies ; in certain cases there certainly is a connexion between the two, but generally speaking this is not so.

It is quite certain, from the content of the psalms in which this phrase occurs, that they were sung liturgically at one of the great festivals. This is to be gathered from the fact that in these psalms ceremonies are referred to which necessarily imply liturgical usage. First, there is this phrase " Yahweh is become King " ; a proclamation such as this must, from its very nature, have been uttered in reference to something that had just taken place ; in other words, it refers to the ceremony of Yahweh having ascended his throne. However we may envisage the actual performance of this ceremony (see below), the words of Ps. 47[5, 8] point to a ceremonial rite : *God ascendeth with a shout, Yahweh with the blast of the ram's-horn* ; that the ascent upon his throne is here referred to is seen by the words : *Yahweh is become King over the nations, he sitteth upon his holy throne.* The mention of the " shout " and " the blast of the ram's-horn " point to an accompanying rite ; similarly in Ps. 98[6] : *With trumpets and the blast of the ram's-horn make a joyful noise before the King.* That a ceremonial procession took place goes without saying, for this was the usual accompaniment to religious celebrations ; some commentators take the words *God ascendeth with a shout* to be in reference to a procession ascending Mount Zion ; it may be so, but the context seems to point to the ascent upon the throne. Another very important part of the ceremony

---

[1] Ebeling, in Gressmann's, *Altorientalische Texte zum alten Testament*, p. 109 (1926).
[2] *Ibid.*, p. 147.   [3] Erman, *Die Religion der Ägypter*, p. 51 (1934).

was the commemoration of Yahweh as Creator; this was extremely appropriate; and in connexion with this it was natural enough that other elements in the Creation-story, as traditionally handed down, should be sung. Thus, the primeval combat of Yahweh with the waters of the great deep, conceived of as the embodiment of the evil powers, and his victory over them, receive notice; and the mythical picture is adapted and made to apply to God's victory over the nations. That this is eschatologically interpreted does not admit of doubt, hence the emphasis laid on Yahweh as Judge.

We must seek next to answer the question : *What was the point and object of the ceremony of Yahweh's Enthronement?* And here we come to the central part of our whole discussion; for, as we have insisted, this ceremony was the initial rite at the celebration of one of the great feasts. We have first to inquire what feast this was. It would necessarily have been a feast at which the Enthronement ceremony was appropriate; a feast which brought before the worshippers the thought of Yahweh's power and supremacy. There is plenty of evidence, though space forbids our going into details, to show that this feast was the *New Year Festival, celebrated by the Israelites concurrently with the feast of Tabernacles.*[1] That these two coincided is sufficiently well known,[2] and need not detain us; our main concern is to examine their nature and significance, and the connexion that the Enthronement ceremony had with them. To do this it is necessary to go back to origins.

In both ancient Egypt and Babylonia there was, in the celebration of the New Year Festival, a " ritual pattern ", as Hooke appropriately designates it, representing " the things which were done to and by the king in order to secure the prosperity of the community in every sense for the coming year ".[3] The central feature was thus the importance of the king who, both in Egypt and Babylon, was regarded as divine, and represented the god in the great seasonal rituals. This does not, however, mean to say that the god himself was not worshipped; we have, for example, a very striking psalm sung at the Near Year Festival in honour of the god Horus, who has overcome his enemies, and ascended upon his throne; this is worth quoting :

> Come, shout, ye gods of the land,
> Come, rejoice, ye men and people,
> Come, sing praise with gladness of heart,
> Horus hath ascended his throne . . .
> He will refresh what lay waste,
> He will gladden the downcast hearts,
> He will save all men.
> Regard ye Horus, he weareth his crown . . .
> He strideth far and wide o'er the land.

---

[1] For details see Volz, *Das Neujahrsfest Jahwes*, pp. 12 ff. (1912).
[2] Oesterley, in *Myth and Ritual* (ed. S. H. Hooke), pp. 122 f. (1933).
[3] *Myth and Ritual*, p. 8.

The ' Nine gods ' kiss the ground before him . . .
Regard ye Horus, ye gods and men,
And rejoice because of his crown . . .
He hath crushed the heads of his foes . . .
Regard ye Horus, ye gods and men,
How he entereth the conflict and conquereth,
Like a blaze in the time of the storm,
When it rageth in the midst of the thorn-bush,
Consuming, and nothing is left.[1]

Here a word must be said about the question of the ascription of divinity to the earthly king. That, as just remarked, the king was looked upon as divine in both Egypt and Babylon is indisputable. Thus, the Pharaoh of Egypt was identified with Ra [2]; in some of the titles applied to him he is called the god Horus; in one song he is called " our Horus " [3]; a reflection of this may be seen in the Tell-Amarna letters, where the Palestinian rulers address their Egyptian suzerain as " My Sun " (Šamaš). In much later times the Assyrian kings Ashurna-sirpal and Shalmaneser II call themselves " the Sun of the peoples ", whereby they wish to indicate their illimitable power.[4] That the idea of the king-god was not unknown in Israel even as late as the time of Ezekiel is evident from what the prophet says : " Son of ,man, say unto the prince of Tyre, Thus saith the Lord Yahweh : Because thine heart is lifted up, and thou hast said, I am a god, I sit in the seat of God, in the midst of the seas ; yet thou art man, and not God, though thou didst set thine heart as the heart of God." We even find in two of the psalms an identification of the king with God : Ps. 45[6], 110[2]. We have drawn attention to this to show how the Israelites were influenced here by extraneous ideas. This is seen, further, when we compare the ritual of the New Year Festival, as celebrated in Egypt [5] and Babylon [6], with what is said in some of the psalms in references to the same Festival, and which coincides, as we have said, with the Feast of Tabernacles (Sukkôth). First we may point out that, with regard to Egypt and Babylon, while many gods are believed in, one stands out as creator and as the giver of the fruits of the earth ; and the earthly king is identified with him. Among the Egyptians this highest god was Osiris, among the Babylonians he was Marduk. At the annual New Year Festival held in honour of these deities, in each case he was proclaimed king, the earthly king representing him ; and this was realistically set forth by the rite of his ascent upon his throne ; this was the opening ceremony at the celebration of the New Year Festival, and it was accompanied by the

[1] Translated from the German rendering of Erman, Die Religion der Ägypter, p. 372 (1934).
[2] Moret, Du caractère religieux de la Royauté Pharaonique, p. 310 (1902).
[3] Erman, op. cit., p. 51.
[4] Jastrow, Die Religion Babyloniens und Assyriens, i, 221 (1905).
[5] As described in the Ramesseum Papyrus (Myth and Ritual, p. 27).
[6] As celebrated at the Akitu Festival (Myth and Ritual, p. 46).

recitation of the Creation drama. Just as in the beginning the god had created all things, so at the beginning of the New Year it was believed that he would repeat the act of creation so far as the fruits of the soil were concerned. The rite, with its various accompanying details which we need not dilate upon here, not only symbolized, but was believed actually to bring about, the revivification of Nature. Its supreme importance in the eyes of the people will, therefore, be realized.

Now, we have more than once insisted, and the fact will not be disputed, that the Israelites were to a considerable extent dominated by extraneous influences, and this in the religious as well as in other spheres. Here we have a striking illustration of this. What Osiris was to the Egyptians and what Marduk was to the Babylonians, Yahweh was to the Israelites. Each nation had its King-God. The New Year Festival of the Israelites was celebrated on the first day of the Feast of Tabernacles, when the Kingship of Yahweh was proclaimed, and when he was honoured as Lord of Creation by recalling his work of Creation at the beginning. Faith in his power gave the conviction that the produce of the soil during the coming year would be abundant. It is here that we see the significance of the references to the Kingship of Yahweh in the psalms sung at this festival; we need not quote from them, the relevant passages have been given above (p. 45).

We have already mentioned that at the New Year Festival in Egypt and Babylon an essential element was the recitation of the Creation Epic in order to honour the god as creator. That this was done during the Israelite celebration cannot be doubted when we recall some of the passages occurring in the psalms sung on this occasion; one or two quotations may be given. A reference to Yahweh's creative power, and faith in the continuance of the exercise of that power in the coming year, is clear in Ps. 65^{9-13}:

Thou visitest the earth, and waterest it,   thou greatly enrichest it.
The brook of God is full of water,   thou providest their corn, thus thou
          preparest it :
Thou waterest her furrows, levelling the ridges,   dost soften it with rain and blessest its
          growth.

See also Ps. $104^{13\,\text{ff.}}$, and various other passages.

Further, in the Creation Epic a prominent element is the combat and victory of Marduk over Tiamat, the personification of the watery deep. This, too, we find in the psalms sung at this festival; but Yahweh is now represented as the Victor; thus, in Ps. 74^{12-14} it is said:

But thou, O God,   art my King for ever,
Working triumph   in the midst of the earth.
Thou didst defeat   the sea by thy might,
The heads of the monsters   didst crush on the waters ;
Thou didst shatter   the heads of Leviathan,
Gavest him as meat,   as fodder to jackals.

The theme appears in many other passages.

Then, finally, there was the formal procession which was an important part of the ceremony; and this, too, receives frequent mention in the psalms; one passage may be quoted, Ps. 68[24-26]:

> Behold ye the processions of Yahweh,
> Thy processions, my God,   my King, in the sanctuary;
> The singers go before,   the minstrels follow after,
> In the midst are the maidens beating the timbrels.

One more question suggested itself which we must seek briefly to answer : why did the psalmists embody eschatological material in the psalms sung at this festival? That such material does appear in the psalms in question needs no insisting on; but we shall give some illustrations. In Ps. 47[2-8] (Hebr. [3-9]) it is said :

> For Yahweh, the Most High,   is terrible,
> A great King   over all the earth,
> He subdueth peoples under us,   and nations under our feet . . .
> For Yahweh is become King over all the earth,   sing to God a choice-song,
> Yahweh is become King over the nations,   he sitteth upon his holy throne.

Such words cannot conceivably refer to the present; after the prophetic style, the future is envisaged as present, as an act of faith; but the actual present is not referred to. What is in the psalmist's mind is the return of the primeval time of bliss at the end of the present world-order (see further on this Ps. 85, intr. section). Again, in Ps. 96, where "Yahweh is become King" occurs (v. 10), we read :

> . . . Yahweh, for he cometh,   for he cometh to judge the earth;
> He judgeth the world in righteousness,   and the people in his faithfulness (v. 13).

The Judgement is another of the outstanding events in the Eschatological Drama. In Ps. 97, which begins with "Yahweh is become King", apocalyptic traits occur in vv. 2-5. In Ps. 98[9] the Judgement is again referred to. In Ps. 99, too, a condition is envisaged which is applicable only to the time when, at the end of the present world-order, Yahweh reigns in righteousness (vv. 3, 4):

> Let them praise his name, great and terrible,   holy is he, and a mighty King;
> Thou hast established equity in Jacob,   justice and righteousness hast thou ordained.

It is unnecessary to give further illustrations of the fact that in the psalms sung at the New Year Festival, i.e., the Feast of Tabernacles, eschatological thought played a prominent part (see also 46[6], 47[2-9], 48[4-8], 76[4-12], 149[7-9]).

Now, there must have been some special reason why the psalmists should have made such a point of bringing eschatological themes into the psalms written to be sung at the New Year Festival, celebrated at the Feast of Tabernacles, and especially at its opening ceremony of the Enthronement of Yahweh. As is to be expected, opinions differ here. Mowinckel explains it by saying that all that was originally expected to happen during the coming year as the direct result of what was envisaged during the ritual of the annual celebration of Yahweh's Enthronement was assigned to an indefinite future time, as something that would ultimately come to pass when Yahweh finally ascended his throne for ever, when his enemies would be overcome and the Judgement take place, and when he would fulfil all the hopes and expectations of his people, and abide among them as the Light, and the eternal source of life. And he goes so far as to say that the entire Eschatological Drama originated in the ritual of what he calls the Festival of Yahweh's ascent upon his throne.[1] Needless to say that, with the evidence of the "ritual pattern" of Egypt and Babylonia before us, and for various other reasons which could be adduced, we disagree *in toto* with this view. Scarcely less astonishing is Hans Schmidt's contention that an eschatological interpretation of these psalms is out of the question.[2] On this view we refrain from commenting. *The majority of scholars agree with Gunkel in recognizing the presence of eschatological thought in the psalms, whatever other elements they may contain.* But in other directions we find ourselves unable to agree with Gunkel. We have already drawn attention to his view that the "Yahweh is become King" psalms were adaptations of secular songs composed in honour of the earthly king; in doing so, the psalmists, he goes on to say, "naturally thought of Israel as the dominion of Yahweh, and believed in a *present* kingdom of God. . . . But the contradiction between believing and seeing in the evil times of alien rule, led to the belief in a *future* kingdom of Yahweh."[3] This belief, he holds, the psalmists took over from the prophets, and together with it their eschatological teaching.

In view of what has been said about the "ritual pattern" so frequently reflected in the psalms, it will be gathered that we can agree with this theory only in so far that the psalms in question must be understood in an eschatological sense. *It may well be that the psalmists were influenced by prophetical teaching here;* but not necessarily, and certainly not wholly. When one remembers the world-wide belief in the return of the "Golden Age", whether we think of it as embodied in the "ritual pattern" or whether we speak of it in the Hebrew form of the "Day of Yahweh", it is not a great stretch of the imagination to suppose that the psalmists were aware of the hope apart from anything contained in the prophetical writings. The general familiarity with it among the people, however misunderstood, is amply shown by what we read in, *e.g.*, Am. 5[18-20].

We have now attempted to answer the questions we set ourselves, though we fully realize that many points of detail have had to be left aside. There is so much to be said, and space is limited.

---

[1] *Psalmenstudien*, ii, 226.   [2] *Die Thronfahrt . . .*, pp. 5 ff.
[3] *Einleitung . . .*, p. 98.

A few words are, however, called for regarding the date of the type of psalms with which we have been dealing. It should first be remarked that there is reason to believe that they all belong to approximately the same period; but whatever that period may have been, the bulk of the material they contain goes back in origin to very early times. The celebration of the New Year Festival, for which the psalms in question were composed, was observed, in some form, long before the time of the monarchy; indeed, there is every reason to believe that soon after the settlement in Palestine, when the Israelites came under the influence of Canaanite worship, the celebration of this festival came into vogue among them. It follows, therefore, that so far as the references to the celebration of the Enthronement of Yahweh, and the other ceremonies connected with it, are concerned, the writers of the psalms in question utilized ancient material. Then, again, the large amount of eschato- logical detail contained in these psalms goes back in origin to earlier times. These considerations point to the fact that the New Year Festival psalms are adaptations of earlier forms; for that psalms had always been sung on this occasion there is no reason to doubt. From what has been said it might be gathered that we are contending for a very early date for these psalms; this, however, is not our purpose, so far as their *present form* is concerned; we have been referring only to the utilization of early material on the part of the writers of these psalms. Upon the whole, however, we should be inclined to suspect that these psalms have a pre-exilic basis, being adapted later to the simpler and purer *cultus*, which, as we may suppose, prevailed in the age when Israel's religion was dominated by " P ". This may, moreover, be the reason for some of the metrical irregularities which appear in these psalms.

Some other facts have next to be considered.

The fact that prophetical utterances regarding the occurrences which are to take place at the end of the present world-order were laid under contribution by the writers of these psalms, in their present form, undoubtedly indicates the approximate time of their composition; but it must be remembered that, as just hinted, the material utilized by the prophets was of hoary antiquity. These psalms in their present form belonged, then, at any rate, to the post-prophetical period. Further, the marked indebtedness of the psalmists in question to the thought and diction of Deutero-Isaiah points to a post-exilic date for their composition as we now have them. But the post-exilic period extended to over five centuries prior to the beginning of the Christian era. The question, therefore, is whether there are any indications which may help towards a more definite time within this long period to which these psalms may be assigned. It must be confessed that such indications are few and uncertain. The psalms themselves

E

assume an elaborate resuscitation of the temple-worship such as is hardly likely to have taken place during the times of either Nehemiah or Ezra ; this would imply a date for them about the middle of the fourth century B.C. On the other hand, there is absolutely nothing that points to a Maccabæan date of any of them. The apocalyptic literature with its *fully developed eschatology* began to take shape towards the end of the third century B.C. ; so that our psalms are likely to be earlier than this ; for although full of eschatological material, this is not so developed as in the eschatological literature proper. Again, the marked universalism of these psalms, though undoubtedly largely due to Deutero-Isaiah, is likely to have received a further impetus as a result of the spread of Greek influence. Upon the whole, therefore, it was during the early part of the Greek period, about 300 B.C., that these psalms, as we now have them, are most likely to have been written.

Something must be said, in conclusion, regarding the religious teaching in general contained in these psalms. There is, first, the religious significance of the myths from which the conception of the Kingship of Yahweh was derived. Myths, the pictorial embodiment of ideas and beliefs, were, in the early history of mankind, one of the normal methods accorded to man of divine self-revelation, so far as this could be apprehended by man in an undeveloped stage of culture. They must, therefore, be regarded as embodying the germs of living truths which, with the gradual development of the religious sense, approximated more and more to reality. The idea of the Kingship of Yahweh, derived from the Egyptian and Babylonian myths of the king god, was the attribution to Yahweh of what to human ideas was the highest expression of power and authority ; the king was supreme ; therefore to attribute Kingship to Yahweh was to honour him to the utmost. But kingship assumes rule ; at first the rule was over Israel, then it became world-wide dominion ; and thus by degrees the steps led upward, reaching ultimately the Christian conception of the Kingdom of God. In these "Enthronement" psalms we see the process of development. Again, the frequent references in them, direct and implied, to the enmity between Yahweh and the waters of the sea, is the adaptation of the myth of Marduk's victory over Tiamat, the Great Deep, the personification of all harmfulness, to Yahweh. But his enemies are now the nations of the world who do not acknowledge him. What was originally merely harmfulness develops, with the growth of the religious sense, into wickedness. Yahweh overcomes his enemies, and they bow down before him in humble recognition of his supremacy.

Then, as to belief in Yahweh and the conceptions regarding him. There is no doubt that the most prominent feature here is his illimitable power, and that therefore praise and worship are due to him ; the reiterated call to praise him is unquestionably the most outstanding element in these psalms. On the other hand, an absolute monotheism is not taught; the references to other gods, though of deep inferiority to Yahweh, show that their existence was believed in; and therefore monotheism in the strict sense cannot be said to be taught in these psalms. In another direction, however, the conception of Yahweh is very exalted—namely, the emphasis laid on his ethical righteousness; this is constantly proclaimed among the peoples of the world, and it receives its highest expression in the pronouncement that he comes to judge the world in righteousness. From this it follows naturally that Yahweh's holiness should be insisted on, and if this is not often expressed, it is because such an attribute is taken for granted.

An universalistic outlook is prominent; where eschatological beliefs play so great a part this is to be expected. The absence of all mention of sacrifices will also be noted; the exhortation to " bring gifts " (96[8]) does not refer to sacrifices.

We hope that the various questions connected with the complicated subject of the Kingship of Yahweh have now been sufficiently dealt with.

CHAPTER VIII

SAINTS AND SINNERS IN THE PSALMS

THE large number of psalms in which antagonism between the righteous and their enemies is described, often in much detail, is common knowledge, for it is one of the most distinguishing marks occurring in the Psalter. In some cases it may well be that quarrels of the ordinary kind, common to mankind, form the subject-matter of the psalms in question. It is not this that we have in mind. We are thinking of cases in which, though antipathy between individuals may lurk, the kind of enmity expressed suggests something more deep-seated and extended than merely personal quarrels. We do not for a moment deny that in some of the psalms in question other elements than that with which we are particularly concerned may have entered in. Thus, Mowinckel's very ingenious arguments in support of his theory that the enemies of the saints were magicians are full of interest; and the illustrative Babylonian material adduced in support is distinctly impressive. That there is an element of truth in his contention we would not deny; but we cannot get away from the conviction that Mowinckel over-estimates the presence of magical elements. The subject is dealt with in his *Psalmenstudien* I (1921). Of much interest also is Nicolsky's *Spuren magischer Formeln in den Psalmen* (1927).

The frequent mention of antagonism between the righteous and their enemies gives the impression that the strife between the two was of a permanent, or at least recurrent, character, and recorded a condition of rift within the community which was fundamental in its nature. To discover the cause, or causes, of this state of affairs is a complicated matter, and involves some investigation into the history of the nation during more than one period. Our first task must be to examine the terms applied, respectively, to those between whom this state of conflict endured; but it will be understood that the terms are not necessarily always employed, the allusion being sufficiently clear without them.

    i. *Ḥasid*,[1] plur. *Ḥasidim*: " godly one ", " godly ones " (E.VV.

---

[1] From the root meaning " to be kind ", which is, however, used only in a reflexive sense, " to show oneself kind ". The noun, *ḥesed*, with which it is connected, has various meanings, according to the context, " kindness ", " mercy ", " love ", " piety ". The adjectival form, *i.e.*, that under consideration, *Ḥasid*, is passive in idea, as though in reference to the recipient of mercies; but its usage shows that it is active *in sense*, in reference to one who is zealous in his practice of devotion to God, pious, or saintly, and who thereby shows his love for God; hence our rendering of " godly one ", for *Ḥasid*, in preference to " saint ", which has come to have a somewhat different connotation.

" saints "). It is important to note that the mention of antagonism between the God-fearing and the wicked is not confined to the *Psalms*; it is referred to, *e.g.*, in Mal. 3$^{13-16}$; and that it existed in pre-exilic times can be seen by such passages as Jer. 12$^{1-3}$, Zeph. 2$^{1-3}$. It must also be noted that these terms *Ḥasid*, *Ḥasidim* are likewise not confined to the *Psalms*, though they occur there far more frequently than in other books. Thus, in Mic. 7^2, *e.g.*, it is said : " The godly man (*Ḥasid*) is perished out of the land, and there is none upright among men " ; see also 2 Chron. 6^{41}, Prov. 2^8; and the expressions " men of *ḥesed* " (Isa. 57^1), " man of *ḥesed* " (Prov. 11^{17}), connote much the same idea. Again, it must be observed that in the *Psalms* themselves *Ḥasid* is not always used in a restricted sense ; in 145^{17} it is applied to Yahweh (the same is found in Jer. 3^{12}), and in 89^{19} to the prophet Nathan. Further, there are some passages in which these terms are used in a general sense, not necessarily in reference to a particular body of men ; thus, in 32^6 it is said : " Let everyone that is godly (*Ḥasid*) pray unto thee " ; that applies to anyone in the community ; similarly in 79^2, " thy godly ones " and " thy servants " are parallel ; it can hardly be contended that the " servants " of God applies only to a restricted body ; again, in 85^8 " his godly ones " is parallel to " his people " ; clearly the term is used in a general sense here ; so, too, in 148^{14} " all his godly ones " is parallel to " his people " ; instructive, too, is 139^9, where " his priests " and " his godly ones " are parallel ; it is not to be supposed that the latter were confined to the priesthood ; nor could this be the case if the term were used in a restricted sense in this passage. Finally, there is the unusual expression, in 43^1, a " nation not-godly ". In all these passages, then—and there may be some others—*Ḥasid*, or *Ḥasidim*, are used in a general sense.

But there are, on the other hand, a larger number of passages in which these terms are used in a restricted sense as applying to a particular body of men, or, as we should say, a party or sect ; for in these passages, which deal with the antagonism between the " godly ones " and their enemies, it is not simply a question of quarrels, and the like, that arise between individuals in the ordinary vicissitudes of life ; the expressions used, and the procedure described, point to party strife. This will be best illustrated by examining the characteristics of the " godly ones ", and then by noting the type of men who are their enemies, and the methods used by the latter in their attacks upon their victims.

The *religious* character of the *Ḥasid*, whether applied by the psalmist to himself, or as representing the body of the " godly ones ", may be briefly set forth as follows : although, as we have seen, there are certain passages in which " thy godly ones ", or " his (Yahweh's) godly ones ", are evidently used in a general sense, there are others, and more in number, in which this use of the possessive pronoun indicates those who are marked off from the generality of their fellows; and this suggests a body, or party, characterized by special devotion to God. This is further illustrated by descriptive epithets applied to the Ḥasid; he is spoken of as "righteous" (e.g., 7[9], 11[3, 5]); similarly as "upright of heart" (e.g., 164[10], cp. 14[5]); he is "perfect", a term meaning innocence from all evil (e.g., 18[23], 37[18], 64[4]); and various other epithets of a like import are applied to him. So that the Ḥasid is one whose outstanding characteristic is loyalty to Yahweh.

Then, as to Ḥasid and Ḥasidim being used in the restricted sense of adherents to a party. It is true that "thy godly ones" is sometimes used, as we have seen, in a general sense; but in certain passages in which this expression occurs the context points to its use in a more restricted sense. Thus, in 52[9] the psalmist says: "I will declare [emended text] thy name, for it is good, in the presence of thy godly ones"; the words "in the presence of thy godly ones" suggest a gathering of a particular kind. Again, in 50[5] it is said: "Gather my godly ones together unto me, those that have made a covenant with me by sacrifice". Suggestive also is the mention of "the assembly of the godly ones" in 149[1], which quite evidently refers to an exclusive gathering. And there are a number of other passages from which the impression is gained that the Ḥasidim were a compact body standing aloof not only from those who were avowedly the enemies of religion, but also distinctive as compared with their own people generally.

To sum up, then: the terms Ḥasid and Ḥasidim are not confined to the Psalms, though used there more frequently than elsewhere. In the Psalms the term Ḥasidim is sometimes used in a general sense applying to all those who acknowledge God and worship him; but more frequently it is used in a restricted sense denoting a special body of the godly in the community. In this latter use the outstanding characteristic of the Ḥasidim is their very devoted and strict loyalty to Yahweh, and ardent observance of his commandments; so that they are religious in a more definite and fuller sense than others.

ii. 'Ebyon ,'Aniy, 'Anaw: these three terms, meaning respectively "poor", "downtrodden", "humble" (the last two sometimes confused together), are referred to because they are applied to the Ḥasidim in a number of passages. A few of these may be given by way of illustration. In 86[12] the psalmist, speaking of himself, but as representing others too, says: "I am poor and downtrodden, preserve my soul, for I am a godly one [Ḥasid]", cp. 40[17], 70[5], 109[22]; in 109[16] it is said that the wicked man "persecuted the downtrodden and the poor man"; similarly in 37[14]: "The wicked have drawn out the sword and have bent their bow, to cast down the poor and the downtrodden". They are, however, spoken of as being specially under Yahweh's care, and are thus to be identified with the godly; in 35[10] it is said that Yahweh

" delivereth the downtrodden from him that is too strong for him,
and the poor from him that spoileth him "; see, too, 140^{13}; and
again in 9^{18} : " For the poor shall not always be forgotten, nor the hope
of the humble perish for ever ". The usage in general of these terms
shows them to refer to the humbler classes (*e.g.*, Isa. $3^{14, 15}$, 10^2, Am. 2^7),
and this applies, as a rule, to their use in the *Psalms*, though in some cases
it may well be that no social distinction is intended.

    iii. *Rašaʿ*, plur. *Rᵉšaʿim* : " wicked man ", " wicked ones ". We
have taken those terms as those used in reference to the enemies of the
Ḥasidim because they are the ones which occur most frequently,
but others occur [1]; *ʾOyeb*, " enemy ", or " foe ", is also often used,
and there are various other terms applied to them. In order to get
some idea of the characteristics of these enemies, and of their methods
of attack upon the *Ḥasidim*, it will be necessary to give some quotations.
It must be noted first, that, as in the case of *Ḥasidim*, the " wicked "
are referred to both in a general sense and in a more restricted sense ;
in this latter they seem to be thought of as forming a special body
in the community. For the former we have, *e.g.*, $7^{8, 9}$, where the
wicked are spoken of quite generally, being mentioned in the same
context as " the peoples " ; similarly in 9^{17} : " Let the wicked turn
away to Sheol, all the nations that forget God " (see also $11^{5, 6}$, $58^{1 ff.}$,
where the wicked are spoken of generally as " the sons of men ") ;
in 73^{1-12}, again, the wicked in general are spoken of : it is unnecessary
to give further references. On the other hand, various passages deal
with the wicked in a way which points to their being a particular body
of men. A clear instance is 1^1 : " Happy is the man that walketh not
in the counsel [*i.e.* advice] of the wicked . . . nor sitteth in the seat
[or circle] of scorners " ; a somewhat similar thought occurs in 64^2,
where the " secret counsel " of evil-doers is mentioned ; that must
refer to some special gathering, not to the wicked in general. In
the same way, when in 86^{14} the phrase " the assembly of violent men "
occurs, this can hardly be understood in a general sense. There
are many other passages to the same effect. So that, as in the case of
the *Ḥasidim*, so too in that of the *Rᵉšaʿim*, the term is used sometimes
in a general, at other times in a restricted, sense. We realize that to
any careful reader of the *Psalms* this is self-evident ; but there is a
special reason for drawing attention to the fact, as will be seen. Our
next point must be to describe the character of the " wicked " as
portrayed in the *Psalms*, and to observe their methods of attack against
the " godly ". These methods are of two kinds, and that fact is, perhaps
not without significance. There is, first, frequent mention of verbal
vituperation ; the forms of abuse and accusation are bitter, deceitful,
and untruthful : " they have whet their tongue like a sword, they have

---

[1] Strictly speaking, the opposite to *Rašaʿ* is *Ṣaddiq*, " righteous ".

sharpened like arrows bitter speech " (64^3); in metaphorical speech they are said to hide a snare, to spread a net, to set gins (140^5, 64^3); they speak lies and are deceitful (5^6, 120^2), adder's poison is under their lips (140^3). But their mo:le of attack is not confined to slander and lying; they are accused further of using physical violence. Thus, in 86^{14} they are referred to as " violent men " (cp. $140^{1, 4}$); their type is spoken of as being " like a lion that is greedy of his prey, as it were a young lion lurking in secret places " (17^{12}); they are described as bloodthirsty and murderous (5^6, 55^{23}); " in the covert places doth he murder the innocent " (10^8; cp. 14^4). Fully in accordance with this it is to be noted that they are the enemies of God as well as of men; thus, in $10^{3, 4}$ it is said: " He revileth Yahweh ", " all his thoughts are, There is no God " ; in 14^1, 53^1: " The fool hath said in his heart, There is no God " ; in 37^{20} they are spoken of as " the enemies of Yahweh " ; so, too, in 68^1, where it is also said that they " hate " God. Their irreligious character is thus clear. One more thing to be noted about them is that they belong to the higher grades of society; their being spoken of as " the haughty ones " (86^{14}), and " the proud ones " (140^5, cp. 94^2) points to this; in 101^5 the man that has " an high look and an arrogant mind " must evidently belong to the upper classes; this is implied, too, in 82^2, where those are blamed who " respect the persons of the wicked " ; and that they are spoken of as having riches and being in prosperity ($73^{3, 12}$) similarly shows that they belong to wealthy circles.

The opponents of the *Ḥasidim* are thus slanderous in their accusations, violent in their attacks, irreligious, and they belong to the powerful and wealthy circles among the people.

Our next task must be to consider the question of the causes which led to the enmity between the *Hasidim* and the *Reša'im* ; for this purpose it will be necessary to glance at the history during three periods.

i. The Pre-exilic Period.

We have seen that in the *Psalms* both these terms are used now in a general, now in a restricted, sense, and that the antagonism between the two was due both to religious and social causes. Now the prophetical books make it abundantly clear that already in the eighth century, and indeed earlier, the prophets championed a pure Yahweh-worship as against the syncretistic tendencies of the mass of the people arising from the influences of Canaanite religion. That the prophets had their special following, though composed of a small minority, needs no insisting on (see, *e.g.*, 1 Kgs. 18^{13}, 19^{18}, Isa. 1^9, Am. 3^{12}, $5^{3, 15}$). Thus the causes of differences of religious outlook go back to times long before the Exile. Further, a very cursory reading

of the prophetical books shows that a wide separation existed between
the powerful rich and the helpless poor; the latter were frequently
the victims of cruel maltreatment (see, e.g., Isa. $3^{14, 15}$, $32^{6, 7}$, Jer. 2^{34},
Am. $2^{6, 7}$, 4^1, $5^{11, 12}$, 8^6); but they are spoken of as those for whom
God cares, i.e., those who were faithful to him (e.g., Isa. 11^4, 29^{19},
Jer. 20^{13}). So that social as well as religious differences existed in
pre-exilic times. It follows, therefore, that the use, in the *Psalms*,
of the terms *Ḥasidim* and *R^eša'im* in a general sense can be readily
understood, for religious and social differences among the people
had existed long before causes arose which led to the formation of parties,
in reference to which the terms are used in the restricted sense.

But attention must now be drawn to another cause of division among
the people, a religious-political one, which played an important part
in the ultimate formation of parties. This may, or may not, have been
in the minds of some of the psalmists; direct evidence does certainly
not appear; but it is highly probable that they refer to it implicitly.
The matter is a somewhat complicated one, but the bare outline of the
argument will suffice for our present purpose.[1] It is clear that the
official priesthood centred in the house of Zadok (2 Sam. 8^{17}, 15^{24}, 19^{11},
20^{25}, I Kgs. $1^{34, 39}$); but long before that time the priestly functions were
exercised by the house of Ithamar, who was descended from Aaron (Exod.
6^{23}, 28^1, Num. 3^{2-4}, I Chron. $6^3 [5^{29}] 24^{1-6}$)[2]; the Zadokites, therefore,
displaced the Ithamar priesthood from the position of precedence; and
they introduced certain changes, while their rivals clung to ancient
usage. The earliest echoes of these changes, it is true, are not heard
of till much later times (e.g., contrast Lev. 21^{14} with Ezek. 44^{22})[3];
but such echoes are sufficient to prove earlier existing differences.
At any rate, the main point is that the upholders of ancient tradition
were overborne by the innovators; this, in the nature of things, brought
about, if not the formation of parties, at any rate opposed points of
view. In this connexion Jer. 6^{16-20} is very instructive; it bears
witness to the existence of these tendencies: "Thus saith Yahweh,
stand ye in the ways and see, and ask for the old paths, where is the
good way, and walk therein, and ye shall find rest for your souls;
but they said, We will not walk therein. And I set watchmen over
you, (saying), Hearken to the sound of the trumpet; but they said,
We will not hearken. Therefore hear, ye peoples, ye shepherds of the
flocks.[4] Hear, O earth: Behold, I will bring evil upon this people,
even the fruit of their thoughts, because they have not hearkened unto

---

[1] For details see Aptowitzer, *Parteipolitik der Hasmonäerzeit* . . ., pp. xxii ff.
(1927).
[2] See further, Desnoyers, *Histoire de Peuple Hébreu*, III, 212 ff. (1930).
[3] Aptowitzer, *Spuren des Matriarchats im jüdischen Schrifttum*, Exkurs v, "Endo-gamie" (in Hebrew Union College Annual V).
[4] Following the Septuagint.

my words ; and as for my law, they have rejected it.   To what purpose
cometh there to me frankincense from Sheba, and the sweet calamus
from a far country ?   Your burnt offerings are not acceptable, nor
your sacrifices pleasing unto me."   Here we must quote Skinner's
excellent comment on the prophet's words : " Two methods he had
tried in vain.   He had appealed to the conservative principle which is
essential to sound religious development.   He had called the people
to pause and consider the diverse tendencies of their age, and to follow
that which was in harmony with the historic faith of Israel.   The
' old paths ' are the genuine ethical principles of the Mosaic revelation
embodied in the traditional Tôrā or teaching of Yahweh (v. 19).   These
are contrasted with the new-fangled costly refinements in cultus—
'frankincense from Sheba,' and 'sweet calamus from a far country'—
through which their new spiritual guides held out the delusive promise
of peace of mind . . . the second method was 'the sound of the
trumpet '—the warnings of providence interpreted by prophecy.
To both appeals the people had turned a deaf ear, and their refusal
is accepted as final : judgement can no longer be averted (vv. 18 f.)." [1]
Of the attitude of the people in general we have no indications, but that
in course of time they took sides is shown by the subsequent history.

ii. The Exilic and Post-exilic Periods.

Our sources give unmistakable evidence of the fact that during the
Exile the priestly circles cultivated an intensive study of the Scriptures,
and especially those parts in which the Law was set forth.   The presence
of prophetical influence is equally in evidence ; Ezekiel at the beginning
and Deutero-Isaiah towards the end of the Exile, are sufficient guarantee
of this.   The religion of Yahweh was, therefore, preserved and taught
during the Exile by both priest and prophet.   But there are indubitable
signs of the existence of a very different tendency among some of the
exiles ; one cannot read such passages as Ezek. 14^{1-8}, Isa. 40^{18-25},
42^{17}, 44^{9-20} without recognizing that the ancestral religion had lost its
hold upon many who were dazzled by the gorgeous displays and impressive ritual of Babylonian worship.   This cannot have failed to
bring about a great cleavage among the Jewish exiles, the echoes of
which, as well as its continuance, may be heard in such passages as
Zeph. 2^{1-3}, Mal. 3^{13-18}.   A cleavage brought about by such a cause
as this was justified and righteous ; but, unfortunately, the subsequent
history shows that the germs of a cleavage of a different character were
also at work.

The records which deal with the earlier period after the return
from the Exile are somewhat confused and contradictory.   It is evident

[1] Prophecy and Religion, Studies in the Life of Jeremiah, pp. 116 f. (1922).

that passages which reflect the conditions of later times have been inserted in the text of the books of *Ezra* and *Nehemiah*, thereby somewhat obscuring things. Nevertheless, two important facts emerge clearly enough: the first is that the High-priesthood was still Zadokite (Zech. 3$^{1-10}$ 6^{11}, " Joshua, the son of Jehozadok the high-priest," see also 1 Esdras 5^{48}); and the second is that a section of the people was entirely out of sympathy with the high-priestly party (Ezra 10^1 Neh. 13$^{4ff.}$ $^{10ff.}$); and they were strengthened in their opposition by both Nehemiah and Ezra on account of the marriages contracted by members of that party with non-Israelite women (Ezra 9$^{1-4}$); the sons of Joshua the son of Jehozadak, are specifically mentioned (Ezra 10^{18}). It is said in Ezra 9^2 that " the hand of the princes and rulers hath been prominent in this trespass "; that is to say, that what we may describe as the " upper classes " and their following were entirely in favour of this. Thus, we have a continuation of much the same conditions as had obtained in earlier times: the Zadokites, supported by the wealthier classes, on the one hand; and those who clung to the older traditions, on the other. As to these latter, it is of importance to note that " the sons of Ithamar " are mentioned among those " who went up " with Ezra " from Babylon " (Ezra. 8^1). Of the antagonism between the two sections within the community during the century or so after the Exile there is sufficient evidence (Isa. 57^{20}, 58^9, 59$^{1-15}$, Mal. 2$^{14-16}$, 3^7-4^6 [3^{24} in Hebr.]).

iii. The Greek Period.

During this period the rift between the upholders of traditional orthodoxy and their opponents became intensified. The reasons for this may be briefly indicated. One of the results of Alexander's conquests was a large intermingling of peoples. Important in the present connexion is the fact that the fall of the Persian Empire resulted in the emigration of many Jews from Persia to the west, where they settled down in Greek centres of civilization. We have evidence showing that, before long, communities of Jews were to be found in almost every part of the civilized world.[1] That Greek cities arose in Palestine, which contained a considerable Jewish element, during the third century B.C. is well known.[2] The result being that there was a direct contact of the Jews with Greek-speaking peoples, Greek thought, culture, customs, and, above all, with Greek religious ideas; this could not fail to affect the Jews in a variety of ways. In these circumstances we must recall what has been said above about the opposition

[1] Schürer, *Geschichte des jüdischen Volkes* . . ., III, 12 ff., where many references to authorities will be found.
[2] Alexander himself settled Macedonians in Samaria; see further, Tarn, *Hellenistic Civilization*, pp. 73–116, 129 ff. (1930).

between those who walked in the old paths and those who were affected by extraneous religious beliefs. Politically, too, the advent of Hellenism, with its founding of new cities and the transformation of older ones, must have resulted in a changed outlook among the Jews. " Wherever Hellenism penetrated, and especially on the Philistine coast and the eastern boundaries of Palestine beyond Jordan, the country districts were grouped around single large cities as their political centres. Each of such communities formed a comparatively independent whole, managing its own internal affairs; its dependence upon the rulers, whether of Egypt, or, later, of Syria, consisted only in the recognition of their military supremacy, the payment of taxes, and certain other performances. At the head of such a hellenistically organized community was a democratic senate of several hundred members.[1] It cannot be doubted that the organization on Greek models of the local government of Jewish cities must have brought a new mental outlook to the Jews. ' [2]   It needs no insisting upon that these conditions offered ample scope for political quarrels, with all the bitterness of spirit engendered thereby.

We have, thus, in Israel from pre-exilic times until well into the Greek period causes of religious and political feuds; and we contend that these are reflected in those psalms in which the antagonism between the *Ḥasidim* and the *Rešaʿim* finds expression. The intermingling of religious and political strife is too obvious to need emphasizing. That numbers among the poorer classes to whom the religion of their forefathers was their most precious possession, should often have been victims of the more powerful, cannot cause surprise.

But to follow out to its bitter end the story of the antagonism of those designated under the comprehensive terms *Ḥasidim* and *Rešaʿim* it will be necessary to say something about a later part of the Greek period.

The breach between sections of the people to which attention has been drawn is now seen to be more pronounced than ever; for the all-pervading spirit of Hellenism had exercised its fascination on large numbers of the Jews, whose adherence to the faith of their fathers had, in consequence, become weaker and weaker. Opposed to them were those who clung with ever-greater tenacity to traditional belief and practice. These two sections corresponded, in general, to those of earlier days: the High-priesthood with its following, supported by the more influential and wealthy classes, as against the larger numbers of ordinary folk, led by the guardians of the faith as handed down. It is important, however, to note that the hellenizing elements among the people existed before the attempt of Antiochus Epiphanes was made

[1] Cp. Schürer, *op. cit.*, II, 95.
[2] Oesterley and Robinson, *A History of Israel*, II, 180 (1934).

to stamp out Judaism altogether, an attempt which brought about the Maccabæan revolt. A very significant passage in the first book of *Maccabees* brings this out with ominous clarity: " In those days ", it is said, " came there forth out of Israel transgressors of the law, and persuaded many, saying, Let us go and make a covenant with the Gentiles that are round about us ; for since we were parted from them many evils have befallen us. And the saying was good in their eyes. And certain of the people were forward herein, and went to the king ; and he gave them authority to act in accordance with the customs of the Gentiles. And they built a gymnasium in Jerusalem according to the usage of the Gentiles. And they made themselves uncircumcised, and forsook the holy covenant, and joined themselves to the Gentiles, and sold themselves to do evil " (1^{11-15}). Nothing could be clearer than this ; we would only stress one point ; the words, " for since we parted from them ", *i.e.*, the Gentiles, show that the " making of a covenant " with them was nothing new ; in other words, we have here a continuation of what had taken place in earlier days.

The only other point to which it is necessary to draw attention in the present connexion is the further mention of the Ḥasidim. It is after the first catastrophe had befallen those who remained true to their faith that we hear of the Ḥasidim: " Then were gathered unto them a company of Asidæans [this is the Greek form of the term], mighty men of Israel, every one that offered himself willingly for the law. And all they that fled from the evils were added to them, and became a stay unto them " (1 Macc. $2^{42, 43}$). Here it is to be noted that the way in which mention of the Ḥasidim is made, without a word of explanation as to who they were, shows plainly enough that the name was familiar ; in other words, they had formed a party within the Jewish community long before Maccabæan times ; for the formation of a party, separate and distinct from those of their surroundings, takes time. The passage shows us, further, that though the Ḥasidim were men of special piety who offered themselves willingly for the law, yet outside of their ranks there were plenty of faithful Jews who were bitterly opposed to those of their race who had " joined themselves to the Gentiles, and sold themselves to do evil ". The Ḥasidim are mentioned again in 1 Macc. 7^{13-17}, where it is recorded that sixty of them were slaughtered, and Ps. $79^{2c, 3}$ is quoted as prophetic of this (a point apparently overlooked by those who regard this psalm as Maccabæan !) ; the way in which it is quoted is significant ; the quotation is almost verbal, but not quite, suggesting that the psalm was, more or less, known by heart, and not copied out by the writer ; a *general* familiarity would point to long-continued use. Their religious ardour and patriotism are again referred to in 2 Macc. 14^{6-8}.

For our present purpose it is unnecessary to follow out the history further; it need only be added that ultimately the Zadokites and the *Ḥasidim* became, respectively, the parties of the Sadducees and the Pharisees.

It is, now, in the light of what has been said that all that we read about the *Ḥasidim* in the *Psalms* must be studied.

CHAPTER IX

THE QUESTION OF MACCABÆAN PSALMS

THE majority of commentators hold that a certain number of psalms belong to the Maccabæan period; as to how many are to be assigned to this late date, opinions differ; the minimum number is four—viz., 44, 74, 79, 83. We desire to offer some considerations which, we do not say definitely disprove a Maccabæan date for any psalms, but which suggest that such a date is improbable.

Without going into too much detail, we may begin by mentioning some reasons why many scholars assign a Maccabæan date to these four psalms; with others it does not seem necessary to deal. With regard to Ps. 44, it is held that what is said in *vv.* 17, 18 (18, 19) could be true only of Maccabæan times : . . . *yet have we not forgotten thee, neither have we dealt falsely in thy covenant : our heart is not turned backward, nor our step declined from thy way.* This is said in reference to the *nation*, see *vv.* 5 (6), 9 (10); but in view of 1 Macc. 1¹¹⁻¹⁵, how could these words refer to Maccabæan times? It illustrates the danger of picking out verses for a particular purpose without taking the context into consideration. Again, *v.* 22 (23) is confidently explained as referring to the religious persecution which caused the Maccabæan uprising : *For thy sake we are slain all the day, we are accounted as sheep for the slaughter.* Anyone reading 1 Macc. 1²⁹⁻⁶³, which gives the account of what this persecution really meant, cannot but feel that if this is what the psalmist was referring to, he must have been strangely lacking in the sense of proportion. That a persecution is being referred to in the psalm in question is certain, but not one on the scale of the Jewish–Syrian one, in which Jews had taken the initiative (see 1 Macc. 1¹¹⁻³⁴). There are some other passages in this psalm which make a Maccabæan date practically impossible (see the Intr. to this psalm, p. 244 f.).

Coming next to Ps. 74; a superficial comparison between *vv.* 3–9 of this psalm and 1 Macc. 1³⁸, 2 Macc. 1⁸, suggests the possibility of the same event being referred to in each; but as soon as details are considered, it is seen that this is unlikely to be the case. In *v.* 3 the destruction of the temple is described; it is in *perpetual ruins*; and *v.* 7 says : *They have set thy sanctuary on fire.* This does not agree with what is said about the attack on the temple in Maccabæan times; so far from its being in perpetual ruins, the only parts that were actually destroyed were the " priests' chambers " (1 Macc. 4³⁸); in the account of its re-dedication, nothing is said about its having been rebuilt. Again, so far from its having been set on fire, only the gates were burned (1 Macc. 4³⁸, 2 Macc. 1⁸, 8³³). But the most convincing argument against the contention that both accounts refer to the same event is that in the psalm the crowning horror of the whole tragedy, the building of " an abomination of desolation upon the altar ", is never even hinted at. That omission would be quite incomprehensible if the Maccabæan tragedy were being referred to. Once more, it is held by some commentators that *mô'ădēy-ēl*, "appointed times (or assemblies) of God" (*v.* 8), means " synagogues ", and that, therefore, Maccabæan times must be referred to—we confess that we cannot follow the argument— the expression cannot, however, refer to synagogues; *mô'ēd* is an abstract noun; the earliest name for " the synagogue " is *ha-Keneseth.* Moreover, all the evidence shows that synagogues did not exist in Palestine as early as Maccabæan times; the archæological evidence on this point is quite convincing.[1]

Another argument supposed to be in favour of a Maccabæan date for Ps. 74 is that in *v.* 9 it is said : *There is no more any prophet* ; this would certainly apply to Maccabæan times (see 1 Macc. 4⁴⁶, 9²⁷, 14³¹), but it would apply equally to most of the post-exilic period. Ps. 79 contains some passages (*vv.* 1–4) which appear at first sight to be distinctly reminiscent of Maccabæan times (see 1 Macc. 1²⁹⁻³⁹, ⁴⁶, 2⁷, and 2 Macc. 8²⁻⁴) ; but two facts must be pointed to which are fatal to a Maccabæan date. If this psalm had been written at that time, is it conceivable that it should be absolutely silent on the prime and central cause of the Maccabæan rising—the attempt to crush out the religion of the Jews ? There is no need to stress the obvious fact that to the psalmists religion was all-absorbing. The silence of the deeply religious writer of our psalm (see *vv.* 8, 9, 13) regarding this attempt makes it quite certain that he cannot have written it in reference to the Maccabæan struggle. The other fact has already been referred to—viz., that this psalm was quoted as a prophecy by the writer of 1 *Maccabees* (7¹⁷).

Lastly, we come to Ps. 83. We confess that we find it difficult to take seriously the contention that this psalm is Maccabæan. The idea arose owing to the parallelism between *vv.* 3, 4 (4, 5) of our psalm and 1 Macc. 5² ; in the former it is said : *They take crafty counsel against thy people, and consult together against thy treasure (or " treasured ones ").   They have said, Come and let us cut them off from being a nation ;* [2] *that the name of Israel be no more in remembrance.* The

---

[1] See Sukenik, *Ancient Synagogues in Palestine and Greece,* especially chap. I (1934).
[2] This is a quotation from Jer. 48².

latter runs: "And they took counsel to destroy the race of Jacob that was in the midst of them, and they began to slay and destroy among the people ". We have here another illustration of the precariousness of cutting off verses from their context, and of explaining them without taking the context into consideration. In the psalm the context contains the names of Israel's enemies, among them Assyria (*vv.* 6–8 (7–9)), and God is called upon to destroy them (*vv.* 13–17 (14–18)); but there is not a hint of these enemies having all been defeated. On the other hand, 1 Macc. 5³⁻⁶⁸ is a long and detailed account of the victories of Judas Maccabæus: "And the man Judas and his brethren were glorified exceedingly in the sight of all Israel, and of all the Gentiles, wheresoever their name was heard of; and men gathered together unto them, acclaiming them " (*vv.* 63, 64). How, in view of this fundamental difference in the conditions described in these two writings, respectively, can it be contended that they refer to the same series of events ?

We hope, therefore, that we may claim to have shown that there are reasons for doubting a Maccabæan date for these four psalms. We must, however, add some further general considerations, which will tend to show the improbability of *any* of the psalms in the Psalter having been written as late as the Maccabæan period.

Mention has already been made of the fact that hellenizing tendencies, which find expression in various psalms, do not necessarily point to a Maccabæan date, since hellenistic influences had been exercised among the Jews long before that time. Similarly with regard to the *Ḥasidim*, the mention of whom in some psalms and in 1 *Maccabees* is thought to mark a point of contact between the two; we have already shown that the way in which they are spoken of in the latter implies that they had been long in existence; so that the psalms in question cannot on this ground be claimed as of Maccabæan date.

The persecution under Antiochus Epiphanes began in 167 B.C., and the desecration of the temple took place in December of that year. The re-dedication of the temple was celebrated in December 164 B.C.[1] The fighting that went on during the intervening time was by no means unfavourable for the Jews. But it was during these years that " Maccabæan " psalms must have been written, most probably during the year 166 B.C., for the Jewish successes which almost uniformly marked the subsequent years would not have offered any *raison d'être* for the composition of the psalms in question. On the supposition of their having been written some time during the earlier part of this period, they could not have been used in the wor-

---

[1] For these dates see the very careful work of Kolbe, *Beiträge zur syrischen und jüdischen Geschichte*, pp. 95 ff. (1926).

ship of the temple (see, *e.g.*, 1 Mac. 3$^{35,\ 36,\ 45}$); this could have taken place only after the re-dedication of the temple. Now, the question which we have to ask ourselves is this: Is it likely that psalms of the sorrowful and despairing nature of the "Maccabæan" ones would have been used in the worship of the temple at any time during the succeeding half-century, a period of frequent Jewish triumphs? We fail to see *when* these psalms could have been used. If, on the other hand, the psalms in question had for long been incorporated in the national hymn-book, continued use would have brought them within the same category as many another psalm of similar type, plaintive, penitential, and the like, for which no Maccabæan date is claimed.

Another question, arising out of the foregoing, suggests itself. Seeing that, but for the first few months or so, the Maccabæan period was one of the most glorious in Jewish history, how comes it that, on the assumption of "Maccabæan" psalms, these should all be of a mournful character, and none of a jubilant tone? That, however, by the way.

An argument, of a different character, against the existence of any Maccabæan psalms must now be put forth. It will not be denied that the earliest possible date for any "Maccabæan" psalm is 167 B.C. The question then arises: Would any new psalms have been admitted into the temple hymn-book as late as this? Though no certain answer can be given to this question, two matters deserve to be mentioned which bear upon it. In the Prologue to *Ecclesiasticus* in Greek, the writer (in 132 B.C.) says that his grandfather (Ben-Sira, living about 200 B.C. or a little later) had "much given himself to the reading of the law, and the prophets, and the other books of our fathers"; and later on he again refers to "the law and the prophets, and the rest of the books" studied by his grandfather. While there is no question here of a Canon of Scripture in the later sense, the phrases used certainly point to the existence of three definitely recognized bodies of religious literature of an authoritative character about 200 B.C. This is confirmed, so far as the *Psalms* are concerned, by what Ben-Sira himself says about David: "In all his doings he gave thanks unto God Most High with words of glory; with his whole heart he loved his Maker, and sang praise every day continually. Stringed instruments and song before the altar he ordained, to make sweet melody with their music. He gave comeliness to the feasts, and set in order the seasons to perfection, while they praised his holy name; before morning it resounded from the sanctuary" (Ecclus. 47$^{8-10}$). What is here said gives, we submit, the impression that the book of *Psalms* was by that time completed. The Law (*i.e.*, the five books of Moses), for reasons into which it is not necessary to enter here, and the *Psalms*, because of their sacred use in worship, occupied positions of special sanctity.

The second matter, though belonging to somewhat later times, has a bearing on the present discussion because of the conception held as to what constituted " canonicity ". Josephus writes (*Contra Ap.* 38–41): " We have not myriads of books disagreeing with, and antagonistic to, one another, but two and twenty only,[1] which contain the record of all time (past), and are rightly believed in.[2] And of these five belong to Moses. . . . From the death of Moses till the reign of Artaxerxes, king of Persia, who reigned after Xerxes, the prophets who came after Moses wrote down the things that were done during their time in thirteen books. The remaining four contain hymns to God, and precepts for men's conduct of life. But from Artaxerxes to our times all events have, it is true, been written down ; but these later books are not thought to be worthy of the same credit, because the exact succession of prophets was wanting." The main point here is that no authoritative book of Scripture was written after the time of Artaxerxes I (464–424 B.C.), the " prophetical period ". This was a theory, quite artificial, but it was also the early Rabbinical view, or approximately so ; for they, too, held that the true books of Scripture were written within the " prophetical period " ; for them this period was from Moses to Ezra.[3] With the reasons for framing this, manifestly erroneous, theory we are not here concerned. We mention it because stress is laid in 1 *Maccabees* on the absence of a prophet ; in 4[45–46] it is said that " they pulled down the altar, and laid up the stones in the mountain of the house in a convenient place, until there should come a prophet to give an answer concerning them ". In 9[27] we read : " And there was great tribulation in Israel, such as was not since the time that no prophet appeared unto them ". And, again, in 14[41] : ". . . the Jews and the priests were well pleased that Simon should be their leader and high priest for ever (*i.e.*, in his house) until there should arise a faithful prophet ". If, according to the writer of 1 *Maccabees*, this was a period during which there was no prophet, and therefore no prophetical writings, is there not some justification for thinking that the same would apply to psalmists and psalms ?

Another argument against the existence of " Maccabæan " psalms has been dealt with by Buttenwieser [4]—namely, " the passing of Hebrew as a spoken language in post-exilic times, and its gradual replacement by Aramaic ". He maintains that the literary perfection of those psalms held by many scholars to belong to Maccabæan times is such that they must have been written while Hebrew literature was

---

[1] Josephus reckons *Ruth* and *Lamentations* as belonging, respectively, to *Judges* and *Jeremiah*.
[2] The addition of " as divine " is probably a later addition.
[3] For details, see Hölscher, *Kanonisch und Apokryph*, pp. 36 (1905).
[4] *The Psalms*, pp. 10 ff. (1938).

still at its height; that, presumably, was at any rate prior to the second century B.C. The argument, it is true, is not conclusive; Buttenwieser's criticism of Ben-Sira's Hebrew is a little over-stated, and it is certain that the Hebrew manuscripts of *Ecclesiasticus* have suffered much corruption. If we had the Hebrew originals of 2 (4) *Esdras* (the main part), and of the books of *Tobit, Judith*, 1 *Maccabees*, and, above all, of the *Psalms of Solomon*,[1] we should be in a better position to judge of the literary Hebrew of post-Biblical writings. Nevertheless, what Buttenwieser says offers a further argument against the " Maccabæan " psalms contention.

One, final, point. There is a consensus of opinion among commentators that a number of collections of psalms are incorporated in the Psalter. In many instances the collection to which a psalm belonged is indicated in the title. Twelve belonged to the Asaph collection, according to the titles both in Hebrew and the Septuagint; three of these (74, 79, 83) are held, as already indicated, to be " Maccabæan ". Is it likely that the Asaph collection was not completed until about the middle of the second century B.C. ? The titles of the psalms are confessedly later additions, but it may well be doubted whether any of them are as late as this. While it is not claimed that any of the reasons here put forth against a Maccabæan date for any of the psalms is in itself conclusive, we submit that the cumulative effect of the arguments is against such a date.

The contention as to the existence of Maccabæan psalms is due, of course, to the mention of the destruction or desecration of the temple, and of religious persecution, contained in those psalms. It is asked, To what can these refer (the destruction of the temple in 586 B.C. being out of the question) if not to what happened at the beginning of the Maccabæan struggle ? Ignoring, for the moment, the objections raised against Maccabæan psalms, it must be granted that the question is not without force. But our scant knowledge of Jewish history during the fourth and third centuries B.C. should forbid dogmatism here. Even if history does not record any events to which the psalms in question might refer, it does not necessarily follow that the writers were unacquainted with events which may have happened, and the record of which has not come down to us. Of one such event, indeed, we have knowledge ; and it has often been pointed out that the reference in the psalms of which we are thinking is to this event. In 351 B.C. a revolt on the part of Phœnicia broke out against Artaxerxes III Ochus, the Persian king ; it was of a serious character, for it was not quelled for three years. The references to it in ancient literature give

---

[1] The great majority of those in a position to judge hold these books to have been Hebrew, not Aramaic, in their origin.

but scanty details, but they show that the whole of Syria was involved, Egypt, too, joining in.[1] Owing to this general uprising against Persia, the Jews threw in their lot with the revolters. But when the Persians had once more gained the ascendant, the Jews suffered severely. The city of Jericho was destroyed, and many Jews were carried away captive to Babylonia, and to Hyrcania on the shores of the Caspian Sea. It is difficult to believe that Jerusalem, so near to Jericho, was left unmolested. Hecatæus of Abdera (306–283 B.C.) says that " the Persians formerly carried away many ten thousands of our people to Babylon ".[2] This captivity, as Robertson Smith says, " implies a revolt, and the long account given by Diodorus [3] (xvi. 40 ff.) of Ochus' doings in Phœnicia and Egypt shows how that ruthless king treated rebels. In Egypt the temples were pillaged and the sacred books carried away (ibid. c. 51). Why should we suppose that the temple at Jerusalem and the synagogues fared better ? Such sacrilege was the rule in Persian warfare ".[4] Thus the possibility, at any rate, must be recognized that in the psalms in question it is not the desecration of the temple in 167 B.C. that was in the mind of the writers.

While, therefore, we would not deny that insertions may have been made in some of the psalms as late as Maccabæan times, and perhaps even later, we cannot but feel that, for the reasons given, " Maccabæan Psalms ", as such, have not been incorporated in the Psalter.

---

[1] Eusebius, Chronicon, ed. Schoene, II, 112, 113 (1866). Schürer (Geschichte des jüdischen Volkes . . ., III, 7 (1909) quotes also from Syncellus, ed., Dindorf, Vol. I, p. 486, and from Orosius, III, 7.

[2] Quoted by Josephus, Contra Ap. I, 194.

[3] Second half of the first century, B.C.

[4] The Old Testament in the Jewish Church, p. 438 (1895). The archæological evidence regarding the late date of synagogues in Palestine has only recently become available.

CHAPTER X

In dealing with the individual psalms, we have, in most cases, added a section on its religious teaching; but it will be well to summarize all that is said, and thus to get a general view of the religion and theology of the Psalter as a whole. It will be understood that we can give here no more than a summary; for to deal adequately with such a widely ranging subject would require a volume for itself.

As has been pointed out (pp. 1 f.), the periods during which the psalms were written cover many centuries; therefore the religious conceptions and beliefs set forth in them necessarily differ greatly in spirit and content. Extraneous religious thought is often reflected, and among the Hebrew thinkers themselves differing points of view find expression. But this only enhances the interest of the whole great subject, since it illustrates the profound truth that divine revelation is progressive, in accordance with man's capacity for apprehending the mind and will of the Almighty.

i. The Doctrine of God

Here we have first to consider the question of *monotheistic belief*. It must be recognized that a pure monotheism, such as is expressed, for example, in Isa. 45[21, 22], 46[9], occurs but rarely in the psalms. In Ps. 115[3-7], where idols are described as nothingness, a true monotheism is implied, though not definitely expressed, and the same is true of Ps. 135[15-17]; but these two passages stand alone. Loyalty to the God of Israel is abundantly illustrated in almost every psalm that appears, but again and again we come across passages in which the recognition of the existence of other gods is outspokenly stated; obviously they are not to be compared with Yahweh the God of Israel; but naturally every national god was conceived by his worshippers to be superior to other gods; that is just where the difference between monolatry and monotheism lies. That the psalmists believed in the reality of other gods comes out only too clearly in many passages; thus, to give but a few illustrations; in Ps. 77[13] it is said: "Who is a great god like our God?" That assumes the existence of other gods; more pointed are the words in Ps. 81[9]: "There shall no strange god be in thee, and thou shalt not worship a foreign god". Similarly: "There is none

74

like thee among the gods, Yahweh " (86[8]) ; " For Yahweh is a great God ; and a great King above all gods " (95[3]) ; " For I know that Yahweh is great, and that our Lord is above all gods " (135[5]) ; and there are many other passages to the same effect. But though a pure monotheism is but rarely enunciated in the psalms, that does not in any way impugn the belief in the uniqueness of Yahweh ; and, taking the Psalter as a whole, we can see how the change was gradually taking place in the way in which other gods were regarded ; sometimes they are viewed as inferior deities, sometimes apparently as evil spirits, elsewhere as abominations, and finally as nonentities, figments of the imagination. In fact, within the relatively small space of the Psalter we find mirrored the stages of belief presented during the history of the religion of Israel as a whole. What has been well said by W. T. Davison of the Old Testament in general is true also of the book of the *Psalms* taken by itself : " The lesson of the Old Testament ", he says, " is the establishment of the worship of one God, unique, incomparable, the one God that matters. The main light shines clear, whatever vague forms flit and glimmer in the twilight around it. The history of revelation in the Old Testament is a history of the way in which this light was seen to shine more purely and more powerfully till all the shadows of lesser deities fled away." [1] That is the final development which, as we have seen, does also appear in the psalms, though rarely. And therefore it can be no matter of surprise to find that sometimes in the psalms *undeveloped conceptions* of Yahweh are to be met with. To some of these we must now draw attention. In many instances there can be no doubt that, when human emotions are attributed to God, they are to be understood figuratively ; if, even so, they sound irreverent to modern ears, it must be remembered that they are Oriental modes of expression, and the Oriental clothes his thoughts in realistic guise. When, for example, it is said in Ps. 2[4] : " He that abideth in the heavens laugheth, Yahweh doth have them [*i.e.*, the kings of the earth] in derision ", this may be nothing more than an attempt to portray the contemptible insignificance of men in the sight of God who set themselves in opposition to him ; they are, in the forcible French phrase, *pour rire*. Similarly, when in Ps. 35[23] the psalmist says : " Stir up thyself, arouse thee for my cause, my God, for my plea ", the words sound very irreverent to our ears ; but it is merely an exaggerative Oriental mode of expressive ardent prayer. And many other illustrations of a similar character could be given. On the other hand, anthropomorphisms occur which, however figuratively they may have been interpreted in later days, were in their origin conceived literally. For example, in several passages " refuge " is sought " under the wings " of Yahweh (Ps. 17[8], 36[7], 57[1], 63[7], 91[4]) ; the idea may have

---

[1] *Encycl. of Religion and Ethics*, VI, 253 *b* (1913).

been originally borrowed from the " Horus-hawk ", the symbol of Horus, which by identification with the sun's disk gave rise to the winged disk, the symbol of the deified Pharaoh. When, therefore, the Hebrews first borrowed this idea, and adapted it to Yahweh, it may reasonably be supposed that they understood it literally. Again, in many passages Yahweh is represented as a man of war ; thus, in Ps. 24[8] it is said : " Yahweh strong and mighty, Yahweh mighty in battle " ; and Ps. 35 [1–3] : " Strive, Yahweh, against them that strive with me, fight against them that fight against me ; take hold of shield and buckler, and rise up for my help ; and unsheath spear and battle-axe, to meet my pursuers " ; particularly striking is Ps. 44[9] : " But thou hast cast us off, and brought us to shame, and thou wentest not forth with our hosts " ; so, too, Ps. 60[10]. The frequency of this representation of Yahweh elsewhere in the Old Testament makes it difficult to believe that passages like these are not meant literally. That Yahweh was not thought of as visibly present would not affect belief in his invisible presence. An instructive passage in this connexion occurs in 2 Kgs. 6[8 ff.] ; even though this be but a legendary narrative, it reflects ancient belief : Elisha's servant, on seeing the Syrian host, says to the prophet, " Alas, my master, how shall we do ? " Elisha then prays that his servant's eyes may be opened, then he sees the mountain " full of horses and chariots of fire round about Elisha ". In much later times, during the Maccabæan wars, we have another story of the intervention of superhuman warriors in the battle : " But when the battle waxed strong, there appeared out of heaven unto their adversaries five men on horses with bridles of gold, in splendid array ; and, leading on the Jews, they took Maccabæus between them, and covering him with their own armour, guarded him from wounds, while on the adversaries they shot forth arrows and thunderbolts . . ." (2 Macc. 10[29, 30]). Here again we have a legend ; but it cannot be denied that such old-world stories have a history behind them. They reflect the ancient belief of the actual intervention of supernatural beings ; and though in these two stories Yahweh himself does not appear, it is not difficult to see, from the psalms passages quoted, that in earlier days it was believed that he himself intervened. This anthropomorphic conception, then, in the psalms, it may be justifiably contended, was meant literally, Yahweh being believed to be invisibly present. At the same time it is fully recognized that it is by no means always possible to feel sure whether a literal or a figurative sense is to be postulated in the passages in question. The *trust in Yahweh* thus affirmed is brought out in more spiritual directions in a very beautiful way ; indeed, this is the most prominent element in the doctrine of God as set forth in the Psalter. A few illustrations of this must be given. What may perhaps be called the classical passage setting forth this very lovely relationship of man to God is Ps. 23 ; the familiar words lose none of their beauty by repetition : " Yahweh is my shepherd, I shall not want ", more literally, " I lack nothing ". The experience of life has taught the psalmist that trust in God is all in all. In one form or another this central element of religion appears throughout the Psalter. The psalmists describe the many ways in which troubles assailed them : sickness, misfortune, envy, and ill-treatment on the part of many among their own people ; the victims of slander by unscrupulous adversaries ; the violence of pagan Gentiles ; and sometimes even the fear that they were forsaken by God —but in every trial, in every emergency, in every danger, material or spiritual, there is the conviction that God can and will help : " Why art thou bowed down, my soul, and groanest within me ? Wait for God, for I will yet thank him, the help of my countenance, and my God " (Ps. 42⁵). The whole of Ps. 121, again, offers a beautiful illustration of the conviction that God is very near at hand in any and every emergency. It is unnecessary to illustrate this further, but this witness of God as man's helper, so prominent all through the psalms, is of the greatest importance in considering the religious teaching set forth in them. Then, not unconnected with this, we have the teaching concerning the *worship of God*. This expression of man's relationship to God is such an obvious element in religion that it would seem hardly necessary to dwell upon it ; nevertheless, it belongs so intimately to the content of the psalms that it cannot be altogether passed over in silence. Praise, prayer, and thanksgiving—in other words, man's communion with God—is more vividly and insistently set forth in the psalms than anywhere else in the Bible. That, of course, is to be expected in a book of hymns ; but let us briefly consider the conception of worship as presented in the psalms. The *duty* of praise, incumbent upon every true believer, though usually taken for granted, is sometimes expressed by the psalmists when they invite men to come and worship ; thus, in the familiar words of the *Venite* (Ps. 95⁶)—the Hebrew differs slightly from the Prayer-Book Version—we have : " Let us enter in [*i.e.*, into the temple], let us worship and bow down, let us kneel before our Maker ". Again, in 96⁹ it is said, " Worship Yahweh in holy array, entreat his favour, all the earth " ; and, once more, in 99⁹ : " Exalt Yahweh, our God, and worship at his holy hill, for holy is Yahweh our God ". Then we get some touching passages in which the true lover of God expresses his yearning to come into the sanctuary to worship : " As the hart panteth for water brooks, so panteth my soul for thee, O God. My soul thirsteth for God, the living God ; when shall I come and behold the face of God ? " (42¹, ²). Another psalmist, far away from his native land, recalls the time when he worshipped in the sanctuary, and longs to be present there again : " Yahweh, my God, I seek thee ; my soul thirsteth for thee in a dry land where no water is ;

even as when in the sanctuary I beheld thee, to see thy might and thy majesty; for better than life is thy love; my lips shall praise thee" (63[1-3]). Such, and other similar passages, tell of a yearning for worship which is very inspiring. Very often we get expressions of the joy felt in worship, and these, too, are very beautiful: "Rejoice, O ye righteous, in Yahweh; for the upright praise is fitting. Give thanks to Yahweh with harp, sing praise with a ten-stringed lute. Sing to him a new song, play skilfully, with a shout of joy" (33[1-3]). That "shout of joy" is a kind of liturgical technical term, characteristic of Oriental unrestraint. Something similar occurs in Ps. 81[1, 2]: "Shout aloud unto God our strength, and make a joyful noise before the God of Jacob. Lift up a song of praise [*i.e.*, lift up the voice in praise], sound the timbrel, the pleasant harp with the lyre." And, once more, the spirit of joy in worship is expressed in the words: "I was glad when they said unto me, 'We are going to the house of Yahweh'" (Ps. 122[1]); it is the description of pilgrims going up to Jerusalem to keep the feast.

One other thing in this connexion must be noted—namely, the stress laid on sincerity of worship; the whole of Ps. 15 is concerned with this, teaching that only those who are genuine and faithful servants of Yahweh are fit to worship in his sanctuary: "Yahweh, who may sojourn in thy tabernacle? Who may abide upon thy holy hill? He that walketh uprightly, and worketh righteousness"; and then the psalmist enumerates the various types of men from whom the sincere worshipper must differ. A similar thought occurs in Ps. 118[20]: "This is the gate of Yahweh, the righteous shall enter therein", *i.e.*, this is the gate leading into Yahweh's sanctuary, the righteous, and no others, have the right to enter. Finally, very significant is what is said in Ps. 141[2-4], where sincerity in worship is insisted on: "Let my prayer be set forth as incense before thee, the lifting-up of my hands as an evening oblation; set, Yahweh, a watch o'er my mouth, a guard on the door of my lips. . . ."

These few illustrations, then, will suffice to give us some idea of the conception of worship set forth in the psalms.

And now we must refer to another subject, another form of worship, which is also directly connected with the conception of God, and which, therefore, comes under the heading of the Doctrine of God: the subject, namely, of *sacrificial worship*. Purely spiritual worship, such as we have just been considering, which is not concerned with the materialistic ideas involved in the offering of sacrifices, obviously conceives of the Personality of God in a very different way from that which thinks of him as being pleased with the gifts of animals, or of the fruits of the earth. Now, as we shall see, there are but very few passages in the psalms in which the whole idea of sacrifices is directly repudiated; on the other hand, it is evident from many other passages that sacrificial worship was regarded as normal; a fact which is amply witnessed to elsewhere. Nevertheless, we are bound to ask ourselves, in view of the high ideal of worship which we have seen to have been prevalent among the psalmists, whether many of them did not in their heart of hearts look upon the offering of sacrifices as involving a somewhat unsatisfying conception of God. To repudiate altogether the traditional and time-honoured mode of worship would have required exceptional boldness, and might have been misapprehended as lacking in loyalty to Yahweh, seeing that sacrifices were ordained in the Law. Besides, there were the masses to be thought of, who could not conceive of worship without the offering of sacrifices. If, therefore, reticence was felt to be needful, it was prompted by laudable motives. But that would not have suppressed the inner convictions of many of the psalmists whose conception of God was of a more spiritual nature. We are therefore led to believe that the thought of spiritual worship was more widely held by many of the psalmists than appears upon the surface. That this was not, however, the case with all the psalmists, we must now proceed to show by a few quotations. In Ps. 20[3] the devout wish is expressed that Yahweh may " remember all thy meal-offerings, and accept thy burnt sacrifice "; four technical sacrificial terms are used here. Again in Ps. 50[5] the psalmist cries, putting the words into the mouth of God: " Gather to me my godly ones that have made covenant with me with sacrifice "; and in Ps. 54[6] it is said: " With a free-will offering will I sacrifice to thee, I will praise thy name, for it is good "; and to give but one more illustration out of many, in Ps. 66[13-15] the psalmist glories in the thought of how he is going to fulfil all his vows made in gratitude for having been delivered from trouble: " I will enter into thy house with whole burnt-offerings, I will pay my vows unto thee, which my lips did utter, and my mouth did speak, when I was in trouble; whole burnt-offerings of fatlings will I offer unto thee, with the incense of rams [i.e., the smoke rising from the burning of the sacrifice], I will offer bullocks together with goats ". That will suffice to show the normal mode of worship often spoken of in the psalms. In contrast to this we have instances, and they are but few, in which the idea of sacrifice is directly repudiated; they are well known, but their importance demands our notice of them. First we have in Ps. 40[6] the psalmist's words addressed to the Almighty: " Sacrifice and meal-offering thou desirest not, whole burnt-offering and sin-offering thou dost not ask"; clearly it is here implied that God has no pleasure in receiving sacrifices; the fulfilment of the Law and witnessing to the righteousness of God are, as the context says, of vastly greater importance. But more striking is what is said in Ps. 50[8-14], words imputed to God: " Not because of thy sacrifices do I reprove thee, thy burnt-offerings are always before me. I desire no bullock out of thine house, nor he-goats out of thy fold. . . . If I were hungry I would not tell thee, for mine is the world and its fulness ; do I eat the flesh of bulls, or drink the blood of goats ? Sacrifice thanksgiving unto God, and pay to the Most High thy vows." Again, in Ps. 51[16, 17] it is said : " For thou delightest not in sacrifice, though I brought a whole burnt-offering thou wouldst have no pleasure therein. My sacrifice is a broken spirit ; a heart broken and crushed, O God, thou wilt not despise." And, once more, the spiritual conception of worship is expressed in Ps. 69[30, 31] : " I will praise the name of God with a song, and I will magnify him with thanksgiving ; and it will please Yahweh better than an ox, a bullock with horns and hoofs ". These few passages, then, express the beauty of spiritual worship apart from sacrifices, and therefore a more exalted conception of God ; they are the only ones which directly discountenance sacrificial worship.

Our next subject for brief consideration in dealing with the doctrine of God in the *Psalms* is the very beautiful way in which the psalmists describe the Almighty as the *God of Love.* The Hebrew word *hesed* has various meanings, according to the context of the passages in which it occurs, but in its most exalted sense it expresses " love ", together with all that this connotes. It is one of the great words of the Hebrew language, and no one word in English will carry its full meaning. It may be an attitude of equals towards one another, it may be felt by the inferior for the superior, it may be shown by the superior to the inferior. Nor is it merely a mode of action or an emotion. It is an essential quality of soul, a spiritual endowment which goes deep down into the very nature of him who has it. It implies a full recognition of the value of personality, and adds to that recognition a consecration of one to another. No other word means so much to the Hebrew ear, and its cultivation in the human heart is the highest demand of the prophetic morality. In all its completeness it can be seen only in Yahweh. Nothing shows more convincingly the psalmists' apprehension of God than the way in which they attribute to him the quality of *hesed.* The fulness of its content is nowhere more beautifully set forth than in Ps. 86[15] : " But thou, Yahweh, art a God full of compassion, and gracious, slow to anger, and plenteous in mercy and truth " ; compassion, graciousness, long-suffering, mercy, truth, are all embraced in " love " ; very similar to this passage are Pss. 103[8], 145[8, 9]. The illimitability of divine love is expressed in the words : " For as high as the heavens above the earth, so high is his love over them that fear him " (Ps. 103[11]). No wonder that it was said : " For better than life is thy love " (Ps. 63[3]). Another psalmist in the depth of his gratitude to God reiterates the refrain in every verse of the well-known Ps. 136 : " For his love (*hesed*) endureth for ever ". This could be illustrated to any extent ; suffice to say that the word *hesed* occurs in twenty-three passages in the *Psalms*, in addition to the many more in which the various attributes of love occur; all in reference to God. Then we have the very frequent mention of Yahweh as the *God of law, of righteousness and justice* ; this, however, does not need further illustration.

But something must be said of the teaching that Yahweh as the Creator is the *God of Nature*. There is the frequent assertion that Yahweh brings about all that happens in Nature, according to his will. What we understand as the laws of Nature and their working is ascribed to individual and separate acts of God. Thus, in $65^{9, 10}$ we read : " Thou hast visited the earth, and watered it, greatly dost thou enrich it ; the brook of God is full of water, thou preparest the corn thereof (*i.e.*, of the earth) ; yea, thus thou preparest it : watering the furrows thereof, levelling the ridges thereof ; thou makest it soft with shower, thou blessest the growth thereof ". Much to the point, too, is $135^{6, 7}$: " All that he willed hath Yahweh done in heaven and earth, in the seas and all deeps ; he bringeth up mists from the ends of the earth ; he maketh lightnings for the rain, he bringeth forth wind from his treasures " (cp. Jer. 10^{13}, 51^{16}). So in many other passages. Then we have the teaching that Yahweh is the *God of History* ; and here prophetical influence is very marked ; in proof of this the following passage from Isa. 14^{24-27} is well worth quoting : " Yahweh of hosts hath sworn, saying, Surely as I have thought, so shall it come to pass ; and as I have purposed, so shall it stand : that I will break the Assyrian in my land, and upon my mountains tread him under foot. . . . This is the purpose that is purposed upon the whole earth ; and this is the hand that is stretched out upon all the nations. For Yahweh of hosts hath purposed, and who shall disannul it ? And his hand is stretched out, and who shall turn it back ? " (see also Isa. 7^{18-20}). In the same way the psalmists teach that historical events are ordained and directed by God. One or two illustrations, of many, may be given. In 44^{1-3} we read : " O God, with our ears have we heard, our fathers have told unto us, the work that thou didst in their days, in the days of old by thy hand. Nations thou didst drive out, and planted them (*i.e.*, our fathers) in, didst afflict peoples, and settle them down ; for not by their sword did they possess the land, and not was their arm victorious for them ; but thy right hand, and thy strong arm, and the light of thy countenance, for thou didst favour them." Again, in 111^6 it is said : " The power of his works he made known to his people in giving them the heritage of the nations ". Many other passages to the same effect could be quoted ; but this is not necessary.

What has been said will, it may be hoped, have given all the important matters concerning the psalmists' doctrine of God.

Finally, there is the teaching on *Universalism*. Here, once more, it is seen how some of the psalmists were influenced by prophetical teaching. That the subject is not mentioned more often is due to the nature of the contents of most of the psalms ; but here and there the thought of the universal recognition of God by all nations receives expression ; thus Ps. 66 opens with the words : " Shout for joy unto God, all the earth, sing praise to the glory of his name . . . Let all the earth worship thee, sing praise to thee, sing praise to thy name " ; and again in verse 8 : " Bless, O ye peoples, our God, make the sound of his praise to be heard ", cp. Isa. 44[22, 23], 54[5] ; a similar thought occurs in 67[2-5], 86[9, 10], 96[10], 148[11]. Of special interest is 47[8, 9], where the Gentiles are thought of as joining together in worship with Israel : " Yahweh is become king over the nations, he sitteth upon his holy throne ; the princes of the peoples are gathered together with the people of the God of Abraham ; for to God belong the rulers of the earth ; he is greatly exalted ". It is hardly necessary to add that this conception of the universality of God's rule, and the union of all nations with his people in worshipping him, has a direct bearing on the doctrine of God.

ii. Belief in Supernatural Beings

We do not include here the belief in the existence of the gods of the nations, as this was necessarily considered when we dealt with monotheistic belief. But in a number of the psalms reference is made to supernatural beings of a very different order. Of these something must be said. First, there is the belief in heavenly beings, who are always represented as the ministers of Yahweh, and therefore as wholly inferior to him. The belief in the heavenly hierarchy appears again and again ; thus, in Ps. 89[5-7] praise is offered to Yahweh by the hosts above ; the passage is a very striking one : " The heavens give praise for thy wondrous acts, Yahweh, yea, for thy faithfulness, the assembly of holy ones ; for who in the skies can compare with Yahweh, [who] is like Yahweh among the sons of gods ? God, who is fearful in the assembly of the holy ones. . . ." There can be no doubt that the angels are here referred to, although in the Old Testament they are usually designated *mal'akîm*, " messengers ", *i.e.*, of God, cp. Ps. 91[11], " For he shall give his angels charge over thee ". The term " sons of gods " (cp. Ps. 29[1]) was originally used in a polytheistic sense, but here it is intended to indicate that the angels were divine beings ; elsewhere they are called " sons of God " (Gen. 6[2, 4], in reference to the fallen angels ; Job 1[6], 2[1]). They are also spoken of as " in the skies ", and in *v.* 8, where it says : " Yahweh of hosts, who is like unto thee ", the word " hosts " refers to the hosts of heaven ; but under this term, as Ps. 148[1-3] shows, the heavenly luminaries are meant : " Praise Yahweh from the heavens, praise him in the heights ; praise him, all ye his angels (*mal'akîm*), praise him, all ye his host ; praise him sun and moon, praise him all ye stars of light " ; in Ps. 103[20, 21], too, " his angels " (mal'akîm) is parallel to " his host " (cp. Ps. 19[1], 50[6], 97[6]). Their creation is spoken of in Ps. 33[6] : " By his word were the heavens made, and by the breath of his mouth all their host " (cp. Gen. 2[1], Isa. 40[26], 45[12]). The primary duty of the angels, as all these passages tell, is to worship the Almighty in the spheres above ; but in a few other passages it is seen that they had duties to perform also on earth. Here we may note, first, an old-world echo according to which, as God's ministers, the angels accompany him when he leaves the heavenly spheres to come down on to the earth. Clouds, wind, and fire were all in ancient belief conceived of as animated beings ; in later Hebrew thought these were represented as subordinate ministers of God, of the angelic nature, whom he used for his special purposes ; thus, in Ps. 104[3, 4] it is said : " Who maketh clouds his chariot, who goeth forth on the wings of the wind, who maketh winds his messengers (mal'akîm), fire and flame his ministers ". In this connexion we may refer to Ps. 68 [17] : " The chariots of God are twenty thousand even thousands upon thousands ", which means that in his going forth the train of the Almighty which followed him was composed of a mighty host of angels in chariots, an innumerable company. A curious idea, which has an old-world ring about it, is that which imputes to angels the eating of material food ; in Ps. 78[24, 25] it is said : " He rained down manna upon them to eat, and gave them of the corn of heaven ; man did eat the bread of the mighty, he sent food to the full ". That by " the mighty " ('abbîrîm) angels are meant is seen from Ps. 103[20], where they are called " mighty ", though a different word is used in Hebrew : " Bless Yahweh, ye angels of his, ye, mighty in strength (gibborê koah), that fulfil his command ". In Ps. 105[40] the manna is called " bread from heaven ". This idea of the angels eating food goes back to ancient times. As a rule angelic functions are spoken of as being exercised in the heavenly spheres ; but in a few cases they are thought of as active on earth ; thus, in Ps. 34[7] we read : " The angel (mal'ak) of Yahweh encampeth round about them that fear him, and delivereth them " ; and in Ps. 57[3] the same thought occurs, though the angel is not directly mentioned : " He shall send from heaven and save me " ; but most pointed is Ps. 91[11] : " For his angels he will give charge over thee, to keep thee in all thy ways ; they shall bear thee up, on their hands, lest thou dash thy foot against a stone ". Here the function of angels is that of guardianship, but elsewhere they are spoken of as God's instruments of punishment ; thus, in Ps. 35[5, 6] it is said in reference to the psalmist's enemies : " Let them be as chaff before the wind, with the angel of Yahweh pursuing them ; let their way be dark and slippery, with the angel of Yahweh driving them on ". And in Ps. 78[49], where the Egyptians are spoken of, it is said : " He cast upon them the fierceness of his anger, wrath and indignation and trouble, a band of harmful angels ". Here we have the personification of wrath, indignation, and trouble, conceived of as destructive angels; the counterpart of this personification occurs in Ps. 43³, where light and truth are angelic persons leading the psalmist, according to his prayer, to God's holy hill, *i.e.*, to the temple to worship : " O send out thy light and thy truth, let them lead me ; let them bring me to thy holy hill, and unto thy dwelling-places " (cp. also 25²¹, 57³, 85¹³).

A different class of supernatural beings, though of the angelic order, which are mentioned three times in the psalms, are the *Cherubim*. Of these it is not necessary to say much here ; that the conception of them was of Babylonian origin there is no doubt. The first mention of them is in Ps. 18¹⁰, which contains mythical elements ; it is there said of Yahweh that " he rode upon a cherub, and did fly ", *i.e.*, the cherub flew ; it reflects a very undeveloped conception of Yahweh. In Ps. 80¹ it is said : " Thou that sittest upon the cherubim, shine forth " ; the thought is evidently that of Yahweh sitting upon his heavenly throne, from which he rules the world ; the Cherubim are the guardians of the throne (cp. Ezek. 28¹³, ¹⁴, ¹⁶). The same picture is presented in Ps. 99¹ : " Yahweh is become king, let the peoples tremble, he sitteth upon the cherubim, let the earth shake ". This echoes the early Israelite belief that the Cherubim were, in effect, the divine chariot, the bearers of Yahweh's throne in its progress through the world (cp. 1 Sam. 4⁴, 2 Sam. 6²). The belief in them must have been very real, for they figure largely in post-Biblical Jewish literature.

The last of the supernatural beings of which something must be said are the *Demons*. Here again we have a belief which goes back in its origin to very early times, and plays a great part in later days. In the *Psalms* the mention of them is very rare, but though only incidentally referred to it is certain that belief in their activity was deep-seated. In Ps. 106³⁶⁻³⁸, in reference to the Israelites after their settlement in Canaan, it is said, " And they served their idols [*i.e.*, of the nations], and they became a snare unto them ; and they sacrificed their sons and and their daughters to demons (*šēdîm*), and they poured out innocent blood, and the land was polluted with blood ". It is in Ps. 91, however, that we get the most striking allusions to demons, though the term for " demons " (*šēdîm*) is not actually used ; but for the details we must refer to the notes on this psalm. It is worth noting that in the Talmud (*Sebuoth* 15ᵇ) this psalm is called " a song for evil encounters ", *i.e.*, of demons, and its use in the event of demoniacal onslaughts is recommended. In Ps. 58⁴, ⁵ the mention of " serpent " and " adder " refers, in all probability, to demons, for serpents were regarded as the incarnations of demons.

This concludes, then, what is said in the *Psalms* about supernatural beings.

iii. THE DOCTRINE OF SIN

Based on the teaching of the prophets, the doctrine of sin in the *Psalms* centres on the truth that what constitutes sin is the doing of something which is contrary to the divine commands ; an act is sinful because it is against the will of God. If this definition of sin, as implied in the prophetical *dictum*, " your iniquities have separated between you and your God " (Isa. 59²), is not quoted in so many words, it is because it has become axiomatic. This may sound self-evident, but it must be remembered that in pre-prophetic times " sin is almost invariably presented to us as nothing more than disobedience to the statutes regulating religious, social, and civil life in Israel, and the violation of the good customs in vogue among this people." [1] But probably the earliest idea of sin was connected with ritual offences, for such things as lying (Gen. 20²), deception (Gen. 27⁹), drunkenness (Gen. 9²¹), adultery (Gen. 16³), suicide (1 Sam. 31⁴), are mentioned without any hint of their being sinful acts. It is thus impossible to exaggerate the enormous advance in ethical teaching due to the prophets. It is to them that the psalmists were primarily indebted for their doctrine of sin. Further, while it is fully recognized by the psalmists that the consequences of sin entail sickness and misfortune, it is not merely on that account that sin is to be avoided, but because sin involves a break in the relationship between a man and his God. And again, it is not because divine help is withdrawn from him who sins that a good man refrains from sin, rather it is because a sinner cannot have communion with God. When sin has been committed, or when, as a result, sickness or adversity overtakes the sinner, in one way or another the yearning is expressed of entering again into communion with God—in other words, of re-establishing the relationship with him. When, therefore, a psalmist has suffered for sin and confesses it, his comfort centres in his renewed communion with God in prayer : " My sin I made known to thee, and mine iniquity I hid not . . . therefore unto thee shall every godly man pray " (32⁵, ⁶) ; similarly in 51, after confession of sin, the psalmist says, in *v*. 11 : " Cast me not from thy presence, and take not thy spirit from me ". This need not be further illustrated, for it occurs over and over again in many of the psalms. The deep sense of sin, so often expressed by the psalmist, appears in a twofold way : the horror expressed at sin in others, and the whole-hearted recognition of sin in the psalmists themselves, their confession, and the consequent certitude of forgiveness. How genuine and deep-seated was this sense of sin is shown by the conviction that even when sin is not discerned it may yet lurk within, though unrecognized : " Who can discern his errors ? Clear thou me from hidden faults " (19¹²) ; and this is further

[1] Schultz, *Old Testament Theology* (Engl. Transl.), II. 281 (1892).

G

emphasized by the realization of the truth that God is all-knowing, that nothing is hidden from him : " Thou, O God, knowest my foolishness, and mine offences are not hid from thee " (69^5).

While the existence of sin is taken for granted, no theory as to its origin is put forth by the psalmists ; it is part of man's nature from birth, but no attempt is made to account for this ; thus, in 51^5 the psalmist says : " Behold, in iniquity was I brought forth, and in sin did my mother conceive me " ; this is not intended to offer an excuse for having been guilty of sin, it is simply a statement of fact. In 50^3, again, it is said : " The wicked are rebellious, from the womb they go astray, from the belly they speak lies " ; an exaggerated statement, but expressing the same fact. There is no thought here of a doctrine of original sin through the fall of Adam ; that is never taught in the Old Testament and has never been held in Judaism. There can be little doubt that, according to the belief of the psalmists, sinning was purely a matter of human action ; to commit sin or to avoid sin lay with man's free-will, hence, though in exaggerated language, another psalmist could say : " Yea, thou wert my strength from the womb, my trust [when I was] upon my mother's breasts ; on thee did I cast myself from the womb, thou art my God from my mother's belly " ; in other words, the psalmist protested that he had put his trust in God from birth ; that he should have exercised his free-will thus as a new-born babe is poetical hyperbole, but the words illustrate the belief of all the psalmists that sinful acts and good acts are alike a matter of human free-will. The traditional doctrine is expressed in the words of Ben-Sira : " If thou desirest, thou canst keep the commandment, and it is wisdom to do his [God's] good pleasure ; and if thou trust him, of a truth thou shalt live. Poured out before thee are fire and water, stretch forth thine hand unto that which thou desirest. Life and death are placed before man, that which he desireth shall be given him " (Ecclus. 15^{15-17}).

iv. THE DOCTRINE OF RETRIBUTION

This subject is closely connected with the foregoing. It is unnecessary to illustrate in detail the well-known fact that in ancient Israel in pre-prophetic times the idea of tribal solidarity accounted for the belief that the sin of one member of a family or community necessarily involved all the members (see, e.g., Josh. $7^{1,\ 24,\ 25}$, 2 Sam. 21). With the prophets this teaching underwent a transformation ; while concerned with the nation as a whole, they also taught, at first but occasionally, the responsibility of the individual (e.g., Am. 7^{17}, Hos. 1-3, Isa. $22^{22,\ 23}$). It is with Jeremiah and Ezekiel that the fuller development appears, e.g., Jer. 31^{19}, and especially Ezek. $18^{1ff.}$: " What mean ye, that ye use this proverb among the sons of Israel, saying : ' The fathers have eaten sour grapes, and the children's teeth are set on edge ' ?   As I live, saith Yahweh, none shall use this proverb in Israel any more.   Behold, all souls are mine ; as the soul of the father, so also the soul of the son is mine ; the soul that sinneth, it shall die. . . ."   It is the following of the prophets that the psalmists base their teaching on individual responsibility.   But according to the traditional teaching, so fully illustrated in the book of *Job*, all suffering and adversity were sent by God upon the sinner, whereas prosperity was the lot of the righteous.   Thus theoretically the sinner was always the victim of sickness or misfortune, while the righteous always enjoyed health and prosperity.   But the experience of life showed that this was far from being the case ; again and again the sinner was prosperous, and the righteous in distress.   The question, therefore, forced itself upon thinkers in Israel : Is God just in letting the wicked prosper and the righteous suffer adversity ?   We are concerned here only with the way in which the psalmists faced this problem and sought to solve it. Most of them simply accepted the traditional belief in spite of its perplexity.   Thus, in Ps. 1 this is fully set forth ; of the righteous it is said " He is like a tree planted by the water . . . whatsoever he doeth it prospereth " (*v.* 3) ; but the wicked are " like the chaff which the wind driveth away . . . the way of the wicked shall perish " (*vv.* 4–6).   The same teaching occurs over and over again.   But in a few cases attempts are made to grapple with the problem ; with these we must deal a little more fully.   First, however, it is worth noting that an attitude is sometimes adopted which, it may be safely assumed, was common : we mean the attitude of resigned acceptance of facts which can be neither understood nor altered.   In Ps. 39, for example, the words with which the psalmist begins suggests that the sight of the wicked in prosperity had prompted doubts as to the justice of God in permitting this ; the expression of such doubts encouraged the wicked in their disbelief ; of this he now repents, saying : " I said, I will take heed to my words, that I sin not with my tongue ; I will put to my mouth a bridle because of the wicked before me ".   If he cannot understand the ways of God, he will, at any rate, not impugn their justice.   Then he gives expression to the thought of the transient character of the life of all men, good or bad ; implicitly, therefore, he concludes that what is, must be ; it is not for him to question the ways of God, nor to worry about what he cannot understand ; far more important is it for him to trust in God : " And now, what is my hope, O Lord ? my waiting is for thee ".   It is an attitude of reverent resignation, but forgoes any attempt to solve the problem.   With some other psalmists it is different ; here and there real attempts at a solution are made.   Ps. 37 seems to have been written primarily with the object of showing that the prosperity of the wicked was merely apparent, or at best but short-lived.   The whole psalm should be read in order to see what sincere efforts the psalmist made to convince others that there was no need to be perplexed about the well-being of ungodly men, which was but a passing phase; it will be sufficient to quote the first two verses, which in substance is repeated again and again: " Be not enraged because of evil-doers, and be not envious of the workers of unrighteousness; for like grass do they speedily wither, and fade away like the green herb ". Of the righteous, on the other hand, it is said: " He knoweth the ways of the perfect, and their inheritance abideth for ever " (v. 18). An optimistic outlook, though again no real solution of the problem; but the difficulty of reconciling the justice of God with the prosperity of the wicked and the adversity of the righteous was so far mitigated in that the duration of the former was held to be fleeting, while that of the latter was lasting. True, it was but *faute de mieux*, for the experience of life must have taught that, while in some instances the contention held good, it was far from being the rule.

In Ps. 49 two solutions are attempted; the first follows in the lines of Ps. 37; but in the second the psalmist touches upon a real solution—namely, that the ungodly at death, according to their deserts, go to Sheol; but the righteous, represented by the psalmist, are received by God. Here the implication is that, in the world to come, the incongruities of this life will be put right; life on the earth is but an unfinished episode; the righteousness and justice of God will be vindicated in the hereafter: " Like a flock of Sheol are they destroyed, death is their shepherd, hath dominion over them . . . but God will redeem my soul from the power of Sheol, for he will receive me " (vv. 14, 15). Finally, we come to Ps. 73. As we deal with this again on p. 91, it will suffice to quote here what the psalmist says of the latter end of the ungodly and of the righteous, respectively; of the former he says: " Surely in slippery places thou settest them, in beguiling thou bringest them down; how are they a waste in a moment, through terrors are finished and ended! " (vv. 18, 19). But of the righteous: " With thy counsel thou leadest me in the way, and afterwards wilt gloriously take me; whom have I in the heavens? In the earth I have no delight save in thee; my flesh and my heart cease to be, but my portion is God for ever " (vv. 23–26). Here again, then, it is taught that to judge only of what takes place in this life is to misconceive of the ways of him who is eternal, and to mistake man's final destiny. Final retribution for the wicked, the endless abiding in God's presence for the righteous; that is the psalmist's solution of the problem.

v. Belief in the After-Life

This leads us to consider more fully what is taught by the psalmists regarding the life to come. As in other directions, it is the traditional belief that appears most prominently here, namely, the Sheol belief; in three passages (88^{10}, $106^{28,\ 37}$) the primitive popular ideas of the departed seem to be referred to, but this is very exceptional, and need not detain us. There are good grounds for the contention that the Sheol belief became the official doctrine concerning the hereafter owing to the influence of the eighth-century prophets [1]; so that here again the psalmists were ultimately indebted to prophetical influence for their teaching. In accordance with what had become traditional belief, it is held that Sheol is situated under the earth; in 22^{29} the departed are spoken of as " they that go down to the dust "; it is a place of darkness : " he causeth me to dwell in dark places " (143^3); silence reigns there : " the dead praise not Yahweh, nor all that go down into silence " (115^{17}); all things are forgotten there, it is called " the land of forgetfulness " in 88^{12}; but it is conceived of as a great city, its " gates " are spoken of in 9^{13}, 107^{18}; it is synonymous with death ($18^{4,\ 5}$, 49^{14}), with the " Pit " (28^1, 30^3 and elsewhere), with " corruption " (30^9), and with 'Abaddôn, " destruction " (88^{11}). For the godly the most terrible thing is that in Sheol there is no communion with God : " For in death there is no remembrance of thee, in Sheol who will give thanks unto thee ? " (6^5), " Shall the dust praise thee ? shall it declare thy truth ? " (30^9, cp. 88^5, 143^7).

We have next to consider those few passages in which a development of belief is to be discerned ; not all commentators are agreed on the interpretation of these passages, but we submit that there are good grounds for the view here held. First, we have two passages in which the psalmists, while not yet realizing the truth of life hereafter, express thoughts which come very near to this. Ps. 16^{9-11} reads as follows : " Therefore my heart rejoiceth, and my soul is glad, my flesh also shall dwell in safety ; for thou wilt not leave my soul to Sheol, neither wilt thou suffer thy godly one to see the Pit. Thou showest me the path of life, fulness of joy is in thy presence, at thy right hand there are raptures for ever." Here we may be permitted to give the following quotation : [2] " As the earlier part of the psalm shows, this passage must be taken as referring to belief in the After-life. Nevertheless, though this life is not to be thought of as eternal in the literal sense, since it terminates with the close of human existence, the conception of life as the psalmist experiences it, living in loyalty to God and feeling his nearness, thus making life very exalted and glorious, may in a true sense be said to anticipate life eternal. For the ideal of life held by the psalmist, that its value depends solely upon its being lived in communion with God, could not fail, sooner or later, to necessitate further thought. The

[1] For details, see Oesterley and Robinson, *Hebrew Religion, its origin and development*, pp. 318–327 (1935).
[2] Oesterley, *A Fresh Approach to the Psalms*, p. 265 (1937).

sense of close union with God, which the psalmist so beautifully sets forth, with him who is omnipotent, to whom time is nothing, leads inevitably to the question : How can such a union cease ? And there we are on the very threshold of the belief in its continuance hereafter." Our psalmist was coming very near to the beautiful truth expressed in Wisd. 15³ : " For to know thee is perfect righteousness, yea, to know thy dominion (τὸ κράτος) is the root of immortality ".

Our next passage is 17¹⁵ : " As for me, in righteousness I behold thy face, I shall be satisfied, when I awake, with thine appearance ". It is difficult to understand these words in the sense of awakening from natural sleep ; the psalmist shows that he is in constant communion with God, and experiences the unceasing nearness of God ; he never contemplates separation from God ; why, then, should he be satisfied with the divine appearance only on awaking from natural sleep ? It should also be noted that the word for " appearance " or " form ", in reference to Yahweh, is extremely rare, occurring elsewhere only in Num. 12⁸, Deut. 4¹², in each case under very special circumstances. Death is spoken of as " sleep ", e.g., in Ps. 76⁵, Jer. 51³⁹, ⁵⁷ and possibly Ps. 90⁵ ; in Isa. 26¹⁹ it is said : " Awake and sing, ye that dwell in the dust ". It can scarcely be doubted, therefore, that the psalmist is here thinking of awaking from the sleep of death, and thus expresses belief in the life hereafter.   In Ps. 39⁶, ⁷ the psalmist says : " Surely as a vapour doth every man stand, surely as a shadow man doth walk . . . And now, what is my hope, O Lord ? My waiting is for thee." The emphasis laid here on the transience of human life, with which is contrasted " my hope ", " my waiting is for thee ", justifies the contention that the psalmist is thinking here of life with God, i.e., life unending. Opinions differ on the meaning of the passage, but we range ourselves with Duhm,¹ who says in reference to it : " It appears to me that no other explanation is possible than that of assuming that the poet in silent thought hoped for the continuance of life after death, though without being able to base this hope on any demonstrable proof, or on any teaching that had been put forth. . . . Therefore, since he is unable, or unwilling, to rely upon any general doctrine of immortality, which might solve the riddle of the forlornness of human existence, whereby to still his perplexity, he pleads sadly, and with hesitation, ' What is my hope ? Everything depends on thee.'   It is a silent prayer, the prayer of one sighing in this fleeting life for that which is abiding."

This belief receives more definite expression in Ps. 49, quoted in part above ; here the psalmist contrasts the lot of the wicked hereafter with that which, in his ardent trust in God, he is convinced is reserved for him ; there can, therefore, be no doubt as to his meaning ; in

¹ *Die Psalmen*, p. 115 (1899).

reference to the former he says : " Like a flock of Sheol are they destroyed, death is their shepherd, hath dominion over them ; in the field of Abaddon is their resting-place, in the belly of Sheol is their dwelling ". As for himself, on the other hand, he can say : " But God will redeem my soul from the power of Sheol, for he will receive me ".

Coming now to Ps. 139, the psalmist begins by setting forth the omniscience of God ; then he goes on to speak of God's omnipresence ; this unique conception of God, so far as the psalmists are concerned, justifies the contention that this psalmist did contemplate some form of real life hereafter. What is of special significance is the belief that God is present in Sheol : " If I descended to Sheol, lo, thou art there " (v. 8). As already pointed out, the normal Sheol doctrine taught that God was wholly unconcerned with that place whither the departed descended, as with the departed themselves ; but if God was thought of as being present there—present, that is, among the departed—that must imply a changed outlook regarding the hereafter. Even if the psalmist did not envisage life after death in its fulness, what he says shows at any rate the dawning of this in his mind ; and it is prompted by his developed conception of the Personality of God.

Finally, there is the following passage in 73^{23-26} : " Nevertheless, I am ever with thee, thou holdest my right hand. With thy counsel thou leadest me in the way, and afterwards wilt gloriously take me. Whom have I in the heavens ? In the earth I have no delight save in thee ; my flesh and my heart cease to be ; but my portion is God for ever." Here again the primary condition of belief in a future life is expressed : communion with God ; but in this psalm what that communion finally results in is more fully realized. Union with the eternal, unchanging God cannot be interrupted by death. As in life on this earth God is with his servant, so in the world to come God will be with him. In the presence of God there is life.

Among some modern commentators there appears to be a disinclination to recognize any signs of belief in a life hereafter in the *Psalms*. It may, however, be pertinent to ask whether sufficient consideration is given to the possibility of the influence of Zoroastrian belief on some of the deeper thinkers among the Jews, such as these psalmists were. The dates of those psalms in which, as we submit, belief in a life hereafter is contemplated, are post-exilic ; so that there was ample time for such influence to have been exerted. The intercourse with Persia was undoubtedly considerable. In other directions Zoroastrian influence on Jewish thought is demonstrable ; so that the possibility, to say the least, of such influence in the domain of the subject under consideration should be recognized.

vi. ESCHATOLOGY

In Ps. 85[1] there occurs the technical term šᵉbûth, which, as pointed out in the commentary, was adopted from prophetical usage, and means the " restoration " in reference to the " bringing back " of the primeval time of happiness, i.e., the return of the " Golden Age ". In Jer. 33[11] the prophet says, in the name of Yahweh : " I will cause the restoration (šᵉbûth) of the earth to return as at the first (or, ' as in the beginning ') saith Yahweh ". This is the thought which lies at the base of the eschatological hope so often referred to by the psalmists. The way in which this is spoken of shows that the various ideas connected with it were familiar, and therefore needed no explanation. That for the whole picture of the Eschatological Drama as presented in the Psalter the psalmists were indebted to the prophets is as clear as anything could be ; the thoughts expressed and the very words used are in almost every detail taken from the prophetical writings. To illustrate this would involve a lengthy dissertation. We must therefore restrict ourselves to just a few of the many references to the prophetical books which could be given.

The belief in the looked-for " restoration " is thus expressed, e.g., in Ps. 53[6] : " O for the salvation of Israel from Zion, when God bringeth back the restoration of his people " (cp. Jer. 30[18], Am. 9[11]) ; and in 126[1] the psalmist feels that it will be so glorious that he says : " When Yahweh bringeth back the restoration of Zion we shall be as those who dream " ; and he pleads, " Bring back, Yahweh, our restoration as streams in the Negeb " (for the force of these words see the Commentary). The time of restoration is believed to be near : " Of a truth, nigh to them that fear him is his salvation, that his glory may abide in our land " (85[9], cp. Isa. 10[25], Hab. 2[3]). Not only so, but, again in the prophetic mode, so certain is the belief in its near approach that it is sometimes envisaged as present : " Love and Truth are met together, Righteousness and Peace kiss each other ; Truth sprouteth forth from the earth, and Righteousness looketh down from heaven " (85[10, 11], cp. Isa. 33[10]). The supreme glory and central significance of this renovation of the earth is that it will be inaugurated by the coming of Yahweh himself : " Thou wilt arise and have mercy on Zion, for the time is come to be gracious unto her " (102[13], cp. Isa. 35[4]) ; and he will come in glory : " For Yahweh doth build up Zion, and shall appear in his glory in the midst of her " (102[16], cp. Isa. 60[1–3]) ; and in wondrous terror will he appear : " Clouds and darkness are round about him, righteousness and justice are the foundation of his throne ; fire goeth before him, and burneth his adversaries round about. His lightnings lighten the world, the earth seeth it, and trembleth, the mountains melt like wax before the Lord of all the earth " (97[2–5], cp. Nah. 1[5]). The convulsions of Nature which take place at Yahweh's appearance find frequent mention, *e.g.*, 93[3, 4]: " The floods rose up, Yahweh, the floods raised up their roar, the floods raised up their crashing. More glorious than the roar of many waters, more glorious than the raging of the sea, is Yahweh, glorious on high (cp. Isa. 24[19, 20], Hab. 3[10]). It is the time of the great assize, for Yahweh comes forth as Judge: " For he cometh to judge the earth ; he judgeth the world in righteousness, and the peoples in his faithfulness " (96[13], see also 9[7, 8], 98[9], cp. Joel 3[12]). The nations rise up in opposition to Yahweh, but they are overwhelmed by him: " Nations rage, kingdoms are moved ; he uttereth his voice, the earth is dissolved " (46[6], cp. Jer. 25[30], Joel 2[11]); " For, lo, kings assembled, united together ; they beheld ; then were they terrified, dismayed, put in fear . . ." (48[4–6], cp. Isa. 13[8], 24[21]). As a result they acknowledge Yahweh as their God: " Yahweh is become king over the nations ; he sitteth upon his holy throne ; the princes of the people are gathered together with the people of the God of Abraham ; for to God belong the rulers of the earth ; he is greatly exalted " (47[8, 9], cp. Isa. 66[18]). This world-dominion of Yahweh finds frequent mention: " For Yahweh, the Most High, is terrible ; a great king over all the earth " (47[2] and elsewhere, cp. Mal. 1[14]); it brings Israel gladness and joy : " Light ariseth upon the righteous, and joy to the upright of heart. Rejoice in Yahweh, O ye righteous, and give thanks to his holy name " (97[11, 12]) ; " Then shall be filled our mouth with laughter, and our tongue with shouting. Then will they say : ' Yahweh hath done great things for them. Yahweh hath done great things for us, we are joyful ' " (126[1–3], cp. Isa. 25[1, 8]). Ultimately Israel will rule over all nations : " He subdueth peoples under us, and nations under our feet ; he enlargeth for us our inheritance, the pride of Jacob whom he loveth " (47[3, 4], cp. Isa. 49[2, 3]).

That some mythological *traits* appear in the eschatological picture presented by the psalmists illustrates again the presence of prophetical influence. Mention has been made of the terrors accompanying the advent of Yahweh—fire before him, the melting of the mountains, the roaring of the seas ; these are of mythological origin. One or two other points may be referred to. Thus, in 82[1] there is the mention of the " divine council ", cp. Isa. 24[21]. In 68[16] there is an adaptation of the mythological " mountain of God " ; so, too, in 36[6], cp. Isa. 14[13, 14].

This, then, is a brief account of the psalmists' utilization of eschatological material. It could, of course, be much developed by further quotations both from the *Psalms* and from the prophetical books ; but the main points have been mentioned. It is noticeable that there is no reference to the Messiah ; but this, too, is in accordance with the predominant teaching of the prophets. On the question of Messianic prophecy in the *Psalms* see next chapter.

CHAPTER XI

THE use made of the *Psalms* in the New Testament, whether directly quoted or only alluded to, is a subject full of interest from several points of view. First and foremost there is Christ's use of them, which raises some important questions. Then there are the various instances in which the Evangelists quote the psalms as in reference to Christ; some of these suggest difficulties. This applies, too, to the use of the psalms in *Acts*, where a considerable number of quotations appear. Among the Pauline epistles more use is made of psalms in *Romans* than in any of the others. In the epistle to the *Hebrews*, as would be expected, quotations are numerous; sometimes their appropriateness may be questioned. In *Revelation* there are allusions rather than quotations.

To deal exhaustively with the subject would involve too extended a dissertation; we must, therefore, restrict ourselves to some of the more important illustrations.

In considering our Lord's use of the psalms we begin by noting the instances in which he quotes them in reference to himself. In Matth. 21[16], in answer to the protest of the chief priests and scribes against the children crying out " Hosanna to the son of David ", Christ rejoins : " Yea, did ye never read, *Out of the mouth of babes and sucklings thou hast perfected praise* " (Ps. 8[2]). It must be noted that the quotation is from the Septuagint, which makes it appropriate to the occasion; had the Hebrew been quoted, where " strength " occurs instead of " praise ", the quotation would have lost its force. The question naturally suggests itself as to why, in addressing the Jewish religious leaders, Christ should be represented as quoting the Septuagint form of the text rather than that familiar to his hearers. To this we shall have to return later. The quotation occurs only in the first Gospel, though the episode is recorded in Mk. 11[15-18] and Lk. 19[45, 46]. According to the Matthæan form of the passage, then, Christ applies the title " son of David " to himself; so that the fact that the quotation has been messianically interpreted is comprehensible; though in the psalm itself there is nothing that supports this interpretation.

We turn next to Matth. 21[42] (= Mk. 12[10], Lk. 20[17]), where at the end of the parable of the Wicked Husbandmen Christ adds : *The stone which the builders rejected, this is become the head of the corner ;*

this is from the Lord, and it is marvellous in our eyes (Ps. 118[22, 23], in *Luke* the second verse is omitted). The quotation is again from the Septuagint. The " stone " is interpreted by Christ in reference to himself, and according to Acts 4[11] (cp. Rom. 9[33], Ephes. 2[20], 1 Pet. 2[6n.]), the early Church—and the same is true of the Jewish Church—interpreted the passage in a Messianic sense; but in the psalm there is no reference to the Messiah.

Again, in Matth. 22[41-45] (= Mk. 12[36, 37], Lk. 20[42-44]) Christ quotes Ps. 110[1]: *The Lord said unto my lord, Sit thou on my right hand, till I put thine enemies underneath thy feet* (*Mark* and *Luke* " till I make thine enemies the footstool of thy feet "). Without going into several points which arise here (see the Commentary), it will suffice to say that Christ is represented as interpreting the whole psalm as Messianic, and as applying it to himself; he had asked the question : " How say the scribes that Christ is the son of David ? " Then the psalm is quoted and followed by the further question : " David himself called him Lord and whence is he his son ? " Naturally enough, no one was able to give an answer; but what was implied by our Lord was that the Messiah—applied to himself—was not only the son of David, and therefore a human ruler, but also the Son of God, and therefore a divine ruler.

In Matth. 27[46] the utterance of our Lord from the Cross is recorded : *Eli, Eli, lama sabahthani.* In Mk. 15[34] it is : *Eloi, Eloi . . .* In the parallel passage in Lk. 23[44n.], these words do not occur, but only : "; Father, into thy hands I commend my spirit." The quotation, from Ps. 22[1], is in each case partly Hebrew, and partly Aramaic. There are other verses in this psalm which, though not quoted by our Lord, were made to refer to him by the evangelists. With their intimate knowledge of the psalms, the earliest disciples could not fail to observe the extraordinary similarity between some words of this psalm and what was happening during this dark hour; thus, in *v.* 18 : *They apportion my garments among them, and upon my vesture do they cast lots* (cp. Mk. 15[24], Jn. 19[23, 24]); similarly between *v.* 15 : *My strength* [probably we should read " throat "] *is dried up like a potsherd, and my tongue cleaveth to my jaws*, and what is said in Jn. 19[28, 29]; and, again, between the words of *v.* 17 : *They gaze and look at me*, and Lk. 23[35], " And the people stood beholding."

In a few other instances quotations from the psalms by the evangelists are given as applying to our Lord. Thus, in the account of the Temptation, Matth. 4[6], Lk. 4[10], the words of Ps. 91[11, 12], *He shall give his, angels charge concerning thee; and on their hands they shall bear thee up, lest thou dash thy foot against a stone* (from the Septuagint), are put into the mouth of Satan. And, to give one other illustration, Ps. 78[2] is quoted in reference to Christ's teaching by parable (Matth. 13[35];

I will open my mouth in parables, I will utter things hidden from the foundation of the world ; the form of the text varies somewhat).

In the Synoptic Gospels, then, there are perhaps not so many quotations from the psalms as might have been expected. A few examples may be given, .iext, of the use of the psalms in the Fourth Gospel. In Jn. 10[34] the words of Ps. 82[6], *I said, Ye are gods*, are quoted as though from the Law, to prove the divinity of Christ. It is a strange piece of exegesis. Again, in Jn. 15[25], *They hated me without a cause* (Ps. 35[19] = 69[5]) is quoted as in reference to Christ. It is possible that the passage in Jn. 10[1ff.] about the Shepherd of the sheep was thought by the evangelist to be reminiscent of Ps. 95[7] : *For he is our God, and we are the people of his pasture, and the sheep of his hand.* It must be confessed that the use of the psalms in the Fourth Gospel is not very pointed.

In Acts 1[20] two psalms are quoted, but loosely : *Let his habitation be made desolate, and let no man dwell therein* (Ps. 69[26]) ; *His office let another take* (Ps. 109[8]) ; these are taken as a prophecy of Júdas. Again, in Acts 2[25-28] the Septuagint of Ps. 16[8-11] is quoted, but the crucial words are *vv.* 9, 10 : *Therefore my heart is glad, and my glory rejoiceth; my flesh also shall dwell in safety. For thou wilt not leave my soul to Sheol; neither wilt thou suffer thine holy one to see corruption.* The passage is taken as in reference to Christ's resurrection. This is an illustration of the way in which isolated passages are interpreted in an arbitrary manner without taking the context into consideration, and thereby entirely missing the meaning of the passage. Other instances occur of a similar character.

We will consider next a few cases of St. Paul's use of the psalms. It is in *Romans* that this is most conspicuous. Much of this epistle is of an argumentative nature, adopted with a view to combat Jewish controversialists. For this purpose the Apostle often utilizes quotations from the psalms (mostly from the Septuagint), following a method which was Jewish in character. Thus, in chap. 3, in support of his contention that the Jews are sinners like the rest of men, and that they can claim no exemption from the consequences of sin, he quotes from half a dozen psalms, all of which, as he maintains, point to the general sinfulness of mankind (51[4], 14[1-3] = 53[1-3], 5[9], 140[3], 10[7], 36[1]; it will not be necessary to quote these). The central point of the whole argument is to show that no man is righteous in the sight of God, and that no amount of works of the Law can make him so. Hence man's redemption must be acquired in some other way. The string of quotations which St. Paul gives here is quite in the style of the Jewish teachers ; as Edersheim [1] says : " A favourite method was that which derived its name from the stringing together of beads (*Haraz*), when a preacher,

---

[1] *Life and Times of Jesus the Messiah*, I, 449 (1883).

having quoted a passage or section from the Pentateuch, strung it on to another and like-sounding, or really similar, from the Prophets and the Hagiographa ". One other illustration; in Rom. 15[9, 11], St. Paul quotes Pss. 18[49], 117[1], and in applying them to Christ, interprets them Messianically. From the Christian point of view this is very forced exegesis; but from the Jewish standpoint there was more justification in regarding them, especially 18[49], as Messianic prophecies; thus, in the Midrash on the *Psalms* it is said, in reference to this passage, including *v.* 50, which belongs to it, that at " the gathering of the Israelites " David will give thanks unto the Lord among the nations; this is in reference to one of the great episodes of the Messianic Drama, according to Jewish tradition, viz., the ingathering of Israel, to which reference is made in Isa. 27[13] (cp. Isa. 49[22], 60[4, 9], 66[20]), where it is said (according to the Midrash) that the Gentiles will themselves escort the exiles to their home. Passages from the psalms, like the one under consideration, exercised a great influence on Jewish Messianic ideas; the exaltation of Israel among the nations, with their idolatrous beliefs, would have had the effect of enhancing the glory of Israel with their Messianic king. That this passage was interpreted in Jewish Messianic sense is seen, further, by the Midrashic comment on the words, *And sing praises unto thy name*; these praises, it is said, are those which will be offered at the advent of the Messiah. The traditional Jewish Messianic interpretation of the psalms, much of which is undoubtedly pre-Christian, has an interest and significance for us, since there is every reason to believe that the early Christians, *i.e.*, Jewish-Christians, were influenced by that interpretation, and applied it to our Lord.

From this point of view the use made of the psalms in the epistle to the *Hebrews* is particularly instructive. We will restrict ourselves to the first chapter, though other illustrations could be given; in this chapter there is a string of quotations somewhat similar to what we find in Rom. 3, though in this latter epistle the quotations are all from the psalms. Ps. 2[7] is first quoted: *Thou art my Son, this day have I begotten thee* (see also Hebr. 5[5]); this is interpreted as in reference to Christ's resurrection and Kingship. Then, in *vv.* 8, 9, Ps. 45[6, 7], *Thy throne, O God, is for ever and ever . . .*, are applied to Christ as pointing to his divinity; similarly in *vv.* 10–12, where Ps. 102[25–27] are quoted and interpreted as proving his divinity and eternity; this is immediately followed by Ps. 110[1], *Sit thou on my right hand . . .*, in reference to Christ's session on the divine throne. These quotations are thus used for dogmatic purposes. The same is true of the quotation from Ps. 110[4]: *Thou art a priest for ever after the order of Melchizedek*, in 5[6] (cp. 7[17]), in evidence of Christ's Priesthood; also of the words of Ps. 40[6–8], *Sacrifice and offering thou wouldest not . . .* in 10[5–7], as showing the uselessness of sacrifices, since Christ was the one true

Sacrifice. Lastly, there is in 13^6 the quotation from Ps. 118^6: *The Lord is my helper, I will not fear ; what shall man do unto me?* in reference to the love of Christ. Thus, in this epistle all the quotations from the psalms are used for dogmatic purposes in regard to the Person of Christ.

In the book of *Revelation* direct quotations from the psalms rarely occur ; but there are frequent incidental allusions to them ; thus, *e.g.*, in 2$^{26, \ 27}$, 12^5, 19^{15}, Ps. 2$^{8, \ 9}$ is quoted : *He shall rule them with a rod of iron* . . ., in reference to Christ's world-rule.

It must be recognized that, speaking generally, and apart from the Synoptic Gospels, the use of the *Psalms* in the New Testament follows Jewish methods. According to this, when a passage is used for illustrative or dogmatic purposes, it is chosen for its verbal form irrespective of its real meaning.

CHAPTER XII

THE PSALMS IN THE JEWISH CHURCH

WE are concerned here only with the use of the *Psalms* in the Jewish community from the time at which they became part of the worship of the Synagogue; their earlier use is dealt with in the Commentary. This may be dated, so far as Palestine is concerned, as having begun soon after the end of the Maccabæan Wars, towards the end of the second century B.C.; there is no evidence for the existence of synagogues in Palestine prior to this date.[1] This, of course, is not to say that gatherings for worship other than in the temple were not held; that was obviously the case, see, *e.g.*, 1 Macc. 3[46]; but we are referring to the Synagogue as an institution with an official liturgy. How far the *Psalms* were used in the worship of the Synagogue while the temple was still standing is a matter of uncertainty; but there are a few indications forthcoming which throw some light on the subject. Thus, after the daily morning sacrifice in the temple, the Levites sang Ps. 105[1-15], and after the daily evening sacrifice Ps. 96; these—and probably in course of time others were added—were taken over and used in the daily services of the Synagogue.[2] Again, in the Mishnah, *Tamid* vii. 4, it is said that the special psalm for each day of the week was sung by the Levites in the temple; this custom was taken over by the Synagogue; these are, for the seven days respectively: 24, 48, 82, 94, 81, 93, 92. With the exception of the third and fifth, what is here said is corroborated by the Septuagint titles to these psalms. Then, again, Pss. 145-150, which as early as the middle of the second century A.D. were an integral part of the daily synagogal service, were similarly sung daily in the temple.[3] And once more, the *Hallel* psalms (113-118, the word means " Praise "), were taken over from the temple Liturgy and sung in the synagogues after morning prayer on eighteen days of the year, including those of the New Moon.[4] These do not exhaust the indications that could be given to show how in many respects the Synagogue took over from the temple-worship the use of

---

[1] Synagogues in the lands of the Dispersion undoubtedly existed long before this date; on the subject in general see Oesterley, *A Fresh Approach to the Psalms*, pp. 153–165 (1937).
[2] *Seder Olam* xiv, mentioned by Elbogen, *Der Jüdische Gottesdienst in seiner geschichtlichen Entwickelung*, p. 82 (1913).
[3] *Sopherim* XVII, 11, this is one of the so-called " smaller treatises " of the Talmud; see further below.
[4] Elbogen, *op. cit.*, p. 249.

the psalms.   It is true that nowhere is it directly said that these various psalms were used in the Synagogue while the temple was still standing; but there is good reason for believing that this was the case; it is recorded, for example, that Joshua ben Chananiah (he died in A.D. 130), a member of the Levitical choir in the temple, used to go with the choristers in a body to the synagogue from the orchestra by the altar, and so take part in both services.[1]

In the many passages in the Gospels and *Acts* in which synagogues are referred to, mention is made only of teaching and of reading the Scriptures in them, but that is simply because there was no occasion to speak of the singing of psalms there; that was taken for granted; where there was worship psalms obviously had their place.   Once, however, there is a definite reference to the singing of psalms; in 1 Cor. 14[26] it is said: " When ye come together, each hath a psalm; hath a teaching . . ." (cp. Eph. 5[19], Col. 3[16]); it is a Christian assembly that is here in question, but as the first Christian congregations followed the procedure of the Synagogue in their form of service, this may justifiably be regarded as indirect evidence of what occurred in the Synagogue, in this respect, while the temple was still standing.

Turning now to times after the destruction of the temple, a great deal of information regarding the use of psalms in the ancient Synagogue is contained in the tractate *Sopherim* x–xxi.[2]   According to Zunz,[3] this important tractate belongs to the period of the *Geonim*,[4] A.D. 589 onwards; it gives details of the traditional use of the *Psalms* in the Synagogue, and therefore what it says applies to the previous centuries. Some of the details given are worth recording, for they tell us what psalms were used on special occasions, why they were chosen, and other points of interest; we shall, of course, not restrict ourselves here to this tractate.

First, mention may be made of the use of the *Hallel* (Pss. 113–118); in the Jewish liturgy it is treated as a single composition; it was known also as the " Hallel of Egypt ", from the opening words of Ps. 114, " When Israel went forth from Egypt ", in order to distinguish it from the " Great Hallel ", Ps. 136.   The ancient way of reciting this was for the leader to begin with " Hallelujah ", which was repeated by the congregation; then after each half-verse the congregation fell in with " Hallelujah ", which was thus said 123 times.[5]   In course of time this method of recitation was altered in different countries.[6]

---

[1] Bab. Talmud, *'Arakhin*, 11 b.
[2] The text, with notes, has been published by Joel Müller, *Masseket Soferim, der Talmudische Traktat der Schreiber* . . . (1878).
[3] *Die gottesdienstlichen Vorträge der Juden*, p. 101 (1892).
[4] The plural of *Gaon*, " excellency "; this was the title given to the heads of the two leading Academies of Babylonia, namely Sura and Pumbeditha; the period is reckoned as lasting to the early part of the eleventh century.
[5] Cp. *Sopherim* xvi. 11, 12.   [6] Elbogen, *op. cit.*, p. 496.

We are told that the " Hallel ", as well as other psalms, was known by heart by the congregation.[1] It has always occupied a place of peculiar importance in the Jewish Church, and the custom of singing it at the great festivals was, as we have said, taken over from the temple-worship to that of the synagogue. But in addition to the " Hallel ", proper psalms were appointed to be sung at these festivals, and these psalms were chosen because in each case they contained something appropriate to the occasion; thus for *Pesaḥ* (" Passover ") [2] the special psalm was 135, and this was chosen on account of *vv.* 8, 9, " He smote the first-born of Egypt . . ." The festival of *Shabuôth* (" Weeks " = Pentecost) [3] was regarded as the Feast of the Revelation of the glory of God, Ezek. i. being one of the special lessons; hence the proper psalm was 29, where " the voice of Yahweh " is explained as the manifestation of " the God of glory ". For the festival of *Sukkôth* (" Tabernacles ") [4] the special psalm was 76, chosen on account of *v.* 2 (3): " In Salem also in his tabernacle " (*Sukkah*), for this festival was celebrated, according to Lev. 23 [42, 43], in commemoration of the way in which the Israelites dwelt in " booths " (*Sukkôth*) during their journey through the wilderness. The eighth day of this feast was of special importance, the proper psalm for which was 12; mention is also made of 111 as an alternative; as the whole period of this festival was regarded as " the season of our rejoicing ", the former was probably chosen on account of *vv.* 5 and 7, where Yahweh's guardianship is spoken of; in the case of the latter, the whole psalm is thoroughly appropriate to a time of rejoicing. In the celebrations of each of these great festivals some other psalms were also sung or said; but the more important details have been indicated. Then, as to the lesser feasts, the special psalms for the New Moon [5] were 98 and 104; the former on account of the reference to the *shôphar* (" ram's-horn ") in *v.* 5, which, according to Num. 10[10], was to be sounded " in the beginnings of your months "; the whole of Ps. 104 is appropriate to this occasion, but *v.* 19 is particularly pointed: " He made the moon for appointed seasons ". At the feast of Dedication (*Ḥannukkah*), called also the " feast of the Maccabees " (see 1 Macc. 4[59], 2 Macc. 1[18]), Ps. 30 was appointed; [6] it is probably owing to this that the title " A Song at the Dedication of the House " was added; [7] the appropriateness of the psalm for this occasion is obvious. At the feast of *Purim* (" Lots ", cp. Esther 9[24]) the special psalm was 7, chosen because it speaks of vengeance on the adversary [8] (*vv.* 6, 11–16, and see Esther 9[13x]); in the Midrash *Tehillim*, " Cush the Benjaminite ", mentioned in the title of this psalm, is said to refer to Saul.

[1] Müller, *op. cit.*, p. 263.
[3] *Sopherim* xviii. 3.
[5] *Sopherim* xvii. 11.
[7] Elbogen, *op. cit.*, p. 130.

[2] *Sopherim* xviii. 2.
[4] *Sopherim* xix. 2.
[6] *Sopherim* xviii. 2, see also xx. 8.
[8] *Sopherim* xviii. 2.

Coming now to the Sabbath, as we should expect, psalms occupied an important part in the services. From early times the Sabbath has been specially connected with the work of creation, and with the deliverance from Egypt, when Israel became a nation. In all the special Sabbath psalms, therefore, verses occur in which, either directly or indirectly, reference is made to one or other of these. It cannot be said for certain which these psalms were in the earliest days of the Synagogue; but there can be little doubt that traditional usage has, in the main, been followed. Unfortunately, the tractate *Sopherim* gives no details on this subject. In the earliest rituals, however, the special Sabbath psalms for the Morning Service are : 19, 92, 93, 100, 135, 136, not necessarily in this order; for the Evening Service, 67 and 144. In addition there was, and is, the service for the Sanctification (*Qiddush*) of the Sabbath, with Pss. 29, 92, 95–99 ; and the service for the Conclusion (*Habdalah*, lit. " Separation ") of the Sabbath, when Pss. 67 and 144 are again used.

Turning now to the fast-days ; there is first the Day of Atonement (*Yôm Kippûr*, see Lev. 22²³⁻³², 23³¹, ³²) ; one of the appointed psalms was 130 ("Out of the depths have I cried unto thee, Yahweh"),[1] and here again the appropriateness is evident; the other was 103, containing several verses which would greatly appeal on this day, the last of the annual "ten days of penitence",[2] namely, vv. 3, 8–13. As in the case of the festivals, early usage has undergone much modification in the choice of psalms, as in other respects, during subsequent centuries. There are certain other lesser fast-days which have been observed by the Jewish Church for many centuries, and for which special psalms were used. It is not possible to say for certain what these psalms were, especially because of the fact that custom varied here in different countries ; but in indicating the use of the modern synagogue it is highly probable, we may feel sure, that traditional use has been followed. First, there is the *Fast of Gedaliah* (Tisri 3), observed in memory of Gedaliah, the son of Ahikam, who was murdered by Ishmael (Jer. 41²) ; at the Morning Service on this day the special psalms are 20, 25, 83, at the Evening Service 20, 25, 102 ; in each of these verses occur which may be regarded as appropriate to the occasion. The *Fast of Tebeth*,[3] the tenth day of this month commemorates the beginning of the siege of Jerusalem, the special psalm being 74, which opens with the words : "O God, why hast thou cast us off for ever ? " The Fast of *Tammuz*, on the seventeenth day of the month, is observed in memory of the first breach made in the wall during the siege,

---

[1] *Sopherim* xix. 2.
[2] The Jewish Year opens with a penitential period consisting of " ten days of penitence " ('*asārāh yĕmē teshûbah*), a kind of Advent season.
[3] From the Babylonian *Tebetu*, the tenth month, described as the month of violent rains.

the special psalm is 79, beginning : " O God, the heathen are come into thine inheritance ; thy holy temple have they defiled ; they have laid Jerusalem in heaps ". And lastly the, *Fast of Ab*, on the ninth day of the month ; according to Rabbinical tradition, both the first and the second temples were destroyed on this day, hence its observance ; the special psalm is 137 : " By the waters of Babylon, there we wept, when we remembered Zion ".

In addition to what has been said, it has always been the custom for verses from different psalms to be used in various parts of the services as versicles.

It will thus be seen that in the Jewish Church the liturgical use of the *Psalms* has been, as we should expect, of quite outstanding importance. A matter of considerable interest must, however, be added. It has always been recognized that not all the psalms, owing either to their form, or content, or spirit, were adapted to public worship, and that, indeed, many of them were never intended for this purpose. As a result, the psalms used in the Synagogue-worship—and it may be confidently asserted that the same applied to the Temple-worship—were, and still are, restricted in number. In the modern Synagogue only about one-half of the psalms are used ; such psalms as 35, 37, 45, 58, 78, 109, for instance, not being regarded as acceptable for public worship. There is every reason to believe that the early Church exercised similar discrimination (see below).

We have so far dealt with the public use of the *Psalms* in the Jewish Church ; it will not be without interest if we consider, quite briefly, the place of a number of psalms in private, or quasi-private, use. How far back, in the cases to be mentioned, the use of a psalm, or psalms, goes, cannot be stated ; but it is certain that Jewish usages in these matters have a long history behind them ; so that although we shall give the custom of the Jewish Church at the present day, we may feel confident that it reflects that of ancient times. There is a certain amount of difference of usage between the two divisions of orthodox Jews, the *Sephardim* and the *Ashkenazim*,[1] but this is not of great importance. At the ceremony of a circumcision the Sephardic Jews use Ps. 128 : " Happy is everyone that feareth Yahweh, that walketh in his ways " ; while the Ashkenazic Jews say Ps. 12, chosen, no doubt, because of the words of *vv.* 6, 7. The Marriage Service opens with the versicles : " Blessed is he that cometh in the name of Yahweh, we bless you from the house of Yahweh " (118²⁶) ; " O come, let us worship and bow down, let us kneel before Yahweh our maker " (95⁶) ; and : " Serve Yahweh with fear, and rejoice with trembling " (2¹¹).

---

[1] The term *Sephardim* comes from Sepharad (Obad. 20), identified with Spain, and referred originally to the Spanish and Portuguese Jews ; that of *Ashkenazim*, from Ashkenaz the son of Gomer (Gen. 10³), was first used in reference to the Jews of Germany. Both terms date from mediæval times.

These are followed by Ps. 100, and at the conclusion of the ceremony Ps. 150 is said. It is a touching custom according to which the husband recites frequently Ps. 128 when the time is drawing near for his wife to be delivered of a child; the appropriateness of this is pointed (see *vv*. 3, 4). Then, again, the special psalm for the Burial Service is 16: " Preserve me, O God, for in thee do I put my trust ". In the Sephardic ritual, when the coffin is lowered into the grave, Ps. 91 is said: " He that dwelleth in the secret place of the Most High shall abide under the shadow of the Almighty ". In the house of mourning Ps. 49 is said; and the Sephardic Jews have the curious custom of reciting those sections of the acrostic Ps. 119 of which the letters make up the name of the departed.

The echo of an extremely ancient custom is observed by holding a service at the consecration of a house. At this service Pss. 15, 30, 101, 121 are said, and if there are children in the family, Pss. 127, 128, are added, the reason being obvious (see 127³⁻⁵, 128³⁻⁶). In addition to these, the four sections of Ps. 119 are said, the initial letters of which make up the Hebrew word for " Blessing ", viz., *vv*. 9–16, 153–160, 81–88, 33–40, in this order. The Sephardic Jews, on the other hand, use only Pss. 30, 134.

A few points of minor interest may be added. In the Talmud (*Berakhoth* 4 *b*) it is written: " He who says Ps. 145 three times daily may rest assured that he will inherit the life eternal "; the reason given being that this psalm is regarded in the light of a prayer for all flesh; and the material blessings granted by the Almighty (*vv*. 8, 9, 15, 16) are an earnest of the far greater spiritual blessings to be enjoyed hereafter. Again, Ps. 30 is said by many devout worshippers while " laying the Tephillin " before divine service; this is the technical term used for binding on the head- and hand-Tephillah or "phylactery" (cp. Matth. 23⁵); the psalm is presumably chosen on account of the words of *v*. 11 (12): " Thou hast loosed my sackcloth, and girded me with gladness ". The phylacteries were worn in accordance with what was understood to be commanded in Deut. 6⁸: " And thou shalt bind them [*i.e.*, the words of God] for a sign upon thine hand, and they shall be for frontlets between thine eyes " (cp. Deut. 11¹⁸, Exod. 13⁹, ¹⁶).

Psalms have been used for the most diverse purposes, but the most curious has been their magical use. Nowhere is this shown forth in more detailed fashion than in the *Sepher Shimmush Tehillim*,[1] " *The Book of the use of the Psalms* "; to deal with this in any detail would be out of place here; but a few illustrations may be offered to show the belief in the efficacy of reciting psalms, held in past days. Under Ps. 3 it is said: " Whosoever is subject to severe headache and

---

[1] Edit. Heldenheim (1852); see also Blau, *Das Altjüdische Zauberwesen* (1898).

backache, let him pray this psalm . . . over a small quantity of olive oil; anoint the head and back while in the act of prayer; this will afford immediate relief ". As a cure for sick boys Ps. 9 is recommended; it has to be written on pure parchment, with a new writing instrument, and hung round the neck of the sufferer. A sovereign remedy against an evil spirit is Ps. 10; "let him fill ", it is said, "a new earthen pot with water from the spring, and, in the name of the patient pour into it pure olive oil, and pronounce over it this psalm nine times . . ." The belief that demons have a horror of water is extremely ancient, the reason being that it is the cleansing element (cp. Matth. 12⁴³). To give but one other illustration; concerning Ps. 109 it is said: " If you have a mighty enemy, who plagues and oppresses you, fill a new jug with new sparkling wine, add some mustard to it, then repeat this psalm three days consecutively; at the same time keep in mind the holy name of *El*; afterwards, pour the moisture before the door of your enemy's dwelling. But be careful that you do not sprinkle a single drop upon yourself when in the act of pouring it out; " this will effectually cause the enemy to cease worrying.

Further illustrations would be wearisome; but every single one of the psalms is recommended to be recited as a cure for evils of one kind or another. Pathetic as this all is, it does witness to an extraordinary belief in the efficacy of the mere recitation of psalms; so that even in the secular affairs of life they played an important part.

CHAPTER XIII

THE PSALMS IN THE CHRISTIAN CHURCH

As the first Christians (Jewish-Christians) worshipped in the temple or in the synagogue, it must be assumed that they followed the traditional usage of the Jewish Church in the singing or reciting of psalms. But this can have lasted only as long as the Christian community was confined to Jerusalem. Not later than the year 50, when the apostolic missionary activities brought them into the Gentile world, the psalms would necessarily have been said in Greek; and this took place first of all in Antioch: " The disciples were called Christians first in Antioch " (Acts 11^{26}, cp. *v.* 20). Greek was then the universal language.[1] In the Septuagint the daily psalm is indicated in the respective titles. As the Septuagint was the Bible of the early Church, and was repudiated by the Jewish Church, it is permissible to assume that the daily psalm thus indicated (they do not all correspond with the Hebrew titles) was in accordance with the usage of the Church, at any rate at first. But otherwise we have no information about the use of psalms in Christian worship in the earliest age. Apart from this daily psalm, however, it is probable that no definite system of dividing the psalms into daily, weekly, or monthly, portions was in existence; for all the evidence, as soon as it becomes available, shows that there was much variety in this in different localities; this is hardly likely to have been the case if any fixed method had been adopted by the Church of the first century. When Tertullian says (*Apologia* xxxi. 3) that the psalms were taken over from the Synagogue by the Christians in their worship, and used in all parts of the world, he is speaking of the psalms in general, not to any systematic method of recitation.

There are certain indications which support Tertullian's statement in an interesting way. In the account of the Sunday Vigil Service, which occurs in the *Peregrinatio Etheriæ* (it is quoted below), the component parts of the service are: alternate praise (a psalm) and prayer; then the central prayer portion, the " commemoration of all " ; after that the reading of Scripture, concluding with praise (a psalm) and prayer; then the final blessing. This corresponds in the main outline with the earliest form of service in the Synagogue service.

---

[1] Tertullian (end of second century) refers to the fact that the Jews of Egypt used the Septuagint in their synagogues there (*Apologia* xviii).

When it is realized that the *Peregrinatio* is describing the form of service as held in Jerusalem in the fourth century, it is difficult to believe that we have here a mere coincidence. It seems far more likely that we may discern a confirmation of what Tertullian says. In another respect it is probable that the use of the psalms in the early Church was taken over from the Synagogue. A very ancient element in the Synagogue-worship, adapted almost certainly from the Temple-worship, was the use of versicles from the psalms. Similarly in different parts of the early Church Liturgies appropriate verses from psalms were said. For instance, Cyril, in his *Catecheses* (xix–xxiii), delivered in 348, gives some account of the Syrian Liturgy, and tells us, among much else, that during the communion of the worshippers the verse was sung: " O taste and see . . ." (Ps. 34[8]). In the Gallican Liturgy, three verses from this psalm were sung at this part of the service (*vv.* 8, 1, 22), after each of which followed a threefold " Hallelujah ". This was called by Germanus the *Trecanum*, and expressed, according to him, the doctrine of the Holy Trinity.[1] Or again, in the various ancient Liturgies, after the Bishop has proclaimed the " Holy things for holy persons ", a response is made which contains quotations from Ps. 118[25–27]. The use of these and other phrases from the *Hallel* psalms, which have also suggested much other liturgical language, support Bickell's theory that the *Anaphora* was originally modelled on the *Hallel*.[2]

Interesting again is the definite statement of Socrates (*Hist. Eccles.* vi. 8) that Ignatius (end of first century) introduced antiphonal singing of the psalms in accordance with a tradition of the Church of Antioch ; but nothing is said about the number of psalms to be recited daily. How abundant their use was, however, may be gathered from the words of Chrysostom (*circa* 345–407): " If we keep vigil in the Church, David comes first, last, and midst. If, early in the morning, we seek for the melody of hymns, first, last, and midst is David again. If we are occupied with the funeral solemnities of the departed, if virgins sit at home and spin, David is first, last, and midst. . . . In the monasteries, amongst those holy choirs of angelic armies, David is first, last, and midst. In the convents of virgins, where are bands of them that imitate Mary ; in the deserts, where are men crucified to this world and having their conversations with God, first, midst, and last is he." [3] The expression used regarding the saying, or singing of psalms (" first, last, and midst "), is perhaps to be understood in the light of what was ordered by the seventeenth canon of the Council of Laodicæa

[1] Duchesne, *Origines du Culte Chrétien*, p. 215 (1908).
[2] *Messe und Pascha*, Engl. transl. by Skene, *The Lord's Supper and the Passover Ritual*, pp. 86 ff. (1891).
[3] Quoted by Neale and Littledale, *Commentary on the Psalms*, p. 1 (1860).

(fourth century) to the effect that the psalms were to be sung interspersed with Scripture lessons instead of being sung consecutively.
With this we may compare the somewhat different usage recorded in
the *Peregrinatio Etheriæ* (fourth century) ; it is taken from the Sunday
Offices, *Vigil* : " And when the people have entered in, someone among
the priests says a psalm, and all respond ; after this prayer is made.
Then someone among the deacons says a psalm, and similarly prayer
is made.   Then a third psalm is said by one of the clerics, and a third
prayer is made, and there is a commemoration of all. . . . Then, the
Gospel having been read, the bishop goes out, and is led with hymns
to the Cross, and all the people with him.   There again one psalm is
said, and prayer is made.   Thereupon he blesses the faithful, and
the Dismissal takes place (*et fit missa*)." [1]   The psalms here alternate
with prayer, not with lessons ; but it bears out the principle that
during divine service psalms should not be said consecutively.   At
other times, however, the recitation of a number of psalms, no doubt
said consecutively, was considered an act of meritorious piety, for
Cassian (died 435) tells us—and this illustrates the variation in local
usage—that in the choice of the number of psalms to be said daily
in monasteries there was a difference of twenty and thirty ; while in
monasteries in Egypt as many as fifty, or even sixty, were read in a
day (*Institut. Coenobit.*, ii. 2, v).   In the early Western Church (sixth
century) the system of Gregory—and the same is true of the Benedictine rule (sixth century)—was carried out, the whole of the Psalter
being gone through in the course of seven days.   This is found, too,
in somewhat later times ; among mediæval Service Books was the
Psalterium, containing the *Psalms* divided into different portions,
according to variations in different localities ; but in all cases the
Psalter was read through in the course of a week ; they were said at
the Hours services. [2]   It may be added that candidates for ordination
were required to know the whole Psalter by heart ; Gennadius, Patriarch
of Constantinople (494), refused to ordain anyone who could not recite
the Psalter by heart.   Canons to the same effect were passed at the
Eighth Council of Toledo (653), and at the Council of Orviedo (1050).
Nothing could show more eloquently the immense importance attached
to a knowledge of the psalms by the Church.   And this may be illustrated by one further detail : the mediæval Church, in its use of the
seven penitential psalms, referred each to what were held to be the
seven deadly sins ; the saying of each of these psalms was believed
to act as a deterrent against committing these sins ; thus Ps. 6, *contra
iram* ; Ps. 32, *contra superbiam* ; Ps. 38, *contra gulam* ; Ps. 51, *contra
luxuriam* ; Ps. 102, *contra avaritiam* ; Ps. 130, *contra invidiam* ; Ps. 143,

---

[1] Quoted from Duchesne, *op. cit.*, pp. 473 f. (1889).
[2] Maskell, *Monumenta Ritualia* . . ., I, xli. (1882).

contra acediam. These psalms were not regarded as penitential by the Eastern Church.

The most complete and regular recitation of psalms began when the "Canonical Hours" of Prayer were introduced, in their final form, in the Christian Church. It is not known when this first took place; but the system originated in the Eastern Church, from which it was taken over by the Western Church probably some time during the sixth century. At each of the eight services psalms were read: at *Nocturns*, probably a night service, but corresponding to the *Matins* of later days, twelve psalms were read in course; at *Lauds, Prime, Tierce, Sext, Nones*, fixed psalms were said: at *Vespers*, the evening service, four or five psalms were read in course, while at *Compline*, the bed-time service, several fixed psalms were read. The "Canonical Hours" were for the monasteries and the clergy; but devotional books for the laity were not wanting; they went under the name of *Horæ*, the most popular being the "Hours of the Blessed Virgin". The devotional books varied much in content, but psalms always occupied a prominent place. These *Horæ* became in later days the basis of the devotional book for the laity known in the fourteenth century as the *Prymer*. So far as psalms were concerned, this book contained the seven penitential psalms, the "fifteen" psalms (120–134), and what are called "the psalms of Commendations" (119, the divisions being regarded as separate psalms).[1] When this *Prymer* is compared with that of the *Prymer* of Henry VIII (1545), it may be said that "for one hundred and fifty years preceding the Reformation, and probably for a much longer period, *the* Prymer was the book authorized by the English Church for the private devotion of the people".[2] We have drawn attention to this in order to emphasize the fact that the *Psalms* had an important place in the devotional life not only of the clergy, but also of the laity.

These details, being but a few of a great number that could be offered, will suffice to give some idea of the abundant use of the *Psalms* in the Christian Church. It is unnecessary to discuss their use in the ·Reformed Churches, as this is sufficiently well known. But a final word may be said about the Psalter in the *Book of Common Prayer*, since among English-speaking people this Version is probably the most familiar.

In his important account of the Old Latin Version,[3] Burkitt says that "Latin versions of the Scriptures can be traced back into the second century"; but he continues: "No *tradition* of the origin or literary history of the Latin versions seems to have been known even

---

[1] Maskell, *op. cit.*; III, 90 ff.
[2] Procter, *A History of the Book of Common Prayer*, p. 15 (1889).
[3] *Encycl. Bibl.*, IV, 4992 ff. (1903).

to Augustine or Jerome; it remains an open question whether the first translation was made in Roman Africa, in Italy, or in Gaul. What is certain is that by the middle of the fourth century, Latin Biblical MSS. exhibited a most confusing variety of text. . . . In classifying our Old Latin authorities each group of books must be treated separately." In the *Psalms*, he says, "we find a maze of aberrant texts". The Old Latin version, a daughter-version of the Septuagint, was revised by Jerome (383); but of the Psalter he made, at different times, three versions, known as the Roman, the Gallican, and the Hebrew; the second of these ultimately superseded the others, and became the Psalter of the Western Church. It was translated by Jerome from Origen's *Hexapla*, when he was living at Bethlehem (389), and was brought to Gaul by Gregory of Tours; later it was brought over to England, where it superseded the older Latin Psalter, and was used ultimately throughout the Church in England. The Prayer-Book Psalter is a translation of this Gallican Psalter, but not wholly, for a number of translations were made of it into Anglo-Saxon and mediæval English at different times, until at last an authorized edition of the Bible was issued (Cranmer's Bible or the "Great Bible," 1540); the *Psalms* were, however, with some slight revision, taken from the Gallican Psalter. This will explain why the Prayer-Book version of the *Psalms*, beautiful as it is in the main, differs in many passages from the Hebrew text.

CHAPTER XIV

THE HISTORY OF THE EXEGESIS OF THE PSALMS

So far as the New Testament is concerned, this subject is dealt with in Chap. XI. We begin, therefore, with the method of exegesis of the teachers of the second century A.D. It will be readily understood that nothing in the shape of a commentary is to be looked for during this early period. The method of exegesis adopted by the early Church Fathers must be gathered from their incidental use and explanation of passages from the *Psalms* which occur in their writings. They used, of course, the Septuagint Version—the Bible of the early Church. It is somewhat surprising to find how very little use is made of the *Psalms* by these writers as compared with their use of the other books of the Old Testament. The reason for this may have been that inasmuch as the Psalter, from the earliest times, was the hymn-book of the Church, used during divine service, it was, as it were, outside the category of Biblical books in the ordinary sense. The lack of the use of the *Psalms* in the writings of the early Church Fathers may also be due, in part, to the fact that Scripture was primarily an apologetic weapon, and though there was a good deal in the *Psalms* which, later, was used in a Messianic sense, this did not at first appear. However this may be, among the second-century Church writers, with the exception of the *First Epistle of Clement*, and the *Epistle of Barnabas*, there are hardly any quotations from the *Psalms* in their writings; none in the so-called *Second Epistle of Clement* or in the *Didaché*, only two in the *Epistles of Ignatius*, and two in the *Epistle of Polycarp*; there are incidental references to passages in the *Shepherd of Hermas*, but very rarely actual quotations. For illustrations of exegesis we must, therefore, have recourse to the *First Epistle of Clement* and the *Epistle of Barnabas*. In the great majority of cases in the former quotations from the *Psalms* are given in illustration of precepts of a practical nature, whether exhortations to right living or warnings against wrong-doing; so that a passage is taken in its literal sense, and explained accordingly. On the other hand, in about a dozen instances passages are explained as in reference to our Lord; for example, Ps. 3^5, *I laid me down and slept; I awaked, for Yahweh sustaineth me*, is interpreted as referring to our Lord's resurrection (xxvi. 2). Again Ps. 34^{11-17}, *Come, ye children, hearken unto me . . .*, is explained as the utterance of our Lord himself, which he spoke "through his Holy Spirit" (xxii. 1). Similarly, it is stated that our Lord said in reference to himself: *But I am a worm and no man . . .* (Ps. 22⁶⁻⁸), and it is added: "Ye see, beloved, what is the example that hath been given to us; for if the Lord was humble-minded, what shall we do who, through him, have come under the yoke of his grace" (xvi. 15–17). In the *Epistle of Barnabas* much the same line is followed; but here and there passages are explained in support of doctrinal teaching. Thus, *And he shall be like a tree planted by the streams of water . . .* (Ps. 1³⁻⁶) is interpreted as referring to baptism (xi. 6–8). A quaint piece of exegesis occurs in x. 1, 9, 10, which is worth quoting because it illustrates the arbitrary method of exegesis whereby a text could be made to mean anything required, a method which was widely adopted as time went on. It is in explanation of Ps. 1¹: first a summary is given of the food laws in Lev. xi; then it continues: "Now, in that Moses said, ' Ye shall not eat swine, nor an eagle, nor a hawk, nor a crow, nor any fish which hath no scales on itself ', he included three doctrines in his understanding"; then, in reference to this it is said a little further on: "Moses received three doctrines concerning food, and thus spake of them in the Spirit; but they [*i.e.*, the Israelites], according to the lust of the flesh, received them as concerning [material] food. But David received knowledge concerning the same three doctrines, and said: ' Blessed is the man that hath not walked in the counsel of the ungodly ', as the fishes go in darkness in the deep waters; and, ' and hath not stood in the way of sinners ', like those who appear to fear the Lord, but sin like the swine; and ' and hath not sat in the seat of the scorners ', like the birds who sit and wait for their prey". That gives some idea of the fantastic kind of exegesis which becomes increasingly prevalent; at the same time, the principle of explaining scripture by the Scriptures is a sound one when rationally employed; and in later times was often adopted with good effect. In general, however, in regard to the earliest post-Biblical writings, it may be said that two central purposes are to be observed in the use of the *Psalms*, and their exegesis : (*a*) to discern, wherever possible, a prophecy of our Lord, or an allusion to him; and (*b*) to use them as an authoritative guide for conduct of life.

Here a brief reference must be made to the exegetical methods of Philo on account of the great influence which they had on the Church Fathers;¹ he lived during the first half of the first century A.D. Philo sought to harmonize Greek wisdom with Hebrew religion; though scorned by the orthodox among his own people, his work came to be highly regarded by Christian exegetes. He dealt mainly with the

¹ See Siegfried, *Philo von Alexandria als Ausleger des Alten Testaments . . .*, pp. 303 ff. (1875).

Pentateuch, but his rules of exegesis applied, of course, to all the Scriptures. According to his teaching, the literal sense of a passage must, in the first instance, be determined; but it is of far greater importance that it should be interpreted allegorically, for therein lies its true meaning; he compares the literal and the allegorical with the body and soul of man.[1] Philo's influence appears especially in the writings of the Alexandrian Christian teachers. Pantænus (*circa* A.D. 200), the founder of the celebrated School of Alexandria, was, according to Eusebius (*Eccles. Hist.* v. 10), the first to write a commentary on the *Psalms*. The same authority tells us that there followed next a commentary by Origen (vi. 24), who became the father of the allegorical method in the Church. , Of all the Church Fathers, however, none exercised such a lasting influence on the writers who followed him as Augustine; he adopted the seven exegetical rules of Tyconius.[2] Allegorical interpretation naturally played a very important part, but Augustine frequently explains a passage in a figurative sense. An illustration of his exegetical method may be offered: in explaining Ps. 51^{18-20} (50^{16-18}, in the Septuagint), he remarks that when the psalmist said "that God did not require one kind of sacrifice, he showed that he required another kind. For he does not require the sacrifice of a slain beast, but the sacrifice of a sorrowing heart. The sacrifice, therefore, that God does not demand, *i.e.*, the slain beast, is merely the symbol of the sacrifice which he does demand, *i.e.*, the sorrowing heart. God does not require sacrifices, then, to gratify his own pleasure, as some are foolish enough to imagine; and had he not wished that the sacrifice of a sorrowing heart should be symbolized by the sacrifices of slain beasts, the latter had never been ordered by the Law. Moreover, the passing and temporary nature of these old covenant sacrifices is a proof of their symbolical nature, and is a warning to us not to imagine that the sacrifices themselves, rather than the things symbolized by them, were acceptable to God" (*De Civ. Dei*, x, 5). Other passages would, of course, demand different methods of interpretation, literal, historical, allegorical, in accordance with the rules adopted from Tyconius, but space forbids our giving illustrations of these. Augustine's methods were, in the main, followed by all the Church teachers during the Middle Ages. It will not be necessary to go into details regarding the work of these; as has been pointed out by various modern writers on the subject, the fourfold meaning of Scripture discerned by mediæval scholars in general is succinctly expressed by the following saying: *Litera gesta docet, quid credas allegoria, moralis quid agas, quo tendes anagogia,* which may be freely paraphrased: " The literal sense teaches facts,

---

[1] See further, Siegfried, *op. cit.*, pp. 168 ff., **196 f.**
[2] Dealt with by Burkitt, *The Book of the Rules of Tyconius*, pp. xv ff. (1894).

allegory dictates belief, the moral sense guides as to right living, spiritual elevation is the final goal ".

In the field of Jewish exegesis mention must be made of the labours of the " Masoretic " (Masora = " tradition ") scholars who prepared the way for a closer and more literal exposition of the Biblical text. Though great care had always been taken in preserving a correct Hebrew text of the Old Testament Scriptures by the Scribes, exegetical studies received a powerful impetus in the seventh century, when vowel-signs were introduced. Henceforward Masoretic studies steadily developed, and the body of Masoretic tradition—all concerned with the exact determination and preservation of the Biblical text—steadily grew for centuries. It must, however, be noted that as early as about A.D. 800 great opposition arose against all Rabbinical interpretation and tradition on the part of the heretical Karaite [1] sect. The Karaites undertook a most minute and critical study of the Biblical text; and in order to oppose and refute the Karaite teaching, the Rabbis had to undertake a similar task. This dual critical study developed into a very keen contest between Rabbinic and Karaite champions; and there is no doubt that the bulk of the work of a final and authoritative text must be assigned to the heretical Karaites. That this ultimately contributed powerfully to the whole study of exegesis among both Jewish and Christian scholars needs no emphasis. We need but add that the " Masoretic " text is that of the Hebrew Bible at the present day; and it is also that from which the Old Testament in English is translated.

A brief reference may be made next to some outstanding mediæval Jewish exegetes, since their work was not without influence on Christian scholars. First, there was Saadia ben Joseph (died A.D. 942), who, while not altogether ignoring tradition, laid special stress on *reason* as the basis of interpretation and exegesis; hence he insisted, among other things, that Scriptural passages must be explained in the light of their context. Self-evident as this appears to us, it must be realized that this method was a great advance on what had preceded; and even at the present day it is not always followed, as when isolated texts are sometimes torn from their context and given a meaning which would be seen to be false if the context were taken into consideration. Saadia translated, with commentary, the whole of the Old Testament into Arabic; Margulies, in his dissertation published in 1884, has translated the *Psalms* portion into German.

Somewhat later there was the celebrated exegete Solomon bar Isaac, better known as Rashi (an abbreviation of *Rabbi Shelomo Izchaki*, the Hebrew form of his name); he died in A.D. 1105. He,

---

[1] The Hebrew form of the name is *Beni Miqra*, " Sons of Reading ", *i.e.*, of the Scriptures.

too, respected the traditional exegesis, making much use of the Targums; but, like Saadia, he sought for the plain, straightforward meaning of a text, and did not ignore its context. His special contribution, however, was the stress he laid on the need of bringing linguistic knowledge into account in seeking to explain Scripture. He wrote a commentary on the *Psalms*, which Breithaupt published in 1713.

Here mention must be made of the *Midrash* on the *Psalms*; it is approximately of the same time as Rashi, *i.e.* belonging to about the eleventh century, and known as *Midrash Tehillim*; it is also called *Shocher Tob* (" He that diligently seeketh good ", Prov. 11[27]), from the opening words of the book. Although comparatively late in date, it contains a great deal of extremely valuable ancient material, its special interest being that it has preserved much of the traditional Palestinian exegesis of the *Psalms*. The homiletic method of exegesis characteristic of it may not appeal to us, yet it is not without interest; the following illustration gives a parable by way of explaining Ps. 2[12], *Kiss the son lest he be angry, and ye perish from the way*: " Whereunto is this to be compared ? It is like a king who was wrath against the inhabitants of a city; these, therefore, went unto the king's son and made their peace with him, in order that he might go to the king and make peace on their behalf. So he went and pacified the king. When the inhabitants of that city knew that the king had been propitiated, they desired to sing a song (of thanksgiving) to him; but he answered and said: ' Do ye wish to sing a song (of thanksgiving) to me ? Nay, but go and sing it unto my son, for had it not been for him, I should have destroyed the inhabitants of the city '."

This illustrates the essential tendency of homiletical exegesis, which is characteristic of this *Midrash*. Another comment occurring in this *Midrash* may be quoted as giving a good insight into a somewhat different line of interpretation; the passage Ps. 8[4-6] is thus explained: " *What is man that thou art mindful of him ?* This refers to Abraham, as it is written in Gen. 19[29], ' When God destroyed the cities of the Plain, God remembered Abraham '. *And the son of man that thou visitest him ?* This refers to Isaac, as it is written in Gen. 21[1], ' And Yahweh visited Sarah, as he had said '. *For thou hast made him but little lower than Elohim.* This refers to Jacob, as it is written in Gen. 30[39], ' And the flocks conceived before the rods '; Jacob was able to cause the flocks to bring forth ringstraked, speckled, and spotted, thus possessing almost divine power, but he was a little lower than Elohim because he could not give them souls. *And crownest him with glory and honour.* This refers to Moses, as it is written in Exod. 34[29], ' Moses wist not that the skin of his face shone by reason of his speaking with him '. *Thou madest him to have dominion over the works of thy hands.* This refers to Joshua, as it is written in Josh. 10[12, 13], ' Then spake Joshua . . . Sun, stand thou still upon Gibeon, and thou, Moon, in the valley of Aijalon . . .' *Thou hast put all things under his feet.* This refers to David, as it is written in 2 Sam. 22[43], ' Then did I beat them small as the dust of the earth, I did stamp them as the mire of the streets '. *All sheep and oxen.* This refers to Solomon, as it is written in 4[33] (Hebr. 5[13]), ' He spake also of beasts '. *Yea, the beasts of the field.* This refers to Samson, as it is written in Judg. 15[4], ' And Samson went out and caught three hundred foxes . . .' *The fowl of the air.* This refers to Elijah, as it is written in 1 Kgs. 17[6], ' And the ravens brought him bread and flesh in the morning . . .' *And the fish of the sea.* This refers to Jonah, as it is written in Jon. 2[1], ' Then Jonah prayed unto Yahweh his God out of the fish's belly '. *Whatsoever passeth through the paths of the seas.* This refers to the Israelites, as it is written in Exod. 15[19], ' The children of Israel walked on dry land in the midst of the sea '."

We have quoted this in full as illustrating the kind of exegetical ingenuity whereby Scriptural texts may be made to mean anything that is desired. It is a method not restricted to Jewish exegesis. But that by the way.

Not long after the time of Rashi arose the eminent scholar Abraham Ibn Ezra (he died in 1167). His exegetical methods followed those of his great predecessor, his special contribution being that by his intimate knowledge of the Hebrew language he was able to throw much fresh light on Biblical texts. " In his commentaries ", says Israel Abrahams, " he rejected the current digressive and allegorical methods, and steered a middle course between free research on the one hand, and blind adherence to tradition on the other. . . . He never for a moment doubted, however, that the Bible was in every part inspired, and in every part the word of God." [1] He, too, wrote a commentary on the *Psalms*, though restricted to the first ten (published by Fagius in 1542). A contemporary of Ibn Ezra was David Kimchi, who likewise sought primarily for the natural meaning of Scripture, laying great stress on the help afforded by grammatical knowledge. His commentary on the first book of the *Psalms* was published by Schiller-Szinessy in 1883 ; this is in Hebrew.[2]

These Jewish exegetical scholars are mentioned because of the use made of their works by mediæval Christian scholars, and even more by those of later times.

We come next to the Reformation period. It is unnecessary to enumerate the various commentaries on the *Psalms* which appeared

---

[1] *A Short History of Jewish Literature*, p. 69 (1906).
[2] For much information on the Jewish exegetes, see Bacher, *Die Jüdische Bibelexegese* . . ., pp. 68 ff. (1892).

during this period. The outstanding names are Luther and Calvin, both of whom wrote commentaries on the *Psalms* which influenced, more or less, all the teachers of the sixteenth and seventeenth centuries. The main characteristics which mark the exegetical methods of scholars during these centuries are : a reaction against the allegorical interpretation of Scripture; concentration on the literal meaning of the text, aided especially by its grammatical sense; and the principle that Scripture must be explained by Scripture. Luther, for example, strongly contended that the teaching as to the fourfold meaning of Scripture (see above) was a delusion; only the literal, grammatical sense was decisive; he conceded an allegorical interpretation only where the inspired writers themselves employed it. Protestant scholars had the great advantage over those of the Roman Church in that they took the Hebrew text as the basis of their study, whereas the latter relied on the often faulty translation of the Vulgate. It was no doubt inevitable that the successors of the Reformers should have interpreted Scripture in a dogmatic sense in accordance with their point of view; this was, of course, again and again fatal to scientific exegesis.

A new point of view—and this applies to the *Psalms* especially—was presented by Lowth in his *Prælectiones de Sacra Poesi Hebræorum* (1753), where he deals with the metrical forms of Hebrew poetry. In later days he was followed by other scholars, who further developed his principles ; of outstanding importance here were the works of Ley, especially *Leitfaden der Metrik der Hebräischen Poesie* (1887) ; but the whole of this subject is dealt with in Chap. IV. Here exegesis is affected by metrical considerations ; this is often illustrated in the following Commentary.

Of the highest importance for the study of the Old-Testament and its exegesis was the work of Kennicott in the eighteenth century ; in his *Vetus Testamentum Hebraicum cum variis lectionibus* (1776–1780) he collated, with the assistance of other scholars, over six hundred Hebrew manuscripts, together with sixteen Samaritan codices ; for the textual critic, and for a resultant scientific exegesis, this work was of inestimable value, though not, of course, in itself exegetical.

Finally, we come to the labours of the scholars of the nineteenth and twentieth centuries, which has done so much for the fuller understanding of the *Psalms*. Of these, however, we need say but a few words here, for our indebtedness to them will be found to be acknowledged again and again in the Commentary (see also the Bibliography). Archæological research during the last generation has been of immense value to Biblical students ; new light has been thrown on the early religious beliefs and ritual of the Hebrews ; philological studies have been greatly forwarded ; historical, geographical, and ethnical knowledge

I

have been increased. Much of this bears on the study of the *Psalms*, and modern commentators, as a whole, have made good use of the new material offered. In addition, greater attention has been paid to the criticism of the text, especially in the light of the ancient Versions; and the metrical form in which the *Psalms* were written has received the recognition it deserves. Differences of opinion on many matters necessarily exist; but this is to be welcomed, for final decisions and ultimate truth can be reached only by the frank exchange of varying points of view.

PSALM 1

THIS psalm is in the nature of a Preface to the Psalter. The main
theme, often dealt with by other psalmists, centres in the doctrine of
retribution; and it will be recognized that this theme in a " Preface "
of this kind is wholly appropriate. The psalmist sees that, broadly
speaking, his people are divided into good and bad, godly men and
evil-doers. As observers of the Law the former are prospered by God,
while the evil perish. The psalmist knew well enough that the facts
of life did not always bear this out; but he maintains that, generally
speaking, the man who was faithful to the Law was rewarded; but
that the wicked suffered for their wickedness. The psalmist presents
this great division among his people without taking account of the
various views urged by other psalmists (see, further, Ps. 73); nor does
he speak of the oppression of the godly by the wicked, which is an
outstanding theme in so many psalms. He says nothing on the subject
of worship, or sacrifices, and of other matters of religious importance.
The omission of such subjects in what is in the nature of a Preface is
a matter of common sense; we mention the point only because it is
sometimes stated that the writer of this psalm is lacking in the
presentation of important truths. It is true that his religious outlook
does not seem to partake of the deep spirituality of so many of the
psalmists; but this is simply due to the fact that he was writing an
introductory preface.

In all that he says the psalmist has only his own people in mind;
the " wicked " are those of his own race, not Gentiles.

As to date, the psalm may be assigned to the Greek period;
roughly, about the middle of the third century B.C.; this is suggested
by the fact that the psalmist belonged to the circle of the Sages, and
by the emphasis laid on the Law; a somewhat earlier date is, of
course, quite possible; but its character of " Preface " makes the later
date more probable because the whole Psalter was presumably in
existence (see further, pp. 70 f.) before this psalm was written.

The metre is somewhat variable, but the changes are effective in
bringing out thoughts for special emphasis.

1.   O the blessedness of the man
                that doth not walk
              in the counsel of the wicked,
And in the way of sinners doth not stand,   and in the seat of scorners doth not sit.
2. But in the Law of Yahweh is his delight, and in his Law doth he meditate day and
                                    night.

3.
          He is like a tree
          planted by ° the water,
          the fruit of which
          it bringeth forth in its season,
          and its leaf fadeth not.
       ° And whatsoever he doeth it prospereth.°

4. Not so are the wicked, ° not so °,   but like the chaff which the wind
                                      driveth away are they.

5.
      Therefore ° they shall not hold their own,°—
    the wicked,—in the judgement,
  Nor sinners in the assembly of the righteous.

6.
         For Yahweh knoweth
         the way of the righteous ;
    But the way of the wicked shall perish.

Text-critical Notes

3. Om. פַּלְגֵי, " the streams of ", which disturbs the rhythm, and does not occur in Jer. 17⁸ on which this verse is based. On the last line see exeg. note. 4. Repeat, with G, לֹא־כֵן, demanded by the rhythm. 5. Lit. " they shall not arise ", see exeg. note.

1. The psalmist describes the avoidance of fellowship with evil-doers in three directions if a man would be blessed ; the word is a noun, *blessedness,* which connotes here spiritual happiness (cp. Ps. 34⁸) ; but it is also used of material benefits (*e.g.*, Ps. 127⁵). The way in which this is expressed is in the style of the Wisdom-writers (cp., *e.g.*, Prov. 3 ¹³, ¹⁴), and marks the psalmist as belonging to the circle of Wise-men (*Ḥakamim*). The three terms used of evil-doers, following their usage in the Wisdom literature, are in a rising scale : *the wicked* is a general term ; *sinners* are lit. those who " miss " the right way, purposeful in wrong-doing ; while *scorners* are the worst type, for they mock not only men, but God. With such the godly man will not *walk, stand,* nor *sit.* This negative action on the part of the godly man is followed by what is his positive conduct : *delight* in fulfilling *the Law of Yahweh,* and *meditating* therein *day and night.* This stress on the observance of the Law is another characteristic of the Wisdom writers (see, *e.g.*, Prov. 3¹⁻³ and elsewhere). 3. The comparison of the godly man with *a tree planted by the water . . . ,* is clearly taken from Jer. 17⁵⁻⁸ ; but the prophet may well have been indebted to the Egyptian Wisdom book, " The Teaching of Amen-em-ope," where it is written :

  " But the truly silent one [in contrast to the passionate man], when he standeth
    aside,
  He is like a tree that groweth in a plot ;
  It groweth green, and the fruit thereof increaseth ;
  It standeth in the presence of its lord ;
  Its fruits are sweet, its shade is pleasant,
  And it findeth its end in the garden."

In details the two are naturally divergent, but it is the central idea of the comparison which is significant. In our psalm we have omitted " the streams of " before *the water,* as this does not figure in the prophetical passage referred to, and interferes with the two-beat rhythm here. It is probable, as several commentators remark, that the words *And whatsoever he doeth it prospereth* were not part of the original form of the psalm; they are prosaic, and uncalled-for after the poetical way in which the prosperity of the godly man has been described. 4, 5. In contrast to the happy lot of him who observes the Law of Yahweh, *the wicked* (spoken of in the plural), with the ruinous fate that awaits them, are held up as a warning. The emphatic repetition, *Not so are the wicked, not so*, is taken from the Septuagint; but the extra beat is required to correspond with the beats in the second half-line, so that the Septuagint evidently represents the original form of the Hebrew text. Very graphic is the picture of *the wicked* being *like the chaff which the wind driveth away*: when the threshers had gathered the corn on to the threshing-floor, usually situated on an elevated exposed spot, they tossed it up into the air with four- to five-pronged forks; thus the wind blew the chaff away, and the corn remained to be gathered and sifted from the straw in a sieve (cp. Am. 9⁹). This was always done late in the afternoons when the western sea-breeze blew with sufficient force to disperse the chaff, but was not so boisterous as to damage the corn. The picture portraying this familiar scene was particularly impressive because it displayed so pointedly the ineffectiveness and uselessness of the wicked. The words which follow, 5, illustrate this; but it is difficult to give a good translation of the Hebrew when seeking to reproduce the order of the words as they stand: *therefore they* (*i.e.*, the wicked, which comes in the second member of the verse) *shall not hold their own—the wicked—in the judgement*; this is confessedly a paraphrase in order to bring out the force of the Hebrew, " they shall not arise "; for the picture is that of a court of justice, where, in turn, accuser and accused stand up to plead. In this case God is the Accuser; but the thought is not that of the final Judgement; the psalmist is dealing with present conditions, not with the world of the future, which belongs to Eschatology. Just as the wicked are silenced in the presence of the Almighty, so too shall *the sinners* not be able to assert themselves *in the assembly of the righteous*. 6. Finally, the psalmist sums up all that has gone before: *For Yahweh knoweth the way of the righteous*, *i.e.*, Yahweh takes note of the manner of life of the righteous, and rewards them accordingly; *But the way of the wicked shall perish, i.e.*, the usage or mode of action of the wicked leads to nothing. " Way " (*derek*) in Hebrew has a variety of meanings according to the context.

Religious Teaching

The central theme is the doctrine of retribution; but, as this has already been dealt with in some detail (pp. 86 ff.), we shall refer to it

only indirectly now. Apart from this, however, there are one or two
other matters of deep religious interest, suggested by the psalm, to
which attention may be drawn. We have, first, the teaching, implicit,
not directly stated (v. 6), that the reward of the righteous and the
punishment of the wicked are brought about by divine action. To be
sure, each, reward and punishment, is the result of a man's way of
life; but these, it is taught, do not follow as the necessary sequence
of cause and effect; they are brought about by the act of God.
Closely connected with this there is, in the next place, the teaching on
human free-will which underlies all that the psalmist says; this
sounds like a contradiction of what has just been said; it is not so in
reality. We must distinguish between the divine will and divine
grace. The psalmist fully recognizes the former; he also stresses the
action of human free-will; but there is no hint of divine grace. The
tendency to lay stress on the former rather than on the latter is, in
general, characteristic of Judaism; not that the action of divine grace
is lost sight of; that is not the case; but it is no injustice to say that
it does not receive the same emphasis as that laid on human free-will.
It is not to be denied that the true balance between divine grace and
human free-will does sometimes find expression in Jewish authoritative
writings; but it is exceptional.

One other matter: intercourse between the godly and sinners is
directly discountenanced. Two thoughts strike one here: if the
wicked never come into contact with the godly, what chance have they
of learning better things and improving? We must suppose that the
psalmist was actuated by the principle that they that touch pitch will
be defiled! Perhaps that is sometimes the only way (cp. 1 Cor. 5[11]);
yet we cannot help thinking of our Lord's way (Mk. 2[15-17]).

PSALM 2

THE main difficulty in the interpretation of this psalm is to decide
who the speakers are; on this there are differences of opinion. The
difficulty is increased by the abrupt opening of the psalm, which reads
as though some words preceding had been uttered by a speaker, and
are now lost. We hope to show that the whole psalm was recited by
the king; if, as some hold, it is the court-poet who speaks in the name
of the king, his words come, at any rate, as from the king. The
nations are represented as speaking in v. 3, Yahweh in vv. 6, part of 7,
8, 9, but these are words put into the mouths of others by the king.
It was on the occasion of his enthronement that the king in question

recited the psalm. Contrary to the opinion of some commentators, the psalm, as we shall show, is thoroughly logical and consistent throughout. It is a magnificent confession of faith in God at a time when the newly anointed king, entering upon his position of great honour and responsibility, finds that his country is menaced by a confederation of external foes.

Nothing could be more natural than that the psalm should have been interpreted in a Messianic sense : " his anointed ", " my king ", " my son ", the possessive pronoun being in each case in reference to God, as well as the king having been begotten by Yahweh, would seem to demand a Messianic interpretation. In spite of this, however, we shall give reasons to show that the psalm is not Messianic. The expressions mentioned will be seen to refer to the earthly ruler, not to the Messianic king. It is only by reading-in later ideas that a Messianic interpretation is suggested. That *v.* 7 is quoted in Acts 13[33], Hebr. 1[5], 5[5] as in reference to Christ cannot be urged in support, for Old Testament passages are often utilized by New Testament writers for illustrative purposes without taking their context into consideration ; it is worth noting that our Lord never quotes this verse, yet there were occasions on which it would have been so appropriately quoted had he believed it to have had a Messianic sense ; see, *e.g.,* Lk. 22[70,] Jn. 5[17, 18].

As to the date of the psalm, apart from the fact that it is obviously pre-exilic, there is nothing in it which enables us to point to anything more definite. The conditions portrayed in the first two verses clearly reflect some actual historical event ; but we are unable to find in the Old Testament any *data* whereby this can be identified. When, however, one considers that, dating from the beginning of the monarchy to its disappearance, a period of, roughly, four centuries is covered in the comparatively short Biblical record, many events must have happened of which we have no details. The two or three Aramaisms which occur in the psalm are no indication of date ; they could have been inserted at any time. As to the contention of some commentators that the psalm is Maccabæan, we can only suggest that some little attention should be paid to Jewish history during the last two pre-Christian centuries.

The metre, with the exception of *vv.* 5, 7, 8, 12, is 3 : 3 ; these are, respectively, 2 : 2 : 2, 3 : 3 : 3, 2 : 2 : 3, 3 : 3 : 3.

1. Why do the nations rage, and the peoples imagine a vain thing ?
2. The kings of the earth ° conspire together °, and the princes take joint counsel
   Against Yahweh and against his anointed :
3. " Let us tear their bands asunder, and let us cast away from us their cords."
4. He that abideth in the heavens laugheth, ° Yahweh ° doth have them in derision ;

5.   then shall he speak
           unto them in his wrath,
           and in his fierce anger terrify them :
6. " Yea, I have set up my king   on Zion my holy hill ! "
7.   I will speak concerning Yahweh's decree :
   He said unto me : " My son art thou ;   this day have I begotten thee ;
8.   Ask, and I will give
           nations for thine inheritance,
         And for thy possession the ends of the earth ;
9. Thou shalt break them with a rod of   and dash them in pieces like a potter's
   iron,   vessel ! "
10. And now, O ye kings, be wise ;   be instructed ,O ye judges of the earth ;
11. Serve Yahweh in fear,   ° and with trembling kiss his feet °,
12. Lest he be angry, and ye perish in the
   way,   for his wrath may soon be kindled.
         O the blessedness of all that seek refuge in him !

Text-critical Notes

2. Read יִתְיָעֲצוּ (cp. Ps. 83³) for יִתְיַצְּבוּ, " set themselves ". 4. Read,
with many MSS., יהוה for אֲדֹנָי, " my Lord ". 8. Om. מִמֶּנִּי, " from me ",
for the rhythm's sake. 11. Read, with Bertholet, וְנִשְּׁקוּ בְרַגְלָיו בִּרְעָדָה for
וְגִילוּ בִּרְעָדָה נַשְּׁקוּ־בַר " and rejo:ce with trembling kiss son ".

1, 2. The psalm opens in a somewhat abrupt manner, and records,
as will be seen from the context (v. 6), the words of a newly enthroned
king. The reason for this unusual beginning is that the words express
what was foremost in the mind of this king, namely, the menace of a confederation of rebellious subject-states who were taking the opportunity
of the advent of a new ruler to assert their independence. The
frequency of this procedure in the history of the ancient eastern
kingdoms is sufficiently well known not to need further illustration.
The mention of *nations* and *peoples*, *kings* and *princes*, sounds very
imposing to modern Western ears ; but we are dealing with ancient
Oriental modes of speech ; we find, *e.g.*, in the Tell el-Amarna tablets
that even the ruler of a mere city is called a king. In the ancient
East " king " (Hebr. *melek*) had not the same connotation that it has
now. The reference in our psalm is to such states as Edom, Moab,
Ammon, and the like. The interrogative form with which the psalm
opens is, on the one hand, an expression of surprised contempt, but,
on the other, an implicit expression of faith, as the context again
shows. The purpose of these nations was so utterly foolish in view
of the fact that the king against whom their action was directed was
Yahweh's representative, that it could be referred to only by a contemptuous query : *Why do the nations rage, and the peoples imagine a
vain thing ?* The Hebrew word rendered " rage," which occurs here
only (the noun in Ps. 64²), must, in view of the context, be understood
in the sense of angry feelings, not in that of tumultuous demonstration ;
for the imagining of " a vain thing ", together with what is said in the
next verse, points to secret machinations, which had come to the
king's ears. This the king then describes more fully. The slight
emendation of the Hebrew text (following Ps. 83³), whereby we read

conspire together for *stand up together*, is justified both because of the parallel *take counsel together*, and also because it gives the requisite sense ; for standing up together and thereby revealing their purpose, is just what they would not do ; the conspiracy is as yet only in preparation. It is because they are conspiring *against Yahweh and against his anointed*, that their purpose is so utterly foolish. In those days, when each people had their own national deity, to attack the nation was to defy the god. In this case, these peoples had been subdued by Yahweh, who had thereby shown his power ; what folly, therefore, to contemplate fighting against him and his anointed king. The implicit faith in God which the king here exhibits will be noted. 3. He then puts into the mouth of the kings and princes the words which he assumes them to be uttering : *Let us tear their bands asunder, and let us cast away from us their cords* ; *i.e.*, they intend to throw off their state of vassalage under Judah.

It will be noted, in passing, how impossible, in view of what has been said, a Messianic interpretation of the psalm is. The nations spoken of have hitherto been subject to Yahweh and to his anointed king, thereby acknowledging him as their ruler ; but never in Messianic teaching does such a *trait* occur ; the nations of the world are the enemies of the Messiah, and never anything else until the Messianic kingdom is set up. But that by the way. 4. The threat of the nations calls forth, first, the mockery of Yahweh : *He that abideth in the heavens laugheth* ; to our ears it sounds irreverent, but anthropomorphic expressions of this kind are inevitable where there is still an undeveloped conception of God. But this is followed by his wrath. 5, 6. The cause of Yahweh's wrath is that in spite of the fact that it is *he* who established the king on the throne, yet it is against *Yahweh's* representative that the nations conspire : *Yea, I* (emphatically expressed in the Hebrew) *have set up my king on Zion my holy hill.* These words the king puts into the mouth of Yahweh ; 7. then, addressing the assembled courtiers again, he says : *I will speak concerning Yahweh's decree* ; he claims to have received a divine oracle. However we may conceive of the way in which such divine utterances were communicated, there is no sort of doubt that it was believed that to kings they were vouchsafed (cp. 1 Sam. 11[6], to Saul ; 2 Sam. 23[2, 3], to David ; 1 Kgs. 3[5], 9[2 ff.], to Solomon, and elsewhere). 8, 9. The words of the decree then follow, the king asserting that they had been spoken to him : *He said unto me.* That the words which follow were Messianically interpreted by the early Church is an illustration of the way in which later thought read a meaning into passages which originally they did not have (cp., *e.g.*, Isa. 7[14] in Matth. 1[18-23], Gal. 4[27], Hebr. 1[8 ff.], and elsewhere). *My son art thou*; in the ancient East the belief in the divine origin of the king was widespread.

Numerous illustrations could be given, did space permit; but it is more to the purpose to show that a similar belief was held by the people of Israel. Nothing could be more pointed than the words put into the mouth of Yahweh by the prophet Nathan; they are spoken to David in reference to Solomon : " I will establish the throne of his kingdom for ever; I will be his father, and he shall be my son." Similarly, in reference to David it is said in Ps. 89²⁶, ²⁷: " He shall call me, ' My father art thou . . .', yea, I have made him my firstborn, most high among kings of the earth." In its origin the divine sonship of the king was conceived of in a literal sense; but this was utterly alien to Hebrew thought, where the idea is purely that of adoption; on the enthronement of the king Yahweh adopted him as his son. This is fully brought out by the words which follow in the psalm : *this day have I begotten thee*; " this day " is the day of the king's enthronement. He is to have *nations* for his *inheritance*, and *the ends of the earth for* his *possession*; this is in the Oriental poetical style, similarly as in Ps. 72⁸. The destruction of the peoples, 9, is again not intended literally, as the words which follow show. Here the king speaks again in his own name, 10-12 : *And now, O ye kings, be wise ; be instructed, O ye judges of the earth*; these words express, of course, the royal wish, for obviously they could not have been addressed directly to the kings and judges who were busy conspiring together. By the words *Serve Yahweh in fear*, are meant, " Be subject to me," *i.e.*, Yahweh's representative. The text of the second half of this verse is confessedly difficult; as it stands, the Hebrew text reads : " And rejoice with trembling. Kiss the son, lest he be angry . . ."; read in connexion with their context, and without preconceived notions, it must be granted that the words raise doubts as to their genuineness. To begin with; the metre requires three beats in each half of the verse, thus :

    " Serve Yahweh in fear,   and rejoice with trembling, kiss-son ";

" kiss-son " is joined together as one word in the Hebrew. Then it must be noted that " rejoice with trembling " is an impossible combination according to Hebrew usage; one has but to look up the passages in which these two words, respectively, occur to see the truth of this. Again, as the text stands, there is no parallelism, which is so characteristic of the rest of the psalm. And finally, the use of the Aramaic word for " son " (*bar*), after the Hebrew, *ben*, has been used previously (*v.* 7), is unprecedented. It is evident that the Versions did not all have before them the text as it now stands; the Septuagint and the Vulgate have, instead of " kiss the son," the rendering, " take hold of correction "; similarly the Targum. Jerome had the present text before him, but translated it *adorate pure*, taking *bar* in an adverbial sense from the root *barar* " to purify ". It will thus be seen

that there is every justification for emending the text; we are indebted
to Bertholet[1] for the rendering: "and with trembling kiss his feet",
which involves but little alteration of the text.   The phrase " to kiss
the feet " means to acknowledge subjugation, cp. Isa. 49²², Ps. 72⁹,
Mic. 7¹⁷, and occurs in Egyptian and Babylonian documents.   In
the final verse of our psalm, *Lest he be angry . . .* , refers therefore as
we should expect, to Yahweh.   The final words, *O the blessedness of
all that seek refuge in him,* held by some commentators to be a later
addition, make an extremely appropriate conclusion to the psalm, since
they are uttered in reference both to the king and to the nations who
have been adjured to " be wise ".

Religious Teaching

   The conception of God portrayed in this psalm does not reach the
same high level as that of so many other psalms.   There are some old-
world ideas expressed which betray a somewhat undeveloped apprehension of the Divine Personality.   Anthropomorphisms do not, it is
true, necessarily denote primitive conceptions, as they may be, and
often are, in the Old Testament, figurative expressions; but in this
psalm the references to the Almighty are somewhat crude.   At the
same time, it must be recognized that belief in God, and trust in his
power, appear prominently.   Moreover, the thought of God adopting
the king as his son, so different in conception from the similar belief
among other nations of antiquity, witnesses at any rate to a far higher
religious stage among the Hebrews.

PSALM 3

THIS beautiful little psalm tells of one who is in grave danger from
the malice of enemies; the cause of their animosity is not indicated;
but from their mocking words: " No help for thee in thy God!" we
may gather that religious differences were largely in question.   This
is substantiated by the psalmist's superb faith in God, through whose
protection he feels perfectly safe from his enemies, who are also the
enemies of God.
   In the title the psalm is attributed to David, and is brought into
connexion with the narrative contained in 2 Sam. 15; but this cannot
be taken seriously; when one reads this narrative the conviction is
forced upon one that various *traits* would necessarily have been reflected

[1] *ZAW*, for 1908, pp. 58, 59, 193.

in the psalm had there been any connexion between the two. There
is not sufficient reason to deny a pre-exilic date to the psalm, but
anything more precise cannot be postulated, as indications in the psalm
itself are wanting.

The metre is mainly 3 : 3, but in *vv*. 3, 7, 8, we have, respectively,
2 : 2 : 3, 2 : 2 : 3 : 3, and 2 : 2.

1. *A Psalm. David's; when he fled from the face of Absalom his son. (But see 2 Sam.*
1 8³¹⁻³³.)

1 (2). Yahweh, how many are mine
adversaries,   many are they that rise up against me ;
2 (3). Many are they which say to my   " No help ° for thee ° ° in thy God ° ! "
soul :   Selah.
3 (4).   But thou, Yahweh,
art a shield about me,
My glory, and the lifter-up of my head.
4 (5). With my voice unto Yahweh do I   and he answereth me from his holy hill.
cry,   Selah.
5 (6). I laid me down and slept,   I awoke, for Yahweh sustaineth me.
6 (7). I have no fear of ten thousands of   that set themselves against me round
people   about.
7 (8).   Arise, Yahweh,
save me, my God ;
For thou dost smite all mine enemies
on the cheek-bone,   thou dost break the teeth of the wicked.
8 (9).   To Yahweh belongeth help,
upon thy people be thy blessing.   Selah.

Text-critical Notes

2. Read, with S, לֹה‎ for לֹו‎ " for him ". Read, with S, בֵּאלֹהָיו‎ for
בֵּאלֹהִים‎ " in God ".

1, 2. The psalmist gives no indication as to the cause of the
perilous position in which he finds himself ; but as to a friend he
pours out his heart to *Yahweh*, telling him of the many *adversaries*
who *rise up against* him, and of their wicked words : *No help for thee
in thy God, which they say* to his *soul*, a Hebrew way of expressing the
individual self. 3, 4. But he sees how foolish is the threat of his
enemies, for he knows him in whom he trusts : *But thou, Yahweh, art
a shield about me*, so that the missiles cast at him, whether literal, or
slanderous words, fall harmless to the ground ; for he knows that
Yahweh is his *glory*, or " honour," *and the lifter-up of his head*. 4.
This implicit faith is unshakeable, for his happy experience is that
whenever he lifts up his *voice* and cries unto *Yahweh*, *he answereth me
from his holy hill*. By the " holy hill " is meant Zion (cp. Ps. 2⁶).
5, 6. His sublime faith in the ever-watchful care of Yahweh over him
night and day he expresses further in words, the simple beauty of
which is very inspiring : *I laid me down and slept*, implying a conviction
of the loving presence during the hours of darkness ; *I awoke, for
Yahweh sustaineth me* ; his first thought on awakening is of Yahweh.
That inspires him with fearless courage, come what may : *I have no
fear of ten thousands of people that set themselves against me round about.*

7, 8. The note of triumphant faith peals out in the final words : *Arise, Yahweh, save me, my God,* is an exclamation denoting the psalmist's affirmation of trust, rather than in the nature of an appeal; this is evident from the statement of Yahweh's action in the words which follow; the *smiting on the cheek-bone* is not elsewhere imputed to Yahweh (cp. 1 Kgs. 22²⁴, Job 16¹⁰), but for the thought of Yahweh *breaking the teeth of the wicked,* cp. Ps. 58⁶; distasteful as such anthropomorphic expressions sound to our ears, it must be remembered that when uttered by spiritually-minded men like our psalmist, they are used figuratively. In the closing words the psalmist identifies himself with his people, attributing *help to Yahweh,* and calling for his *blessing* upon his *people.* It is unnecessary to regard these words, as some commentators do, as a later liturgical addition.

Religious Teaching

This has been brought out in the exegetical notes. It needs but to be added that for the expression of sublime trust in God this psalm is not surpassed in the Psalter.

PSALM 4

THE variety of ways in which this psalm is explained by commentators witnesses to the difficulty of interpreting it. This difficulty arises largely owing to the fact that references to persons and events occur without any clear indication as to who the persons are, and what events are in question. The interpretation which we have to offer differs in some particulars from those of other commentators; it may, or may not, be the right one; but we venture to hope that it will be found to explain the various obscurities. For its justification we must refer to the exegetical notes. But our interpretation is, briefly, as follows: Owing to the failure of the harvest, the people, or a large section of them, are disheartened and discontented; they not only blame Yahweh for this, but even turn, in consequence, to the worship of another god. The psalmist, firm in his trust in God, in spite of all, is mocked for his belief and faithfulness. He reproves the people for their unstable belief, testifying from his own experience that God always helps in time of need. His prayer on behalf of the wavering people, implied in the opening words of the psalm, is seen to be answered by what he says in the concluding verse.

There is no sufficient reason for doubting that the psalm belongs to pre-exilic times; but it is not possible to assign a more exact date, as indications are wanting.

The second half of *v.* 1 has three beats to each half-line; in the rest of the psalm we have indicated the metre as 2 : 2 : 2 : 2, which may, however, also be denoted as 4 : 4.

1.   *For the Precentor : With stringed instruments. A Psalm. David's.*

1 (2).   When I cry, answer me,
                 O God of my righteousness;
      When I was in trouble thou didst set   be gracious unto me, and hear my
         me at large;   prayer.

2 (3).   O ye sons of men, how long
                 shall my glory be for dishonour?
                 Ye love vanity,
                 Ye seek falsehood. Selah.

3 (4).   ° But know that Yahweh
                 did wondrously show his mercy to me °;
                 Yahweh ° doth hear me °
                 when I call unto him.

4 (5).   Be perturbed, but sin not;
                 Commune with your heart
                 on your couch, and be silent. Selah.

5 (6).   Bring righteous offerings,
                 and trust in Yahweh.

6 (7).   Many say:
                 " Who showeth us good?
                 ° Departed from us
                 is the light of his countenance ! " °

7 (8).   ° Yahweh ° hath given
                 joy in my heart,
                 ° greater than ° when their corn
                 and their wine were abundant.

8 (9).   Altogether in peace
                 will I lie down and sleep;
                 For thou, Yahweh,°
                 makest me to dwell in safety.

Text-critical Notes

3. Read וְדְעוּ כִּי־הִפְלָא יְהוָה חַסְדּוֹ־לִי for the present Hebr. text: " But know that Yahweh hath set apart a godly one to him ". Read, with G, יִשְׁמָעֵנִי for יִשְׁמַע " he heareth ". 6. Read, with Gunkel:

נָס מֵעָלֵינוּ אוֹר פָּנָיו :

7. Add יהוה from the previous verse. Lit. " more than at the time ". 8. Om. לְבָדָד " alone ", for the rhythm's sake.

1. At a time of distress the psalmist appeals to Yahweh, addressing him as *God of my righteousness*, by which is meant that whatever righteousness there is in the heart of the psalmist is from God. His present appeal is prompted by the experience of divine mercy in the past: *When I was in trouble thou didst set me at large*; the force of these words is difficult to bring out adequately in translation; the root-idea of " in trouble " is that of restriction, or of being hemmed in, so that there is much significance in this being followed by " thou didst set me at large ". The psalmist, then, recalls this act of divine mercy in the past, and in the strength of it now pleads, *be gracious unto me, and hear my prayer*. What is the purport of his prayer?

That is just where, at first sight, this psalm is so puzzling. 2. **Instead** of saying what he is praying for, thereby continuing to address his words to God, which is what would naturally be expected, the psalmist suddenly puts a question to the more influential class of men, as the expression *benê 'iš* implies, saying: *O ye sons of men, how long shall my glory be for dishonour?*   The point here is that these men had scoffed at his trust in Yahweh in which he had gloried; hence they had turned his glory to shame, from their point of view.   They, on the other hand, had forsaken the worship of Yahweh, and had been guilty of idolatry: *Ye love vanity,* lit. " emptiness," *ye seek falsehood (kazab)*, a word used in reference to false worship in Am. 2⁴, Hos. 7¹³, 11¹² (12¹), cp. Isa. 44²⁰, Ps. 40⁴. 3. In contrast to this, the psalmist bids them take knowledge that *Yahweh* had shown *his mercy* to him in wondrous wise, in reference to what he had said in *v.* 1, and that *Yahweh doth hear me when I call unto him,* implying that he will do the same for them. He grants that they have reason to be worried—he explains why later: 4. *Be perturbed,* but that is no excuse for their sin of turning from Yahweh; let them think out the matter for themselves, *Commune with your heart on your couch, and be silent, i.e.,* from calling upon some other god; let them be faithful in their duty to Yahweh: 5. *Bring righteous offerings, and trust in Yahweh.* 6. Then he quotes their words, describing their lack of faith in Yahweh: *Who showeth us good? Departed from us is the light of his countenance;* they think that they have been forsaken by Yahweh . 7. Then, at long last, the psalmist reveals what is the *raison d'être* of the whole psalm; through his faith Yahweh *hath given joy in my heart,* which is greater than all the satisfaction they had enjoyed at former harvests, *when their corn and their wine were abundant;* here we have the explanation of all that has gone before: there has been a bad harvest, in consequence of which the people had lost their faith in Yahweh, and had looked to some other god, no doubt Baal, for help; we are reminded of the words of the prophet: " But she did not know that it was I that gave her the corn, and the wine, and the oil, and gave her much silver and gold which she made (into an image of) Baal " (Hos. 2⁸). The psalmist, by his magnificent faith in God, even when times were distressful, sets an example to his people; and his final words of peaceful repose suggest that his example was not in vain.   It is, we hope, not fanciful to see in these closing words the answer to the prayer uttered at the opening of the psalm: *When I cry, answer me, O God of my righteousness.*

Religious Teaching

Apart from the earnest faith in God in time of distress which is characteristic of all the psalmists, there is one element in this psalm which rarely, if ever, finds expression elsewhere in the Psalter. Written at a time when there was famine, or at any rate shortage of food, in the land owing to a bad harvest, the psalmist glories in the spiritual satisfaction of joy within him through his love and faithfulness to God; compared with this, material wants do not trouble him. He recognizes, of course, that men need food and drink; but he knows that the Giver of all good gifts will supply all that is needful: " Thou, Yahweh, makest me to dwell in safety." With him it is first things first; it is the victory of the spiritual over the material. We are reminded of the gracious words: " Your heavenly Father knoweth that ye have need of all these things; but seek ye first his kingdom, and his righteousness; and all these things shall be added unto you " (Matth. 6[32, 33]).

PSALM 5

WE have here the prayer of a faithful servant of Yahweh, uttered during the offering of the morning sacrifice; the ceremonial for this is described in Exod. 29[39, 40], Lev. 6[12-18] (in the Hebrew 6[5-11]), Num. 28[4-7]. The psalmist is menaced by many enemies, but he nowhere gives any indication of the cause of their enmity; they are evidently men of his own race, for, had they been Gentiles, the fact would have been brought out. On the whole subject of the frequent mention of the enemies of the psalmists, see above, Chap. VIII.

One cannot but recognize that the psalmist's prayer suffers interruptions because his mind is so full of the thoughts of his enemies; this occasions a certain incongruity; but the simple-hearted way in which the alternations are uttered is an interesting illustration of the unrestrained outpouring of one who has experienced the love of God in full measure, and feels that he can unburden his heart as to a friend. The psalm is difficult to date, but the type of the enemies suggests that it is post-exilic.

The metre is 3 : 2 throughout.

1.   *For the Precentor : To the Nehiloth. A Psalm. David's.*

1 (2). Give heed to my words, Yahweh,   consider my musing;
2 (3). Hearken unto the sound of my
        cry,   my King, and my God;
        For to thee do I pray ° at morn,   3 (4). mayest thou hear my voice;
        At morn I make ready for thee,   and watch ° for thee.°
4 (5). For thou delightest ° not in wicked-
        ness,   an evil man sojourneth not with thee;
5 (6). The arrogant stand not up   before thine eyes;

Thou hatest all workers of iniquity,
The man of blood and deceit

7 (8). As for me, because of the greatness of thy love,
I worship in thy holy temple

8 (9). Yahweh, lead me in thy righteousness;
Make straight before me thy way.

9 (10). For there is no understanding ° in their mouth °,
An open sepulchre is their throat,

10 (11). Hold thou them guilty, O God,

Because of the multitude of their transgressions repel them,

11 (12). But let them that trust in thee rejoice,
° And let them continually exult in thee,

12 (13). For thou dost bless the righteous man,
And dost cover him as with a shield,

6 (7). ° all ° them that speak lies ;
° thou dost abhor,° Yahweh.

I enter thy house,
in the fear of thee.

because of mine adversaries,

their inward part is destruction,
they make smooth their tongue.
may they fall through their own plannings,

for they have rebelled against thee.

let them ever shout for joy,

all that love thy name.

Yahweh, with peace,

dost crown him with favour.°

Text-critical Notes

2. Om. יהוה and place the stop after בֹּקֶר, for the rhythm's sake. 3. Add אֵלַי for the rhythm's sake. 4. Om., with many MSS., אֵל, " God ". 6. Om. הָאָוֶד for the rhythm's sake; insert כָּל־ with G. Read תְּתָעֵב for יְתָעֵב "he abhorreth". 9. Read, with the Versions, בְּפִימוֹ for בְּפִיהוּ, " in his mouth ". 11, 12. The text is here clearly out of order, and there is no metrical arrangement as it stands ; read, with several commentators :

וְיַעְלְצוּ בְךָ תָּמִיד כָּל־אֹהֲבֵי שְׁמֶךָ :
כִּי־אַתָּה תְּבָרֵךְ צַדִּיק יְהוָה בַּשָּׁלוֹם
וְתָסֹךְ עָלָיו כַּצִּנָּה רָצוֹן תַּעְמְרֶנּוּ :

On the difficult and uncertain meaning of the expression " To the Nehiloth " in the title, see pp. 11 ff.

1–3. The prayer which the psalmist addresses to Yahweh is described in a threefold manner: *Give heed to my words*, in reference to the content of the prayer : *consider my musing*, referring to the thoughts which have prompted the *words*, cp. Ps. 39[3], at first mentally expressed ; the prayer is then uttered aloud : *Hearken unto the sound of my cry*. For the address to Yahweh as *my King and my God*, cp. Ps. 44[4], 68[24], 74[12], 84[3]. The prayer is offered *at morn*, cp. Ps. 88[13], and that it was uttered during the offering of the daily morning sacrifice is made clear by the expression *I make ready* ; this is a technical sacrificial term, meaning lit. " to set in order ", in reference to the wood for the fire to burn the sacrifice (cp. Gen. 22[9], 1 Kgs. 18[33], the term is also used in Lev. 1[8, 12], 6[12] [6[5] in Hebrew]) ; its use here suggests that the psalmist was a priest, for the term is used in connexion with priestly functions. The sacrifice, during which the prayer was said, would naturally be thought to make the prayer more efficacious, for sacrifice was in the nature of inviting the divine presence ; hence the psalmist's words that he *watches for* Yahweh (cp.

K

Isa. 21⁶, Mic. 7⁷). 4–6. The prayer is interrupted here, for the psalmist's mind is so full of the thoughts of his enemies—because of whose menacing attitude he utters his prayer—that he breaks off in order to open his heart to God about them. That these enemies are men of his own race is shown by the way in which the psalmist repudiates the idea of their coming to worship, a thing which would not be contemplated in the case of Gentiles : *the arrogant stand not up before thine eyes, i.e.,* do not present themselves in the presence of God (cp. Josh. 24¹, 1 Sam. 10¹⁹, Zech. 6⁵). The type of these enemies is of the worst kind ; they are *arrogant, workers of iniquity,* they *speak lies,* are *men of blood,* and full of *deceit,* all terms occurring in other psalms in describing other psalmists' enemies of a similar type. Such *Yahweh doth abhor.* 7. In contrast to these the psalmist says of himself that owing to *the greatness of* God's *love (ḥesed)* for him, he is enabled to *enter* his *house,* and, in holy *fear of* him, to *worship in* his *holy temple.* 8–10. The psalmist then takes up his prayer again : *Yahweh, lead me in thy righteousness,* lest his *adversaries* should tempt him into wrong ways ; and he adds : *Make straight before me thy way,* in order that he may see clearly how he ought to walk. But the thought of his adversaries again predominates, and the bitter things said about them can be justified only because they are reckoned as God's enemies : *they have rebelled against thee.* 11, 12. More edifying is the final part of the prayer ; the text in these verses has suffered in transcription, for the order of the clauses is not quite logical, and the metre, which is regular in the rest of the psalm, disappears here. For the rendering given above we are largely indebted to several commentators ; it will be seen that it reads smoothly, and the metre conforms to that of the rest of the psalm. The passage is the most beautiful part of the psalm. The psalmist prays both for himself and for those like-minded with him, that they who *trust* in God may *rejoice* ; and closes with an affirmation of faith : God does *bless the righteous man with peace,* and *cover him as with a shield,* the word used is that of the large shield which covers the whole body, and *crown him with favour* (cp. Ps. 103⁴).

Religious Teaching

This has been sufficiently dealt with in the exegetical notes.

PSALM 6

THE psalm presents us with a picture, one of the most vivid of its kind in the Psalter, of a sufferer prostrate on his bed of sickness. So

severe is the nature of his malady that a fatal outcome is contemplated.
That the psalmist conceives his suffering to be inflicted because of sin
is evident from his mention of the divine wrath.   Towards the end of
the psalm reference is made to the sufferer's adversaries ; but, as in so
many other psalms of a like nature, it is not said who they are or why
they are envenomed against him.   The sudden change from plaintive
grief to the triumphant denunciation of his enemies, together with the
declaration that God has heard his prayer, suggests that the last three
verses may have been added a little later, but by the same writer.

As to the date, the pronounced sense of sin points to the post-
exilic period ; but a more exact indication of date is not possible.

The metre is 3 : 3, with the exception of *vv.* 2, 4, 8 ; in the first
half of each of these it is 2 : 2, the second half having again three beats.

1.   *For the Precentor : With stringed instruments.   On the eighth.   A Psalm.   David's.*

1 (2). Yahweh, rebuke me not in thine   and in thine indignation chasten me
          anger,   not.
2 (3).   Have mercy on me, Yahweh,
                               for I am withered away,
                 Heal me, ° for my bones ° are dried up.°
3 (4). My soul is greatly terrified,   but thou, Yahweh, how long ?
4 (5).   Turn thee, Yahweh,
                                deliver my soul,
                 Save me for thy lovingkindness' sake.
5 (6). For in death there is no remem-   in Sheol who will give thanks unto
          brance of thee,   thee ?
6 (7). I am weary with my sighing ; °
          I flood my couch every night,   with my tears I deluge my resting-place.
7 (8). Mine eye wasteth away for grief,   groweth weak ° because of all ° ° my
                                                    distress °.
8 (9).   Depart from me,
                                all ye workers of iniquity,
                 For Yahweh hath heard the sound of my weeping ;
9 (10). Yahweh hath heard my supplica-
          tion,   Yahweh hath accepted my prayer.
10 (11). Let all mine enemies ° be greatly   let them turn away and be put to shame
          terrified,   suddenly.

Text-critical Notes

2. Om., with G, יהוה for the rhythm's sake.   Read, with Perles (*Analecten* ii.
51 f.), נִבְלוּ for נִבְהֲלוּ, " are terrified ".   6. Some part of the text seems to have
fallen out here.   7. Read, with S, מִכָּל־ for בְּכָל־, " in all ".   Read, for the better
parallelism, צָרְתִי for צוֹרְרָי, " mine adversaries ".   10. Om. וְיָשֻׁבוּ for the
rhythm's sake : the word occurs in the next half-line.

For the meaning of the expressions used in the title, see above,
pp. 11, 12.

1. The psalmist's pleading that God's *anger* may not crush him is
an implicit confession of sin, cp. Ps. 38[1].   2. He cries for *mercy*, for
the sickness from which he is suffering has left his body in an
emaciated state ; in somewhat exaggerated language he cries, *I am
withered away*, and speaks of his bones as being *dried up* ; for this
latter expression cp. Ezek. 37[11] ; it is an emendation of the Hebrew
" terrified ", which can hardly be used in reference to bones, and the

word occurs immediately after, 3. *My soul is greatly terrified.* The
pitiful mental condition of the sufferer is poignantly expressed in the
unfinished exclamation, *how long?* It can refer either to Yahweh's
anger—how long will it last?—or to the sufferer's sickness; probably
both are included. That his sickness is a punishment for sin is not
definitely stated, but it is implied in the petition, 4. *Turn thee—i.e.,*
from thy wrath—*Yahweh,* and in the appeal: *Save me for thy lovingkindness' sake.* 5. His sickness has brought him near to death, and
here we get one of the most pointed illustrations in the Psalter of an
undeveloped belief in the Hereafter: *For in death there is no remembrance of thee, in Sheol who will give thanks unto thee?* Cp. Ps. 30⁹,
88¹⁰⁻¹², 115¹⁷ (see further pp. 88 ff.). 6. In what follows: *I am weary
with my sighing,* something seems to have fallen out of the text, cp. Ps.
69³. The tendency to exaggeration, already noted, comes out again
in what the psalmist says about the abundant outpouring of his tears,
and 7. of the consequent effect on his eyes; but such modes of
expression come naturally to the Oriental. 8–10. The very sudden
change of subject in the concluding verses reads strangely, for they
deal with *the workers of iniquity,* who are bidden to depart from the
presence of the sufferer, the reason given being that *Yahweh hath
heard the sound of my weeping* . . . It may, of course, be inferred that
the thought of these sinners, *all mine enemies,* was at the back of the
psalmist's mind in his utterances in the earlier part of the psalm.
This is possible, but his entire silence on the subject hitherto does not
support this; it seems more likely that these concluding verses (8–10)
were added by the psalmist to his psalm at a subsequent period, when,
having recovered from his sickness, through the mercy of Yahweh, he
could stand forth as his forgiven servant, and denounce all those who
were unfaithful to the God of their fathers.

Religious Teaching

Of high importance in this psalm is the teaching on the doctrine
of sin. The sense of sin, though not explicitly enunciated, is very
evidently implied; there is, first, *the recognition of sinfulness,* for sin
calls forth the divine anger; then there is the truly *penitential spirit*
which throws itself upon the mercy of God, and weeps in sorrow for
sin; and, finally, *the assurance of forgiveness,* expressed by trust in
God's lovingkindness. It is the first of the seven penitential psalms
of the Church.

Of a negative character is the teaching concerning the After-life.
The Sheol doctrine is the normal belief in the psalms, with but few
exceptions. On the whole subject, see pp. 88 ff.

PSALM 7

THIS psalm must be described as one of the less inspiring in the Psalter. It gives a vivid picture of the hatred engendered by religious strife, a hatred which is mutual. The self-righteousness of the psalmist is very different from the humble-mindedness so characteristic of most of the psalm-writers. The sudden introduction of the eschatological scene in *vv.* 6–10 comes in strangely, and may possibly not be part of the original psalm. Much use is made of earlier psalms, which may in part account for the irregularity of the metre. The text has suffered in some verses, though it would appear that here and there unnecessary emendations are made by some commentators.

The date is probably that of the Greek period.

1. *Šiggaion. David's, which he sang to Yahweh because of the words of Kush the Benjamite.*

1 (2).   Yahweh, my God,
                              in thee do I trust;
               save me ° from my persecutor °, and deliver me,

2 (3). Lest he tear my soul like a lion,   rending, and none delivereth.

3 (4).   Yahweh, my God,
                             if I have done this,
                 if there be iniquity in my hands,

4 (5). If I had requited evil to him that —but I delivered him that was without
      was at peace with me,   cause mine adversary—

5 (6). Then let the enemy persecute my ° and let him tread down my life to the
      soul,   ground,
            and lay my glory in the dust. Selah.

6 (7). Arise, Yahweh, in thy wrath,   lift up thyself against the rage of mine
                              adversaries,
            awake, my God, for judgement °;

7 (8). And let the assembly of ° the   and over it ° be thou seated ° in the
      gods ° encompass thee,   height.

8 (9). Yahweh judgeth the peoples;   judge me, Yahweh, according to my
                            righteousness,
         and according to mine integrity ° reward me °.

9 (10). May the ° wickedness ° of the
      wicked ° come to an end °,   ° and may righteousness be established,°
      For he that trieth the hearts and
      reins   is a righteous God.

10 (11). My shield is with God,   who saveth the upright of heart.

11 (12). God judgeth the righteous,   yea, a God that hath indignation every
                            day;

12 (13). If he turn not, he will whet his he hath bent his bow, and made it
      sword,   ready;

13 (14). For him hath he prepared the
      instruments of death,   he maketh his arrows fiery shafts.

14 (15).   Behold !
                 He travaileth with iniquity,
                 he conceiveth mischief,
                 he bringeth forth falsehood.

15 (16). He dug a pit, and burrowed it out, and is fallen into the hole he made.

16 (17). His mischief shall return upon and upon his crown shall his violence
      his own head,   descend.

17 (18). I will give thanks to Yahweh and I will sing praise to the name of
      according to his righteousness,   Yahweh Most High.

Text-critical Notes

1. Read מְרֹדְפִי, in view of the context, for מִכָּל־רֹדְפִי, "from all my persecutors". 5. The Hebrew adds וְיַשֵּׂג, "and let him overtake", in reference to "my soul"; we have tentatively omitted it because it overloads the half-line. 6. Om. צִוִּיתָ, "thou hast commanded", for the rhythm's sake. 7. Read (cp. context) אֱלֹהִים (Ps. 82¹) for לְאֻמִּים, "peoples". Read, with several commentators, שׁוּבָה for שֻׁבָה, "return". 8. Read, with Kittel, גָּמְלֵנִי for עָלַי, "upon me". 9. Read רֹעַ for רַע, "wicked". Read יִגָּמֵר for יִגְמָר. Read, with Jerome (*et confirmetur justitia*), וְתִכּוֹנֵן צְדָקָה (Gunkel), for יִתְכּוֹנֵן צַדִּיק, "and mayest thou establish the righteous man".

For the title see pp. 12 ff.

1, 2. The psalmist prays for deliverance from his persecutor; the context shows that we must read the singular here; his savage fierceness is compared with that of a lion; *my soul* is, as often elsewhere, used of the individual self. 3–5. A protestation of innocence follows: *if I have done this*, i.e., the evil which is then described, the psalmist is ready to suffer at the hands of his persecutor. 6. He therefore calls upon God to *arise* in his *wrath* for the *judgement* of his *adversaries*; here the plural is used, showing that his particular adversary is one of many. In praying that *Yahweh* will *arise for judgement*, the thought of the psalmist is directed to the final Judgement, which is developed in 6–10, where the Almighty is pictured as seated on his throne above, and surrounded by the host of heaven; before that tribunal *Yahweh judgeth the peoples*; then *may wickedness come to end*, and *righteousness be established*. That the psalmist should here speak of the peoples, on the one hand, and of himself individually, on the other, certainly reads strangely; it is difficult to believe that the text is in order; indeed, it may well be, as a number of commentators contend, that *vv.* 6–10 belonged originally to another psalm. 11 ff. follow logically after *v.* 5; *God judgeth the righteous*, the psalmist is referring to himself and to those like-minded with him; opposed to him is his enemy, and here again a particular individual is referred to; against him *God hath indignation every day*; in what follows, 12, 13, we have an illustration of the way in which a psalmist, in the bitterness of wrath against his enemy, becomes guilty of imputing to Yahweh action which is wholly human, and therefore altogether unseemly. No doubt the words are figuratively intended; but they are, none the less, distasteful. It is in reference to the wicked man that it is said: *If he turn not, he*—i.e., Yahweh—*will whet his sword*, as though Yahweh were a human warrior; *he hath bent his bow and made it ready*, just in the way that men prepare to meet their enemies. Sword and bow are *the instruments of death*, especially as in this case the *arrows are fiery shafts*, elsewhere equivalent to lightning (Ps. 18¹⁴), which strike a man dead on the spot. This fate of the wicked man the psalmist feels justified in envisaging because of the innate wickedness of the former. He then goes on, 14, to describe the origin and full development of the ungodly man's wickedness; it must be confessed that the comparison here with a woman in childbirth is extremely distasteful; allowance must, however, be made for the Oriental's want of delicacy, according to Western standards. Figurative language of a harmless character is used by the psalmist when he says of the wicked man, 15, that *He dug a pit, and burrowed it out,* just as a hunter does in order to entrap his prey; this is in reference to libellous accusations, the untruth of which recoils upon the head of the false accuser: *His mischief shall return upon his own head, and upon his crown shall his violence descend.* Retribution having thus fallen upon the psalmist's enemy, thanksgiving and praise are offered to Yahweh: *I will give thanks to Yahweh . . . and will sing praise to the name of Yahweh Most High.* From these concluding words we may gather that the psalmist's rectitude in the sight of God was vindicated.

The subject-matter of the psalm does not offer material for a section on religious teaching.

PSALM 8

THIS psalm, one of the most inspiring in the whole of the Psalter, was written by one who was both a poet, a devout servant of God, and a believer in man, whether as a child or as the lord over created things.

All too short as this beautiful little psalm is, it contains teaching and subject-matter for thought which are truly great. Brief reference is made to these below, but in a commentary it is hardly possible to do justice to the fulness of its content, as this would require more space than can here be devoted to it. Of the pre-exilic date of this psalm we are convinced, in spite of the arguments of some commentators.

The metre is very interesting; it is indicated in the translation; the short lines have two beats, the rest either 3 or 3 : 3.

1.   *For the Precentor : On the Gittith.   A Psalm.   David's.*
1 (2).   Yahweh, our Lord,
                  how excellent is thy name
                  in all the earth !
          ° Thou hast set ° thy glory above the heavens.
2 (3).   From the mouth of children °
                  dost thou establish strength,
                  because of thine adversaries,
          To still the enemy ° and the rebellious.°
3 (4).   When I behold thy heavens,
                  the work of thy fingers,
          The moon and the stars which thou hast prepared,—

4 (5). What is man that thou shouldest   or the son of man, that thou shouldest
        think of him,   give heed to him?
5 (6). Thou madest him a little lower   and dost crown him with glory and
        than gods,   honour;
6 (7). Thou makest him to have dominion
        over the works of thine hands,   all things thou hast put under his feet,
7 (8). Sheep and oxen, all of them,   and also the beasts of the field,
8 (9).   Birds of the heavens,
                          and the fish of the sea,
          All that passeth through the paths of ° the waters °.
9 (10).   Yahweh, our Lord,
                          how excellent is thy name
                          in all the earth.

Text-critical Notes

1. Read נָתַתָּה for תֶּנָה, "set". 2. Om. וְיֹנְקִים, "and sucklings" (=עוֹלְלִים), which overloads the half-line. Read, with Duhm, וּמְהִתֹקוֹמֵם for וּמִתְבַקֵם, "and the avenger", cp. Ps. 17⁷. 8. Read, with Jerome, מָיִם for יַמִּים, "seas".

1, 2. In simple, but beautiful, words the psalmist raises his voice in praise to *Yahweh, our Lord* (*'Adon*), whose *name is excellent in all the earth*; very pointed is "*our* Lord"; the psalmist stands there in solitude, but unites with himself his people. The *name* is identified with Yahweh, as in Ps. 148¹³; his work of creation is seen *in all the earth*, and men see the excellence of the work of the Creator though they cannot apprehend the Creator himself. Not merely the earth, but *the heavens* are of Yahweh's creation, and *above* them his *glory* abides (cp. Ps. 113⁴). Even *children* witness to the glory of Yahweh, thereby silencing his *enemies* and those who are *rebellious* against him; in that sense the children exhibit divinely-given strength; the Hebrew text is, however, somewhat uncertain. 3-8. It is at eventide that the psalmist gazes up at the illimitable expanse of the heavens with the mysterious glory of the moon, and studded with stars; and an overpowering sense of the greatness and might of God takes hold of him. With holy self-contempt at the thought of the insignificance of humanity in the sight of God, he cries: *What is man that thou shouldest think of him . . .?* And yet—and here the psalmist is implicitly uttering praise and thanksgiving to God—it had seemed good to the Almighty to create man in wondrous fashion: *Thou madest him a little lower than gods* (cp. Gen. 1²⁷), thereby *crowning him with glory and honour*; it must be noted that the mention of *gods* here in no way impugns monotheistic belief; according to ancient Hebrew belief, the assembly of the gods, or the heavenly host, were wholly subordinate to, and of entirely different nature from, Yahweh (cp. Ps. 7⁷, 82¹); they were conceived of as angelic beings—*i.e.*, as the messengers of God who carried out his will.

The honour and glory with which Yahweh has deigned to crown man are then described by the psalmist: *Thou makest him to have dominion over the works of thine hands . . .*, evidently an echo of

Gen. 1²⁶, 2¹⁹, ²⁰ slightly developed. The repetition of the opening words of praise makes a fitting and noble conclusion to the psalm.

Religious Teaching

The expression of the majesty and glory of God, compressed as it is in Hebrew into little more than half a dozen words, is wonderfully impressive. Prompted by the recognition of God's creative power in contemplating the glorious moon-lit sky, it teaches that one of the most compelling aids to belief is to observe the world of Nature. Very appropriately in this connexion does Kittel quote the words of Kant: " Two things fill the mind with ever-renewed wonder and reverence the more often and persistently thought is occupied with them : the star-lit heavens above me, and the moral law within me."

Unique in the Psalter is the teaching that within the hearts of little children lies enshrined divine strength which has the power to subdue everything; the deep significance of this is only realized when our Lord's words are recalled : " Whosoever shall not receive the kingdom of God as a little child, he shall in no wise enter therein " (Mk. 10¹⁵, Lk. 18¹⁷).

Full of instructive beauty is the twofold thought of man's insignificance in the sight of God, and yet of man's dignity as God's highest creation. Of this we refrain from saying more; it would require an essay for itself.

PSALMS 9, 10

MOST modern commentators are agreed that in their original form these two psalms constituted a unity. The reasons for this contention are that in some Hebrew MSS., in the Septuagint and the Vulgate, and in the other Latin Version of Jerome, they appear as a single psalm. Pointing in the same direction is the fact that, taken together, the two psalms form an acrostic ; that in a few cases, especially in Ps. 10, the alphabetical letters are wanting is fully explained by the disorder of the text itself in some of the verses. Then it is also to be noted that the " Selah ", which never appears at the end of a psalm, occurs in 9²⁰, showing that this cannot originally have been the end of the psalm. But the most convincing reason for regarding these psalms as forming a unity is gained by reading them through without a break ; there are throughout the same lines of thought, sometimes identity of expression in the two parts, and the same alternations of subject-matter. Even on the assumption that there are here two distinct psalms, both would have to be assigned to the same writer.

The lack of logical sequence may be due to want of care in transcription; this may also account for the way in which at one time foreign enemies are spoken of, at another time enemies among the people of the land.

The text, especially in the latter part (Ps. 10), is frequently corrupt; in many cases where we have ventured to emend the text the emendation is fairly obvious; in other cases, while fully realizing that the text is not in order, we have rendered the Hebrew as it stands because, however emended, there is much uncertainty as to the emendation being correct, the attempts made by commentators being many and various.

It is difficult to believe that, in its present form, the psalm was used in the temple worship; it has certainly never appeared in the Liturgy of the Synagogue. The date is late post-exilic, as indicated both by the acrostic form and by the contents. The metre, owing to the reasons given, is very uncertain.

1.   *For the Precentor : 'Almuth labben. A Psalm. David's.*

1 (2). א   ° I will give thanks to thee,° Yahweh,
          with all my heart,
      א   I will tell of all thy wondrous works.

2 (3). א I will rejoice and exult in thee,   א I will sing praise to thy name, O
                                        Most High.

3 (4). ב When mine enemies turn
          backward,   they stumble and perish before thee.

4 (5).   For thou hast ° upheld ° my right and my plea,
          Thou satest on the throne
          judging righteously.

5 (6). ג   Thou hast rebuked the nations,
          thou hast destroyed the wicked,
          their name thou hast blotted out
          for ever and ever.

6 (7).   The enemies are come to an end,
          ° their remembrance is perished ;
          Destructions for ever,
          ° Their cities ° hast thou rooted out ! °

7 (8). But Yahweh sitteth for ever,   establishing his throne for judgement ;
8 (9). ו And he judgeth the world in he doth minister judgement to the
          righteousness,   peoples with equity.

9 (10). ו Yea, Yahweh ° is become °
          a defence for the oppressed,
          a defence in times of ° trouble °.

10 (11). ו And they trust in thee,
          they that know thy name,
          for thou dost not forsake
          them that seek thee, Yahweh.

11 (12).   Sing praise to Yahweh,
          who sitteth in Zion,
          Declare among the peoples his works.

12 (13).   For he avengeth blood,
          he remembereth them,
          He doth not forget the cry of the afflicted.

13 (14). ח Yahweh ° had mercy upon me °,
          ° he saw ° mine affliction,
          ° lifting me ° ° above °
          the gates of death,

14 (15).   that I may show forth
          all thy praises
          in the gates of the daughter of Zion ;
          I will rejoice in thy salvation.

15 (16). ט   The nations are sunk
       in the pit they made ;
       in the net which they hid
       is their foot taken.

16 (17).   Yahweh hath made known
       that he executeth judgement ;
       in the work of his hands
       is the wicked ° ensnared °. Higgaion. Selah.

17 (18). May the wicked ° turn away °
       to Sheol,   all the nations that forget God.

18 (19). כ   For not for ever
       shall the needy be forgotten,
       nor the hope of the afflicted
       perish continually.

19 (20).   Arise Yahweh,
       let not man prevail,
     let the nations be judged before thee.

20 (21).   Give, Yahweh,
       ° fear ° unto them,
       let the nations know
       that they are but men. Selah.

Ps. 10. 1. ל   Wherefore, Yahweh,
       dost thou stand afar ?
     ° Thou hidest thyself ° in the times of ° trouble °.

2.   ° In his pride ° the wicked
       doth hotly pursue the afflicted,
       ° he taketh him ° in the devices
       which ° he hath conceived °.

3.   For the wicked boasteth
       of his heart's desire,
       and the covetous ° . . .

4. ו The wicked ° contemneth °, in the pride of his countenance,
     Yahweh,   seeketh (him) not ;
       " There is no God "
       are all his imaginings ;

5.   ° he prospereth ° in his ways at all times.
     Thine ordinances are ° far
     from his sight °,   all his enemies,—he puffeth at them.

6.   He saith in his heart : " I,—from generation to generation (I shall
     shall not be moved,   be) ° without harm.° "

7. פ   His mouth is full
       of deceits and oppression,
       under his tongue
       mischief and iniquity ;

8.   He sitteth in ambush in
     villages,   in hiding-places, ° to slay ° the innocent,
   ע   His eyes are directed against ° the poor °.

9.   He lurketh in a hiding-place,
       like a lion ° in a thicket °,
       ° to catch the afflicted °,
       ° to draw him ° into his net.

10.   He croucheth, he boweth down,
       and he falleth by his strong ones °.

11.   He saith in his heart ;
       " God hath forgotten,
       He hath hidden his face,
       he will never see it."

12. ק   Arise, Yahweh,°
       lift up thine hand,
       forget not the afflicted ;

13.   Wherefore should the wicked
       contemn God ;
       he hath said in his heart :
       " He will not search it out ! "

14. ר Thou hast seen ° trouble and thou beholdest (it) ° that thou mightest
     grief,   requite it with thine hand.°
     To thee doth the orphan °
     leave it,   thou art ° his helper °.

15. שׁ   Break the arm of the wicked,°   ° seek out ° his wickedness °(till) it be
                                             not found.°

16.   Yahweh is King
          for ever and ever,
          the nations are perished from his land.

17. ת   The desire of the afflicted
          thou hearest, Yahweh,
          ° thine heart ° giveth heed,
          thine ear hearkeneth,

18.   To vindicate the orphan and the oppressed ;
          that man of the earth
          should terrify no more.°

Text-critical Notes

1. Read, with G, אוֹדֶה for אוֹדֶה, " I will give thanks ". 4. Lit. " done "
or " fulfilled ". 6. Read the fourth member after the first, as the sense demands.
Read עָרִים for עָרִים, " cities ". Om. הֵמָּה, " they ". 9. Read וַיְהִי for וִיהִי,
" shall be ". Read הַצָּרָה for בַּצָּרָה, " in trouble ". 13. Read, with Baethgen,
חָנְנֵנִי for חַנְנֵנִי, " have mercy upon me ". Read רָאֵה for רְאֵה, " look upon ".
Read, with one MS., מְנַשְׂאָי for מִשֹּׂנְאָי, " from them that hate me ". Read, with
Gunkel (Marti), מְרוֹמְמִי for מְרוֹמִי, " lifting me up ". 16. Read נוֹקֵשׁ for נוֹקֵשׁ,
" ensnaring ". 17. Read יֻשַׁבּוּ for יְשׁוּבוּ, " they shall turn away ". 20. Read,
with many MSS., מוֹרָא for מוֹרֶה, " thou makest to hide ". Ps. 10. 1. Read, with T, תִּתְעַלֵּם for תַּעֲלִים,
" thou makest to hide ". Read הַצָּרָה as in 9⁹ for בַּצָּרָה, " in trouble ". 2. Read
בְּגַאֲוַת for בְּגַאֲוַת, " in the pride of ". Read יִתָּפְשׂוּ for יְתָפְשׂוּ, " they are
taken ". Read חָשָׁב for חָשָׁבוּ, " they had conceived ". 3. Om. בֵּרֵךְ " blesseth " ;
the text is quite out of order. 4. Add נָאֵץ from preceding verse. 5. Read, with
several commentators, יָחִילוּ for יָחִילוּ, " they ? ". 5. Lit. " above from before
him ". 6. Read, with G, בְּלָא רָע for אֲלֵה. Om. אֲלֵה, " he hath sworn ". 8. Read,
with the Versions, יַחֲרֹג for לַחֲרֹג, " he doth slay ". Read, with the Versions,
חֶלְכָּה for חֵלְכָה. 9. Read בְּסֻכֹּה for בְּסֻכֹּה. Om. יֶאֱרֹב. Om. יַחֲטֹף עָנִי as
redundant. Read לְמָשְׁכוֹ for בְּמָשְׁכוֹ, " when he draweth him ". 10. Om.
חֶלְכָּאִים ? the text defies emendation. 12. Om. אֵל, " O God ". 14. Om.
כִּי־אַתָּה, " for thou ". Lit. " to give with thine hand ". Om. חֶלְכָה, " the
poor ", which overloads the half-line. Read עֹזֵר for עֹזְרוֹ, " helping ". 15. Om.
וָרָע, " and evil ", which overloads the half-line. Read דְּרוֹשׁ for תִּדְרוֹשׁ, " thou
wilt seek out ". Read, with S, תִּמְצָא for תִּמְצָא, " thou wilt (not) find ". 16. Read
לְבָם for לִבָּם, " their heart ". 18. Om. עוֹד, " yet ".

For the title see p. 13.

1–3. Thanksgiving, praise, and rejoicing fill the heart of the
psalmist because of the downfall of his enemies. In describing the
final destruction of the wicked, 4–8, an eschatological picture is
presented ; the final judgement is symbolically conceived of as present
(cp. Ps. 7⁶ ᶠᶠ·). The constant reference to *the nations* points to the
overthrow of foreign enemies. 9, 10. The acknowledgement of
Yahweh's help in this critical time of trouble, is followed by (11, 12),
the exhortation *to praise Yahweh, who sitteth in Zion,* an implicit
reference to the temple where Yahweh abides. The subject then
changes, and (13, 14), the psalmist speaks of his personal experience.
He tells of how Yahweh had *had mercy upon* him, and had saved him
from *the gates of death,* a phrase which occurs also in Ps. 107¹⁸ ; *death*

here is a synonym for Sheol (cp. Isa. 28[18]), which, according to one
conception, was pictured as a great city, hence the gates (cp. Isa. 38[10]).
In his deliverance from death the psalmist sees the divine purpose of
making him a witness, *that I may show forth all thy praises in the gates
of the daughter of Zion.* The curious expression " the gates of the
daughter of Zion " is unique in the Psalter (but cp. Isa. 1[8], Mic.
1[13], Zech. 2[10 (14)]); Zion is synonymous with Jerusalem, each of which
is sometimes symbolically represented as the mother of the people
(see, *e.g.*, Isa. 37[22], Ps. 87), so that by " the daughter " of Zion here
is meant the nation united with its " mother." 15–18. The psalmist
then reverts to the subject of the nations, but this is interspersed with
the theme of the ungodly sinners among the people, for such expressions
as *the pit they made*, cp. Ps. 7[15], *the net which they hid*, cp. Ps. 31[4],
may the wicked turn away to Sheol, cp. Ps. 31[17], *that forget God*, cp. Ps.
50[22], all occur in psalms the subject of which is the persecution of the
godly—often the individual psalmist—by the wicked renegades within the
nation itself; so that here, when *the needy* and *the afflicted* are spoken
of, it is not the nations who maltreat them, but the wicked among the
Jews.   In 19, 20, however, the main subject of the enemy *nations* is once
more taken up, and Yahweh is called upon to judge them, and to inspire
them with fear, in order that they may realize their insignificance in
his sight as mere men.

   In Ps. 10 the subject of the nations is left aside, and the psalmist
concentrates on that of the wicked among his own people who persecute
the innocent in the land.   The psalmist is himself suffering at their
hands, and is in grievous trouble; he feels forsaken by Yahweh, and
in words which betray a spirit of despair, he cries, 1, *Wherefore,
Yahweh, dost thou stand afar? Thou hidest thyself in the times of
trouble*; perhaps the note of interrogation should come at the end of
the verse. A long description of *the wicked* then follows, 2–11;
though spoken of in the singular the word is collective; the picture
here presented of the wicked and their course of action may be thus
summarized: they glory in their power of being able to plunder the
poor; they are not only blasphemous, but they go so far as to deny
altogether the existence of God; as so often happens in the case of
the wicked, they prosper, and scoff at those who dare protest against
their mode of living; relying on the power of wealth, they are
persuaded of the permanence of their prosperity. They use every
underhand and unscrupulous means of oppressing and getting the
better of the less fortunate of their own race, scoffing at the idea that
God has any care for them, *God hath forgotten, he hath hidden his face,
he will never see it—i.e.*, the cruelty of their actions. In *v.* 10, *he
falleth* refers to the *afflicted* in *v.* 9. The picture is a very
dreadful one, and were it not for some ominous passages in the

prophetical writings, it might be thought that the psalmist was somewhat over-stating things; but if, for example, one reads such passages as Isa. 1[4-6, 21-23], Mic. 3[10, 11], Jer. 5[1-9, 25-28], among many others, it becomes evident that there is no over-statement here. It is owing to this unrestrained evil-doing of the wicked that the psalmist gives way to the almost irreverent outburst, 12, 13, *Arise, Yahweh, lift up thine hand, forget not the afflicted* . . . Yet his faith remains firm; 14, he does not doubt God's knowledge of the present *trouble and grief*, and knows that God will *requite* it; *to thee doth the orphan leave it, thou art his helper*; this *v.* (14) is difficult; the text can hardly be in order, but the general sense seems clear. Then, once more (15), the psalmist prays that the *wickedness* of the ungodly may be brought to an end. In *v.* 16 there is a sudden mention of *the nations* again; this is quite out of harmony with what has preceded and with what follows: *Yahweh is King for ever and ever, therefore the nations are perished out of his land*; it seems as though this verse had become misplaced. On the term Higgaion see p. 13.   17, 18. The psalm concludes with an expression of certitude that *Yahweh* will *give heed* to the cause of *the afflicted, the orphan and the oppressed*.

The points in the religious teaching will come before us in dealing with that of other psalms, the central theme of which is the same as in this psalm.

PSALM 11

COURAGE, supported by faith, is the burden of this psalm. Here is one in grave peril from violent enemies who seek his life. As in so many other psalms of a like nature, nothing is said as to who his enemies were and what was the reason of their enmity; but this is natural enough, for both were matters of common knowledge. His friends counsel flight, urging the murderous intent of his enemies; but for two reasons he scorns their advice; one is his unshakeable trust in Yahweh, the other is the need of his presence in order to champion and support the orthodox among his people. We recognize that this interpretation of one part of the psalm is not usually held; facts in the history of Israel compel us, however, to adopt it (see the exegetical notes). The psalmist's attitude is strengthened by his firm belief in the presence of Yahweh in the temple, and who is yet enthroned in heaven.

There is no reason to doubt that the psalm is pre-exilic.

For the most part the psalm consists of short lines 2 : 2.

For the Precentor : David's.

1. In Yahweh do I trust ;
    How say ye to my soul :
    ° " Flee ° ° to the mountain ! °
2. For, behold, the wicked
    do bend their bow,
    they make ready their arrow upon the
    string   to shoot ° at the upright of heart."
3. If the foundations be destroyed,
    what shall the righteous do ° ?
4. Yahweh is in his holy temple,   Yahweh, his throne is in the heavens ;
    His eyes behold,
    his eyelids scrutinize,
    the children of men.
5. Yahweh trieth
    both righteous and wicked,
    him that loveth violence
    doth his soul abhor ;
6. He raineth upon the wicked
    ° coals of ° fire,
    a burning wind
    is the portion of their cup.
7. For Yahweh is righteous,
    he loveth righteous acts,
    ° the upright ° shall behold ° his face °.

Text-critical Notes

1. Read, with many MSS. and the Versions, נוּדִי for נוּדוּ. Read הָרָה, cp.
Gen. 14¹⁰, for הַרְכֶם, " your mountain ", and om. צִפּוֹר, " bird " (marg. gloss).
2. Om. בְּמוֹ-עֹפֶל, " in darkness ". 3. Read יִפְעָל for פָּעָל, " hath done ". 6.
Read פַּחֲמֵי for פַּחִים, " snares "; and om. וְגָפְרִית, " and brimstone ". 7. Read
יְשָׁרִים for יָשָׁר, " an upright one ". Read פָּנֵיו for פָּנֵימוֹ, " their face ".

1–3. Protesting against the advice of his friends that he should
take to flight, the psalmist affirms that *In Yahweh do I trust* ; he then
quotes their words giving the reason for their advice ; first they say :
Flee to the mountain ; there he will find plenty of hiding-places where he
will be safe from his enemies. The Hebrew text adds the word " bird ",
but with the one exception of Prov. 26², the verb for " flee " (*nūd*) is
never used of birds, and in the *Proverbs* passage it is used artificially to
make a word-play with *nūph*, to " fly ". A bird would fly into a tree,
not to a distant mountain. The comparison is inept ; moreover, the
serious position in which the psalmist found himself would make what
is, after all, a playful comparison, inappropriate. The addition of
" bird ", which stands isolated from the sentence, must be regarded
as a marginal gloss, inserted later by a copyist in the text. The
psalmist's friends then go on to explain why he should flee : *the wicked
do bend their bow . . .* ; it is not indicated who these *wicked* are, nor
why they are seeking the life of the psalmist (but see below) ; they are
compared with hunters who shoot at the upright of heart (plural) ;
the Hebrew text adds " in darkness ", but how can they see to shoot in
the dark ? Either the text is corrupt, or it is a glossator's thoughtless
addition ; the text reads more smoothly by omitting it. To this the

psalmist replies, giving the reason why he will not think of fleeing, and enabling us to understand the whole position : *If the foundations be destroyed, what shall the righteous do ?*   We have here a cryptic reference to the religious-political strife which in different forms broke out during most periods of the history of Israel ; for the causes of this and other details we must refer to the chapter on " Saints and Sinners in the Psalms " (pp. 56 ff.).   Here it will suffice to say that this strife centred in the opposition between the upholders of ancient tradition and the innovators who introduced changes in traditional usages (cp. Jer. 16^{16}, 17).   In the psalm the former are appropriately designated *the foundations* ; if these are *destroyed, what shall the righteous do ?*   The " righteous " are, of course, those who cling to ancient custom as handed down ; " the wicked " (*R^{e}ša'im*) are the innovators.   This strife is referred to again and again in the psalms ; that it was at times attended by violence is evident from what the psalmists say ; at the same time, a little over-statement must sometimes be allowed for on the part of those who were not infrequently the victims of unscrupulous antagonists.

4–6.   The psalmist then replies further to the fears of his friends. He reminds them, first, that *Yahweh is in his holy temple*, i.e., he is in their midst ; the scene is thus laid in Jerusalem ; but more than that, for though the divine presence is often in the sanctuary, *his throne is in the heavens,* high above the earth, whence he looks down and sees all that happens, and all that is done by men, on earth : *His eyes behold, his eyelids scrutinize, the children of men* ; he tests *both righteous and wicked,* and as the All-righteous, he *doth abhor him that loveth violence.* The punishment for such is then described in words no less terrible for being metaphorical : *He raineth upon the wicked coals of fire ; a burning wind is the portion of their cup* ; here we have echoes of the theophany, cp. Ps. 18$^{12, 13}$.   For this meaning of " cup " in the sense of " destiny ", cp. Ps. 16^5. (7).   In contrast to the terrible lot of the wicked that of the righteous is briefly indicated ; the prophetical teaching on the ethical righteousness of Yahweh as one who *loveth righteous acts,* is here echoed, cp. Ps. 33^5 ; the reward of *the upright* is that they *shall behold his face,* cp. Ps. 17^{15} ; the meaning here is perhaps that they shall apprehend his presence in the sanctuary ; see Ps. 3$^{3-7}$, 63^2 ; but the expression is sometimes used in a more literal sense (cp. Exod. 24^{11}).

Religious Teaching

The primary subject in the religious teaching of this psalm—namely, trust in Yahweh, be the adverse conditions what they may—is a fundamental religious element which is taught in a great many psalms.   As this will come before us again and again, we shall say no more about it here.   Another matter, very briefly hinted at in the psalm, is the difficult question as to how far innovations or modifications, whether in doctrinal expression or in the cultus, are advisable and justified. The psalmist, influenced as it would seem by Jeremiah, implicitly insists on following in the " old paths ", as the prophet expresses it. We can do no more here, it will readily be realized, than merely mention this very controversial and vast subject. But it is of much interest to find that the religious principles involved—principles which have so often exercised the minds of men in the history of religion—should be hinted at in this psalm, though it be in but very few words.

PSALM 12

THE psalmist depicts a condition of deplorable degeneracy among a section of his people. The main indictment which he brings against them is that of lying and false speaking, which may well reflect conditions similar to those referred to in Ps. 11. The reference to the ill-treatment of the poor in the community who clung to traditional usages points to this. The words put into the mouth of the tyrants, " Who is our master ? ", together with the insistence on the pure words of Yahweh, mark them as religious renegades, probably the innovators referred to in Ps. 11. The main purpose, however, of the psalmist is to declare that Yahweh is about to put an end to all this.

Like Ps. 11 this, too, is pre-exilic.

The metre again consists of the short half-lines, as in Ps. 11, with two beats.

1.	*For the Precentor : On the eighth. A Psalm. David's.*
1 (2).	Help, Yahweh, for ° love ° hath ceased, for faithfulness ° is no more ° among the sons of men ;
2 (3).	They utter ° falsehood ° each to his neighbour, flattering lip, a double heart.°
3 (4).	May Yahweh cut off all flattering lips, the tongue that speaketh great things ;
4 (5).	they that say : " ° With ° our tongue will we prevail, our lips are ° our own °, who is our master ? "
5 (6).	" Because of the ° oppression ° of the afflicted, Because of the sighing of the poor, now will I arise ", saith Yahweh, " ° I will give (him) the help ° he panteth for."
6 (7).	The words of Yahweh are pure words, tried silver,° purified seven times.

L

7 (8).   Thou, Yahweh, ° wilt keep us,°
                          thou wilt preserve us from a generation
                          ° worthless and unrighteous ° ;
8 (9).   The wicked walk around
                          when worthlessness is exalted
                          among the sons of men.

Text-critical Notes

1. Read חָסָד for חָסִיד, " godly one " ; the verb גמר is not used in reference to men, cp. Pss. 57³, 138⁸. Lit. " hath come to an end ", read אָסְפוּ, cp. Isa. 16⁴, since the verb פסס is otherwise unknown. 2. Lit. " vanity ", cp. Pss. 41⁶, 144⁸' ¹¹. Om. the repetition of יְדַבְּרוּ, which overloads the line. 4. Read בְּ for לְ, " to ". Lit. " with us ". 5. Lit. " destruction ". Lit. " I will set (him) in safety ". 6. Om. בַּעֲלִיל לָאָרֶץ, " in a furnace on the earth ", which overloads the line ; probably a marg. gloss. 7. Read, with some MSS. and the Versions, תִּשְׁמְרֵנוּ for תִּ —" wilt keep them ". Read, with many commentators, זוּ לְעוֹלָם for זֻלָל וְעַגֻּל, " which is for ever ".

For the title see p. 12.

1, 2. Yahweh's help is called for because *love* and *faithfulness* have disappeared from *among the sons of men* ; this, as *vv.* 5, 6, show, is an over-statement prompted by the psalmist's righteous indignation at the action of a section among his people. The indictment is that *they utter falsehood* (lit. " vanity " or " nothingness ", cp. Ps. 41⁶, 144⁸' ¹¹), speak with *flattering lip*, and are guilty of harbouring *a double heart*. These expressions bear out exactly what the sequel (*vv.* 3, 4) shows to have been the cause of the psalmist's cry for help ; they refer to the attitude of a party in the land, led by the ruling class, and therefore the more wealthy among the people, who did not hold firmly to traditional belief and practice ; what they urged in support of their views the psalmist describes as *falsehood* ; the *flattering*, lit. " smooth ", *lip* refers to the way in which they sought to persuade others, their *neighbours*, that their teaching was right ; and the *double heart* points to their holding partly to the traditions handed down, but mainly to their advocacy of newfangled ideas and practices. The conditions are, in fact, the same as those reflected in Ps. 11 (for details see pp. 56 ff.). 3, 4. As one of the orthodox who clung to the " old paths " (Jer. 6¹⁶), the psalmist desiderates that *Yahweh* would *cut off all flattering lips*, and *the tongue that speaketh great things*, *i.e.*, the extolling of their point of view, and their lofty superiority in insisting that what they taught was right and edifying : *with our tongue will we prevail* ; they scoffed at the orthodox who maintained that they must be guided by traditional ordinances and precepts as handed down by their forefathers : *our lips are our own, who is our master ?* 5. The words which the psalmist then puts into the mouth of Yahweh point to the fact that the wealthier classes referred to maltreated their poorer and helpless brethren because they clung to the time-honoured and familiar beliefs and practices. 6. By *the words of Yahweh* are meant the traditional Law and teaching of the Mosaic revelation ; these must stand, for they *are pure words, tried silver, purified seven times.* 7. Yahweh, from whom such words come, will *preserve* his faithful ones *from a generation worthless and unrighteous.* The final words, it must be granted, make a disappointing conclusion ; the text may well be corrupt ; but the emendations suggested are somewhat drastic ; it is possible that they are a copyist's remark placed originally in the margin.

For the religious teaching see the final section to Ps. 11.

PSALM 13

THIS psalm is a beautiful instance of the intimate relationship felt by a sufferer between himself and his God ; the outpouring of the innermost feelings of the heart tells of one for whom God is a loving Friend. However protracted his suffering may be, it does not affect his deep conviction that ultimately God will help him. The enemy spoken of would seem to be a personal one ; there is nothing in the psalm which suggests the type of enemy referred to in the two preceding psalms ; nor does the psalmist call upon God to take vengeance on his enemy, or enemies (*v.* 4). There is no mention of sickness ; the psalmist's suffering seems to be purely mental.

It is impossible to assign a date to the psalm, either pre- or post-exilic.

The metre, but for the first line of *v.* 5, is 2 : 2.

1.	*For the Precentor : A Psalm. David's.*
1 (2).	How long, Yahweh, wilt thou ever forget me ? How long wilt thou hide thy face from me ?
2 (3).	How long shall I harbour ° sorrows ° in my soul, grief in my heart, day ° and night ° ? How long shall mine enemy be exalted over me ?
3 (4).	Look upon me, answer me, Yahweh, my God ; Lighten mine eyes lest I sleep in death ;
4 (5).	Lest mine enemy say : " I have prevailed against him " ; Lest mine adversaries rejoice because I am moved.
5 (6). As for me, in thy love do I trust, may my heart rejoice in thy succour ; I will sing to Yahweh, for he dealeth bountifully with me.	

Text-critical Notes

2. Read צְבָאוֹת (cp. Prov. 15¹⁸) for עֵצוֹת, " counsels ". Add, with G, וְלַיְלָה.

1, 2. Wearied with ceaseless menaces from his enemy, the psalmist pathetically cries: *How long, Yahweh?* The fourfold repetition: *How long?* tells of the despair of a worried heart. To the psalmist it seems as though Yahweh had forgotten him, had *hidden his face from* him, so that *day and night* he pines over the *sorrows* and *grief* that overwhelm him. *How long* is this *enemy* going to lord it over him? he asks 3, 4. Then, in his disconsolate state, he lifts up his prayer: *Look upon me, answer me, Yahweh, my God*; in his dejection he even fears the approach of death, and therefore pleads: *Lighten mine eyes lest I sleep in death*, cp. 1 Sam. 14[27] (the expression " lighten mine eyes " is used in a different sense in Ps. 19[8]); for the thought of death as a sleep cp. Job 3[13]. And he thinks how grievous it would be if those who were against him should mock at his trust in Yahweh, and boast of having *prevailed against him*, and should rejoice at his downfall. 5. But, in spite of all, the psalmist's faith in Yahweh holds firm; he *trusts* in his *love*, and believes that his *heart* will *rejoice* because of the *succour* that shall be accorded him; and he looks forward in confidence to the time when he *will sing to Yahweh*, for he knows by past experience that he *deals bountifully* with him; a similar expression occurs in Pss. 116[7], 119[17].

Religious Teaching

Very short as this psalm is, it brings out forcibly the great truth that trouble, though long-drawn-out, does not mean that God has no care for those who trust in him. The reason why relief does not come is doubtless often hidden; in many cases it will be the sufferer's own fault, which in his blindness he does not realize; in other cases it may be for his own ultimate good, as many a sufferer has found. But the psalm teaches the beautiful lesson that the true believer in God will not be shaken in his faith, however severe the stroke: " For I am persuaded, that neither death nor life . . . shall be able to separate us from the love of God, which is in Christ Jesus our Lord " (Rom. viii. 38, 39).

PSALM 14—see Psalm 53

PSALM 15

THIS psalm presents us with the scene of one coming up to the temple to worship; at the entrance to the sanctuary the priest, appealing to Yahweh, asks who is worthy to enter into his place of worship. The worshipper gives the reply, in which he describes what must be the moral condition of him who is worthy to enter, implying that he fulfils the divine requirement. Thereupon the priest assures him that " he that doeth these things shall never be moved."

It may well be that we have here the echo of earlier custom, according to which worshippers were questioned as to their ritual fitness to enter the sanctuary, a custom known in all probability in Israel, even though we have no direct mention of it, for it was certainly in vogue among other peoples. But in this psalm we have the reminiscence of the custom, not the account of a ritual which took place in the psalmist's day ; had that been the case, some mention of the worshipper's entry into the sanctuary could hardly have been omitted, as that would have formed part of the ceremony ; whereas our psalm ends with a pious ejaculation, in which there is not even any intimation that the worshipper may now proceed into the " tabernacle ".

The psalm refers to man's duty to God and his neighbour, and is thus in the nature of a commentary on Deut. 6⁵, Lev. 19¹⁸, and this stress on the moral law is very striking ; but to argue from this that the psalmist depreciates the ceremonial law is quite beside the mark, for the entry into the temple was for the purpose of taking part in sacrificial worship ; that was the *raison d'être* of the sanctuary.

The post-exilic date of the psalm is shown by the psalmist's know-ledge of the Deuteronomic Code and the Code of Holiness, from the latter he quotes Lev. 25³⁷ in *v*. 5.

The metre alternates between 3 : 3 and short half-lines of two beats, 2 : 2.

1.
A Psalm. David's.

1 (2). Yahweh, who shall sojourn in thy
       tabernacle ?
                             who shall dwell on thy holy hill ?
2 (3).   He that walketh uprightly,
                and worketh righteousness ;
                and speaketh truth,°
3 (4).   and slandereth not with his tongue,
   that doeth no harm to his neighbour,   and taketh not up a reproach against
                               his near one ;
4 (5). Despised in his eyes is the reprobate, but he honoureth them that fear
                                Yahweh,
                that sweareth ° to his neighbour °,
                and changeth not ;
5 (6). His money he putteth not out on and a bribe against the innocent he
    usury,   receiveth not.
                He that doeth these things
                shall never be moved.

Text-critical Notes

2ᵥ Om. בְּלְבָבוֹ. 4. Read, with G, לְרֵעֹה.

1. The psalm opens abruptly with a twofold question put to Yahweh *Who shall sojourn in thy tabernacle? Who shall dwell on thy holy hill?* This is a form of address to God which occurs

elsewhere only in Ps. 10[1], 13[1], 22[1], 74[1]. The use of "tabernacle"
for the temple is an archaism as in Ps. 61[4], and accords with
the ancient custom which the psalm echoes (see above). The
"dwelling" on the holy hill, *i.e.*, of Zion, may well reflect, as Kittel
points out, the custom of pilgrims who came for the feasts and
pitched their tents in the vicinity of the temple. In what follows the
psalmist puts into the mouth of the supposed worshipper a description
of the moral state of one who may be deemed worthy to enter the
sanctuary. 2. First, there is his duty to God : *he that walketh uprightly* refers to a manner of life lived in accordance with the will of God
(cp. Isa. 33[15], Prov. 28[6, 18]) ; *and worketh righteousness* refers to the
fulfilling of the divine laws (cp. Isa. 56[1]) ; the whole duty of man to God
is thus included in these two short sayings. The duty to his neighbour
is described in more detail because the psalmist takes up the *rôle* of
a moral teacher rather than that of a spiritual guide. Speaking the
truth and (3) refraining from slander are parallel with *doeth no harm to
his neighbour*, and *taketh not up a reproach against his near one* ; sins
very prevalent, as so many psalms illustrate. 4. The next thing required
is that he should *despise the reprobate* ; this, in view of the *honouring of
them that fear Yahweh*, must mean the renegade who denies Yahweh ;
with these renegades, again, many psalmists deal ; they were a danger to
the community. Then, the faithful worshipper must be one who keeps
an oath made to his neighbour, and does not *change* his mind ; the
keeping of an oath thoughtlessly taken might often involve disagreeable
consequences, but it must be kept under all circumstances, especially
as the oath was often taken in Yahweh's name. 5. He must, moreover,
be strictly honest in money matters, and may *not put his money out on
usury* ; this sin was evidently a very common one, judging from such
passages as Exod. 22[25], Lev. 25[37], Deut. 23[20], Ezek. 18[8], 22[12], and the
same applies to the receiving of *bribes*, cp. Exod. 23[8], Deut. 27[25], Isa.
1[23], Ezek. 22[12], and often elsewhere. The words are then put into the
mouth of the priest : *He that doeth these things shall never be moved*,
i.e., he will continue in prosperity, cp. Pss. 10[6], 16[8], 112[6], and elsewhere.
The absence of any reference to more heinous forms of sin is because
those guilty of such would not have the effrontery to seek to enter the
sanctuary.

Religious Teaching.

The psalm teaches the indissoluble connexion which should exist
between ethics and religion. The moral law is to be observed not
only for its intrinsic excellence, but primarily because it is based on
divine precepts. The motive force of doing what is right must be a
true perception of the relation between man and God, together with a

realization of the truth that human perfection can be attained only by acting in accordance with the will of God (cp. Matth. 5⁴⁸).

PSALM 16

THIS psalm is a beautiful example of a psalmist's communing with God. It is an outpouring of gratitude, and portrays vividly the sense of contentment with his lot felt by the psalmist; he cannot sufficiently express his soul-felt recognition of the fact that his happy state is solely due to the lovingkindness of God. He contrasts this with the pitiable plight of those who worship any deity other than Yahweh. The proneness to idolatry among the people is ominously illustrated, e.g., in Isa. 57³⁻⁸, especially vv. 5, 6, which the psalmist seems to have in mind. But this thought is fleeting; and he speedily reverts to his main theme of joyful recognition of the favour shown to him by Yahweh; his sense of gratitude is increased by the certitude that this loving mercy will continue, and that he will be kept from all harm.

That the psalm is of post-exilic date is suggested by the evident reminiscence of Isa. 57⁵, ⁶.

The metre is mainly 2 : 2 half-lines, interspersed here and there with three beats to the half-line.

Miktam.   David's.

1. Preserve me, O God,
   for I trust in thee.
2. ° I said ° to Yahweh ° :
   " Thou art ° my welfare °,
   ° it all resteth on thee." °
3. As for the holy ones in the land,
   they ° all are my delight.°
4. Their sorrows ° are increased °
   ° that choose ° another (god)';
   I will not pour out their drink-offerings
   of blood,   nor take their names upon my lips.
5. " Yahweh, ° thou allottest °
   my portion and my cup,
   ° thou holdest ° my destiny."
6. The lots are fallen unto me in pleasant
   places,   yea, ° mine heritage ° is beautiful to me.
7. I bless Yahweh
   who hath given me counsel,
   yea, at nights ° he instructeth me ° in my ° inmost being °.
8. I set Yahweh
   before me always ;
   if ° he ° is at my right-hand I shall not be moved.
9. Therefore my heart is glad,
   and ° my very self ° rejoiceth,
   yea, my flesh doth dwell in safety.
10. " For thou wilt not abandon
    my soul to Sheol ;
    thou wilt not suffer thy godly one
    to see the Pit ;
11. Thou wilt show me the path of life,   in thy presence is fulness of joy,
    raptures at thy right-hand are for evermore."

Text-critical Notes

2. Read, with some MSS. and the Versions, אָמַרְתִּי for אָמַרְתְּ, "thou hast said". Om. אֲדֹנָי "my Lord", for the rhythm's sake; Lit. "my good", cp. Ps. 106⁵. Lit. "all of it is on thee", read, with Kittel, כֻּלָּה for בַּל, "not". 3. Om. וְאַדִּירֵי, "and the excellent ones of", and om. בָּם, "among them"; the text seems to have been worked over. 4. Read, with ST, יִרְבּוּ for יִרְבּוּ. Read, with Kittel, בָּחֲרוּ for מָהֲרוּ, "they exchange". 5. Read, with Gunkel, מְנָת for מְנָת, "the lot". Read, with some MSS., cp. Gunkel, תָּמֵךְ, lit. "holding" (cp. Prov. 31¹⁹), for תּוֹמִיךְ, "thou maintainest". 6. Read, with GS, נַחֲלָתִי for נַחֲלָת, "an heritage". 7. Read, with some MSS., יִסְּרֵנִי for יִסְּרוּנִי, "they instruct me". 8. Add הוּא for the rhythm's sake. 9. Read, with Gunkel, כְּבֵדִי, lit. "my liver", for כְּבוֹדִי, "my glory".

1. The prayer with which the psalm opens, *Preserve me, O God*, is, as the following verse shows, for the continuance of the happy conditions under which the psalmist is living. It is the prayer of faith : *for I trust in thee*. 2. The psalmist realizes that it is to Yahweh alone that he owes his present prosperous state, *Thou art my welfare*, and that its continuance depends solely on Yahweh, *it all resteth on thee*. 3, 4. In accordance with his close walk with God is his companionship with those only who are like-minded with himself, his *delight is in the holy ones in the land*; the term used here for " holy ones " (*q'dōšîm*) occurs in 34⁹ and Deut. 33³. With these are contrasted those *that choose another god*; the text here is somewhat uncertain, and the suggested emendations vary considerably ; but the sense of our rendering, based on the context, is clear enough ; for the expression " another god " (" god " being understood) see Isa. 42⁸, while in Exod. 34¹⁴ the full term " another god " occurs. The psalmist says of these idolaters that *their sorrows are increased*, a statement based doubtless on observation (cp., on the other hand, Ps. 147³), and he repudiates the very idea of partaking in their idolatrous worship : *I will not pour out their drink-offerings of blood*; the reference is to what is said in Isa. 57⁵⁶, where the prophet inveighs against them " that slay the children in the valleys, under the clefts of the rocks " ; to idols have they " poured a drink-offering ". His detestation of those who are guilty of such abominations is such that the psalmist will not even *take their names upon his lips*. The mention of these worshippers of a false god in such a very different context is distressing evidence of the influence which contact with alien peoples had upon many of the Jews during the Persian period (cp. Isa. 58³⁴). But the psalmist does not permit these distasteful things to dwell in his mind. He turns to the main theme of his psalm, and again delights in acknowledging Yahweh as the source of all his happiness ; 5, 6 : *Yahweh, thou allottest my portion and my cup, thou holdest my destiny*, i.e., it is in the hands of Yahweh ; the use of these three words emphasizes the psalmist's full apprehension of the fact that all the material benefits which he enjoys are vouchsafed

by the bounty of Yahweh ; and he further enlarges on this by referring
to the land which he possesses : *the lots*,—a different word from that
used for " destiny " which also means " lot ", and is often' used in
reference to land, *e.g.*, Ps. 105¹¹—*the lots are fallen unto me in pleasant
places, yea, mine heritage is beautiful to me.* 7. But greater than material
benefits is the spiritual blessing of divine guidance ; and the psalmist
tells of his communing with Yahweh in the silent night-time, when
God reveals his will to him : *who hath given me counsel, yea, he instructeth
me in my inmost being* ; this last expression is lit. " my kidneys ", used
in Hebrew in reference to what was conceived of as the most sensitive
and vital part of man, cp. Pss. 73²¹, 139¹³. 8. Acting in accordance with
this guidance, the psalmist says : *I set Yahweh before me always* ; he
knows that he will *not be moved* ; 9, and therefore his *heart is glad, and
my very self rejoiceth* ; the word we have rendered " very self " is lit.
" liver ", conceived of as the centre of human feelings, cp. Lam. 2¹¹ ;
the Hebrew has " my glory ", but a parallel to " my heart ", is more
appropriate ; the consonants are the same in the Hebrew words, so that
the confusion arose easily; the following mention of *my flesh* also points to
the correctness of the emendation. 10, 11. Finally, the psalmist expresses
his conviction that God *will not abandon* his *soul to Sheol*, nor *suffer his
godly one to see the Pit* ; meaning that God will preserve him in life, and
will guide him in his *path* through *life* ; walking with God is *fulness of
joy*, at his side there are ever *raptures*, the rendering " pleasures " is
not strong enough. There is no reference here to life hereafter ;
the psalmist is speaking of his present life ; *evermore*, as often elsewhere,
means " constantly ", or " always ", cp. Ps. 15⁵.

Religious Teaching

First must be noted, as already pointed out, the teaching that man's
destiny is in the hands of God. This does not, of course, deny human
free-will ; it is when this is exercised in accordance with God's will
that man's lot is shaped by God. The psalm teaches, further, that the
enjoyment of prosperity in life is greatest when it is recognized that
this is granted by God. And, lastly, there is the expression of deep
trust in God, characteristic of all the psalmists, which knows that
where he is guide all is well.

PSALM 17

THE psalmist, conscious of his innocence and uprightness of life,
appeals to God for protection and deliverance from the enemies by
whom he is beset. As in so many other psalms in which the writers

appear as the victims of bitter enmity, no indication is given as to the
cause of this.   That the enemies here spoken of are not aliens, but of
the same race as the psalmist himself, may be regarded as certain ;
had they been Gentiles, the fact would have been made clear, see, *e.g.*,
Pss. 43¹, 83³, ⁴ and elsewhere.   It will be noticed that while " enemies "
are spoken of, the singular is used in *v.* 13 ; the same occurs in some
other psalms of this character, and points to some particular adversary
among many.   The subject of these enemies of the psalmists is dealt
with on pp. 56 ff.

The text in some verses is very corrupt, and some of our renderings
are necessarily uncertain.   There are cases in which the Hebrew as it
stands is meaningless.

The date is post-exilic ;   more than that cannot be said.   The
metre is mainly 2 : 2 : 2 : 2, but 3 : 3 also occurs, and sometimes a single
three-beat line.

A Prayer.   David's.

1.   Hear, ° O God of my righteousness,°
                      hearken unto my cry,
                      give ear to my prayer
                      from lips not deceitful.
2. Let my cause   come   forth   from   thy
          presence,   let ° mine eyes ° behold equity.
3.   Thou hast proved mine heart,
                      thou hast visited me at night,
                      thou hast tried me, and findest not
                      ° wickedness in me °.
                      My mouth shall not transgress
4.   after the deeds of men ;
                      ° the command of ° thy lips
                      do I observe.
                      ° From ° the ways of the violent
5.   ° thou holdest ° my goings,
                      in thy paths my footsteps are not moved.
6.   I cry unto thee,
                      for thou hearest me, O God ;
                      incline thine ear to me,
                      hearken to my speech.
7.   Show wondrously thy lovingkindnesses,
                      thou that savest them that trust,
                      with thy right-hand, from them that rise up.
8. Keep me as the apple of the eye,   in the shadow of thy wings hide me,
9.   From the face of the wicked that despoil me,
                      my deadly enemies,
                      they compass me about.
10. ° With fat their heart ° they close,   with   their   mouth   they   speak   with
                                                                     arrogance ;
11.   Now ° they advance,° they surround me,
                      ° their heart ° they set,
                      ° to cast down ° to the ground.
12.   ° Their intent against me ° is like a lion
                      that is eager to rend,
                and like a young lion lurking in secret.
13.   Arise, Yahweh,
          come before him, cast him down,   save my soul from the wicked one ;
                      with thy sword 14. ° slay them °,
                      with thine own hand, Yahweh ;
                      ° destroy them ° from the world,
                      ° snatch them from life °.

> With thy treasure fill their belly,
>   let them be sated ° therewith °,
> and let them leave their residue to their babes.
>
> 15.   As for me, in righteousness
>   will I behold thy face,
> I shall be satisfied when I awake with thine appearance.

Text-critical Notes

1. Read אֶל־צִדְקִי (cp. Ps. 4²) for יְהֹוָה צֶדֶק, " Yahweh, righteousness ".
2. Read, with G, עֵינַי for עֵינֶיךָ, " thine eyes ". 3. Read זַמָּה בִי for זַמֹּתִי, " I have devised ". 4. Read דְּבַר for בִּדְבַר, " in, or by, the command of ". Add מָ. Read תִּרְמֹךְ for תָּמֹךְ, " to hold ". 10. Read, with Kittel, חֵלֶב לְבָּמוֹ (cp. Ps. 73⁷, 119⁷⁰) for חֶלְבָּמוֹ, " their fat ". 11. Read אַשֻּׁרוּ for אַשֻּׁרֵינוּ, " our footsteps ". Read לְבָבָם for עֵינֵיהֶם, " their eyes ". Read, with Buttenwieser, לִנְטֹשׁ for לִנְטוֹת, " to bend ". 12. Read, with Gunkel, דְּמוּ־לִי, lit. " they devise against me " (cp. 2 Sam. 21⁵), for דִּמְיֹנוֹ, " his likeness ". 14. Read, with Gressmann, quoted by Gunkel, חַלְּצֵם מֵחַיִּים, הַרְתְּמֵם, הֲמִיתֵם, הֲמִירֵם. Read, with Hans Schmidt, בָּזֶה for בָּנִים, " sons ".

The designation " A Prayer " is in this case very appropriate. On the name of David in so many titles, see p. 10.

1. The danger, as the sequel shows, confronting the psalmist prompts his urgent appeal to God : *Hear, hearken, give ear* (cp. Ps. 4⁴, 5², ³). For the address to the Almighty as *God of my righteousness* meaning that his righteousness is of God, cp. Ps. 4²; this is the rendering of the Septuagint, and commends itself in view of the protestation of innocence which follows. The psalmist urges the sincerity of his prayer by saying that it is *from lips not deceitful*, lit. " in not lips of deceit," a pregnant phrase in Hebrew difficult to render adequately without paraphrasing. In 2, the expressions are forensic ; God is thought of as on the judgement-seat, and the psalmist's cause has come before him ; therefore he prays that his vindication may come forth from the divine *presence*, and that he may see the justice of God : *let mine eyes behold equity.* 3–5. The way in which these verses are divided in the Hebrew text is clearly wrong ; the text has suffered considerable corruption ; emendations cannot but be tentative. Of the general meaning, however, there is no doubt : it is a protestation of innocence on the part of the psalmist in a somewhat boastful strain ; but it must be remembered in extenuation that there is at the back of his mind the constant thought of the wickedness of his enemies. He confidently addresses the Almighty in words expressive of a sense of innocence ; God has *proved* his *heart*, witnessing to the psalmist's intimate communion with God, especially when in the silence of night there is nothing to distract his thoughts : *thou hast visited me at night* (cp. Ps. 16⁷). The divine scrutiny has been, the psalmist feels, searching ; he uses three expressions in regard to it : thou hast *proved*, *visited*, *tried* ; nevertheless, he can say that God *finds not wickedness in*

him. As in the past, so shall it be in the future : *my mouth shall not transgress after, i.e.,* in imitation of, *the deeds of men,* in reference to the slanderous attacks of his enemies ; far from that, he *observes the command of thy lips* (for the anthropomorphism cp. Ps. 89³⁴). But it is noteworthy that the sense of his own righteousness does not prevent the psalmist from recognizing to whom this is due ; it is God who *holds* him *from the ways of the violent* ; and following *in thy paths my footsteps are not moved,* a figurative way of saying that he who lives in accordance with divine guidance is safe from harm. 6–9. The psalmist then raises again the voice of prayer with which he began, and now says definitely what has called forth his petition, namely the menace of those *that rise up*—*i.e.,* his enemies. In 7, the Hebrew is difficult to translate, more especially when seeking to reproduce the rhythm ; but the general sense is clear ; the psalmist prays : *Show wondrously thy lovingkindnesses* (cp. Ps. 31²¹) ; in what follows the text has suffered some corruption, and there seems also to have been some displacement of the words ; our rendering reads awkwardly owing to the desire to keep as closely as possible to the Hebrew ; the meaning is clearer if the words are arranged thus : *thou that savest with thy right-hand them that trust (in thee) from them that rise up.* 8. Very graphically does the psalmist then express his longing for divine protection : *Keep me as the apple of the eye* ; for the expression cp. Deut. 32¹⁰, Prov. 7² ; the word rendered " apple " is in Hebrew *îsh,* " man " with the termination *-ôn,* signifying a diminutive, thus " little man " ; this must originally have had reference to the widespread belief that the soul resided in the pupil of the eye ; the reflection of anyone looking into the eye of another suggested the presence there of a " little man," *i.e.,* the soul. This is the origin of the expression, though to the psalmist it may merely have meant something very precious. Another old-world conception is reflected in the words : *in the shadow of thy wings hide me* ; this is probably of Egyptian origin ; representations of the " winged solar disk " are frequent ; for the winged sun-god Horus see Erman, *Die Religion des Ägypter,* pp. 28 f. (1934). 9–12. How urgent the need is for him to be protected *from the face of the wicked that despoil me,* the psalmist then sets forth by the description of his *deadly enemies* (lit. " mine enemies against the soul ", *i.e.,* life), who *compass him about.* He says of them : *with fat their heart they close* ; the expression is a strange one, meaning that they shut their heart to all feelings of compassion (cp. Job 15²⁷) ; *with their mouth they speak with arrogance,* so that both inwardly and outwardly they are cruel. The next *v.* 11 is again difficult ; the text cannot be in order, as it stands it reads : " our steps now have they surrounded me " ; our emendation involves but a slight alteration ; the psalmist is describing the approach of his enemies, and says : *Now they advance, they surround* *me.* The rest of the verse is very variously emended and explained by commentators; the Hebrew verb for " they set " is never used in connexion with " eyes ", but frequently with " heart " in the sense of setting the mind to do something (*e.g.*, Ps. 48, Prov. 22¹⁷ and elsewhere); we have, therefore, emended the text so as to read " their heart " for " their eyes "; somewhat drastic, we admit, but at any rate it gives sense; the enemies are bent on *casting* him *to the ground, i.e.,* on destroying him. This is supported by what follows, 12, *their intent against me is like a lion,* lit. " they devise against me," a slight emendation for the meaningless " his likeness." The comparison with *a lion* occurs several times elsewhere (Pss. 7², 10,⁹ 17¹², 22¹³). 13, 14. The psalmist then calls upon Yahweh to *arise,* and *cast down* his enemy, *the wicked one;* the use of the singular is probably in reference to the leader among his adversaries. In what follows we have an illustration of the bitterness of a revengeful spirit which to our ears is distasteful. The text is again corrupt in parts, and the precise meaning of the last part of the verse is very difficult to determine; we suggest tentatively that *thy treasure* is used here, as the verb in Job 21¹⁹, in the sense of " retribution " or the like; the psalmist expresses the wish that his enemies and their children may be overtaken by divine vengeance. In contrast to this the psalmist (15) says that he *will behold* God's *face in righteousness,* adding : *I shall be satisfied when I awake with thine appearance.* Taken in contrast with what is said in *v.* 14, there is some justification for the view that the psalmist envisages, though it be but vaguely, awaking from the sleep of death; this would be prompted by his sense of close communion with God as exhibited in the opening verses of the psalm; his unexpressed thought may well have been : How can communion with the ever-living God be broken by death? This view is not held by all commentators.

Religious Teaching

Of this, apart from the opening and concluding verses, there is not much to be said. The psalm teaches, it is true, implicit faith in God and in his justice. But apart from this, the exaggerated sense of righteousness, and the terrible feeling of revenge expressed, are distasteful elements. As warnings such things may have their uses. The teaching, however, in the last verse is very different. If, as may well be the case, there occur here the beginnings of the apprehension of a fuller life hereafter, then we have in this psalm one of the few instances of this in the Psalter, a fact not to be lightly passed over.

PSALM 18

THIS psalm occurs also in 2 Sam. 22. Probably both go back independently to an earlier form, the differences being due to the vicissitudes of transmission. That each has some textual corruptions, as in
the case of most of the psalms, is only to be expected; the one can,
however, be corrected by the other in a number of passages. The
psalm has been worked over and added to both for doctrinal and
liturgical purposes; but in its original form it is certainly one of the
most ancient in the Psalter. The occasion is clearly indicated at its
conclusion; it was composed to commemorate the victory of a king
over his enemies. While Davidic authorship cannot be claimed
for it as it stands, there is no reason to doubt that in some early form of
it, David may, at any rate, have inspired it. Some commentators are
inclined to cut it up rather unnecessarily, as it appears to us; that
there are unevennesses and some lack of logical sequence is not to be
denied, and some additions have clearly been made; but, taking it as a
whole, the psalm forms a unity.

After some opening words of praise and thanksgiving for having
been rescued from the hands of enemies, the writer launches forth into a
description of the theophany. There follows a further recognition of
deliverance from foes, a deliverance which the psalmist—either the
king or a court-poet in his name—feels is according to his deserts,
since his faithfulness to Yahweh has always stood firm. Then there is a
renewed expression of praise and gratitude to Yahweh who has helped
him to overcome his enemies, namely " foreign nations "; and their
utter defeat is described.

The date of the psalm, *as we now have it*, is probably late pre-
exilic, excepting for a few later additions. In this form there is good
reason to believe that Josiah is the king in question.

The metre is almost uniformly 3 : 3.

1. *For the Precentor : David's, the servant of Yahweh ; who spake unto Yahweh the
words of this song in the day that Yahweh delivered him from the grasp of all his
enemies and from the hand of Saul ;*
2. *and he said :*

1 (3).   I love thee, Yahweh, my strength;
2 (4). ° My rock, my stronghold, and
           my deliverer,   my God, my refuge, in him do I trust;
          My shield, and the horn of my safety °;
3 (5). Worthy to be praised is he; I   and from mine enemies I have been
          called upon Yahweh,   delivered.
4 (6). ° The waves of ° death encom-   and the floods of destruction terrified
          passed me,   me;
5 (7). The cords of Sheol surrounded me, and the snares of death came upon me.
6 (8). In my trouble I called on Yahweh, and unto my God I cried;
          He heard my voice from his
          sanctuary,   and my cry came ° into his ears.
7 (9). The earth shook and trembled,   the foundations of the mountains
                                             quaked,
                    They reeled to and fro because he was wrath;

8 (10). Smoke went up from his nostrils, and fire from his mouth devoured,
coals kindled because of him.

9 (11). He bowed the heavens and descended, and darkness was under his feet;

10 (12). And he rode upon a cherub, and flew, he swept onwards on the wings of the wind;

11 (13). He made darkness his hiding-place, his tabernacle round about him,
° a gathering of ° the clouds of the skies.

12 (14). ° Brightness from his presence passed forth °, hailstones and coals of fire;

13 (15). Yahweh thundered ° from ° the heavens, yea, the Most High uttered his voice °;

14 (16). He sent forth ° arrows ° and scattered them, ° he shot forth lightning ° and discomfited them;

15 (17). The stream-beds of the ° sea ° were disclosed, and the foundations of the earth were revealed,
Because of thine anger, Yahweh, at the blast of the breath of thy nostrils,

16 (18). He sent from on high, and took me, he drew me out of mighty waters,

17 (19). He delivered me ° from my fierce foes,° and from them that hated me, for they were too strong for me.

18 (20). They overcame me in the day of my distress, but Yahweh became my support;

19 (21). He brought me forth into a wide place, he delivered me, for he delighted in me.

20 (22). Yahweh rewarded me according to my righteousness, he recompensed me according to the cleanness of mine hands;

21 (23). For I kept the ways of Yahweh, and sinned not against my God;

22 (24). For all his judgements were before me, and I put not his statutes from me;

23 (25). Yea, I was perfect with him, and kept me from mine iniquity;

24 (26). And Yahweh rewarded me according to my righteousness, according to the cleanness of mine hands ° before him °.

25 (27). With the merciful thou art merciful, with the perfect ° thou art perfect;

26 (28). With the pure thou art pure, and with the perverse thou art tortuous.

27 (29). ° An afflicted people thou savest, but haughty eyes thou humblest;

28 (30). For thou art my lamp, Yahweh, my God that lighteneth my darkness.

29 (31). For with thee ° I will shatter a wall,° and with my God I will leap o'er a fence.

30 (32). O God,—perfect is his way; the word of Yahweh is pure,
a shield ° to all that trust in him.

31 (33). For who is ° God ° save Yahweh, and who is a Rock but our God?

32 (34). The God that girdeth me with strength, and maketh my way perfect;

33 (35). He maketh my feet like hinds' feet, and setteth me up on ° the heights °;

34 (36). He teacheth my hands to war, ° and placeth ° ° a bow ° ° in mine arms.°

35 (37). Thou gavest me the shield of ° my safety °, and ° thy encouragement ° ° strengtheneth me ° ° ever °.

36 (38). Thou enlargest my footsteps under me, so that my ankle-bones do not give way.

37 (39). I pursued mine enemies, and overtook them, and turned not till they were consumed;

38 (40). I shattered them so that they could not rise, they fell underneath my feet.

39 (41). Thou didst gird me with strength for the battle, thou didst bow down beneath me those that rose up against me.

40 (42). Yea, mine enemies turned the back to me, and as for them that hated me, ° thou didst destroy them °.

41 (43). They cried out, but there was no helper, ° unto ° Yahweh, but he answered them not;

42 (44). I crushed them like the dust of ° the earth °, like the mire of the streets ° did I stamp on them °.

43 (45). Thou didst save me from the strivings of ° the people °, thou didst set me at the head of the nations,

a people that I knew not served me,

44 (46). When they heard me they obeyed me,

the sons of strangers cringed before me.

45 (47). The sons of strangers fainted away,

they came trembling out of their strongholds.

46 (48). Yahweh liveth, and blessed be my Rock,

and exalted be the God that helpeth me ;

47 (49). The God that granteth me vengeance,

° and subdueth ° the peoples under me,

48 (50). Who delivereth me from mine angry enemies,

and lifteth me from them that rise up against me,

and saveth me from violent men.

49 (51). Therefore will I laud thee among the nations,

Yahweh, to thy name will I sing praise,

50 (52). Who maketh great the deliverance of his king,

and showeth lovingkindness to his anointed,

to David and to his seed for evermore.

Text-critical Notes

2. Om. יהוה to avoid the repetition ; also for the rhythm's sake. Om. מִשְׂגַּבִּי for the rhythm's sake. 4. Read, as in 2 Sam., מְשֻׁבָּרֵי for חֶבְלֵי, which occurs in the next verse. 6. Om., as in 2 Sam., לְפָנָיו. 11. Read, as in 2 Sam., הִשְׁרַת for חֶשְׁכַת, " darkness of " ; om. מָיִם. 12. Read, with Gressmann, quoted by Gunkel : מִפְּנֶה נֶגְדּוֹ עָבְרוּ for נֹגַהּ נֶגְדּוֹ עָבָיו עָבְרוּ, " at the brightness before him clouds passed over ". 13. Read מ for בָ, " in ", as in 2 Sam. Om., with G, as in 2 Sam., בָּרָד וְנַחֲלֵי־אֵשׁ, " hailstones and coals of fire ". 14. Read, with G, as in 2 Sam., חֵצָיו for חִצָּיו, " his arrows ". Read וַיִּבְרַק בָּרָק, cp. 2 Sam., and G for וּבְרָקִים רָב, " and lightnings great ". 15. Read, as in 2 Sam., יָם for מַיִם, " waters ". 17. Read, with the Versions, מֵאֹיְבַי הָעֲזִים for מֵאֹיְבִי עָז, " from my fierce foe ". 24. Read לְנֶגְדּוֹ for לְנֶגֶד עֵינָיו, " before his eyes ", for the rhythm's sake. 25. Om. גֶּבֶר " man ", for the rhythm's sake. 27. Read, as in 2 Sam., אֶת for כִּי־אַתָּה, " for thou ". 28. Om., as in 2 Sam., תָּאִיר, " thou dost light ". 29. Read אָרֻץ גֶּדֶר for בְּדוּד אֶרֶץ, " I will run upon a troop ". 30. Om. הוּא, " (is) he ", for the rhythm's sake. 31. Read, as in 2 Sam., אֱלוֹהַ for אֵל. 33. Read בָּמוֹת for בָּמוֹתַי, " my heights ". 34. Read וַתִּנַּח for וְרִחַתָה, " and it bendeth ". Om. נְחוּשָׁה, " brass ", for the rhythm's sake. Read בְּזַלְעָתִי. 35. Read, with G, יִשְׁעִי for יִשְׁעֶךָ, " thy safety ". Read, as in 2 Sam., צַלְהֶךָ, lit. " thy answering ", for עֲנוֹתְךָ, " thy humbleness ". Om., as in 2 Sam., וִימִינְךָ תִסְעָדֵנִי, " and thy right-hand supporteth me ". Read, with Gunkel תְּנַבְּרֵי for תַּרְבֵּנִי, " thou dost increase me ". Add, with G, לָנֶצַח. 40. Read, with GV, תַּצְמִיתֵם for אַצְ־, " I destroy them ". 41. Read, as in 2 Sam., אֵל for עַל, " upon ". 42. Read, as in 2 Sam., אֶרֶץ for עַל־פְּנֵי־רוּחַ, " upon the face of the wind ". Read, as in 2 Sam., אֲרִיקֵם for אֲרִיקֵם, " I emptied them out ". 43. Read עַמִּים for עָם, " a people ". 44. Read, with GS, יְכַחֲשׁוּ for יְכַחֵשׁוּ, " they deceived ". 47. Read, as in 2 Sam., וַיַּדְבֵּר for וּמוֹרִיד, " and putteth to flight " (?).

For the title see p. 14.

1–3. In his gratitude for deliverance from grave dangers, detailed later, the psalmist begins with a heartfelt acknowledgement to Yahweh for his love and protection. Some commentators regard the opening words, *I love thee, Yahweh, my strength*, as a later addition ; it is true that the word for " love " here used is late Hebrew, and is never used in reference to God ; but in Ps. 116[1], where this line is quoted, the corresponding word is often used of man's love to God, and may well have stood here originally. Gunkel and others suggest that it is a corruption, and should be read, " I exalt thee ", as in Pss. 30¹, 145¹, and there is something to be said for this ; in any case, these opening words are wholly appropriate, and the more striking for being an independent half-line, and thus in the nature of a key-note to the psalm, for the might and power of Yahweh resound again and again. The reiterated figures of speech expressing Yahweh's strength as *deliverer* and protector reveal the intensity of the psalmist's feelings. The expression the *horn of my safety* does not occur elsewhere ; it means that the psalmist's safety is set on high, and therefore out of harm's way. So, in exultation, he cries : *Worthy to be praised is he ; I called upon Yahweh, and from mine enemies I have been delivered.* 4, 5. In highly coloured, figurative language the psalmist then describes how near he had come to death ; he uses four phrases all expressing ancient thought of how death was envisaged : *the waves of death* (cp. Ps. 42⁷) and *the floods of destruction*, reflect the old-world idea of the all-devouring waters of the great deep ; *destruction* here is lit. " Belial ", used in this sense in Ps. 41⁸, Nah. 1¹¹, 2¹ ; *the cords of Sheol*, and *the snares of death* present a different picture in which death, synonymous with *Sheol*, is personified, and thought of as setting a trap and ensnaring men. 6. In this perilous danger of death the psalmist had *called upon Yahweh*, who *from his sanctuary heard* his *cry* ; the word for " sanctuary " used here is *hēkal*, and refers mostly to the earthly temple ; but in Ps. 11⁴, Isa. 6¹, 29⁹, 63¹⁵, Mic. 1², Hab. 2²⁰ it is used of the heavenly temple ; this may well be its meaning here, in which case the description of the theophany follows appropriately (see *v.* 9). This description (7–15) is held by some commentators to be a later insertion ; an unnecessary assumption, for the psalmist's purpose is to set forth the stupendous power of Yahweh, and he utilizes ancient material with great effect. The details are gathered together from various sources, and one must recognize the skill with which they have been woven together into a consistent whole. The advent of Yahweh causes the very earth to *shake* and *tremble* for fear ; for he comes in *wrath* against those enemies (*v.* 3) on account of whom the psalmist had appealed to him. His wrath burns, realistically described : *Smoke went up from his nostrils, and fire from his mouth devoured*, so that everything he approached caught fire : *coals kindled because of him.* It is in response to his servant's call to him in his sanctuary (*v.* 6) that (9) *He bowed the heavens and descended* to the earth ; in contrast to the blazing light of fire before him, all is dark beneath, *darkness was under his feet* ; 10, and he swoops down, riding *upon a cherub* ; the word is used collectively, they were the guardians of the divine throne (cp. Ezek. 1²⁶) ; here, they are thought of as synonymous with *the wings of the wind* (cp.

M

Ps. 104[3, 4]).   11. But the majestic and terrible figure of Yahweh remains shrouded within *a gathering of the clouds of the skies* (cp. Ps. 97[2]), for it would be fatal for mortals to behold him (cp. Exod. 33[20]), therefore *he made darkness his hiding-place, his tabernacle round about him.*   12. But the *brightness* within the clouds, emanating *from his presence*, is so dazzling that it raises a whirlwind of *hailstones and coals of fire.*   13. Then came the terrific sound of the rumbling and crashing of the divine voice : *Yahweh thundered from the heavens, yea, the Most High uttered his voice* (cp. Ps. 29[3–9]) ; and his enemies (14) *scattered* by his *arrows*, *i.e.*, the lightning (cp. Ps. 77[17, 18]), are *discomfited* (cp. Ps. 144[6]). 15. Then, once again, there is a cataclysm of Nature, terrified at Yahweh's *anger : the stream-beds of the sea were disclosed, and the foundations of the earth were revealed.*   16–19. Thus did Yahweh come *from on high* to the help of his servant, and *drew* him *out of mighty waters*, figurative for his enemies, and *delivered* him from those *fierce foes*, who without the help of Yahweh were *too strong* for him.   They had, indeed, actually overcome him, but Yahweh brought him into a place of safety, *a wide place*, and *delivered* him, *for he delighted in* him.   Thus, the psalmist, in order to express the intensity of his feelings, gathers together these ancient and awe-inspiring pictures, and applies them to his own experiences of peril, and his deliverance from them.   20–24. He then makes the assertion that *Yahweh rewarded* him thus *according to* his *righteousness* ; he sets forth the integrity of his character in somewhat overstated terms, ending with the claim that he was *perfect* with Yahweh, *i.e.*, complete in all that Yahweh required of him ; and he repeats that it was for this reason that Yahweh rewarded him.   The Deuteronomic expressions occurring in these verses show that they have been worked over by a later editor.   In 25, 26 the attitude of Yahweh towards men, according to their variable qualities, which the psalmist describes, witnesses to an undeveloped conception of God, and marks these verses as ancient.   With 27 a new subject is momentarily taken up ; the thought of his people comes into the mind of the psalmist ; they had been *afflicted*, but Yahweh had saved them, and had *humbled* the *haughty eyes* of their enemy.   And now (28, 29) he speaks again of his own experience of Yahweh's loving care for him : *For thou art my lamp, Yahweh, my God that lighteneth my darkness*, a similar figure of deliverance from perplexing danger occurs in Job 29[3], cp. Ps. 132[17] ; on this verse is based the evening collect in the Prayer Book, " Lighten our darkness . . ."   The quaint thought of Yahweh helping to *shatter a wall* and to *leap o'er a fence*, or rampart, is possibly a reminiscence of David's escape from Keilah (1 Sam. 23 [12, 13]).   In what follows (29–36) there is much that betrays a *naïve* and old-world conception of Yahweh, interspersed with more exalted thoughts, which again points to the fact that this ancient poem has been worked over in later days.

The main theme is that Yahweh has helped his anointed, as the sequel shows him to have been; the psalmist, therefore, proceeds (37–48) to give a description of how he overcame his enemies, and gained a complete victory. There is nothing in these verses which calls for special comment; they seem to recall episodes in the life of David whose constant wars were an outstanding element during his reign. 49–50. These last two verses show that it is a king who is the speaker, or a court-poet in his name, in the whole of the psalm; he concludes by declaring that, in gratitude for all that Yahweh has done for him in overcoming his enemies, he will *laud* him *among the nations*, for it is Yahweh *who maketh great the deliverance of his king, and showeth loving-kindness to his anointed, to David and to his seed for evermore.*

Religious Teaching

This psalm illustrates a great religious truth in a way which is unparalleled in the Psalter. We mean the truth that God spoke in old time " by divers portions and in divers manners," as it is expressed in Hebr. 1[1]; in other words, that the self-revelation of God to man is granted only in accordance with man's capacity of apprehension; and that, therefore, revelation is a gradually progressive process. The psalm presents us, on the one hand, with a conception of God which is very undeveloped, though it does exhibit a striving towards envisaging the Deity in the greatness of his power. On the other hand, there gleams through the darker shades of the picture a conception of God as taught by the inspired prophets, his justice, his purity, his mercy, and his unity. That these wholly incompatible ideas of God should appear, as it were, side by side, shows how the psalmist, all unconsciously, was placing on record, and illustrating, the great truth that divine revelation is progressive; and that God, in his mercy, does not ask of man more than man, with his limited mental and spiritual capacities, can give. From this point of view the psalm is one of the most helpful in the Psalter.

PSALM 19

THE very different subject-matter comprised in verses 1–6 and 7–10, respectively, justifies the contention that we have here two originally independent psalms. As will be seen from the quotations given in the exegetical notes, the *former* of these is an adaptation of Babylonian mythological elements. Skilfully and finely as the poet has constructed his little poem, it must nevertheless be recognized that it comes strangely from the pen of a Hebrew writer. Doubtless at the back of his mind the thought of Yahweh as the Creator was present; but he never mentions the name of the God of Israel; his use of *El* in the opening words of the poem could refer to any god. In view of this, the action of some later psalmist in attaching to it something which was more in the spirit of Hebrew psalmody is fully comprehensible. His seven-fold repetition of the name of Yahweh (including its mention in the final verse) is significant. This second psalm, *vv.* 7–10, takes the form of a hymn in praise of the Law of Yahweh. In its whole-hearted recognition of, and gratitude for, the divine gift, it is far more edifying than the poem, pagan in form if not in spirit, that precedes it.

The dates of these two compositions are, of course, different; the former is certainly pre-exilic; the few Aramaisms which it contains do not necessarily point to a late date. The second psalm is seen by its content to have been written after the time of Ezra, during the fourth, or even the third, century B.C.

The metre differs in each case; in the former it is mostly 2 : 2, with 3 : 3 in *vv.* 4 and 6. In the latter it is uniformly 3 : 2, but in the concluding verse, which, as often in the psalms, differs from the rest, it is 3 : 3 : 3.

1.   *For the Precentor : A Psalm. David's.*

1 (2).   The heavens declare
            the glory of God,
            and the work of his hands
            doth the firmament proclaim.

2 (3).   Day unto day
            poureth forth speech,
            and night unto night
            showeth forth wisdom ;

3 (4).   Neither speech nor words,
            not heard is their voice ;

4 (5). In all the earth °goeth forth°   °and to the end of° the world their
        °their voice°,   utterances.

            For the sun is set
            a tabernacle ° in the sea ° ;

5 (6).   and he, like a bridegroom,
            cometh forth from his chamber ;
            he rejoiceth like a champion
            to run his course ;

6 (7). From the end of the heavens is his
        going forth,   and his circuit ° unto ° their end,
            and nought is hid from his heat.

                *   *   *

7 (8). The law of Yahweh is perfect,   refreshing the soul ;
       The testimony of Yahweh is
          trustworthy,   making wise the simple ;

8 (9). The precepts of Yahweh are up-
          right,   rejoicing the heart ;
       The commandment of Yahweh is
          pure,   enlightening the eyes ;

9 (10). ° The word of ° Yahweh is pure,   standing fast for ever ;
        The judgements of Yahweh are
          Truth,   they are altogether righteous,

10 (11). They are preferable to gold,   yea, to much fine gold,
         Yea, sweeter than honey,   and the dripping from the honey-comb.

11 (12). Thy servant also is instructed by them,

12 (13). Errors,—who discerneth them?

13 (14). Also from purposeful sins keep thy servant,
Then shall I be perfect and innocent

14 (15). Let the words of my mouth be acceptable,

in observing them is great reward; from un-intended sins keep me innocent;

let them not master me,

of great transgression.
and the meditation of my heart, before thee,
Yahweh, my Rock and my Redeemer.

Text-critical Notes

4. Read יָצָא for יֵצֵא, "hath gone forth". Read קוֹלָם for קַוָּם, "their measuring-line". Read וְלִקְצֵה for וּבִקְצֵה, "and in the end of". Read בַּיָּם for בָּהֶם, "in them". 6. Read עַד for עַל, "on". 9. Read אִמְרַת. cp. Ps. 119³⁸, for יִרְאַת, "the fear of".

1. The psalm opens abruptly with a statement of fact; a certain number of psalms begin in this way, but it is exceptional; usually a psalm opens with words addressed to the Almighty, or in reference to him. The mention of *God* in this verse is not in reference to the God of Israel, though doubtless so interpreted in later days; but in its origin it was, as *vv.* 5, 6 show, in reference to the Sun-god. The verbs *declare* and *proclaim* are, in Hebrew, invariably used in the literal sense of utterance; that this is not the sense, however, in which they are here used is obvious. The psalmist is expressing some such thoughts as occur, for example, in the following Babylonian hymn to the Sun-god, Shamash:

" O Shamash, on the horizon of the heavens
The bolt of the glorious heavens
The gates of the heavens
O Shamash, thine head hast thou raised
O Shamash, the glory of the heavens,
Light hast thou granted
Life's course on the earth
All creatures that live
O Shamash, like a father and a mother

hast thou risen ablaze,
hast thou unlocked,
hast thou opened!
o'er the land;
thou coverest the lands;
to the face of the land!
dost thou guide,
thou dost quicken;
thou showest care." [1]

2. In a similar metaphor the psalmist continues: *Day unto day poureth forth speech*, i.e., each day, as the sun rises, has its message to give of the god's glory; *and night unto night showeth forth wisdom, i.e.*, the god's wise forethought in providing rest for the creation is shown forth night by night. 3. No sound is heard; yet their palpable eloquence is apprehended throughout the world. So far the psalmist has merely implied, though plainly enough, that the thought of the Sun-god was in his mind; now he directly asserts this: 4. *For the sun is set a tabernacle in the sea*; the emendation "in the sea", for the meaningless "in them", is too obvious to need discussion. The idea that a tabernacle, or tent, is set up in the sea for the sun, is ancient and *naïve* (though paralleled by the modern expression of the sun sinking in the

[1] Gressmann, *Altorientalische Texte zum alten Testament*, p. 243 (1926).

west !) ; representations of Shamash in his " tabernacle " occur on ancient seals (see, for illustrations of this, Gressmann, *op. cit.* i, nos. 101, 102). 5. The daily rising of the sun is then compared with a *bridegroom* coming forth *from his chamber* ; who *rejoiceth like a champion to run his course* ; and here again Babylonian conceptions regarding the Sun-god are echoed ; in a prayer to him, one of many that have come down to us, mention is made of his bride, Ai, and he is spoken of as a hero, or champion : " O warrior, champion, Shamash, and thou, Ai, the bride, look ever favourably upon my pious deeds . . ." [1] So, too, in the concluding lines, the words : *From the end of the heavens is his going forth, and his circuit unto their end, and nought is hid from his heat*, we have a thought reminiscent of another Babylonian prayer to the Sun-god, in which it is said :

> " The mighty mountains hath thine awesome glance covered,
> Thy light hath filled the expanse of the lands ;
> Thou regardest the hills, beholdest the earth . . .
> O'er the wide earth is thy daily course,
> O'er sea and ocean, o'er hills, o'er earth and heaven. . . ." [2]

That the Hebrew poet utilized Babylonian material in composing his poem is thus abundantly clear. For a poem of this character to have been included among the Hebrew psalms may, indeed, cause surprise, even though adapted, and made to apply to Yahweh ; and we can fully understand why a later psalmist felt impelled to counteract its distasteful pagan atmosphere, as it was to him, by adding a psalm more in accordance with the Hebrew conception of praise. This brings us to *vv.* 7-14. The first point to note here is the significant seven-fold utterance of the name of Yahweh ; in protest, as it were, to its omission in the other poem. 7-10. The absence of parallelism in most of the psalm will be noticed ; this is exceptional, but does not interfere with its beauty. It is a finely constructed series of utterances in praise of the Law, all the terms used being different aspects of the Law. The manifest delight which the psalmist has in the Law shows that there was nothing burdensome in observing it ; in later days, owing to Pharisaism, it was different, and became a " yoke " (cp. Gal. 1 [5]) ; but in the time of the psalmist the observance of the Law was a source of happiness. The meaning of these verses is clear and straightforward, comments are therefore not called for. 11-14. The psalmist then applies what he has said about the Law to himself personally. He has learned by experience that in observing the Law *great reward* accrues : a clear conscience and the certitude of living according to the divine will. Then, with the sensitiveness of a truly religious man, he recognizes that no one is wholly free from sin ; there are *un-intended sins*, and he prays that he

---

[1] Jastrow, *Die Religion Babyloniens und Assyriens*, i. p. 400 (1905).
[2] Gressmann, *op. cit.*, pp. 244 f.

may be kept innocent from these. He knows, too, the weakness of human nature, and prays that he may not give way to temptation : *from purposeful sins keep thy servant, let them not master me*; then, with divine help, he will at least be *innocent of great transgression.* And he concludes with the prayer that in word and thought he may be right in the sight of God. These final verses are of deep import for personal religion.

Religious Teaching

This has been dealt with in the exeg. notes.

PSALM 20

THIS psalm is unique in the Psalter. It is in the nature of a prayer for victory, uttered on the eve of battle, after sacrifices have been offered ; the scene presented is, therefore, in the temple. Confidence in the favourable outcome of the impending conflict is expressed, for all has been committed to the hands of Yahweh in whose might implicit trust is placed. This ceremony was customary in Israel from early times ; it is implied in Judg. 4^{14}, 5^{11}, and directly described in 1 Sam. 7^9, 13^9, cp. 1 Kgs. $8^{44, 45}$; the rite was common to all peoples of antiquity. The prayer is offered by the priest on behalf of the king. Thus encouraged and fortified, the king expresses his conviction that in answer to the prayer the victory will be his. The psalm closes with another short petition, uttered by the assembled worshippers, that Yahweh will answer the prayer which has been offered. The mention of the king is an obvious indication that the psalm is pre-exilic ; he is the ruler of the southern kingdom (*v.* 2) ; but otherwise there is nothing in the psalm which helps in fixing a more exact date.

The metre is mostly 3 : 3, with occasional two-beat half-lines.

1.   *For the Precentor : A Psalm.   David's.*

1 (2).   May Yahweh answer thee
                                          in the day of trouble,
                                          may the name of the God
                                          of Jacob ° defend thee ° ;

2 (3). May he send thee help from his
            sanctuary,   and from Zion uphold thee.

3 (4). May he remember all thine offerings,   and ° have respect unto ° ° thy whole
                                                        burnt sacrifices ° ; Selah.

4 (5). May he grant thee ° thy heart's
            desire °,   and fulfil all thy purpose.

5 (6). We will shout for joy at thy victory,   and in the name of our God ° will we
                                                        delight °

                          May Yahweh fulfil all thy requests.

6 (7). Now ° I know of a certainty °   that Yahweh giveth victory to his
                                                        anointed ;

            He will answer him from his holy   with the mighty acts of his right-hand
            heavens,   will he help him.

7 (8).
    These in chariots
    and those in horses,
    but we in the name of °
     our God,° are strong °;
8 (9). They stumble and fall,   but we rise up and stand firm.
9 (10). O Yahweh, save the king,   ° and answer us ° in the day we call.

Text-critical Notes

1. Lit. "set thee up on high". 3. Read, with Ehrlich, יְדְרְשֶׁנָּה, lit. "seek favourably", (for this use of the word see Deut. 11¹²) for יְדַשְּׁנֶה, "make fat". Read, with some MSS. and ST, עוֹלֹתֶיךָ for the sing. 4. Lit. "according to thy heart". 5. Read, with Cheyne, נָגִיל for נִדְגֹּל, "we will set up our banners"; the parallelism is demanded. 6. Read, with Budde, יָדֹועַ יָדַעְתִּי, as required for the rhythm. 7. Om., with some G MSS., יְהוה. Read, G MSS. S, נַגְבִּיר (cp. Ps. 12⁴) for נַזְכִּיר, "we will cause to remember". 9. Read, with the Versions, וַעֲנֵנוּ for יַעֲנֵנוּ, "he will answer us".

1-4. The prayer with which the psalm opens is spoken by the priest, and supplements that which had already been uttered by the king : *May Yahweh answer thee in the day of trouble* ; the sequel shows that "thee" has reference to the king, and "the day of trouble" refers to the impending battle. Faith in *the name of the God of Jacob* will *defend* him, cp. Ps. 46⁷, ¹¹, 54³ and elsewhere. This *help* will be sent *from his sanctuary*, *i.e.*, the temple on mount *Zion*, conceived of as Yahweh's dwelling-place when among his people ; the king in question ruled, therefore, over the southern kingdom of Judah. It is further pleaded that Yahweh *may remember all thine offerings, and have respect unto*, *i.e.*, take note of, *thy whole burnt sacrifices* ; the types of sacrifices here spoken of are the *minḥah* and the *'olah* ; the former was a general term for any kind of offering, as here, but in post-exilic times it was restricted to the meal-offering ; the *'olah* was the common designation for a burnt-offering, burned on the altar in its entirety. It will be noted how the ancient belief in the acceptability of sacrifices by Yahweh appears here. Finally, the priest prays that God will grant the king his *heart's desire*, *i.e.*, victory, *and fulfil all his purpose*, *i.e.*, prosper all his plans for the coming battle. **5.** At this point the assembled worshippers burst out in joyful strain and express their confidence in the victory of the king : *We will shout for joy at thy victory* (lit. "salvation," but cp. e.g., 1 Sam. 14⁴⁵), *and in the name of our God will we delight*, a confidence which is further emphasized in the words : *May Yahweh fulfil all thy requests*. **6-8.** And now the king himself speaks ; all has been done which duty to God demands : prayer, sacrifice, and the expression of earnest trust in him, so that he can confidently affirm : *Now I know of a certainty that Yahweh giveth victory to his anointed* (cp. Ps. 2²). But the king speaks of the divine answer as coming *from his holy heavens*, not from Zion, as in *v.* 2 ; there is, of course, no contradiction here ; sometimes Yahweh is thought of as present in the sanctuary, at others as dwelling in the heavens. For the phrase *the mighty acts of his right-hand*, cp. Ps. 106². The king then, speaking both in his own name and in that of his warriors, contrasts the vain trust *in chariots* and *in horses* on which the enemy relies, with those who *are strong* by virtue of *the name of our God* ; in the one case, *they stumble and fall*, but he and those who follow him in the strength of God, *rise up and stand firm.* 9. The ceremony closes with a final petition uttered by the whole body of worshippers : *O Yahweh, save the king, and answer us in the day we call.* " In the day " means here : at the present time. The verse makes a most fitting and appropriate conclusion ; it is difficult to understand why some commentators regard it as a later addition.

Religious Teaching

The old-world belief that God directs the issue of battles, together with that of the acceptability of sacrifices, find natural expression in such an ancient psalm as this.   Nevertheless, the ardent faith expressed must be recognized.   But otherwise the religious teaching belongs to a distant age.

PSALM 21

In this psalm, one of the " royal " psalms, there occurs what, at first sight, seems to present an incongruity.   Verses 1–6 contain a thanksgiving that the prayer, offered no doubt during the sacrifice which has preceded it (cp. Ps. 20), has been answered ; but *vv.* 8–12 contain wishes that the king may be victorious over his enemies, showing that the victory has not yet been gained.   How, then, can *vv.* 1–6 be a thanksgiving for victory ?   This apparent incongruity is such only at first sight.   We have here an illustration of one of the finest elements in Israelite religion, namely, faith in the efficacy of prayer so deep and living that the·certitude of prayer being answered is expressed by the affirmation that it *is* already answered.   It is worth pointing out here that this religious element appears in some of the prayers of the Synagogue Liturgy.   As is well known, in a certain number of instances these prayers go back in their origin to pre-Christian times ; and even among those of later date, there is no reason to doubt that the spirit and essence of ancient prayers has often been preserved.   An illustration of faith in the efficacy of prayer, such as has been referred to, may be offered. One of these prayers concludes thus : " Blessed art thou, Yahweh, our God, our Father, our King, who art good, and dealest kindly with all ; thou hast dealt kindly, dost deal kindly, and wilt deal kindly with us ; thou hast bestowed, thou dost bestow, thou wilt ever bestow upon us grace, lovingkindness, and mercy." In this connexion it is impossible not to recall the words of our Lord : " Therefore I say unto you, All things whatsoever ye pray and ask for, believe that ye have received them, and ye shall have them " (Mk. 11[24]). This, then, we submit, is the way in which this psalm is to be understood ; faith in the efficacy of prayer envisages it as answered before its actual fulfilment.

The psalm is pre-exilic, but it is not possible to say who the king in question was.

The metre of the first part of the psalm is almost uniformly 2 : 2, that of the latter part 3 : 3.

1.

For the Precentor : A Psalm. David's.

1 (2).
Yahweh, in thy strength
doth the king rejoice,
and because of thy help
° he is full of joy ;

2 (3).
the desire of his heart
hast thou granted him,
and the request of his lips
thou hast not denied ; Selah.

3 (4).
Yea, thou didst meet him beforehand
° with choice benefits °,
thou didst place on his head
a crown of gold !

4 (5).
Life he asked °,
thou gavest it him,
length of days
for ever and ever !

5 (6).
Great is his glory
because of thy help,
honour and majesty
hast thou laid on him ;

6 (7).
Yea, thou dost ° grant ° him
blessings for ever,
Thou makest him glad with the joy of thy presence.

7 (8). For the king trusteth in Yahweh,   and, with the love of the Most High, he will not be moved.

8 (9). May thine hand light upon all thine enemies,   may thy right-hand ° shatter ° all them that hate thee ;

9 (10). Mayest thou make them like a furnace of fire,   in the time of thy wrath ° ° mayest thou destroy them °, and may the fire consume them ;

10 (11). Mayest thou destroy their ° offspring ° from the earth,   and their seed from the sons of men.

11 (12). For they ° purposed ° evil against thee,   they imagined a device,—° in vain ° ;

12 (13). For thou makest them (turn) the ° back °,   ° thy bow-strings thou preparest against the face of them.

13 (14). Arise, Yahweh, in thy might,   we will sing, and praise thy power.

, Text-critical Notes

1. Om., with the Versions, מַה־, " how ", for the rhythm's sake. 3. Lit. " with blessings of goodness ". 4. Om. מִמְּךָ, " of thee ", for the rhythm's sake. 6. Lit. " appoint ". 8. Read, with Kittel, תִּמְחַץ to avoid the repetition of תִּמְצָא. 9. Om. פָּנֶיךָ יהוה, " thy presence, Yahweh ". Read תְּבַלְּעֵם for יְבַלְּעֵם, " may he destroy them "; for בלע in this sense see 2 Sam. 20[19, 20]. 10. Lit. " fruit ". 11. Lit. " spread out ", cp. Judg. 4[11]. Lit. " they were not able ". 12. Lit. " shoulder ". Om. בְ " with ".

1–6. With unflinching faith the conviction is expressed that the prayer which has been offered will be answered; indeed, so rooted is the certitude that Yahweh will grant what has been pleaded for, that the petition is regarded as fulfilled. It has been pointed out above that this is an element in some of the prayers of the Jewish Liturgy, and there is no reason to doubt its existence in earlier days. Both the spirit and wording of many synagogal prayers echo far earlier usage. This explains what at first sounds strange in this psalm, namely that the answer to prayer is recorded before the prayer has been fulfilled. It is difficult to determine by whom the different parts of the psalm were uttered, or rather sung; but in view of the words in the concluding verse, " we will sing and praise thy power," it would seem that, with the exception of *v.* 7, the whole psalm was sung by the temple choir. The note of joy is first struck because of the king's faith in the *strength* of *Yahweh*; for in that faith the king knows that his prayer, *the desire of his heart, is granted*, and *the request of his lips not denied.* This faith is the stronger in that already Yahweh had granted *choice benefits* before they were asked for; *thou didst meet him beforehand*, a difficult word in Hebrew to render adequately; perhaps it is best expressed by the word " prevent," as used in the Prayer Book collect : " Prevent us, O Lord, in all our doings with thy most gracious favour." In the present case it was the *crown of gold*, conceived of as having been *placed on* the king's *head* by Yahweh at his coronation. Further, he had prayed for a long *life* and this had been granted; in the Oriental mode of speech, *For ever and ever*; not, of course, to be taken literally, cp. 1 Kgs. 1 [31], Dan. 2 [4], 3 [9], etc. And because of Yahweh's *help* the king enjoyed *great glory*; for *honour and majesty* had Yahweh *laid on him*; but most blessed of all was the happiness granted to him by *the joy* of Yahweh's *presence, i.e.*, by the sanctified happiness experienced through the conviction of God's nearness to him. There follows now (7) what seems to be a link joining together the two parts of the psalm. The first part, the thanksgiving, has been addressed to Yahweh; the second part records the good wishes of the worshippers present, and is addressed to the king. Between the two parts come the words, sung by a single voice, affirming the faith of the king : *The king trusteth in Yahweh*, and expressing the conviction that, shielded by the love of the Most High, he will not be moved. And now (8–13) the whole temple-choir sings again, recording the wish that the king may wholly overcome all his enemies : *May thine hand light upon all thine enemies*; more is implied by the expression " light upon " than the rendering would seem to indicate; it means lit. " find "; for the sense in which it is here used, *i.e.*, " crush " or " annihilate ", cp. Isa. 10 [10, 14]; the same word is repeated in the second half of the verse, and as such repetition is against Hebrew poetical usage, it is evidently a case of dittography;

the emendation adopted " shatter " (root MHZ) occurs fairly frequently
in reference to the total overthrow of enemies (*e.g.*, Num. 24⁸, Ps.
18³⁸). The next verse (9) is difficult; the text has clearly undergone
some corruption, the general sense shows that the name of Yahweh has
got in by mistake, for the whole section is in reference to the king;
the words, *Mayest thou make them like a furnace of fire*, taken in conjunction with the parallel in the second half of the verse, are probably
intended to be a picture of destruction which is to be the lot of the
enemies; but it must be confessed that the state of the text makes any
interpretation uncertain. With the cruel thought of the extermination
of *offspring* and *seed*, cp. Josh. 6²¹. This is to be the vengeance on the
enemies for their evil designs. Finally, Yahweh is called upon to con-
summate the victory so that the people may *sing, and praise* his *power*.

Religious Teaching

See intr. section.

PSALM 22

THIS psalm is one of those which record the antagonism between the
orthodox section of the people, who continued faithful to the religion
and worship of their forefathers, and those who, dominated largely
by extraneous influences, were anti-traditionalist, and lax, both in regard
to belief and practice, in their attitude towards the religion that had
been handed down (see further on this, pp. 56 ff.). As so many of the
psalms in which this struggle is reflected show, the behaviour of the anti-
traditionalists must at times have been as cruel as it was unscrupulous.
Our psalmist would appear to have been one of the leaders of the
orthodox party judging from the numbers and characters of those
opposed to him; and they had evidently gained some notable, if
temporary, success; ultimately, however, he regained his position
of influence among the true worshippers of Yahweh. This seems to be
the general state of affairs as presented by the psalm.

The alternating outbursts of plaint and praise realistically reflect
the conflicting emotions of the psalmist. Unlike some other psalms
of a similar character, nothing is said about sin being the cause of the
sufferer's troubles, though there is no vaunt of righteousness. Notable,
too, is the fact that the psalmist nowhere calls for divine vengeance to
be visited on his adversaries. The psalm forms a unity; to deny this
is to misapprehend the mental and spiritual state of the psalmist;
logical thought-sequence is not to be looked for in one who is at first

so overwhelmed with perplexity and worry, and ultimately spiritually exalted by unexpected deliverance.

In some of the verses the text has suffered corruption.

To assign a date to the psalm is difficult; but the conditions portrayed may well point to the Greek period.

The metre is very varied, reflecting doubtless the mental condition of the psalmist : short two-beat lines interspersed with those of three beats.

1.   *For the Precentor : ' The Hind of the dawn.'   A Psalm.   David's.*

1 (2).   My God, my God,
                  Why hast thou forsaken me ?
                  Why ° art thou far ° ° from my cry °,
                  from the words of my ° clamour ° ?

2 (3).   ° I cry in the day-time,
                  but thou answerest not,
                  and in the night I am not silent.

3 (4).   But thou abidest ° in the sanctuary,°   ° the praise of ° Israel.

4 (5).   In thee did our fathers trust,   they trusted, and thou didst deliver
                                                  them ;

5 (6).   Unto thee did they cry, and were   in thee did they trust, and were not
            rescued,   put to shame.

6 (7).   But I am a worm, and no man,
                  the reproach of men,
                  and despised of the people.

7 (8).   All that see me laugh me to scorn,
                  they shoot out the lip,
                  they shake the head :

8 (9).   " He ° cast ° himself on Yahweh,   let him rescue him, for he delighteth in
            let him deliver him,   him ! "

9 (10). But thou art ° my strength ° from   ° my trust ° while on my mother's
            the womb,   breasts ;

10 (11).   On thee have I been cast from the womb,
                  from my mother's belly
                  thou art my God.

11 (12).   Be not far from me,
                  for trouble is nigh,
                  but there is no helper.

12 (13). Mighty bulls surround me,   strong ones of Bashan encompass me ;

13 (14). ° He openeth upon me his mouth °,   a lion ravening and roaring.

14 (15). Like water am I poured out,   my bones are all out of joint ;
         My heart is become like wax,   melting within ° mine innermost parts ° ;

15 (16). Dried up like a potsherd is ° my
            throat °,   and my tongue cleaveth to my palate,
                     ° and the dust of ° death is ° on my lips °.

16 (17). For ° many ° dogs surround me,   the assembly of evil men gather round
                                                  me,
                     ° they bind ° my hands and my feet ;

17 (18). I proclaim all ° my pains °,   they gaze and look at me ;

18 (19). They apportion my garments
            among them,   and upon my vesture do they cast lots.

19 (20). But thou, Yahweh, be not far,   my Helper, haste to mine aid ;

20 (21). Rescue my soul from the sword,   ° my life ° from the power of the dog ;

21 (22). Save me from the mouth of the   and ° mine afflicted one ° from the
            lion,   horns of the wild-oxen.

22 (23). I will declare thy name unto my   in the midst of the congregation will I
            brethren,   praise thee ;

23 (24). Ye that fear Yahweh, praise him,   all ye seed of Jacob, glorify him,
                  and stand in awe of him, all ye seed of Israel ;

24 (25).   For he hath not despised,
                  he hath not ° spurned °,
                  the affliction of the afflicted one ;

         And he hath not hidden his face   and when he cried unto him he
            from him,   hearkened.

25 (26).   ° From him ° is my praise
in the great congregation ;
my vows will I pay
in the presence of them that fear him.
26 (27).   The meek shall eat and be satisfied,   they that seek him shall praise Yahweh,
May your heart live for ever.
27 (28).   Let them recall it and turn,°
all the ends of the earth,
and let them worship ° before him °,
all the kindreds of the nations.
28 (29).   For the Kingship is Yahweh's,
and ° his rule ° is over the nations.
29 (30).   ° Of a truth, him ° shall they worship,
all that ° sleep ° in the earth,
before him shall they bow down,
all they that go down to the dust,
° and the soul that liveth not
30 (31).   shall glorify his power °.
It shall be told ° about Yahweh °
° to a generation 31 (32) that cometh ° ;
and they shall declare his righteousness
to a people that shall be born,
that he hath done it.

Text-critical Notes

1. Read תִּרְחַק for רָחוֹק, "distant". Read, as a better parallel, with Gunkel, מִשַּׁוְעָתִי for מִשׁוּעָתִי, "from my salvation". Lit. "roaring". 2. Om. אֱלֹהַי for the rhythm's sake. 3. Read, with G, בַּקֹּדֶשׁ for קָדוֹשׁ, "holy". Read, with many MSS. and the Versions, תְּהִלָּה for תְּהִלּוֹת, "the praises of". 8. Read, with the Versions, גֹּל, lit. "rolled", for גֹּל imperat. 9. Read, with Duhm, עֹזִי for גֹּחִי, "that bringeth me forth". Read, with the Versions, מַבְטִיחַ for מַבְטִיחִי, "that causeth me to trust". 13. Read, as the sense demands, פָּצוּ עָלַי פִּיהֶם for פָּצָה עָלַי פִּיהוּ, "they opened their mouth upon me". 14. Lit. "my bowels". 15. Read, with many commentators, חֵפִּי for כֹּחִי, "my strength", as a better parallel to "my tongue". Read, with Gunkel, וְלַעֲפַר for וְעָפָר "and to the dust of"; and תִּשְׁפְּתֵנִי for בִּשְׁפָתַי, "thou layest me". 16. Add, with GT, רַבִּים as demanded by the rhythm. Read, with some commentators, כָּאֲרִי for אָכְרוּ, "like the lion". 17. Lit. "recount". Read, עַצְמוֹתַי for עַצְמוֹתָי, "my bones". 20. Lit. "mine only one". 21. Read, cp. G, עֲנִיתִי for עֲנִיתַנִי, "thou hast answered me". 24. Lit. "made detestable". 25. Read מֵאִתּוֹ for מֵאִתֶּךָ, "from thee". 27. Om., לְפָנָיו for לְפָנֶיךָ for the rhythm's sake. Read, with the Versions, לְפָנָיו "before thee". 28. Read מָשְׁלוֹ for מֹשֵׁל, "ruling". 29. Read אַךְ לוֹ for אָכְלוּ, "they eat". Om. וְ before יִשְׁתַּחֲווּ. Read יְשֵׁנֵי for דִּשְׁנֵי, "the fat ones of". 30, 31. Read, with Gunkel, וְנֶפֶשׁ לֹא־חִיָּה זַרְעוֹ יַעַבְדֶנּוּ for וְנַפְשׁוֹ לֹא חִיָּה: זֶרַע יַעַבְדֶנּוּ "and his soul he hath not preserved alive, a seed shall serve him". 30. Read לַיהוה for לַאדֹנָי, "about the Lord". Read, with G, לְדוֹר יָבֹא.

For the title see p. 14.

1, 2. The mental and spiritual state of the psalmist is poignantly expressed by the words of despair with which he begins. He feels himself forsaken by God, for although he has cried *in the day-time and at night*, no answer has come. The repeated *My God, my God*, is very impressive. One or two textual emendations are offered in these verses ; *my cry* in place of " my salvation " (the two words are very similar in Hebrew, see text-crit. note) gives the proper parallel to *my clamour*, lit. "my roaring", a strong expression indicating the intensity of suffering and yearning for relief. The omission of " My God " at the beginning of *v.* 2 is for the sake of the rhythm. But in spite of his despair the psalmist does not lose faith ; he knows that God is near (3) *in the sanctuary* (as the Septuagint reads), where he is wont to be, and where *praise* is offered to him. 4, 5. For his own comfort the psalmist recalls how in the past the *fathers trusted in* God, and were delivered ; and in saying so he implicitly asks why this is not the case with him. 6, 7. But his humility and sense of unworthiness rebuke him ; and he reflects upon what an object of contempt he is : *I am a worm, and no man* (for the term cp. Isa. 41¹⁴) ; he feels bitterly the way in which he has been treated by his opponents, reproached, despised, and laughed at ; and (8) what doubtless hurt him most of all, because there seemed to be some truth in it, was that he had called upon Yahweh, but in vain, the words are those of his enemies : *He cast himself on Yahweh*, a very expressive term, lit. " he rolled " on to Yahweh, meaning whole-hearted abandonment. The words : *for he delighteth in him*, are, of course, ironical. 9–10. Then, however, the psalmist's innate faith gains the mastery ; from birth he has been very close to Yahweh ; he claims to have acknowledged God from the very beginning of his life : *from my mother's belly thou art my God.* 11. He therefore feels his right to claim Yahweh's help in his present straits, for apart from Yahweh, *there is no helper.* 12–13. And now the psalmist describes his foes, and the pitiable state he is in owing to their cruel enmity. As we have seen, he was a man of deep feelings, and given to use strong expressions. He speaks of his enemies as *mighty bulls*, intimating both their strength and fierceness, *strong ones of Bashan*, the broad and fertile tract of country north-east of the Jordan ; here the cattle were turned loose, and became wild and ferocious. The leader of these enemies is compared with *a lion ravening and roaring* (cp. Pss. 10⁹, 17¹²), ready to tear the poor victim to pieces, *he openeth upon me his mouth* ; a slight emendation is here called for ; the text as it stands, " they open upon me their mouth," makes the bulls the subject, whereas it is the " lion " that is the subject. 14, 15. With a characteristic sudden change of thought, the psalmist then contemplates his own helpless state, both bodily and mental, and speaks of himself as near to death. Here again, exaggerated utterances reflect a condition of intolerable strain on the part of the sufferer. His feeling of utter helplessness he describes in an extremely graphic picture as being *poured out like water*, likening his body to water splashed on the ground and spreading aimlessly, his *bones* being *all out of joint*. Similarly with his state of mind, or *heart*, which, according to the Hebrew conception, was the seat of the emotions (cp. Ps. 25¹⁷, 73²¹) ; this, he says, *is become like wax, melting within* him (cp. Deut. 20[8], Josh. 2[11], Nah. 2[10]), a picture of helpless fear. He speaks further of his bodily suffering, perhaps in reference to burning fever : *Dried up like a potsherd is my throat* ; the Hebrew text has, " my strength," but the parallel *my tongue cleaveth to my palate,* makes *my throat* more appropriate ; the two words are again very similar in Hebrew, and easily confused (see text-crit. note). In this state of weakness he feels the hand of death upon him : *the dust of death is on my lips* ; the Hebrew text here has : " and to the dust of death thou layest me " ; but this cannot be correct, for God is not being addressed, the psalmist is describing his state ; the two words, " thou layest me " and " on my lips " are almost exactly alike in Hebrew. The mention of " dust " with " lips," where death is referred to, is peculiarly appropriate ; " death," as often, is synonymous with *Sheol*, the abode of the dead ; the Hebrew conception of this place was the same as that of the Babylonians : it is a place of darkness where dust covers all things ; dust is on bolt and bar, and dust covers the shades of men as they silently glide through the dust-laden streets of this city of the dead ; their only food is dust, and their drink is black, murky water. It will thus be seen that the psalmist's words, *the dust of death is on my lips*, are very significant. The thought of death then further occupies his mind, 16–18. In likening his enemies to *dogs*, he is thinking of the scavengers that devour corpses, see 1 Kgs. 21[43], 2 Kgs. 9[36] ; like these, the enemies *gather round* him, and already treat him as a dead body : *they bind my hands and my feet*, according to Oriental usage (see John 11[44], " bound hand and foot with grave-bands "). The Hebrew text here reads, " Like a lion my hands and my feet," a corruption recognized by the early translators, as the Versions show ; they suggest various emendations, none of which is satisfactory. A number of emendations are also proposed by modern commentators ; but there can be no certainty as to the right reading. Some authorities read " they bind ", the letters of which in Hebrew come near to those of " like a lion " ; we have adopted this as giving the best sense. Although he cries out on account of the pain they are causing him, they simply *gaze and look at* him, regarding him as already destined to death. According to custom, the clothes of a criminal, who suffered quite naked, were the perquisite of the executioner : *They apportion my garments among them* . . . . Thus, the psalmist envisages the approach of death. But even in the hour of deepest peril he still looks for help (19–21) and calls upon Yahweh : *Rescue my soul from the sword, my life from the power of the dog* ; the rendering " my life " is lit. " mine only one ", meaning the psalmist's very self, and thus a synonym for " soul ", as in Ps. 35[17]. The terms *dog* and *lion* are again applied to the enemies, and he prays that Yahweh may save *mine afflicted one from the horns of the wild-oxen* ; here again an emendation is called for ; the Hebrew text reads " thou hast answered me from the horns of the wild-oxen ", which is meaningless; in Hebrew the two words " thou hast answered me " and " mine afflicted one " are almost identical (see text-crit. note), and it is easy to see how the corruption arose. " Mine afflicted one " is in reference to the psalmist himself, being synonymous with " my soul " and " mine only one ". The expression *the horns of the wild-oxen*, again in reference to the enemies, is descriptive of strength and ferocity; the psalmist pictures himself as entangled in the cruel onslaught of his powerful foes. Then (22–26) without any words as to how it was brought about, the psalmist indicates that he has been delivered, in consequence of which he says : *I will declare thy name unto my brethren, in the midst of the congregation will I praise thee*; he will, in other words, give thanks and praise to God for his deliverance. He, further, calls upon all them that *fear Yahweh*, namely, the *seed of Jacob*, and the *seed of Israel*, to join with him in glorifying and worshipping him. Significant are the echoes here of what is said in the earlier verses of the psalm ; thus, when the psalmist says : *For he hath not despised, he hath not spurned*, there is an implicit reference to his humble description of himself as a " worm " (*v.* 6); and *the affliction of the afflicted one* is a point of attachment with *v.* 21 ; as marking the unity of the psalm this is worth mention. In gratitude the psalmist continues : *And he hath not hidden his face from him* (*i.e.* the afflicted one). . . . 25. The *praise* that he therefore offers *in the great congregation*, he recognizes to be *from him, i.e.,* inspired by God. The *vows*, made in the time of peril, he will now fulfil, and thus witness to God's loving-kindness *in the presence of them that fear him.* In saying that *the meek shall eat and be satisfied*, the psalmist is referring to the sacrificial feast which takes place after the offering of the sacrifices in ful-filment of his vows, to which he invites his friends (cp. 1 Sam. 9[19, 22-24]) ; *the meek*, or " humble," is one of the technical terms applied to the Ḥasidim, the " godly ones," *i.e.,* the faithful upholders of traditional belief and practice (see further pp. 56 ff.). He encourages his friends and followers with the words : *May your heart live for ever*, thus expressing the wish for their continued prosperity after the troublous times now past. The universalistic note then sounded (27, 28) reflects prophetical influence ; it is not enough that the faithful should praise God ; *all the ends of the earth* are called upon to recognize what God had done for his servant, and to *turn, i.e.,* be converted ; then shall *all the kindreds of the nations worship before him, for the Kingship is Yahweh's, and his rule is over the nations*, an element belonging to prophetical eschatology (cp. Isa. 62[3], Obad. *v.* 21, Zech. 14[9]). A remarkable thought then follows (29) which adumbrates a developed belief in the After-life ; the verse is a very difficult one on account of the corruption of the text, but there can be no doubt as to its general sense, namely that the departed will join in worshipping God for the manifestation of his power in delivering his

servant. As the Hebrew text stands it is impossible to make sense out of
it; the emendations which we have adopted, and for which we are
mainly indebted to Gunkel, are very convincing; a glance at the text-
critical notes will show how closely the emended form resembles the
Hebrew text, and how the corruptions arose owing to faulty transcribing.
Finally (30) the psalmist declares that those now living will hand on *to a
generation that cometh, to a people that shall be born*, the way in which
God's *righteousness* was vindicated by the accomplishment of this
wondrous deliverance and reinstatement of his servant.

From all that is recorded in this psalm, especially in *vv.* 22–30, we
are justified in believing that it embodies, in outline reference, some
episode in Jewish internal history which was of far-reaching importance.
It tells of one of the decisive victories, gained after a severe struggle, of
the orthodox party in the long drawn-out conflict between them and
those whose attitude towards the traditional faith threatened to under-
mine the Jewish religion (on this see further pp. 56 ff.). The importance
of this victory is graphically portrayed in this psalm. It is, we submit,
no exaggeration to say that this victory constituted one of the decisive
steps which led ultimately to the permanent establishment of Jewish
orthodoxy in the supremacy of Pharisaism. Much that later Pharisaism
developed was alien to Judaism at its best, yet it must in fairness be
recognized that it preserved, in face of opposed tendencies, the fundamental tenets of the Jewish religion. The victory recorded in this
psalm may well have been epoch-making. Our knowledge of the
history of the Jews during the fourth and third centuries B.C. is unfortunately meagre, owing to the scantiness of historical records; but if,
as we believe, this psalm has preserved a reminiscence of a vital victory,
it is, both historically and religiously, of deep interest and importance.

Religious Teaching

The outstanding religious element contained in this psalm is its
witness of one whose indomitable faith, in face of overwhelming forces,
according to human standards, stood firm to the very verge of martyr-
dom. That he was ready to die for his religious belief is quite clear.
His deliverance at the eleventh hour vindicated his trust in God. The
only other point to be noted here is the psalmist's communing with God
which upheld him in his direst need. No dilating on these sublime
facts is required; they call for thought, not words.

The quotation of some of the verses in this psalm in the Gospels is
dealt with on p. 95.

PSALM 23

THIS exquisite little psalm, probably the most familiar of all the psalms,
tells of one whose **sublime trust** in God has brought him peace and

contentment. The close relationship to God felt by the psalmist is expressed by the two pictures representing: the protecting Shepherd and the loving Host. The brief reference to his enemies indicates that he had not been free from trouble by the malice of the evil-disposed among his people; but the mention of them is cursory. Unlike so many other psalmists who are the victims of unscrupulous foes, and who pour out their grief in bitterness of spirit, this happy and loyal servant of God has only words of grateful recognition of the divine lovingkindness. The whole psalm breathes a spirit of calm, and peace, and contentment, brought about through faith in God, which makes it one of the most inspiring in the Psalter.

There is no adequate reason for denying a pre-exilic date for the psalm. The metre is 3 : 2, with the exception of *vv.* 1, 2, which have 3 : 3.

A Psalm. David's.

1. Yahweh is my Shepherd, I lack nothing;
2. in green pastures he maketh me to lie down,
3. he refresheth my soul;

Beside still waters doth he lead me,
He guideth me into paths of righteousness

for his name's sake.

4. Yea, though I go through a valley of darkness,
° With me is thy rod and thy staff,

I fear no evil,
° they guide me °.

5. Thou spreadest out a table before me,
Thou anointest my head with oil,

in the presence of mine enemies;
my cup overfloweth;

6. Yea, goodness and lovingkindness shall follow me
° And I will dwell in the house of Yahweh.

all the days of my life;

for length of days.

Text-critical Notes

4. Om. פִּי־אַתָּה. Read, with several commentators, יַנְחוּנִי (cp. Ps. 43³) for יְנַחֲמֻנִי, " they comfort me ". 6. Read, with S, וְיָשַׁבְתִּי for וְשַׁבְתִּי, " and I return ".

1–3. The picture of *Yahweh* as *Shepherd* is one in which the central thought is that of his loving care for the helpless. It is used here in reference to the individual psalmist, but elsewhere Yahweh is thought of as the " Shepherd of Israel " (Ps. 80¹, cp. 79¹³, 95⁷, 100³); so that while in such passages as these it is the flock that he shepherds, here he tends a single member of the flock. This is not without significance; for it points to the growing sense of the importance of the individual in contrast to the traditional conception of the community as the unit of divine solicitude (cp. the teaching of Jeremiah and Ezekiel). The peace and contentment of body and mind is exquisitely portrayed in the picture of restful repose *in green pastures* beside the refreshing coolness of *still waters* (cp. Isa. 49¹⁰). But greater than material comforts is the spiritual happiness of being led *into paths of righteousness.* That Yahweh leads him thus *for his name's sake* means that it is not the psalmist's own doing which enables him to walk righteously, but that for the honour of his

name Yahweh leads him ; this implicit teaching on divine grace should
be noted (cp. Isa. 63¹⁴). 4. It is not fanciful to see in what follows the
recalling of a peril through which the psalmist had passed in days gone
by ; he speaks of it as going *through a valley of darkness* ; as the Hebrew
now stands the word for " darkness " is pointed *zalmaweth*, lit.
" shadow of death " ; but compound nouns, excepting as proper names
hardly ever occur in Hebrew ; as has long been recognized, the word
should be pointed *zalmuth*, from *zelem* " shadow " (Arabic *zalima* " to
be dark "), with the noun-termination -*uth* (see GK. 86 *k*).   It should
also be noted that " shadow of death " is out of harmony with the picture
presented, the reference being simply to one of those dark ravines which
abound in Palestine.   With Yahweh as his guide, the psalmist says, there
is nought to fear in passing through such a dark valley, in reference no
doubt to wild beasts, or evil spirits, for Yahweh guides and protects him
with his *rod* and *staff* (for the shepherd's rod cp. Mic. 7¹⁴).   5, 6. The
picture then c'.anges, and Yahweh is thought of as a loving Host, who
spreadest out a table before me in the presence of mine enemies, the idea being
that they may see the reward of one whose whole trust is in Yahweh.   For
the anointing of the guest's *head with oil*, according to the custom of the
times, cp. Ps. 45⁷, Lk. 7⁴⁶.   *My cup overfloweth*, lit. " my cup is satiety,"
is a figurative expression here, meaning that he is fully supplied with
his needs.   In the fulness of his trust the psalmist knows that Yahweh's
goodness and lovingkindness shall follow him *all the days of* his *life* ; and
that goodness and lovingkindness is shown forth not only in the
bestowal of temporal benefits, but by the far greater spiritual blessing of
dwelling in the house of Yahweh for length of days—parallel with *all the
days of my life*—for there he is in the presence of Yahweh, and partakes
daily of the joy of worship.

In connexion with a psalm like this, where the exegetical notes
necessarily deal with all its religious teaching, a special section on this is
not called for.

PSALM 24

IN reading this psalm the impression which is at first gained is that three
fragments belonging originally to different psalms, now no longer extant,
have been put together to make a single psalm.   This conclusion is
suggested by observing the differing subject-matter of each of the three
fragments.   *Vv.* 1, 2 speak of the creation of the earth ; *vv.* 3–6 describe
what must be the character of those who would worship Yahweh ; and
vv. 7–10 contain a summons to the gates, personified, to admit the king
of glory.   The psalm is, therefore, regarded by some commentators as a

piecing together of three disjointed fragments. Judged by modern canons of composition this conclusion has much to justify it. But can we apply these to an ancient poem, written by one with a vivid imagination, who is not bound by literary niceties, and who writes for those to whom his allusions are familiar? Much depends upon the occasion for which the psalm was written; but here again opinions differ, and the force of the arguments put forth must be recognized. We venture, however, to suggest that the psalm was written to be sung at the great feast, the feast of Tabernacles. Outstanding elements proper to this festival were: the worship of Yahweh as the Lord of Creation, the proclamation of him as King, and as one mighty in battle; and one of the central ritual acts was the great procession which accompanied the chariot of the Hero-King. In our psalm all these elements appear, whether directly or indirectly expressed. Thus in *vv.* 1, 2, the creation of the earth is spoken of; a very appropriate introduction to the psalm; the procession, consisting of many pilgrims from all quarters, is formed at the foot of mount Zion; then one of the priests addresses the assembled worshippers, putting the heart-searching question: "Who may ascend on to the mount of Yahweh?" Another priest takes up the answer. This preliminary completed, the great procession ascends the holy mount. On reaching the temple gates, a halt is called, and in antiphonal song the Levitical choir and the crowd of worshippers sing their triumphal song. There the psalm ceases, and we must picture to ourselves the entry of the joyful throng into the hallowed precincts. It is thus quite possible for the psalm to be regarded as a unity.

As to the date of the psalm, some authorities assign it to the time of David, others to the Maccabæan era; the former is out of the question seeing that the gates of the temple are described as "ancient"—there is not the slightest justification for regarding the gates as those of the city— and a post-exilic date, let alone a Maccabæan one, is excluded by the antique ring resounding through the psalm. Everything points to a pre-exilic date, though anything more precise cannot be postulated owing to the lack of the requisite *data*.

The metre varies; in *vv.* 1–6 it is in part 3 : 3, and in part short lines with two beats; *vv.* 7–10 are almost uniformly 3 : 3 : 3, with a slight variation at the end of *v.* 10. The difference of metre between the parts is no argument against unity, as this occurs also in psalms in which diverse authorship is out of the question.

David's. A Psalm.

1. The earth is Yahweh's, and the fulness thereof,   the world and the dwellers therein;
2. For he founded it upon the seas,   and upon the streams did he firmly set it.
3. Who may ascend on to the mount of Yahweh,   and who may stand up in his holy place?

4.   He that hath innocent hands,
            and a pure heart,
            who hath not lifted up
            ° his soul ° to wrong-doing,
            nor sworn deceitfully;
5.   He shall receive a blessing
            from Yahweh,
            and prosperity from the God of his help.
6. Such is the generation of them that   that seek ° the face of the God of °
   enquire after ° Yahweh °,   Jacob. Selah.
7.   Life up your heads, O ye gates,
            and be ye lift up, ye ancient doors,
            that the King of glory may come in !
8.   Who is the King of glory ?
            Yahweh, a strong and mighty one,
            Yahweh, a mighty one in battle !
9.   Lift up your heads, O ye gates,
            ° and be ye lift up °, ye ancient doors,
            that the King of glory may come in !
10.   Who is he, the King of glory ?
                  Yahweh of hosts,
            he is the King of glory ! Selah.

Text-critical Notes

4. Read, with many MSS., נַפְשׁוֹ for נַפְשִׁי, " my soul ".   6. Add, with G,
יהוה.   Read, with G, פְּנֵי אֱלֹהֵי.   9. Read, with many MSS. as in v. 7, וְהִנָּשְׂאוּ
for וּשְׂאוּ, " and lift up ".

As to the title, the Septuagint adds " for the first day of the week ";
doubtless this indicates what was customary at one time.   In later days,
however, it was sung on the Sabbath while the procession with the roll of
the Law marched from and to the " Ark " in which the roll was kept.

1, 2. The psalmist begins by proclaiming the creative power of
Yahweh: *The earth is Yahweh's, and the fulness thereof*, because he
created it.   This reference to the creative act of Yahweh is significant,
since the recitation of the Creation-Drama was ·one of the central
elements belonging to the celebration of the feast of Tabernacles.   That
the earth was *founded upon the seas, and firmly set upon the streams*, is a
strange conception; it is, however, taken almost verbally from the
Babylonian Creation-myth, the idea being that the earth rose up out of
the primeval waters.[1]   The very brief mention of the Creation in these
opening verses is to be explained by the fact that the subject found more
detailed expression later during the celebration of the festival; we have
here only the opening ceremony.   The assembled worshippers from far
and near who have come to celebrate the feast are on the point of ascending mount Zion on their way to the temple.   A temporary halt is called,
and one of the priests accompanying the pilgrims raises his voice : *Who
may ascend on to the mount of Yahweh, and who may stand up in his holy
place ?* i.e., the temple, showing that they are gathered at the foot of the
hill.   The words are not addressed directly to the throng; it is a question of general application, but especially appropriate now.   4, 5. The

---

[1] See Jeremias, *Handbuch der altorientalischen Geisteskultur*, pp. 122 f. (1929).

reply is made by another priest, and contains a heart-searching picture
of the man whose spiritual state and manner of life are such as to make
him worthy of offering worship to God : *innocent hands and a pure heart,*
i.e., outwardly and inwardly of upright life ; *who hath not lifted up his soul*
to wrong-doing, i.e., who has not arrogantly and of set purpose been
guilty of evil courses; it is possible that there is also a reference to
idolatry here, for the word rendered " wrong-doing ", lit. " vanity ", is
sometimes used in reference to idols (*e.g.*, Ps. 31^6, Jer. 18^{15}, Jon. 2^8) ;
and, finally, *nor sworn deceitfully, i.e.*, has not infringed the sacredness of
an oath.   5.   Such a one is indeed worthy to enter the house of worship,
thereby receiving *a blessing from Yahweh*, and *help* in his walk in life.
Thereupon the priest who had first raised his voice addresses the
assembled worshippers : *Such is the generation of them that enquire after*
Yahweh, that seek the face of the God of Jacob ; the implication is that the
priest regards those addressed as coming under this description.   The
ascent of mount Zion then proceeds ; that this is not stated in so many
words is for the simple reason that it was obvious.

7-10.   Arrived at the temple gates there is again a halt, and a short
triumphal hymn is sung; it is rendered antiphonally, two bodies of
singers taking part, with a solo voice intervening : first, the Levitical
choir, in the mode of Oriental poetry, addresses the temple gates,
personified : *Lift up your heads, O ye gates, and be ye lift up, ye ancient*
doors ; it is, of course, a command to the gate-keepers to open the gates
as the procession is now ready to enter the sanctuary ; but, with the
Oriental love of the dramatic, the command is clothed in this forceful
style.   And it continues : *that the King of glory may come in.*   Here two
points must be briefly dealt with.   On the basis of an entirely different
interpretation of the psalm from that here put forth, it is held that the
" gates " are those of the city, and that the Israelite army, returning from
a victory, stands before the city gates demanding entry.   This curious
view hardly needs refuting ; apart from other matters, is it likely that the
army, flushed with victory, would be kept waiting outside the gates ?
And why should the gates be closed against such a throng ?   There is
not a word in the psalm which suggests that the city gates are in question.
The temple gates, though not as ancient as those of the city, could, at
any rate, claim a respectable antiquity,[1] unless we are to regard the psalm
as Davidic !   A claim which is not to be taken seriously in view of vv.
3-6.   The other point is in connexion with the words : *That the King of*
glory may come in.   This has been interpreted as in reference to the Ark
of the Covenant, with Yahweh conceived of as enthroned upon it ; 1 Sam.
$4^{4\,ff.}$ is pointed to as an illustration of the ark of the covenant, with Yahweh
of hosts, " which dwelleth between the cherubim," being taken with the

[1] See Hollis *The Archæology of Herod's Temple*, passim (1934), which deals with
the whole subject of the temple gates.

Israelite host to ensure victory, on to the battle-field ; the words of our psalm, *Yahweh, a strong and mighty one, Yahweh, a mighty one in battle,* are, of course quoted in support.   If *vv.* 7–10 are regarded as a separate fragment, without any connexion with the rest of the psalm, it must be granted that this view has a great deal in its favour.   But in that case an objection suggests itself ; if these verses are independent of the rest of the psalm, they cannot be other than a fragment, as stated ; they obviously imply something that has preceded.   How comes it, then, that the remainder of the psalm to which it belonged is lost ?   It would, on account of its antiquity, have been a psalm of high value ; and to cut off a part of it in this way without preserving the rest would be difficult to account for.   It is true that we have cases in which fragments of psalms have been pieced together ; but they are not of the character or age of this, supposed, psalm, judging from the " fragment ".   We contend that unless there are stronger reasons than any that have been put forward, there is no justification for cutting up our psalm.   On our view that the psalm, a decidedly ancient one, was sung during the festival of Tabernacles, the New Year feast, the psalm presents a perfectly logical unity.

But to return ; when it is said : *that the King of glory may come in,* the reference is not to the bringing of the Ark of the Covenant, for, as has been pointed out, the psalm was sung during the celebration of the feast of Tabernacles, and in the midst of the festal procession about to enter the sanctuary was Yahweh's chariot in which he was conceived of as present.[1]   After the Levitical choir have sung their address to the temple gates (*v.* 7), a solo voice puts the question : *Who is the King of glory?* the whole assembly of worshippers reply : *Yahweh, a strong and mighty one; Yahweh, a mighty one in battle !*   The reference is again to the Babylonian Creation-myth, the *rôle* of Marduk, as in numerous other Old Testament passages, being adapted to Yahweh, see, *e.g.*, Pss. 74[12-15], 89[8-10].   The whole is repeated in *vv.* 9, 10, with the exception that in *v.* 10 the chorus of the worshippers varies slightly : *Yahweh of hosts, he* (emphatic) *is the King of glory !*

Religious Teaching

This has been dealt with in the exegetical notes.

[1] See, further on this, *Myth and Ritual*, ed. S. H. Hooke, pp. 126—133 (1933).

PSALM 25

THIS is one of the acrostic psalms consisting largely of self-contained sayings, though thought-sequence is to be observed here and there. The need of following out the alphabetical order for the beginning of each verse accounts for the somewhat artificial style. The psalm is, nevertheless, full of spiritual guidance. The enemies of the psalmist, of whom mention is twice made, point, as in the case of so many other psalms, to the existence of religious party strife. That the psalm is an "individual," *i.e.*, one in which the psalmist all through speaks of himself personally, and does not represent his people, is undoubted, in spite of the contention of some commentators that he writes on behalf of others. The last verse does not belong to the psalm (see exegetical note).

The date, like all the acrostic psalms, is late post-exilic; pointing in the same direction is the Wisdom style which occurs in several of the verses (4, 5, 12–14, 21).

The metre is 3 : 3, with the exception of *vv.* 1, 15.

David's.

1 א. Unto thee, Yahweh,
     do I lift up my soul ;

2 ב. In thee have I trusted, let me not be shamed,   may mine enemies not ° laugh me to scorn °.

3 ג. In truth, none that wait for thee shall be shamed,   shamed shall they be that deal faithlessly to no purpose.

4 ד. Thy ways, Yahweh, make me to know,   ° and ° thy paths teach me.

5 ה. Guide me in thy truth, and teach me,   for thou art the God of my help,
 ו. ° And on thee ° do I wait every day,   7° ° because of thy goodness, Yahweh °.

6 ז. Remember thy tender-mercies ° and lovingkindnesses,   for they are from of old ;

7 ח. The sins of my youth ° remember ° not,   in accordance with thy mercy remember me °.

8 ט. Good and upright is Yahweh °,   he instructeth ° sinners ° in the way ;

9 י. He guideth the meek with justice,   and teacheth ° the poor ° in his way.

10 כ.   All the ways of Yahweh
     are mercy and truth
     for them that keep his covenant and his testimonies.

11 ל. For thy name's sake, Yahweh,   forgive me mine iniquity, for it is great.

12 מ. Who, then, is the man that feareth Yahweh ?   he will teach him in the way that he chooseth ;

13 נ. His soul shall abide in prosperity,   and his seed shall inherit the land.

14 ס. The friendship of Yahweh is for them that fear him,   and his covenant is for them to whom he maketh it known.

15 ע. Mine eyes are continually unto Yahweh,   for he bringeth my feet out of the net.

16 פ. Look unto me, and be gracious unto me,   for alone and afflicted am I.

17 צ. The troubles of my heart ° are increased °,   bring me out of my distresses ;

18 ק. ° Give heed ° to mine affliction and my trouble,   and forgive all my sins.

19 ר. Behold mine enemies, for they are many,   with bitter hatred do they hate me.

20 ש. Preserve my soul, and deliver me,   let me not be put to shame, for I trust in thee.

21 ת. Let integrity and uprightness cover me,   for I wait for thee, ° Yahweh °.

[22.   Redeem Israel, O God, from all his troubles].

Text-critical Notes

2. Read יַלְעֲגוּ for יַעַלְצוּ, which never takes לְ after it. **4.** Add, with G, וְ. **5.** Read, with some MSS., וְאוֹרְתְךָ, for the sake of the acrostic. A half-line is wanting in this verse, while *v.* 7 is overloaded. **6.** Om. יהוה for the rhythm's sake **7.** Om., with S, וּפְשָׁעַי, "and my transgressions", for the rhythm's sake. See *v.* 5. **8.** Om. עַל־כֵּן, "therefore", for the rhythm's sake. **8.** Read חֹטְאִים for חַטָּאִים, "sins". **9.** Read אֶבְיֹנִים instead of the repetition of עֲנָוִים. **17.** Read, with the Versions, רַבּוּ for הִרְחִיבוּ, "are enlarged". **18.** Read שָׁב for רְאֵה, "behold", for the sake of the acrostic. **21.** Add, with G, יהוה for the rhythm's sake.

The simple and straightforward series of sayings of which this psalm is composed do not call for much in the way of exegetical notes.

1, 2. An expression of trust in Yahweh, on the strength of which the psalmist pleads that his enemies may *not laugh* him *to scorn*; on the need for the emendation here see the text-crit. note. The *enemies* are those opposed to the orthodox circles to which the psalmist belongs; **3-5,** these are they that *wait for* Yahweh, they will not *be ashamed* like those *that deal faithlessly to no purpose*, *i.e.*, their underhand dealings bring them no advantage; the reference is to party strife. The prayer for guidance is offered in confidence both because the psalmist looks daily to Yahweh, in reference to the daily worship, and because he knows Yahweh's *goodness*; the last half-line of *v.* 7 is added here because a half-line has fallen out, whereas in *v.* 7 there is a half-line too much. **6, 7.** Though he faithfully seeks to do the will of God, the psalmist is too honest to deny his shortcomings; but he throws himself upon the mercy of God, praying that his sins may not be remembered, *i.e.*, that they may be forgiven; for (8, 9) in his goodness Yahweh *instructeth* even *sinners*, so that they may walk in the right *way*. **10.** His ways *are mercy and truth*, ever granted to those who *keep his covenant and his testimonies*. **11.** With a sudden change of subject the psalmist reverts to the thought of his sin, *for it is great*, and prays again for forgiveness. **12-14.** Then, in the style of the Wisdom-writer, he puts a question, and gives the answer: *Who then, is the man that feareth Yahweh?* The answer is indirect: he that feareth Yahweh is one who walks *in the way* that Yahweh *chooseth*, and whom therefore Yahweh will *teach*. Such a one shall not only himself continue to live *in prosperity*, but *his seed*, too, *shall inherit the land*; it is taken for granted that the children of a good man will follow the example of their father. The psalmist continues: *The friendship of Yahweh is for them that fear him*; the word " friendship " is full of significance; it means intimate intercourse, such as exists between friends; in this sense it is used in Ps. 55[14], where the English Versions beautifully render it " sweet counsel ". **15-20.** After these sayings of general application the psalmist speaks of his enemies of whom brief mention had been made in *v.* 2. He begins with an affirmation of faith: *Mine eyes are continually unto Yahweh, i.e.*, he ever looks to Yahweh for guidance, and is therefore confident that *he bringeth my feet out of the net, i.e.*, the deceitful entanglements in which his enemies involve him by their intrigues, the simile occurs several times (Pss. 9^{15}, 31^4, 35^8, 57^6). There is special need for this confidence now, for the psalmist is *alone and afflicted*; and for the third time he speaks of his *sins*, thus regarding *the troubles* of his *heart*, and his *distresses*, as due to sin. So he prays for forgiveness and deliverance from his *many* enemies, who *hate* him *with bitter* (lit. " violent ") *hatred*. His final prayer is that *integrity* and *uprightness* may *cover* him, a forceful expression; he desires to be enveloped, as we might almost say, in the " whole armour of God " (Eph. 6^{13}).

22. This verse does not belong to the psalm; it is outside the alphabetical sequence. A later copyist added it, desirous of making the psalm apply to Israel, thus generalizing it.

Religious Teaching

Very inspiring here is the teaching on the *persistence* of communion with God, in face of continued troubles, set forth by the psalmist; the stress laid on such words as " trust ", " wait for ", " make known ", " teach ", " guide ", " instruct ", " remember " (and " remember not "), in reference to himself in the case of the first two, in reference to the Almighty in the case of the rest, witnesses to a personal religion which is most impressive. If the psalm taught nothing but this, its value would be incalculable; it is the most outstanding element in its religious teaching; others, however, occur, but these have been referred to in the exegetical notes.

PSALM 26

THIS psalm is one of the many which refer to religious strife among the Jews (see pp. 60 ff.). The psalmist, in all probability a priest, protests his innocency of life in contrast to the ways of the wicked, *i.e.*, those who are renegades. The assertion of his righteousness, somewhat strongly claimed (*v.* 2), has led some commentators to regard this as an unlovely *trait*; this we believe to be unjustified (see the exeg. note on *vv.* 2, 3). The psalm is clearly an individual one, the writer speaks of himself personally, not as the representative of his party.

There is no direct indication of date, but the conditions reflected point to the Greek period.

The metre is 3 : 3, excepting in the opening verse, which has 2 : 2 : 3.

David's.

1. Vindicate me, Yahweh,
   For in mine integrity have I ° walked ;
   And ° in thee ° have I trusted, I shall not slide.
2. Try me, Yahweh, and prove me,   test my reins and my heart,
3. For thy lovingkindness is before mine
   eyes,   and I have walked in thy truth.
4. I do not sit with worthless men,   nor go with dissemblers,
5. I hate the assembly of evil-doers,   and do not sit with the wicked.
6. I wash mine hands in innocency,   and encompass thine altar, Yahweh,
7. That I may cause the sound of thanks-
   giving to be heard,   and may declare all thy wonder-works ;
8. ° I love the habitation of thine house,   the place of thy glory's abiding.
9. Snatch not away my soul with sinners,   and my life with bloodthirsty men,
10. In whose hands is evil-purpose,   and their right-hand is full of bribes.
11. But I walk in mine integrity,   redeem me, ° Yahweh °, and be gracious
    unto me ;
12. My foot standeth in a level place,   and in the assemblies do I bless thee °,
    Yahweh.

Text-critical Notes

1. Om. אֲנִי for the rhythm's sake. Read בְּךָ, cp. Ps. 25², 143⁸, for בַּיהוה, " in Yahweh " 8 Om. יהוה for the rhythm's sake. 11. Add יהוה for the rhythm's sake. 12. Read, with G, אֲבָרְכֶךָ for אֲבָרֵךְ, " I bless ".

1. The circumstances under which this psalm was written, namely, the controversy and conflict between the orthodox upholders of the traditional faith, and the innovators who endangered its purity, are reflected in the contrast which the psalmist sets forth between himself as a loyal upholder of the former, and the wicked (*Reša'im*) representing the latter (see, on the whole subject, pp. 56 ff). As a champion of the right cause, he calls upon *Yahweh* to *vindicate* him, *i.e.*, to justify him in the face of his enemies ; for he is conscious of having lived wholly in accordance with the commandments of God : *in mine integrity have I walked* ; the word rendered " integrity " connotes the idea of complete-ness in Hebrew. He can with the greater confidence appeal to *Yahweh*, inasmuch as he has always trusted in him : *in thee have I trusted*, in consequence of which he feels safe from the danger of erring from the right way : *I shall not slide*, *i.e.*, from God's way, see Ps. 37³¹ where the same word is used. 2, 3. Then, in words of great boldness, prompted by his sense of loyalty to Yahweh, the psalmist, as it were, challenges Yahweh to see if he is not truly righteous ; the terms used are very searching : *Try me, prove me, test my reins* (lit. " kidneys " the seat of the emotions) *and my heart*. The words sound like an assertion of self-righteousness which no man has a right to claim ; but to understand the words in this way would be doing an injustice to the psalmist. The words which follow must be given due weight : *For thy lovingkindness is before mine eyes, and I have walked in thy truth* ; the psalmist here indicates that his walking in the truth is owing to Yahweh's loving-kindness ; in other words, it is owing to divine love that he is enabled to walk in truth ; so that his way of living is, as we should express it, due to

divine grace.   Then, in fairness to the psalmist, it must be remembered
that the thought of the contrast between himself and the renegade Jews,
his enemies, is ever present; it is not necessarily in any spirit of self-
righteousness that one, striving to live a godly life, contrasts with this
the arrogant, ungodly life of those opposed to him.   The idea of
associating with such is abhorrent to the psalmist, so that he can feelingly
aver, 4, 5: *I do not sit with worthless men, i.e.,* those who are vain and
unreliable, *nor go with dissemblers, i.e.,* those who conceal their motives;
I hate the assembly of evil-doers, this points to a particular body of men
(see pp. 63 ff.); *and do not sit with the wicked,* in reference to Jewish renegades.   Altogether opposed to, and different from, men of this type, is
the psalmist's devotion to the worship of Yahweh (6–8) and the stress
laid on this may imply that the " worthless men " and " dissemblers "
refer to idolaters, or, at any rate, to a syncretistic form of worship due to
contact with aliens.   The psalmist says: *I wash my hands in innocency,
and encompass thine altar, Yahweh*; whether the washing of the hands
here is to be taken literally, in reference to Exod. 30$^{17-21}$, is questionable,
for in that case there should be mention of the washing of the feet as
well; and the addition of " in innocency " suggests a symbolical phrase,
as in Pss. 24 and 73^{13}.   The encompassing of the altar refers probably to
a procession around the altar of which there is mention elsewhere, see,
e.g., the note on Ps. 118^{27}.   In the temple he will lead the psalm of
thanksgiving and declare Yahweh's *wonder-works*; this is doubtless in
reference to his deliverance from his enemies.   These verses indicate
the psalmist as a priest who was constantly present in the temple;
hence his words: *I love the habitation of (i.e.,* abiding in) *thine house,*
which is the place of the divine presence (cp. Ps. 27^4).   9, 10. The
psalmist then prays that Yahweh *will not snatch* him *away with sinners*;
this is the force of the Hebrew word which is difficult to render in
English.   It is a prayer against sudden death, and shows that religious
strife was sometimes very bitter.   11, 12. But this fear of death does
not really trouble the psalmist, for he walks in uprightness of life, and his
petition, *redeem me, Yahweh, and be gracious unto me,* is a prayer of
certitude, since Yahweh has placed him in safety, *My foot standeth in a
level place,* and he will *bless Yahweh* in *the assemblies* of the faithful.

Religious Teaching

The psalm brings before us the figure of one who, in the consciousness of his rectitude, prays that on that account God will justify him.
That is one side of the picture, and taken by itself there lurks therein a
grave spiritual danger, which in the Judaism of later days assumed
ominous proportions (cp. Rom. 4$^{1-5}$, 11^6, Gal. 2^{16}).   But there is
another side to the picture: spiritual pride, arising out of a sense of self-
righteousness, is not a characteristic of the psalmist, because he imputes

to God his rectitude of life, " in thee have I trusted, I shall not slide ",
he says. This is a very different attitude from that of the Pharisee in
the parable (Lk. 18[11, 12, 14]). For a man to recognize, in a spirit of true
humility, that he is striving to live according to the will of God, need not
generate spiritual pride, but should be a source of sanctified joy. While,
on the one hand, to confess sin is a supreme duty for man, the recognition of his virtues, when rightly envisaged, is, on the other hand, to
acknowledge the action of divine grace.

PSALM 27

THIS psalm consists of two parts (*vv.* 1–6, 7–14) ; but the content and
spirit of each, respectively, are so different that most commentators
agree that we have here two originally distinct psalms. *V.* 7 clearly
begins a new psalm, while *v.* 6 is an appropriate conclusion. The
enemies mentioned in each part offered a point of attachment between
the two ; this may account for their having been joined together.

The first of the two psalms presents us with the figure of one whose
faith and trust in Yahweh are such that he can defy any danger that
confronts him. His ardent desire is to abide in Yahweh's presence, and
to worship in his temple. In the second we have the description of one
in deep despair ; thus, in striking contrast to what has preceded. Both
psalmists are, however, alike in this, that their trust in Yahweh is
unshakeable.

A date cannot be indicated, other than that both psalms are post-
exilic. The metre of the first psalm is 3 : 2, but in the last verse, 6, it is
2 : 2 : 3 ; that of the second is similarly 3 : 2, but some serious corruption in the text makes the metre in some verses uncertain.

David's.

1. Yahweh is my light and my salvation,   of whom should I be afraid ?
   Yahweh is the stay of my life,   of whom should I be in terror ?
2. When evil-doers draw nigh against me   to devour my flesh,
   Mine adversaries and they that are mine
       enemies,   they stumble and fall.
3. Though an host encamp against me,   my heart doth not fear ;
   Though war arise against me,   even so do I trust.
4. One thing have I asked of Yahweh,   that have I sought :
   To dwell in the house of Yahweh   all the days of my life,
   To behold the delightfulness of
       Yahweh,   and to contemplate his sanctuary ;
5. For he hideth me in his tabernacle,   in the day of trouble,
   He covereth me in the covert of his
       tent,   he setteth me up upon a rock.
6. And now is mine head lifted up   o'er my foes round about me,
       And I will offer in his tabernacle
       Sacrifices of joy ;
       I will sing and praise Yahweh.

*   *   *   *   *

7. Hearken, Yahweh, to my voice   ° in the day ° that I call ;
   ° Be gracious unto me and answer me,
8. ° my God °,   ° for my heart is bitter ° ;
   Thy face do I seek, Yahweh,   9. hide it not ° from me ;
   Reject not thy servant in wrath,   mine help art thou,
   Cast me not off, and forsake me not,   O God of my salvation,
10. For my father and my mother have for-
   saken me,   but Yahweh will receive me.
11.   Show me, Yahweh, thy way,
   And lead me in a level path,   because of them that lie in wait for me.
12.   Abandon me not to the will of my adversaries,
   For false witnesses are risen up against
   me,   ° and they breathe out ° violence.
13. Had I not believed to see   the goodness of Yahweh
     in the land of the living . . . °
14. ° Stand fast, and let thine heart take
   courage,   and wait on Yahweh.

Text-critical Notes

7. Add בְּיוֹם for the rhythm's sake. Om. ו with many MSS. and the Versions.
8. Add אֵלֶי for the rhythm's sake. Read, with Gunkel, כִּי מַר לִבִּי for לְךָ אָמַר
לִבִּי, " to thee hath my heart said " ; and om. בַּקְּשׁוּ פָנָי, " seek ye my face ".
9. Om. פָּנֶיךָ, " thy face ". 12. Read, with S, וְיָפֵחַ " and they breathe out ",
for וִיפֵחַ, " and he breatheth out ". 13. The end of the verse seems to have
fallen out. 14. Om. קַוֵּה אֶל־יהוה which occurs at the end of the verse.

1-3. The exultant strain with which the psalm opens, proclaiming
unshakeable trust in Yahweh, is called forth, as the sequel shows, owing
to the triumph of the psalmist over his enemies. What has been
achieved is due to Yahweh's guidance : *Yahweh is my light*, which has
led him (cp. Ps. 43³), *and my salvation, i.e.*, the state of security granted to
him by Yahweh through the victory over his enemies. *Of whom*, then,
need he *be afraid?* His life, being now upheld by the strength of
Yahweh, *the stay of his life*, there is no cause for *terror*, intimating, however, that this had been the case previously. But he has now seen the
downfall of his bloodthirsty *enemies*, compared with wild beasts, who had
sought to *devour* his *flesh*. So strong is his confidence in Yahweh that he
feels he could face an army without fear : *though an host encamp against
me, my heart doth not fear* ; and should *war* break out against him, *even
so* his *trust* would uphold him. The language is purposely forceful in
order to express the psalmist's feelings of triumph and safety. 4, 5.
From what follows it is clear that the psalmist is distant from Jerusalem,
though there is nothing to show that he was in a foreign land ; his
adversaries are those of his own race, whom he regards as the enemies of
God also. As a faithful and loyal worshipper of Yahweh his one ardent
desire is to be back in his native city, so that he can again *dwell in the
house of Yahweh*, adding, *all the days of my life*, in reference to the daily
worship in the temple. It is here that he will *behold the delightfulness of
Yahweh, and contemplate his sanctuary* ; these words are a little difficult,
and, not unnaturally, are differently interpreted by commentators. It
may be pointed out, however, that the Hebrew word for " to behold " is

used in the sense of " to experience " in Job 15^{17}, 24^1, 27^{12}, and there is
no reason why it should not be so understood here; in this case we
might paraphrase the first part of the line thus: " to experience the
sense of happiness and peace at being in Yahweh's presence ". The
word rendered " delightfulness ", or pleasantness, occurs in Ps. 135^3 in
reference to Yahweh's name, cp. also 90^{17}. As to the words, *to contemplate his sanctuary*, they offer an excellent parallel to the first half of
the line; the word for " to contemplate " is used, as here, in Prov. 20^{25}
of reflecting upon something; and what the psalmist is referring to is
that which, in the sanctuary, witnesses to Yahweh's presence, the Holy
Place, and the altar; in contemplating these the psalmist realizes, indeed,
that in the sanctuary he will be in Yahweh's presence. It is here, *in his
tabernacle*, that he will be in safety should a *day of trouble* arise again.
Tabernacle and *tent* are used of the temple, as elsewhere (Pss. 31^{20}, 61^4,
76^2); such archaisms were dear to the poet. 6. Now that he has
triumphed over his foes who had been *round about* him—the expressive
phrase is: *now is mine head lifted up*—his earnest wish is to show forth
his gratitude in the *tabernacle* by offering *sacrifices of joy*, doubtless in
fulfilment of vows made in time of peril; the expression " sacrifices of
joy ", lit. " of shout ", may well be equivalent to the " sacrifices of
thanksgiving " spoken of in Ps. 107^{22} for, as the psalmist adds, in his joy
and gratitude he *will sing and praise Yahweh*. This forms a very fitting
conclusion, which justifies the contention that we have here a psalm
which is independent of what follows; the change of metre, so often
characteristic of the last verse of a psalm, points in the same direction.

In striking contrast to the psalm just considered is the pathetic outpouring contained in that which follows. 7–10. The opening words
mark the beginning of another psalm, as comparison with that of many
other psalms shows (*e.g.*, 55^1, 61^1, 64^1, etc.): *Hearken, Yahweh, to my
voice in the day that I call*. In *v.* 8 the text is hopelessly corrupt; but in
comparing the Hebrew of the emended text (see text-crit. note), for
which we are indebted to Gunkel, with that now extant, it will be
seen that there is much similarity between the two; when it is remembered that originally there was no division between the words
of a line and no vowel-points, it will be realized how easily confusion
could arise through careless copying.[1] The psalmist was clearly
in great trouble; his *heart* is *bitter*, he prays that *Yahweh* will
not hide his face from him; *reject not thy servant*, he says; *cast me
not off ; forsake me not*; petitions which only too plainly reveal his
piteous state. He has been forsaken even by his *father and mother*,
due doubtless to the false witnesses to whom he refers later. Yet, in
spite of all, his trust does not give way; he can still affirm that *Yahweh*

---

[1] See, *e.g.*, the plates in Kahle's *Masoreten des Westens* (1927), and they are re-
productions of Hebrew MSS. of late date.

will receive him.   11, 12. The cause of all his trouble he then describes: *adversaries* who *lie in wait for* him (cp. Ps. 5[8], where the same word occurs), *false witnesses,* who *breathe out violence.* Help from these can come only from Yahweh; therefore the psalmist prays: *Show me, Yahweh, thy way, and lead me in a level path, i.e.* a place of safety. In *v.* 13 some words have fallen out, but clearly they must have been to the effect that he would have given up all hope of life, had he not believed to see the goodness of Yahweh in the land of the living. His last words are those of encouragement addressed to himself in self-communing.

Religious Teaching

In each of the two psalms the central point in its religious teaching is the same, though presented from different points of view. In the former, faith in God, which has sustained the sufferer through his trials and brought him triumphantly through them, has thereby become deeper. In the latter the victim, in a piteous state of despair, surrounded by dangers, and plunged in sorrow, is borne up solely by his faith in God. Thus, whether in joy or sorrow, in prosperity or adversity, it is the certitude of God's presence and his love which dominates all things. " Who shall separate us from the love of Christ? shall tribulation, or anguish, or persecution, or famine, or nakedness, or peril, or sword? . . . Nay, in all these things we are more than conquerors through him that loved us " (Rom. 8[35-37]).

PSALM 28

THIS psalm is, in the main, a prayer for help against foes who are represented as godless (*v.* 5). To this is added an appeal to Yahweh to destroy them. In the latter part of the psalm all danger appears as past, and *vv.* 6, 7 form a short hymn of praise and thanksgiving for deliverance. The conditions reflected are the same as those of several other psalms with which we have dealt: strife between the champions of the faith handed down and those whose religion is contaminated by the infusion of alien influences. It is possible that in some cases the passionate feelings of the psalmists may have led them to represent their antagonists as worse than they really were; but there can be no doubt that the latter constituted a grave menace to traditional faith and practice. That politics became mixed up with religion (see pp. 64 f.) naturally made things worse. In this, as in other psalms of a like nature, it is an individual who is in personal danger; this points to his having been one of the leaders of the orthodox party.

o

To indicate a date is impossible; but there is nothing in the psalm to exclude it from being pre-exilic.

The metre, but for the last verse, is 3 : 2.

David's.

1. Unto thee ° do I cry, O my Rock,   be not deaf unto me,
   lest thou be silent unto me, and I be like   them that go down to the Pit.
2. Hear the voice of my supplication   when I cry unto thee,
   when I lift up mine hands, ° Yahweh °,   to thine innermost sanctuary.
3. Drag me not away with the wicked,   and with the workers of iniquity,
   that speak peace with their neighbours,   but evil is in their heart.
4. Recompense them according to their doing,   and according to the wickedness of their acts,
   according to work of their hands °
   render   their desert unto them ;
5. ° They heed not ° the work of ° Yahweh,   nor the doing of his hands ;
   may he cast them down, and not build them up.
6. Blessed be Yahweh, for he hath heard   the voice of my supplication ;
7. Yahweh is my strength and my shield,   mine heart trusteth in him.
   ° I was holpen, and my flesh revived,   and from my heart I gave him thanks.°
8. Yahweh is the strength ° of his people °,   the protection and help of his anointed °.
9.   Save thy people,
   and bless thine inheritance,
   Nourish them and bear them up for ever.

Text-critical Notes

1. Om. יהוה for the rhythm's sake. 2. Add יהוה for the rhythm's sake. 4. Om., with some MSS., תֵּן לָהֶם, "recompense them", repeated from the previous line. 5. Om. כִּי, "for". Read, with some MSS., פְּעֻלָּת for ־ת, plur. 7. Read, following GS (Duhm, Gunkel):

נֶעְזָרְתִּי וַיַּחֲלֹף שְׁאֵרִי   וּמִלִּבִּי אֲהוֹדֶנּוּ

instead of the present Hebrew text : "And I was holpen, and mine heart exulted, and from my song I gave him thanks". The rendering of the Versions was evidently based on a different, and purer, form of the Hebrew text. 8. Read, with many MSS. and the Versions, לְעַמּוֹ for לָמוֹ, "to them". Om. הוּא, for the rhythm's sake.

1, 2. The extreme peril in which the psalmist finds himself is indicated by the intensity of his appeal. In the Hebrew text "Yahweh" is inserted after *Unto thee*; but this is evidently not original as it breaks the rhythm. The Almighty is addressed as *my Rock*, an ancient designation expressive of the safety accorded to those who call upon him (cp. Pss. 18², 19⁴, and elsewhere). How urgent the psalmist's need is appears from his fear that if God is deaf to his appeal his life will be endangered; he will *be like them that go down to the Pit*, a synonym for *Sheol* (cp. Pss. 30³, 88³, ⁴), but the lowest part of it. The prayer was offered up in the temple, for the psalmist lifts up his hands in front of the *innermost sanctuary, i.e.*, the Holy of Holies (*debir*); the rendering "oracle" conveys a wrong idea as though it were a place whence utterances proceeded. 3–5. The cause of the psalmist's peril is the action of *workers of iniquity*, deceitful in word and deed; they are the enemies of God, for *they heed not the work of Yahweh*; the psalmist, therefore, prays that Yahweh may *recompense them according to their doing*. They are thus the same type of "enemy" as depicted in so many other psalms, namely, renegades; men who are unfaithful to the religion of their fathers. The psalmist, having thus set forth his peril, and the cause of it, then goes on to show that it is now past, and makes his acknowledgements to Yahweh for having delivered him (6, 7); *Blessed be Yahweh, for he hath heard the voice of my supplication*; the psalmist addresses him as *my strength and my shield*, expressive of Yahweh's power to deliver and to protect (cp. Ps. 3³). For the rendering of the line which follows, see the text-crit. note; it is based on the Septuagint and Syriac Versions, and is more pointed than the Hebrew text in its present form, telling of how both in body and mind he had experienced Yahweh's help and protection. 8, 9. These verses can hardly be an original part of the psalm; they represent the *people* and the king, the *anointed*, as the objects of Yahweh's solicitude; whereas in the rest of the psalm it is the individual psalmist. The probability seems to be that these verses were taken from some ancient psalm and added here in order to adapt it to liturgical worship.

Religious Teaching

The main theme, trust in God in the midst of danger, has already been dealt with in several other psalms.

PSALM 29

THIS fine and ancient hymn of praise is unique in the Psalter. It was doubtless inspired, in the first instance, by the awesome descriptions of the theophany on Mount Sinai (Exod. 19¹⁶⁻¹⁹), and the divine presence on Mount Horeb (1 Kgs. 19¹¹, ¹²). The psalmist's aim is to proclaim Yahweh's supremacy in the heavens and on earth. The heavenly powers are described as " sons of gods ", and subordinate to Yahweh; a witness to monotheistic belief in contrast to the polytheism of the nations which regarded the highest god as different in rank, but not in nature, from the rest of the gods. The old-world conception of the thunder being the voice of Yahweh appears here in pronounced form (cp. Pss. 18¹³, 46⁶, 68³³, 77¹⁸). The belief was not unnatural, and was paralleled among other peoples who had their storm-gods and the like. It is easy to understand the awe-inspiring effect of thunder and lightning, accompanied by gale and shower, on men in those compara-tively early times, unaware of their whence and why.

The psalm is certainly one of the earliest in the Psalter. It is perhaps owing to its age that the text has suffered some corruption, and that the metre is somewhat irregular. Most of the verses have two beats to the half-line; but *vv.* 3, 4, 6 have 3 : 3, and *v.* 10 has 3 : 2 : 2.

A Psalm. David's.

1.   Ascribe unto Yahweh,
             O ye sons of gods,
             ascribe unto Yahweh
             glory and might ;
2.   Ascribe unto Yahweh
             the glory of his name ;
             worship Yahweh
             in holy array !

3. The voice of Yahweh is upon the
      waters °,   of Yahweh upon many waters,
4. The voice of Yahweh with power,   the voice of Yahweh with splendour.
5.   The voice of Yahweh
             shattereth cedars,
             yea, Yahweh shattereth
             the cedars of Lebanon.

6. He maketh Lebanon to ° skip ° like a
      calf,   and Sirion like a young ° wild-ox °.
7.   ° The voice of Yahweh ° heweth out
             flames of fire.
8.   The voice of Yahweh
             shaketh the wilderness,
             Yahweh shaketh
             the wilderness of Kadesh.
9.   The voice of Yahweh
             maketh hinds to calve ;
             ° the voice of Yahweh °
             strippeth bare the ° forests °.
             And in his temple ° everyone °
             saith : " Glory ".
10.   Yahweh sitteth over the flood,
             And Yahweh abideth
             King for ever.
11.   May Yahweh grant
             strength to his people,
             May Yahweh bless
             his people with peace.

Text-critical Notes

3. Om. אֶל־הַכָּבוֹד הִרְעִים, " the God of glory thundereth ", which overloads
the line, and is out of harmony with the context. 6. Read וַיִּרְקֵד for וַיַּרְקִידֵם,
" he maketh them to skip ". Read רְאֵם for רְאֵמִים, " wild-oxen ". 7. קוֹל־יְ
with maqqeph, one beat. 9. Add קוֹל־יהוה which seems to have fallen out, but
the text is uncertain ; יְעָרוֹת with fem. plur. does not occur elsewhere, it is a
masc. noun. Read הַבַּל for כֻּלוֹ.

1, 2. With a boldness prompted by his intense zeal for the honour
and glory of Yahweh, the psalmist calls upon the heavenly hosts to
ascribe unto Yahweh glory and might. It is to the *sons of gods* that the
exhortation is made ; only once elsewhere in the Psalter do we find a
similar address, Ps. 97[7], though the existence of these heavenly beings
is spoken of in 89[6, 7] (and cp. the Seraphim in Isa. 6[2, 3]). That the *name*
of Yahweh should, in a sense, be differentiated from Yahweh himself,
though a vital part of him, is in accordance with ancient thought.
The expression *sons of gods* (cp. Deut. 4[19]) indicates that the supernatural beings which were originally conceived of as independent gods
were now held to be subordinate to Yahweh, thus emphasizing monotheistic belief. They are bidden to *worship Yahweh in holy array* ;

just as men put on *holy array* when they worshipped (see 2 Chron. 20²¹, where the same expression is used), so the psalmist conceives of the heavenly host as robed in special garments for worship.   3–9. The conception of Yahweh's presence on earth, made known by the sound of his voice, is then dealt with in a unique manner; quaint as the thoughts are, the poetic vigour of the passage is very striking.   *The voice of Yahweh is upon the waters* presents the awe-inspiring experience of the psalmist, as we may surmise, when standing on the sea-shore and listening to the roar of the thunder reverberating over the watery expanse; the sound is deafening, *with power*, but majestic, *with splendour.* Then, again, the psalmist may be recording what he had seen when he says that *the voice of Yahweh shattereth cedars*; the trees struck by lightning he believes to be the result of the thunder; that he was familiar with the *Lebanon* district is likely enough.   A thunder-storm was doubtless sometimes accompanied by earthquake (cp. Exod. 19¹⁷, ¹⁸, where both are mentioned), and the psalmist, with pardonable exaggeration, compares the trembling of Lebanon and Sirion (see Deut. 3⁹) with the antics of cattle.   The text of *vv.* 7, 8 has suffered some corruption; various emendations are offered by commentators, but there is an element of uncertainty about them.   In *v.* 7 *the voice of Yahweh* is an addition, but the rhythm seems to require it; we have followed the text as it stands in rendering *heweth out flames of fire*; but the verse may not be an original part of the psalm; the meaning would presumably be in reference to the lightning splitting a tree and setting it on fire. The mention of *the wilderness of Kadesh*, brings us to the south of Palestine; Kadesh, or Kadesh-barnea (Num. 34⁴), lay about fifty miles south of Beersheba.   *The voice of Yahweh* is thought of as rolling over the widespread *wilderness* just as it resounded over the many waters, hence it *shaketh.*   In *v.* 9 the text is again uncertain; the beginning is clear enough; the statement that *the voice of Yahweh maketh hinds to calve*, may well be in accordance with fact.   What follows is quite uncertain; in place of, *the voice of Yahweh strippeth bare the forests*, already, in effect, spoken of in *v.* 5, one would rather expect something parallel with the preceding couplet; there is, therefore, much to be said in favour of Gunkel's suggested emendation : " scareth away the wild-goats with flames of fire ", *i.e.*, the lightning.   Further, the sudden change of subject, making mention of the temple, gives the impression that it was originally preceded by another couplet.   At any rate, when the psalmist says : *And in his temple everyone saith :* " *Glory* ", the reference is to the worship of men, following the example of the heavenly hosts. Very appropriately does the psalmist conclude with the reference to the Kingship of Yahweh; he is enthroned *over the flood*, the word " flood " (*mabbūl*) refers otherwise always to the Flood in the days of Noah; but here it is obviously an echo of *v.* 3.   The final verse (11) expresses a noble, patriotic wish for the welfare of the nation ; but it may well be, as many commentators hold, a later addition, for *v.* 10 makes a very fine conclusion ; the thought of Yahweh is the fittest in ending the psalm.

Religious Teaching

The central thought here of Yahweh as the God of Nature, is dealt with on p. 81.

PSALM 30

THIS beautiful psalm, somewhat in the nature of an autobiographical sketch, is the joyful thanksgiving of one who has been delivered from grievous sickness which had brought him near to death. It is composed of two more or less parallel parts (*vv.* 1–5 and 6–12). The *second* of these is in the nature of a retrospect, recalling the time of quiet happiness, which was, however, suddenly broken. But the appeal to Yahweh brought peace and contentment once more. Subordinate as the reference to sin is, as the cause of his sickness, it nevertheless does find a passing expression in each part. The *first* part recounts the return of the time of happiness, though here, too, there is a reference to the past.

The psalm is so obviously the record of the experiences of an individual that it is difficult to understand the contention of some commentators that the writer represents the nation.

The date of the psalm we believe to be pre-exilic, against the view of some commentators. The metre is mainly 2 : 2, interspersed here and there by 3 : 3.

1.   *A Psalm. A Song at the Dedication of the House. David's.*

1 (2). I will exalt thee, Yahweh, for thou   and didst not suffer my foes to rejoice
          didst draw me up,   over me.
2 (3).   Yahweh, my God,
                         I cried unto thee,
                         and thou didst heal me.
3 (4).   Yahweh, thou broughtest up
                         my soul from Sheol,
          Thou didst keep me alive ° from them that go down ° to the Pit.
4 (5). Sing praise to Yahweh, O ye godly
          ones,   and give thanks to his holy ° name °
5 (6).   ° For there is suffering when he is wrath °,
                    but life in his favour ;
                    in the evening ° weeping,
                    but joy at morn.
6 (7).   As for me, I said in my prosperity :
               " I shall never be moved ! "
7 (8).   ° Through thy favour I was made to stand
               upon my strong mountain ° ;
               thou didst hide thy face,
               I became dismayed.
8 (9). Unto thee, Yahweh, I cried,   and unto my God ° I made sup-
                                        plication :

9 (10).   What profit is there in my blood
                  if I go down to corruption ?
                  Should dust give thee thanks,
                  should it declare thy truth ?
10 (11).   Hear, Yahweh, and have mercy on
                  me,   Yahweh, be thou my helper.
11 (12).   Thou hast turned my mourning
                  to dancing for me ;
                  thou hast loosed my sackcloth,
                  and hast girded me with joy,
12 (13).   that ° my heart ° may sing praise to thee,
                  and not be silent ;
                  Yahweh, my God,
                  I will give thanks to thee for ever.

Text-critical Notes

3. Read, with *K^ethib* and the Versions, מִיּוֹרְדִי for מִיָּרְדִי, " that I should not
go down," an anomalous form for מֵרִדְתִּי (see GK. 69*m*). 4. Lit. " memorial ",
cp. Ps. 97¹², and see Exod. 3¹⁵. 5. Lit. " For a stroke is in his wrath ", reading, with
Halévy and Gunkel, נֶגַע for רֶגַע, " a moment ". Om. יָלִין which overloads the
half-line. 8. Read, with Gunkel :

בִּרְצוֹנְךָ הֶעֱמַדְתִּי   עַל־הַרְרִי עֹז

(omitting יהוה which overloads the half-line). 8. Read, with G, אֱלֹהַי for
אֲדֹנָי, " my Lord ". 12. Read, cp. G, כְּבֵדִי, lit. " my liver ", for כָּבוֹד,
" glory ".

For the title, see p. 14.
1–3. In thanksgiving for his recovery from very serious illness, the
psalmist praises God : *I will exalt thee, Yahweh,* and he uses a significant
expression, *for thou didst draw me up,* in reference to his having been,
as it were, lifted up from slipping down into the depth of *Sheol,*
mentioned subsequently. The *foes* of whom the psalmist speaks must
refer to evil-disposed persons who mocked at his trust in Yahweh, and
would have been glad to see his faith unavailing ; unbelievers of this
kind existed in every period of Israel's history. Hence the psalmist's
words : thou *didst not suffer my foes to rejoice over me.* He then recalls
how he *cried unto Yahweh,* and how he was healed of his sickness ;
this must have been very severe since he came nigh to death ; but
Yahweh brought him up as he felt he was going down to *Sheol,* and was
thus kept from joining those who *go down to the Pit,* the lowest part of
Sheol (cp. 28¹, and " the lowest pit " 88⁶). 4. It is not enough that he
should personally praise Yahweh for his recovery ; he, therefore, calls
upon those like-minded with himself, the *godly ones, to sing praise to
Yahweh,* and *to give thanks to his holy name,* lit. " memorial," cp.
Exod. 3¹⁵ : " this is my name for ever, and this is my memorial unto all
generations ". 5. The psalmist then implicitly acknowledges that his
sickness had been sent to him because he had, through sin, aroused
the *wrath* of Yahweh ; for the emendation of this sentence see the text-
crit. note. But he feels that he has been forgiven, for by Yahweh's
favour he now enjoys *life* ; it had been a time of sorrow, but that is
past : *in the evening weeping, but joy at morn.* This concludes the first

part of the psalm. The subject-matter of the second part is similar to what had already been said. This repetition, in substance, is fully comprehensible if one reflects upon the deeply stirred emotions of the psalmist. Moreover, it will be noticed that in the first part one stage of the psalmist's experiences is not mentioned, namely, that which preceded the period of his sickness. To make this good, he now indicates three stages. The first, 6, 7ª, tells of his state of well-being before he was struck down with sickness; at that time he had said to himself in a boastful spirit: *I shall never be moved*; true, his innate religious sense ascribed this to Yahweh: *Through thy favour I was made to stand upon my strong mountain* (for the necessary emendation see text-crit. note), *i.e.*, through Yahweh's favour he lived in unassailable prosperity. But, as *v.* 5 shows, he had overlooked a fatal fact, that of his sin; hence his significant words, 7ᵇ, *thou didst hide thy face, I became dismayed*; why should Yahweh turn from his servant except for his having been unfaithful to the divine precepts? And so he *became dismayed*, for his sickness had the effect of opening his eyes. This is the second stage of his experiences. In his state of sickness (8) he *cried* unto Yahweh, and *made supplication* unto God. 9, 10. His plea, it must be confessed, is *naïve*, and betrays a somewhat undeveloped conception of God: *What profit is there in my blood (i.e.,* life) *if I go down to corruption?* he asks; as though it were to the advantage of the Almighty to preserve his servant's life; for the *dust* cannot *give thanks* nor *declare* his *truth*! The psalmist urges that his death will be the loss of a devout worshipper to Yahweh, and thus a reason why *Yahweh* should *have mercy on* him, and *be* his *helper*. If, on the one hand, this reveals a very inadequate apprehension of the Divine Personality, it offers, on the other hand, a touching picture of the psalmist's childlike intimacy and communion with God. 11. In his mercy, God grants him health and strength again. Thereupon the psalmist tells of the third stage of his experiences: *Thou has turned my mourning to dancing for me*; the reference here is to the festivities which took place after the sacrifice of thanksgiving had been offered; this feast, given by the offerer to his friends, is referred to, *e.g.*, in 1 Sam. 1⁴, 9¹², ¹³, ²²⁻²⁴, see also Exod. 32⁶, ¹⁹. This, therefore, the psalmist recalls, and thinks of how he rose from his bed of sickness, for God had *loosed* his sackcloth, and in place thereof had *girded* him *with joy*; and of how his *heart* (see text-crit. note) *sang praise* to God, and was *not silent*. His deep gratitude he expresses once more in his final words: *Yahweh, my God, I will give thanks to thee for ever*.

Religious Teaching

Trust in God's mercy, gratitude for answer to prayer, and consequent " rejoicing in the Lord ", are the outstanding features of the psalm.   If the conception of God is revealed as somewhat undeveloped, it is compensated for by the intimacy of the psalmist's walk with God.

PSALM 31

THIS psalm is one of many in which an individual servant of Yahweh, menaced by the bitter enmity of unscrupulous foes, pours out his complaint to God; at the same time his unceasing prayer brings him the certitude of deliverance from his troubles.   The somewhat irregular composition of the psalm has led some commentators to postulate composite authorship, especially as with v. 9 a new beginning seems to be made.   This supposition we believe, however, to be unnecessary. When the dire state of peril in which the psalmist finds himself is taken into account, the fear of his enemies, alternating with trust in God, the fear of death, with the conviction of divine help, it is surely natural enough that a logical thought-sequence should be wanting.

Indications in the psalm suggest a post-exilic date.

The metre is very variable, which may also reflect the psalmist's mental state.

1.   *For the Precentor : A Psalm.   David's.*

1 (2). In thee, Yahweh, I seek refuge,   let me never be put to shame,
                In thy righteousness deliver me, ° and save me °.
2 (3). Bow down thine ear unto me,   haste thee, ° Yahweh °, save me;
                Be to me a strong rock,   a house of defence to preserve me;
3 (4). For my rock and defence art thou;   for thy name's sake lead me and guide
                                                    me.
4 (5). Bring me out of the net they have
                hid for me,   for thou, ° Yahweh °, art my refuge.
5 (6). Into thy hand I commend my   thou dost redeem me °, O God of
                spirit,   truth.
6 (7). ° Thou hatest ° them that cleave to
                false-idols,   but as for me, I trust in Yahweh.
7 (8). Let me rejoice and be glad in thy
                lovingkindness,   thou who didst see mine affliction,
                And knewest the troubles of my soul.
8 (9). Thou didst not deliver me into the   thou didst set my feet in a large
                hand of the enemy,   place.
9 (10). Be gracious unto me, Yahweh, for
                I am in trouble,   mine eye wasteth away for grief °;
10 (11). For my life is spent with sorrow,   and my years with sighing,
                My strength faileth ° through
                affliction °,   my bones consume away.
11 (12).   Because of all mine adversaries
                I am become a reproach,
                To my neighbours ° a terror °,
                A fear to mine acquaintance;
                They that see me without
                Flee away from me.
12 (13). I am forgotten as one dead, out of
                mind,   I am become like a destroyed vessel.
13 (14). For I hear the defaming of many,   terror all around,
                While they take counsel together
                against me,   to take my life they plan.
14 (15). As for me, in thee do I trust °,   I say, My God art thou:

15 (16). In thine hand are my times, deliver me   from the power of mine enemies and persecutors.

16 (17). Make thy face to shine on thy servant,   save me in thy lovingkindness.

17 (18).   Yahweh, let me not be ashamed, for I call on thee,
      Let the wicked be ashamed,
      Let them be silent in Sheol.

18 (19). Let the lying lips be dumb,   that speak ° with pride and contempt.

19 (20). How great is thy goodness, ° Yahweh °,   which thou hast laid up for them that fear thee,
Which thou hast wrought for them that trust thee,   before the children of men ;

20 (21). Thou hidest them in the covert ° of thy wings °,   ° from the calumnies ° of men,
Thou treasurest them ° in thy shelter °,   from the strife of tongues.

21 (22).   Blessed be Yahweh,
      For he hath shown wondrously his lovingkindness
      ° In the time of trouble °.

22 (23). As for me, I said in my fear,   ° I am cut off ° from before thine eyes ;
      Nevertheless, thou didst hear
      The voice of my supplications,
      When I cried unto thee.

23 (24). O love Yahweh, all ye his saints,   the faithful doth Yahweh keep ;
      But he plenteously requiteth
      him that acteth proudly.

24 (25). Be strong, and let your heart stand firm,   all ye that wait for Yahweh.

Text-critical Notes

1. Add with G, וְהַצִּילֵנִי. 2. Add with 1 MS. יחוה. 4. Add יהוה for the rhythm's sake. 5. Om. יהוה, which gives a beat too much. 6. Read שָׂנֵאתָ for שָׂנֵאתִי, " I hate ". 9. Om. נַפְשִׁי וּבִטְנִי, " my soul and my body ", which overloads the line. 10. Read with GS, בְּעָנְיִ for בַּעֲוֹנִי, " because of mine iniquity ". 11. Read מֹרָא for מְאֹד, " very ". 14. Om. יהוה, which gives a beat too much. 18. Om. עַל־צַדִּיק עָתָק, " against the righteous man insolently ", which overloads the half-line. 19. Add with 3 MSS. G יהוה. 20. Read בְּנָפְךָ for פָּנֶיךָ, " before thee ", cp. Ps. 61⁴. Read, with Duhm, מְרִיכֵלֵי for מֵרֻכְסֵי, " plottings ". Read בְּסֻכָּתְךָ for בְּסֻכָּה, " in a shelter ". 21. Read, with Kittel, בְּעֵת מָצוֹק for בְּעִיר מָצוֹר, " in a defenced city ". 22. Read, with many MSS., נִגְרַזְתִּי, cp. Ps. 88⁵, for נִגְרַזְתִּי.

1–5. These pening verses are largely identical with Ps. 71¹⁻³. Trust in Yahweh conditions the petitions which follow. The inter-mingling of prayers and utterances of faith is entirely natural for one in trouble ; a logical thought-sequence is not to be looked for in such a case. The metaphor of the *net* for the entanglement brought about by plotting opponents is familiar to the psalmists (see 9¹⁵, 37⁷, 57⁶, 140⁵). That the foes of the victim are idolaters (6) is an additional reason why Yahweh's help should be accorded to one whose sole trust is in him ; and past experience of deliverance from *affliction* prompts the prayer : *Let me rejoice and be glad in thy lovingkindness . . .* (7, 8).

With *v.* 9 we have what looks like the beginning of a new psalm ; on the other hand, there is no reason why *vv.* 1–8 should not be re-garded as an introduction to the main portion of the psalm (9–13). These verses describe in fuller detail the sorry plight in which the psalmist finds himself. His sufferings are of long standing, *my life is spent with sorrow, and my years with sighing*; the words recall the prophet Jeremiah's plaint : "Wherefore came I forth out of the womb to see labour and sorrow, that my days should be consumed with shame?" (20[18]). As a result of the defamation on the part of his enemies (13) the psalmist has become even to his friends *a reproach* and *a terror*; here again we are reminded of Jeremiah's experience : "I am become a laughingstock all the day, everyone mocketh me . . . because the word of Yahweh is made a reproach unto me, and a derision all the day. . . . For I have heard the defaming of many, terror on every side" (20[7-10]); indeed, the whole of Jer. 20[7-13], compared with our psalm, is very instructive, though the relationship between the two is difficult to determine. 14-16. A further asseveration of trust in God, followed by petitions, shows affinity of style with the first part of the psalm, and therefore suggests unity of composition. In the words, *In thine hand are my times*, we have a somewhat unusual expression, *times* is used of fate or destiny, cp. Isa. 33[6]. Some antique conception must lie behind the expression, *Make thy face to shine on*, meaning, "Show that thou hast pleasure in"; it occurs only in the later literature, Num. 6[25] (P), and is used frequently in post-exilic psalms (67[1], 80[3, 7, 19], 119[135]). 17, 18. As so often in the psalms, the beauty of a passage is marred by a malediction on the enemies : *Let the wicked be ashamed, let them be silent in Sheol*; silence reigns in the abode of the departed, cp. Pss. 94[17], 115[17]. The psalm closes with words of praise and an acknowledgement of Yahweh's goodness to those *that trust* in Him (19-24). In a number of instances words and phrases in these verses are echoes from other psalms. The triumphant exhortation with which the psalm ends is particularly fine : *Be strong, and let your heart stand firm, all ye that wait for Yahweh.*

Religious Teaching

The religious elements in this psalm are largely similar to those in a number of other psalms. Trust in God when in trouble is the dominating note. The intimate relationship which the psalmist feels to exist between him and his God is very beautifully brought out : he knows that God knows all his grief, therefore he can pour out his heart to one who feels for him; though all his friends forsake him, he has a Friend who is ever mindful of him; his destiny is in God's hands, therefore he is convinced that ultimately all will be well. As containing the words hallowed by being uttered by the Saviour on the Cross, the psalm must ever stand out as one of peculiar sanctity : "Into thy hands I commend my spirit" (Lk. 23[46]).

PSALM 32

THIS psalm is reckoned among the seven penitential psalms by the Church, though the penitential element is less pronounced than those of joy and gratitude at the obliteration of sin. It is the utterance of one who, in the conviction of the forgiveness of past sin, experiences the happiness of the peace of God. The nature of the sin of which the psalmist has been guilty is not indicated; but he has been brought to acknowledge it through the stroke of sickness which, as he believes, is the mark of divine displeasure. His recovery is to him the assurance that his sin has been forgiven. The sense of righteousness, engendered by the conviction of freedom from sin, induces the psalmist to act as instructor and guide in the way of righteousness to others. The noticeable style of the Sage in the latter part of the psalm is distinctly reminiscent of the Wisdom Literature, a fact which points to the post-exilic period; a more exact date cannot be assigned to it.

The text has undergone some corruption here and there; to this, at any rate in part, may be due the somewhat irregular metre; 2 : 2 and 3 : 2 predominate.

David's. Maskîl.

1. Blessed is he whose transgression is forgiven,   whose sin is covered;
2. Blessed is the man to whom Yahweh doth not impute iniquity, And in whose spirit there is no deceit.
3. When I kept silence my bones waxed old,   as I moaned all the day.
4. For day and night lay heavy   thy hand upon me; My life-sap was ° dried °   ° like ° the summer drought. Selah.
5. My sin I made known to thee,   and mine iniquity I hid not, I said, I will confess,   concerning my transgression, to Yahweh; And thou forgavest   ° mine iniquity ° and my sin. Selah.
6. Therefore unto thee   shall every godly man pray; ° In the time of distress °,   at the flowing of many waters,— Unto him they shall not come nigh.
7. Thou art a hiding-place for me,   thou preservest me from trouble, With shouts of deliverance dost thou encompass me. Selah.
8. I will instruct thee and teach thee,   in the way thou shouldst walk; I will counsel thee, ° will guide thee °,   on thee is mine eye.
9. ° Be not ° like a horse, like a mule,   without understanding, ° Which is brought unto thee °   with bridle and bit.
10. Many are the pangs of the wicked; But he that trusteth in Yahweh,   lovingkindness encompasseth him.
11. Rejoice in Yahweh,   and be glad, O ye righteous. Shout for joy, all ye upright of heart.

Text-critical Notes

4. Lit. "was changed". Read כ for בָ, "in". 5. Read עֲוֹנִי for עֲוֹן, "iniquity". 6. Read, with Duhm, לְעֵת מָצוֹק for לְעֵת רַק מְצֹא, "at a time to find, howbeit". 8. Add, with G, אֲעָצָה for the rhythm's sake. 9. Read תְּהִי for תִּהְיוּ, "be ye". Lit. "to bring unto thee"; read, with Duhm, לְהָרִיב אֵלָיךָ for בַּל קְרֹב אֵלֶיךָ (=לְהָחֲרִיב), "not to come nigh unto thee"; and om., as a late gloss, עֶדְיוֹ לִבְלוֹם, "to curb its trappings"; בלם is an Aramaic word which does not occur elsewhere in the O.T.

1, 2. In expressing the blessedness of him *whose transgression is forgiven, whose sin is covered*, the psalmist confesses, by implication, that he has been guilty of sin in the past; he does so explicitly later. The three words *transgression, sin, iniquity*, express different aspects of the concept of wickedness: "transgression" (*pešā'*) contains the idea of rebellion against God; "sin" (*ḥāṭā'āh*) is equivalent to the Greek ἁμαρτία, "a missing of the mark", thus, not of the nature of wilful sin, as the preceding; and "iniquity" (*'āwōn*) means lit. a "turning off" from the way, and, therefore, again deliberate going wrong. Similarly with the three words used for the obliteration of sin: to "forgive" (*nāṣā'*) is lit. to "lift up", or "carry away", the burden of sin; to "cover" (*kāsāh*) expresses the idea of covering over sin, and thus putting it out of sight, overlooking it; while not to "impute" (*ḥāšab*) is, in effect, the equivalent of imputing righteousness, cp. Rom. 4[6] ". . . unto whom God reckoneth righteousness", followed by the quotation of these two verses. Some commentators regard the clause, *And in whose spirit there is no deceit*, as a gloss, for metrical reasons; but an isolated hemistich of this kind is of frequent occurrence in the *Psalms* (e.g., 2[12]). The psalmists were not bound by rigid metrical rules; in this case the words, as an expression of sincerity, are wholly appropriate. 3, 4. In these verses the psalmist, looking back, records his conviction that as long as he refrained from confessing his sin, *when I kept silence*, the mark of divine displeasure, *i.e.*, his sickness, abode with him; his *bones waxed old*, lit. became "worn out"; by the *bones* are meant his whole bodily frame (cp. Pss. 22[14], 31[10], 102[3]); his very *life-sap* seemed to "change", as the Hebrew word means literally, its very moisture became *dried up*; and he thinks of the *summer drought*, the parched land; he was suffering from severe fever. The ancient Hebrew belief that all suffering is the visible sign of God's wrath for sin appears here again. Then, in 5, the definite confession of sin is made, in reference of course, to the past, together with the assurance of forgiveness. Out of his own experience the psalmist adds (6, 7), *Therefore unto thee shall every godly man pray*, for then there is the certitude of deliverance from trouble. For the metaphor of *the flowing of many waters*, *i.e.*, dangers, cp. Pss. 18[16], 69[1, 2], 144[7]. The psalmist's words are continued in 8, 9; they are not words put into the mouth of Yahweh, as might be gathered from: *on thee is mine eye*, cp. Ps. 33[18], Jer. 32[19]; the whole passage is in the style of the Wisdom teacher, the verbs occur frequently in the Wisdom Literature; *in the way thou shouldst walk* refers to the way of the Law; *mine eye* refers to the eye of the teacher; with *Be not like a horse, like a mule*, cp. Prov. 26[3]. For the textual difficulty in 9 see the text-critical notes. The closing note of triumphant happiness, 10, 11, reflects the conscience-cleared joy of the forgiven sinner.

Religious Teaching

This is brought out in the exegetical notes; but there is one matter
which demands some further consideration. While we must recognize
the whole-hearted gratitude and loyalty to God so beautifully expressed
by the psalmist, there is no disguising the fact that to him the act of
confession *per se* acquires forgiveness; that confession is a condition of
forgiveness goes without saying; but if that alone procures forgiveness
it means that this is attained by the act of man; in other words, that
a good work acquires justification in the sight of God. Unless it is
recognized that forgiveness is of divine grace, quite apart from anything
that man can do, there is the danger of the belief in the efficacy of
works. Forgiveness is something more than the result of human action.
While, then, it is fully recognized that the religious teaching of this
psalm insists on the need of penitence and confession, it must be said
that, from the Christian point of view, it is lacking in the recognition of
divine grace. This, to be sure, is to be expected; nevertheless, in
some other psalms there is a distinct, even though only implicit,
acknowledgement of divine guidance whereby the sinner is turned to
penitence.

PSALM 33

A HYMN of praise and thanksgiving, this psalm, as its contents show,
was written in commemoration of deliverance from some threatened
national peril. The thought-sequence brings this out clearly: the call
to rejoice and give thanks because of Yahweh's righteousness and mighty
acts; this is illustrated, above all, in his creative power; further, he
it is who frustrates the plans and overrules what nations intend;
he observes the doings of men and discerns their purposes; armies and
all the paraphernalia of war are of no avail against his will; and those
who trust in him are delivered. Hence the final note, like that at the
opening, is one of rejoicing. The separating of the psalm into independent divisions, thereby obscuring this thought-sequence, has prevented
some commentators from recognizing the *raison d'être* of the composition. Opinions differ, as usual, with regard to date; some assign
it to pre-exilic times, others to the Maccabæan era. There is nothing
at all in the psalm which suggests the latter; more is to be said for
the former view, though one or two considerations make this doubtful
too: its thought-contact with some of the later literature, its general
style; and especially the non-mention of a king of Judah in contra-
distinction to a Gentile king in *v.* 16; during the monarchical period

reference would surely have been made to Yahweh's anointed in contrast to a king whose armies were of no avail. The psalm probably belongs to the Persian period.

The text has been extraordinarily well preserved, another indication of late date. The metre is uniformly 3 : 3, with the exception of *vv.* 10, 12, which are 4 : 3.

1. Rejoice, O ye righteous, in Yahweh, — for the upright praise is fitting.
2. Give thanks to Yahweh with harp, — sing praise with a ten-stringed lute;
3. Sing to him a new song, — play skilfully, with a shout-of-joy.
4. For righteous is the word of Yahweh, — and all his doing is in faithfulness;
5. He loveth righteousness and justice, — the earth is full of ° his lovingkindness°.
6. ° By his word ° were the heavens made, — and by the breath of his mouth all their host;
7. He gathereth ° as in a bottle ° the sea-waters, — he placeth the deeps in treasure-houses;
8. All the earth feareth Yahweh, — all the dwellers of the world stand in awe of him;
9. For he spake, and it was done, — he commanded, and it stood fast.
10. Yahweh counteracteth the purpose of nations, — he frustrateth the plans of the peoples;
11. ° His purpose ° standeth fast for ever, — the intents of his heart from generation-to-generation.
12. Blessed is the nation whose God is Yahweh, — the people whom he hath chosen for his inheritance.
13. From heaven Yahweh looketh down, — he seeth all the children of men;
14. From the place of his dwelling he looketh forth — on all the dwellers on the earth;
15. He fashioneth altogether their heart, — he discerneth all their works.
16. No king is saved by a mighty-host, — by great-strength no warrior is preserved;
17. Vain is the horse for victory, — by its mighty strength it protecteth not.
18. Behold, the eye of Yahweh is on them that fear him, — on them that look for his love,
19. To deliver their soul from death, — and to keep them alive from famine.
20. Our soul doth wait for Yahweh, — our help and our shield is he,
21. For in him our heart rejoiceth, — ° in his holy name we trust.
22. May thy love, Yahweh, be upon us, — even as we have waited for thee.

Text-critical Notes

The Versions have the title " David's ", possibly it stood in the Hebrew text originally as in the preceding and following psalms. 5. Read חַסְדּוֹ for חֶסֶד יהוה, " the lovingkindness of Yahweh ", for the rhythm's sake. 6. Read, for a similar reason, בִּדְבָרוֹ for בִּדְבַר יהוה, " by the word of Yahweh ". 7. Read כַּנֹּאד, as in Job 38³⁷, for כַּנֵּד, " like a heap ". 11. Read עֲצָתוֹ for עֲצַת יהוה, " the purpose of Yahweh ", for the rhythm's sake. 21. Om. the repetition of כִּי, " for ".

1–3. A call to the righteous to rejoice in Yahweh, and to praise him ; gratitude goes together with joyfulness, hence the psalmist's exhortation : *Rejoice, Give thanks, Sing a new song* ; this last (cp. Pss. 40³, 96¹, 98¹) points to a special occasion for which the psalm was composed. Hand and voice are to join in giving praise ; for the *shout-of-joy* (*tĕru'āh*) cp. Ps. 47⁵, and for the musical instruments used in worship see the notes on Ps. 150. The psalmist sets forth the right way of praise thus : first, the extolling of Yahweh's *righteousness, faithfulness, loving-kindness*, and *justice*, the visible proofs of which *the earth is full.* 4, 5·

Then follows the confession of faith in Yahweh's acts of *righteousness* and *lovingkindness*. 6–9; His mere utterance brings the heavenly spheres into existence, cp. Gen. 1⁶⁻⁸; it required but *the breath of his mouth* to create *all their host, i.e.,* the stars, conceived of as personalities; here we recall Job 26¹³, where it speaks of his breath making the heavens beautiful; the expression is really synonymous with the utterance of the word, which involves the giving forth of breath; it connotes also the energy of life, see Job 27³, 33⁴. Further, in reference to Gen. 1⁷, the psalmist speaks of the gathering of the waters of the sea; this is compared with the pouring of water into a bottle (lit. " skin "), in order to emphasize the stupendous power of the Creator; the Hebrew text has, " He gathereth as an heap ", but the thought is taken from Job 38³⁷, " Who can pour out the bottles of heaven? " Similarly, *he placeth the deeps in treasure-houses,* is suggested by Job 38²², " Hast thou entered the treasuries of snow, or hast thou seen the treasuries of the hail? " The thought of Yahweh's creative power inspires fear in *all the earth, For he spake and it was done, he commanded, and it stood fast.* Having thus offered praise to Yahweh, the psalmist now turns to contemplate his action on earth (10–19); and here, in the following of the prophets, he enunciates the doctrine of Yahweh as the God of History; and this with special reference to the event which prompted the composition of the psalm; what this event was is not indicated, but the principle set forth is of universal application; whatever nations may plan and purpose is brought to nought unless it is in accordance with the purpose of Yahweh, which, like the eternal heavens, *standeth fast for ever.* Therefore, *Blessed is the nation (i.e.,* of Israel) *whose God is Yahweh.* The remaining verses of this section speak of Yahweh's intimate knowledge of the thoughts and doings of all men. The event commemorated is again referred to in the words *No king is saved by a mighty-host . . . ,* for Yahweh delivers those *that fear him,* and *that look for his love, from death and famine,* the results of an enemy's victory. The concluding verses, 20–22, proclaim trust *in the holy name of* Yahweh, which makes the *heart rejoice*; and the psalm ends with the prayer: *May thy love, Yahweh, be upon us, even as we have waited for thee.*

The religious teaching has been brought out by what has been said, so that a special section on this is not called for here.

PSALM 34

THIS is another of the so-called acrostic psalms, each verse beginning with a letter of the Hebrew alphabet, in order; the sixth letter has, however, fallen out, doubtless through the carelessness of a copyist; and a final line has been added which does not belong to the original alphabetical scheme. The psalm is divided into two clearly distinct parts; the first (*vv.* 1–10) is the psalmist's thanksgiving for deliverance from evil; in the second (*vv.* 11–21), written in the style of the Wisdom Literature, he gives an instruction on honouring Yahweh. Thus, while the first part is an expression of gratitude, the second tells of something done to show forth that gratitude in practical form. Some commentators hold that the psalm was written in the name of the community collectively; but that cannot be the case, for in *v.* 3 it is said : " O magnify Yahweh with me "; and the whole of the second part, written in the first person, is addressed to " my sons ", the Wisdom Teacher's regular form of address. On the doctrine of retribution taught in the psalm see the section on Religious Teaching, pp. 86 ff. The date is sufficiently indicated by its Wisdom Literature form as post-exilic. The metre is, with few exceptions, 3 : 3.

David's ; when he changed his behaviour before Abimelech ; and he drove him out and he departed.

1	(2) א.	I will bless Yahweh at all times,	continually shall his praise be in my mouth.
2	(3) ב.	In Yahweh shall my soul glory,	the humble shall hear, and be glad.
3	(4) ג.	O magnify Yahweh with me,	let us exalt his name together.
4	(5) ד.	I sought Yahweh, and he answered me,	and from all my fears he delivered me.
5	(6) ה.	° Look ° unto him and be lightened °,	and ° your faces ° shall not be ashamed.
6	(7) ז.	This afflicted one cried, and Yahweh heard,	and saved him out of all his troubles.
7	(8) ח.	The angel of Yahweh encampeth	around them that fear him, and delivereth them.
8	(9) ט.	O taste and see that Yahweh is good,	blessed is the man that trusteth him.
9	(10) ·	O fear Yahweh, ye his saints,	for there is no want to them that fear him.
10	(11) כ.	° Wealthy men ° lack, and suffer hunger,	but they that seek Yahweh lack not °.
11	(12) ל.	Come, ye children, hearken unto me,	the fear of Yahweh will I teach you.
12	(13) מ.	Who is the man that desireth life,	that loveth days, and to see prosperity i
13	(14) נ.	Keep thy tongue from evil,	and thy lips from uttering deceit;
14	(15) ס.	Depart from evil, and do good,	seek peace, and pursue it.
15	(16) ע.	The eyes of Yahweh are toward the righteous,	and his ears toward their cry;
16	(17) פ.	The face of Yahweh is against evil-doers,	to cut off their remembrance from the earth.
17	(18) צ.	They cry, and Yahweh heareth,	and from all their ills he delivereth them.
18	(19) ק.	Near is Yahweh to the heart-broken,	and he helpeth the crushed in spirit.
19	(20) ר.	Many are the distresses of the righteous one,	but from all of them Yahweh delivereth him ;
20	(21) ש.	He keepeth all his bones,	not one of them is broken.
21	(22) ת.	Evil slayeth the wicked one,	they that hate the righteous shall be punished.
22	(23).	Yahweh redeemeth the soul of his servants,	and none that trust in him shall be held guilty.

P

Text-critical Notes

5. Read, following the Versions, הַבִּיטוּ אֵלָיו וּנְהָרוּ for הִבִּיטוּ אֵלָיו וְנָהָרוּ,
" they looked unto him and were lightened ".   Read פְּנֵיכֶם for פְּנֵיהֶם, " their
faces ".   10. Read, with G, כְּבֵדִים (cp. Gen. 13²) for כְּפִירִים, " young lions ".
Om. כָּל־טוֹב, " all good ", for the rhythm's sake.

The utter inappropriateness of the title must be due to its having
been placed in its present position by mistake.   The reference is to
1 Sam. 21¹⁰⁻¹⁵, " Abimelech " should, of course, be Achish.

1, 2.   The psalmist expresses his gratitude to Yahweh for deliverance
from trouble, which is mentioned in *vv.* 4, 6.   In the fullness of his
thankful heart he calls upon others to join with him in *magnifying*
Yahweh.   3.   Just as he had *sought Yahweh* when in distress, and was
answered, so he exhorts all to *Look unto him and be lightened* (4–6),
the expression means that their faces will beam with joy (cp. Isa. 60⁵).
7.   The mention of *the angel of Yahweh* encamping *around them that*
fear him, may be in reference to 2 Kgs. 6¹⁷; but it is more probable
that we have here an indication of the developed angelology of post-
exilic times due to Persian influence.   8–10.   There follows a further
invitation to trust in Yahweh who provides for all who fear him.
For the term for " saints " (*qādōš*) used here, cp. 16³, see also Deut. 33³.
In this context the reference to " young lions " in the Hebrew text
comes in strangely when men are being spoken of (see, however, 35¹⁷);
the Septuagint rendering *Wealthy men*, so often synonymous with the
wicked, is more likely to represent the original reading.

Vv. 11–18 are wholly in the style of the Wisdom Literature : *Come,*
ye children, or sons, is the mode of address of the Wisdom Teacher, see
Prov. 4¹, 5⁷, 7²⁴ and often.   The teaching of *the fear of Yahweh* was the
basic subject of the instruction of the Sages, see Prov. 1⁷, 9¹⁰, 15³³,
etc. ; that through this a man's days were prolonged is taught in
Prov. 10²⁷; for the keeping of the tongue from evil, cp. Prov. 13³,
21²³.   It is unnecessary to indicate this further ; every verse in this
part of the psalm has its parallel, sometimes verbal, in one or other of the
Wisdom books.

Religious Teaching

Gratitude to, and trust in, Yahweh runs through the psalm, as in
so many of the psalms ; we need not dwell on that here.   What demands
attention is the doctrine of retribution insisted on by the psalmist.
While the godly may suffer bad treatment and troubles of various
kinds, they are ultimately delivered ; but not so the wicked, upon
whom destruction comes.   That this theory did not square with the
facts of life was realized by some of the Sages ; but our psalmist persists
in the erroneous theory.   He holds, further, the view that the ideal

reward for a godly man is a long life, indicating an undeveloped belief
in a future life.   These points are worth noting, for it is well to recognize
that, in some respects, the psalmists, with all their beauty and religious
fervour, had not attained to the fullness of truth.

PSALM 35

IN studying this psalm the impression is gained that, while it shows
unity of authorship, it was not all written at the same time, and that it
deals with two episodes in the life of the writer.   This is suggested by
the fact that in the first portion of the psalm (*vv.* 1–10) the psalmist is
seen to have been the object of physical violence by his enemies which
has endangered his life;   whereas in the second portion (*vv.* 11–27)
he speaks of " false witnesses " who have testified against him, the scene
being that of a court of law.   The two situations differ the more in that
in the former the attacking opponents are, and have been, nothing but
inveterate enemies ;   but in the latter, those who are now opponents had
formerly been friends,   The psalm gives a vivid picture of the conditions under which God-fearing men often lived in those days ;   the
prophets, too, bear ample witness to this, the rich and powerful often
subjecting their less fortunate brethren to cruel and unjust treatment ;
and there is plenty of evidence to show that in later times, too, the
" meek " in the land suffered.   Bitter enmity between the orthodox
and the hellenistically-minded Jews began to show itself during the
third century B.C., allusions to this occur in a number of psalms ;   it is
possible that we have an echo of this here ;   but religious strife between
those faithful to Yahweh and renegades existed in earlier times (see
pp. 60 ff).   On the other hand, there is the possibility that the original
basis of this psalm is a piece of ritual which might be used in serious
legal cases.   For the Israelite, God was the supreme court of appeal ;
and cases which were " too hard " (see Deut. 1¹⁷) for ordinary human
decision had to be taken to the sanctuary, where the divine verdict was
given through the priestly lot.   We may be sure that a ritual of some
kind developed for this purpose, and, before the lot was cast, the
defendant will have had to state his case and make his plea.   His
language will naturally have been of the kind presented in this psalm.
Some of the expressions used suggest that the implied physical violence
may be metaphorical, intended to emphasize the spontaneous malice
of the accusers.   They seek his ruin, though he has done no wrong to
them or to any other.   They charge him with crime (" witnesses of
violence " *v.* 11), and he stands in the mourning garb of the defendant

to make his great appeal (*v.* 13). Yahweh is his only defence and his only hope ; Yahweh knows the truth, and will vindicate him (*vv.* 23–27).

That the psalmist speaks as an individual, and not as representing his people, is suggested by most of what is said in the psalm ; *v.* 22 is an exception, " those peaceful in the land " ; but elsewhere the individual note is clearly sounded.

There is a good deal of textual corruption ; the psalm has clearly been worked over ; *v.* 18 would suggest for liturgical purposes ; but it is not used in the Jewish Liturgy. The corruptions in the text have to some extent interfered with the metre ; in its original form it may well have been, in the main, 3 : 2.

David's.

1. Strive, Yahweh, against them that strive with me, fight against them that fight against me.
2. Take hold of shield and buckler, and rise up for my help ;
3. And unsheathe spear ° and battle-axe,° to meet my pursuers ;
    Say to my soul,
    " Thy help am I ",
4.   Let them be ashamed and dishonoured,
    That seek after my soul,
    Let them be turned backward and confounded, who purpose evil against me ;
5. Let them be as chaff before the wind, 6ᵇ with the angel of Yahweh pursuing them,
6ᵃ Let their way be dark and slippery, 5ᵇ with the angel of Yahweh driving them on.°
7. For without a cause have they hidden ° their net for me, ° a pit ° have they dug ° ;
8. ° And their net ° which ° they hid,° ° may it catch them °, ° into the pit may they fall °.
9. But may my soul exult in Yahweh, may it rejoice in his saving power ;
10. Let all my bones say : " Yahweh, who is like thee,
    Who delivereth the afflicted from him that is too strong for him.
    ° and the poor from his spoiler ! "
11. Witnesses of violence arise, of that which I know not they accuse me ;
12. They reward me evil in place of good,
    ° They bring to ruin ° my life.
13. But I, when they were sick, put on sackcloth,
    I humbled ° my soul,
    And my prayer returned to ° my mouth °,
14.   As though for my friend and brother ;
    I went about as one mourning for a mother, black and bowed down.
15. And when I stumbled they rejoiced and gathered together, gathered together against me,
    ° Like strangers ° whom I know not, ° they cry °, and are not silent ;
16. ° Like the godless ° ° they mock continually °, ° they gnash ° their teeth.
17. Lord, how long wilt thou bear· the sight ? rescue my soul ° from them that roar,°
    Mine only one from the young-lions.
18. ° [I will give thee thanks in the great congregation, among a mighty people will I praise thee].°
19. Let them not rejoice over me that are deceitful enemies, ° that wink with their eyes.
20. For they speak not peace ° to ° those peaceable in the land ;
    Words of deceit do they conceive, 21. they open wide ° their mouth,
    They say, " Aha, aha, our eyes have seen it ! "

22. Thou sawest it, Yahweh, keep not
silence,
23. Stir up thyself, arouse thee for my
cause,
24. Judge me according to thy righteousness, Yahweh,°
25. Let them not say in their heart,
Let them not say, " We have swallowed him up ! " ;
26. Let them be ashamed and dishonoured
altogether,
Let them be clothed with shame and
disgrace,
27. Let them shout for joy ° that delight in
my triumph,
" Magnified be Yahweh, who hath
pleasure
28. And let my tongue declare thy
righteousness,

° be not far from me ;

my God, ° for my plea ;

and let them not rejoice over me.
" Aha, our desire ! "

that rejoice at my hurt,

that magnify themselves against me.

and let them say continually,

in the peace of his servant " ;

thy praise all the day.

Text-critical Notes

3. Read וְסֹגֵר for וּסְגֹר " and stop the way ". 5[b] and 6[b] have been misplaced.
as the sense shows. 7. Om. with S שַׁחַת " a pit ". Read שַׁחַת for חִנָּם
" without a cause ". Om. לְנַפְשִׁי " for my soul ", for the rhythm's sake. 8. Om.
תְּבוֹאֵהוּ שׁוֹאָה לֹא־יֵדַע " let destruction come upon him he knoweth not ",
a marginal gloss based on Isa. 47[11]. Read וְרִשְׁתָּם for וְרִשְׁתּוֹ " and his net " ;
and בַּשּׁוּחָה (cp. S) for בְּשׁוֹאָה " into destruction " ; and יִפְלוֹ for יִפָּל־בָּהּ
" let him fall into it ". These emendations, following largely Duhm and Gunkel, are
demanded by the context. 10. Om. וְעָנִי, " and an afflicted one ". 12. Read, with
Cheyne, הַכְשִׁילֹה for שְׁכוֹל " childlessness ". 13. Om. בַּצּוֹם, " with the fast ",
an explanatory gloss. Read חִכִּי (lit. " my throat " or " my palate ") for הָיָתְי,
" my bosom ". 15. Read כְּנָכְרִים for נֵכִים " smiters ", and קָרְעוּ for קָרְאוּ, " they
rent asunder ". 16. Read כְּחַנְגִּים for בְּחָנְפֵי " with the profane ". Read, with
G, יִלְעֲגוּ לַעַג (lit. " they mock, a mocking ") for לַעֲגֵי מָעוֹג, " mockers of a
cake ". Read חָרְקוּ for חָרֹק, " to gnash ". Om. עָלַי " against me ", for the
rhythm's sake. 17. Read, with Duhm, מִשּׁוֹאֲנִים for מִשֹּׁאֵיהֶם, " from their
destructions ". 18. This verse is wholly out of harmony with the context ; it
should perhaps come before v. 28. 19. Om. שֹׂנְאֵי חִנָּם, " that hate me without
a cause ", for the rhythm's sake. 20. Read עַל for וְעַל, " and to ". 21. Om. עָלַי
" against me ", for the rhythm's sake. 22. Om. אֲדֹנָי for the rhythm's sake. 23.
Om. וַאדֹנָי, and in 24, אֱלֹהַי for the same reason. 27. Om. וְיִשְׂמְחוּ, " and let
them rejoice ", for the same reason.

1-8. Doubtless the psalmist's words must not be taken too literally ;
at the same time, there is no disguising the fact that Yahweh is here
conceived of in an unedifying way. The antique conception of him
as a warrior-God reappears ; in the first instance, Yahweh was thought
of as leading the armies of Israel just as he was leader of the heavenly
hosts (Yahweh Zebaoth) ; this idea is here adapted to apply to an
individual, and Yahweh is called upon to *strive against* the personal
enemies of the psalmist ; the term used, *rib*, means originally to fight
in battle (*e.g.*, Judg. 11[25]), and then to contend with words, often in a
forensic sense ; in this latter the noun is used in our psalm (*v.* 23).
Even if meant metaphorically (which is never elsewhere the case), such
words as *Take hold of shield and buckler, and unsheathe spear and battle-*

axe, in reference to Yahweh, are unseemly.   In fact, we must not hesitate to recognize that in some of the psalms an undeveloped conception of God is manifested.   A toning-down of the representation of Yahweh as a warrior may be discerned in that his *angel* is thought of as *pursuing* and *driving on* those *who purpose evil against* the psalmist.   His thought is then turned (9, 10) to the help which he is confident will be afforded him by Yahweh.   With the quaint expression, *Let all my bones say, Yahweh, who is like thee . . .*, cp. Ps. 51[8], what is meant is the entire being or bodily frame, as in Ps. 6[2].   But the psalmist's mind is so filled with thoughts about the maltreatment which he is suffering from his enemies that he soon reverts to that subject.   11–12. The incident referred to in this second part of the psalm would seem to be a different one from that dealt with in the first part.   For here the psalmist's enemies charge him with violence, though at one time they had been his friends, for whom he had evinced the deepest sympathy *when they were sick.* Putting on *sackcloth* and *humbling the soul* were the outward signs of mourning (cp. Ps. 30[11]); to humble the soul was the technical term for fasting, see, *e.g.*, Isa. 58[3, 5], cp. Ps. 69[10]; *prayer* for them constantly *returned* to his *mouth* (lit. " palate "), *i.e.*, he prayed for them repeatedly as he was wont to pray for a *friend and brother* ; and he grieved for them in their distress like *one mourning for a mother, black and bowed down* (cp. Ps. 38[6]), *black* means lit. " squalid ", going negligently clad, another outward sign of mourning.   In spite of the sympathy thus shown they behave in the most heartless manner to him who had been their friend (15, 16); and the psalmist again (17) calls upon Yahweh to *rescue* him *from them that roar* at him like *young lions* ; the expression *Mine only one*, parallel with *my soul*, means the very self (cp. Ps. 22[20]).   19–20 describe further the cruel and deceitful actions of these enemies, followed, 22–26, by a reiterated prayer to be delivered from them.   Finally, (27, 28) in the conviction that deliverance is at hand, the psalmist utters the confident cry that all those who *delight* in his forthcoming *triumph* may *shout for joy*, saying, *Magnified be Yahweh, who hath pleasure in the peace of his servant.*

Religious Teaching

Though it is not to be denied that there are elements in this psalm which fall below the religious standard of most of the psalms, one must recognize that in one respect, at any rate, a true religious spirit is manifested.   In spite of grievous wrong suffered by the psalmist, he nowhere expresses the intention, or even the wish, of taking personal revenge upon his enemies and traducers ; that he should desire their punishment is natural enough; but this is left wholly in the hands of the Almighty; we recall Rom. 12[19]: " Vengeance is mine, saith the Lord, I will repay," cp. Deut. 32[35].   This wholehearted placing of his cause in the care of the all-knowing God witnesses to a true sincerity of religious belief. In various other psalms this renouncing of personal revenge, however justified from a worldly point of view, will be found to be present.

PSALM 36

THE personification of Transgression, as here set forth, is unique in the *Psalms*. It is represented as a demon who whispers temptation into the heart of him who is prepared to listen, *i.e.*, the sinner. The reference here is not to atheism, as in Ps. 53[1]: "The fool hath said in his heart, There is no God" (= Ps. 14[1]); it is even worse, for while the existence of God is acknowledged, disregard for his own honour is imputed to him (see, further, the exegetical notes). It is assumed, evidently as the result of observation and experience, that many have succumbed to this kind of temptation; against such the words of indignant protest are uttered.

The psalmist's own conception of, and belief in, Yahweh is proclaimed in words of much beauty.

The contention of some commentators that the psalm is of composite authorship is quite unnecessary when the true nature of the psalm is grasped. The psalm may be assigned to the Greek period.

The metre in the first part of the psalm (*vv.* 2–4) is partly 3 : 2, and partly 3 : 3 ; the second part is all 3 : 3.

1.   *For the Precentor : David's, the Servant of Yahweh.*

1 (2). Oracle of Transgression to the wicked,
"There is no fear of God
 in the depth of ° his heart : °
 before his eyes,

2 (3). ° For he maketh his eyes to over-look it,°
 ° so as not to discern the iniquity of his tongue ".°

3 (4). The words of his mouth are wickedness and deceit,
 he hath ceased to deal wisely, to do good,

4 (5).   He deviseth wickedness on his bed ;
He setteth himself on a way that is not good,
 evil he abhorreth not.

5 (6). Yahweh, unto the heavens is thy love,
 thy faithfulness unto the skies ;

6 (7). Thy righteousness is like the mountains of God,
Man and beast thou preservest,
 ° The children of men come unto thee,°
 thy justice ° like the great deep ; °
 7 (8). Yahweh, how precious is thy love.
 in the shadow of thy wings they seek refuge ;
 thou makest them to drink of the torrent of thy delights.

8 (9). They are sated with the fatness of thine house,

9 (10). For with thee is the well-spring of life,
 in thy light shall we see light.

10 (11). Continue thy love to them that know thee,
 and thy righteousness to the upright of heart.

11 (12). Let not the foot of pride approach me,
 nor the hand of the wicked shake me.

12 (13). May evil-doers ° be appalled,° may they fall,
 may they be thrust down, and unable to rise.

Text-critical Notes

1. Read, with some MSS. and the Versions, לָבּוֹ for לִבִּי, "my heart". 2. Read, with Gunkel, כִּי־הֶחֱלִיק אֵלָיו בְּעֵינָיו for כִּי־הֶחֱלִיק עָלָיו עֵינָיו, "for he flattereth unto him with his eyes"; and read לִמְצֹא עֲוֹנוֹ לִשְׂנֹא for מִמְצֹא עֲוֹן לִשְׂנֹא, "to seek his iniquity, to hate" (see, further, the exegetical note). 6. Read תְּהוֹם רַבָּה for כְּהַרֲהוֹם רַבָּה "the great deep". 7. Read, with Duhm, אֵלֶיךָ יָבֹאוּ for אֱלֹהִים וּ, "God and". 12. Read, with Gunkel, שַׁמֵּמוֹ for שָׁם "there".

1-2. The intepretation of these two verses is difficult, as is recognized by all commentators. We take the meaning to be as follows : the psalmist represents *Transgression*, personified, as whispering an oracle into *the depth of* the *heart* of the *wicked* man, just as Yahweh whispered oracles into the heart of his prophets. The words of the oracle then follow ; but the Hebrew text here is meaningless ; many emendations have been suggested. The R.V. rendering is merely a paraphrastic guess, and does not even represent the corrupt Hebrew text. As it is Transgression that gives the oracle, it must be a temptation to the wicked man to do, or think, something evil ; and it takes the form of suggesting to him a conception of God which recalls the words of Ps. 50²¹, " Thou thoughtest I was like thee " (cp. also Ps. 94⁷), namely, the blasphemous conceptior that God takes no more notice of sin than the wicked man does : *There is no fear of God before his* (i.e., God's) *eyes*, meaning that God is indifferent to the reverence and fear that men should entertain towards him ; *For he* (i.e., God) *maketh his eyes to overlook it* (i.e., iniquity), so that he does *not discern the iniquity of his tongue* (i.e., of the wicked man who hates God) ; in other words : God closes his eyes to iniquity, and takes no notice of the sins that wicked men who hate him commit. The implication is that inasmuch as it is immaterial to the Almighty whether men sin or not, they can sin as much as they like with impunity. That, then, is the oracle which Transgression whispers as a temptation to the wicked man. It follows (3, 4) that his words are all evil, and any good to which he may have been inclined is left undone ; even as he lies on his bed at nights he *deviseth evil*. In contrast to all this, the psalmist proclaims Yahweh as he really is, and tells of the blessedness of those who come unto him (5-10). First, he speaks of the illimitable sway of the love and faithfulness of Yahweh, reaching unto the heavens (cp. Pss. 57¹⁰, 103¹¹). In the words, *His righteousness is like the mountains of God*, the psalmist is making use of an ancient mythological conception of the divine mountain abode " in the uttermost parts of the north " (Isa. 14¹³¹⁴). The comparison of Yahweh's *righteousness* with *the mountains of God* expresses its reliable, enduring nature. A further mythological *trait* appears in the phrase : *thy justice is like the great deep* ; the reference is to the waters under the earth (cp. Gen. 1⁶, 7¹¹, Am. 7⁴), and the comparison is intended to express the unfathomable depth of Yahweh's justice. So that these two verses (5, 6) extol the divine attributes of love, faithfulness, righteousness, and justice, as filling the heavens above, the earth beneath, and the waters under the earth; a clear mark of prophetic influence. Further, special stress is laid on Yahweh's love ; *precious*, because through it both *man and beast* are preserved (8). For the thought of the *refuge* to be sought under the *shadow of* Yahweh's *wings* cp. Pss. 57¹, 61⁴, 91⁴. A difficulty is presented in the words : *They are satisfied with the fatness of thine house.* This is usually interpreted as referring to the sacrificial meals enjoyed in the temple by the worshippers of Yahweh; but inasmuch as the subject, *They*, includes *the children of men* in general, and not only the worshippers of Yahweh, this interpretation is hardly satisfactory; moreover, the parallel clause, *thou makest them to drink of the river of thy delights*, cannot well refer to the drink enjoyed during the sacrificial meals. Gunkel would read the *fatness of thy goodness*, for which there is much to be said ; but, like the other expression, it is otherwise unknown ; we have, therefore, followed the Hebrew text as it stands, unsatisfactory though it is. With the parallel between *life* and *light* (9), cp. Ps. 56¹³, Job 33³⁰. A prayer for the continuance of Yahweh's *love to them that know* him (10) is appropriately added ; and the psalmist concludes with a petition that he may be defended against the approach of wickedness which overwhelms the evil-doers.

Religious Teaching

This psalm is not without interest from the point of view of the Jewish doctrine of sin. It teaches that men are under the influence of evil spiritual powers just as they are under the influence of God. That is to say, evil is external to man. On the other hand, since it is " the wicked man " who is open to the evil influence, the implication is that evil is already present in him, which is the reason for his succumbing to temptation (cp. Gen. 6⁵). The problem of sin, here only adumbrated, exercised the minds of Jewish thinkers in an increasing degree during the post-exilic period ; and it centred, as it was bound to do, on the question of the origin of sin. If sin is external to man, who or what is it that causes it ? If, on the other hand, sin is innate in man, how did it come to be so ? The attempted answers to these questions, put forth by Jewish thinkers, are of much interest ; we can but briefly indicate them, as the general subject of the origin of sin and its prevalence is far too large a one to enter upon here: The theories, or dogmas, as the case may be, the evidence for which, whether in the Bible or in post-Biblical Jewish literature, is abundant, are the following :

(1). The theory, based on ancient mythology, that fallen angels brought sin into the world.

(2). The dogma of the Fall; the danger of dualistic conceptions was simply ignored.

(3). The dogma of the creation of good and evil tendencies in man, the two *Yetzers*.

(4). The theory that sin originated in man, and was of his making.

(5). The theory that God created evil.

So far as our psalm is concerned, none of these theories or dogmas come into consideration; the existence of sin is taken for granted without seeking to explain its origin. We are thus led to surmise that the psalmist, all unconsciously, was influenced by Persian Dualism; but that he did not realize the danger to monotheistic belief which this involved.

PSALM 37

WE have here another acrostic psalm, which, with one exception, differs from the others of this character in that each letter of the Hebrew alphabet begins alternate lines, two lines going to each letter. Similar to this are Pss. 9, 10, which constitute a single psalm. Our psalm belongs to the Wisdom type; each couplet is, as a rule, self-contained, and the style is that with which we are familiar in the book of *Proverbs*. The happy lot of the righteous is again and again contrasted with that of the wicked, so that the central theme of the psalm is the doctrine of retribution. That the realities of life did not support the optimistic outlook of the Sage did not trouble him; he insists that, in spite of appearances, the upright enjoy prosperity, the godless the reverse. This conviction is based on an unshakeable trust in divine providence; according to him, if the godly suffered, and the wicked prospered, that was merely temporary; a little patience, and the final outcome will be seen. The inordinate length of the psalm, and its repetitions, are due to its artificial alphabetical construction.

As a product of the Wisdom Literature, the psalm belongs, in all probability, to the third century B.C.

The metre is for the most part 3 : 3; but some variations occur.

David's.

1 א.   Be not enraged because of evil-doers,
        ° and ° be not envious
        of workers of unrighteousness;

2.   For like grass do they speedily wither,   and fade away like the green herb.

3 ב   Trust in Yahweh, and do good,   be the land thy dwelling, fidelity thy pasture;

4.   And delight thee in Yahweh,
        that he may grant unto thee
        the requests of thine heart;

5 ב. Commit thy way unto Yahweh, and trust him, and he will do it,
6. And he will bring forth thy
 righteousness as light,   and thy rectitude as the noon-day.
7. ד.   Be still before Yahweh,
      and wait patiently for him.
 Be not angered at him whose way
  doth prosper,   at the man who performeth evil-devices.
8 ה.   Cease from anger,
    and forsake wrath,
  Be not angered (it leadeth) only to evil-doing;
9.   For evil-doers will be cut off,
    but they that wait on Yahweh
    ° shall inherit the land.
10 ו. Yet a little, and the wicked is no thou wilt consider his place, but he is
 more,   no more.
11. The meek shall inherit the land, and shall delight them in abundance of
           peace.
12 ז. The wicked plotteth against the
 righteous,   and gnasheth against him his teeth.
13. The Lord doth laugh at him, for he seeth his day is coming.
14 ח.   The wicked have drawn the sword,
    they have bent their bow,
   To cut down the afflicted,
    to slay the upright of life.
15. Their sword shall enter their heart, and their bows shall be broken.
16 ט. Better is a little that the righteous
 hath   than ° great ° ° wealth ° of the wicked.
17. For the arms of the wicked shall be
 broken,   but Yahweh upholdeth the righteous;
18 י. He knoweth the days of the perfect, and their inheritance abideth for ever;
19. They shall not be ashamed in the and in the days of want they shall be
 evil time,   sated;
20 כ.   But the wicked shall perish,
    and the enemies of Yahweh,
    ° Like the burning of furnaces °
    shall they vanish like smoke.°
21 ל. The wicked borroweth, and re-
 payeth not,   but the righteous is gracious, and giveth.
22. For they whom he blesseth shall but they whom he curseth shall be cut
 inherit the land,   off.
23 מ From Yahweh are the steps of man, ° he establisheth him in whose way ° he
          delighteth;
24. Though he fall he shall not be cast
 headlong,   for Yahweh upholdeth his hand.
25 נ. I have been both young and old, but have not seen the righteous for-
          saken,
   Nor his seed begging for food;
26. He is ever gracious and lendeth, and his seed ° shall be ° for a blessing.
27 ס. Depart from evil, and do good, and dwell ° in the land ° for ever;
28.   and will not forsake his godly ones.
 ע. ° The godless ° ° shall be destroyed ° and the seed of the wicked shall be cut
 for ever,   off.
29. The righteous shall inherit the land, and shall dwell thereon for ever.
30 פ. The mouth of the righteous mur-
 mureth wisdom,   and his tongue discourseth justice;
31. The law of his God is in his heart, his footsteps ° shall not totter.°
32 צ. The wicked spieth upon the
 righteous,   and seeketh to slay him;
33. But Yahweh will not abandon him nor condemn him when he stands in
 to his power,   the judgement.
34 ק.   Wait for Yahweh,
    and keep his way,
 And he will exalt thee to inherit the when the wicked are cut off thou shalt
 land;   see it.
35 ר. I saw the wicked ° exultant,° ° and raising himself up like the cedars
         of Lebanon °;
36. ° I passed by,° and behold, he was I sought him, but he was not to be
 not,   found.

37 שׁ. Keep °integrity,° °and foster up-
         rightness,°
38.   But transgressors shall be destroyed
         altogether,
39 ת. The salvation of the righteous is
         from Yahweh,
40.   And Yahweh doth help them and
         deliver them

for the latter end °of the upright ° is
   peace ;

the end of the wicked be cut short.

their refuge in the time of trouble ;
   °from the wicked °; for they trust in
   him.

Text-critical Notes

1. Add וְ with many MSS. and the Versions. 9. Om. חֵמָה for the rhythm's
sake. 14. Om. וְאֶבְיוֹן for the rhythm's sake. 16. Read רָב for רַבִּים, " many "
(in reference to " the wicked "). Read מֵהוֹן for מֵהַמוֹן, " than the abundance ".
18. Om. יהוה for the rhythm's sake. 20. Read, with Baethgen, בִּיקֹד כָּרִים for
בִּיקַר כָּרִים, " like the preciousness of lambs ". Om. the second כָּלוּ. 23. Read,
with Duhm, כּוֹנְנוּ וְדַרְכּוֹ for כּוֹנָנוּ בְּדַרְכּוֹ, " be ye established and his way ". 26.
Add יִחְיֶה for the rhythm's sake. 27. Add בָּאָרֶץ for the rhythm's sake. 28. Add,
with G, עַוְלִים. Read, with G, נִשְׁמְדוּ for נִשְׁמָרוּ, " they shall be preserved ". 31. For
the fem. sing. with the subject in the plur. (תִּמְעַד אֲשֻׁרָיו) see GK. 145k. 35.
Read, with Duhm (cp. G), עָלִיץ for עָרִיץ, " ruthless ". Read, with G, וּמִתְעַלֶּה
for וּמִתְעָרֶה כְּאֶזְרָח רַעֲנָן כְּאַרְזֵי הַלְּבָנוֹן, " and uncovering himself like a green
native (tree) ". 36. Read, with the Versions, וְאֶעֱבֹר for וַיַּעֲבֹר, " and he passed
by ". 37. Read, with the Versions, תֹּם and יֹשֶׁר, nouns, in place of the adjectives
תָּם, " perfect ", and יָשָׁר, " upirght "; and read וּרְאֵה for וְרָאֵה, " and observe ".
Read, with Gunkel, יֹשֶׁר for לְאִישׁ, " for a man ". 40. Om. יְפַלְּטֵם and וַיּוֹשִׁיעֵם,
" he delivereth them and saveth them ", which overload the line.

Most of the sayings of which the psalm is composed are of such a
straightforward and simple character that not much in the way of
exegesis is called for. Here and there a few comments may be offered ;
but, on the whole, the thoughts are expressed with such transparent
simplicity that their meaning is self-evident.

1–11. The psalm opens abruptly with an exhortation to the God-
fearing *not to be enraged*, lit. " heated " with anger, nor *envious*, because
they see evil-doers going unpunished and living in prosperity (cp.
Prov. 24[19]), for this is but transient (cp. Prov. 24[20, 22]); very soon *workers
of unrighteousness* will be seen to *wither like grass, and fade away like
the green herb* (cp. Ps. 92[7]). The godly man has but to possess his soul
in patience, and he will see the wicked *cut off*. The great requisite is
to *Trust in Yahweh, and do good* (cp. Prov. 3[5]); he will vindicate those
who *commit* their *way* to him, lit. " roll " their way upon Yahweh
(cp. Prov. 16[3]), the expression occurs also in Ps. 22[8], and contains the
thought of whole-hearted flinging of oneself upon God, knowing that
his will prevails. So that, even though the wicked prosper and the
godly suffer, one must *be still before Yahweh*, i.e., submit in silence to
what he ordains, and it will soon be seen that *the wicked is no more*
(cp. Job 24[24], see further the section on Religious Teaching to Ps. 44),
but that *the meek shall inherit the land* (cp. Matth. 5[5]). The psalmist
is here thinking of the wealthy landowners who grind down their
poverty-stricken dependents ; these latter are encouraged by the prospect

that ultimately it is they who will possess the land.   This is insisted on several times (*vv.* 22, 27, 29, 34).   This, then, constitutes the main theme of the psalm, as so often in the Wisdom Literature; in spite of appearances, the ungodly, who in their pride and prosperity oppress the righteous, will soon be humiliated; but they who trust in Yahweh will enjoy permanent peace and quietude.   In one form or another this is reiterated all through the psalm.

12–24.   The wickedness of the ungodly is intensified by their bitter enmity *towards the righteous*; this is manifested not only by their plotting, *i.e.*, devising evil machinations, but also by actual attempts on the lives of the righteous; they *draw the sword, bend*, lit. " tread ", *the bow*, and seek to *slay the upright of life*, lit. " of way " (cp. Ps. 7^{10}); retribution, however, soon follows, and as the wicked intended, so shall it be done unto them (15); so that their wealth, which is their all in all, is vain, and becomes of less value even than the *little* possessed by their victims : *Better is a little that the righteous hath than great wealth of the wicked*; this thought is suggested by Prov. 15^{16}, 16^{8}; the rendering is that of the Versions, which is preferable to that of the Hebrew : ". . . . than the wealth of many wicked ".   In contrast to this, the righteous are upheld by Yahweh, who will see to it that *they shall not be ashamed in the evil time, and in the days of want they shall be sated*. In *v.* 20 there is an obvious corruption in the Hebrew text; for the suggested emendation, see the text-critical note.   A further count against the wicked man is that *he borroweth, and repayeth not*, while the righteous man is *gracious, and giveth* spontaneously; therefore he has the authority which makes his words effective, so that they whom he blesses *inherit the land*, and they whom he *curses are cut off*.

25–40.   Here the psalmist gives what has been his experience through a long life : *I have been both young and old, but have not seen the righteous forsaken, nor his seed begging for food*; and he proceeds to repeat the main theme of the psalm, interspersed with exhortations to the righteous to persevere in the right way, and certifying them that *Yahweh doth help them and deliver them from the wicked; for they trust in him*.

Religious Teaching

This is so abundantly and clearly set forth throughout, that further remarks are not called for.   The psalmist's teaching on retribution has been referred to; here it may merely be added that his point of view on the subject, which is an erroneous one, is precisely the same as that of Job's friends; Job himself is at pains to refute it.

PSALM 38

THERE is probably no psalm, with the one exception of the fifty-first, which is of such a deeply penitential character as this; and it is naturally numbered among the seven penitential psalms of the Church. It is possible that part of it at any rate, may have been, as Mowinckel contends, in the nature of a counteraction to a magical spell cast upon the psalmist by his enemies. But, in the main, it is the outpouring of one suffering grievous sickness, and who is convinced that this is a punishment inflicted upon him because of sin. This transgression he confesses with unflinching candour, expressing his contrition in words of poignant feeling. His friends, seeing in him one struck down by the hand of God, and therefore guilty of some secret sin, turn from him, and become his enemies; their reviling he submits to in silence. His one recourse is to plead with Yahweh for his help.

Like Ps. 37, this psalm belongs, in all probability, to the Greek period. It shows numerous traces of dependence on earlier writings. The metre, with few exceptions, is 3 : 3.

There is so much in this psalm which is reminiscent of Babylonian psalms of a similar type, that it will not be out of place if we give some extracts from one of these. It is a psalm addressed to the goddess Ishtar by a penitent, who is suffering from sickness, and feels that this is inflicted as a punishment for sin. It is far too long to quote in full, but the following extracts will sufficiently illustrate its nature :—[1]

" I call upon thee,

Have regard unto me, O my goddess,
Look upon me in mercy,
O tell thou forth my forgiveness,
The forgiveness of my careworn body,
The forgiveness of my sickly heart,
The forgiveness of mine innermost self,
I moan like a dove,
I am bowed down,
With pain and travail
I cry to thee, yea, to thee,
Pardon my guilt, my transgression,
Forget my ill-doing,
Loosen my bands,
Guide my footsteps,

Let me tread down mine enemies,
They that are wrathful against me cast
    down,
My prayer and my supplication,
May thine abundant mercy

I, thy wretched, pitiful, and suffering
    servant;
give heed to my supplication;
hearken unto my prayer.
O may thy heart be softened,—
full of discomfort and restlessness,
full of tears and sighs,
full of discomfort and restlessness . . .
day and night,
and weep in bitterness;
is my spirit tormented . . .
release me from the spell;
my misdeeds and my sin,
receive my supplication;
and grant me freedom;
that I may walk among the living in
    gladness . . .
as upon the ground;

let them grovel at my feet.
let them come unto thee,
abide on me."

1.   *A Psalm. David's.* To Commemorate.

1 (2). Yahweh, punish me not in thy   ° and in thy fierce-anger ° chasten me
        wrath,   not.

---

[1] They are taken from the German translations of the original by Jastrow, *Die Religion Babyloniens und Assyriens,* ii. 66 ff. (1912), and Gressmann, *Altorientalische Texte zum Alten Testament,* pp. 257 ff. (1926).

2 (3). For thine arrows pierce me,   and thine hand ° is heavy ° upon me.
3 (4).   There is no soundness in my flesh,
    because of thine indignation,
    nor ° wholeness ° in my bones,
    because of my sin.
4 (5). For mine iniquities are gone over   like a ° burden, they are too heavy for
my head,   me.
5 (6). My wounds stink, they fester,   because of my foolishness.
6 (7). I am bowed down and prostrated
greatly,   all the day I go about mourning;
7 (8). For my loins are full of burning,   and there is no soundness in my flesh.
8 (9). I am faint and greatly bruised,   I cry out for the groaning of my heart.
9 (10). O Lord, before thee is all my
longing,   and my sighing is not hid from thee.
10 (11).   My heart throbbeth,
    my strength hath failed me,
    the light of mine eyes ° is not with me.
11 (12). My lovers ° draw off from before
me,°   and my neighbours stand afar off,
12 (13). And they lay snares,° they utter
destructive-things,   and meditate evil-devices all the day.
13 (14). And as for me, I am like a deaf   and like a dumb man that openeth not
man ° that heareth not,°   his mouth;
14 (15). Yea, I am like a man that heareth   and in whose mouth there are no
not,   reproofs;
15 (16). But in thee do I hope, Yahweh,   thou wilt make answer,° my God;
16 (17). ° I said: "Lest they rejoice   and ° boast over ° me when my foot
against me,   slippeth;
17 (18). For I am on the verge of giving
way,   for my pain is continually with me;
18 (19).   ° Mine iniquity I confess,
    I am harassed because of my sin.
19 (20). And mine enemies assail me   and they that hate me falsely are
° without cause,°   many;
20 (21).   They render me evil
    instead of good,
    They are mine enemies because
    I follow after good.
21 (22). Forsake me not, Yahweh,   my God, be not far from me,
22 (23).   Haste thee to help me,
    O Lord, my salvation."

Text-critical Notes

1. Read, with many MSS. and the Versions, וְאַל־בַּחֲמָתְךָ for וּבַחֲמָתְךָ.
2. Read, with Duhm, וַתִּכְבַּד for וַתִּנְחַת. 3. Read, with Duhm, שָׁלֵם for שָׁלוֹם,
a better parallel to "soundness". 4. Om. כָּבֵד, "heavy", for the rhythm's sake.
10. Om., with G, גַּם־הֵם, "even they". 11. Read מִפְּנֶגְדִּי נָגְשׁוּ for וְרֵעַי מִנֶּגֶד
נִגְעִי יַעֲמֹדוּ, "and my friends stand aloof from my stroke (plague)", which overloads the line; the same verb occurs in the next half-line. 12. Om. as overloading
the line, מְבַקְשֵׁי נַפְשִׁי וְדֹרְשֵׁי רָעָתִי, "they that seek after my soul and they that
seek my hurt". 13. Read יִשְׁמַע לֹא for לֹא אֶשְׁמַע, "I hear not". 15. Om.
אֲדֹנָי for the rhythm's sake. 16. Om. כִּי, "for". Read יַגְדִּילוּ for הִגְדִּילוּ.
18. Om. כִּי, "for". 19. Read חִנָּם for חַיִּים, "are living".

For the title, see p. 15.
1. Self-condemnation is implicit in the opening words of the psalm.
The psalmist, quoting Ps. 6¹, feels that he has aroused the wrath of
Yahweh, and deserves punishment, because of his sins; so that the
prayer that this may be averted is in itself a confession. This, there-

upon, receives explicit expression, and in 3-10 the penitent, in acknowledging his sins, describes the scourge of which they are the cause.
For the metaphorical sense of the *arrows* of the Almighty cp. Job 6[4];
and for that of Yahweh's hand resting heavily on the sinner cp. Pss.
32[4], 39[10]; they are the marks of his *indignation*, to which is attributed
the malady from which the penitent is suffering : there is no *soundness*
in his flesh (possibly a reminiscence of Isa. 1[6]), and no *wholeness* in his
bones. Flesh and bones constitute the material part of the human
body (cp. Lk. 24[39]), the spirit the intangible part; it will be noticed
that blood, the seat of life, is not mentioned. A fuller confession then
follows : *mine iniquities are gone over my head*, i.e., they have overwhelmed
him like a flood of waters (cp. Pss. 69[2, 15], 124[4]), and with a sudden change
of metaphor he continues : *like a burden, they are too heavy for me*;
the very incongruity in this change of metaphor is full of significance,
for it tells of the entirely natural variableness of thought in the troubled
mind of a sufferer ; first the rushing flood of sins, then the burden of
them ; what a realistic picture these two wholly incompatible ideas
present of the mental condition of one who, because of his sins, is sunk
in the sea of despair, and bowed down with their weight ! Then the
penitent goes on to describe in fuller detail the nature of his malady ;
from what is said the impression is gained that it was some form of
leprosy from which he was suffering ; his *wounds stink* and *fester* (again
cp. Isa. 1[6]), *because of* his *foolishness*, synonymous with sin (cp. Ps.
69[5]); but he is not on a bed of sickness, for he *goeth about all the day
mourning* (cp. Ps. 42[9]), lit. " black ". The description of the sickness
is followed (9, 10) by some very touching words which reveal the depth
of the realization of the psalmist's relationship with God ; such an
opening of the heart, as is here set forth, is an inspiration of enduring
value : *O Lord, before thee is all my longing, and my sighing is not hid from
thee*; only where there is the deepest confidence and trust in the divine
Friend can one say : *My heart throbbeth, my strength hath failed me,
the light of mine eye is not with me*, in the full conviction that divine
sympathy will be forthcoming ; it is at the same time an implicit
appeal for mercy. 11-16. This need for help from on high is the more
urgently felt because the sufferer's *lovers* and *neighbours* will have nothing
to do with him ; *they draw off from before me, and stand afar off*;
believing him to be stricken of God they turn from him as one to be
avoided (cp. Ps. 88[18], and especially Isa. 53[3, 4]). But more, these
friends, as they had once been, now maltreat him ; they have become
his enemies, *they lay snares* (cp. Ps. 141[9]), *they utter destructive-things*,
a very strong expression, meaning that what they say is intended to result
in his destruction (cp. Ps. 52[2]), and *they meditate evil-devices all the day*,
i.e., their machinations are done in secret so that they may assail him
unawares (cp. Ps. 35[20]). In face of all this the victim simply takes no

notice, he is *like a deaf man that heareth not, and like a dumb man that openeth not his mouth* (cp. Isa. 53⁷), and makes *no replies*, lit. " reproofs ", *i.e.*, he does not attempt to refute their lying words, for there is one in whom he trusts, *But in thee do I hope, Yahweh.* Finally (17–22) the penitent in his dire distress, again makes his confession : *Mine iniquity I confess, I am harassed because of my sin* ; let his enemies do their worst, he has done what he ought to do, and is following after what is good ; therefore he can pray in certitude that his prayer will be heard : *Forsake me not, Yahweh, my God, be not far from me* (cp. Pss. 22¹¹, ¹⁹, 35²²), *Haste thee to help me, O Lord, my salvation* (cp. Pss. 40¹³, 27¹).

As in some other instances, the religious teaching of this psalm is necessarily dealt with in the exegetical notes.

PSALM 39

In order to appreciate the essential significance of this psalm attention must be directed first to *v.* 10, which gives the key to the whole of it : " Take away from me thy stroke, through the smiting of thine hand I am perishing ". Sickness has overtaken the sufferer, and it is of so severe a character that he fears a fatal outcome. As in the case of the preceding psalm, here too, the stricken one realizes that his suffering is a divine visitation, a punishment for sin ; hence the primary duty of making confession : " From all my trangressions deliver me ". That puts him in the fitting condition to appeal to God : " Hear my prayer, give ear to my cry ". The psalm is, therefore, in the fullest sense, of a penitential character, though at first sight it does not appear to be so, and is, therefore, not reckoned among the penitential psalms. Now, what is particularly noteworthy in this psalm is that the nature of the sin of which the penitent has been guilty is indicated in the clearest manner. In all the other penitential psalms, where there is also a full recognition and confession of sin, the actual nature of what has been done amiss is not indicated. In this case it is different. The stroke of sickness which had fallen upon him was not, at first, recognized by the sufferer as a just retribution for sin, and he had been guilty of adopting an attitude towards God of a character somewhat similar to that urged upon Job by his wife : " Dost thou still hold fast thine integrity ? Renounce God, and die ! " (Job 2⁹). In the bitterness of spirit engendered by long-drawn suffering, impatience and irritability had possessed him, and he had sinned with his tongue by speaking against God, hence the opening words of the psalm which are at once a confession of past sin, and a resolution of amendment : " I said, I will take heed

Q

unto my words, that I sin not with my tongue ", followed by a detailed confession of the nature of his sin (see, further, the exegetical notes).

The date of the psalm, like that of the preceding one, is the third century.

The metre is somewhat variable, which is, however, fully to be accounted for by the troubled state of mind of the writer.

1.   *For the Precentor. Jeduthun's. A Psalm. David's.*

1 (2). I said, I will take heed unto ° my
                words,°
                                              that I sin not with my tongue ;
        ° I will put ° to my mouth a bridle   ° because of ° the wicked before me ;
2 (3).   I was dumb in silence,
                                I held my peace from what was good.
                                ° But my feelings ° were stirred,
3 (4).   my heart was hot within me,
                                while I mused the fire kindled,
                                I spake with my tongue :
4 (5).   " Let me know, Yahweh, mine end,   and the number of my days, what it is,
                                that I may see how transient I am ;
5 (6).   Behold, handbreadths
                                hast thou made my days,
                                and my life is as nought before thee ;
        Surely as ° a vapour ° doth every   6 (7). surely ° as a shadow ° man doth
        man stand. Selah.   walk,
        ° Riches ° he gathereth, but knoweth not who will gather them."
7 (8). And now, what is ° my hope °, O
                Lord ?   my waiting is for thee ;
8 (9). From all my transgressions deliver   the reproach of the foolish make me
        me,   not.
9 (10). I am dumb, and open not my
        mouth,   for thou didst do it ;
10 (11). Take away from me thy stroke,   ° through the smiting ° of thine hand I
                                             am perishing ;
11 (12).   With rebukes for iniquity
                                thou chastenest man ;
        Thou destroyest like a moth ° his   surely a vain thing, is every man.
        beauty,°   Selah.
12 (13).   Hear my prayer,°
                                Give ear to my cry,
                                Be not deaf to my weeping ;
                                For a stranger am I with thee,
                                A sojourner like all my fathers.
13 (14). ° Look away ° from me that I may
        be cheered,   before I go hence and am no more.

Text-critical Notes

1. Read דְּבָרַי, as demanded by the context, for דְּרָכַי, " my ways ". Read, with G, אָשִׁימָה f.r אֶשְׁמְרָה, " I will take heed ", or " keep ", repeated from the previous line. Read בַּעֲבוּר for בְּעֹד, " while ". 2. Read, with Gunkel, וּכְבֵדִי, lit. " but my liver " (the seat of the feelings, according to ancient Hebrew thought), as a better parallel to לִבִּי, " my heart ", for וּכְאֵבִי, " but my pain ". 5. Read, with S, כְּהֶבֶל for כָּל־, " every vapour ", and 6. בְּצֶלֶם for בְּ, " in a shadow ". Read הָמוֹן for אַךְ־הֶבֶל יֶחֱמָיִן, " surely they are disquieted in vain ". 7. Read, with GS, תִּקְוָתִי for מָה־קִוִּיתִי, " what wait I for ? " 10. Read, with G, מִגְּבוּרַת, lit. " through the strength of ", for מִתִּגְרַת, " through the conflict of ". 11. Read, with some MSS, חֲמוּדוֹ for חֲמוּדוֹ, " his delight ". 12. Om., with G, יְהוָה, " Yahweh ". 13. Read שְׁעֵה for הָשַׁע, lit. " besmear (thine eyes) " cp. Isa. 6¹⁰.

For the title, see p. 15.

1–6. With his conscience overburdened with the sense of sin the penitent plunges at once into a full acknowledgement of the nature of the sin of which he has been guilty : *I said, I will take heed unto my words, that I sin not with my tongue.* The general content of the psalm shows that this sinning with the tongue had been the uttering of *words* displeasing to the Almighty. The Hebrew text has " ways " instead of *words*, but the context, with the mention of *tongue* and *mouth*, shows that " words " must have been the original reading ; the similarity between the two (see text-critical note) easily accounts for the copyist's error. The nature of these *words* is described later ; but this is preceded by a passage which is a little difficult ; it may, however, be explained thus : the opening word of the psalm, " I said ", applies to the whole of *v.* 1, viz., *I said, I will take heed unto my words . . ., (I said) I will put to my mouth a bridle . . .*; so that both clauses refer to the past ; they describe the right state of mind to which the psalmist had been brought, while implicitly recalling the prior evil state of his mind. What he had first said would appear to have been doubting of divine justice, in permitting the *wicked* to prosper ; therefore, having come to a better frame of mind, he had said, *I will put a bridle to my mouth because of the wicked before me*, even though this resulted in *holding his peace from what was good.* The passage, it must be confessed, is somewhat involved ; but this is easily accounted for when one considers the psalmist's varying emotions.

Then the penitent reverts to his confession with which he began the psalm ; he now, therefore, describes what he had been guilty of in fuller detail : *But my feelings* (lit. " my liver ") *were stirred*; the context demands this emendation ; the Hebrew text has " my pain " (the two words are again somewhat similar, see text-critical note) ; *my heart was hot within me*, in the sense of being angry ; both expressions are extremely rare ; *while I mused the fire kindled*, lit. " in my meditation ", in late Hebrew the verb means also " to argue ", and the noun here may well have the sense of mental argument. Weary, impatient, and irritable through much suffering, the sick man asks himself what is the meaning of it all ; why is he suffering ? What has he done to deserve it ? Why does God not help him ? Does God care ? Is life worth living ? The inner struggle becomes intolerable, and rage bursts forth, *the fire kindled*; then, in desperation he speaks *with his tongue*, and in the words then uttered lay the essence of his sin (*vv.* 4, 5). At first sight there does not seem to be anything particularly reprehensible in those words ; but the evil of them lies in what they imply. *Let me know, Yahweh, mine end, and the number of my days, what it is . . .*: that is an entirely unseemly request, and reveals an altogether wrong spirit ; the ways of divine providence are not for man to know. Then, the desire to go hence, which is implied, is an evil one because it

points to a refusal to trust in God ; moreover, it manifests an indifference
to relationship with God, for in death there is no remembrance of
him (Ps. 6⁵).   Further, to say that *my life* (*i.e.*, duration of life) *is as
nought before thee* is to ignore a great truth (see Ps. 90⁴).   And, finally,
to depreciate man by speaking of him as *a vapour*, and *a shadow*, is an
insult to God who made man " in his own image " (Gen. 1²⁷).   Thus,
the whole passage betrays a spirit which in its attitude towards God is
deplorable.   But that is all in the past.   The psalmist then turns to
the present :   7, *And now, what is my hope, O Lord?   my waiting is for
thee* ;   8, and he prays to be delivered from all his *transgressions* which
he has just recalled.   The *foolish* would naturally *reproach* him for his
conversion to God.   9–11. In humble submission, and in striking
contrast to his former wrong-headed utterances, he is now *dumb* before
God, and *openeth not his mouth* ;   for he has come to understand that his
suffering was God's doing, and that his chastening was the just punishment for his *iniquities*.   He speaks of man as *a vain thing* (it is the same
word as that for "vapour") in a very different spirit now ;   not as
contemptible, but as powerless under the hand of God.   12, 13. His
one recourse is to *prayer*, and in fitting humility he speaks of himself as
a *stranger* in the sight of God, and in his deep sense of unworthiness
prays that God may *look away from* him, *i.e.*, in his sinfulness, and thus
be cheered before he *goes hence and is no more*.

   In this psalm, again, the religious teaching has been dealt with in
the preceding notes.

PSALM 40

THAT we have here two independent psalms which have been combined
would be obvious, even if we did not know that one of them occurs
elsewhere as Ps. 70.   The difference in the type of psalm as well as in
subject-matter between the two parts (1–11 and 13–17) shows that they
do not belong together (on *v.* 12 see exegetical note).   The former is an
expression of gratitude for recovery from sickness (see *v.* 2), while the
other is a prayer to be delivered from enemies.   In each it is an individual who writes in his own name ;   that he represents the community
as some commentators hold, is an untenable view in face of what is
said in *vv.* 9–11 in the first psalm and in *v.* 17 in the other.   Both
psalms are post-exilic, the former because of the repudiation of sacrifices
(on this see the exegetical notes on *v.* 6), and because of what is said
about the Law ;   the latter because the enemies are contrasted with
" those that seek thee " (*v.* 16), *i.e.*, the enemies are hellenistic Jews.

   The metre is mostly 3 : 2, but there are some variations from this,

which may, however, be due to textual corruption occurring here and
there.

1.   *For the Precentor : David's.   A Psalm.*

1 (2). I waited patiently for Yahweh,   and he inclined unto me,
       ° [With my voice unto him I cailed],° and he heard my cry.
2 (3). He brought me up from the pit of
       ° Sheol,°   from the miry clay ;
       He set my feet upon a rock,   making firm my footsteps ;
3 (4).   And he put in my mouth
                   a new song,
                   a hymn-of-praise to our God ;
       Many saw it and feared,   and trusted in Yahweh.
4 (5). Blessed is the man who maketh   Yahweh his trust,
       And turneth not unto vain things, falling away to falsehood.
5 (6). Many hast thou wrought ° for us,°   Yahweh,° of thy wondrous-works,
       And thy purposes to us-ward,—   there is none to compare with thee ;
       Should I declare and speak (of
       them),   they would be too many to number.
6ª (7ª). Sacrifice and meal-offering thou   6ᶜ (7ᶜ). Whole burnt-offering and ° sin-
       desirest not,   offering ° thou askest not ;
6ᵇ (7ᵇ). ° Mine ears hast thou perfected for
       me ° ;   7 (8). then said I, lo, I come—
       In the roll of the book it is
       written °—   8 (9). to do thy will ° I delight,
                   Thy Law is within my heart.
9 (10).   I proclaim thy righteousness
                   in the great assembly ;
                   Behold, my lips
                   I do not restrain,
                   Yahweh, thou knowest ;
10 (11).   Thy righteousness I hide not
                   within my heart,
                   Thy faithfulness and succour I declare ;
       I do not conceal thy lovingkindness
       and mercy   before the great assembly.
11 (12). Thou, Yahweh, wilt not withhold   thy tender-mercies from me ;
       Thy love and thy truth
       Will ever preserve me.

Text-critical Notes

1. A tentative addition : קוֹלִי אֵלָיו צָעָקְתִּי, cp. Ps. 77¹, to supply what seems
to have fallen out of the text. 2. Read, with Gressmann, שָׁאוֹל for שָׁאוֹן, " tumult ".
5. Read, with most commentators, אִתָּנוּ for אַתָּה, " thou ". Om. אֱלֹהַי as
overloading the half-line. 6ᶜ. Read חַטָּאת for חֲטָאָה, " sin ". 6ᵇ. Read אָזְנַי
גָּמַרְתָּ לִי (cp. G ὠτία δὲ κατηρτίσω μοι), cp. Ps. 138⁸, for אָזְנַיִם כָּרִיתָ לִי,
" ears hast thou dug for me ". 7. Om. עָלַי, " of me ". 8. Om. אֱלֹהַי as
overloading the line.

1, 2. Expressive of the dominating emotion of the psalmist's heart,
that of gratitude, the psalm begins with the recognition of Yahweh's
response to him who *waited patiently* for him : *He inclined unto me, and
he heard my cry.* The words in brackets are no part of the text ; they
are merely an attempt to supply what may have stood in the text
originally ; that some words have fallen out seems likely as they are
wanted for the balance of the line. The psalmist then proceeds to
state what it was that called forth his gratitude. This is expressed in
metaphorical language ; through God's mercy he has recovered from a
severe sickness which had brought him near to death. *He brought me*

up from the pit of Sheol; the emendation *Sheol* is demanded because the Hebrew reads, "the pit of noise", or "tumult" (see text-critical note), which does not give adequate sense. For the pit as synonymous with *Sheol*, see Pss. 30³, 88³⁻⁵ Isa. 14¹⁵; the thought of the pit as being of *miry clay* occurs also in Ps. 69¹⁴, ¹⁵. That the psalmist is referring to recovery from sickness is evident, as may be seen from the parallel passage Ps. 30², ³, where the sufferer is "healed" by Yahweh, and "brought up from Sheol", see also Ps. 116¹⁻³. His recovery is described metaphorically as having his *feet set upon a rock* (cp. Ps. 27⁵), and as having his *footsteps made firm* (cp. Ps. 37²³), whereby he triumphantly proclaims the completeness of his recovery.   3. Very significant is the way in which the psalmist ascribes to divine inspiration the psalm which he composes : *And he put in my mouth a new song, a hymn-of-praise to our God*; it is a *new song* (cp. Pss. 33³, 96¹), for in his grateful happiness it is insufficient for him to sing one of the older psalms of thanksgiving; he must utter, through divine prompting, the feelings of his own heart.   He sings it in the sanctuary among his fellow-worshippers, and many of those who were watching him *feared, i.e.*, were filled with reverential awe, and *trusted in Yahweh*; faith is strengthened in others by this manifest proof of God's power and loving-kindness.   4. This leads the psalmist to insist on how *Blessed is the man who maketh Yahweh his trust*, in contrast to idol-worshippers; the expressions here used are a little difficult; the expression " to turn unto " is used in a technical sense of turning unto idols in Lev. 19⁴, Deut. 31¹⁸, ²⁰ the word rendered " vain things " (*rᵉhābîm*) does not mean " proud " or " arrogant " here; it is the plural of Rahab, the name of the primeval monster known under the more familiar name of Tiamat, the great opponent of Yahweh (see Job 26¹², Ps. 89¹⁰, Isa. 51⁹.)[1]   That the word was understood in the sense of " idols " or *vain things* by the Septuagint is significant, and justifies our rendering : *And turneth not unto vain things, falling away to falsehood* (καὶ οὐκ ἐνέβλεψεν εἰς ματαιότητας καὶ μανίας ψευδεῖς).   The root from which the word *falling away* comes (שׂטה, *satah*) means, in its cognate form in the Targum (שׂטא, *sata'*), " to apostatize ".   Our psalmist is, thus, insisting on the blessedness of the man who trusts in Yahweh and not in idols.   And he goes on (5) to declare that *there is none to compare with* him, who has *wrought wondrous works* for his people; they are innumerable.   In vv. 6–8 the Hebrew text seems to have got into some disorder; we have sought to give a logical sequence to the lines; but the text is corrupt in parts.   Generally speaking, in the *Psalms* the sacrificial system is taken for granted, which makes the passage before us all the more remarkable (see also 50⁸⁻¹⁴, 51¹⁶, ¹⁷, 69³⁰, ³¹).   Four terms are used of sacrifices which are unacceptable to Yahweh: the first, *sacrifice* (*zebah*) is a

---

[1] See Gunkel, *Schöpfung und Chaos*, pp. 30–40 (1895).

general term, meaning lit. " slaughter " (for sacrifice) ; the *meal-offering*
(*minhah*) was, in post-exilic times, a cereal offering, though in earlier
days it was also a general term for any kind of gift-offering to Yahweh ;
it was offered every evening ; the *whole burnt-offering* (*'ólāh*), called also
kalîl (" holocaust "), is the most usual term applied to the offering of
the entire victim ; it was offered every morning ; and the *sin-offering*
(*hatā'th*), which in post-exilic times was an expiatory sacrifice. That
the thank-offering (*tódāh*) is not mentioned is because it was included
under the *zebah*-sacrifices. The psalmist thus insists that, as expressions of gratitude to Yahweh, all such offerings are unacceptable to
him. This repudiation of the sacrificial system was doubtless due,
in the first instance, to the influence of prophetical teaching. But an
advance on this must be noted in what is said here and in the other
psalms referred to. It is customary to take a few passages from some
of the prophetical books, and to draw from them the deduction that the
prophets advocated the entire abrogation of sacrifices ; while many
other passages in which the offering of sacrifices is taken for granted
are ignored. The fact is, however, that while the prophets strongly
condemned sacrifices when offered in the wrong spirit, they did not
condemn them if offered in sincerity of motive. Jeremiah was the one
exception, and with him, in the psalms mentioned, sacrifices *per se* are
repudiated, and a purely spiritual worship is advocated. This was an
advance in religious belief and practice which was especially characteristic of certain circles during late post-exilic times.[1]

Having thus expressed his disbelief in the need of sacrifices, the
psalmist declares what he holds to be truly acceptable to God. Just
as he had ascribed as due to divine inspiration the utterance of his
" new song ", so does he now ascribe to the same source his apprehension of what the practice of true religion consists : 6[b], *Mine ears
hast thou perfected for me* ; the Hebrew text has, " Ears hast thou dug
for me ; " and it is, of course, possible to extract some sense from
this ; but it is an extraordinary mode of expression, and the text is
regarded as corrupt by the great majority of modern commentators.
Our rendering is based on G (see text-critical note), which gives
excellent sense : Yahweh has so perfected the ears of his servant,
i.e., the faculty of apprehending his will (cp. Isa. 50[4, 5]), that the
servant discerns at once what is truly acceptable to him, *i.e.*, that which
is written (7) *in the roll of the book*, in other words, his Law, expressive
of his will : 8, *to do thy will I delight, thy Law is within my heart.*
9-11. Then, like every true and zealous servant of God, he is impelled
to bear witness before others : *I proclaim thy righteousness in the great
assembly*, *i.e.*, of worshippers ; and, in his conviction of acting in

---

[1] On the whole subject see Oesterley, *Sacrifices in Ancient Israel*, chaps. xiv, xv
(1937).

accordance with the divine will, he can say : *Behold, my lips I do not restrain, Yahweh, thou knowest ; thy righteousness I hide not within my heart . . .*; and he again glories in his championship of Yahweh : *I do not conceal thy lovingkindness and mercy before the great assembly.* The beautiful psalm ends appropriately with a declaration of faith in Yahweh : *Thou, Yahweh, wilt not withhold thy tender-mercies from me ; thy love and thy truth will ever preserve me.*

The deep religious feeling expressed throughout the psalm has been emphasized in the notes above ; a special section on the religious teaching is, therefore, not required.

20.   *Verses* 13–17 (14–18) = *Ps.* 70.

° [12 (13). For troubles encompass me   beyond number,
        Mine iniquities have overtaken me,
        I am unable ° to bear ° them.
        They are more than the hairs of
        my head,   and my heart hath failed me.] °

13 (14). Be pleased, Yahweh, to deliver
        me,   ° haste thee to help me.

14 (15). Let them be put to shame and
        confounded together,   that seek after my soul,°
        Let them turn themselves back-
        wards and be brought to dis-
        honour,   that desire my hurt ;

15 (16). ° Let them turn away ° in
        consequence of their shame-
        fulness,   that say ° Aha, Aha ;

16 (17). Let them rejoice and be glad in
        thee,   all that seek thee,
        Let them say,° Yahweh be
        magnified,'   that love thy salvation.

17 (18). But I am poor and needy,   ° O God, haste thee to me,°
        ° My helper ° and my deliverer
        art thou,   my God, tarry not.

Text-critical Notes

12. See exegetical note. Read, with Duhm, לִשְׁאַת for לִרְאוֹת, " to see (them) ". 13. Om. יהוה " Yahweh ", the repetition overloads the half-line. 14. Om., as in Ps. 70², לִסְפּוֹתָהּ, " to snatch it away ". 15. Read, as in Ps. 70², יָשׁוּבוּ for יָשֹׁמּוּ, " let them be desolated ", or " appalled ". Om., as in Ps. 70², לִי, " to me ". 16. Om. תָּמִיד " continually ", for the rhythm's sake. 17. Read, as in Ps. 70⁵, אֲדֹנָי יַחֲשָׁב־לִי for אֱלֹהִים חוּשָׁה־לִי, " my Lord hath regard unto me ". Read עֹזְרִי, partic. cp. Ps. 70⁵, for עֶזְרָתִי, " my help ", to correspond with " my deliverer ".

12. This verse is so entirely out of harmony with the whole spirit of the preceding psalm that it cannot have been part of it ; and there is nothing corresponding to it in Ps. 70. It must, therefore, have been inserted by the redactor in order to form a link between the two psalms. But the link was inappropriately chosen ; for the content of the verse presupposes circumstances differing from those of the psalm which follows. In the former, which is but a fragment, the penitent pours out his confession, recognizing that his troubles are the consequence of his iniquities ; while the psalm is a prayer to Yahweh for deliverance

from enemies ; and there is no hint that the petitioner is conscious of
sinfulness ; all that he says about himself is that he is poor and needy.
The thoughts and expressions of the interjected verse are taken largely
from other psalms (88³, 38⁴, 69⁴, 73²⁶).

13. The prayer for deliverance from enemies takes an unusual
form : *Be pleased, Yahweh* . . .; in such a connexion the expression
does not occur elsewhere. The sense of close relationship to Yahweh
emboldens the psalmist, in his perilous position, to urge Yahweh to be
speedy with his help, *haste thee to help me* ; so, too, in the concluding
verse ; it is a mode of address which would be unseemly on the part
of man to God, were it not for the childlike, trustful sense of closeness
to him which fills the psalmist's heart (cp. Pss. 22¹⁹, 38²², 71¹², 141¹).
14, 15. The petition against the enemies expresses itself in a threefold
form : *Let them be put to shame and confounded together* . . . (cp. Ps.
35⁴, ²⁶) ; how this is to be brought about is not indicated, as it is in
Ps. 35¹⁻³. The second petition is difficult to render adequately without a paraphrase ; the verb, *let them turn themselves backwards*, is often
used in the sense of apostatizing from Yahweh, see especially Ps. 78⁵⁶, ⁵⁷ ;
so that what is implied is that the enemies may become renegades to their
faith, and thus *be brought to dishonour*. Parallel with this is the third
petition, where again the verb *Let them turn away*, in one of its various
meanings, has the sense of turning from Yahweh (*e.g.*, Ps. 78⁴¹, 1 Sam.
15¹¹, 1 Kgs. 9⁶, etc.). The rendering given above is that of Ps. 70¹⁴,
which is a better parallel than that of the Hebrew word here, " let
them be desolated ", or " appalled ". The interjection *Aha, Aha* expresses the delight of the enemies at the downfall of a godly man ; it
is not for such to rejoice ; this is reserved (16) for *all that seek* Yahweh,
and magnify him. 17. The psalm closes with a final appeal to Yahweh
from his *poor and needy* servant (cp. Pss. 86¹, 109²²).

PSALM 41

THE opening verses of this psalm speak of the blessedness of the man
who helps those who are in want. An abrupt change of subject then
occurs, namely, a confession of sin, followed in the rest of the psalm
by an account of the evil words and acts of the enemies of the psalmist,
of which he has been made the victim. Another abrupt change of
subject occurs at the end of the psalm where the psalmist makes an
assertion of his integrity. There seems, thus, to be some incongruity
in the way in which the subject-matter is presented. Nevertheless,
having regard to the various emotions called forth owing to the circum-

stances in which the psalmist finds himself, this apparent incongruity
is wholly natural. The absence of a strictly logical sequence of thought,
noticeable in some other psalms of a similar nature, is a mark of realism,
and shows how very human the psalmists were. Here we have one who,
by acts of kindness to his less fortunate neighbours, had fulfilled the
commandment in spirit and in act: " Thou shalt love thy neighbour as
thyself " (Lev. 19^{18}); hence the very natural and justified feeling of a
sense of righteousness, and the conviction that God's blessing is upon
him. But then there is the fact that he is suffering sickness, and that
many enemies are seeking his harm; this calls forth the feeling that he
must in some ways have been lacking in his duty to God, in consequence
of which troubles have come upon him as a punishment for sin; and
therefore he confesses that he has sinned against God. But then,
again, in considering the altogether uncalled-for and vindictive behaviour of his enemies, he becomes convinced that they cannot be
the instruments of punishment for sin, and that he is justified in calling
upon God for help in rendering to his enemies due requital. He can,
thus, revert to the thought with which he began his psalm, and boldly
maintain that " in mine integrity thou upholdest me ".

The text has undergone some corruption, and in one or two cases
emendation is difficult and uncertain.

The general content of the psalm suggests a late post-exilic date.

The metre is, generally speaking, 4 : 4, but the textual corruptions
make this uncertain in several cases.

For the Precentor : A Psalm. David's.

1 (2). Blessed is he that considereth the poor ° and needy,° · in the day of trouble Yahweh delivereth him ;

2 (3). ° He preserveth him, and keepeth him alive,° that he may prosper ° in the land, ° and giveth him not over ° to the desire of his enemies.

3 (4). Yahweh upholdeth him on his bed of languishing, °·all his pain thou turnest to strength.°

4 (5). As for me, I said, Yahweh, be gracious unto me, heal my soul, for I have sinned against thee ;

5 (6). Mine enemies speak evil concerning me ° : " When shall he die, and his name perish ? "

6 (7). And when one cometh to see me he speaketh falsehood,° he gathereth mischief ° and uttereth it abroad.

7 (8). All that hate me whisper together against me, against me do they devise evil for me ;

8 (9). A base thing ° do they pour out ° ° against me ° : " ° Now ° that he lieth down let him rise up no more."

9 (10). Even my familiar friend whom I trusted, who ate of my bread, hath magnified himself against me.°

10 (11). But thou, Yahweh, be gracious unto me, and raise me up, that I may render to them ° requital °.

11 (12). Hereby shall I know that thou favourest me, that mine enemy exult not over me.

12 (13). As for me, in mine integrity thou upholdest me, and settest me up before thy face for ever.

13 (14). Blessed be Yahweh, the God of Israel, from henceforth now and for ever.

Amen, and Amen.

Text-critical Notes

1. Add, with G, וְאֶבְיוֹן, as demanded by the metre. 2. Om. יהוה which overloads the half-line. Read, with some MSS., יֶאְשַׁר for יְאֻשַּׁר, " he shall be happy ". Read, with G, וְלֹא יִתְּנֵהוּ for וַאַל תִּתְּנֵהוּ, " and give him not over ". 3. Read, with Gunkel, כָּל־מִכְאֹבוֹ הָסַבְכָּ לְחָיִל for כָּל־מִשְׁכָּבוֹ הָפַכְתָּ בְחָלְיוֹ, " all his bed thou turnest in his sickness "; the verb, הָפַךְ, cannot be used in this sense. 5. Read עָלַי for לִי, " to me ". 6. Om. לָבּוֹ, " his heart ", and לוֹ יֵצֵא, " to himself, he goeth forth ". But the whole verse is so overloaded that emendations, of which many are proposed by commentators, are very uncertain. 8. Read יְצֹקוּ for יָצוּק, " he poureth out "; and read, with G, בִּי for בּוֹ, " against him ". Read בַּאֲשֶׁר for וַאֲשֶׁר, " and which ". 9. Om. עָקֵב, " heel ". 10. Add עָקֵב from the preceding verse (cp. Ps. 19¹³).

1–3. In these opening verses the psalmist, in reference to himself, describes what is the lot of him *that considereth the poor and needy*; he is rewarded by *Yahweh*, who, *in the day of trouble delivereth him* (cp. Ps. 37¹⁹), and *keepeth him alive* (cp. Ps. 30³), so *that he may prosper in the land* (cp. Ps. 112²), and who protects him from *the desire of his enemies* (cp. Ps. 27¹²), and upholds him in sickness (cp. Ps. 30²). He then turns (4–11) to the experience through which he has passed, the vindictiveness of his enemies, and the sickness he had suffered ; from both of which Yahweh had delivered him. 4. *As for me, I said*; thus, he refers to the past ; at that time, when he was ill (*v.* 8), and when his enemies were maturing all kinds of evil against him, he felt that these were scourges whereby God was punishing him for sin ; so he confessed : *I have sinned against thee*, yet praying that *Yahweh* will *be gracious unto* him, and *heal* him. And then he opens his heart to God, and describes the nature of the machinations which his enemies weave in order to encompass his destruction. This is contained in *vv.* 5–8. Why it is that these enemies have risen up against him, the psalmist does not say ; it is, however, to be noted that there is no indication of their being actuated by religious motives, as, *e.g.*, in Ps. 31, or by political rancour, as, *e.g.*, in Ps. 140. It is personal animosity that prompts their action, and, as the expressions occurring in these verses show, it is by means of a magical spell that his enemies seek to compass his destruction.[1] Thus, to *speak evil*, to *speak falsehood*, to *gather mischief*, to *whisper, a base thing*, lit. " a word of Belial ", are all terms used in connexion with sorcery ; though it is granted that they also occur in a more general sense ; but the use of them all here together points rather to the former. That among his enemies there should be numbered (9) his *familiar friend* (lit. " the friend of my peace ") *whom* he had *trusted*, and who *ate of* his *bread*, was particularly distressing (this verse is

[1] See Mowinckel, *Psalmenstudien I, Awān und die individuellen Klage-psalmen*, pp. 17 ff., 105 (1921) ; and for the subject in general, Blau, *Das altjüdische Zauberwesen* (1898), Nicolsky, *Spuren magischer Formeln in den Psalmen* (1927).

quoted in John 13[18]). In his bitter indignation, aroused by the cruel
treatment to which he has been subjected, the psalmist utters the very
human, but unseemly, request (10, 11) that Yahweh will help him to
take vengeance. That ends the account of the past sufferings of the
psalmist. He then takes up his opening thought, convinced that (12)
in his *integrity* God will *uphold* him, and *set him before his face for ever*.
The last verse (13) is not part of the psalm, it is the benediction which the
final redactor of the Psalter placed at the conclusion of each of the five
books into which it was divided, in imitation of the five books of Moses.
     For the religious teaching of the book, see the introductory section.

PSALMS 42, 43

IN many MSS. these two psalms are treated as one ; that they formed a
unity originally does not admit of doubt ; the identical refrain occurs in
each (42[5, 11], 43[5]), similar thoughts appear, and the phrase in 42[9] is
repeated in 43[5]. With most commentators, therefore, we deal with
both parts as forming a single psalm.
     The psalm is one of the most touching in the Psalter ; both thought
and word, as well as the conditions under which it was composed, stamp
it as, in some respects, unique. It was written by one living far from
home in a foreign land ; why he had left his home is not told, probably
it was against his will, for the strangers among whom his lot is cast treat
him with contempt and roughness. He yearns for home. His home-
sickness is made the more bitter through a very grievous illness from
which he is suffering. Mind and body are thus plunged in agony.
Nevertheless, in sanctified self-communing he gains comfort and spiritual
strength by recalling the happy days of the past when he went with the
throng of worshippers into the house of God. But, above all, he waits
in hope and trust, for in his living faith he is confident that, by the
mercy of God, the time will yet come when he will once more enter
into the presence of God, and give him thanks for deliverance.
     As in the case of so many psalms, to assign a date is difficult ;
opinions, as so often, vary. One or two considerations may be offered
which may help in suggesting a date. That the writer's home was in
northern Palestine seems clear from his mention of " the Hermons "
(v. 6) ; and the fact that Jerusalem is never mentioned points in the
same direction ; that the writer speaks of God's " dwelling-places ", in
the plural, would mark the psalm as pre-exilic. The " house of God "
(v. 4) does not necessarily refer to the temple, cp. Bethel ; and the
expression, " the tent of the glorious one " (v. 4), which has naturally

occasioned much difficulty, is very ancient. On the other hand, " thy holy hill " (43³) cannot refer to anything but mount Zion ; we have " the hill of Samaria " in 1 Kgs. 16²⁴, but there was assuredly nothing holy about it. In view of these various points, we suggest, but quite tentatively, that this psalm was originally written by one of those carried away captive after the fall of Samaria, 721 B.C., but that, in later days, it was used, and slightly worked over.

The metre is, with quite a few exceptions, 3 : 2.

1.　　　　For the Precentor : Maskil.　　Of the Sons of Qorah.

1 (2). As the hart panteth / ° for ° water-brooks,
So panteth my soul / for thee, O God.

2 (3). My soul thirsteth for God, / the living God ;
When shall I come ° and behold ° / the face of God ?

3 (4). My tears have been for me my food / day and night,
° While they say ° to me all the day : / " Where is thy God ? "

4 (5). These things I recall, and pour out / my soul upon me :
How I went ° into the tent ° ° of the Glorious One °, / into the house of God,
With the sound of joy and praise, / ° the clamour of the pilgrims °.

5 (6). Why art thou bowed down, my soul, / and groanest within me ?
Wait for God, for I will yet thank him, / ° the help of my countenance, 6 (7) and my God °.
My soul is bowed down within me, / therefore I think of thee
From the land of Jordan and the Hermons, / from the hill of Mizar.

7 (8). Deep calleth unto deep / at the sound of ° their rushing ° ;
All their waves and their billows / have passed over me.

8 (9). In the day-time ° I watch for Yahweh °, / ° and for his mercy at night ° ;
Within me (my) ° meditation ° is a prayer / ° to the living God ° ;

9 (10). I say unto God, my Rock : / " Why hast thou forgotten me ?
Wherefore go I mourning, / while the enemy oppresseth ? "

10 (11). ° Like ° a shattering in my bones,
Mine enemies revile me,
While they say unto me all the day : / " Where is thy God ? "

11 (12). Why art thou bowed down, my soul, / and ° groanest within me ?
Wait for God, for I will yet thank him, / the ° help ° of my countenance, and my God.

XLIII.

1. Judge me, O God,
and champion my cause,
against an ungodly nation,
From men of deceit / and injustice deliver r:..
2. For thou art the God of my strength, / why hast thou cast me off ?
Wherefore go I mourning / while the enemy oppresseth ?
3. O send out thy light and thy truth, / let them lead me,
Let them bring me to thy holy hill, / and into thy dwelling-places,
4. That I may go unto the altar of God, / to the God of ° my joy,°
° That I may rejoice ° and praise thee with harp,
O God, my God.
5. Why art thou bowed down, my soul, / and° groanest within me ?
Wait for God, for I will yet thank him, / the ° help ° of my countenance, and my God.

Text-critical Notes

1. Read אֶל (lit. "unto ") for עַל, "upon " or " by ". 2. Read, with some MSS. and S, וְאֵרָאֶה for וְאֵרָאֶה, "and be seen ", or " appear ". 3. Read, as in *v.* 10, בְּאָמְרָם for בֶּאֱמֹר, "while one saith ". 4. Read בְּסֹךְ for בְּסָךְ; and cp. G (see Ps. 8¹⁽²⁾) for אֶדַּדֵּם, " I led them "; and הֲמוֹן חוֹגְגִים for אַדִּיר, "a multitude keeping holy-day ". 5. Read יְשׁוּעֹת פָּנַי וֵאלֹהָי for חֲמוֹן חוֹגֵג, יְשׁוּעֹת פָּנָיו : אֱלֹהָי, " the helps of his countenance. O my God ". 7. Read צַוָּארֶיךָ for יַד ——, " thy rushing ". 8. Read, with Gunkel, יְצַוֶּה אֶצְפֶּה בַּיהוה for יְהוה, " Yahweh commandeth "; and וְהַסְּדוֹ בַּלַּיְלָה for חַסְדּוֹ וּבַלַּיְלָה, " his mercy and in the night "; and (cp. G) שִׂיחָה for שִׁירָה, " song "; and לְאֵל חַי (see *v.* 2) for לְאֵל חַיָּי, " to the God of my life ". 10. Read בְּ for בִּ, " in ". 11. Om. מַה־ (see *v.* 6); and read יְשׁוּעַת for עֵת ——. xliii. 4. Read שִׂמְחָתִי for שִׂמְחַת. Read וְאָגִילָה for גִּילִי " my joy ". 5. Read as in xlii. 5, 11.

1. With a picture as graphic as it is realistic, the psalmist, without preamble, pours out the yearning of his heart for communion with God : *As the hart panteth for water-brooks, so panteth my soul for thee, O God.* The simile is immensely expressive when one pictures a hart parched with thirst, gasping for the one thing that can give relief, the water-brooks, wherein flowed the running or " living " water, as it was called (*e.g.*, Lev. 14⁵, ⁶). 2. And the *soul* of the psalmist *thirsteth for the living God.* The way in which his " thirst " must be assuaged he puts in the form of a question : *When shall I come and behold the face of God?* which at the same time expresses a longing. The point of these words is, not that his " thirst " will be allayed by his appearing before God, but by his beholding God ; it is the psalmist, athirst, who seeks God. The Hebrew as now pointed can, it is true, be translated : " When shall I come and appear (lit. " be seen ") before God ? " but in the Hebrew it is bad grammar, and cannot possibly be original. The present pointing, involving a passive instead of an active sense (" when shall I be seen " instead of " when shall I see "), was put in for the purpose of counteracting an erroneous conception of the Almighty ; the same alteration has been made in Deut. 16¹⁶ and Isa. 1¹². In earlier times it was believed that God could be seen, Gen. 32³⁰, cp. Judg. 6²², ²³, 13²², Isa. 6⁵, and especially Exod. 33²⁰, where the words are put into the mouth of God : " Thou canst not see my face ; for man shall not see me and live ", implying the possibility in the mind of Moses of seeing the face of God. This belief was expressed by the psalmist, but, with the development of more spiritual ideas concerning God, the need of altering the sense of the words under consideration was recognized. 3. The thought of being far from God, in a foreign land, fills the psalmist with bitter sorrow, so that his *tears* are to him as *food*, a hyperbolic way of expressing the depth of grief ; and this grief is aggravated by the mockery of those about him : *Where is thy God?* they ask him. 4, 5. Under these circumstances there is, at any rate, one thing that can give him comfort : he *recalls* the past in self-com-

muning, or, as he expresses it: *I pour out my soul upon me,* meaning that he presents to himself the flood of happy memories of long ago. He was wont to go into *the tent of the Glorious One,* that is, *the house of God,* with *joy* in the company *of pilgrims.* The expression *tent* for the house of God is archaic; it is used, in the first instance, of the tabernacle in the wilderness (Exod. 26$^{9\,n.}$, 39$^{32\,n.}$), but also of other places of worship (Ps. 78^{60}, 1 Chron. 16^1, 2 Chron. 1^4), so that, unlike Ps. 76^2, the temple in Jerusalem is by no means necessarily meant. The expression " the Glorious One " (*'Addir*), represents an emendation suggested by the Septuagint, as the Hebrew text can hardly be correct; it is true that, as applied to God, its occurrence is rare; nevertheless, it does occur (Isa. 10^{34}, 33^1, cp. Ps. 8^1). These thoughts so cheer the psalmist in his sorrow that, in the words of the thrice repeated refrain, he reproaches himself for being so downcast; he will yet be able to *thank* God for deliverance; and he thinks again of his homeland, *the land of Jordan*; the river rises to the north of the various Hermon peaks (hence " the Hermons ") and flows slightly eastwards round the foot of these; hence the expression *the land of Jordan,* though it also applies to the whole of Palestine. The locality of *the hill of Mizar* is not known.

From these thoughts the psalmist turns abruptly to his perilous position. **7.** He has been brought very near to death, and this he expresses in realistic, but poetical, language; he has been engulfed in the waters of the underworld; the use of *Tehom* for " Deep " proves that this was in the mind of the psalmist, similarly as in the psalm in Jon. 2, where Jonah speaks of the waters which compassed him, and of " Tehom round about " (*vv.* 5, 6). **8–11.** Nevertheless, his faith in Yahweh is not shaken; his thought of God becomes a prayer, *within me my meditation is a prayer to the living God*; even though he utters his plaint because God seems to have forgotten him, and the mental anguish caused by the *reviling* of his *enemies* is like *a shattering* in his *bones*—even so, in self-adjuration he repeats his refrain; his soul need not be bowed down, for he will yet thank God for deliverance. **43^1.** Another abrupt change of thought then finds utterance; in his conviction that God is on his side, the psalmist experiences a sense of uprightness, so that he can boldly appeal to God to uphold him against his enemies: *Judge me, O God, and champion my cause against an ungodly nation*; this last is not to be understood in a literal sense; it is one of several somewhat exaggerated modes of expression which occur several times in the same psalm. The final verses (2–5) of the psalm illustrate the alternating emotions which in turn dominate the psalmist's being: firm faith, *thou art the God of my strength*; the puzzled thought that God seems to have forsaken him, *why hast thou cast me off?*; then the prayer for divine guidance, *O send out thy light and thy truth, let them lead me*; followed by the joyful looking forward to

praise God with harp; and, finally, the reiteration of the refrain proclaiming the certitude that the time will soon come when he will *thank*
God for deliverance.

It is impossible not to recognize the extreme naturalness of these
conflicting emotions of one in the position in which the psalmist found
himself; the outpouring of his inner self on the part of this saintly
singer which is here presented is as instructive as it is touching.

Religious Teaching

There are two directions in which the religious element of this psalm
is particularly impressive. The earnest longing to be in communion
with God, so uniquely but realistically expressed, is, in various degrees,
characteristic of most of the psalmists, and will come before us again
and again. Of this, therefore, we shall say no more here. But the
other subject, though occurring sometimes elsewhere in the *Psalms*, is
nowhere presented with quite the same open-hearted candour and
straightforwardness as here. We mean the act of religious self-
communing. In its most pointed form this comes out in the thrice-
repeated refrain, but it occurs also in one or two other verses (4, 8).
The psalmist addresses his soul as though it were distinct from himself,
and yet, almost in the same breath, identifies himself with it. He takes
his soul to task for its despondency, but immediately protests his own
faith in God. It is this self-communing, when honestly and devoutly
practised, which is one of the most necessary and helpful elements in
personal religion; and it could not be more simply, yet instructively,
illustrated than in the psalm before us. Religious difficulties and problems of faith have confronted men in all ages; in many ways help may
be afforded, and light shed in dark places; but ultimately, under God,
the believer must unflinchingly commune with his individual self;
he must be the final arbiter; that is the condition of the divinely given
free-will. The responsibility is great, but it may not be shirked; and
the psalmist teaches so beautifully how courageous self-communing
issues; there may be some waiting, but assuredly in the end divine
grace will help.

PSALM 44

THIS psalm presents us with the picture of the mental struggle of one
who through the calamity which has overcome him and his people
seems to have somewhat lost his spiritual balance; for what is said in
the latter part of it sounds like a rebuke to the Almighty. The redeem-
ing quality of the psalm lies in the psalmist's ardent belief that God can

help in time of trouble; but this belief is marred by an irreverent approach to the Almighty which is without parallel in the Psalter. That the psalm is not used in the worship of the Synagogue is comprehensible. Various indications point to the psalm having been written in late post-exilic times. It is held by some commentators that it belongs to Maccabæan times, and v. 22, e.g., is quoted as pointing to a religious persecution; but to isolate a verse in this way without taking the context into consideration may lead to erroneous conclusions. One has but to read, e.g., vv. 11–14, and compare what is said in them with the account of the Maccabæan struggle given in 1 Maccabees to see how impossible it is to regard this psalm as belonging to the Maccabæan period. At what time during this period could it be said that the Jews were scattered amidst the nations, or that they were a byword among the nations? But for the short-lived success of the Syrians, within quite a restricted area, at the beginning of the struggle, the Maccabæan wars were, with one or two set-backs, a series of Jewish triumphs. Even at the initial catastrophe, so far from there being any question of succumbing to the nations, Mattathias says: " And take ye unto you all the doers of the Law, and avenge the wrong of your people. Render a recompense to the Gentiles, and take heed to the commandments of the Law " (1 Macc. 2[67, 68]). Whatever episode it was to which our psalm refers, it could not have been to that of the Maccabæan struggle.[1] It must be remembered that, owing to lack of details, our knowledge of Jewish history during the early part of the Greek period is limited.

The metre, with the exception of v. 21, is uniformly 3 : 3.

1.   *For the Precentor : Of the Sons of Qorah. Maskil.*

1 (2). O God, with our ears have we heard,   our fathers have told unto us,

The work that thou didst in their days,   in the days of old 2 (3) ° by thy hand.°

Nations ° thou didst drive out,° and plantedst them in,   didst afflict peoples, ° and settle them down °;

3 (4). For not by their sword did they possess the land,   and not was their arm victorious for them;

But thy right-hand ° and thy strong arm,°   and the light of thy countenance, for thou didst favour them.

4 (5). Thou art my King and ° my God,°   ° thou commandest ° the victories of Jacob;

5 (6). Through thee do we push back our adversaries,   and in thy name do we tread down those that rise up against us.

6 (7). For not in my bow do I trust,   my sword doth not gain me the victory;

7 (8). But thou makest us victorious over our foes,   and bringest to shame them that hate us.

8 (9). We praise ° God ° every day,   to thy name will we give thanks evermore. Selah.

9 (10). But thou hast cast us off, and brought us to shame,   and thou wentest not forth with our hosts;

10 (11). Thou madest us turn back from the foe,   and they that hate us took spoil for themselves;

11 (12). Thou gavest us for food like sheep,   ° amidst the nations ° hast thou scattered us;

---

[1] On the whole question of Maccabæan psalms, see pp. 67 ff.

R

12 (13). Thou hast sold thy people °for nought,° — and madest no profit by their prices.

13 (14). °We are become ° a reproach to our neighbours, — a scorn and derision to those around us ;

14 (15). Thou hast made us a byword among the nations, — a wagging of the head among the peoples.

15 (16). Every day is my dishonour before me, — and shame ° hath covered ° my face,

16 (17). Because of the voice of the scorner and reviler, — because of the presence of the enemy and avenger.

17 (18). All this is come upon us, yet have we not forgotten thee, — neither have we dealt falsely in thy covenant ;

18 (19). Our heart is not turned backward, — nor ° our step ° declined from thy way ;

19 (20). Yet °hast thou thrust us ° into the place of ° dragons,° — and hast covered us with darkness.

20 (21). Had we forgotten the name of our God, — and stretched out our hands to a strange-god,

21 (22). Would not God have searched out this ? For he knoweth the secrets of the heart.

22 (23). Yea, for thy sake are we slain all the day, — we are accounted as sheep for slaughter.

23 (24). Awake, °Yahweh,° wherefore sleepest thou ? ° — arise, cast us not off for ever !

24 (25). Wherefore hidest thou thy face, — and forgettest our affliction and oppression ?

25 (26). For our soul is bowed down to the dust, — our belly cleaveth to the ground.

26 (27). Arise as a help for us, — and redeem us for thy love's sake.

Text-critical Notes

2. Read, for the rhythm's sake, בְּיָדְךָ for יָדְךָ אַתָּה, "thou, thy hand ". Read גֵּרַשְׁתָּ (cp. Deut. 33²⁷) for הוֹרַשְׁתָּ, "thou didst cause to inherit ". Read, with several commentators, וַתִּשְׁתָּלֵם, lit. "and thou didst transplant them " (cp. Ezek. 19¹³). 3. Read, for the rhythm's sake, עֻזְּךָ וּזְרוֹעַ, as in Ps. 89¹⁰, for וּזְרוֹעֲךָ, "and thine arm ". 4. Read, with GS, וֵאלֹחַי for אֱלֹהִים, "God ". Read, with GS, מִצְוֶה for צַוֵּה, "he commanded ". 8. Read בֵּאלֹהִים for בֵּאלֹהִים, "in God ". 11. Read בֵּין גּוֹיִם for וּבַגּוֹיִם, "and among the nations ", for the rhythm's sake. 12. For the phrase בְּלֹא־הוֹן, see GK 152a, Rem. i. 13. Read הֵיבֵנוּ, as in Ps. 79⁴, for תְּשִׂימֵנוּ, "thou makest us ", the same word occurs in the next verse. 15. Read כִּסְּתַה for כִּסְּרַנִי, "hath covered me ". 18. Read, with some MSS., אֲשֻׁרֵנוּ for אֲשֻׁרֵינוּ, "our steps ", as the verb is in the sing. 19. Read, with Budde, הִדַּחְתָּנוּ for דִכִּיתָנוּ, "thou hast crushed us ". Read, with some MSS., תַּנִּים for תַּנִּים, "jackals ". 23. Read, with many MSS., יהוה, and om. אֲדֹנָי, "O Lord ".

1–3. These introductory verses set forth the reason why divine help is to be looked for in view of the perilous circumstances in which the people find themselves, and which are described in what follows. The psalmist, identifying himself with his people, records how they had *heard* what their *fathers* had *told* them of the *work* which *in the days of old* had been wrought *by the hand* of God. The reference is, of course, to the conquest of Canaan, when God *drove out nations*, and *planted them*, *i.e.*, the fathers, *in the land*. The history as recorded in the book of *Joshua* is envisaged rather than that of *Judges*. But, as the psalmist goes on to say, the possession of the land was not gained by their *sword*, nor was it *their arm* which won them the victory; it was by God's *right-hand* and by his *strong arm*, and by *the light* of his *countenance*, because his *favour* was with them. For the expression *the light of thy countenance*, meaning the sign of divine favour, cp. Ps. 4⁶. Two matters in these verses demand brief notice. When it is said: *With our ears have we heard, and our fathers have told us*, we have a clear reference to the oral tradition, the handing down of which is enjoined in Deut. 6²⁰⁻²³, and which is kept up to the present day by Jews at the annual *Seder* Festival, *i.e.*, the Home-Festival part of the Passover feast. The recounting of past history by word of mouth, rather than by the reading of the written word, was necessitated in days when copies of the Scriptures would not be in the hands of many. One result of this, however, was that a number of historical details would be passed over; so that, and this is the second matter to be noted in these verses, nothing is said of the long-drawn-out struggles whereby the promised land was at long last gained. That the possession of the land was imputed to the divine act alone witnesses to a very living faith, which is seen also in the *Deuteronomy* passage referred to; but the history shows that human action, too, was demanded. 4-8. Just as in the days of old trust was placed in divine help, so now faith in God is expressed: *Thou art my King and my God, that command-est the victories of Jacob* (for " Jacob " used in reference to the whole people, cp., *e.g.*, Exod. 19³, Am. 3¹³, though the phrase is usually " the house of Jacob "). The personal note struck by the psalmist, *For not in my bow do I trust . . .* , when he is otherwise speaking in the name of his people, is striking; it witnesses to his sense of unity with his people; this is a *trait* frequently occurring in the psalms. A realistic picture is envisaged where it is said: *Through thee do we push back our adversaries*; it is doubtless taken from Deut. 33¹⁷: " And his horns are the horns of the wild-ox, with them shall he push peoples, all of them . . . " (cp. 1 Kgs. 22¹¹); and just as the wild-ox tramples upon those whom he has " pushed back ", so do the people *tread down them that rise up against* them. This is done *in thy name*, *i.e.*, by invoking the divine name, see Ps. 20¹. In this faith *praise* and *thanks* are daily offered to *thy name* (cp. Ps. 34¹⁻⁴).

So far, the psalmist has been recalling past history upon which is based the conviction that divine help is ever-present. From this he turns (9–16) to contemplate the melancholy condition in which the people find themselves at the present time. A battle has been fought, and lost; and this is ascribed to the absence of the divine presence: *thou wentest not forth with our hosts* (see, on the contrary, Ps. 60¹²); indeed, the defeat of his people the psalmist believes to be directly due to God: *thou madest us turn back from the foe*; this naïve conception of God as the God of battles was, of course, world-wide, though held in regard to various gods; and it appears often in the Old Testament

(e.g., Judg. 4^{14}, 2 Sam. 5^{24}). But further, in his desperate frame of
mind the psalmist goes on to express thoughts in reference to the
Almighty which are of an unseemly character : *Thou gavest us for food
like sheep,* as though the people were, in the sight of God, of no more
value than sheep (cp. *v.* 22) ; God has *sold* them for *nought,* and has
made *no profit by their prices* ; the verse contains a parallelism, and the
thought is that of a slave-dealer who has made a bad bargain ; but the
implication is that although God has favoured the enemies of his people,
he has not thereby gained any who will acknowledge him. Such
irreverent sarcasm is without parallel in the psalms, and must be
ascribed to the writer's despairing pessimism, engendered by the present
apparently hopeless conditions. The people had been reduced to a
position of deep humiliation, to describe which expressions are literally
piled up : *a reproach* to their *neighbours,* friendly countries are meant ;
a scorn and derision (cp. Ps. 79^{4}) ; a *byword* (lit. " a proverb ", cp. Ps.
69^{11}, Job 17^{6}) ; *a wagging of the head* (cp. Jer. 18^{16}). Then once more
(15, 16) the psalmist identifies himself with his people : *dishonour* and
shame are his lot, because of the reproaches and revilings hurled against
him, for *the enemy and avenger* is before him (cp. in general Ps. 89 $^{38-51}$).
The unseemly tone of the psalmist's complaint is increased by the
assertion of injured innocence (17–19) ; unlike the far more fitting
attitude of many other psalmists when in trouble, whose sense of unworthiness bows their head in humility, we have here the claim of
righteousness, and the implication that God has not been dealing fairly
with his people : they *have not forgotten* God, it is claimed, *nor dealt
falsely in thy covenant, our heart is not turned backward, i.e.,* from God,
nor our step declined from thy way ; yet in spite of all this vaunted
righteousness he has *thrust* his people *into the place of dragons, i.e.,* as
though God were treating his people as he treated Tiamat and her
brood, identified with the sea, and conceived of as the embodiment of
wickedness (cp. Isa. 51$^{9, 10}$), and *covered* them *with darkness,* lit. " the
shadow of death " (see note on 23^{4}), cp. Job 38$^{16, 17}$, where the sea is
parallel with the shadow of death. 20–22. The further plea of self-
justification is put forward by the claim that the people had not forgotten God by appealing to any *strange god* ; on the contrary, *for thy
sake we are slain all the day.* 23–25. The height of irreverence is
reached when the psalmist dares to say : *Arise, Yahweh, why sleepest
thou ?* We are reminded of Elijah's words in reference to Baal, when he
mockingly cried to the Baal-worshippers : " Cry aloud ; for he is a
god, either he is musing, or he is gone aside, or he is on a journey, or
peradventure he sleepeth and must be awaked ! " (1 Kgs. 18^{27}). Only
at the very end of this part of the psalm is there a sign of a more fitting
frame of mind, when the psalmist appeals to God for his love's sake.

Religious Teaching

From what has been said it is clear that the religious teaching of this psalm is largely of a negative character. It witnesses doubtless to a very real belief in the divine guidance of history, and to a reliance on God's help, which is in the best spirit. But there are other elements which betray a very undeveloped conception of the divine Personality. The thought of Yahweh himself taking part in battle by going forth with Israel's hosts is an antique way of conceiving of the manner in which divine guidance was accorded on such occasions (see Judg. 4¹⁴, 2 Sam. 5²⁴). It may be urged that in our psalm this is merely a poetical mode of expression, not meant literally, as would have been the case in earlier days, and that the psalmist is echoing ancient traditional belief without actually sharing it himself. That is probably the case. Other passages naturally sound unfitting to our ears ; the idea of God bartering with the people's enemies, and the gibe that nothing is gained by the bargain, the urging of God to wake up from sleep, and the implied reproach conveyed in the words : " Wherefore hidest thou thy face, and forgettest our affliction and oppression ? " Such thoughts doubtless strike us as unseemly ; but there are two considerations here which must not be lost sight of. In the first place, the psalmist's heart is overwhelmed with grief at the desperate plight in which his people found themselves ; that this should have occasioned some temporary loss of the sense of proportion is so intensely human as to be pardonable. But still more to be urged is the fact that just this very condition of his suffering people was so incomprehensible to him ; the first part of the psalm has shown what God's power was, and his solicitude for his people which had always been in evidence ; how, therefore, was the present state of affairs to be accounted for ? The people had done their duty to their God, they had not forgotten him, they had not turned backward from him, nor had they declined from his way. What, therefore, does it all mean ? The psalmist is utterly puzzled. His mental condition reveals the same bewildered perplexity as that felt by Job in his words : " Show me wherefore thou contendest with me ; is it good unto thee that thou shouldest oppress, that thou shouldest despise the work of thine hands, and shine upon the counsel of the wicked ? " (Job 10², ³) ; and again : " I will speak in the anguish of my spirit, I will complain in the bitterness of my soul. Am I a sea or a sea-monster, that thou settest a watch over me ? " (Job. 7¹²). Job was a righteous man, faithful to his God, and yet he was afflicted with sore sickness and poverty ! He cannot understand it ; it is wholly incomprehensible to him. And so with our psalmist. The theology in which he had been brought up had taught him that God upholds the righteous, and punishes the wicked ; and here were facts of experience

in glaring contrast with this! Who dare fail to sympathize with him in
his perplexity ?   In spite of all, his faith did not give way, and his final
words are a prayer to him in whom he believed : " Arise as a help to us,
and redeem us for thy love's sake."

PSALM 45

THAT this psalm, if it may be so called, found a place in the Psalter
is to be explained on grounds somewhat similar to those which ultimately permitted the admission of the *Song of Songs* into the Canon ;
though, unlike that, it is purely secular in origin, but was, in later
days, interpreted in a Messianic sense by the Jewish Church. The
king, who plays the leading part, was conceived of as representing the
Messiah, and the queen, as the princess was about to become, as the
Jewish people of the Messianic era. That this interpretation was
taken over, and adapted, by the early Christian community is shown
by Hebr. 1 [8, 9] to have been the case.
    The poem offers an illuminating picture of a royal wedding in
ancient Palestine. A religious note is sounded, it is true, when the
singer assures the royal bridegroom of God's continued blessing on
him, and designates him as God's chosen one. This would be confidently assumed, since the king was, in a real sense, looked upon as
God's representative among the people ; so much so that the king is
actually addressed by the divine title. This it doubtless was which
in later days, when the early conception of kingship was a thing of
the past, prompted the Messianic interpretation.
    Opinions differ as to who the royal personage may have been in
whose honour this poem was composed ; as, however, the only known
case of an Israelite king marrying a " daughter of Tyre " is that of
Ahab marrying Jezebel (1 Kgs. 16[51]), there is a strong argument in
favour of the contention that this is the king in question. If this is
the case, then we have here one of the earlier of the psalms ; Ahab
reigned 874–852 B.C. ; the fact that it contains several late words
merely points to its having been worked over in subsequent periods.
To its early date, and to the vicissitudes of transmission must be
ascribed the corrupt state of the text. In several cases emendation
presents very considerable difficulty ; in comparing the various
attempts at reconstruction we are impressed by the often convincing
suggestions offered by Gunkel, to whom we are largely indebted.
    In spite of textual difficulties there seems little doubt but that the
metre is four beats to a line ; in various cases the lines are self-contained, so that we have doubts as to a 4 : 4 metre. A 2 : 2 metre is
not excluded, but some authorities would disagree here

1.   *For the Precentor : Set to " Lilies ".*
            Belonging to the Sons of Qorah.   A Maskil.   A Song of Loves.

1 (2).   My heart is astir with goodly thought ;
            I will sing, even I, ° my song ° for the king—
            My tongue is the pen of a skilful scribe— :

2 (3).   " ° Fairer art thou ° than the sons of men,
            Poured-forth is grace upon thy lips ;
            Therefore hath God blest thee for ever.

3 (4).   Gird thee thy sword on ° thy side °, O mighty one ;
            ° With thy pomp and splendour be-mantle thy loins °,

4 (5).   For the cause of truth, ° and for righteousness' sake °.
            And may thy right-hand ° show forth ° terrible things ;

5 (6).   May thine arrows so sharp ° strike-with-fear ° the peoples,
            ° May the heart of thine enemies falter, O king °.

6 (7).   Thy throne, O God, is for ever and ever,
            A sceptre of right is the sceptre of thy rule,

7 (8).   Thou hast loved justice and hated wickedness,
            Therefore hath God, thy God, anointed thee,
            With the oil of gladness ° in the presence of ° thy companions.

8 (9).   Myrrh and aloes ° are all thy garments ;
            ° Harps of ivory,°—° their strings ° give thee joy ;

9 (10).   ° The daughter of kings cometh forth to greet thee °,
            A queen at thy right-hand in gold-gear from Ophir."

10 (11).   " Hearken, O daughter °, incline thine ear,
            ° Forget ° thy people and thy father's house ;

11 (12).   ° Let him desire ° thy beauty, for he is thy lord.

12 (13).   ° Let him kneel before thee, Tyre's-daughter °, with gifts,
            Let the wealthiest of ° peoples ° give honour to thee,

13 (14).   ° Give-thee-homage with corals in settings of gold °."

14 (15).   ° Clad in gay-garments are the maidens behind her,
            Her companions who lead her before the king,

15 (16).   Who conduct her with gladness and joy to the palace °.

16 (17).   " In place of thy fathers thou shalt have sons,
            Thou shalt make them princes in all the earth.

17 (18).   I will keep-in-memory thy name in all generations,
            Therefore the peoples will praise thee for ever °."

Text-critical Notes

1. Read מַעֲשָׂי (lit. " my work ", see exegetical note) for מַעֲשַׂי, " my works ".
2. Read, with GS, יְפִי יָפִיתָ (lit. " beauty, thou art beautiful ") for יָפְיָפִיתָ, an anomalous form. 3. Read, with GS, יְרֵכֶךָ for יְרֵךָ, " side ". Read, with Gunkel, בְּהוֹדְךָ וַהֲדָרְךָ חֲלָצֶיךָ כַרְבֵּל (for כַּרְבֵּל see 1 Chron. 15¹⁷) for : הוֹדְךָ וַהֲדָרְךָ צְלַח רְכַב, " thy pomp and thy splendour, and thy splendour, prosper, ride on ". 4. Read וְעַנְוָה־צֶּדֶק for וְיֵעַן הַצֶּדֶק, " and meekness, righteousness ". Read וְתֹרֵא for וְתוֹרֶךָ, " and may . . . teach thee ". 5. Read, with Gunkel, עַמִּים תַּחְתֶּיךָ for עַמִּים תַּחְתֶּיךָ, " peoples under thee " ; and read, following Gunkel in part : יִפֹּל בְּלֵב אוֹיְבֵי הַמֶּלֶךְ for יִפֹּל לֵב אוֹיְבֵי הַמֶּלֶךְ, " may the enemies of the king falter (lit. " fall ") in heart ". 7. Read לִפְנֵי for מִ, " more than ". 8. Om. קְצִיעוֹת, " cassia ", which overloads the line. Read כְּלִי שֵׁן (lit. " instruments of . . .") for מִן־הֵיכְלֵי שֵׁן, " from palaces of ivory ". מִנִּי is an abbreviated form of מִנֶּנּוּ, see GK 87 f. 9. Read נִצְּבָה בַת מְלָכִים לִקְרָאתֶךָ for בְּנוֹת מְלָכִים בְּיִקְּרוֹתֶיךָ נִצְּבָה, " the daughters of kings are among thy honourable women, she stands ". 10. Om. וּרְאִי, " and see ", which overloads the line. Read שִׁכְחִי omitting the וְ. 11. Read יִתְאָו omitting the וְ. Om. הַמֶּלֶךְ which overloads the line. 12. Read וְהִשְׁתַּחֲוִי־לוֹ for וְיִשְׁתַּחֲוֶה לָךְ בַּת־צֹר, " and worship him and the daughter of Tyre ". Read עַמִּים for עַם, " people ". 13-15. In place of the corrupt text of these verses we have adopted Gunkel's emendation :

13. יְכַבְּדוּךָ פְּנִינִים מִשְׁבְּצוֹת זָהָב
14. לִבְגֹשֶׁת רִקְמוֹת בְּתוּלוֹת אַחֲרֶיהָ
     רֵעוֹתֶיהָ מְבִיאוֹת לָהּ לַמֶּלֶךְ
15. תּוּבַלְנָה בְּשִׂמְחַת וָגִיל בְּהֵיכָל :

17. Om. וָעֶד, " and ever ", which overloads the line.

For the title, see p. 16.

1. The poet begins his poem with some introductory words telling of his heart's impulse to sing in honour of the king : *My heart is astir,* lit. " bubbling over ", *with goodly thought,* lit. " a good word ", or " matter " ; but the Hebrew word *dābār* has various meanings according to the context in which it stands ; *thought,* rather than " word " is suggested here because it comes from the *heart,* the seat of the emotions and thoughts, according to the Hebrew conception. The song which this court-poet *sings,* lit. " utters ", is *for the king, i.e.,* in honour of the king. *My song* is lit. " my work ", but this word, too, has various meanings, *e.g.,* in Exod. 26[1] it has the sense of " a work of art " ; so that in its present context it can be rendered *song.* His *tongue* is ready to pour forth words just as *a skilful scribe* (cp. Ezra 7[6]) writes copious words on a papyrus-roll with his *pen.* 2. The king is then addressed. The poet begins by extolling his personal beauty ; in saying that his royal master is *fairer than the sons of men,* it is implied that he is of super-human, *i.e.,* divine, beauty ; that this is not merely exaggerated adulation in the Oriental mode (cp. Acts 12[22]), is seen from *v.* 6, where the king is directly addressed as " God ". Further, the poet says : *Poured forth is grace upon thy lips* (cp. Prov. 22[11], though the text there is uncertain) ; the previous line would suggest that what is implied is that the king's utterances are divinely inspired, and thus a divine attribute. But the divinity ascribed to the king (see further under *v.* 6) is, of course, of a wholly different nature from that of God Himself, from whom whatever is divine in the king is der ved ; so that the virtues he possesses are all the outcome of God's blessing on him : *Therefore hath God blest thee for ever* ; the last expression is not to be taken literally, but must be understood in the sense of " long-continuance ", as, *e.g.,* in Pss. 22[26], 61[7], cp. Am. 1[11]. 3–5. The text of these verses is very corrupt, but the general sense is clear. The poet extols the king as victorious in battle ; this is natural enough since leadership in war was a primary duty of the king in ancient Israel (cp. 1 Sam. 8[20]) ; but the words are in reference to the future, for, as a young man about to marry, the king in question is hardly likely yet to have fought battles. Nevertheless, he is addressed as a *mighty one, i.e.,* in battle, and bidden to *gird on* his *sword.* But the king is mighty in more than a merely physical sense, for the royal robes in which he is *be-mantled* symbolize *truth and righteousness,* of which he is the champion. Then the poet comes back to the earlier thought, and expresses the hope, equivalent to conviction, that in battle the *sharp arrows* of the royal warrior may *strike his enemies with fear,* and cause them to lose heart. 6, 7. The poet now addresses the king directly as *God,* and says his throne is to last *for ever and ever,* to be understood again in the sense of a long time. The context (7),

which says, *therefore hath God anointed thee*, shows that in *v.* 6 the words, *thy throne, O God*, are addressed to the king.　If not precisely paralleled elsewhere, there are many passages which suggest the idea of deity in the king; in Isa. 9⁵, *e.g.*, the Messianic king is called *'El gibbôr*, " God of a hero "; something very near regarding the king as divine occurs in 2 Sam. 7¹⁴, 14¹⁷, ²⁰, and then there are such passages as Pss. 2⁷, 89²⁶, ²⁷, where the king is spoken of as Yahweh's son.　There can be little doubt that just as in Egypt and Babylonia, so in ancient Israel, the king was regarded as divine (see p. 49).　But this conception did not, even in the minds of the prophets, endanger belief in Yahweh as the only God for Israel, because in whatever sense divinity was believed to be attached to the king, it was, and could be, only by the will and act of Yahweh, that this was brought about.　Hence, his *sceptre*, the symbol of kingship, is one of *right*, or " equity " (cp. Ps. 67⁴, where the same word is used in reference to the rule of God), he has *loved justice and hated wickedness*, and his God has *anointed* him (cp. Ps. 89²⁰, 1 Sam. 10¹) with the oil of gladness (cp. Isa. 61³), *i.e.*, the oil that gives joy or exultation; the anointing of the king takes place *in the presence of* his *companions*, cp. 1 Sam. 16¹³ : " Then Samuel took the horn of oil and anointed him in the midst of his brethren."　The poet then (8, 9) concludes his words to the king, recalling how, in preparation for the joyous ceremony, his garments had been perfumed so abundantly that he can say, *myrrh and aloes are all thy garments*.　The text of the line which follows offers some difficulty; the Hebrew reads : " From palaces of ivory (cp. 1 Kgs. 22³⁹, Am. 3¹⁵, " house of ivory ") strings rejoice thee ", which is a curious phrase—in any case it could be a question of only one palace—and implies that the sound of the strings reached the king from within; but obviously on such an occasion as this the music would take place in the presence of the king; for the emendation *harps* (lit. " instruments ") *of ivory*, we are indebted to Gunkel; the Hebrew words for " palaces " and " instruments " are very similar.　And, finally, the poet points to the royal bride, *the daughter of kings*, in reference to a long line of kings, who has *come forth to greet him*, and now stands in the place of honour at the king's *right-hand*; a *queen*, apparelled in *gold-gear from Ophir*.　This leads the poet to address the royal bride.

10–13.　The import of his opening words here may strike us as hardly becoming, considering the respective positions of the singer and the royal personage addressed; to this there is, however, a twofold reply : the court-poet would naturally be one who was held in high honour, and who could, therefore, speak in terms which in the mouth of anyone else would be unseemly; that he was also privileged as being comparatively advanced in years may be gathered from the words : *Hear, O daughter*.　But more important is the fact that he is expressing the thoughts of the king in saying: *Forget thy people and thy father's house*; and especially when, seeing the queenly bride somewhat abashed by the royal bridegroom's ardent glances, he adds: *Let him desire thy beauty, for he is thy lord.* Having, then, spoken, as it were, on behalf of the king, he goes on to offer words of homage on his own part to the queen; let her deign to accept the royal gifts, and the costly offerings from foreign lands. The text of the next two verses, 14, 15, is very corrupt; for our rendering we are indebted to Gunkel's emendation, though even this does not entirely overcome all the difficulties; presumably the poet's words are addressed in-directly to the maids-of-honour in attendance on the queen. Finally (16, 17), the poet turns once more to the king, and, in ancient Oriental fashion, which sounds a little indelicate to our ears, heralds the advent of the royal progeny, whom the king will *make princes in all the earth*, a poetical exaggeration quite natural to the Oriental. In his closing words the poet glories in the thought that by means of his song *the peoples will praise* the king *for ever.*

The subject-matter of this psalm does not call for a section on religious teaching.

PSALM 46

JUST as some psalms are seen by their form and content to be of the Wisdom type of literature, so some others, by their thought and phraseology, show themselves as belonging to the apocalyptic or eschatological type. Of these latter the psalm before us is a striking example. In so far as apocalyptic ideas and pictures appear in the Old Testament they are confined almost wholly to the prophetical books; and their various occurrences in the *Psalms* must be regarded primarily as signs of the influence of prophetical teaching. It is noteworthy that in our psalm familiarity with apocalyptic ideas is taken for granted. As is well known, these were taken over and adapted by the prophets from Babylonian mythology, and in later days modified and added to in accordance with Iranian beliefs; in our psalm, however, no signs of the latter appear. The adapted apocalyptic *traits* which occur are the following: the destruction of the earth at the end of the present world-order, this is preparatory to the bringing back of the primeval "Golden Age"; the combat between the gods and the powers of evil, *i.e.*, Tiamat and her helpers, identified with the sea; and the final victory of the gods headed by Marduk. The prophets, while accepting these as foreshadowing what would actually take place, inter-preted them as follows: the destruction of the earth was necessary because it was polluted by wickedness; Tiamat and her helpers symbolized the wicked nations; the rôle of Marduk was transferred to Yahweh; the return of the " Golden Age " meant the setting-up of the rule of Yahweh on a renovated earth. It is worth observing how in the later apocalyptic literature the fundamental ideas of this eschatological drama receive expression, though some modifications, due to other extraneous influences, appear. For example, in the " Vision of the Man from the Sea ", Ezra Apocalypse (2 (4), Esdras in the Apocrypha) 13¹⁻¹³, the Seer relates: " And I beheld, and, lo, this wind caused to come up from the midst of the sea as it were the likeness of a man; and I beheld, and, lo, that man flew with the clouds of heaven." This is the heavenly Messiah, God's representative, whose coming up from the midst of the sea implies his victory over the powers of evil. Against him there is gathered " a multitude of men, out of number, from the four winds of heaven, to make war against the man that came out of the sea "; these are the nations of the world, and they are destroyed by " the flaming breath " of the man from the sea. Thereupon the heavenly Messiah ascends upon a great mountain, *i.e.*, the abode of the divine ruler in the kingdom. And, finally, a " peaceable multitude " comes unto the divine ruler, indicating those subjects who are worthy of the kingdom. Thus, though in form the apocalyptist's vision differs from the psalmist's picture, the underlying conceptions are the same.

That in their transfigured form the psalmist believed in the literal fulfilment of these happenings at the end of the world is not to be doubted; as well contend that the apocalyptists did not believe what they prophesied. It was just because the psalmist was so convinced that these things would come to pass that he encouraged and heartened his people during a present emergency by reminding them of the ultimate victory of Yahweh; hence the triumphant refrain: " Yahweh Zebaoth is with us, our strong-tower is the God of Jacob ". What particular emergency was in question the psalm gives no help in determining.

The developed form of the eschatological picture points to a late post-exilic date; but the underlying traditional conceptions are, of course, ancient.

The metre is somewhat irregular, but short two-beat half-lines predominate.

For the Precentor : Belonging to the sons of Qorah. According to ' Alamoth. A Song.

1 (2).	God is our refuge and strength,	a help in troubles,
	° fully proved °;	
2 (3).	Therefore we fear not	
	if the earth ° be dissolved °,	
	And the mountains be cast	
	into the midst of ° the sea °;	
3 (4).	° The sea roareth °,	
	its waters are troubled,	

Mountains quake at its haughty pride;
° Yahweh Zebaoth is with us, our strong-tower is the God of Jacob.°
Selah.

4 (5). A river ! its streams
make glad God's-city,
Holiest of the dwellings of the Most High;
5 (6). God is in the midst of her, she shall not be moved,
God will help her
before the morn.
6 (7). Nations rage,
kingdoms are moved;
He uttereth his voice,
the earth is dissolved.
7 (8). Yahweh Zebaoth is with us, our strong-tower is the God of Jacob.
8 (9). Come, behold,
the works of Yahweh,
Who hath brought desolations on the earth,
9 (10). Causing wars to cease
to the end of the world;
He breaketh the bow,
and knappeth the spear,
° The shields ° he burneth with fire.
10 (11). " Let be, and know that
I am God,
Exalted among the nations,
exalted on the earth.
11 (12). Yahweh Zebaoth is with us, our strong-tower is the God of Jacob.
Selah.

Text-critical Notes

1. Lit. " to be much found ". 2. Read הָמוֹג for הָמִיר, " changed ". Read
הַיָּם for יַמִּים, " waters ". 3. Read יֶהֱמֶה הַיָּם for יֶהֱמוּ, " they roar ". Add,
following most commentators, the refrain. 9. Read, with G, עֲגִילוֹת for עֲגָלוֹת,
" carts ".

1, 2. The dominant thought of the psalm is expressed in the
opening words: *God is our refuge and strength*, an affirmation of faith
in him who is the one reliable stay and support in adverse times, *a
help in trouble*; the Hebrew phrase which we have rendered *fully
proved* is difficult to reproduce in translation, but this seems to be the
sense intended; experience had shown how often God's help had
been forthcoming. The psalmist, representing his people, *our refuge
and strength*, thus indicates that a national emergency has arisen;
and, like a true patriot, generates confidence in his people by directing
their thoughts to the one infallible source of strength and help. In
doing this he recalls the prophecies, uttered in the past, concerning
the world-catastrophe which is to take place at the end of the days,
and pictures the time when the God of Israel, in overwhelming might,
will manifest his power over all creation. Just as in that day Israel
will have no need to fear, so now fear is excluded, for it is their God
who is their help both then and now. The psalmist thereupon repeats
some of the ancient conceptions regarding the final world-catastrophe
(2, 3); these had been utilized by the prophets, and it is their words
which the psalmist takes as the basis for his own; to realize this, one
has but to read such passages as Isa. 24[5, 6, 19, 20], Hag. 2[6, 21]; cp.

also Ps. 89[9]. But the cataclysm pictured can have no terror for the people of God, for *Yahweh Zebaoth is with us, our strong-tower is the God of Jacob*; in the Hebrew text this refrain does not figure here, but that its omission is a copyist's oversight is exceedingly probable; the strophic balance of the psalm demands it. For the title *Yahweh Zebaoth*, the "Lord of Hosts", cp. Ps 24[10], Mal. 1[14]; the hosts meant originally the heavenly hosts, later they were made to refer to the armies of Israel.

4, 5. A new picture now rises up before the psalmist's mental vision; it is also eschatological, but has its bearing on the present. The sudden and abrupt exclamation, *A river*, was full of meaning to those of the psalmist's day, and they were many, who were conversant with the prophetical writings. There is in this connexion a striking eschatological passage in Isa. 33[18-24]; it has some cryptic allusions, and the text appears to have been worked over; but the central thought is clear enough, for it tells of the kingdom of righteousness and peace when Yahweh will be judge and law-giver and king; then "thine eyes shall see Jerusalem a quiet habitation . . . a place of broad rivers and streams." This is the picture which was in the psalmist's mind; a strange picture indeed when one thinks of the position of Jerusalem on a hill; it was, however, a familiar eschatological conception which occurs in other prophetical books, see especially Ezek. 47; in another eschatological passage, Joel 3 (4), it is said that "a fountain shall come forth of the house of Yahweh, and shall water the valley of Shittim" (*v.* 18). How this conception persisted among the apocalyptists is evident from the striking words in Rev. 22[1, 2]: "And he showed me a river of water of life, bright as crystal, proceeding out of the throne of God . . ."; that is in "the holy city, new Jerusalem" (21[2]). This, then, is the *river* of which the psalmist thinks, whose *streams make glad God's-city, holiest of the dwellings of the Most High.* 5. That city is invulnerable, *for God is in the midst of her* . . .; 6. in vain do the *nations rage*, for God *uttereth his voice, the earth is dissolved* (cp. Ps. 76[8], Jer. 25[30, 31], Joel 2[11], 3 (4)[16]). 7. The refrain follows. 8, 9. A further eschatological picture describes the end of war, and with that the beginning of the reign of eternal peace is implied, though not actually stated (cp. Isa. 2[2, 3]). Then the Almighty speaks: *Let be, and know that I am God, exalted among the nations, exalted on earth* (cp. Isa. 2[11, 17], 33[10]). With the exultant refrain the psalm closes.

Religious Teaching

Eschatological *traits* occur in some of the psalms already dealt with (2, 9, 18), but we have here for the first time one which is definitely eschatological throughout.

To the Jewish teachers the fundamental significance of eschatological beliefs centred in the final victory of Yahweh over all the
nations of the world, and in their subjection to him and their acknowledgement of his sovereignty. Whatever meaning the catastrophic
elements may have had originally in the extraneous centres from
which they were borrowed, to the prophets, and following them, to
the psalmists, the destruction of the world was interpreted as a necessary condition of, and prelude to, Yahweh's universal rule; and this
because of the innate evil believed to exist not only in the bulk of
humanity, but also in all creation (cp. Rom. 8[20-22]); the spirit of the
powers of evil permeated the material world as well as the hearts of
men. That the Dualism inherent in this conception (cp. the Iranian
belief in Ahura Mazda and Angra Mainyu) never affected Jewish
monotheistic belief was simply due to the fact that the Jewish teachers
ignored the obvious deduction to be drawn from the belief in the
existence of the two opposed powers of good and evil. But the
instinct which ignored this deduction was a right one; for however
difficult it was to account for the origin of evil, its presence was indisputable; and the belief in its final destruction by Yahweh proclaimed
the eternal truth that he in whom is centred the divine attribute of
righteousness must gain the ultimate victory. This is the essence of
the religious teaching of this psalm.

PSALM 47

THIS psalm, like that which precedes it, belongs to the " Enthronement " group, and is eschatological in content, though it deals only
with the culminating act of the eschatological drama.[1] It pictures
the time when, after the elimination of all evil elements, the Kingdom
of God will be established on earth; Yahweh, having ascended upon
his throne amid the shouts of praise of all nations, is become King
over all the world. Such a psalm would be appropriately sung at
the festival during which was celebrated Yahweh's ascent upon his
throne (see further on this, pp. 48 f). As in the preceding psalm,
the actual present is envisaged in the light of the ideal future.
Like all the psalms the subject-matter of which is eschatological, the
influence of prophetical teaching appears prominently (see further,
p. 92).

In conception, as probably in its original composition, the psalm
is pre-exilic, though it has undergone some slight modification in

---

[1] According to *Sopherim* xix. 2, it was the special psalm for the New Year Festival.

course of time; in its present form, however, it may be assigned to the Greek period.

The metre is variable, with telling effect.

1.   *For the Precentor : Of the Sons of Qorah.   A Psalm.*

1 (2).   O clap your hands, all ye people,
                    Shout unto God
                       with the voice of triumph;
2 (3).   For Yahweh, the Most High, is terrible,
                    A great King
                       over all the earth;
3 (4). He subdueth peoples under us,   and nations under our feet;
4 (5). ° He enlargeth ° for us our in-   the pride of Jacob whom he loveth.
       heritance,   Selah.
5 (6). God ascendeth with a shout,   Yahweh with a blast of the ram's-horn.
6 (7). Sing praises to God, sing praises,   sing praises to our King, sing praises;
7 (8). For ° Yahweh is become King °
          ° over ° all the earth,   sing to God a choice-song;
8 (9). ° Yahweh ° is become King over the
          nations,   ° he sitteth upon his holy throne;
9 (10). The princes of the peoples are   ° with ° the people of the God of
          gathered together   Abraham;
                    For to God belong
                    ° the rulers ° of the earth;
                    He is greatly exalted !

Text-critical Notes

4. Read יַרְחֵב for יִבְחַר, " he chooseth ". 7. Read מֶלֶךְ יְהֹוָה for מֶלֶךְ, " king "; add with many MSS., עַל. 8. Read יְהֹוָה for אֱלֹהִים, " God ". Om. אֱלֹהִים. 9. Add, with GS, עַם. Read נְגִידֵי (cp. G), for מָגִנֵּי, " shields ".

1-4. The eschatological character of the psalm is announced in the opening sentence; for *all peoples* would not be called upon to *clap* their *hands* and *shout unto God* unless they had all been subdued by Yahweh (see *v.* 3), and this is just one of the main themes of the eschatological drama (cp. Ps. 66[1-4]). The future is, in the usage of the prophets, envisaged as present. The clapping of the hands was, in the first instance, an accompaniment to the ritual dance (cp. the primitive cymbals mentioned in the notes to Ps. 150); in later times the phrase was used figuratively as an expression of joy, *e.g.*, Ps. 98[8], and Isa. 55[12], " and all the trees of the fields shall clap their hands ". In this latter sense it is used here. But the triumphant joy, in the circumstances pictured, is not incompatible with holy awe, for *Yahweh, the Most High, is terrible,* i.e., awe-inspiring (cp. Ps. 66[3]). For the thought of Yahweh as a great King over all the earth, cp. Zech. 14[9], Mal. 1[14]. The supremacy of Israel in the last times, indicated in the words, *He subdueth peoples under us, and nations under our feet,* is a frequent theme in prophetical eschatology (*e.g.*, Isa. 49[23], 60[10-16]); similarly the prophecy of the extension, beyond the land of Canaan, of Israel's *inheritance, the pride of Jacob* (*e.g.*, Isa. 26[15], 54[3], Zech. 10[10]); but both of these ideas are later eschatological *traits.*

5-9. That this psalm was sung during the festival of Tabernacles in celebration of Yahweh's ascent upon his throne comes out clearly in the words, God *ascendeth with a shout*, and in *v.* 8; the " shout " is a technical ritual term, used like *the blast of the horn, i.e.*, the ram's horn, on the occasion of the ascent upon his throne of an earthly king (*e.g.*, 1 Kgs. 1[39]). The repetition of the call to *sing praises* is very effective; in a less pointed form such repetitions occur in Pss. 57[1], 75[1, 4, 5]. The term *choice-song* (*maskil*) occurs in the titles of fourteen psalms. Most fittingly does the psalm conclude with the picture of Yahweh sitting *upon his holy throne*, before which the *princes of the peoples*, joined to *the people of the God of Abraham, are gathered together;* there is but one Ruler on earth, and to him are subject all other *rulers*, thus *he is greatly exalted.*

Religious Teaching

On the significance in general of the eschatological-apocalyptic elements in the *Psalms,* see the last section of the preceding psalm, and also pp. 92 ff.

PSALM 48

THE nature and content of this psalm have been differently interpreted by commentators; and it must be recognized that there is a good deal to be urged in favour of each of the two main interpretations put forward. The glorification of Jerusalem, with which the psalm opens, and the dispersal of foes who had assembled against it, which is then dealt with, suggest that some historical event prompted the composition of the psalm. Jerusalem, " the city of the great King ", has been delivered from some impending danger, and its protection is ascribed to Yahweh, who is " great ", and who has manifested himself as its protector; hence, as the psalmist says, " God doth establish it for ever ". This seems to echo the prophet Isaiah's teaching on the inviolability of Jerusalem: " As birds flying, so will Yahweh Zebaoth protect Jerusalem; he will protect and deliver it, he will pass over and preserve it " (Isa. 31[5]). But these words are uttered in reference to the defence against the Assyrian attack, for in *vv.* 8, 9 it is said further: " Then shall the Assyrian fall with the sword, not of man; and the sword, not of men, shall devour him; and he shall flee from the sword, and his young men shall become tributary. And his rock shall pass away by reason of terror, and his princes shall be dismayed at the ensign, saith Yahweh, whose fire is in Zion, and his furnace in Jerusalem." The prophet is here referring to the siege of Jerusalem by the army of Sennacherib

(701 B.C.), of which it is said further (Isa. 37$^{33-37}$): " Therefore thus
saith Yahweh concerning the king of Assyria, He shall not come unto
this city. . . . By the way that he came, by the same shall he return,
and he shall not come unto this city, saith Yahweh. For I will defend
this city to save it, for mine own sake, and for my servant David's
sake. And the angel of Yahweh went forth, and smote the camp of
the Assyrians. . . . So Sennacherib king of Assyria departed. . . ."
Read in the light of this, as it appeared, miraculous deliverance of
Jerusalem, and of the prophet's conviction of its inviolability, there
is much in favour of a historical interpretation of our psalm, and
there are various incidental allusions which support this (see the
exegetical notes). On the other hand, there is a good deal in the
psalm which justifies an eschatological interpretation. Thus, the
presence of the divine ruler on his holy hill (Jerusalem), and the
onslaught of the nations and their discomfiture, are regular eschatological themes; in the apocalyptic literature we have a parallel, for
example, in the " Vision of the Man from the Sea ", in the *Ezra
Apocalypse* (2 (4) Esdras 13$^{1-13}$); see further on this the introductory
section to Ps. 46, cp. Mic. 4^{11}, Zech. 3^8. Again, the idea of the mount
of God lying in the farthest north is a mythological *trait* taken over
by the apocalyptists; it finds an echo, *e.g.*, in Isa. 14^{13}, cp. Isa. 2^2,
Mic. 4^1. And once more, the description of Zion as " the joy of all
the earth " transcends any conceivable historical conditions; it is
another apocalyptic conception. It cannot, therefore, be denied that
the psalm contains eschatological elements. There is, thus, justification
for each of the interpretations mentioned.

If it be asked, then, in what sense the psalm is to be understood,
it must be said that to adopt one of the interpretations mentioned to
the exclusion of the other is a mistake; both interpretations must be
accepted; an actual historical event forms the basis, and this is idealized
and presented as a picture of what will take place at the final consummation. In principle it may be compared with Ps. 46 and Isa. 14.

The last three verses of the psalm bear out the historical interpretation, for they evidently refer to a procession round the city as
an act of thanksgiving for its deliverance from the enemy. To assign
a date is difficult; we are inclined to regard it as a pre-exilic psalm
worked over in post-exilic times.

The metre is mostly 3 : 2, but in *vv.* 1, 2 it is 2 : 2 : 2 ; in the last
lines of *vv.* 2 and 8 it is 3 : 3.

1.   *A Song. A Psalm. Of the Sons of Qorah.*

1 (2).   Great is Yahweh,
                         And highly to be praised
                         In the city of our God,
                         ° on ° his holy hill,

S

2 (3). A beautiful height,
        the joy of all the earth;
    The hill of Zion, farthest-limit of
        the north,   the city of the Great King.
3 (4). God within her palaces   hath made himself known as a refuge;
4 (5). For, lo, the kings assembled,   ° united ° together,
5 (6). They beheld; then were they
        terrified,   dismayed, put in fear;
6 (7). Trembling took hold of them
        there,   anguish, as of a woman in travail;
7 (8). ° As the east wind ° ° wrecketh ° the ships of Tarshish.
8 (9). Like as we have heard, so have we
        seen,   ° in the city of our God,
    In the city of Yahweh Zebaoth °,   God doth establish it for ever. Selah.
9 (10). We have thought, O God, of thy
        love,   in the midst of thy temple:
10 (11). ° As that which we have heard of so is thy praise, ° to ° the ends of the
        thee °, O God,   earth;
    Thy right-hand is full of righteous-
        ness,   11 (12). let the hill of Zion rejoice;
    Let the daughters of Judah be
        glad,   because of thy judgements.
12 (13). Go round about Zion, and en-
        compass her,   tell the number of her towers.
13 (14). ° Take well heed of ° ° her
        rampart °,   go through her palaces,
    That ye may tell to a future
        generation   14 (15). that this is God,
    Our God for ever and ever,   he will guide us °.

Text-critical Notes

1. Add עַל. 4. Read הָבְרוּ for עָבְרוּ "they passed by." 7. Read, with some MSS. 'כְּרוּחַ for בְּ. Lit. "breaketh in pieces." 8. The rhythm demands that these two half-lines should be transposed as above; the Hebr. text has them in the reverse order. 10. Read כְּשִׁמְעֲךָ for כְּשִׁמְךָ, "as thy name". Read עַד for עַל, "upon", 13. Lit. "set your heart". Read, with many MSS., cp. G, הֵילָה for הֵילָהּ. "a rampart". 14. Om. עַל־מוּת, "concerning death"; see title of Ps. 9.

1, 2. The close association of Yahweh with the holy city naturally enough finds frequent expression both in the psalms and elsewhere, see, *e.g.*, Pss. 9[9-11], 14[7], 46[4-7], 76[1-4], Isa. 12[4-6], Jer. 17[12, 13]. Here the special significance of that association lies in the fact that the psalmist commemorates the deliverance of Jerusalem from peril through what was believed to have been the intervention of Yahweh, as the context indicates. Hence the opening words: *Great is Yahweh, and highly to be praised in the city of our God* (cp. Pss. 46[4], 87[2, 3], Isa. 60[14]); it is his presence there which sanctifies and beautifies the very hill on which the city stands; so that besides being *holy*, it is *a beautiful height*. The description of it as *the joy of all the earth* may be merely poetical hyperbole; but it is much more likely that current eschatological thought in regard to it was employed; for it is further spoken of as being in *the farthest-limit of the north*. The reference here is to a widely-spread apocalyptic conception (cp. Isa. 14[13], Ezek. 1[4]); one of the most striking accounts of it occurs in the *Book of Enoch* 24, 25; the mountain lies in the north (cp. 18[6-10], 24[2]), and the Seer is told by the archangel Michael that "this high mountain which thou hast seen, whose

summit is like the throne of God, is his throne, where the holy Great One,
the Lord of Glory, the eternal King, will sit, when he shall come down
to visit the earth with goodness " (25³). This is the conception which
the psalmist envisages, and applies to the hill of Zion, identified with
Jerusalem, *the city of the Great King*, for this title cp. Pss. 47², 95³,
and see Gunkel, *Schöpfung und Chaos* . . ., pp. 307 f. (1895). 3–7. In
these verses again, eschatological ideas are brought to bear, present
history being coloured by the prophetical conceptions of the last times.
The historical event in the psalmist's mind may well have been the
siege of Jerusalem in 701 B.C. by the army of Sennacherib, of which
mention has been made above. The sudden and wholly unexpected
withdrawal of the enemy from before the walls of the city was a sure
proof to the psalmist that *God* was *within her palaces*, and had shown
his power, having *made himself known as a refuge*, or protection. The
eschatological picture is then applied to the enemy that had surrounded the city. It would be unreasonable to look for exact correspondence here ; traditional eschatology pictured *the kings* of the earth
who would *assemble* and join themselves together to fight the divine
ruler (cp. Isa. 13⁴) ; in the present event only the Assyrian king was
in question, and apparently he was not present in person at the siege.
But such differences in detail would not affect the central fact. The
description of the terror of the oncoming foes is partly eschatological,
and partly the product of the psalmist's vivid imagination. According
to the former, the very sight of the divine conqueror inspires the
enemies with terror and dismay (cp. 2 (4) Esdras 13⁸) ; to this the
psalmist adds the prophetical picture of their *anguish* being *as of a
woman in travail* (cp. Isa. 13⁸). Not altogether *à propos* is the psalmist's
own conception of the broken enemy with the *ships of Tarshish* wrecked
by the east wind ; but his desire is to present a picture of entire destruction. *Tarshish* was the Phœnician colony in Spain ; ships of
special build were required for making this long journey. 8–11. In
these verses the historical picture alone is presented, without eschatological allusions. The prophetical utterances concerning Jerusalem
were those which had been handed down and *heard* by the people
(*e.g.*, Am. 1², Isa. 2²⁻⁴, Mic. 4¹⁻³, cp. also 1 Kgs. 11³², 14²¹), they
have now been *seen* to be true ; this was indeed a city which *God*
had *established for ever*. The divine act of deliverance compelled
pondering upon God's love, especially when the people gathered
together for worship ; in their name, therefore, the prophet says :
We have thought, O God, of thy love in the midst of thy temple ; in
accordance with what they had heard of him, so is their offering of
praise to him ; and that not only in Jerusalem, but also *to the ends
of the earth* ; this may be an eschatological echo ; but if so, it is adapted
to apply to the chosen people wherever they may be. The thought

impels the psalmist himself to utter the words of praise: *Thy right-hand is full of righteousness*, *i.e.*, the right-hand, which is the instrument of action, brings about righteous deeds (cp. Pss. 77¹⁰, ¹¹, 98¹); therefore it is fitting that not only *the hill of Zion* should *rejoice*, but also all the *daughter*-cities of *Judah* (cp. Pss. 69³⁵, ³⁶, 97⁸); the divine *judgements* are right decisions. 12, 13. Finally, the grateful people are called upon to form a procession, the ritual act of thanksgiving, *round about Zion*, and thus convince themselves that though the enemy had been before it, by the mercy of God no harm had been done; *towers, rampart, palaces*, all are intact. This is something to be told *to a future generation*, for it is God's doing, *our God for ever and ever*; all confidence must ever be placed in him, for *he will guide us*.

Religious Teaching

The two central themes are the place of eschatological thought in the beliefs of Israel, which has been dealt with under Ps. 46; and the prophetical doctrine of Yahweh as the God of History; for this latter see pp. 81 ff.

PSALM 49

THIS is a psalm of the Wisdom type. Its central theme is the denunciation of the wealthy, regarded as ungodly. Not that the Sage describes the possession of wealth, as such, to be sinful; what he denounces is its misuse and the bad effect it has on so many by engendering self-indulgence, with its accompanying vices, a false sense of security, and pride. While the evidence suggests that the rich were but too often of godless character, it is impossible to believe that those of the type of Zacchæus did not exist (see Lk. 19⁸). But it is only the former that the Sage has in mind.

That the text has undergone some serious corruption is evident; the thought-sequence is not always logical, and that some additions have been made to the original text does not admit of doubt.

The metre is 3 : 3.

1.   *For the Precentor : Of the Sons of Qorah. A Psalm.*

1 (2). Hear this, all ye peoples,   give ear, all ye inhabitants of the world,
2 (3). Both of low degree and high degree,   rich and poor together.
3 (4). My mouth shall speak wisdom,   my heart's musing is of understanding.
4 (5). ° Incline your ear ° to a parable,   I will solve my dark saying with the harp.
5 (6). Wherefore should I fear in the evil days,   (when) the iniquity of ° mine enemies ° encompasseth me,
6 (7). Who trust in their wealth,   and boast of the abundance of their riches ?

7 (8). ° But ° no man ° can buy himself off °,

nor pay a ransom to God,

8 (9). ° [Precious is the redemption of ° his soul °,

he must cease from that for ever.] °

9 (10). And live ° for ever and ever,°

and never see the Pit.

10 (11). For he seeth that wise men die,

both the foolish ° and intelligent ° perish,
And leave their wealth to others.

11 (12). ° Graves ° are their houses ever-more,

their dwelling-places for ever and ever.
They call ° their lands their own °.

12 (13). But man abideth not in honour,

he is like the beasts that perish ;

13 (14). This is ° the fate ° (of them) that are so confident,

and ° their latter end ° (of those) ° who boast with their lips °. Selah.

14 (15). ° Like a flock of Sheol are they destroyed,
In the field of Abaddon is their resting-place,

death is their shepherd, and hath dominion over them ;

in the belly of Sheol is their dwelling ° ;

15 (16). But God will redeem my soul

from the power of Sheol, for he will receive me. Selah.

16 (17). ° Look not ° upon one if he become rich,

if ° he increase ° the glory of his house,

17 (18). ° For at his death he will take nothing away °,

his glory will not descend after him.

18 (19). Though while he liveth he blesseth his soul,

° and men praise him because it goeth well with him °,

19 (20). ° He will go ° to the generation of his fathers,

and ° he shall never see ° light.

20 (21). Man ° abideth not ° in honour,

he is like the beasts that perish.

Text-critical Notes

4. Read הַטּוּ אָזְנֵיכֶם for אַטֶּה אָזְנִי, " I will incline mine ear ". 5. Read עֲקֹבַי, lit. " they that over-reach me " for עֲקֵבַי, " my heels ". 7. Read, with many MSS., אַךְ for אָח, " brother ". Read יִפְדֶּה lit. " will redeem himself," for פָּדֹה יִפְדֶּה, " will by any means redeem ". 8. This is a marginal note which has found its way into the text. Read נַפְשׁוֹ for נַפְשָׁם, " their soul ". 9. Read לְעוֹלָם וָעֶד for עוֹד for the rhythm's sake. 10. Read וְנָבוֹן for וָבַעַר, " and brutish man ". 11. Read, cp. GS, קְבָרִים for קִרְבָּם. Read, cp. G, עַל אַדְמוֹתָם קָרְאוּ שְׁמוֹתָם (see exeg. note) for קָרְאוּ בִשְׁמוֹתָם עֲלֵי אֲדָמוֹת, " they call with their names over lands ". 13. Lit. " way ". Read אַחֲרִיתָם for אַחֲרֵיהֶם, " after them ". Lit. " they are pleased with their mouth ". 14. The hopelessly corrupt state of this verse necessitates a somewhat drastic emendation ; the following is suggested :

כְּצֹאן לִשְׁאוֹל נִשְׁחָטוּ   מָוֶת יִרְעֵם וַיֵּרְד בָּם
בְּשָׂדֶה אֲבַדּוֹן מַרְבְּצָם   לְבֶטֶן שְׁאוֹל מִזְּבֻלָם :

For the expression בְּטֶן שְׁאוֹל, see Jon. 2³.

16. Read אַל־תֵּרֵא, lit. " look not ", *i.e.*, with envy, for אַל־תִּירָא, " be not afraid ". Read יַרְבֶּה for יִרְבֶּה. 17. Read כִּי לֹא־יִקַּח בְּמוֹתוֹ הַכֹּל. 18. Read וְיוֹדֻהוּ כִּי יִיטַב לוֹ for וְיוֹדְךָ כִּי־תֵיטִיב לָךְ, " and men praise thee because thou causest to do well to thyself ". 19. Read יָבֹא for תָּבֹא, " thou wilt go ". Read לֹא יִרְאֶה . . . for לֹא יִרְאוּ . . ., " they shall . . .". 20. Read בַּל־יָלִין (*v.* 12) for וְלֹא יָבִין, " and he understandeth not ".

1–3. Since in this psalm the subject dealt with is one which is universally applicable, the psalmist addresses himself to *all ye peoples*, and to those of every degree. He is about to *speak wisdom*, for his thoughts have been concentrated on that which is *of understanding*. 4. To all men it is, therefore, said : *Incline your ear* (cp. Ps. 78¹) ; they are to listen to a *parable*, or *mashal*, a word which in Hebrew has a wide sense, such as a popular saying (*e.g.*, 1 Sam. 10^{12}), or wise advice (*e.g.*, 1 Kgs. 20^{11}), or a universal truth (*e.g.*, Prov. 16^9), in fact, what we ordinarily understand as a " proverb "; but it is also used in reference to prophecy (*e.g.*, Num. 24$^{3-9}$), and even of an allegory (*e.g.*, Ezek. 17$^{2-10}$); all these in addition to " parable " as ordinarily understood. The psalmist continues : *I will solve my dark saying with the harp*; the " dark saying " is lit. " a riddle ", though not necessarily in our sense ; it is often used as a parallel to " parable ", as here (cp. Ps. 78^2). *I will solve* is lit. " I will open ", which can mean either that he will " begin " his dark saying, or that he will " explain " it, to the accompaniment of the *harp*. Nowhere in the Wisdom Literature, or indeed elsewhere in the Old Testament, is there mention of wise sayings being thus accompanied ; but it may well have been the practice on special occasions ; the words of a song are not less effective for being accompanied by mu⸱ i⸱, much the contrary ; the same is true of musical accompaniment to narratives (cp. the Troubadours). The mention of the *harp* here is thus of distinct interest. 5–14. The introductory words to the " parable " which now follow are difficult. We have followed the Hebrew text, but it must be confessed that the words of *v.* 5 do not read altogether appropriately. At any rate, those whom the psalmist has in mind are they *who trust in their wealth*, and he is concerned to impress upon them the folly of boasting in *the abundance of their riches*, because death will come upon them, as on all others. The words : *But no man can buy himself off, nor pay a ransom to God*, must be understood as a sarcasm ; but it was necessary to utter the taunt, and to remind the godless wealthy that death was their lot, because they never called that to mind in the midst of all their worldly enjoyments. *V.* 8 is an obvious addition to the original text ; it is the kind of thought that a pious copyist would have written in the margin of his MS. ; a later copyist then inserted the words in the text. The psalmist then brings before the minds of the rich that *graves are their houses for evermore, their dwelling-places for ever and ever*, in glaring contrast to their brief tenure of *their lands* which *they call their own*, lit. " lands over which they call their name ", meaning lands of which they have taken possession. Like all men who *abide not in honour* (cp. Ps. 39^5), and are *like the beasts that perish* (cp. Eccles. 3^{19}), this is also the fate, lit. " way ", of the self-confident wealthy *who boast with their lips* (a free rendering, see text-critical note). The next verse is hopelessly corrupt ; its emendation is at best tentative ; no two commentators agree on any emended form ; we have tried to keep as closely as possible to the Hebrew text (see text-critical note), but we regard our emendation merely as *faute de mieux* ; all that can be claimed is that in a general sense it probably approximates to what was originally meant. The next verse, 15, reads like words put into the mouth of the psalmist by a copyist. 16–20. These closing verses, addressed apparently to a disciple of the psalmist, are merely a repetition of the thoughts already expressed. The text, with the exception of the last verse which repeats *v.* 12, is again very corrupt, and commentators are not in agreement as to how they should be emended. The possibility cannot be excluded that these verses were added by a sage at a later date.

Religious Teaching

As to this, all that can be said is that it proclaims a very necessary truth which is more pointedly set forth in the Parable of the Rich Fool (Lk. 12[16-21]).

PSALM 50

EVEN a cursory reading of this psalm shows how profoundly the writer was influenced by prophetical thought and diction. This will be illustrated by references to the prophetical books in the exegetical notes. Attention may, however, be drawn here to some outstanding prophetical themes which the psalmist utilizes. The mention of the divine utterance with which the psalm opens, the description of the theophany which follows, the relative unimportance of sacrifice as compared with spiritual worship, and the denunciation against the wicked man in the latter part of the psalm ; all these are thoroughly in the prophetic vein, and show that our psalmist was wholly in the following of the prophets. This is the most important element in the psalm, and cannot be too strongly emphasized. In the latter part of the psalm there is an earnest protest against reliance on the outward observance of legal precepts without regard to the spirit of their teaching. As a pre-exilic date for the psalm is, for various reasons, out of the question, and as the re-building of the temple has clearly taken place, the psalm must have been written at any rate later than 516 B.C. ; indeed there are indications which point to a considerably later date for its composition.

The metre is, with but few exceptions, 3 : 3.

A Psalm. Asaph's.

1. ° Yahweh hath spoken,
   And called the earth,
   From the rising of the sun,
      Unto the going down thereof.
2. From Zion, the crown of beauty   hath God appeared,
3. Our God cometh,
   And is not silent.
   A fire before him devoureth,   around him it rageth mightily.
4. He calleth to the heavens above,   and to the earth, to judge his people :

5. " Gather to me my godly ones, that have made a covenant with me with sacrifice."

6. Let the heavens ° declare ° his righteousness,
for a God that judgeth is he.

7. " Hear, O my people, and I will speak, God, thy God, am I.
O Israel, and I will testify against thee,

8. Not because of thy sacrifices do I reprove thee,
thy burnt-offerings are always before me.

9. I desire no bullock out of thine house,
nor he-goats out of thy fold,

10. For mine are all the beasts of the forest,
the cattle on the mountains of ° God ° ;

11. I know all the fowls of ° the air °,
and whatsoever moveth in the fields is mine ;

12. If I were hungry I would not tell thee,
for mine is the world and its fulness ;

13. Do I eat the flesh of bulls,
or drink the blood of goats ?

14. Sacrifice thanksgiving unto God,
and pay to the Most High thy vows ;

15. And call upon me in the day of trouble,
I will deliver thee, and thou shalt glorify me."

16. But to the wicked man saith God :
" Is it thine to declare my statutes,
and to take my covenant on ° thy lips °,

17. Thou that hatest correction,
and hast cast my words behind thee ?

18. When thou seest a thief ° thou favourest him °,
and with adulterers is thy portion ;

19. Thy mouth thou givest to evil,
and thy tongue frameth deceit ;

20. ° Shamefully ° dost thou speak against thy brother,
thy mother's son thou dost slander.

21. These things hast thou done, and I was silent,
thou thoughtest that I was ° like thee ° ;
I will reprove thee, ° and set it before ° thine eyes.

22. Give heed to this, ye that forget God,
lest I rend you, and none delivereth.

23. He that sacrificeth a thanksgiving he honoureth me,
° and he that walketh uprightly, ° I will show him ° my salvation °."

Text-critical Notes

1. Om. אֶל אֱלֹהִים, not only because it is out of harmony with the metre, but also because it is an extremely unusual expression for the Deity ; it occurs elsewhere only in Josh. 22²², where it is written twice over. The rendering of the RV. marg. " the God of gods " is questionable. 6. Read, with the Versions, וְיַגִּידוּ for . . . וְ. 10. Read אֶל for אֶלֶף, " a thousand," or " cattle ". 11. Read, with the Versions, הַשָּׁמַיִם, lit. " the heavens " for הָרִים, " mountains ". 16. Lit. " thy mouth ". 18. Read תִּרְצֵהוּ for וַתִּרֶץ עִמּוֹ, " thou consentedst with him ", which makes the half-line too long. 20. Read, with several commentators, בֹּשֶׁת, lit. " shame," for תֵּשֵׁב, " thou sittest ". 21. Om. הֱיוֹת, " to be " ; and read with S, וְאַעֶרְכָה, expressing the pronoun, for וְאֶעֶרְכָה. 23. Read, with several commentators, וְשָׂם דֶּרֶךְ for וְשָׂם דֶּרֶךְ, " he that prepareth a way " Read יִשְׁעִי for בְּיֵשַׁע אֱלֹהִים. " with the salvation of God ".

1-6. The conception of the theophany here described is derived, in the first instance, from Exod. 22, especially vv. 16-18 ; there are also various points of contact with Deut. 32, 33. From east to west (cp. Mal. 1¹¹) Yahweh has *called the earth*, i.e., the inhabitants of the earth, to hear the words which he is about to utter to his people. It is noticeable that only the *earth* is called, as in Mic. 1², 6² ; in other passages in which Yahweh is represented as uttering a judgement against his people, such as Deut. 4²⁶, 32¹, Isa. 1², the heavens also are called, cp. Isa. 48¹³ ; this omission is not without reason ; it is a universalistic *trait* ; though Israel alone is addressed, all men are to be listeners ; the Almighty thus proclaims that he is the God of all the human race ; the mention of the heavens would, therefore, be inappropriate.

The theophany is transferred from Sinai to Zion, *the crown of beauty*, an expression which occurs in Lam. 2^{15} in reference to Jerusalem. When it is said : *He calleth to the heavens above* this does not gainsay the remark just made because it is a new train of thought with which the psalmist is now occupied. The words : *Gather to me my godly ones* are not addressed to the heavens and the earth, but to the *godly ones* themselves ; here we have again the mention of the *Ḥasidim* (see further, pp. 56 ff.), *that have made a covenant with me with sacrifice* ; the covenant was originally made at Horeb (Exod. 24^{5}), but it was confirmed by all lovers of Yahweh whenever they came to worship him with their offerings. The favourable acceptation of sacrifice here must be read in connexion with what is said in the verses which follow. 7–15. The people are called upon to *Hear*, a thoroughly prophetical mode of address when an indictment uttered by Yahweh is recorded (*e.g.*, Isa. 1$^{2, 10}$, 28^{14}, 48^{1}, Jer. 2^{4}, Mic. 3^{1}) ; it is solemnly added : *God, thy God, am I* (cp. Isa. 42^{8}, 43^{15}). It must be noted that it is the wrong motive in offering sacrifices that the psalmist condemns here, not sacrifices as such : *Not because of thy sacrifices do I reprove thee*, and see *v.* 5 ; the real point of condemnation is contained in the words of *v.* 13 : *Do I eat the flesh of bulls, or drink the blood of goats?* By these words the psalmist repudiates the traditional belief that the Deity consumed his share of a sacrifice. The purpose of their being burned was that the ascending smoke should reach the heavens, and the essence of the flesh was thus thought to be consumed ; the blood, again, was poured out at the foot of the altar, or sprinkled upon it, with the idea that the Deity, invisibly present in or on the altar, somehow absorbed it. One of the fundamental purposes of sacrifices was thus to give nourishment to the Deity, and, through the blood, to convey to him the life-principle (Lev. 17^{11}). To eradicate the quaint old-world materialistic conception of God was what the psalmist was aiming at ; hence all that is said in *vv.* 9–13. The time had not yet come for the abrogation of the sacrificial system ; but this psalmist was preparing men's minds for this ; hence his words : *Sacrifice thanksgiving unto God*, *i.e.*, the contemplation of purely spiritual sacrifice ; it is sufficient to *call upon God* when in trouble, he *will deliver*, and the thankful recipient of God's mercy will *glorify* him. 16–23. Having thus exhorted those who worshipped God, though in an inadequate way, the psalmist now turns *to the wicked man*, and in burning words enumerates the sins of which he is guilty ; how dare such a one pretend to be righteous : *Is it thine to declare my statutes, and to take my covenant upon thy lips?* The type of Jew whom the psalmist here rebukes was he who by outward observance of legal precepts held that he did all that was needful, and was therefore free to give rein to all his evil passions : theft, adultery, lying, and slander. It may be that, in his righteous indignation, the psalmist has a little over-stated the

guilt of the hypocrite; but this type was a terrible danger to true religion, and drastic condemnation was called for.   We see here the
beginnings of the tendency to regard the fulfilling of the Law in its
outward form as procuring justification in the sight of God—an
indication, among others, of the comparatively late date of this psalm—
this, as is well known, was one of the results of an exaggerated authority
accorded to the Law.   When the psalmist speaks of God being *silent*
he means that no punishment was inflicted on the sinner in question,
who, in consequence, assumed that *I was like thee*; obviously, from his
point of view, there was no reason why he should be punished; but
this just shows the low ebb to which religion had fallen among many;
and the superb merit of this and other psalmists, following in the line of
the prophets, is that they set their face against spurious, self-deceptive
substitutes for religion; sooner or later, in one form or another, the
inevitable would come: *I will reprove thee, and set it before thine eyes.*
The concluding verse expresses once more the psalmist's ideal of spiritual
worship.

Religious Teaching

The central points have already been indicated; they may, however,
be briefly recapitulated.   The theophanic details of a long-past age
cannot, of course, appeal to us as it did to men of bygone times; but it
must be recognized that, however weird and erroneous these old-world
ideas about the divine appearance on earth may be, they do witness to a
very real belief in the might and terribleness of the Almighty.   Then
we have the ardent advocacy of spiritual worship as distinct from that
in which the offering of sacrifices constituted the central element.   To
champion such an innovation demanded an intensity of religious conviction engendered by a development of conception regarding the Being
of God which is very impressive.   In not more than two or three other
psalms is sacrificial worship contemplated as unnecessary.   The
teaching that sacrifices as an external form of worship endanger
spiritual religion is paralleled by that which protests against the mere
external obedience to the letter of the Law without a corresponding
observance of its spirit.   For its insistence on the true nature of
practical religion this psalm stands out as second to none.

PSALM 51

In this, the most heart-searching of all the penitential psalms, the
penitent concentrates his mind upon his state of sinfulness to the exclusion of all thought of surrounding circumstances external to himself.
In this particular it differs from all other psalms of a similar nature.   For

the realization of the sense of sin, set forth with unflinching candour, it has no equal in the Psalter.

In outward form the psalm is beautifully and skilfully constructed, and reveals most exquisitely the emotions which succeed one another in the penitent's heart: first, the cry to God for mercy; then, confession of sin, uttered in deep contrition; this is followed by prayer for forgiveness, and the resolution of amendment of life; and finally, in certainty that God in his love answers prayer, thanksgiving and praise.

The contention of some commentators that the psalmist is speaking not as an individual, but in the name of the community, can only be described as fantastic; the personal note sounded all through the psalm, culminating in such words as " in iniquity was I brought forth, and in sin did my mother conceive me ", should make it abundantly clear that the whole psalm is the outpouring of an individual in reference to himself.

That the psalm was written by David, as the title states, referring to 2 Sam. 11, 12, cannot have been the case; apart from other reasons, in view of his treatment of Uriah, how could David have uttered such words as: " Against thee, thee only, have I sinned " ? (See, however, the section on *Religious Teaching*.) But it should be obvious, in view of the developed sense of sin so pronounced throughout the psalm, that it must belong to post-exilic times; it was the experience of the Exile which engendered a conception of sin never before realized.

One or two later additions have been made to the psalm; attention to these will be drawn in the exegetical notes.

With two exceptions (*vv.* 1, 11), the metre is uniformly 3 : 3.

1. *For the Precentor : A Psalm. David's ; 2. When the prophet Nathan came unto him after he had gone in to Bath-sheba.*

1 (3).   Have mercy on me, O God, according to thy lovingkindness,
              According to the abundance of thy tender mercies
                      Blot out my transgressions.
2 (4). Wash me throughly from mine iniquity,   and cleanse me from my sin.
3 (5). For ° I acknowledge ° my transgressions,   and ° confess ° my sin continually.
4 (6). Against thee, thee only, have I sinned,   and done that which is evil in thine eyes,
       That thou mightest be justified ° in thy words °,   and vindicated when thou judgest.
5 (7). Behold, in iniquity was I brought forth,   and in sin did my mother conceive me.
6 (8). Behold, thou desirest truth in the inward parts,   and makest me to know wisdom in the innermost being.
7 (9). Purge me with hyssop that I may be clean,   wash me that I may be whiter than snow.
8 (10). ° Fill me with ° joy and gladness,   that the bones which thou hast crushed may rejoice.
9 (11). Hide thy face from my sins,   and blot out all mine iniquities.
10 (12). Create in me a clean heart, O God,   and renew a steadfast spirit within me.
11 (13). Cast me not from thy presence,   and take not thy holy spirit from me ;
12 (14). Restore unto me the joy of thy help,   and sustain me with a willing spirit.

13 (15). Then will I teach transgressors thy ways,
that sinners may turn unto thee.

14 (16). Deliver me °from silence°, O God °,
that my tongue may sing aloud of thy righteousness ;

15 (17). O Lord, open thou my lips,
and my mouth shall show forth thy praise ;

16 (18). For thou delightest not in sacrifice,
though I brought a whole-burnt-offering °thou wouldst have no pleasure therein ° ;

17 (19).   ° My sacrifice ° is a broken spirit ;
A heart broken and crushed,
O God, thou wilt not despise.

18 (20). In thy favour show good unto Zion,
mayest thou build the walls of Jerusalem ;

19 (21). Then shalt thou be pleased with the sacrifices of righteousness °,
then shall they offer bullocks upon thine altar.

Text-critical Notes

3. Read אוֹדִיעַ for אֵדַע, " I know ; " and אַגִּיד for נֶגְדִּי, " before me ". 4. Read, with many MSS. and G, בְּדָבְרֶיךָ for בְּדָבְרְךָ, " when thou speakest ". 8. Read, with S, תַּשְׂבִּיעֵנִי, lit. " thou wilt make me satisfied ", for תַּשְׁמִיעֵנִי, " thou makest me to hear ". 14. Read, with Gunkel, מִדְּמָם (cp. Ps. 94¹⁷, 115¹⁷, see also Ps. 39², 62¹ and especially Hab. 2¹⁹) for מִדָּמִים, " from bloodguiltiness ". Om. אֱלֹהֵי תְּשׁוּעָתִי, "O God of my salvation," which overloads the half-line. 16. Read לֹא תִרְצֶה for לֹא תִרְצֶה, " thou wouldest have no pleasure.". 17. Read זִבְחִי for זִבְחֵי אֱלֹהִים, " the sacrifices of God ". 19. Om. עוֹלָה וְכָלִיל, " a whole burnt-offering and a whole burnt-offering ; " the two words refer to the same type of sacrifice, though in various passages, e.g., 1 Sam. 7⁹, כָּלִיל is used in apposition to עוֹלָה.

For the title, see intr. section.

1, 2. For the true penitent the first impulse is to cry for *mercy* to God against whom sin has been committed. The psalmist's plea has a threefold basis ; it implores an exercise of pure generosity, undeserved but freely bestowed, God's *mercy* ; it claims the *lovingkindness* which, in a certain sense, is to be expected of God in view of his relation to man ; it appeals to the *tender mercies* which are fundamental to his being, as much a part of his spiritual nature as the love of mother or father for the child. The intensity of the psalmist's penitence is shown by the reiterated expressions : *blot out* (cp. Isa. 43²⁵, 44²²), *i.e.*, obliterate, as though recorded in a book ; *wash me throughly* (cp. Jer. 4¹⁴), lit. " increase, wash me ", the word is used mostly of washing garments by treading them (*e.g.*, Exod. 19¹⁰ ¹⁴) ; *cleanse me*, used also of purifying metal by rubbing off impurities (*e.g.*, Mal. 3³). His guilt he expresses by the three words, *transgressions, iniquity, sin*. Thus the consciousness of sinfulness could not be more fully presented.

3–5. The essence of the confession which follows is contained in the words : *Against thee, thee only, have I sinned* ; whatever wrong he may have done to men is primarily a sin against God ; and since he is guilty before God, the divine *words* of condemnation are *justified*, and the sentence pronounced is *vindicated* (the word means lit. " to be pure " or " clear ", cp. Mic. 6¹¹). The sincerity and whole-heartedness of the psalmist's confession is further emphasized by the acknowledgement that from his very birth his being was evil; this is not intended as an excuse, as though he could not help being sinful, but as the recognition of his innate evil nature, cp. the words of Ps. 58³: " The wicked are estranged from the womb, from birth they utter falsehood ". 6–12. The petitions which now follow are prefaced by words which show that the psalmist not only knows what God demands of those who are faithful to him, but also has the conviction that God will grant this : *thou desirest truth in the inward parts,* " truth " must be understood in the sense of faithfulness, as, *e.g.,* in Isa. 38³, and *wisdom,* which God makes known, must be thought of in its highest sense, *i.e.,* the fear of Yahweh. It must, however, be pointed out that some commentators take this verse in connexion with the preceding one, and explain it to mean that the Almighty will reveal to the psalmist the mystery of his sinfulness from birth. The interpretation of the verse is certainly difficult. But, however it is to be understood, the meaning of what follows is plain enough ; it is true, the thought-sequence of 7–12 is not quite logical ; but that is easily accounted for by the alternating emotions of one in the spiritual condition of the psalmist. In the knowledge of his uncleanness in the sight of God he prays that he will *purge* him with *hyssop* ; " purge ", lit. " un-sin ", is a technical term for ritual purification, cp. Ezek. 45¹⁸ ; *hyssop* is a wild herb the leaves of which were held to possess cleansing powers (cp. Lev. 14⁴ ⁿ·) ; and that he may be washed and become *whiter than snow* (cp. Isa. 1¹⁸) ; it is, of course, figurative language that is being used. In such a state of purity the psalmist feels justified in praying : *Fill me with joy and gladness* ; the text reads " make me to hear ", but we have followed the Syriac Version (lit. " satisfy me ") on account of the parallel in Ps. 90¹⁴. Figurative language is again used when it is said : *that the bones which thou hast crushed may rejoice* (cp. Pss. 22¹⁴, 102³). Then the thought of his *sins* again predominates, and he prays that God may *hide* his *face* from them, and *blot out all* his *iniquities,* that his *heart* may be *clean* and his *spirit steadfast.* In such a spiritual condition he will be able to abide in God's presence. But he still feels uncertain of himself, and prays that God will *not cast him away from his presence nor take his holy spirit from him* (cp. 2 Kgs. 13²³, Ps. 102¹⁰, and Ps. 143¹⁰) ; and he recalls the time long ago when he had not fallen away from God, and prays : *Restore unto me the joy of thy help, and,* as of yore, *sustain me with a willing spirit.* 13. As, once more, a faithful servant of God, he will show his repentance by amendment of life, and bear witness for God by teaching *transgressors* and *sinners* to turn unto him. 14–17. The concluding verses deal with praise to God, and self-dedication to him. The Hebrew text reads in 14 : *Deliver me from bloodguiltiness, O God* ; this is so out of harmony with the context that we have adopted Gunkel's suggested emendation, *Deliver me from silence, O God*; for the similarity of the two words in Hebrew see the text-critical note. The psalmist feels, in his happily restored relationship to God, that to keep silence from praising him would be altogether wrong; his *tongue* must *sing aloud* of his *righteousness*; and so he continues: *O Lord, open thou my lips, and my mouth shall show forth thy praise.* The psalm closes (16, 17) with one of the most beautiful utterances regarding spiritual worship in the Psalter. Wholly in opposition to the belief and practice of his times, he repudiates the idea of material sacrifices. The text of these verses is a little out of order; but the emendations are fairly obvious. What the psalmist offers is not the whole burnt-offering which was supposed to atone for sin, but himself with his *broken spirit* and *contrite heart*, which God does not despise. On the subject of the repudiation of sacrificial worship in the *Psalms*, see further, Ps. 40.

That the last two verses (18, 19) formed no part of the original psalm is obvious on the face of it; if in 18 there is any reference to a historical event, and if the verse were part of the psalm, there would assuredly have been some hint elsewhere in the psalm of such a terrible catastrophe (*i.e.*, the destruction of Jerusalem) as had happened. The verse is, however, usually interpreted in an eschatological sense (cp. Isa. 26[1], Pss. 102[13-16], 147[2, 13]), in reference to the time of the restitution of all things; in this case the verse is even more incongruous in its present position. But it is the final verse (19), with its enthusiastic belief in sacrifices, so utterly different from the spirit of the psalm itself, that definitely marks these verses as a later addition.

Religious Teaching

This has been largely dealt with in what has already been said; but a few points, on account of their far-reaching importance, call for special emphasis, even at the expense of some little repetition. The implication contained in the words, " Against thee, thee only, have I sinned," that offences against man are essentially sins against God, is of profound significance. It is a truth only too often lost sight of; yet, were it realized by men in their dealings with one another, how different would be the attitude of even the best towards each other. It is, further, a striking characteristic of this psalm that it contains no word of denunciation against others; its only precise parallel is Ps. 130; very close to it is Ps. 32, but *v.* 9 of that psalm is not quite in the same spirit. The next point is the teaching that sin is inherent in man from birth. For the Jewish doctrine of sin the words of *v.* 5 are of great interest. They have often been taken to imply the doctrine of original sin; that is a mistake; Judaism has never taught this; the idea that Adam's sin in any way affected the status of the human race is quite alien to Jewish teaching. Another important point is that in our psalm, which speaks so much of sin, nothing is said of suffering or adversity being the result of sin (cp. John 9². ³). Finally, the words, few though they be, about sacrifices, are of great religious importance, because the implication is that nothing man can do can effect reconciliation with God when he has been sinned against. This cuts away with one stroke the whole doctrine of the merit of works. Into this subject we cannot go further here, but its far-reaching importance will be realized.

PSALM 52

THERE would seem to have been a twofold purpose which prompted the composition of this psalm. It presents, on the one hand, a graphic picture of the bitter resentment felt by the godly man towards one who had no fear of God. The acrimonious words addressed by the writer to the special object of his wrath are palliated by his conviction that his enemy is also the enemy of God. Numerous individuals are, however, in question, and it is probable that they represent, respectively, opposed sections among the people. In the second place, the writer inculcates, at any rate implicitly, the doctrine of divine retribution. This will be further dealt with in the exegetical notes. The abrupt opening of the psalm, as well as its spirit and content, make it difficult to believe that it was ever used liturgically; in any case, it has never been so used in the worship of the Synagogue, as far as one can judge from the evidence.

The date of the psalm is indicated by its content · it belongs to the Greek period.

The metre is almost entirely 3 : 2, the text is in a few instances uncertain.

1. *For the Precentor : Maskil of David ; 2. When Doeg the Edomite came and reported to Saul, and said to him, David is come into the house of Ahimelek.*

1 (3). Why boastest thou thyself in evil, O powerful one, ° against the godly
                  man ° ?
 All the day 2 (4). thou devisest
  destruction,   thy tongue is like a sharpened razor °.
3 (5). Thou lovest evil more than good, lying ° more than righteousness °.
                    Selah.
4 (6). Thou lovest all destructive words, O deceitful tongue.
5 (7). Yea, God will destroy thee for ever ; he will snatch thee away, and pluck thee
                   from thy tent ;
     and root thee out of the land of the living. Selah.
6 (8). The righteous shall see it and fear ; but at him they will laugh :
7 (9).   " Behold, the man
        who maketh not
       God his strength !
 He trusted in the abundance of his and strengthened himself ° in his
  riches,   wealth ° ! "
8 (10). But, as for me, I am like a green
  olive-tree   in the house of God ;
 I trust in the love of God   for ever and ever.

9 (11). I will thank thee, °Yahweh°, for
    ever,
°And I will proclaim °thy name, for
    it is good,

for °thou °hast done it;

in the presence of thy godly ones.

Text-critical Notes

1. Read אֶל־חָסֶד (for the omission of the ֿ see GK 24 *e–g*) for חֶסֶד אֵל, " the love of God ". 2. Om. עֹשֵׂה רְמִיָּה, " working deceit," which overloads the line. 3. Read מִצֶּדֶק for מִדַּבֵּר צֶדֶק, " than speaking righteousness," for the rhythm's sake. 7. Read with ST, בְּהַוָּתוֹ for בְּהַוָּתוֹ, " in his destruction ". 9. Add יהוה, " Yahweh ", and אַתָּה, " thou ", for the rhythm's sake. Read וְאֲחַוֶּה for וַאֲקַוֶּה, " and I will wait for ".

Title. For the inappropriateness of the reference to Doeg the Edomite, see 1 Sam. 22⁹.

1–4. The verse-division in 1, 2, is somewhat uncertain, and one or two textual emendations are demanded; but in neither case is there unanimity among commentators. We have sought to give what seems to be a logical thought-sequence.

It is exceptional to find a psalm not beginning with words addressed to God, or in reference to him; there are about a dozen of such in the Psalter. In the present case, where we should expect an appeal to God for help against the enemy (as, *e.g.*, in Pss. 7, 12, 25, 35, etc.), the psalm opens abruptly with a challenge to the latter. It is not to be supposed that we have here the record of an actual dispute between the psalmist and a representative of the freethinking section, for in that case some words of the latter would have been quoted and would have given the psalmist further material for rebuke (see, *e.g.*, Pss. 10⁶, 12⁴, 14¹); rather, he is presenting the general attitude of those who were like-minded with himself towards those within the Jewish community among whom the ancestral faith was spurned. The most telling way of expressing this was to adopt the form of utterance to an individual. The quarrel was one of words; other psalms record more violent action (*e.g.*, 54³, 94²¹, 140¹, ⁴, ⁵). That the opposing faction included those of standing in the land is shown by the antagonist being addressed as *O powerful one* (lit. " mighty man "); this is not sarcasm; as a man of abundant wealth (7) he would occupy a position of importance. *Why boastest thou thyself?* he is asked, meaning that he had adopted an attitude of superiority, *against the godly man*, the psalmist is referring here to himself as representing the religiously-minded among his people; the Hebrew text is obviously corrupt; the Revised Version has adopted a paraphrase in order to give sense; but, even so, the two halves of the verse do not read as though belonging together. The evil-disposed mind of the adversary prompts a cruel method of damaging his innocent victims: *All the day thou devisest destruction*, by which is meant slanderous accusations designed to bring disgrace upon the *godly man.* The alteration of the verse-division here is demanded, otherwise the devising of destruction has *thy tongue* for its subject; but the function of the tongue is utterance, not mental activity. Hence we must read: *thy tongue is like a sharpened razor,* and the added words of the Hebrew text, " working deceitfully ", should be omitted, both because they overload the line and because they impute to the tongue that which belongs to the mind. In Ps. 57[4] the tongue of the godless is likened to " a sharp sword ". The word for " razor " has, in Jer. 36[23], the meaning of " knife ". In face of the *destructive* (lit. " swallowing up ") *words* of this deceitful tongue, the psalmist sets forth the doctrine of divine retribution. 5–7. This centred in the belief that upon the ungodly divine wrath was always visited in one form or another, while the godly always enjoyed divine favour, manifested by a prosperous life; though contradicted by the facts of life, this doctrine held sway, and appears here, as in various other psalms (*e.g.,* 37[10, 11], 49[16, 17]). Therefore it is said: *God will destroy thee for ever,* and this is described as taking place in three stages: *he will snatch thee away,* the thought is that of snatching up fire from a hearth (cp. Isa. 30[14]); *and pluck thee from thy tent*: in Deut. 28[63] the word is used of the people being " torn away " from their land; " tent " is sometimes used of an ordinary place of habitation (*e.g.,* Ps. 132[3] " the tent of thy house ", Isa. 16[5], Jer. 30[18]); *and root thee out of the land of the living*; the godless man thought he was safely rooted in the land (cp. Isa. 40[24], Job 5[3]). It is held by some commentators that this verse (5) is in the nature of a magical curse, the utterance of which, it was believed, would *ipso facto* take effect; it may be so (cp. Ps. 109[6 ff.]); but we are inclined to believe rather that the words are intended to be a statement of fact, namely, that divine retribution will descend upon the head of the wicked. Such retribution, which, according to the psalmist, will be witnessed by the righteous, naturally inspires them with awe, the *righteous shall see it and fear,* though the foolish delusion of the wicked man may cause them to *laugh* (cp. Ps. 58[10]), for worthy of contempt, indeed, is the man who repudiates God, and who trusts *in the abundance of his riches* (cp. Ps. 49[6]), and who looks upon his *wealth* as his strength. 8, 9. But if retribution overtakes the wicked, no less certain is the psalmist's conviction that prosperity will be the lot of him who *trusts in the love of God.* He likens himself, as representing the godly men in general, to *a green olive-tree in the house of God* (cp. Ps. 92[13]); this picture of flourishing strength and beauty is metaphorical, it is difficult to believe that trees grew within the temple enclosure (cp. Ps. 92[12, 13]); the whole consecrated area could be spoken of as the *house of God.* Within it, *in the presence of thy godly ones,* the psalmist *will thank Yahweh for ever, i.e.,* continually (cp. Ps. 89[2], etc.), for he knows that all has been brought about by the act of God, *for thou hast done it.* Thanksgiving and praise

T

belong together, hence the proclaiming of the name among those who love him.

The religious teaching of the psalm has already been sufficiently indicated in the exegetical notes.

PSALM 53 (= PSALM 14)

FOR the most part this psalm is identically the same as Ps. 14; the differences are, with one exception, trifling; the exception is *v.* 5 (6); in both psalms the text of this verse is hopelessly corrupt, probably due, at any rate to some extent, to the mutilated condition of the MS.; evidently more than one copy was made of the original psalm, with the result that the corruption was increased. In the light of the context, however, the original text can be tentatively restored—in this we are partly indebted to Gunkel; while the correctness of the emendation cannot of course be guaranteed, it may be claimed that it gives the general sense of what was originally written. We have taken this psalm, in preference to Ps. 14, for detailed study because, although the latter represents the earlier form (mainly on account of the use of *Yahweh* for *Elohim*), the passage which contains the main differences seems in Ps. 53 to have retained more of the original text than the corresponding verse in Ps. 14.

The psalm was written at a period of moral decline among the people in general, and not less so among those who should have been their religious leaders, namely the priests (for the justification of this statement see the exegetical notes). Of such deplorable conditions the prophets had occasion to complain at different times; for example, in Hos. 4[6-9] it is said: " My people are destroyed for lack of knowledge. . . . They feed on the sin of my people, and set their heart on their iniquity. And it shall be, like people, like priest; and I will punish them for their ways, and will recompense them for their doings." In later days another prophet says: " For the priest's lips should keep knowledge, and they should seek the Law at his mouth; for he is the messenger of Yahweh of hosts. But ye are turned aside out of the way; ye have caused many to stumble in the Law; ye have corrupted the covenant of Levi, saith Yahweh of hosts " (Mal. 2[7, 8]); this belongs to about the middle of the fifth century B.C. Still later, about 300 B.C., or thereabouts, another prophet, who was also an apocalyptist, speaks of the final world-catastrophe, saying: " The earth is polluted under the inhabitants thereof; because they have transgressed the laws, changed the ordinance, broken the everlasting covenant "; and he prefaces this with: " And it shall be, as with the people, so with the priest . . ."

(Isa. 24$^{2, 5}$); thus all come under the same condemnation. Our psalmist stands, therefore, in a line with the prophets; and there is reason to believe that he wrote his psalm at about the same period as the prophet from whose writing our last quotation is taken. The atheistic attitude referred to in the opening words of the psalm (cp. Ps. 10^4 which belongs approximately to the same period) points to a time when intercourse among the Gentiles had weakened the faith of many, i.e., during the Greek period; the worldliness of the priesthood, the ruling caste, was characteristic of this period; it was due, at any rate in part, to their political dealings with foreign potentates. In somewhat later times (i.e., during the Maccabæan period) there is ample evidence of this. But that the psalm itself was written in Maccabæan times is quite out of the question. At a time when a great part of the people were fighting and dying for the faith of their fathers, how could it possibly be said: "Every one of them is gone back, they are altogether become abominable; none doeth good, not even one"?

The metre is for the most part 3 : 2.

1.   *For the Precentor : Al-maḥalath. Maskil. David's.*

1. (2).   The fool saith in his heart :
                              " There is no God ! "
        They are corrupt and abominable ° in
                act °,   none doeth good.
2 (3). ° God ° looketh down from heaven   upon the children of men,
        To see if there are any that deal
            wisely,   seeking ° God ° ;
3 (4). Every one of them is gone back,   they are altogether become corrupt,
                None doeth good,
                Not even one.
4 (5). Have the workers of iniquity no
            knowledge ?   they devour my people ;
        They eat the bread of God,   but call not upon ° his name °.
5 (6). ° Is it not a terrible thing !   for God doth scatter his bones ;
                The profane one is brought to shame,
                For God hath rejected him°.
6 (7). O ° for the salvation of ° Israel from   when ° God ° bringeth back the restor-
            Zion,   ation of his people ;
                Jacob shall rejoice,
                Israel shall be glad.

Text-critical Notes

1. Read, with Ps. 14^1, צְלִילָה for עָוֶל, " unrighteousness ". 2. Ps. 14^2 has יהוה. Ps. 14^4 has יהוה, but in this case wrongly. Read שְׁמוֹ for שָׁם, " there ", which has been put into the next verse. 5. For this verse read, following Gunkel :

כִּי־אֱלֹהִים פִּזַּר עַצְמוֹתָיו   הֲלֹא־הָיָה פַחַד
חָנֵף הוֹבִישׁ
כִּי־אֱלֹהִים מְאָסוֹ :

(G = חָנֵף for חֹנְךָ). In order that the corruption of the text of this verse in both psalms may be seen, we quote them as they now stand :

Ps. 53^5 שָׁם פָּחֲדוּ־פַחַד לֹא־הָיָה פָחַד כִּי־אֱלֹהִים פִּזַּר עַצְמוֹת חֹנָךְ הֱבִשֹׁתָה
כִּי־אֱלֹהִים מְאָסָם :

" There they feared a terrible thing, there was no terrible thing, for God doth scatter

the bones of him that encampeth against thee ; thou hast put to shame, for God hath
rejected them ".

Ps. 14[6, 6] שָׁם פָּחֲדוּ פַחַד פִּי־אֱלֹהִים בְּדוֹר צַדִּיק : עֲצַת־עָנִי תָבִישׁוּ כִּי
יְהֹוָה מַחְסֵהוּ :

" There they feared a terrible thing, for God is in the generation of the righteous.
The counsel of the poor ye put to shame ; for Yahweh is his refuge." 6. Read, with
some MSS. and the Versions, also Ps. 14[7], יְשׁוּעַת for יְשׁוּעוֹת, " salvations ", or
" helps "; Ps. 14 has יהוה.

For the title, see p. 17.

1–3. Horror-struck at the wickedness which he sees all around him,
the psalmist begins his denunciation in a manner as terse as it is drastic :
The fool saith in his heart, There is no God. As the verbs in the plural
show, the *fool* is meant collectively. It should also be pointed out that
the verbs, though in the perfect, represent actions the influence of which
extends into the present ; so that while in Hebrew the perfect form is
used, the sense is present ; hence in English they should be rendered in
the present tense. The expression *fool* (*nabal*) connotes not merely
stupidity, but also disgraceful and immoral conduct, in him thus
designated. Those condemned by the psalmist say : *There is no God* ;
their saying so is due to two causes : persistent evil-living results not
only in forgetting God, but, in effect, in denying his existence. In
addition to this, the contact with Gentiles involved many Jews in what
was practically atheism ; true, the Gentiles had their gods, but to the
psalmist, as to the prophet (Isa. 41[24]) they were " nothing ". The
wickedness of those of whom the psalmist speaks is described in a
threefold way : *they are corrupt*, *i.e.*, they are morally ruined (cp. *e.g.*,
Prov. 6[32]) ; *abominable in act*, *i.e.*, what they do is abhorrent ; *none doeth
good*, *i.e.*, there is nothing that mitigates in any way their evil doing It
need hardly be said that the psalmist is not speaking of mankind in
general, but of his own people, see *v.* 4, " my people ". *Naïve* as the
psalmist's conception is in picturing the Almighty as *looking down from
heaven upon the children of men*, this old-world realism enshrines a very
deep spiritual truth ; and if, in saying that *none doeth good, not even one*,
he somewhat overstates the unhappy conditions of the time, such
overstatement is very natural and pardonable in a devout and loyal
servant of God who stands aghast at the sight of evil-living men about
him. 4–5. So far the psalmist has been speaking of his people in
general ; now he particularizes. The change of subject is abrupt, but
there is no mistaking whom he now has in mind ; he uses a phrase which
makes this quite clear : *they eat the bread of God.* Whether by the
expression *the bread of God* is meant sacrifices in general (*e.g.*, Lev. 21[6]),
or the show-bread, called " the bread of God " in Lev. 21[22], cp. Lev. 3[11],
1 Sam. 21[4], see also Matth. 12[3, 4], is immaterial (probably both are
included), the point is that it is the priests whom he now denounces
because they *call not upon his name* ; they are *workers of iniquity* who

have no *knowledge*, *i.e.*, of God (cp. Hos. 1[4, c]); instead of being
spiritual guides, *they devour* the *people*, in reference to the sacrificial
offerings brought by the people, which they consumed for their own
benefit (cp. Ezek. 34). The verse which follows (5), as will be seen from
the text-critical note, is very corrupt; one of the difficulties centres in
the fact that both in this psalm and in Ps. 14, " they ", " them ", as
well as " he ", " him ", occur, so that it is an open question whether
one particular priest or the priests as a whole are referred to. In the
preceding verse, it is true, the priests as a body are clearly meant; both
psalms agree in this; but it is just for this reason that a copyist may have
altered the pronoun. We have taken the reference in the verse before
us to be to one in particular, *i.e.*, the High-priest, for he, as the head of
the priesthood, would be most to blame. We know from somewhat
later history how sometimes the High-priest was far from being what he
ought to have been (1 Macc. 7[21, 22], 9[54-56], 2 Macc. 4[6-10], 13[3-8]).
In the present case an awful fate overtakes him : *Is it not a terrible thing !
for God doth scatter his bones*; that means that he was not accorded
decent burial, a fearful degradation (cp. Jer. 8[1, 2], 2 Chron. 34[5]); so
it is said : *The profane is brought to shame, for God hath rejected him*.
From this terrible picture the psalmist turns to envisage the future (6),
and prays for *the restoration of his people*; the phrase used is *šūb š^rbūth*,
a technical term for the bringing back of the time of primeval happiness
(for the fuller explanation of this see Ps. 85); then *Jacob shall rejoice
and Israel shall be glad.*

On this psalm a section on the religious teaching is not called for.

PSALM 54

A SHORT and simple, but heartfelt appeal to the Almighty for help
against such as had " not set God before them ", *i.e.*, freethinkers.
The psalm is similar in content to a number of others (*e.g.*, 55, 64, etc.).
It is the outpouring of an individual who speaks on his own behalf.
Like all those psalms which deal with the enmity of the freethinking
element in the community against the orthodox, the psalm belongs to the
Greek period.

The metre is irregular, alternating between 3 : 2 and 3 : 3 ; in v. 3 it
is 3 : 3 : 3.

1. *For the Precentor : With stringed instruments. Maskil. David's ; 2. When the
Ziphites came and said to Saul, " Is not David hiding himself with us ? "*

1 (3). O God, by thy name save me,   and by thy power vindicate me ;
2 (4). O God, hear my prayer,   give ear to the words-of-my-mouth ;
3 (5).   For the ° proud ° are risen against me,
                and violent men seek my life ;
                they have not set God before them. Selah.

4 (6). Behold, God helpeth me,

5 (7). May ° he requite ° the evil unto mine enemies,

6 (8). With a free-will-offering will I sacrifice to thee,

7 (9). For it hath delivered me from all trouble,

the ʾLord is ° one that upholdeth ° my life;

in thy faithfulness destroy them.

I will praise thy name,° for it is good;
and mine eye gloateth over mine enemies.

Text-critical Notes

3. Read זֵדִים for זָרִים, "strangers", as being a better parallel to "violent men", עָרִיצִים, see Ps. 86¹⁴.   4. Not as R.V., "of them that uphold", see GK 119*i*, and exeg. note. 5. Read יָשׁוּב. 6. Om. יהוה for the rhythm's sake.

The title, which occurs also in G, may be due to some ingenious copyist who discerned a parallel between the evil machinations of the psalmist's enemies and the episode recounted in 1 Sam. 23¹⁹⁻²³. 1-3.   In accordance with most psalms of this kind prayer is offered before the mention of what is prayed for: *O God, by thy name save me, i.e.*, by means of the name, the utterance of which was all-powerful, hence the words which follow: *and by thy power vindicate me* (cp. Pss. 5¹¹, ¹², 2¹²).   *Name* and *power* are thus parallel, just as *hear my prayer*, and *give ear to the words-of-my-mouth* (one beat in Hebrew), form another parallelism.   Then follows the reason for which the prayer was offered (3).   The psalmist is assailed by those who are described as *proud*, or "arrogant", and *violent*; the former epithet connotes the idea of presumptuousness, the latter that of causing terror, because such men are ruthless in their actions.   The cause of their enmity is a religious one, for *they have not set God before them*, which is just what the psalmist does first and foremost.   He, therefore, affirms with quiet confidence that (4) God *helpeth me*, and *upholdeth my life*.   The Hebrew form of the expression *one that upholdeth* is difficult to render adequately in translation; to translate it literally, as the R.V. does, "of (or marg. "with") them that uphold", as though *the Lord* were one among others, conveys quite an erroneous idea.   The concept of upholding, or preserving, life can be held in regard both to men and to God, without for a moment comparing human with divine action; in the same way, men can help, and *God helpeth*; but there is no kind of comparison between the help of each.   The parallelism in Hebrew poetry is seen here to be of great value for purposes of interpretation.   When the psalmist then goes on to express the wish (5) that God *may requite the evil unto mine enemies* . . ., we are confronted with a distasteful *trait*, but at least he does not retaliate personally, vengeance is left in the hands of God (cp. Ps. 143¹² and elsewhere).   A promise of thanksgiving follows (6): *With a freewill-offering will I sacrifice to thee: and I will praise thy name, for it is good*, reverting to the opening verse.   The freewill-offering (*nĕdābāh*) was a sacrifice which was offered not of obligation, but with the sole purpose of honouring God (cp. Exod. 35²⁹).

The power of the name is again emphasized in the concluding verse (7): *for it hath delivered me from all trouble*; the certitude that its utterance brings about what is desired is such that the psalmist can speak of his trouble as already past. The final words illustrate once more a spirit of vengeful bitterness; the Hebrew expression means more than merely looking upon the enemy, it connotes the idea of rejoicing over him (cp. Pss. 112[8], 118[7]).

The religious teaching of this type of psalm is dealt with in that of others of a similar nature, *e.g.*, 28 and others, especially Ps. 35 (final section).

PSALM 55

THIS psalm presents unusual difficulties, both of text and of interpretation. It is classed by Gunkel as a " Lament of the Individual ", and Hans Schmidt still further specifies it as one of the poems used in legal process by an accused person, who is protesting his innocence and pleading for acquittal in the supreme court—the house of God. But, even if this be admitted, there remain problems whose solution is far from being certain, mainly due to the repeated change in the personal pronouns. Sometimes the opponent is a single individual, in *vv.* 12–14 directly addressed, in *v.* 21 mentioned in the third person. In *vv.* 10–12, again, there seems to be a general complaint, in the prophetic spirit, of iniquity rife in the city as a whole. We cannot invoke the doctrine of corporate personality here, because the adversary (or adversaries) is not a formal group, but a number of individuals who are at one in their attack on the speaker, though they seem to be otherwise independent of each other. In the circumstances, it is not surprising that several commentators hold the psalm to be composite. Thus Briggs makes two psalms, 1–8[a] and 8[b]–23, with a later insertion in 16–19. Gunkel finds a separate piece in 19[c]–22, 24, while Buttenwieser assigns *vv.* 1–11, 16–19, 22 to one poem, and regards 12–14, 20–21 as a fragment, in which there is a gap after *v.* 14. Hans Schmidt thinks that the original poem has been worked over in order to adapt it to a national situation. We may, however, regard the whole as a unity, especially if *v.* 18 is correctly read and interpreted below, and ascribe the swift changes of person to the liveliness of the Hebrew mind. Even so, unless we are to accept drastic alterations of text, there is a gap between *vv.* 14 and 15, the latter part of one line and the beginning of another, with, perhaps, several lines between, having been lost.

Thus regarded, the psalm appears as the plaint of one who is attacked by enemies, public or private. His case makes him long for solitude, for it is his old friends and acquaintances who have made him the object of their assault. One, in particular is singled out, perhaps, on Hans Schmidt's theory, the chief accuser. In the spirit normal among ancient Israelites (though not confined to them), the psalmist prays for vengeance on his enemies.

There is little to indicate date; style and language suggest the post-exilic rather than the pre-exilic period. The author is familiar with the old Israelite stories, *e.g.*, of the Tower of Babel and of the death of Dathan and Abiram. The text is often obscure and uncertain, but help is sometimes given by the Septuagint and by the Peshiṭta.

The metre is 3 : 2, with 2 : 2 in *vv.* 9, 10^{ab}, and, probably, in the last line of all. Anacrusis occurs in *v.* 6.

For the Precentor : On stringed instruments. Maskil. Of David.

1	(2).	Give ear, O Yahweh, to my prayer,	and hide thee not from my petition.
2	(3).	Attend to me and answer me ;	restless am I with anxious thought.
3	(4).	By the voice of the foe,°	
		° And I am distraught °	by the cry of ° the wicked.
		For ° they turn ° evil upon me,	and in wrath they bitterly assail me ;
4	(5).	My heart doth writhe within me,	and terrors ° ° are upon me.
5	(6).	Fear and trembling come over me,	and shuddering hath covered me.
6	(7).	And I said :	
		Oh that I had pinions as a dove,	that I might fly away and make my home !
7	(8).	Behold, afar would I rove,	I would lodge in a wilderness ! Selah.
8	(9).	I would haste to my refuge	° from the blast of the storm ° !
·9	(10).	Confound, O Lord,	divide their speech !
		For I have seen violence,	and strife in the city.
10	(11).	By day and by night	they encompass it upon its walls.
		Evil and pain are within her,	11 (12). ruin ° in her midst °,
		Nor are her spaces free	from violence and deceit.
12	(13).	For it is no foe that insulteth me,	or I could bear ° my shame.
		Not my enemy that hath done great things against me,	or I would hide from him.
13	(14).	But it is thou, a man mine equal,	mine intimate and my friend,
14	(15).	With whom I was wont to have sweet converse	in the house of God.
		We would walk in the sacred throng,	. . . . .
15	(16).	May . . . . . ° deceive,	death ° ° swallow them up °,
		May they go down alive to Sheol, .	for evils ° ° are in their heart.
16	(17).	As for me—unto God will I call,	and may Yahweh save me.
17	(18).	Evening and morning and noon	would I meditate and moan.
		° That he may hear ° my voice,	
18	(19).	° and redeem °	my soul in peace.
		(Redeem) ° from them that are near me, for as adversaries °	have they become to me. .
19	(20).	May God hear ° and afflict them °,	he that dwelleth ° from of old °.
		Which keep no oath,	nor fear they God.
20	(21).	He hath put forth his hand ° against his confederates °,	he hath defiled his covenant.
21	(22).	Smoother ° than butter ° ° is his face °,	but war is ° in his heart °.
		Softer his words than oil,	yet are they drawn swords.
22	(23).	Cast thy burden on Yahweh,	and he shall sustain thee. ‧
		He will not suffer for ever	the righteous to be moved.
23	(24).	But thou, O God, wilt bring them down	° to the pit of doom ° ;
		Men of blood and deceit	shall not live out half their days.
		But I will trust	in thee, ° O Yahweh °.

Text-critical Notes

2. Read, with Duhm, וְאָהוֹמָה for "and I moan". 3. Read, with Olshausen, מִדַּעֲקַת for "pressure of". Read, with G, יָשׁוּ for "they remove". 4. Om., with Gunkel, "of death" and "have fallen".ʹ 8. Read, with S, מֵרוּחַ סָעֲרָה for "from rushing wind, from tempest". 11. Read, with Duhm, בְּתוֹכָה for "within her". 12. Add בְּלִבָּתִי (the verb needs an object; cp. Ez. 16⁶², 36⁶ʼ⁷). 15. Read, with Qᵉʳê, יַשִּׁיא מָוֶת for Kᵉthibh יַשִּׁימוֹת (= desolations). Read, with Brüll, יִבְצָלְמוֹ for "upon them". Om., with S, "in their terror". 17. Read, with G, וְיִשְׁמַע for "and he heard". 18. Read, with G, יִפְדֶּה for "he redeemed". Read (cp. S) מִקְּרָבִים לִי כִּי בְרַבִּים for "from my war" (or "from nearness to me") "for with many". 19. Read, with G, וַיַּעֲנֵּם for "and answer them". Read, with G, יֹשֵׁב מֶקֶּדֶם for "and he that dwelleth in the east" (or "of old"). 20. Read, with G, יָדוֹ for "his hands". Read, with Gunkel, בִּשְׁלְמָיו for "in his peace" (plur.). 21. Read, with Olshausen, מֵחֶמְאָה for "butter-words" (?). Read, with G, פָּנָיו for "his mouth". Read, with Buhl, בְּלִבּוֹ for "his heart". 23. Read, with Buhl, לְבְאֹר for "to the spring of". Add, with G, יהוה.

The psalmist begins, in language appropriate to a hymn of distress, with an appeal to Yahweh to *give ear* and *attend* to him. He has been *restless*, turning this way and that with his *anxious thought*. The trouble comes from the outside, and is due to the *voice of the foe* and the *cry of the wicked*. They control, as it were, the course that *evil* takes, and can "bend" and *turn* its path so that it will meet him. Hence the *writhing* of his heart—a strong metaphor for palpitation—the *fear*, *trembling*, and *shuddering* which have come over him. In words familiarized and enriched by their musical associations, he expresses his longing to get away from all his trouble; even a *wilderness* would be preferable to *the breath of the storm* that rages about him (*vv.* 6–8).

It is not surprising that in such case the poet should pray for vengeance. His mind goes back to the old story of how Yahweh had *confounded* and *divided* the speech of men who, in their arrogance, had sought to reach the heavens. Wherever he looks, he finds iniquity, *violence and strife*, which go round the city walls like watchmen; his trouble is only one example of a general situation (9–11).

Suddenly the psalmist's thought fastens on one aspect of his case. As we gather from 18 (if the reading adopted from the Syriac version be approximately correct), his adversaries are his former intimates. But it seems that there had been one whose hostility and faithlessness had been especially prominent, and it is to him that the psalmist turns. His trouble would have been bearable if it had been caused by a *foe*, but a man cannot *hide* from a *familiar* and a *friend*, especially when their intimacy has been cemented by the *sweet converse* they have had together in the *house of God*. We may suspect that both the psalmist and his adversary were priests attached to the sanctuary, and the language of 14 recalls that of Ps. 42⁴.

Here there is a break, too sudden to be ascribed to a simple change of thought, for it comes in the middle of a line. We are forced to the conclusion that there has been some accidental mutilation of the text, perhaps at the foot of a column of writing. When the poem is resumed, we are near the end of a curse on the enemy. The common term, *swallow them up*, takes the poet's mind back to the story of Dathan and Abiram, and he prays that his enemies too *may go down alive to Sheol* (15, cp. Num. 16³¹⁻³³).

Back comes the poet once more to his own need. At the special hours of prayer—*evening, morning and noon*—he would plead with Yahweh. The times mentioned have been held to suggest a post-exilic date, but, while we know that they were the proper hours of worship in later Israel, we do not know that the custom was instituted after the Return; it may have been ancient. As the sufferer pleads, there rises again the bitter thought that his *adversaries* are those who have been *near* him (18, 19). Their perfidy (*oath* is an unusual sense for the word employed here, but is certified by a cognate Arabic root), and their disregard of the obligations imposed by association and *covenant*, together with the foul hypocrisy which makes their faces *smoother than butter* and their *words* more soothing than *oil* (again the psalmist singles out an individual), while *war* and *drawn swords* (a unique word) are in their *heart*—these things once more provoke a prayer for the punishment of the enemy (20, 21).

Verse 22 reads as though it were the divine answer to the psalmist's prayer. Again we have words which are among the most familiar of those given to us by the Old Testament. The man who *casts* his *burden upon Yahweh* will receive the divine nourishment and sustenance. That is all the assurance he needs, and the poem concludes in 23 with the renewed contrast between the premature fate of the wicked and the psalmist's happy *trust* in *Yahweh*.

Religious Teaching

As so often, the value of the psalm lies not so much in its doctrine as in the spirit it expresses. Here is a man living in a world of violence and treachery which threaten to overwhelm him, longing to escape from it all, and yet confident in the God to whom he has committed himself. Though he would shelter from the storm, and cannot, yet the temple of his life is founded on a rock, the rock of his faith.

PSALM 56

LIKE so many other pieces in the Psalter, this is a cry of suffering and strikes the familiar notes. The poet is in distress, surrounded by malicious and crafty enemies who plot his ruin and seek his life. There is no word of confession or of consciousness of sin, nor, on the other hand, is there any assertion of innocence.   While, then, Gunkel is justified in placing the psalm among the " Laments of the individual ", there is less ground for Hans Schmidt's ascription of the piece to the " prayers of the accused ".   It is, however, apparent that at least one attempt has been made to adapt the psalm to the needs of the community; the latter part of *v.* 7, with its demand for the punishment of the " nations ", has no place in a merely personal appeal.

The structure of the psalm is interesting and suggestive.   It is generally recognized that it falls into two almost equal parts, the division coming after *v.* 7.   In *vv.* 4 and 10–11 we have nearly identical language (*v.* 10 contains an obvious doublet), and, though some moderns (notably Gunkel and Hans Schmidt) regard this as due to textual corruption, it is difficult to avoid the impression that Briggs is right, and that we have a genuine refrain of some kind.   It is possible that such a " refrain " might have been placed in the middle of the section to which it belongs—the earlier champions of the " strophe " often found such medial refrains.   But, on the whole, it seems more probable that it occurred originally at the end of each section and not in the middle. This would mean that it has dropped out after *v.* 7, where its place is taken by the intrusive and obscure reference to the " nations ", and after *v.* 13.   This arrangement would yield four three-line stanzas, each followed by the refrain.   *V.* 9 seems to have been mutilated; possibly the doublet of *v.* 10 ousted the proper conclusion of the verse. There is also, apparently, a word missing at the end of *v.* 13 ; it is easy to understand that it might have suffered the fate of the last refrain.

There is nothing in the psalm, either in style or in reference, which gives the least clue to its date.   The text seems to have suffered seriously in course of transmission, though both the Septuagint and the Peshitta sometimes offer a useful alternative text.

The metre is 3 : 3 throughout, the refrain being 3 : 3 : 3.   Anacrusis occurs in *v.* 1.

1. *For the Precentor : On " The dove of the distant oaks ".   Of David.   Miktam. When the Philistines seized him in Gath.*

1 (2).   ° O God ! °
     Have mercy on me, for man
          trampleth me down,   every day doth the warrior oppress me.
2 (3). Watchers do ever oppress me,   for many war against me.
     ° Uplift me ° 3 (4). in the day that
          I fear;   I will trust in thee.
4 (5). In God ° I will carry my cause to
          its end °,
                    in God do I trust, fearless ;
                         what shall flesh do unto me ?
5 (6). Ever they speak, ° they take
          counsel °,   against me are all their thoughts.
     For evil 6 (7). they lurk, ° they
          spy on me °   they watch my steps.

As they have longed for my life,   7 (8). ° heed ° their iniquity °.   °
° In God I will carry my cause to its
end ;
                                                in God do I trust, fearless ;
                                                what shall flesh do unto me ? °
8 (9). O count thou ° my restless toss-
          ings °   set my tears ° before thee °.   °   °
9 (10). Then shall my foes turn back,   in the day when I cry ° unto thee °.
          This I know, that God is mine, ...
10 (11). In God ° I will carry my cause to
          its end °;   °   °
11 (12).   in God do I trust, fearless,
                                                what shall ° flesh ° do unto me ?
12 (13). Vows to thee are upon me, my God,   thank-offering will I pay unto thee.
13 (14). For thou deliveredst my soul from
          death,   ° thou keptest my feet from stumbling.
          That I might walk in the presence
          of God,   in the light of life .   .   .   .   .
          ° In God will I carry my cause to its
          end ;
                                in God do I trust, fearless ;
                                what shall flesh do unto me ? °

Text-critical Notes

1. Transpose אֱלֹהִים to beginning of verse. 2. Read, with Gunkel, רוֹמְמֵנִי for
" on high ". 4. Read, with Schlögl, אֲכַלֶּה דְּבָרֵי for " I will praise his word ".
5. Read, with Gunkel (cp. S), יְדַבְּרוּ יִנְעֲצוּ for " they pain my words " (or " my
words give pain "). 6. Read, with Gunkel, יַצְפִּינוּ for " they conceal ". 7. Read,
with Ewald, פַּלֵּס for " deliver ". Om. " In anger bring down the nations, O
God " (gloss). Insert, with Briggs, refrain as v. 4. 8. Read, with Duhm, נְדֹד
for " my wandering " (?). Read, with G, לְנֶגְדֶּךָ for " in thy bottle ". Om., with
Briggs, " are they not in thy reckoning ? " 9. Insert, with G, לָךְ. 10. Cp. on v. 4.
Om., with Gunkel, " In God will I praise with a word ". 11. Read (cp. v. 4)
בְּשָׂר for " man ". 13. Read, with Halévy, כְּלֹאת for " is not ? " Insert, with
Briggs, refrain as in v. 4.

For the title, see p. 17.
    The first three stanzas of this psalm are devoted to a description of
the psalmist's plight and a plea for deliverance. In the first (1-4) he
cries out for *mercy*, the free, unmerited, favour of a God on whom he
has no claims, and pleads that he may be *uplifted* from the pit of troubles
into which he has fallen. His enemies are cruel, powerful, and crafty
warriors who *trample* him *down, watchers* who let slip no opportunity of
oppressing him. Yet he is determined to see the matter through to *its
end*, and this conviction that God will at last see him is the refrain which
runs all through the poem.
    The second stanza (5-7) stresses the malicious cunning of the
adversaries. The poet is under constant observation, for at every
corner in the city and behind every bush in the country there *lurks* a
spy, ready to take advantage of anything he may say or do. The world
for him is full of jealous eyes, all *watching* him, that his foes may win
their hope and rob him of *life*.
    In the third stanza (8-11) we have the victim turning to God for

vengeance and deliverance. He begs that God will *count* (a precative perfect, as Buttenwieser has seen) the number of times he has turned and tossed on his bed, kept wakeful by anxiety and fear. He would have his *tears set before* God (the " bottle " of the traditional Hebrew text is a large wineskin, and in no way resembles the little glass " tear-bottles " identified by the archæologist; hence the adoption of the reading attested by G). Then he will win his case, and the defeated enemy will *turn back* in flight.

Such deliverance calls for thanksgiving (12–13). The psalmist is under an obligation, he *bears* his *vows* as a burden to be discharged. So sure is he of the rightness of his cause, and of the divine justice and mercy, that he can speak of his deliverance as an accomplished fact. The confidence of the refrain is justified, and its note of unshaken trust gives a fitting conclusion to the poem.

Religious Teaching

The psalm is but another testimony to the firm belief of the pious Israelite in the justice, mercy, and love of God—a thought so characteristic as to need no further elaboration.

PSALM 57

THIS psalm falls naturally into two parts, *vv.* 1–5 and 6–11, each consisting of seven lines followed by a refrain. *Vv.* 7–11, however, reappear (with some slight textual differences) in Ps. 108 : 1–5. The two sections are alike in tone ; each prays for deliverance from enemies. But, while the first half ends (apart from the refrain) with a description of these enemies, the second is mainly occupied with an exultant outburst of song, due to the sense of God's greatness. *V.* 6, it is true, describes the psalmist's peril, but the poet passes at once to the happier note in *v.* 7.

It is widely recognized that in Ps. 57 we have a combination of two psalms, or rather of sections of two psalms. The division, however, is usually made after *v.* 6, not after *v.* 5, an arrangement which seems at first sight to be supported by the text of Ps. 108 but which fails to take into account the structure of Ps. 57. The presence and position of the refrain strongly suggest that the true line of partition comes after *v.* 5.

Clearly, neither portion is complete. *Vv.* 1–5 obviously form the first " stanza " of a poem which celebrated redemption from the perils actually described, and we may safely assume that the whole originally ended on the note of confidence with which it began. The second part is equally clearly the conclusion of a poem with a similar *motif*; while the refrain in *v.* 5 makes it impossible to attach *v.* 6 closely to the first part, the *Selah* at the end of *v.* 6 makes it appear that this was the closing verse of a section, or stanza, whose earlier portion has not been preserved.

We conclude, then, that the person responsible for the present form of Ps. 57 took these two sections from other psalms. The first was a complete stanza; in attaching the second he included a pair of lines which would give the same number of lines as those in the first extract, and would take up the theme where the first left off. To round off the whole, he added the last line of his first selection at the end of the second; it may have been already a refrain in the psalm from which *vv.* 1–5 were drawn.

In spite of textual differences (some of which disappear in the Septuagint), the " compiler " of Ps. 108 probably borrowed directly from this psalm. This seems to be the most probable explanation of the fact that *v.* 11, which, as we have seen, can hardly have belonged to the poem from which these verses were taken, is also found in Ps. 108[5].

Accurate dating is out of the question; the first part contains in *v.* 3 a reminiscence of Ps. 43[3] and is, then, later than Pss. 42–43.

The text is, on the whole, well preserved. The Septuagint sometimes offers a superior reading, but conjectural emendation is hardly necessary.

Metre: *Vv.* 1–5, 11, 3 : 3, with 2 : 2 : 2 in 4[b]–5[a]; *vv.* 6–10, 3 : 2, with 2 : 2 in 7[c]–8[a].

For the Precentor : " Destroy not ". David's. Miktam. When he fled before Saul into the cave.

1 (2). Grant me favour, O God, grant me favour!   for in thee hath my soul trusted.
And in the shadow of thy wings ° am I secure °   ° till the destruction be passed °.
2 (3). I cry to God Most High,   to God ° who bestoweth good ° on me.
3 (4). May he send from heaven and save me,   ° may he put to shame ° them that crush me. Selah.
May God send
         his love and his truth,
         4 (5), ° and deliver ° my soul.
In the midst of lions I lay me down: blazing (with hate) are the sons of men.
Their teeth are spears and arrows,   and their tongue a sharp sword.
5 (6). Be high over the heavens, O God;   upon all the earth be thy glory.
6 (7). A net have they spread for my feet,   ° they have bent down ˇ my soul.
They have dug before me a pit;   they have fallen therein. Selah.
7 (8). Firmly fixed is my heart, O my God;   firmly fixed is my heart.
I would sing and give praise!   8 (9). awake, ° O my lyre °.
Awake, lute and lyre,   I would waken the dawn!
9 (10). I will praise thee among the peoples, O Lord,   hymn thee among the nations.
10 (11). For thy love is great unto the heavens,   and unto the skies thy truth.
11 (12). Be high over the heavens, O God;   upon all the earth be thy glory.

Text-critical Notes

1. Read, with G, אֶבְטַח for "I will trust". Read עָדִי עֲבֹר for עַד יַעֲבֹר.
2. Read, with G, גֹּמֵל for "who completeth". 3. Read (cp. G) יִתֵּן לְחֶרְפָּה for
"he hath shamed". 4. Insert (cp. G) וַיּוֹשַׁע. 6. Read, with G, כָּפְפוּ for "he
bent down". 8. Read, with G, כְּבוֹדִי for "my glory".

While it is true that portions of two psalms have here been combined,
it is clear that the composite result was intended to be a unified whole.
The compiler deliberately constructed this " prayer of the individual "
to express his own needs and the needs of others in like case with himself.
He opens, then, in *v.* 1, with a plea for *favour*, the free, uncovenanted
grace on which he has no claim, and with an expression of *trust* and
security. Black though the outlook may be, he has no real cause for
anxiety, for he can rely on his God. Then, in *v.* 2, he proceeds to put
his request, basing his demand, as so often, on the fact that God has
bestowed good on him in the past, and demanding that his enemies be
put to shame. He recalls Ps. 43[3], and describes his foes as *lions*, or as
men in a *blaze* of hate. This leads him to the refrain ; the vindication
of his cause will serve as an assertion of God's universal supremacy.

The second part is almost identical, as we have seen, with Ps.
108[1-5]. But *v.* 6 appears only here ; the compiler of the later psalm
did not need it for his purpose, though it forms a good transition from
complaint to confidence. It is true that the enemy has *put a net for
the feet* of the psalmist—the word used for " feet " commonly means
" steps " in Hebrew, but means " feet " in Phœnician—and has *dug a
pit before* him, but it is the offender who suffers, not the intended victim.
This may be an experience already past, or it may be an expression of
complete certainty in the knowledge of divine justice. Whichever it
be, it gives a *heart firmly fixed*, a serene reliance on God. But the
psalmist soon goes further still ; his confidence is not merely passive,
but results in an outburst of song and *praise* (*v.* 7). He must give
utterance to his feeling, and turns to the instruments of music so long
mute and sleeping, and bids them *awake*. So great is his joy that it
must be told abroad to the *nations* (*v.* 9). It is only right that this should
be so, for the *love* of God is as great as the *heavens* which arch over all
men (*v.* 10), and his *glory* should be spread *high* over *all the earth*.

Religious Teaching

We have, once more, the familiar truths that God hears prayer,
that he punishes the wicked, and that he justifies the righteous.

PSALM 58

THIS psalm, like Ps. 82, brings before us certain forms of iniquity and
injustice, which are ascribed either to subordinate deities or to human

rulers who claim divine rank. A fuller discussion of the question will
be found under Ps. 82. Ps. 58 is simple in form, as it falls into two
unequal parts, of which the former, *vv.* 1–5, describes the iniquity
rampant in the world, and the latter, *vv.* 6–11, calls for vengeance.
There is no evidence whatever as to the date of the psalm ; if the rulers
were native Israelites, it might be pre-exilic. But it is not likely that
Israelites would have claimed divine honours at any period, and it is,
therefore, more probable that the sinners are foreigners and the date
post-exilic. There are one or two linguistic peculiarities, including a
few rare words and a preference for the long, poetic forms of certain
prepositions.

Metre : 4 : 3, with 3 : 4 in *vv.* 4 and 8.

For the Precentor : " Destroy not ". David's. Miktam.

1 (2). ° O ye gods ! ° will ye verily   speak righteously,
                                        judge men uprightly ?
2 (3). Surely, with a heart of ° iniquity °   do ye work in the earth ;
                              violence ° do your hands ° weigh out ° !
3 (4). Estranged are the wicked,   from the womb they do err,
                 from birth ° they speak ° falsehood.
4 (5).   They have poison like a ° ° serpent,
         as a deaf cobra   that stoppeth its ears ;
5 (6). That heedeth not   the voice of the charmers,
                      of the skilled weaver of spells.
6 (7). O God, crush   their teeth in their mouth,
             the fangs of the young lion uproot. °   °
7 (8). May they vanish as waters   that pass away,
                 ° as grass by the path ° let them wither.
8 (9).   As the snail that passeth in slime,
         ° as a woman's abortion,°   let them see not the sun.
9 (10). Before they know it,   ° may he cut them down ° as a bramble.
             ° as with wind ° ° in ° fury ° may he sweep them away °.
10 (11). Let the righteous be glad   when he seeth vengeance ;
             let him wash his feet in the blood of the wicked.
11 (12). And let mankind say,   " Surely the righteous hath fruit,
             yea, there is a God that judgeth in the earth ".

Text-critical Notes

1. Read, with Ewald, אֵלִים· for " dumbness ". 2. Read, with S, עָוֶל for
" iniquities " (or " burnt-offerings " ?). Read, with G, חָמָס for " violence of ".
Read (cp. G) תְּפַלֵּסוּן for תִּפַלֵּסוּן. 3. Read, with G, דֹּבְּרֵי for " speakers
of ". 4. Om., with G, " poison of ". 6. Om. " Yahweh " (gloss). 7. Read (?) with
Gressmann (cited by Gunkel), כְּמוֹ חָצִיר בְּדָרֵךְ for " he treadeth on his arrow
as . . . ". 8. Read, with Buhl, כְּנֵפֶל אֵשֶׁת for " a woman's abortion ". 9. Read,
with Gunkel, יַבְרִיתֶם כְּמוֹ for " your cooking-pots ". Read, with Gunkel, רוּחַ
for " living ". Read כְּמוֹ for " like ". Read, with Gunkel, יִשְׂעָרֵם for " may he
sweep him away ".

As has been already pointed out, the first part of this psalm (*vv.*
1–5) gives an account of the iniquities and corrupt government of certain
powers, human or divine. As in Ps. 82, they are addressed as *gods*,
and it is possible that we should take the word *men* at the end of *v.* 1
as a vocative, and not as the object to the verb. That would offer a
pointed contrast, such as we actually find in Ps. 82 : " Ye call yourselves

gods, but ye are only men, after all!" We note the familiar features
in the complaint, *iniquity* and *violence*.

In *v.* 3, the psalmist ceases to address the offenders directly, and
turns to God in prayer. He emphasizes the innate corruption of the
wicked rulers, who *err* and *speak falsehood* as life-long habits. They are
like snakes who will not be *charmed*, even by *the skilled weaver of spells*.
As the language implies, the power of taming snakes was held to be
a species of magic, and even to-day there seems to be something
" uncanny " about the process. In this instance, however, the
serpents are deliberately unresponsive; they themselves *stop* their
ears.

The crimes and wicked nature of the offenders have now been
described and in *v.* 6 the imprecation begins with a new metaphor, that
of the *young lion*, which can be rendered harmless only by having its
teeth crushed and its *fangs* (a rare and late word) uprooted. Other
comparisons follow—the flowing streams, the grass, the snail, the issue
of miscarriage, the bramble (or, more exactly, buckthorn). Most of
these are familiar, but the snail is particularly interesting. The
slimy trail the creature leaves is supposed to be a part of its body, which
thus gradually wears away. In the latter part of *v.* 8 we seem to have a
reminiscence of Job 3[16], and the verb in the last clause is a good example
of the " precative perfect ", so emphasized by Buttenwieser. We must
remember that these parallels are more than mere poetic similes.
The person weaving the spell was making a deliberate attempt to destroy
his enemy thereby. He brought the object of his wrath into some kind of
connexion with these perishing or dead objects, and it might be supposed
that the destruction which had befallen them, or which would befall
them, would involve also the person whom the spell had linked to them
When the poet said " *may they vanish as waters* ", he actually included
them among the waters, and the fate of the *passing* streams would be
theirs. When he classified them with the *snail*, the effect would be that
every movement of theirs would scrape from them a portion of their
substance, and so would, in the end, wear them completely away.
The general principle lying behind words like these is much the same
as that which appears in the familiar magical act of making a wax image
of the person to be injured, and holding it before the fire. Here, it is
true, we have no more than words, but words, to the ancient mind, are
potent instruments for good or evil.

The psalm closes in *vv.* 10, 11 with the joy and relief of the righteous.
It is not merely vindictive triumph that actuates them, but rather the
feeling that, in spite of superficial appearances, the universe lies under
the government of a truly righteous God.

U

Religious Teaching

Here, as so often, we have a demand for the vindication of God's character. He *is* righteous—so the psalmist believes—and in the end the truth will be so proved that men shall have no more doubts in the matter.

PSALM 59

Ps. 59 is the complaint of an individual, oppressed by his enemies, and rings the changes on the familiar *motifs*, prayer for deliverance, confidence in God, and demand for vengeance. It has certain affinities with Ps. 55, but, in the main, shows a fair amount of independence, and exhibits some unique expressions.

The structure of the psalm is curious. It contains twenty lines, with a fragment of a twenty-first. *Selah* occurs at the end of the sixth and fifteenth lines (*vv.* 5 and 13). Lines seven and sixteen (*vv.* 6 and 14) are identical; we may call them Refrain I. Line 10 and the first two words of line 11 (*vv.* 9, 10) are repeated at the end of the psalm (*v.* 17); this we may called Refrain II. The actual structure of the poem as it now stands, then, is :—

> Six lines
> Selah
> Refrain I
> Two lines
> Refrain II
> Four lines
> Selah
> Refrain I
> Three lines
> Refrain II.

These facts suggest three different and mutually incompatible systems of strophic arrangement, none of which yields that metrical symmetry which is indispensable for true strophic organization. In the circumstances it is not surprising that several scholars have found the temptation to more or less drastic surgery irresistible. Sometimes lines are transposed; sometimes lines are eliminated (especially the refrains); sometimes even stranger reconstruction is attempted. Inasmuch as none of them appeals to us as satisfactory, and we can feel no confidence in any restoration of our own, we have allowed the psalm to stand as it is in the traditional text, making only such verbal alterations as are necessitated by the sense of the individual verses, or suggested by the readings underlying the ancient Versions. At the same time, we fully realize that, in all probability, very considerable alterations have been made in the psalm since it was first written.

There is little clue to the date. There are phrases which suggest that the persecution is national rather than individual; if these be followed, the psalm will come from a time when Israel was suffering from foreign oppression. On the other hand, there are expressions which imply that the sufferer is an individual, and, if these are not to be explained by the doctrine of corporate personality, they will leave a very wide range within which to place the composition of the psalm. Unhappily there are few known periods in human history in which man has not had ground for complaint against his fellows.

Metre: 3 : 3, with 2 : 2 : 2 in vv. 6, 12^{a-c}, 13^{b-d} and 14. Vv. 1^b and 7 contain each a word which must count as two verse-units.

For the Precentor : " Destroy not ". David's. Miktam. When Saul sent, and they watched the house to kill him.

1 (2). Deliver me from my foes, O my God ;

2 (3). Deliver me from workers of iniquity ;

3 (4). For behold ! they lie in ambush for my life,
No transgression or sin is mine ;
Rouse thee to meet me, and look,

Awake, to punish all nations,

6 (7). They come back at even,
they growl as dogs,

7 (8). Behold ! they slaver with their mouth ;

8 (9). But thou ° ° dost mock at them,

9 (10). ° O my strength °, to thee will I sing praise ;

10 (11). ° My loving God ° shall meet me ;

11 (12). Slay them not, lest my people forget ;

12 (13). ° Deliver them up °, O Lord,
for the sin of their mouth, the word of their lips,

And for the curse and the spell they repeat,
And let them know that God ruleth in Jacob,

14 (15). ° They come back ° at even,
they growl as dogs,

15 (16). They wander for food ;

16 (17). But I will sing of thy might,
For thou hast been my fortress,

17 (18). O my strength ! to thee will I bring praise,

from them that exalt themselves against me rescue me.

and from men of blood save me.

strong ones ° act presumptuously ° against me.

4 (5). for no ° wrong of mine ° do they array them.

5 (6). seeing that thou art ° ° the God of Israel.
to vile traitors show no favour. Selah.

and go about the city.

° a sword ° is in their lips. ° °

thou holdest all nations in derision.

for ° thou °, O God, art my fortress.

God shall let me look on mine adversaries.

make them totter by thy might and bring them down.

° may they be caught ° in their arrogance ;

13 (14). ° destroy them in thy wrath ° that they be no more.

to the ends of the earth. Selah.

and go about the city.

if they be not sated, ° they murmur °.

exult loudly at morn in thy love.

and a refuge in the day of my affliction.

for ° thou °, O God, art my fortress.
My loving God . . .

Text-critical Notes

3. Read, with S (probably also G), יְזוּדוּ for " stir up strife ".   Om., with Baethgen, " Yahweh ".   4. Read, with Wellhausen, עֲוֹנִי for " wrong ".   5. Om. " Yahweh God (of) Hosts ".   7. Read, with G, חֶרֶב for " swords ".   Om., with Duhm, " for who heareth ? "   8. Om. " Yahweh ".   9. Read, with G and *v.* 18, עֻזִּי for " his strength ".   Insert, with G, אַתָּה.   10. Read, with Q, חַסְדִּי for K חַסְדּוֹ.   12. Read, with Duhm, מִגְּנִמּוֹ for " our shield ".   Om., with S, " and ". 13. Read (cp. S and Buhl) כַּלֵּם בְּחֵמָתְךָ for " destroy in wrath, destroy ". 14. Om., with G and *v.* 6, " and ".   15. Read, with G, וְיָלִינוּ for " and they lodged ".   17. Insert, with G, אַתָּה.

The psalmist begins with a prayer (*vv.* 1–3[b]), which summarizes the whole poem.   He is beset by *foes, workers of iniquity* and *men of blood*, from whom he seeks to be delivered.   The word *rescue* in *v.* 1 is significant ; the idea seems to have been a favourite with this psalmist for he uses the cognate noun three times.   The root-meaning is that of " height "—his enemies *exalt themselves*, but God has a yet more lofty refuge for his servants, far out of their reach.   The attack made by the *nations* is entirely unprovoked by any *transgression* or *wrong* done by the psalmist or his people, and therefore he can appeal to the *God of Israel* to *rouse* himself and *punish* the *traitors* (*vv.* 3[c]–5).   In the first refrain (*v.* 6), the enemy are likened to the dogs the scavengers of an eastern *city*, sleepy and harmless by day, but active and dangerous *at even*, when, as the psalmist paints them, they wander round the city with *slavering* jaws and *sword*-like fangs (*v.* 7).

The thought of divine protection reappears.   After a glance at the *mockery* and *derision* God pours on the nations, the psalmist introduces the second refrain, emphasizing the *strength*, protection, and *love* of God, and the vengeance he secures (*vv.* 8–10).   *V.* 11 offers a strange and subtle prayer ; the psalmist feels for the moment that he would not have his enemies *slain*.   If they were completely destroyed, the nation would forget the triumph of God.   Rather let them be *shaken* and *brought down*, that their desperate state may be a permanent reminder of what God has done in the past and may do in the future.

This mood passes, and is succeeded by a longing for extreme vengeance.   It would seem that the enemy had employed magic—*curses and spells*—against the psalmist ; their *sin* lies in *the word of their lips* (*vv.* 12–13[a]).   With a lack of logic which seems strange to us, the psalm depicts the offenders as learning the universal supremacy of the *God* that *ruleth in Jacob* by their annihilation (*v.* 13[b, c]).

Once more the first refrain recurs, and this time it is followed in *v.* 15 by a picture of the dogs' failure to get food enough for themselves. But the psalmist no longer dwells on them ; it is his own deliverance that makes him *sing* and *exult at morn*, and leads him to a repetition of the second refrain, which, though mutilated, offers a fitting conclusion to the whole.

Religious Teaching

As so often in psalms of this type, we have the belief of the pure monotheist in the divine government of the world, and in the ultimate vindication of God and of his people. Like most of his fellows, the psalmist has not risen above the desire for vengeance; the world still had some centuries to wait before it heard the lesson, " Love your enemies; do good to them that hate you, pray for them that despitefully use you ".

PSALM 60

ONCE again we have a powerful appeal for help against the enemies of the psalmist and of his people. Its form, as Gunkel has seen, is that of a brief " liturgy ", beginning and ending with national complaints, while the central portion consists of a divine word, an " oracle ". It is interesting to note that this oracle is arranged in three-member lines, while the rest has the normal two-member lines The 3 : 3 : 3 is not infrequent as a regular variation of the 3 : 3 (see pp. 30 f.), but when it occurs in blocks, as it does here, it may be assumed that the poet intended to indicate some kind of special quality in the passage so composed. It is possible that this oracle is a quotation from a poem, otherwise lost, which described the triumphs of Yahweh, and it is certainly this part of the poem which has given rise to the historical note which stands at the head of the psalm. Perhaps the *Selah* which now stands at the end of *v.* 4 should be transferred to the following verse.

Like Ps. 57, Ps. 60 was used as a source by the compiler of Ps. 108, and *vv.* 6–12 are identical with 108[6-13]. There are a few very slight differences, but the text in both cases has been unusually well preserved. Unlike Ps. 57, however, Ps. 60 is a single whole, and suggests neither compilation (with the possible exception of the middle section) or mutilation.

As usual, the dating is very uncertain, and estimates range from David (following the heading) to the time of John Hyrcanus, or even Alexander Jannæus. It need not be said that both extremes are highly improbable; the metaphor in *v.* 3 suggests a reference to 2 Isaiah.

Metre: 3 : 3; *vv.* 6–8, 3 : 3 : 3. The last word of *v.* 9 counts as two verse-units.

> *Of the Precentor. On "The Anemone of witness". Miktam. David's. To instruct. When he fought with Aram Naharaim and Aram Zobah, and Joab returned and smote Edom in the Vale of Salt, twelve thousand men.*

1 (3). O God ! thou hast spurned us and broken us; thou hast been wrath with us—turn back to us !

2 (4). Thou hast shaken the earth, rent it open; Oh ° heal ° its breaches for it tottereth.

3 (5).	Thou hast shown thy people a hard fate,	thou hast made them drink wine of reeling.
4 (6).	Grant ° a refuge ° to them that fear thee,	that they may flee before the bow. Selah.
5 (7).	That thy darlings may escape,	save with thy right hand ° and answer me °.

6 (8). God hath spoken in his sanctuary,
    " I will exult, I will divide Shechem as spoil,
        and the Vale of Sukkoth will I measure out.

7 (9). Gilead is mine, and mine Manasseh,
    and Ephraim my chief fortress,
        Judah my marshal's staff.

8 (10). Moab is my wash-pot,
    over Edom will I cast my shoe,
        ° over ° Philistia ° do I raise a shout °."

9 (11).	Oh that one would bring me to a strong city !	Oh that one ° would lead me.° even unto Edom !
10 (12).	Hast thou n⟨ ⟩ ⟨ ⟩ ..rned us, O God ?	and goest not forth ° ° in our hosts ?
11 (13).	Give us help against the adversary,	seeing that man's salvation is vain.
12 (14).	Through our God could we do feats of valour,	and he would trample down our adversaries.

Text-critical Notes

2. רְפָה probably error for רְפָא. 4. Read, with Graetz, מִנֵּס for " standard ". 5. Read, with Q and 108⁶, וַעֲנֵנִי for " and answer us ". 8. Read, with S and 108⁹, עָלַי for " upon me ". Read, with S and 108⁹, אֶתְרוֹעָע for " my shouting ". 9. Read, with G, יַנְחֵנִי for " led me ". 10. Om., with S, " God ".

As has been already remarked, *vv.* 5–12 of this poem are repeated in 108⁶⁻¹³, and a full exposition of them will be found under that psalm. The opening verses however, have been preserved only here. They are a record of manifold disaster, whose root lies in the *wrath* of God— he has *spurned and broken* his people. Later we hear of human enemies, but in *vv.* 2–3 it seems as if Nature were the foe. There has been an earthquake ; the ground has not merely been *shaken*, it has been *torn open*. It is as if some unhappy man had met with a terrible accident, which had shattered his limbs, and the psalmist appeals to God to *heal its breaches, i.e.,* to mend its broken bones. It is, perhaps, the earthquake which has made men *reel*, as if from excess of heady wine, a metaphor which occurs elsewhere in the Old Testament, *e.g.,* in Isa. 51¹⁷, ²², Zech. 12². So the psalmist prays for a *refuge*, where men will be safe. By now it is war that is uppermost in his mind, and it is the *bow* that he fears. The Israelite fear of the bow is significant ; it was the weapon of the professional soldier, and was strange to the simple herdsman and farmer. So it is only as God will *save* that his *darlings may escape* (*v.* 5).

The answer comes in a God-given oracle, which may be older than the rest of the psalm. In practice we may imagine it to have been spoken by a temple prophet, acting as the mouthpiece of God. The theme is the universal power of God. The references to *Shechem* and the *Vale*

of Sukkoth are obscure. The explanation given, *e.g.*, by Gunkel, is
that these districts were in the hands of a foreign power, while those
mentioned in *v.* 7, Gilead, Manasseh, Ephraim, and Judah, were still
under native Israelite government; the date suggested is immediately
after 722 B.C. But there was no period in the history of Israel, till
comparatively late post-exilic times, when such a situation was to be
found. The whole of the country to the east of Jordan (as far south as
the Dead Sea) was organized as an Assyrian province by Tiglath-pileser
II in 732 B.C., ten years before the fall of Samaria. Further, *Shechem*,
is certainly to be included in the *Manasseh-Ephraim* territory, and the
Vale of Sukkoth (the Jabbok district) in *Gilead*. We can only suppose
that the various expressions used are simply ways of claiming ownership
and complete authority. God can do as he pleases, both with the land
claimed as truly Israelite, and with those neighbouring districts which
had been alternately slaves and masters to his people. It is to be
noted that *Moab* and *Edom* are given a lower status; the thought of a
washpot is that of a " vessel to dishonour ", while to *cast* the *shoe* over a
vassal was certainly a sign of contempt (cp. the illustrations cited by
Gunkel *ad loc.*).

Strangely enough, the psalmist is not wholly reassured by the
oracle. He is emboldened to continue his prayer, but the form of his
petition, with its longing for a *strong city* and its desire to be led *even
unto Edom*—not merely power to resist an assault, but also ability to
conquer an enemy is implied—suggests hope rather than confidence.
The past is not so easily forgotten. After all, *God* has *spurned* his people
and refused to *go forth in* its *hosts*. The battle-panic has fallen upon
Israel, not on their foes, and the only possible explanation is the absence
of God from the ranks. But, if only God will *give help against the
adversary*—and none but God can—then all things will be possible,
and the *feats of valour* performed through divine strength would win
complete and overwhelming victory.

Religious Teaching

The psalm expresses the familiar conviction that all suffering,
national or individual, must be traced to the divine anger. Here we
find no attempt to discover the reason for God's displeasure; there is
no confession of sin, no request for information as to the root of the
trouble, no enquiry as to the measures which must be adopted to recover
the divine favour. The psalmist simply appeals for a change in God's
attitude, which will result in a happy reversal of fortune.

PSALM 61

WRITTEN, like Ps. 63, by one in exile, this psalm is a touching appeal to the Almighty for help and comfort. Especially noteworthy is the psalmist's longing to be present again in the temple, and to feel God's protecting care there. In his loneliness he thinks also of the king, and prays for a long and prosperous reign for him, an unusual subject in the Psalter. It is not necessary to assign the verses (6, 7) which speak of the king to a later hand; they come in abruptly, it is true, but in those days of long ago strict thought-sequence is not to be looked for; see, however, the exegetical note on these verses.

That the psalm is pre-exilic goes without saying; but to what particular period it belongs cannot be said; the occasions on which the country was invaded by foreign foes were various, and that on such occasions captives were carried into exile is obvious.

The metre is variable.

1.
       For the Precentor : ° On stringed instruments °. David's.

1 (2). Hear, O God, my cry,   hearken unto my prayer;
2 (3).   From the end of the earth
      unto thee do I cry
      when my heart ° is in despair °;
      ° Set me on high °, on a rock, lead thou me;
3 (4). For thou art my refuge,   a strong tower from the enemy.
4 (5). O that I might ever sojourn in thy   and hide me in the shadow of thy
    tabernacle,   wings! Selah.
5 (6).   For thou, O God, dost hear my vows,
      dost grant the ° desire ° of them that fear thy name.
6 (7). Mayest thou add days to the days of
    the king,   years ° as the days of ° generations;
7 (8).   May he sit (enthroned) for ever
      in the presence of God;
      Mercy and truth
      ° Apportion ° him, may they preserve him.
8 (9). So will I sing praise to thy name for
    evermore,   and daily perform my vows.

Text-critical Notes

Title : Read, with some MSS. and the Versions, עַל־נְגִינֹת, i.e. accompanied by. 2. Lit. "fainteth". 2. Read, with G, יָרוּם מִמֶּנִּי for תְּרֹמְמֵנִי, "it is too high for me". 5. Read, with many commentators, אֲרֻשַׁת for יְרֻשַׁת, "possession". 6. Read כִּימֵי for כְּמוֹ, "like". 7. מַן apoc. piel imper. for מַנֵּה.

1-3. The petition that *God* may *hear* his cry and *hearken unto his prayer*, is offered by one *from the end of the earth*; this is not an exaggerated expression, for such it seemed to be in those days to one who was far from his home in strange surroundings. He gives no hint as to where it was that he had been carried captive; for that was immaterial to one whose *heart* was *in despair* (lit. "fainting") at being forced to live in a distant land away from familiar scenes and friends. His one hope is in God, to whom he prays: *Set me on high on a rock*, a figurative

expression for safety, out of the reach of harm (cp. Ps. 18²). As he had
been led away captive, so he now pleads : *lead thou me* ; for God alone
is his *refuge* and protection *from the enemy* ; his *strong tower.* 4, 5.
The thought of God as his refuge recalls to his mind the place of the
divine presence, *thy tabernacle,* as he calls the temple, using the ancient
term (cp. Ps. 27⁵) of the place whither men went to seek Yahweh (see
Exod. 33⁷). And he longs that he might ever sojourn there, and *hide in
the shadow of thy wings* (cp. Pss. 17⁸, 63⁷). It was here that *vows* were
made, and the *desires* granted to those who *feared the name* of God,
and such vows the psalmist now makes in the certain hope that God will
grant his desire. 6, 7. The abruptness of the change of subject which
follows, namely the prayer for the *king,* has induced some commentators
to regard these verses as out of place. We believe this to be a mistake ;
when it is remembered how close an association was believed to exist
between God and the king (see on this, pp. 250, 253), it will be realized
that the mention of the king after the prayer offered to God is quite
appropriate. The prayer for the length of the king's life is in the Oriental
manner of speech (cp. Ps. 18⁵⁰). But prayer is also made that his rule
may be *in the presence of God, i.e.,* in accordance with divine guidance,
and that *mercy and truth,* apportioned to him by God, may preserve
him. Such thoughts bring comfort to the exile's heart, and he concludes (8) in a happier vein : *So will I sing praise to thy name for evermore,
and daily perform my vows* ; he is thinking of the time when God will
lead him home again.

Religious Teaching

The central point in the religious teaching of this psalm is the longing
for God's presence in the sanctuary, from which the exile is cut off ;
this will come before us again in considering the religious teaching of
Ps. 63. Another element in the religious teaching of the psalm is the
prayer for the king. That in the early days certain conceptions regarding kingship were of an unedifying and superstitious nature there is no
denying ; but to the devout Israelite what was of paramount importance
was that the king was the anointed one of God. A ruler, in other words,
was such because it was, in accordance with the divine will, for the
benefit of men that they should be governed and led by one superior to
the generality. However much, in the history of nations, kingship
may have been degraded through human folly and wickedness, there is
an underlying principle contained in the essence of rulership which is
of the deepest significance and importance : unless men have somebody
to look up to who is superior, in some respect, to themselves, they are
in danger of becoming little demi-gods—a pitiable spectacle ! The
king himself recognizes God, else were he not fit to be a king.

PSALM 62

THE different ways in which this psalm is interpreted is the measure
of the difficulties presented by it; difficulties which are increased by
the uncertainty of the text in several of the verses. At the same time,
it is just possible that in a few cases commentators have dealt with the
text in too drastic a manner. The interpretation necessarily depends
in large measure on the form of the text adopted. While we fully
recognize that the text as we now have it has suffered in one way and
another during the vicissitudes of its transmission, we have kept to it
as it stands; so far as this is possible. Our interpretation of the psalm
is based upon what many passages in the Old Testament writings tell
us of the religious, political, and social conditions of the people during
various periods of their history. These have been briefly referred to
above (pp. 56 ff.); and although the psalm does not give us sufficient
indications for ascertaining the immediate cause of strife referred to, the
recurrence of such strife, as witnessed to in the Old Testament writings,
enables us to form a general idea of its nature. To go into this here is
unnecessary as the whole subject is dealt with above, as indicated. It
will be sufficient to say that our psalmist, who occupies a position of
importance, is a leader of the orthodox party, the upholder of ancient
tradition; he is opposed by innovators whose attitude towards the
ancestral religion was, to say the least, lax. By their unscrupulous
action the psalmist's position was gravely endangered; but ultimately
he was enabled to assert himself.

To assign a date to the psalm is not possible because the conditions
reflected make it appropriate to more than one period.

The metre is very variable, due, in all probability, to the work of
several editors.

1.   *For the Precentor : Jeduthun's.   A Psalm.   David's.*

1 (2).   Of a surety, unto God,—
                         ° Be still °, O my soul,
                         ° For ° from him is my salvation;
2 (3). Of a surety, he is my Rock and my   my safe refuge, I shall not be greatly
       salvation,   moved.
3 (4). "How long will ye set upon a man?   will ye slay (one) like a ° falling °
                                             wall?" °
4 (5).   Yea, from his position they take counsel to thrust him.
                         They delight in lying;
                         ° With their mouth ° they bless,
                         But in their ° heart ° they curse.
5 (6).   Of a surety, unto God,—
                         Be still, O my soul,
                         For from him is ° my salvation °;
6 (7). Of a surety, he is my Rock and my   my safe refuge, I shall not be ° greatly °
       salvation,   moved.
7 (8). ° With ° God is my salvation and   the Rock of ° my strength °, my refuge
       my glory,   is in God;
8 (9).   Trust in him at all times, O ye people,
                         Pour out before him your heart,
                         God is a refuge for us.

9 (10).   Truly, vanity are they of low degree,
                              Deception are they of high degree,
                              In the balances they will go up.°
10 (11).   Trust not in oppression,
                              And on robbery set not false hope,
                              When wealth increaseth,
                                 ° Rely not thereon °.
11 (12). Once hath God spoken,   twice have I heard this,
         That power belongeth unto God.   12 (13). " To thee, O Lord, belongeth
                                                      love ;
                              For thou dost recompense
                              a man according to his work."

Text-critical Notes

1. Read, as in v. 5, דּוֹמִי for דּוּמִיָּה, " silence ". Add פ. 3. Om. כֻּלְּכֶם, " all
of you ", which overloads the half-line. Lit. " inclining ". Om. גָּדֵר הַדְּחוּיָה, " a
tottering fence ", marg. gloss. 4. Read, with the Versions, בְּפִימוֹ for בְּפִיו, " with his
mouth ". Lit. " inward part ". 5. Read, as in v. 1, יְשׁוּעָתִי for תִּקְוָתִי, " my hope ".
6. Add, as in v. 2, רַבָּה. 7. Lit. " on ". Read עֲלֵי for עֲלֵי. 9. Om. מֵהֶבֶל
יַחַד,, " from vanity together ", marg. gloss. 10. Lit. " set not your heart ".
12. Om. ו.

For the title, see p. 15.

1, 2. These verses are repeated in vv. 5, 6; opinions differ as to
how this is to be accounted for. As the opening of a psalm they are
very appropriate, but their repetition in vv. 5, 6 does not strike us as
original, for the text reads more smoothly without them. There are,
again, differences of opinion regarding the interpretation of the opening
words ; in view of the perilous position in which the psalmist finds himself, and the consequent tumult of his emotions, such an unfinished
sentence is very natural ; amid the inner conflict of feelings and thoughts
so perplexing and worrying, his faith asserts itself, and he bursts forth :
Of a surety, unto God—some such words as, " do I look for help ", are
self-evident ; he does not utter them, but communes with himself :
Be still, O my soul; there is no need to worry, for from God is his
salvation, *i.e.*, his help in his present trouble. And he reiterates his
trust in God : *Of a surety, he is my Rock and my salvation.* The
circumstances are doubtless threatening, but, since God is his *safe
refuge*, he need not fear, he will not be greatly moved, *i.e.*, from the
position he holds, though the expression is often used in a more general
sense ; his enemies are taking a mean advantage, for he is but one
against many ; and he shames them in words, pregnant with contempt :
3. *How long will ye set upon a man?* They seek his destruction, for
reasons which he does not disclose, and his position is endangered ;
evidently he is referring to the post of authority in the community which
he occupied ; his simile is very forceful : *will ye slay one* whose position
is *like* that of *a falling wall?* or, in modern phraseology : " will you hit
a man when he is down ? " Then (4) he explains that their intention is
to thrust him from his position. This gives us a hint as to the *mise en
scène* of the whole psalm, *i.e.*, it deals with political troubles, see pp. 56 ff.,

and the words which follow bear this out; political strife is never characterized by what is expressed by the fine French proverb *Noblesse oblige*; so that we can understand the psalmist's words of disgust: *They delight in lying, with their mouth they bless, but in their heart they curse*; in plain language, they are base hypocrites. With the repetition in 5, 6 of the opening verses we have already dealt. As they are in the nature of a self-communing, their position here breaks the sequence of thought. The action and the character of the psalmist's enemies, and his consequent peril, have been described in *vv.* 3, 4, so that it follows logically when, in contrast to this, he goes on to say: *With God is my salvation and my glory, the Rock of my strength, my refuge is in God*; for, as the sequel shows, the outcome of the strife was favourable to him. 8. But as leader of a party, he thinks also of his followers, and has words of cheer and comfort for them: *Trust in him at all times, O ye people* . . . *God is a refuge for us.* 9. The adversaries, he goes on to say, whether gathered from the common people, *they of low degree*, or from the more influential classes, *they of high degree*, are alike contemptible; in the one case they are unreliable, *vanity*, lit. " a breath ", in the other they are *deception*, lit. " a lie ". They are compared with *balances*, the scale in which they are weighed *goes up* (cp. Job 31[6], Dan. 5[27]). 10. The psalmist then adjures his followers, holding up the adversaries as a warning, *not to trust in oppression*, or unrighteous gain, nor to base *false hope* on what is gained by *robbery*; *wealth*, in any case, is not to be relied upon (cp. Ps. 49[6]). 11. The final words are, once more, the recognition of God's *power* and *love* (*hesed*); in the present circumstances the former has been exhibited in the downfall of the adversaries, the latter in the deliverance of the psalmist and his followers from danger. Very significantly does he add: *For thou dost recompense a man according to his work*; the adversaries, God's enemies, have been discomfited; but he stands firm through his trust in God, repeatedly expressed in the psalm.

Religious Teaching

Common to most of the psalms is the faith and trust in God which is so prominent here; but in this psalm this religious element is brought into connexion with political strife; a very noteworthy fact. In politics, and it has been the same through the history of all ages, unfair utterances and unscrupulous dealings are normal tools; it was so in the psalmist's day. But what a revolution in the conduct and solution of political differences would be brought about if politicians recognized the truth that from no sphere of human activity is the eye of the Almighty withdrawn!

PSALM 63

THE psalm of an exile. In words of intense earnestness the psalmist expresses his ardent yearning for the presence of God. He thinks, first, of the time when in the sanctuary he had worshipped God, and, as he believed, had beheld him (on this see the exegetical note). But he has learned in exile that the divine presence is not restricted either to place or time.

That an exile in Babylon should have his enemies is in the nature of things; but these enemies are of a very different order from those spoken of in many other psalms.

The king referred to can only be Jehoiachin, the psalmist's fellow-exile.

With the view taken by some commentators that the verses of the psalm are out of order because of a supposed want of logical connexion, we must confess entire disagreement. Such a view we believe to be due to the failure to grasp the position, and above all, the religious spirit of the psalmist.

The date is early exilic.

The metre is, with one or two exceptions, 3 : 3.

1.   *A Psalm. David's. When he was in wilderness of Judah.*

1 (2). ° Yahweh ° my God, ° I seek thee ;   my soul thirsteth for thee,
    My flesh longeth for thee   in a dry land ° where no water is ;
2 (3). Even as when in the sanctuary I
    beheld thee,   and saw thy might and thy majesty;
3 (4). For better than life is thy love ;   my lips shall praise thee ;
4 (5). Yea, I will bless thee as long as I
    live,   in thy name will I lift up my hands ;
5 (6).   As with fat and marrow
           my soul thou dost satisfy
           ° With joyful lips °
           my mouth shall sing praise.
6 (7). When I call thee to mind upon my   in the night-watches I meditate on
    bed,   thee ;
7 (8). For thou hast been my help,   and in the shadow of thy wings I am
             happy.
8 (9). My soul cleaveth unto thee, °   thy right-hand doth uphold me.
9 (10). But they that seek after my life ° shall go into the lowest parts of the
             earth ;
10 (11). ° They shall be delivered ° ° over
    to the power of the sword °,   they shall be a portion for jackals.
11 (12). But the king shall rejoice in   every one that sweareth by him shall
    ° Yahweh °,   glory,
         But the mouth of them that speak lies shall be stopped.

Text-critical Notes

1. Read יהוה for אלהים, " God ". Om. אתה. Om. וְעָיֵף, " and weary ", for the rhythm's sake. 5. Lit. " with lips of joyful-shoutings "; read בְּ for וְ, " and ". 9. Lit. " soul "; om. לְשׁוֹאָה, " to destroy it ", marg. gloss which disturbs the rhythm. 10. Read, with GS, יַגִּרוּ for יַגִּירֻהוּ, " they shall deliver him ". Lit. " on to the hands of the sword ". 11. Read יהוה for אלהים.

Title. This was doubtless suggested by the words of *v.* 1, *in a dry land where no water is,* and was added in reference to the narrative in 2 Sam. 17 about David's flight from Absalom.

1. The psalmist, writing apparently in exile, yearns for the presence of Yahweh ; according to the belief of the times, Yahweh's presence was in the Holy Land, where alone he could be worshipped, see 2 Kgs. 5[17]. His whole being, *soul* and *body,* is athirst and longing for God, so deep is his love for him (cp. Ps. 42[1]).   2. He then recalls the time when *in the sanctuary* at Jerusalem he had *beheld* God, and had seen his *might* and *majesty.*   An interesting question is raised if it be asked how we are to understand the psalmist's words about beholding God in the sanctuary, and seeing his might and majesty ; this cannot be explained away by saying that " this beholding of Yahweh in his temple was in oral worship " (Briggs, *in loc.*).   When one reads such passages as Num. 10[35, 36], 1 Sam. 4[3-8], it is clear that the divine presence was conceived of as connected with some concrete object.   The commandment, " Thou shalt not make to thyself any graven image ", bears this out.   Our psalm belongs to the early exilic period, before more spiritual conceptions regarding the divine presence had as yet been apprehended by the bulk of the exiles (see Ezek. 14[1-11], Isa. 44[9 *ff*]) ; and there can be no doubt that the Exile was one of the most potent means of helping faithful worshippers of Yahweh to conceive of him in a more spiritual way. 3-5. This is illustrated very pointedly in the person of our psalmist, who, though far from the homeland and from Yahweh's sanctuary, realizes that his *love* is *better than life* itself ; and most significant, as pointing to his realization of Yahweh's spiritual presence are the reiterated expressions of his worship : *my lips shall praise thee ; I will bless thee as long as I live ; in thy name will I lift up my hands.*   And he recalls again the time when he worshipped in the temple and partook of the sacrificial feasts ; just as he was then *satisfied with fat and marrow,* so now is he filled with happiness in his spiritual worship : *with joyful lips my mouth shall sing praise.*   6-8. Then he gives a very touching picture of his intimate communing with God ; lying awake at nights he thinks of how he has been helped and protected by God in the land of exile : *in the night-watches I meditate on thee ; for thou hast been my help, and in the shadow of thy wings I am happy* ; and he expresses his love for his divine Protector, *my soul cleaveth unto thee,* for he has experienced his protection, *thy right-hand doth uphold me.*   9, 10. And though enemies are around him, he does not fear, for they *shall go into the lowest parts of the earth, i.e., Sheol,* and *be delivered over to the power of the sword, i.e.,* their foes will overcome them, contemptible though those foes are ; he calls them by the opprobrious name of *jackals* (cp. Lam. 5[18]).   11. His last thought is of *the king, i.e.,* Jehoiachin, his fellow-exile (2 Kgs. 24[15]) ; he looks forward to his release, though that did not take place until long

after (2 Kgs. 25²⁷⁻³⁰). What is referred to in the words, *for the mouth of them that speak lies shall be stopped*, it is impossible to say ; but evidently some episode was in the mind of the psalmist of which our records make no mention.

Religious Teaching

The earnest yearning for God, and the insight into communion with him on the part of a truly good man, as these are set forth in this psalm, are unrivalled in the Psalter. From one who had been cut off from the loved and familiar scenes of worship in his native land, and was now condemned to live in exile, these expressions of love for God, these words of heartfelt communing with him, have a reality and sincerity which are intensely touching. A friend of the present writer, whose duties had called him away into a somewhat wild part of Australia, said : " I never knew what yearning for worship meant until circumstances prevented me for months from kneeling at God's altar ". Then, another thing which the psalm teaches is the feeling of care-less (ἀμέριμνος) security engendered by the conviction of God's nearness ; the psalmist expresses it in words of inimitable beauty : " In the shadow of thy wings I am happy ". It is not given to all to have such faith ; but even to hear of it is an inspiration, and an incentive to draw nearer to God.

PSALM 64

THIS outpouring of one who is the victim of cruel enemies is similar in content to a number of other psalms. In this case the action of the psalmist's foes is confined to malicious slander ; there is no mention of personal violence as in some other psalms of similar character. The cause of the feeling against the psalmist is not indicated ; but it was doubtless the same as that which prompted animosity against the Ḥasîdîm, described in many other psalms ; on the whole subject see pp. 56 ff.

Short as the psalm is, the text has suffered considerable corruption. The metre varies, due in part to textual corruption.

The subject-matter points to a post-exilic date.

1.		*For the Precentor : A Psalm. David's.*	
1 (2).		Hear, O God,	
		my voice in my complaint ;	
		From the terror of the enemy	
		preserve my life.	
2 (3).	Hide me from the secret-counsel of the wicked,	from the tumult of the workers of iniquity,	
3 (4).	Who whet their tongue like a sword,	who ° sharpen like arrows,° bitter words,	
4 (5).	To shoot in secret places at the innocent,	suddenly do they shoot, when they are not ° seen °.	

5 (6). ° They strengthen themselves ° in
            an evil purpose,   ° they dig ° that they may hide snares ;
                    They say : " Who will see ° us ° ? "
6 (7). °   .   .   .   .   °
7 (8). ° And ° may God shoot them with
            an arrow,   suddenly may they be wounded ;
8 (9). ° And may he cause them to
            stumble   because   of °   their   so that all who see them wag (their
            tongue,   heads).
9 (10). Then shall all men fear,   and recognize the work of God,
                    Yea, they will realize that it is his work.
10 (11). Let the righteous rejoice in   and let all the upright in heart glory.
            Yahweh °,

Text-critical Notes

3. Read, with Graetz and Gunkel, חֵבְרוּ חִצָּם for דָּרְכוּ חִצָּם, " they bend
(lit. tread) their arrow ".   4. Read, with S, יֵרָאוּ for יִירָאוּ, " fear ".   5. Read
יְתַחֲזִקוּ for יְחַזְּקוּ־לָמוֹ," they make strong to themselves ".   Read יְחַפְּרוּ for
יְסַפְּרוּ, " they recount ".   Read, with SV, לָנוּ for לָמוֹ, " them ".   6. The text of
this verse is very corrupt.   Various drastic emendations are proposed, but they do
not inspire confidence.   7. Read, with the Versions, וַ for וְ.   8. Read וַיַּכְשִׁילֵמוֹ
עָלַי for וַיַּכְשִׁילוּהוּ עָלֵימוֹ, " and they caused him to stumble because of them ".
10. Om. וְחָסָה בוֹ, " and trust in him ", a marg. gloss which breaks the rhythm.

1. The psalmist pleads with God to hearken unto his *complaint*, and
to *preserve* his *life from the terror of the enemy*, used collectively. This
reads as though his life were endangered ; but in what follows, there is
not necessarily any reference to physical violence being offered, so that
the prayer that his life may be preserved is probably meant figuratively,
as much else in the psalm.   2–5. The psalmist then proceeds to describe
these enemies and their methods of proceeding.   They are spoken of as
the wicked and as *workers of iniquity* ; in figurative language they are said
to *whet their tongue like a sword* (cp. Pss. 55[21], 57[4]), and to *sharpen* their
bitter words like arrows (cp. Pss. 7[12, 13], 11[2]) ; they mature their plans in
secret, and their attacks on *the innocent* are made *suddenly* from
unexpected quarters, *secret places* (cp. Ps. 10[8]), where *they are not seen*
(cp. Ps. 10[8-10]).   The evil design on which they are engaged is relent-
lessly pursued, and they are figuratively described as *digging snares* which
are *hidden*, so that their nefarious purpose is carried out secretly : *Who
will see us?* they say.   It is thus evident that the reference here is to
secret intrigues schemed and developed with persistent and unscrupulous activity ; the warfare is one of underhand slander in which
the defamers take good care to remain in the background.   That this
should be undertaken by a number of evil-disposed men against a single
individual suggests that the psalmist was one who occupied a position of
influence.   Since no indication is given as to who the enemies are and
why they have taken this action, it is clear that both were matters of
common knowledge.   It can, therefore, hardly be doubted that the
psalm reflects the political-religious strife which persisted intermittently
through various periods of Jewish history.   For the details of this

see pp. 56 ff. The text of the verse which follows (6) is very corrupt; various emendations are suggested, but each presents difficulties; we have, therefore, been constrained to leave it blank. 7–9. These distasteful verses exhibit a spirit of extreme bitterness; they are probably what may be described as a retributive curse, the mere utterance of which was believed to be effective; the evil designed against others rebounds back on the heads of those who conceived it.

A pleasanter note is struck in the concluding verse (10) where, in contrast to the fate called down upon the wicked slanderers, *the righteous* are bidden to *rejoice in Yahweh*, and the *heart* of *the upright to glory, i.e.,* exult in themselves.

For this psalm a section on religious teaching is not called for.

PSALM 65

THIS psalm consists of two parts: *vv.* 1–8 and *vv.* 9–13. The former is a hymn of praise and gratitude to God for his lovingkindness and power, sung by the whole body of worshippers. First, a recognition of the duty of worship, followed by some striking words expressive of the sense of sinfulness. The blessedness of those who enter the house of God is then emphasized; and this part concludes with the contemplation of God's power. The second part is a thankful recognition of God's mercy in having given the autumn rains, so needful for the fruitfulness of the soil; the very pastures are poetically described as shouting in praise to God; spring-time has now come, and the country is clothed with beauty.

It may well be that we have here the joining together of two psalms, the purpose being to illustrate the seemliness of giving praise to God (1–8) by describing the beauty of the earth of his creation (9–13).

The Hebrew is in parts difficult to give in a translation, and some paraphrase is unavoidable.

The date of the first part is post-exilic; but the second part may well be pre-exilic.

The metre in the first part is 3 : 2; in the second it varies between 3 : 3 and 2 : 2.

1.   *For the Precentor : A Psalm. David's. A Song.*

1 (2). Unto thee praise is ° seemly °,   O God, in Zion,
       Unto thee vows are fulfilled,   2 (3). O thou that hearkenest unto
                                                prayer.
       Unto thee doth all flesh ° bring °   3 (4). ° that which concerneth ° iniqui-
                                                ties;
       Our transgressions ° overwhelm
           us °,   thou dost cover them over.

X

4 (5). Blessed is he whom thou choosest
    and ° acceptest °,   that he may dwell in thy courts ;
    ° We will delight ourselves ° with
    the goodness of thy house,   ° the holiness ° of thy sanctuary.
5 (6). By awe-inspiring deeds dost thou
    answer in righteousness,   O God of our salvation,
    Thou that art the confidence of all
    the ends of the earth   and the distant ° isles °.
6 (7). Who setteth fast the mountains by
    his strength,   girded about with might,
7 (8). Who stilleth the roaring of the seas, the roaring of their waves °.
8 (9). They that dwell in the uttermost
    parts are afraid   at thy tokens ;
    The outgoing of morning and evening thou makest to rejoice.

9 (10). Thou hast visited the earth, and
    watered it,   greatly dost thou enrich it ;
        The brook of God
        is full of water,
        Thou preparest ° the corn thereof °,
        Yea, thus thou preparest it :
10 (11).   Watering the furrows thereof,
        levelling the ridges thereof ;
        Thou makest it soft with showers,
        Thou blessest the growth thereof.
11 (12). Thou crownest the year of thy
    goodness,   and thy waggons drip with fatness ;
12 (13). The pastures of the steppe-land
    ° shout for joy °,   the hills are girded with gladness ;
13 (14). The fields are ° covered ° with
    flocks,   and the valleys are ° full ° of corn ;
        They shout for joy, yea, they sing.

Text-critical Notes

1. Read, with the Versions, דֻּֽמִיָּה (from דמה " to be like ", in the extended sense of " to be fitting "; in the Talmud, *Abod. Zar.* 38ᵇ, it is used in the sense of " to be right ") for דֻּֽמִיָּה, " quietude " or " silence ". 2. Read יָבִיא for יָבֹאוּ, " come ". 3. Lit. " the matters of ". Lit. " are too strong for us "; read, with G, מֶפֿוּ for מֶפִֿי, " for me ". 4. Lit. " causest to come near ". Lit. " we will be satisfied ". Read הֹֽדֶשׁ for קָֽדֹשׁ. 5. Read אִים for יָם, " sea " (רְֽחֹקִים). 7. Om. וַֽהֲמוֹן לְאֻמִּים, " and the tumult of the peoples ", a marg. gloss which disturbs the metre. 9. Read, with S, דְּֽגָנָהּ for דְּֽגָנָם, " their corn ". 12. Read, with Gunkel, יְֽרַֽעֲפוּ for יִֽרְעֲפוּ, " they drip ". 13. Lit. " clothed ". Lit. " enveloped ".

1-3. There is a difficulty about these opening verses because three subjects are pointedly mentioned, and one does not see what connexion there is between them : praise, fulfilling vows, grievous sin ; and one wonders what it is all about. Evidently, therefore, some occurrence was in the psalmist's mind ; and it was clearly something of common knowledge. Failing definite indication, we must suppose that the people had been guilty of some act of transgression, of which they had repented and for which atonement was made by vowing offerings to God. With the burden of sin thus removed, they come to the house of God to sing his praise. Hence the beginning of the psalm : *Unto thee praise is seemly, O God, in Zion* ; " seen 'v " is perhaps not strong enough, the thought is that praise to God is demanded ; for he has *hearkened unto prayer*, for forgiveness, as the context shows ; and this is granted because the *vows* which had been made, *are fulfilled, i.e.,* the sacrifices have been offered. Some striking words follow: *Unto thee doth all flesh bring that which concerneth iniquities* ; the meaning is that sinful humanity (" all flesh ") must make confession to God of iniquities committed, whereby the heart is disburdened ; and if, as will sometimes happen, there have been very grave *transgressions,* plunging the sinner into despair, then he must throw himself upon the mercy of God, who will *cover them over, i.e.,* take them away, and forgive. The Hebrew word rendered " cover over " (the root is *kpr*) is a difficult one, but, in the words of Robertson Smith, " there are Semitic analogies for regarding the forgiveness of sin either as ' covering ' or as ' wiping out ' . . . the most important point is that, except in the Priest's Code, it is God, not the priest, who (on the one etymology) wipes out sin, or (on the other) regards it as covered ".[1] The psalmist thus records that the worshippers have been guilty of grievous sin, that they have repented and fulfilled their vows, and that therefore they have been forgiven. This being so, he continues with sanctified joy (4) : *Blessed is he whom thou choosest and acceptest, that they may dwell in thy courts* ; disburdened of their sin, the worshippers can *delight* themselves *with the goodness of thy house, i.e.,* the blessings of forgiveness and divine favour which have been granted ; the *holiness* of the *sanctuary* is imparted to those who enter there with pure hearts. 5–8. Praise to God is then fitly offered. All that God does is done in righteousness ; awe-inspiring deeds witness to his power, so that not only have his own people trust in him, but he is *the confidence of all the ends of the earth,* a universalistic note which is very striking. The awe-inspiring deeds are then recorded : the act of creation in *setting fast the mountains by his strength,* which, on account of their immoveable firmness, are described as *girded about with might* ; then the great power of him *who stilleth the roaring of the seas,* and *of their waves,* with the thought, no doubt, of the primeval combat (see notes on Ps. 89[9,10]). Such manifestations of power cause them *that dwell in the uttermost parts, i.e.,* of the earth, to be *afraid, i.e.,* awe-struck ; the uttermost parts are further described as *the outgoing of morning and evening, i.e.,* east and west (cp. Ps. 75[6]), which are personified ; they, too, are made *to rejoice* (cp. Ps. 98[3], " all the ends of the earth have seen the salvation of our God ").

9–13. In these verses we have a self-contained and beautiful hymn of gratitude for a bounteous harvest. In the spring God had *visited the earth, and watered it* with plentiful rain, thereby *enriching it, i.e.,* making it fruitful ; hence the prosperous year which the psalmist looks back upon with thankful heart. The old-world idea of *the brook,* or river, *of God* (cp. Gen. 1[7], Job 38[25]) finds mention here ; the belief was that God had a river in the heavenly spheres, ever full of water, from which he

---

[1] *The Old Testament in the Jewish Church,* p. 381, note 1 (1895).

dispensed rain for the earth.   Thereby the earth was made fruitful :
thou preparest the corn thereof, *i.e.*, of the earth, not "their corn", as
though the reference were to the corn of the people, the psalmist has not
got them in mind ;   he then goes on to describe how God *prepares* the
earth for bearing corn :   *watering the furrows* (perhaps this should be
rendered " clods ") *thereof*, and, by means of the rain, *levelling* uneven
patches ;   thus the showers soften the soil so that the sown grain may
sprout : *thou blessest the growth thereof*.   It is a happy picture which the
psalmist brings before his mind's eye ;   so that he speaks of the prosperous year as one of God's goodness, which he has " crowned " ;   a
poetic way of expressing what we should call a record year.   The very
waggons, the psalmist calls them *thy waggons* because they carry God's
gift of corn, *drip with fatness* ;   but at the back of his mind there may have
been another old-world idea that God went through the land leaving
marks of fruitfulness wherever he went.   Nature is again personified, so
that it is said that *the pastures of the steppe-land shout for joy, and the hills
are girded with gladness*, *i.e.*, they wear gladness as an ornament of
clothing ;   *the fields* being *covered with flocks, and the valleys full of corn*,
likewise *shout for joy, yea, they sing*.   It is a delightful picture of whole-
hearted happiness, in which the psalmist, cradled in the lap of surrounding beauty, expresses the outcome of what he began by saying :   *thou
hast visited the earth*.

Religious Teaching

This has necessarily been brought out in what has already been said ;
but we may briefly recapitulate the main points ;   and it is especially
noteworthy that these are presented as normal among all professing
believers in God.   There is, first of all, the thought that it is not only a
duty, but a *privilege*, to enter the house of God and to worship him.
Then there is the conviction that God answers prayer, and especially
when the evidence of repentance for sin is shown forth.   This is followed
by the further teaching that where there is repentance, there is also forgiveness.   It is also well worth emphasizing that the forgiven sinner is
encouraged to rejoice.   The knowledge of being brought nearer to God
through his forgiveness must generate happiness and strengthen the
resolution to fight against all that displeases him.

In reading through this psalm a question almost inevitably suggests itself; is it a unity, or have we here a combination of two psalms, viz. *vv.* 1–12 and 13–20? In the former, the early history of Israel is recalled, and all the earth is bidden to praise God for the manifestation of his power on behalf of his people. In the latter the subject-matter is quite different; it speaks of one who is about to enter the house of God for the purpose of offering sacrifices in fulfilment of vows; and he bids his fellow-worshippers listen while he tells them of God's mercy which had been accorded to him. In favour of unity of authorship it can be urged that in the former half the psalmist recalls God's mercies shown towards the people, and in the latter half towards himself, thus offering a kind of parallelism. But it must be confessed that in reading the psalm through this strikes one as forced. The one point of parallelism is only partial; the people have been delivered from enemies; but the deliverance spoken of in the second part is not from enemies. The repeated invitation to the nations of the earth to praise God which occurs in the first part, has nothing corresponding to it in the second; while, on the other hand, the stress laid on offerings in the second part is not paralleled by anything in the first. If both parts had come from the same writer a more definite and pointed correspondence between the two would assuredly have been in evidence. The conclusion is, therefore, forced upon us that we have here two psalms, or parts of them, which have been joined together, as in some other cases (*e.g.*, Ps. 40$^{14-18}$ =Ps. 70). This joining together of literary pieces containing different subject-matter is easily accounted for owing to the vicissitudes of transmission. Material, whether skins, papyrus, or what-not, for writing on was precious; an open space left at the conclusion of a psalm might well have been utilized by filling it in with another psalm, or part of one, if the space was insufficient for the whole; the main thing was to preserve the holy words which had been handed down. We have an instructive illustration of this—though belonging to far later times—in the five " psalms of David " (a Syriac translation), which have been written on an open space in the middle of a treatise of the Nestorian Bishop, Elijah of Anbar (tenth cent.)[1]; obviously an open space in the MS. was utilized for preserving these psalms; a proceeding of which there are plenty of examples. If this was done in these late times, how much more in earlier days when materials were far more scarce.

[1] See Noth, " Die fünf syrisch überlieferten apokryphen Psalmen," in *ZAW* 1930, pp. 1–23. One of these psalms is the 151st in the Septuagint.

The date of *vv.* 1–12 is post-exilic, and the same is true of *vv.* 13–20
(see further, exeg. notes), as the developed sacrificial system referred to
shows.

The metre is for the most part 3 : 3, but that of some verses varies, as
indicated in the translated text of the psalm.

For the Precentor : A Song.   A Psalm.

1.   Shout for joy unto God, all the earth,
2.   Sing praise to the glory of his name,
    Render ° unto him ° ° the praise due to him ° ;
3.   Say unto God :
    " How terrible are thy works !
    Because of the greatness of thy might
    Thine enemies cringe before thee,
4. Let all the earth worship thee,   sing praise to thee, sing praise to thy name ! " Selah.
5.   Come, and behold
    the works of God,
    Terrible in deed
    toward the children of men,
6. ° Turning ° the sea to dry-land,   they went through the river on foot ;
    There ° did they rejoice ° in him ;   7. ruling in his strength for ever,
    His eyes keeping watch on the nations,   that the rebellious exalt not themselves.
8. Bless, O ye peoples, our God,   make the sound of his praise to be heard,
9. Who ° preserveth ° our soul in life,   and suffereth not our foot to be moved.
10. For thou hast tried us, O God,   thou hast tested us as silver is tested ;
11. Thou didst bring us into the net,   didst lay a ° chain ° upon our loins,
12. Thou didst cause men to ride over our head,
        we went through fire and water,
    But thou didst bring us ° into a wide place °.
13. I will come into thy house with whole burnt-offerings,
    I will pay my vows unto thee,
14. Which my lips did utter,   and my mouth did speak, when I was in trouble ;
15. Whole burnt-offerings of fatlings will I offer unto thee,
    with the incense of rams,
    I will offer bullocks with goats. Selah.
16. Come, hearken, that I may tell you,   all ye that fear God,
    what he hath done for my soul :
17. Unto him did I cry with my mouth,   and high praise was under my tongue,—
18. If I had seen iniquity in my heart,   the Lord would not have heard me—
19. But God hath heard me,   he hath hearkened unto the voice of my prayer.
20.   Blessed be God,
    Who hath not withdrawn
    ° his love from me.

Text-critical Notes

2. Add לוֹ, and om. כָּבוֹד, "glory". Lit. "his praise". 6. Read, with G,
הֵפֶךְ הֹפֵךְ for הָפַךְ, "he turned" (cp. מֹשֵׁל, *v.* 7). Read שִׂמְחוּ for נִשְׂמְחָה, "let us
rejoice". 9. Lit. "putteth". 11. Or "sore burden". 12. Read, with the
Versions, לִרְוָחָה for לָרְוָיָה, "a wealthy", or abundant, "place". 20. Om.
תְּפִלָּתִי וְ "my prayer and ".

1–4. In holy zeal the psalmist calls upon *all the earth* to *shout
for joy*—that is the force of the Hebrew word, cp. Isa. 44²³—*unto God*,
and to *sing praise to the glory of his name* (cp. Isa. 42¹²). He puts into
the mouth of the peoples of the earth the words wherewith he would

have them acknowledge God : *How terrible, i.e.,* awe-inspiring, *are thy works !* ; they are made to say that they recognize *the greatness of his might* for which reason his *enemies cringe before* him ; the word means to feign, or make a pretence, the idea being that even though God's *enemies* do not worship him, yet the *greatness* of his *might* compels them to make a show of doing so. 5–7. Still addressing *all the earth,* the psalmist bids the nations *Come, and behold the works of God,* whereby is meant that they should contemplate with their minds' eye the awe-inspiring acts which, in the distant past, God had wrought for his people, spoken of as *the children of men.* The *works of God,* to which the psalmist refers, are mentioned because they had been directly connected with *the nations* : first, there is the divine act of *turning the sea to dry-land,* in reference to Exod. 14[16, 21, 22], " And the children of Israel went into the midst of the sea upon the dry-land " (the passage through the " Red " sea) ; then, suggested by this, the psalmist says that *they went through the river on foot,* in reference to Josh. 3[9-17], where it is told of how " all Israel passed over on dry ground, until all the nation were passed clean over Jordan ". And lastly, when he speaks of *his eyes keeping watch on the nations, that the rebellious exalt not themselves,* the psalmist has in mind the victories of Gideon, Jephthah, and Samson, over the surrounding nations. Thus, in each case *the nations* were, according to the divine will, and with God's help, defeated. Hence the psalmist's appeal to the nations of his day to contemplate *the works of God* in the past, with the implied injunction that they should acknowledge him. Therefore he continues (8, 9) : *Bless, O ye peoples, our God.* But when he goes on to say, *who preserveth our soul in life, and suffereth not our foot to be moved,* it sounds, at first, a little incongruous that the nations should be called upon to *bless God* because of the mercies vouchsafed to the people of Israel ; but the underlying idea is based upon such passages as Isa. 60[3-6], 61[9], 66[19] ; the nations, being joined to Israel, will become worthy of partaking of their blessings. 10–12. The psalmist's thoughts then revert to the past history of his people : *Thou hast tried us, O God* (cp. Jer. 9[7]) ; *thou hast tested us as silver is tested* (cp. Isa. 48[10]) ; *thou didst bring us into the net* (for the thought cp. Ezek. 12[13], 17[20], 32[3], but the word for " net " in the last passage is different) ; *didst lay a chain upon our loins,* the word for " chain " is Aramaic, and occurs here only, it is rendered " chain " in the Targum (Hans Schmidt *in loc.*) ; *thou didst cause men to ride over our head* recalls Isa. 51[23] ; and *we went through fire and water* is clearly taken from Isa. 43[2] ; *but thou didst bring us into a wide place,* must refer to the homeland, Palestine. It would thus seem that the psalmist has the Babylonian Exile and the Return in mind here. The evident references to exilic and post-exilic writings point to the date of the psalm. 13–15. The entire change of subject, without any connecting link with what has preceded is one of the reasons for regarding this second section as being an independent composition, possibly only part of some other psalm. The words of 13-15 are uttered by one who is about to *pay* his *vows* as a thank-offering for deliverance from *trouble*. The abundance of these offerings has led some commentators to suppose that they were brought on behalf of others, but the repetition of the "I" shows this to be untenable. Possibly the words are not to be taken too literally ; or the offerer may have been a wealthy man. By *the incense of rams* is meant the smoke rising from the burning of the sacrifice (cp. Gen. 8²¹). 16-20. The psalmist then calls on *all that fear God* to listen while he tells them what *God hath done for* his *soul, i.e.*, for his personal self, adding in parenthesis that *if* there had been *iniquity* in his *heart*, God *would not have heard* him ; what this was he puts in few, but none the less significant, words : *God hath heard me, he hath hearkened unto the voice of my prayer.* And he concludes with blessing God, *who hath not withdrawn his love* (*hesed*) *from me.*

Religious Teaching

For the universalistic thought of this psalm, cp. pp. 81 f. Three other matters may be briefly referred to, though they will come before us again. The first is the emphasis laid on gratitude for past mercies. The reference is to mercies vouchsafed to the nation ; but it is taught that every generation should recall, and be grateful for the mercies of which the nation as a whole had been the recipients in the past ; and it is implied that each generation benefits by these, and ought therefore to show forth their gratitude for them. This gives food for thought. It is probably true to say that few people realize how much they have to be thankful for owing to the divine guidance of national history in the past. Here we have, then, brought to our minds something which is well worth pondering over.

Another thing which the psalm teaches is the duty of rendering to God, so far as this is possible for man, a return for his many loving-kindnesses. The psalmist does this by offering sacrifices ; but the main thing is the principle involved ; and for Christians this could not be better expressed than in the familiar words of the Book of Common Prayer : " And here we offer and present unto thee, O Lord, ourselves, our souls and bodies, to be a reasonable, holy, and lively sacrifice unto thee."

And, lastly, there is the teaching on prayer. The gratitude felt by the psalmist for the answer to his prayer is such that he is impelled to proclaim it to others. As a rule, people hesitate to speak to others about their innermost religious experiences ; and naturally so ; but it is worth remembering that sometimes, in telling others of answer to prayer, it means witnessing for God and may be the means of strengthening the

faith of others.   One thing more ; the psalmist teaches that if there is
iniquity in the heart prayer cannot be sincere ; how, in that case, can it
be acceptable to God ?

PSALM 67

THIS short, but beautiful, little psalm is pregnant with subject-matter
illustrative of the best in Israelite religion.   Both the occasion on which
the psalm was sung, and therefore its whole interpretation, are indicated
in the words of *v.* 6 : " The earth hath yielded her increase, Yahweh
our God hath blessed us."   This is clearly in reference to the harvest,
the good yield of which calls forth praise and thanksgiving to God from
the psalmist on behalf of himself and his people.   It was therefore, in
all probability, one of the psalms sung during the feast of Tabernacles.
A little puzzling, at first sight, is the way in which the psalm opens :
" O God,—may he be gracious unto us and bless us . . .", which is
re-echoed in the concluding verse : " May God bless us ".   One might
expect that, inasmuch as the harvest was past, the psalmist would be
looking back, and say : " God hath been gracious unto us . . .", " God
hath blest us ".   Indeed, some commentators emend the text to this
effect.   This is unnecessary, and fails to appreciate the spiritual mentality of the psalmist ; see further, the exegetical notes, and the section on
the religious teaching of the psalm.   Very striking is the teaching on
universalism which is so prominent in the psalm ; with this we deal also,
later.   But it is worth noting here that in the Book of Common Prayer
this psalm is appointed to be said, or sung, as an alternative to the
Nunc Dimittis ; this was doubtless done owing to the universalistic spirit
of our psalm, which was in accordance with the words : " To be a light
to lighten the Gentiles ".
    A quaint usage with regard to this psalm by the Jewish mystics of
the Middle Ages may be mentioned as illustrating the various uses to
which psalms were put.   What is called " the period of counting the
' *Omer* ' " (" sheaf ") was forty-nine days, *i.e.*, from Passover to Pentecost; it was observed in accordance with Lev. 23[10, 11,15] ; our psalm,
in Hebrew, contains forty-nine words (including *Selah*, twice) ; therefore this psalm was brought into connexion with the forty-nine days,
one word for each day ; and this word was uttered aloud on its day in the
belief that it would have its beneficial effect on the utterer.
    To interpret the psalm in an eschatological sense is to miss its import
and religious spirit ; it deals with the present.
    The developed religious sense points to a late post-exilic date ; and
this is confirmed by the adoption of the " Aaronic blessing " (Num.
6[24–26]), belonging to the Priestly Code, in the opening verse.

The metre is 3 : 3, with the exception of the concluding verse, which is 2 : 2 : 2.

1.   *For the Precentor : On stringed instruments. A Psalm. A Song.*

1 (2). O God,—may he be gracious unto   may he cause his face to shine upon us.
        us and bless us,   Selah.
2 (3). That ° his ways ° may be known on
        earth,   ° his saving-health ° among all nations ;
3 (4). Let the peoples thank thee, O God,   let all the peoples thank thee ;
4 (5). Let the nations rejoice and shout for   for thou judgest ° the world in
        joy,   righteousness °,
       ° Thou judgest ° the peoples with   and guidest the nations of the earth.
        equity,   Selah.
5 (6). Let the peoples thank thee, O God,   let all the peoples thank thee :
6 (7). The earth hath yielded her increase,   ° Yahweh ° our God hath blessed us.
7 (8).   May God bless us,
                          and may they fear him,
                          all the ends of the earth.

Text-critical Notes

2. Read, with S, דְּרָכָיו for דַּרְכֶּךָ, " thy way " ; and, with S, יְשׁוּעָתוֹ for יְשׁוּעָתְךָ, " thy saving health ".   4. Add, with G, תֵּבֵל בְּצֶדֶק and תִּשְׁפֹּט 6. Read יהוה for אֱלֹהִים, " God ".

1. In devout thankfulness for the blessings of a good harvest (see *v.* 6), the psalmist cries, *O God,*—and the unexpressed words of gratitude welling up from his heart give place to the prayer that both he and his people, joint-recipients of divine mercies, may continue to be worthy of God's lovingkindness :   *may he be gracious unto us, and bless us* ; for the metaphorical expression, *may he cause his face to shine, i.e.,* may he grant his favour, cp. Num. 6[26] and cp. Pss. 4[6], 44[3], 89[15].   This is not the way in which the verse is usually interpreted, but it is difficult to see its point on any other interpretation.   Emending the text by putting the verbs into the perfect tense (so Gunkel) is too drastic, and misses, as we hold, its true import ; and translating the verbs by imperatives (so E.VV.) is too arbitrary, and contrary to Hebrew usage ; and, again, it obscures the meaning of the verse.   Our interpretation of the verse, we submit, is perfectly natural if one takes into consideration the deep spirituality and religious feeling of the psalmist as expressed all through the psalm (see further the final section).   2. This comes out forcibly in the psalmist's prayer that the people of Israel, through the divine favour vouchsafed to them, may be the means of spreading the knowledge of God abroad, *that his ways may be known on earth, his saving health among all nations* ; and this, in the present connexion, has special reference to the blessings of a good harvest ; *saving health,* often translated by " salvation ", is used in various senses, among others, as here, of temporal blessings. Israel is to be Yahweh's witness that he, and he alone, is the giver of the fruits of the earth, so that (3) *the peoples* may *thank* God.   This universalistic note, so prominent in some of the prophetical writings, especially Deutero–Isaiah, witnesses to an exalted conception of God on

the part of the psalmist; he is not only the God of Israel, but the God of all peoples: 4. *Let the nations rejoice and shout for joy, for thou judgest the world in righteousness*; the word " judge " is not to be understood in the sense of " condemn ", but, as often elsewhere, in that of " vindicate " (cp., *e.g.*, Pss. 10^{18}, 98^9). Striking, too, is the thought that God *guides the nations of the earth*, the word is never used elsewhere in reference to the nations. And again (5), the psalmist calls upon the nations to *thank God*. Not until the psalm is almost ended does the psalmist directly make mention of the immediate cause for thankfulness: 6. *The earth hath yielded her increase, Yahweh our God hath blessed us*; this is far from being merely an afterthought; it required no earlier mention because to give thanks for the abundant harvest was the reason why the worshippers had gathered together; it was uppermost in their minds. Temporal gifts are often spoken of as " blessings ", hence *Yahweh our God hath blessed us*. The psalmist closes his all too brief hymn of gratitude with a reiteration of the universalistic note so dear to him; the divine blessing is not only for Israel, but for all men throughout the world who, through Israel, are to be brought to the knowledge of God, and the fear of him: *May God bless us, and may they fear him, all the ends of the earth*; the words are put in this order for the purpose of keeping as closely as possible to that of the Hebrew text.

Religious Teaching

Our first point here is in connexion with the apparent incongruity, to which reference has been made above, in the opening verse. With the thought of the good harvest which has been gathered in, the psalmist says: " O God,—may he be gracious unto us and bless us, may he cause his face to shine upon us "; the words sound as though the harvest had not yet been gathered in. That, however, is not the case. The psalmist presents us here with a religious factor which is of profound significance and beauty: when a divine blessing has been granted, one of the first emotions in a man, like our psalmist, of real religious insight, is a sense of unworthiness; and this is followed by the spontaneous and ardent wish that the blessing may be used aright; this can be the case only if God's graciousness continues to be accorded; hence the cry: " O God,—may he be gracious." Tested by individual experience, everyone will admit that in this respect the psalm presents us with an element in true religion which demands devout consideration.

Connected with this is the further teaching of the psalm on the subject of gratitude. Only too often temporal benefits, especially in regard to " our daily bread ", are taken as a matter of course, without the remotest thought of him who is the Giver of " every good and perfect gift ". Modern life, and modern methods of providing food, are apt to make us forget whence, ultimately, all our sustenance comes; it is well to think sometimes, when enjoying our meals, of the Creator who made the earth and the fulness thereof; and to be thankful to him. Our psalm teaches not only the fitness of being thankful for a good harvest, which meant sufficiency of food, but also how gratitude should be shown forth—namely, by proclaiming among others the goodness of God.

The psalm has teaching on two other subjects which can only be described as illimitable in their importance: Universalism, and the conception of God connected with it; but as these are dealt with in Vol. I, pp. 81 ff., we refrain from discussing them here.

PSALM 68

IT may safely be said that no other piece in the Psalter offers the student difficulties so great as those presented by Ps. 68. The majority of scholars, attempting to find a single (or even a double) thread running through it, are reduced to a theory of textual corruption so extensive as to necessitate a practical rewriting of the whole, and, even so, the results are never quite satisfactory. Gunkel obviously finds it nearly impossible to classify the psalm, and Buttenwieser is driven to the expedient of assuming that two pieces (one of them by the author of Judg. 5) have been closely interwoven with one another. We can solve the problem only on the hypothesis, advanced also by Hans Schmidt, that it is not strictly a single poem at all, but is a collection of sentences and phrases taken from a number of different poems, and strung together haphazard. It is almost as if a page from the index to a hymn-book (though the fragments are seldom taken from the opening lines of their respective poems) had strayed into the text.

It is true that a number of the " quotations " cannot be referred to any known source, but it is only to be expected that the compiler should have access to great stores of Hebrew literature which have not otherwise survived. Some of them were evidently of high poetic quality, and we must be grateful for the little that has come down to us. The psalm contains, too, an abnormal number of words and forms which do not occur elsewhere in the Bible. We realize that we know only a small fraction of a great literature, rich in powerful and imaginative poetry, and with a much larger vocabulary than we should have suspected if we relied solely on the scanty material contained within the limits of the Old Testament.

The purpose of the compilation is far from clear. It can hardly have been intended, as Hans Schmidt supposes, for the Enthronement festival (see Vol. I, pp. 46 ff.); some of the passages are quite unsuitable for such a ceremonial. In fact, none of the recognized occasions would involve the use of all the poems from which extracts have been taken.

It is generally agreed that the text must have suffered considerably in the course of transmission. We must, however, remember that in brief snatches of poetry, such as we have in this psalm, words often appear meaningless when a fuller context would render them intelligible. The Versions help us only in a few instances; even the renderings of the Septuagint seem at times to be pure conjecture, helping us neither to understand nor to correct the traditional Hebrew text.

It is obviously impossible to date a compilation like this. Parts may be very ancient; the " Song of Deborah " is one of the sources. On the other hand, there are indications (mainly philological) of a very late period, and the psalm, in its present form, must be assigned to the latest age permitted by the general history of the Psalter.

The metre is naturally varied, though each extract seems to be uniform within itself. The metre of each fragment is indicated between brackets in the exegetical notes which follow the translation.

1.   *For the Precentor : David's.   A Psalm.   A Song.*

1 (2). God ariseth!   Let his foes be scattered!
        Let them that hate him flee before   2 (3). as smoke ° is driven °.   °   °
        him,
        As wax melteth   before the fire,
        Let the wicked perish   before God.
3 (4). But let the righteous be glad;   let them exult before God.
        And let them rejoice with gladness   .   .   .   .   .

4 (5). Sing unto God, hymn his name,   build a highway for him that rideth
                                                through the wilderness.
        ° Yah ° is his name; exult ye
        before him, ...

5 (6). The orphan's father,   the widow's judge,
                      is God in his holy dwelling.
6 (7). God restoreth the lonely to a home,   bringeth out prisoners into prosperity.
        But the rebellious dwell in the white-hot land,

7 (8). O God, when thou wentest forth,   didst stride through the waste,
                      before thy people,
8 (9). Earth quaked,
                      yea, the heavens dripped,
                                  before God;
        Yon Sinai
                      before God,
                          the God of Israel.

9 (10). Rain, freely given,   ° thou pouredst down °, O God.
         ° The sick ° and the weary   thou ° didst confirm °.
10 (11). ° With thy food are satisfied °   the .   .   .   .   .
         Thou dost establish by thy good-
                      ness   the afflicted, O God.

11 (12). The Lord giveth utterance,   a great host are they that bring glad
                                                tidings.

12 (13). The kings of the hosts   flee—they flee!
                      and the beauty of the house divideth the spoil.

13 (14). (If ye dwell among the ash-heaps . . . .)
Wings of a dove   that is covered with silver,
      and her pinions with green gold.
14 (15). When Shaddai scattered
        kings therein,
          snow fell in Zalmon.

15 (16). The mount of God   is the mount of Bashan;
        The mount of peaks   is the mount of Bashan.
16 (17). Wherefore keep ye jealous watch, ye peaked ° mountains °,
        On the mount where God   loveth to dwell?
        Surely God   shall dwell (there) for ever !

17 (18). Myriads are the chariots of God, thousands twice told.
        The Lord ° came   from Sinai ° in holiness.

18 (19). Thou art gone up on high,   thou madest captivity captive,
        thou tookest gifts among men.

        Moreover, rebels ° shall not dwell before God °
19 (20). Blessed be the Lord day by day. he prospereth us, the God of our
20 (21). The God (who is) God of saving   salvation ;
        acts,   the God of escapes from death.
21 (22). Verily, God shall crush   the head of the wicked,
        The hair-decked pate   of him that walketh in his sins.

22 (23). Yahweh hath said :
        " From Bashan will I restore, I will restore from the depths of the sea.
23 (24). That ° thou mayest wash ° thy foot in blood,
        The tongue of thy hounds ° may drink its fill of thine enemies °.

24 (25).   ° See ye the festal trains of ° God !
        Thy festal trains, O my God, my king, are in holiness.

25 (26). First go the singers,   last the minstrels,
        ° in the midst ° the timbrel-maidens.
26 (27). ° In the assemblies °   bless ye God,
        ° in the convocations ° of Israel.
27 (28). There is Benjamin,   ° whose folk are few °,
        princes of Judah, rich in men.
        Princes of Zebulon,   princes of Naphtali,
          .   .   .   .

28 (29).   O God, ° command ° thy strength
        ° as the strength of ° God, which thou hast wrought for us.
29 (30).   From thy Temple at Jerusalem,
        to thee let kings   bring a gift.

30 (31). Rebuke ° the beasts of ° the reed, the assembly of the mighty,
        ° Lords of ° the peoples ° effemin-
        ate °,   with wheels (?) of silver.
        Scatter the peoples   that delight in wars.

31 (32). Let ? ? ? come   from out of Egypt ;
        Let Kush lift up   her hand unto God !
32 (33). Ye realms of the earth,   sing unto God ;
        Praise ° the Lord °   33 (34). that rideth in the ancient
          heavens. ° ° °
        Behold he speaketh aloud with a strong voice.
34 (35). Ascribe strength unto God, ° ye people of ° Israel.

        His splendour and his strength are 35 (36). terrible is God ° among his
        in the heavens,   holy ones °.
        The God of Israel giveth strength and might to ° his people °.
        Blessed be God.

Text-critical Notes

2. Read פָּחְנְדֹף for כְּהִנְדֹּף. Om. " thou shalt drive " (doublet). 4. Read, with G, יָהּ for " in Yah ". 9. Read, with Lagarde, תָּפִיף for " thou shalt wave ". Read, with Duhm, נַחֲלָה for " thine inheritance ". Read (cp. Buhl) פּוֹנַנְתָּ for " thou didst establish it ". 10. Read, with Graetz, יִשְׁבָּעוּ מִחְיָתָךְ for " thy animal shall dwell|". 16. Read הַרְרֵי for הָרִים. 17. Read, with Olshausen, בָּא מִסִּינַי for " in them, Sinai ". 18. Read. with S, לֹא יִשְׁכְּנוּ לִפְנֵי אֱלֹהִים for " to dwell, Yah (is) God ". 19. בְּרוּךְ אֲדֹנָי יוֹם יוֹם יַחְפְּצֵנוּ הָאֵל יְשׁוּעָתֵנוּ. 20. הָאֵל אֶל לְמוֹשָׁעוֹת אֱלֹהִים לַמָּוֶת תִּשְׁאוֹת. 23. Read, with G, תִּרְחַץ for " thou mayest shatter ". Read יְרֻדֶּה מֵאֹיְבֶיךָ (?) for " from enemies, from him ". 24. Read, with Wellhausen, רָאוּ חֲלִיכוֹת for " they have seen thy festal trains ". 25. Read. (cp. Graetz) בְּתוֹךְ for " in the midst of ". 26. Read בְּמוֹ מְקֹהֵלוֹת (cp. Deut. 33[4]) for בְּמַקְהֵלוֹת. Read, with Buhl, בְּמִקְרָאֵי for " from the fountain of ". 27. Read, with Gressmann (cited by Gunkel), צָעִיר אָדָם for " a small one treading them down " (or " slumbering "). 28. Read, with G, צַוֵּה for " he commanded ". 30. Read, with Gunkel, הַיּוֹת for " beast ". Read, with Matthes (cited by Cheyne) בַּעֲלֵי for " calves of ". Read מִתְרַפִּים (cp. Arab. *tarafa*) for " humbling himself " (?). 32. Read, with G, לַאֲדֹנָי for אֲדֹנָי. Om. " heavens of " (doublet). 34. Read, with Gunkel, עַם for " upon ". 35. Read, with G, בְּקְדוֹשָׁיו for " from thy sanctuaries ". Read, with G, לְעַמּוֹ for " to the people ".

1[b]–2[a]) is taken from a hymn of praise, and the surviving sentences are based on Num. 10[35]. Enough remains to show the familiar contrast, presented, *e.g.*, in Ps. 1, between the fate of the wicked and that of the righteous. The words in *Numbers* are the formula to be recited when the Ark was taken out to battle, but here it does not seem that a foreign enemy is in view. The two metaphors, the *smoke driven* before the wind and the *wax melting before the fire*, are familiar in Hebrew poetic imagery, cp. for the former, Is. 51[6], Hos. 13[3], Pss. 37[20], 102[4], and for the latter, Mic. 1[4], Pss. 22[15], 97[5].

V. 4 (metre : 4 : 3) seems to be the opening verse of another hymn of praise perhaps belonging to the type which embodies a historical retrospect. The phrase *build a highway* has given much trouble to commentators who regard the psalm as a unity, but falls naturally into its place in a poem recalling (or describing) the return from the Exile. We may compare Is. 57[14], 62[10]. The divine name *Yah* occurs here for the first time in the Psalter. It is found fifty times in the Old Testament, rather more than half the number being in the form " Hallelujah " or similar phrases. In the pre-exilic literature it appears in Ex. 15[2], 17[16] (though the text is sometimes disputed in both cases) ; other passages are probably all post-exilic. It seems to be a contraction for Yahweh, though it has been held in some quarters that *Yah* is the primitive form, of which the normal Yahweh is a reduplication.

The third extract, *vv.* 5–6 (metre 4 : 3) is taken from a poem of the same general type as the first, though there are differences in the mode of application. Here we have the contrast between the depressed and helpless classes, the *orphan*, the *widow*, and the *lonely* (a unique, though

obvious sense for the Hebrew word) and the *rebellious*—the wilful and
the headstrong. Two words call for special comment. The meaning
into prosperity, for a form not found elsewhere in Hebrew, is based on
the assumption that it is a late importation from Aramaic; the root
occurs only in Hebrew of the fourth century and later. In Arabic,
however, it implies " breaking ", and the word may be an adverbial
accusative, suggesting the shattering of prison bars and doors. The
word for " white-hot land ", too, occurs only here, and calls up a picture
of a desolate world, whose limestone rocks reflect the burning rays of the
Oriental sun.

The fourth piece, *vv.* 7–8 (metre: 2 : 2 : 2), is taken almost *verbatim*
from Judg. 5⁴, and suggests that that poem may have had a place in
some form of liturgy.

Vv. 9–10 (metre: 2 : 2), like so much else in this psalm, are drawn
from a hymn of thanksgiving for benefits received, especially by the helpless, the *sick*, the *weary*, and the *afflicted*. The parallelism shows that
there is a gap in the first line of *v.* 10; two letters alone remain of the
missing clause, and they hardly offer an adequate basis for conjectural
restoration.

V. 11 (metre 3 : 3) is an isolated line, possibly from a song of victory.
Those who *bring glad tidings* are women, and the term recalls Is. 40⁹.

In the seventh section, *vv.* 12–13 (metre: 4 : 3), we seem to have an
extract from a song of victory similar to Judg. 5. The poem must have
been singularly vigorous and impressive. With the picture of the
beauty of the house dividing the spoil we may compare the reflections
ascribed to Sisera's mother in Judg. 5³⁰. The first clause of *v.* 13 defies
interpretation, though the word *ash-heaps* recalls Judg. 5¹⁶. The text
may be hopelessly corrupt, and in any case a parallel verse-member is
missing. It might have given a clue to the connexion, if any, with the
latter part of the verse. The last line is generally interpreted as describing one item in a list of the spoil, an ornament in the shape of a *dove*,
studded with *silver* and a peculiar greenish *gold*. Such ornaments might
well have been worn by women, originally, perhaps, in connexion with
the cult of Ishtar, and if the line really does belong to the same piece as
v. 12, this may be the correct interpretation.

V. 14 (metre: 2 : 2 : 2), again, is an isolated line from a song of
triumph. If the text be correct, the reference to *snow on Zalmon*, a
mountain in the Shechem district (cp. Judg. 9⁴⁸), would indicate that a
definite historical event was commemorated in the poem from which
this line was taken.

The ninth fragment, *vv.* 15–16 (metre: 2 : 2), is elusive and intrigu-
ing. If the text of *v.* 15 be correct, it appears to be an echo of a conflict
for supremacy between various sacred sites. On the one hand it is
claimed that Yahweh's true home is in *the mount of peaks, the mount of*

Bashan, which probably means a sanctuary on Hermon. But the champions of Zion retort, " *Why keep ye jealous watch?* " implying that all the world knows that Zion is *the mount where God loveth to dwell,* and that the inferior rival is keenly looking for some ground on which to make good a claim. If we had more of this poem, we might gain a very interesting light on one aspect of Israel's religious life.

Another single verse from a triumph-song appears in *v.* 17 (metre 3 : 2, 2 : 2). Again we think of Judg. 5, with its reference to *Sinai.* Here, however, the stress is on *the chariots of God, i.e.,* the thunderclouds. The Hebrew idiom emphasizes the multitude of them; *myriads* upon myriads is what the poet's form implies. The closing phrase of this line is curious; literally it seems to mean " thousands of repetition ", *i.e.,* " thousands repeated ". The text, however, may be corrupt.

V. 18ᵃ⁻ᶜ (metre 4 : 3) is also an isolated line from a song of victory, best known from the quotation in Eph. 4⁸, where, however, St. Paul says " gave ", not " *took* " gifts.

Two pieces in the collection attain to the length of six lines. The first of these is contained in *vv.* 18ᵈ–21 (metre: 18ᵈ–19, 3 : 2; 20–21, 2 : 2). Here again is a contrast between the wicked and the righteous, the *rebels* and those whose *burden* God *beareth.* God *hath issues from death,* ways through which men may escape even when their doom seems inevitable. On the other side we have the *wicked,* whose *head* God *crushes* (again compare Judg. 5²⁶). The *hair-decked pate* is an interesting expression, which may lead us to think of the wild desert tribesman, who let his hair grow as a cultural or religious practice. The custom is widely spread; it was found at Sparta in the fifth century B.C., and is a familiar element in the Nazirite. The " long locks streaming free " of Judg. 5² may refer to the same practice. A form of religious custom, which in Israel denoted sanctity to Yahweh, may well have been common among contemporary peoples as a token of consecration to their own gods. In that case, the enemy will be a foreign, probably a Bedawin, tribe or people.

Vv. 22–23 (metre: 2 : 3, 2 : 2, 2 : 2) come from a poem which promised victory over some enemies unnamed. The mention of *Bashan* as one of the places from which God will *restore,* suggests the border warfare of the ninth century B.C. between Israel and Damascus, while the *depths of the sea* may refer to raids made by Phœnicians and others, undertaken in order to supply the western slave-markets. The vengeance which promises that the Israelite shall *wash* his *foot in blood,* and that his *hounds* shall *drink* their *fill* of their *enemies'* blood, is an expression of feeling which we find elsewhere in the Psalter.

In *vv.* 24–27 (metre: 4 : 3; *v.* 24, 3 : 4) we are transported into Jerusalem on the occasion of some great festival. The *festal train* is

v

winding its way through the streets that lead up to the temple, led by *singers*, with *damsels* beating timbrels following them, and *minstrels* with their harps bringing up the rear.   It is interesting to observe that the *assembly* includes both *Benjamin* and *Judah* on the one hand and *Zebulon* and *Naphtali* on the other.   The inclusion of these two groups is sometimes supposed to indicate a combination of Judah and Galilee, or to suggest the two extremes of the land.   They may be the remains of a much longer list, for the piece is obviously mutilated, or they may be a later insertion based on the special praise given to these two tribes in the Song of Deborah, Judg. 5¹⁴,¹⁸.   No doubt the ideal cherished by the religious authorities was that of a completed nation once more worshipping as a single whole, and, short as it is, this fragment gives us a valuable glimpse of the actual ceremonial observed on some sacred day.

The next fragment, *vv.* 28–29 (metre 3 : 4), is clearly taken from one of those psalms which appeal to God on the basis of his great deeds in the past.   His *strength* is personified as the servant whom he commissions.   It is a little strange to find that *kings* are expected to *bring a gift from* the temple; possibly the preposition has been wrongly transmitted.

V. 30 (metre : 3 : 2, 3 : 2, 2 : 2) suggests a prayer for victory over the Egyptians, typified by the *beasts of the reed*—the crocodile and the hippopotamus.   Some editors would even read " from Patros " for the doubtful form rendered as *effeminate* above.   The luxury of the enemy, whoever it may have been, is emphasized by the fact that their very chariot-*wheels* are studded with silver.

The second six-line extract is preserved in *vv.* 31–34ᶜ (metre : 2 : 2, with 3 : 2 in *vv.* 33ᵇ–34), to which, perhaps, the rest of *v.* 34 and *v.* 35 should be added.   Here, once more, we have a hymn of praise, in which Yahweh's world-wide supremacy is celebrated.   Unfortunately we do not know who or what it is that may *come from Egypt*.   The Hebrew word is obscure and difficult to assign to a known root, and the Greek translators simply guessed that it meant " messengers "—with, apparently, no philological justification.   It seems to be corrupt beyond hope even of conjectural emendation.   From *Kush* worship is demanded, and *vv.* 32–33 summon all *realms* to join the chorus of praise to a God who *rideth on the ancient heavens*.   Universality could not have been more strikingly expressed ; the same sky is spread over all nations, and Yahweh has dominated it since time began.   Even now he *speaketh aloud*, and it is no wonder that all humanity should be summoned to attest his *strength*.

The collection ends with a little piece closely allied to the preceding, *vv.* 34ᵇ–35 (metre : 3 : 3), and probably attached to it because of the similarity between the two.   Some of the terms are repeated ; in both we have mention of the *strength* of God, of the *heavens* (though the words used are different), and of the *people of Israel* to whom their *God giveth strength and might.*

The last word is the familiar doxology, *Blessed be God.*

Religious Teaching

It is obviously impossible to give an account of the leading doctrines in such a medley as this; nearly every psalm-*motif* is echoed in one or other of its pieces.

PSALM 69

THIS psalm presents us with a remarkable picture of one troubled in mind and body, who gives utterance to his conflicting and rapidly alternating emotions without any attempt at co-ordination of thoughts and ideas. Prayer passes into plaint as suddenly as the mention of the groundless hate of enemies is followed by confession of sin; the claim of suffering for God's sake alternates with prayer; then comes a complaint that he has no sympathizers among his neighbours; there follow terrible curses upon his enemies; then prayer once more; finally, recognition of God's care for the oppressed is followed by some concluding words of praise. These varying and unconnected outbursts witness graphically to the worried frame of mind of the psalmist; and he shows, indeed, that there was ample cause for his distress. Here is one involved in violent strife with those within his own surroundings; he suffers, too, from sickness; and, worst of all, he is haunted by the perception of sinfulness within himself, and his efforts to atone for this are mocked at; to this is added perplexity regarding his relationship to God; and here one cannot fail to notice the absence of those earnest affirmations of trust and faith in God which are so insistently uttered by other psalmists; not that these are really wanting, as his appeals to God show, but the whirl of worry seems to have unsettled his normal spiritual state.

The question as to the cause of the enmity whereby he is beset is a perplexing one; the psalmist himself throws no light upon it; presumably it was so obvious as to need no explanation. We have dealt with this subject in Vol. I, pp. 56 ff.; it will, therefore, not be necessary to say more about it here.

Of the date there are no certain indications; we are inclined to assign it to the Greek period, partly on account of what we believe to be the cause of the enmity against the psalmist and partly on account of what is said in *v.* 35 about Zion and the building of the cities of Judah.

The metre is mainly 3 : 3 ; but there are irregularities.

I.   *For the Precentor : To Shoshannim. David's.*

1 (2). Save me, O God, for there are come   the waters unto my soul ;

2 (3). I sink into deep mire,   and there is no standing,
I am come into deep waters,   and the flood floweth over me.

3 (4).   I am weary with my crying, my throat is parched, Mine eyes are exhausted through waiting for my God.

4 (5). More numerous than the hairs of my head   are they that hate me without a cause,
More in number than ° my locks °   are they that are mine enemies without reason ; that which I stole not (even) that I restore.

5 (6).   Thou, O God, knowest my foolishness, And mine offences are not hid from thee.

6 (7). Let them that wait for thee not be put to shame through me,   ° Yahweh Zebaoth,
Let them that seek thee not be brought to dishonour through me,   O God of Israel ;

7 (8). For, for thy sake do I bear reproach,   shame doth cover my face ;

8 (9). I am become a stranger to my brethren,   and an alien to my mother's sons.

9 (10).   For the zeal of thine house hath eaten me up,
And the reproaches of them that reproach thee are fallen on me.

10 (11). ° I humbled ° my soul with fasting,   and it became a reproach to me ;

11 (12). I made sackcloth my clothing,   and I became ° a mockery ° to them ;

12 (13). They that sit in the gate speak against me,   songs of them that drink strong wine !

13 (14). As for me, my prayer is to thee °,   in an acceptable time, O God,
In the multitude of thy mercies answer me,   in the surety of thy salvation.

14 (15). Deliver me out of the mire that I sink not,   ° lift me up ° out of the deep waters ;

15 (16). Let not the water-flood flow over me,   and let not the deep swallow me up,
And let not the ° pit ° shut her mouth upon me.

16 (17).   Answer me, Yahweh, for good is thy mercy,
In the multitude of thy lovingkindnesses turn unto me ;

17 (18). And hide not thy face from thy servant,   for I am in trouble ; haste thee to answer me.

18 (19). Draw nigh unto my soul, redeem it ;   because of mine enemies ransom me ;

19 (20). Thou knowest my reproach,   and my shame ° before ° all mine adversaries.

20 (21).   Reproach hath broken my heart°,
I looked for one that would have pity, but he was not,   and for them that would comfort, but found them not.

21 (22). They put poison in my ° food °,   and in my thirst they gave me vinegar to drink.

22 (23). Let their table be a snare to them,   ° and their sacrificial feasts ° a decoy ;

23 (24). May their eyes become darkened that they see not,   and cause their loins continually to shake ;

24 (25). Pour out upon them thine indignation,   and may the burning of thy wrath overtake them.

25 (26). Let their habitation become desolate,
that there be no dweller in their tents;

26 (27). For ° him ° whom thou hast smitten they persecute,
° and aggravate the pain of him whom thou hast pierced °.

27 (28). Add iniquity to their iniquity,
and let them not ° see ° thy righteousness;

28 (29). Let them be blotted out of the book of the living,
and let them not be inscribed with the righteous.

29 (30). But as for me, I am poor, and in pain,
and let thy salvation, O God, ° protect me °.

30 (31). I will praise the name of God with a song,
and I will magnify him with thanksgiving,

31 (32). And it will please Yahweh better than an ox,
a bullock with horns and hoofs.

32 (33). The oppressed ones ° will see ° it and rejoice;
ye that seek God may your heart be quickened;

33 (34). For Yahweh hearkeneth unto the needy,
and despiseth not ° his godly ones °;

34 (35). Let heaven and earth praise him,
the seas and all that moveth therein;

35 (36). For God will save Zion,
and he will build the cities of Judah,

That they may dwell there and take it in possession;

36 (37). And the seed of his servants shall inherit it,
and they that love his name shall inhabit it.

Text-critical Notes

4. Read, with Gunkel and others, and a number of MSS., מִצְפָּתִי (cp. Isa. 47² lit. "veil" which covers the locks) for מַצְמִיתַי, "my destroyers". 6. Om. אֲדֹנָי, "my Lord", for the rhythm's sake. 10. Read, cp. GS, וָאֶמְכָּה for וָאֶבְכֶּה, "and I wept". 11. Lit. "a proverb". 13. Om. יהוה for the rhythm's sake. 14. Om. אֶנָּצְלָה, "let me be delivered", which overloads the half-line, and read, with Gunkel, נַשֹּאֲנִי for מִשֹּנְאַי, "from them that hate me". 15. Lit. "well". 19. Om. וּכְלִפָּתִי, "and my dishonour" for the rhythm's sake; and נֶגֶד for כֶּגְדְּךָ, "before thee". 20. Om. וָאָנוּשָׁה, "I am sore sick", for the rhythm's sake. Read, with the Versions, לָנֻד for לָנוּד, "to pity". 21. See exeget. note. 22. Read, with T, וְלִשְׁלוֹמִים for וְשִׁלְמֵיהֶם, "and to them that are in peace". 26. Read, with the Versions, אֵת for אַתָּה, "thou". Lit. "and unto the pain of him whom thou hast pierced they add", reading חֲלָלְךָ for the plur.; and, with GS, יְסַפֵּרוּ for יְסַפֵּרוּ, "they tell". 27. Read, with several MSS. 'and G, יְרָאוּ for יָבֹאוּ, "come". 29. Lit. "set me on high". 32. Read, with some MSS. and G, יִרְאוּ for רָאוּ, "they have seen". 33. Read חֲסִידָיו for אֲסִירָיו, "his prisoners".

For the title, see Vol. I, p. 17.

1-3. A vein almost of impatience seems to be discernible in these opening verses. In psalms of this type it will be seen that the first verse is invariably a parallelism, both members of the verse making mention of God, or of some divine attribute. Here the psalmist says simply *Save me, O God*, and then immediately begins his tale of woes. *Waters, mire,* and *flood* are all metaphors for dangers and troubles (cp. Pss. 32⁶, 40²). There seems to be no relief from them; he has cried to God until he is *weary* of doing so, his very *throat is parched*, and he is tired of *waiting for* his God. This is all very human and natural; it is not meant irreverently; the psalmist's frankness demands all sympathy; and it is not as though his outspokenness betrayed any real lack of faith in God; he is simply irritated by the endless annoyance which he has been suffering from so many enemies. A little overstated, no doubt, but (4) they must have been many in number to be compared to the *hairs of his head*; and their false accusations made things worse. Incidentally, it should be noticed that one whose enemies were so numerous must have occupied a position of some importance; the assumption is, therefore, justified that he was one of the leaders, if not *the* leader, of the orthodox party.

The quite admirable sincerity and straightforwardness of our psalmist is then further illustrated; his conscience tells him that he has not been free from sin, and this he frankly acknowledges: 5. *Thou, O God, knowest my foolishness, and mine offences are not hid from thee*; he does not specify, but following upon the frame of mind exhibited by what he has said in the preceding verses, it may well be that he is thinking of what those offences were. It has been remarked that there are reasons for believing that the psalmist stood in the position of a leader; this is certainly borne out by what is now said: (6) those who have been inspired by his teaching, *i.e.*, his followers, are in danger of having to suffer for it; so the word of prayer is uttered that those who *through me might be put to shame* or *brought to dishonour*, may be spared this suffering; (7, 8) for it was solely for God's sake that he was glad to bear *reproach* and *shame*.

9. What had occasioned the immediate animosity of many who were otherwise in close touch with him seems to have been that the psalmist had forcibly prevented some unseemly proceedings in the temple, *thine house*; this, at any rate, was how the verse was understood in the early Church (John 2[17]). He gives us some insight into his forceful character when he says that *the zeal of thine house hath eaten me up*; but like many another reformer he had to suffer for it, the result being that those who had been guilty of this irreverence resented his interference, and vented their wrath on him: *the reproaches of them that reproach thee are fallen on me*. 10-12. A very different thought now arises in the psalmist's mind; doubtless, in repentance for wrongdoing, already recalled, he had *humbled his soul with fasting*, and put on *sackcloth*, marks of repentance as well as mourning (1 Kgs. 21[27], Joel 2[12]); but this had only called forth *mockery* and gibes on the part of those who sat drinking in the public place, *in the gate* (cp. Lam. 3[14]). 13-17. And now the psalmist turns again to prayer; the passage is one of intense feeling, and witnesses to an earnest trust in God, the more striking because of its contrast to the transient impatience exhibited in the opening verses. 18-20. The trouble he is in causes him to return to the subject of his enemies, from whom he prays to be delivered: *Draw nigh unto my soul, redeem it ; because of mine enemies ransom me*; the strong expressions used show the powerful position of his enemies; God alone can help him; he looks in vain for *pity* or *comfort* from man. 21. The particularly vindictive action of his enemies is described in

metaphorical language; he says *they put poison in his food*; the word used here for " food " (*barûth*) is a technical one, and means food that was brought by friendly neighbours to one who was mourning for the death of a relative, by way of offering him some mark of sympathy and comfort (the word occurs in 2 Sam. 12¹⁷, Jer. 16⁷ and elsewhere); so the psalmist assumes here the *rôle* of a mourner to whom this food is brought, but it has had poison put into it! The metaphor is an extraordinary one and is used in order to place on record the outrageously mean conduct of his enemies. Then he says further, again speaking metaphorically, that when he was thirsty *they gave* him *vinegar to drink*; this means that they put vinegar into his drink, so that, so far from assuaging his thirst, it only made him more thirsty! That our psalmist retaliated on his enemies was natural enough; but the series of curses— that is the force of the utterances which follow (22–28) make a painful impression. It will not be necessary to dwell upon them, though a few phrases call for some words of explanation. In 22 it is said: *Let their table be a snare to them*; in its original sense the word for " table " (*šulḥan*) meant the mat, whether of plaited straw or of leather, which was spread out on the ground, and on which the food for a meal was placed. The word we have rendered " sacrificial feasts " is strictly correct, the *šelem*, or " peace-offering ", was one of the most common kinds of sacrifice; part of the victim came upon the altar, the rest was eaten by the worshippers at a sacrificial feast. The point of the psalmist's words, therefore, is that as his enemies had poisoned his food, so their intended crime was to recoil on themselves; the mat on which their food was placed was to be, as it were, a hidden gin, or " snare "; their joyous sacrificial feast was to be a bait-laying trap. It was a kind of curse-formula, the utterance of which, it was believed, would take effect. And this effect is described in the next verse: *May their eyes be darkened*, the first sign that poison is having its effect; this is followed by the trembling of the limbs, *loins*, as the psalmist expresses it. Then, lest this should not prove to be sufficiently effective, the psalmist goes so far as to pray that God will *pour out* on them his *indignation*, and let *the burning of his wrath overtake them*: so that *their habitation* may *become desolate*, and that *there be no dweller in their tents*; in other words, that both they and their families may be exterminated. And this because they had *persecuted* him whom God had *smitten*, as though the divine punishment for his sin—he does not specify what it is, but see *v.* 5—were not sufficient. Particularly distasteful are the words which follow: *Add iniquity to their iniquity*; the horrible desire is here expressed that God would cause them to sin so as to justify the divine chastisement of them; *and let them not see thy righteousness* means, " and let them not be justified by thee "; *righteousness* is used in the forensic sense of declaration of guiltlessness.

And finally there is the cruel petition : *Let them be blotted out of the book of the living*, in reference to the belief that God kept a register of the living ; if the names no longer appeared there it meant that they would die (cp. Exod. 32[32], Isa. 4[3]). These terrible imprecations, and similar utterances occur in some other psalms, sound painful to our ears ; but it must be remembered that they were regarded as a legitimate means of inflicting retribution. Very different are the beautiful words which form the conclusion of the psalm, 29–36. In his sanctified humility the psalmist feels keenly that he is a pitiable object (that seems to be the force of the Hebrew word here), stricken by sickness : *But as for me, I am poor, and in pain* : nevertheless, he knows that God's help (*salvation*) will *protect* him, a word meaning lit. will " set him on high " (cp. Ps. 20[1]), out of the reach of danger. Then (30) he *will praise the name of God with a song*, and thank him. Some very significant words follow (31) to the effect that this will be more pleasing to God than the offering of *an ox, a bullock with horns and hoofs*—the contemptuous strain is apparent ; here we have one of the few passages in the *Psalms* in which sacrifices are belittled (see also Pss. 40[6], 50[8-14], 51[16, 17]) ; it may well be that this attitude of the psalmist contributed to the feelings of enmity displayed against him. But however this may be, he is convinced that this spiritual conception of worship will be shared by others, and it will give them joy and encourage them : *the oppressed ones will see it, and rejoice ; ye that seek God may your heart be quickened* ; they will recognize that Yahweh gives heed to them and does not despise *his godly ones* (*Ḥasîdîm*) ; this last is an emendation, which is, however, justified ; for the text reads " his prisoners " (see text-crit. note), which is not an appropriate parallel to " the needy " (*'Ebyonîm*), whereas *Ḥasidîm* and *'Ebyonîm* often occur together as parallels ; moreover, there is much in the psalm which makes it clear that the psalmist was himself a *Ḥasid*, and a leader of the " godly ones " (on the whole subject see Vol. I, pp. 56 f.). In gratitude he cries : *Let heaven and earth praise him, the seas and all that moveth therein.*

As to the concluding verses, 35, 36, many commentators question whether they really belong to the psalm in its original form ; and it must be conceded that they certainly seem out of connexion with all that has preceded. They contain an eschatological picture, and express the conviction that *God will save Zion*, and *will build the cities of Judah*, and that all the *servants* of God and those *that love his name* will finally *inherit* the land and abide therein.

Religious Teaching

This has been necessarily dealt with in the introductory section and in the exegetical notes.

PSALM 70: *see* PSALM 40$^{13-17}$

PSALM 71

A PSALM written by one, already advanced in years, who has been the victim of much ill-treatment by unscrupulous enemies; the cause of their resentment is not indicated; what, however, is made clear is that the psalmist is one who has ever been faithful to his God, while his enemies are wicked and godless.

The contention that the psalmist represents, and speaks on behalf of, his people, cannot be sustained; indeed, it is difficult to see what could have prompted the idea. Here is one who has trusted in God from his youth, and who from his " mother's womb " has looked to Yahweh for help and protection; in gratitude he sings his hymns of praise; and offers up prayer for the continuance of God's mercy in his old age. This personal note runs through the whole psalm. To interpret all this in a collective sense is to put a forced and unnatural meaning on many passages, and to misunderstand the entire spirit and purpose of the psalm.

Considered from the point of view of composition the psalm is somewhat lacking; the repetitions and absence of logical sequence in subject-matter make it of less excellence than most of the psalms. But for its deep piety and religious spirit it stands among some of the most beautiful productions in the Psalter (see further, the concluding section).

Considerable use has been made of other psalms, sometimes verbally quoted; at other times an inexact quotation is made, showing it to have been made from memory. Towards the end of the psalm there is some corruption in the text, due, in some cases at any rate, to careless copying.

The psalm is certainly post-exilic, on account of the use made of other post-exilic psalms (*e.g.*, Ps. 31); but there is nothing to indicate a more exact date.

The metre is irregular, partly due, in all probability to working-over by later scribes.

1. In thee, Yahweh, do I trust,   let me never be put to shame ;
2. In thy righteousness deliver me and
          rescue me,   bow down thine ear unto me ;
   Yea, save me, 3. and be unto me,   a Rock of ° safety °,
   ° A house of defence °, to save me,   for my Rock ° art thou.
4.   My God, rescue me
               from the hand of the wicked,
          From the clutch of the unrighteous and violent.
5. For thou art my hope, O Lord,   my trust from my youth, Yahweh ;

6. On thee have I upheld myself from the womb,
From the bowels of my mother
thou art ° my strength °,
Of thee is my praise continually.
7. A wonderment to many am I, but thou art my strong refuge;
8. My mouth is full of thy praise, of thine honour all day.
9. Cast me not away in the time of mine old-age, when my strength faileth me forsake me not;
10. For mine enemies speak against me, they that watch for my soul conspire,
11. ° " God hath forsaken him,
Pursue him and take him,
For there is none that delivereth ! "
12. O God, be not far from me, my God, haste thee to help me;
13. Let them be ashamed ° that attack my soul, let them be covered with reproach and disgrace °.
14. But as for me, I will continually ° rejoice °, and add to all thy praise;
15. My mouth shall tell of thy righteousness, all the day of thy salvation,
Yea, the numbers thereof I know not;
16. ° I will declare the mighty deeds ° of Yahweh, I will make mention of thy righteousness, thine alone.
17. O God, thou hast taught me from my youth, and till now do I declare thy wondrous-works,
18. Yea, even to old-age and grey hairs; O God, forsake me not,
So that I may declare thy ° deliverance ° ° to all ° the generation, ° and thy might to a generation to come °.
19. Thy righteousness, O God, is ° everlasting °, thou that doest great deeds;
O God, who is like unto thee!
20. ° Thou didst show me many troubles °, but thou didst keep me alive,
Yea, from the depths of the earth,
thou didst bring me up again,
21. Thou didst increase my greatness,
° and thou didst bring back ° my comfort.
22. I also will thank thee with the harp for thy faithfulness, O my God,
I will praise thee with the lyre,
O holy one of Israel;
23. My lips shall shout for joy °,
For thou hast redeemed my soul.
24. Yea, my tongue all the day
shall discourse of thy righteousness;
For they are ashamed and confounded
That seek my hurt.

Text-critical Notes

3. Read, with many MSS. and the Versions, מָעוֹז for מָעוֹן, "dwelling-place" (see Ps. 31 2(3)). Read, with Ps. 31 3(4), בֵּית מְצוּדוֹת for לָבוֹא תָּמִיד צִוִּיתָ, "to come continually thou hast commanded". 6. Read, cp. G, עוּזִי for גּוֹזִי, "he that bringeth me over". 10. Om. יַחְדָּו "together", it is unnecessary and overloads the half-line. 11. Om. לֵאמֹר, "saying", for the same reasons as the foregoing. 13. Om. יִכְלוּ, "let them be consumed", which overloads the half-line. Om. מְבַקְשֵׁי רָעָתִי, "that seek my hurt", which overloads the half-line. 14. Read, with Gunkel, אָגִל for אֲיַחֵל, "I will hope", as being a better parallel. 16. Read, with Cheyne, אַבִּיעַ גְּבֻרוֹת for אָבוֹא בִּגְבֻרוֹת, "I will come with mighty deeds"; and om. אֲדֹנָי for the rhythm's sake. 18. Lit. "arm" used figuratively. Read, with G, לְכָל־. Read וּלְדוֹר יָבוֹא גְּבוּרָתְךָ. 19. Read עַד־עוֹלָם for עַד־מָרוֹם, "unto the height". 20. Om. אֲשֶׁר, "who" and וְרָעוֹת "and evils", which overload the half-line. 21. Read, with the Versions, וְתָשׁוּב for וְתִסֹּב, "and turn again". 23. Om. כִּי אֲזַמְּרָה־לָּךְ, "for I sing praise unto thee", which overloads the half-line, and om. אֲשֶׁר, "which".

1–3. This opening prayer, coupled with a resolute faith in Yahweh, is almost verbally identical with Ps. 31$^{1,\ 2}$. The prayer is offered with the greater assurance in that the psalmist knows that he is one of godly life, *In thee do I trust*, so that there is an implied sense of innocence in the words, *In thy righteousness deliver·me and rescue me*, because a righteous God helps those who are true to him. The firm faith of the psalmist in his God as one upon whom he can rely, is expressed by the three phrases : *a Rock of safety* (cp. Pss. 18^{31}, 62^{7}), *a house of defence* (as in Ps. 31^{2}, cp. Isa. 33^{16}), *my Rock* (a different word in Hebrew) *art thou* (cp. Pss. 18^{2}, 42^{9}). The cause which has called forth this prayer is (4) that he may be rescued *from the hand of the wicked, from the clutch* (lit. " palm ", but see Ezek. 29^{7}, " grasp with the palm ") *of the unrighteous and violent.* He is, thus, an object of hatred, but he does not say why ; although he does not apply the title to himself, he was, no doubt, a *Ḥasid*, in which case the cause of enmity would be explained (see Vol. I, pp. 56 f.). There is good reason why he should be convinced that God would *rescue* him, for (5, 6) his *hope* and *trust* had been in *Yahweh* from his *youth* ; nay, more : *On thee have I upheld myself from the womb* ; the thought is that of one clinging on to something ; so had he supported himself on Yahweh. This verse is clearly based on Ps. 22$^{9,\ 10}$; but similar words occur also in Isa. 46^{3}, where the reference is to the nation ; and this has been pointed to in support of the collective interpretation of the psalm ; but the psalmist has just said that in Yahweh has been his trust *from his youth*, which could not be said of the nation ; the prophetical passage makes no mention of the nation's youth.

All through his life the psalmist has had the experience of the blessedness of a real trust in God. Since he thus looks back upon his early years, he was evidently now an old man. Then, turning again to the present, (7) he says that he is *a wonderment to many* ; we have rendered the Hebrew word by " wonderment " rather than by the ordinary word " wonder ", which is generally used in a good sense, whereas here the meaning is rather that of a contemptible spectacle causing astonishment ; the reference is probably to some malady from which the psalmist was suffering. But he disregards the surprised contempt of his enemies because God is his *strong refuge* ; therefore (8) his *mouth is full of praise* and *honour* to God. Then (9–13) the thought of his old-age recurs, and he prays : *Cast me not away in the time of mine old-age . . .* : and he refers again to his *enemies*, this time with a little more detail. They are slanderers, they *speak against* him, and *watch* for any opportunity to harm him. In reference, it may be surmised, to his sickness, they maintain that *God hath forsaken him*, so that they can with impunity pursue him and take him. But the psalmist knows that God will deliver him from their evil machinations, and prays for his help, and that those *that attack* his *soul* may *be ashamed*,

and *covered with reproach and disgrace.* The use of the word *soul* (also
in *v.* 10) should be noted ; it is used almost invariably in reference to an
individual, thus showing again, incidentally, the untenability of the
view that the psalmist represents the community. 14–16. That his
prayer had not been in vain the psalmist now shows by his grateful recognition of God's goodness to him, for which he rejoices and praises him.
So many have been these acts of lovingkindness, showing forth the
divine *rightousness*, that they are simply innumerable, *the numbers thereof
I know not* ; therefore he will declare those *mighty deeds*, and *make
mention* of that *righteousness*, emphasized by the expression *thine alone.*
17–19. His faithfulness to God, and his recognition of divine guidance
from his youth, are then beautifully expressed in the words : *O God,
thou hast taught me from my youth* ; and he can claim that he has de-
clared the *wondrous works* of God all through his life, even *till now*, to
old-age and grey hairs, to which he again refers. This he will continue
to do *to all the generation, i.e.,* to all those living around him, who in
their turn will proclaim it *to a generation to come* ; for God's *righteousness*
is *everlasting*, and he ever does *great deeds*. With over-full heart the
psalmist cries : *O God, who is like unto thee !* 20, 21. Then, once more,
reminiscences of the past come into the psalmist's mind : *Thou didst
show me many troubles*, but God preserved him ; he was even near to
death, but the divine mercy saved him : *Yea, from the depths of the
earth thou didst bring me up again* ; and prosperity and comfort were his
lot once more. 22–24. The psalm closes with a triumphant hymn of
praise and gratitude.

Religious Teaching

So far as devout expressions of faith in God are concerned, this
psalm has much in common with many others.   But what is particularly
noteworthy, and almost unique in the Psalter, is the beautiful picture of
one, now well advanced in years, who can look back upon his past life
in the happy conviction that he has done his duty to God ; and that
in spite of troubles, God has been with him and upheld him.

PSALM 72

THIS psalm is differently interpreted by commentators. A number
of passages quite obviously refer to an earthly king, while others express
thoughts which would seem to apply to the Messianic king.   Against
the view that the psalm is to be Messianically interpreted is the fact
that if the psalmist had had the Messianic king in mind he would not,
with his marked familiarity with the prophetical teaching regarding the

Messiah, have omitted the most striking attributes of that wonderful figure as set forth in such passages, among others, as Isa. $9^{6, 7}$, 11^{1-5}, 32^{1-5}. The psalm, we submit, was composed in honour of a king on his accession to the throne; the psalmist, in characteristically Oriental style, idealizes the royal person whom he is honouring, and gives utterance to thoughts which to modern Western ears sound exaggerated; statements are made and wishes are expressed, which give an impression of unreality; but familiarity with Eastern modes of expression, so often illustrated in the Old Testament, will show them to be perfectly genuine.

The psalm is an exceedingly interesting illustration of the way in which a court-poet of those days welcomed the new king on his accession to the throne; and the definitely religious note struck in the opening verses is full of significance; as God's representative among his people, righteousness is to be the guiding principle of his reign.

The psalm was never intended for liturgical worship, and was never used in the worship of the Synagogue. Its inclusion in the Psalter was doubtless due to the religious conception of the king's duties. That the psalm is pre-exilic is obvious on the face of it; a post-exilic psalm would involve a Messianic interpretation, which, as we have seen, is untenable.

The text of *vv.* 16, 17 has undergone some corruption.

The metre is irregular.

Solomon's.

1. O God, ° thy justice °
    give to the king,
    And thy righteousness to the king's son,
2. ° That he may judge ° thy people with
    righteousness,   and thy poor with justice.
3. May the mountains bring peace °,   and the hills ° righteousness °;
4. May he vindicate the poor among the
    people,   and help the sons of the needy,
        And tread down the oppressor,.
5. While the sun ° endureth °,   and the moon, to all generations;
6. May it descend like rain on the land,   like showers that ° water ° the earth,
7. May ° righteousness ° flourish in his   and abundance of peace till the moon
    days,   be no more.
8. May he rule from sea to sea,   and from the river to the ends of the
                                            earth;
9. May ° his foes ° bow down before him,   and his enemies lick the dust;
10. May the kings of Tarshish, and the isles, bring gifts,
    The kings of Sheba and Seba   offer presents;
11. May all kings bow down to him,   all nations serve him.
12. For he delivereth the needy ° from the
    rich °,   and the oppressed that hath no helper;
13. He hath pity on the weak and poor,   and the souls of the poor he helpeth;
14. He redeemeth their soul from
    oppression °,   and precious is their blood in his eyes;
15.   May he live, and may there be given him gold of Sheba;
    May they pray for him continually,   may they bless him at all times.
16. May there be ° abundance ° of corn in   may it ° grow thick ° on the tops of the
    the land,   mountains;
    Like Lebanon may its yield ° flourish °, and ° its sheaves ° like herbs on the
                                            land.
17. May his name last for ever,   as long as the sun ° standeth firm °,
    And may all nations with him be   and ° all the tribes of the earth ° call
    prospered,   him blessed.

18.   Blessed be Yahweh °
                             the God of Israel,
                        Who alone doeth wondrous things ;
19.   And blessed be his glorious name for ever,
                        And may all the earth be full of his glory.
                             Amen and Amen.
20.   ° [The prayers of David, the son of Jesse, are ended.]°

Text-critical Notes

1. Read, with the Versions, the sing.   2. Read, cp. G, וְיָדֵן for יָדִין, "he
shall judge".   3. Om. לָעָם, "to the people" (gloss).   Read, with G, צְדָקָה,
omitting בְּ, "with".   5. Read, with G, וְיַאֲרִיךְ, lit. "while it continueth",
for יִירָאוּךָ, "may they fear thee".   6. Read יַזְרִיפוּ, or, with the Versions, וְזָרְפוּ.
7. Read, with many MSS. and the Versions, צֶדֶק for צַדִּיק, "righteous (man)".
9. Read צָרָיו for צִיִּים, "jackals".   12. Read, with the Versions מֹשׁוֹעַ, lit. "from
the noble (in rank)" for מְשַׁוֵּעַ, "when he crieth".   14. Om., for the rhythm's
sake, וּמֵחָמָס, "and from violence".   16. Read, with Gressmann, פֶּקֶר, for the
otherwise unknown פִּסַּת.   Read, with Gressmann, יַעְשַׁר, lit. "may it be rich",
for יִרְעַשׁ, "may it shake".   Read יָצִיץ for וְיָצִיצוּ, "and they shall flourish".
Read, with Gunkel, וַעֲמִירוֹ (coll.) for מֵעִיר, "from the city".   17. Read יִכּוֹן
(cp. G διαμενεῖ) for יָנִּיו, "it shall bud".   Om. שְׁמוֹ.   Add, with G, כָּל-מִשְׁפְּחוֹת
הָאָרֶץ.   18. Om., with some MSS. and GS, אֱלֹהִים, "God".   20. Om·ted by
a number of MSS. G reads תְּהִלּוֹת, "praises", for תְּפִלּוֹת, "prayers".

The title assigning the psalm to Solomon was doubtless suggested
by the words of *v.* 10 (cp. 1 Kgs. 10¹ ᶠᶠ.).

1, 2. As already pointed out, this psalm was composed in honour of
the king, in all probability on his accession to the throne. With a true
sense of what is primarily demanded in a king, the psalmist begins with
a prayer to God on behalf of the new ruler : *O God, thy justice give to
the king* ; he says *thy justice* both because divine justice is unalterable,
and because God is the source of all justice ; with this is inseparably
connected *thy righteousness,* also of divine origin, and unfailing.   The
new ruler is spoken of as *the king's son,* which would seem to imply that
he was yet young. With divine guidance he will be able to *judge thy people
with righteousness* ; significant is *thy people* and *thy poor* (lit. " afflicted "),
for all the people belong to Yahweh, the king rules on trust ; the poor
are especially God's own, a thought often occurring in the prophetical
writings (*e.g.,* Isa. 3¹⁴, ¹⁵, 14³², 32⁷).   These verses show the untenability
of a Messianic interpretation of the psalm.   3–11. A series of good
wishes for the new king follows.   Thus, the psalmist says, re-echoing Isa.
52⁷, *May the mountains bring peace, and the hills righteousness* (cp. Isa.
55¹²) ; the point of these words is that it is upon the mountains around
Jerusalem that messengers appear (Isa. 52⁷) ; it is a wish, already
expressed in the prayer, that the king *may vindicate the poor among the
people, i.e.,* justify them when wrongly accused, and thus shield them
from *the oppressor,* whom he will *tread down.*   It is a poetical exaggeration when the psalmist adds : *While the sun endureth . . .* An
expressive picture follows : *May it, i.e.,* righteousness, as the next verse

shows, *descend-like rain on the land, like showers that water* (see text-crit. note) *the earth.* The word for " land " is a very rare one, it occurs elsewhere only in Deut. 18[4], Job 31[20], Am. 7[1], and means land on which the grass has fully grown and is ready for mowing. He continues : *May righteousness flourish in his days.* Then (8–11) wishes of another kind are expressed ; they touch upon the political sphere. *May he rule from sea to sea, and from the river to the ends of the earth,* quoted verbally from Zech. 9[10], where they are Messianically interpreted ; the words meant, for one who was living in Palestine; from the Dead Sea to the Mediterranean, east to west, and from the Euphrates to some indefinite part beyond Egypt, north to south (strictly north-east to south-west). 9. In accordance with this wide-spread power the further wish is expressed that *his foes may bow down before him, and his enemies lick the dust,* an Oriental figure of speech to express deep humility before a conqueror ; the expression occurs in Isa. 49[23], Mic. 7[17], but with no reference to the Messianic king, it is before the people of Israel that the nations humble themselves. All the kings of the earth are to be subject to this king, so the psalmist's wish runs next ; they are to bring gifts and tribute to him. *Tarshish* is usually identified with the Phœnician colony of Tartessus, in Spain ; *the isles* refer presumably to those in the Mediterranean sea, but coastlands are also included (cp. Isa. 41[1, 5]) ; *Sheba* was in southern Arabia (cp. Isa. 60[6], Ezek. 27[21, 22]), and *Seba,* or *Saba,* was " a royal city of Ethiopia, which Cambyses afterwards named *Meroe,* after the name of his own sister " (Josephus, *Antiq.* II. 249). These *kings* are all to *bow down to him,* and the *nations* to *serve him* (cp. Isa. 60[5 ff.], [11 ff.], not in reference to the Messianic king). All this is to be the reward of the king, for the psalmist now (12–14) takes for granted that the prayer he had offered on behalf of the king (*vv.* 1, 2) will be answered : *For he delivereth the needy from the rich* (see text-crit. note) *and the oppressed that hath no helper* . . . Therefore (15) the poor will be able to live. *May he live* is collective, and the king will, of his bounty, give him of the *gold of Sheba* ; so the psalmist hopes. Therefore they will *pray for him continually* and *bless him at all times.* Here, again, it will be seen that the thought of the Messianic king was not in the psalmist's mind. But the greatest need of the poor was that they might have their daily bread, therefore the psalmist, in high-flown Oriental style, expresses the wish that not only *may there be abundance of corn in the land,* but that it may even *grow thick on the tops of the mountains* ; and he adds : *Like Lebanon may its yield flourish, and its sheaves like herbs on the land* : it is uncertain whether the reference here is to the luxurious growth of trees on mount Lebanon, or whether *Libanus* is meant, as in Hos. 14[5, 6 (6, 7)], Cant. 4[11], the tree, vigorous and sweet-smelling, from the leaves of which incense was made, hence the Hebrew word, *l'bônah,* " frankincense " ; in any case, like the parallel clause, the language is hyperbolic, but quite in accordance with what would be expected from a court-poet on such an auspicious occasion. A reign during which such prosperity was looked for, would inspire the expectation that the king's *name* would *last for ever*, and *stand firm as long as the sun* ; another Oriental mode of expression, it does not occur elsewhere, though for a somewhat similar thought cp. Ps. 89^{36}. The beneficent reign of this king will be such, according to the psalmist's idealistic wishes, that other nations will partake of his prosperity, *and all the tribes of the earth will call him blessed.* 18, 19. This doxology is not part of the psalm ; it was, no doubt, added when the Psalter was divided into five books (to correspond with the " Five Books of Moses ") ; each book concludes with a similar doxology (41^{13}, 89^{52}, 106^{48}), the place of which is taken by Ps. 150 as the concluding doxology to the whole Psalter. 20 is omitted by a number of MSS.

Religious Teaching

In a psalm so taken up with good wishes for the new king it is not surprising that the religious element is not prominent. But it is significant that the psalm opens with a prayer which, though short, asks for what is of fundamental importance. For a ruler to be guided by just dealing and righteous acts, recognizing that they are of divine inspiration, is a blessing to his country of inestimable value. This conception of kingship was ingrained in ancient Israel ; an ideal for all time.

PSALM 73

Like Pss. 37 and 49, Ps. 73 deals with the problem, first formally stated by Habakkuk and still unsolved, of the principles on which rewards and punishments are distributed among men. The problem could arise only on the basis of such teaching as that given by the eighth-century prophets and their successors—that the world is governed by righteous and infallible Omnipotence. Given that doctrine, however, the further question becomes inevitable, for the facts of life are by no means in harmony with its apparent corollaries. It does not follow that upright conduct always produces happiness, or that the sinner always meets with obvious disaster. The classical discussion of the problem is found in the book of *Job* ; it is raised more than once in the prophets, and is the theme of these psalms. The three, however, handle the matter in different ways. In Ps. 37 the law of mechanical retribution is stated in a somewhat crude form, reminding us of the position taken by Job's friends : the adversity of the righteous and the prosperity of the wicked are alike temporary and evanescent. The writer of Ps. 49,

again, has a totally different line of approach, and dwells on the unreality
of material prosperity in view of the common fate of all humanity.
He has developed a contempt for wealth which suggests the attitude of
the Stoic or even of the Cynic.   Ps. 73 goes deeper, and seeks an answer
to the rankling question through the mystic experience of the thoughtful
saint.

In a sense, then, the psalm has a didactic purpose, and Gunkel's
inclusion of it among the " Wisdom Psalms " has some justification,
though even in that group it is unique.   Like so much of the Wisdom
literature, it comes from a comparatively late date.   Both the teaching
of the psalm and its language point to a time well on in the post-exilic
period.   There are numerous archaisms, apparently intentional, with
unconscious lapses into late form and idiom.

The text has been fairly well preserved, though there are one or two
difficult passages.   The worst case is *v.* 10, which, in any case, badly
interrupts the connexion between *vv.* 9 and 11, and would follow well
after *v.* 5.   Further, Kittel is surely justified in placing *v.* 21 between
vv. 16 and 17.

The metre is mainly 3 : 3, with 2 : 2 : 2 in *vv.* 12 and 18, and anacrusis in *vv.* 2, 11, and 28.   In three instances (*v.* 21, twice, and *v.* 17),
a word heavily charged with meaning must receive two stresses.

1. Surely ° God ° is good ° to the up-
   right °,   Elohim to the pure in heart !
2. But as for me !
   My feet had all but ° slipped °,   a hair's breadth and my steps ° were
                                                      gone °.
3. For I grew hotly indignant at the   as I gazed on the prosperity of the
   ° wealth of the boasters °,   wicked.
4. For no bonds ° have they,   faultless ° and fat is their belly.
5. They are not in the trouble of mortals,   they are not plagued with mankind.
10. ° Thus are they sated with bread °,   ° and for water they have no thirst °.
6. Therefore is pride their necklet,   garb of violence wraps them about.
7. From   fatness   comes   forth   their   the fair schemes of their heart pass all
   ° iniquity °,   bounds.
8. They mock, and speak ill,   ° arrogantly ° they speak in disdain.
9. They have set their mouth against
   heaven,   and their tongue roves through earth.
11. And they say—
    How does God know ?   and is there knowledge in the highest ?
12. Behold ! these are the wicked,
                           and in endless calm
                                                   they increase their wealth.
13. Surely in vain have I kept my heart
    pure,   and washed my hands in innocence !
14. And I have been smitten all day,   ° and chastening was mine ° every
                                                      morning.
15. Had I thought :   I would   ° thus °   I were traitor ° to the generation ° of thy
    tell my tale,   children.
16. So I quested to know this,   a trouble was it in mine eyes.
21. For my heart grew ever more bitter,   and in my reins was a gnawing pain.
22. And I was an ignorant brute,   a very beast I became before thee.
17. Till I entered God's holy places,   understood their latter end.
18. Surely in slippery places
                           thou settest them,
                           in beguiling thou bringest them down.

19. How are they a waste in a moment,
20. As a dream when one waketh, O Lord,

23. Nevertheless—I am ever with thee,
24. With thy counsel thou leadest me
      ° in the way °,
25. Whom have I in the heavens ?

26. My flesh and mv heart ° cease to be,
27. For lo ! they perish that are tar from
      thee,
28. My goodness is nearness to God,

through terrors are finished and ended !
when thou rousest thee thou wilt
    despise their form.
thou holdest my right hand.

and afterwards wilt gloriously take me.
in the earth I have no delight save in
    thee ;
but my portion is God for ever.
all that go a-whoring from thee thou
    destroyest.
I have made in the Lord ° ° my
    refuge. ° °

Text-critical Notes

1. Read, with Graetz, לְיָשָׁר אֵל for " unto Israel ".   2. Read, with Q're G, נָטָיו for K°thib נָטוּי.   3. Read, with Budde, בַּהֲוֹן הוֹלְלִים for "at the boasters".   4. Read with Ewald, לָמוֹ הֵם for '' at their death ''.   10. Read, mainly with Lagarde (cited by Gunkel), כֵּן יְשֻׁבְעוּ לָהֶם for " his people shall return hither ". Read וּמֵיִם לֹא יִצְמָאוּ for " and waters of the full are wrung out ".   7. Read, with G, עוֹנָם for " their eye".   8. Read, with Graetz, עָתֵק for "oppression".   14. Read וְתוֹכַחַת לִי for " my chastening".   15. Read, with Bickell, הִנֵּה for " behold ! ". Read, with Staerk (cited by Gunkel), בְּדוֹר for " the generation ".   20. Read בָּעוּרְךָ for "in the awakening (trans.)".   24. Insert בָּאֹרַח, omitted through similarity with the next word.   26. Om., with Duhm, ''the rock of my heart ".   28. Om., with G, "Yahweh ". The last clause of the verse is a liturgical gloss, still further expanded in G.

" The great Nevertheless " is the descriptive title prefixed by Kittel to this psalm, and its contents justify the phrase.   It opens with a single verse in which the atmosphere of the whole finds expression.   The poet has honestly considered the facts of life, and faces his problems with courage.   Now—as the Hebrew particle at the beginning implies— he is able to state with confidence his general conclusion.   That particle is significant ; it occurs again in *vv.* 13 and 18, " After all, it must be so, in spite of appearances to the contrary, and in spite of desperate inward struggles, *God* (' *el*, as in *v.* 11) *is good to the upright.*"

The psalmist has a right to say this.   It is not the glib statement of an easy and superficial orthodoxy.   He has descended into the depths of torturing doubt, and this side of his experience is set before us in *vv.* 2–11.   His problem is general, but his treatment is his own.   The emphatic pronoun at the beginning of *v.* 2—*As for me*—doubly empha- sized by the anacrusis, serves at once to link the psalmist's account of his case with the general conclusion of *v.* 1.   His experience is described in language which makes us think of a tyro on skates.   His *feet had all but slipped*—flown this way and that without his volition or control— and his *steps* had been within *a hair's breadth* of utter confusion : a strong word, meaning literally " poured out ".   But it is not on level ice that this has befallen him, but on a precipice edge, and there had been a moment when it had seemed that he was actually over the brink.

His danger had not been physical ; he had been stirred by sudden *hot* emotion, jealousy, anger, or a combination of the two, by the peace and prosperity of unworthy men. It is not only their wickedness, but also their bearing and their success that have moved him. Their language is that of *boasters* (*v*. 3), full of arrogant mockery and over-weening pride, counting all others their inferiors, and speaking of them as such (*v*. 8). Nothing on earth commands their respect, and the heavens are not too high, for their criticism (*v*. 9), for they treat God himself as ignorant and stupid (*v*. 11). Yet they are prosperous, and the psalmist's bitter humour finds an outlet in his picture of them. In the East, be it remembered, the first use made of newly-won wealth is to spend it on unlimited food, and it is often literally true that a man's girth varies directly as his income. So wealthy have these men become that they have passed all familiar limits (they have no *bonds*), and seem to be positively globular, with no flaw in the smooth circle of their belly (*v*. 4). The *trouble* that toil brings with it and the strokes whereby *mankind* are *plagued* pass them by ; they have all they can want of the good things of life (*vv*. 5, 10). From their fat heart are schemes of iniquity born, and gorgeous pictures are painted by their extravagant and lawless fancy (*v*. 7). Their language, too, is *arrogant*, and they speak *in disdain*—as the Hebrew idiom has it, " from their lofty posi-tion ", thinking all men beneath them. But God has not said a word.

In the second part of the psalm, *vv*. 12–28, the poet gives the story of the war within himself, and of the victory he finally won. His first reaction had been to succumb to an almost irresistible temptation, and to doubt the validity of his fundamental belief in goodness (*vv*. 12–15). It was here that he had slipped on the brink of the cliff, and all but been dashed to spiritual ruin. " *Behold !* ", he cries, " *these are the wicked* ", and the opening interjection is almost a conditional particle —indeed, it must have had that sound to a writer whose daily vernacular was Aramaic. " *If* that is what wickedness achieves, then, after all (again the particle of *v*. 1), I must have been wrong. All my struggles for purity and innocence have been a failure ; goodness is no good. I have let myself suffer pain and persecution for a phantom and a base-less dream " (*vv*. 13 f.). But from that peril the psalmist had been saved. He knew that he did not stand alone : there were others fighting in the ranks beside him. To allow himself to harbour the doubt would have been to desert to the enemy, and to range himself on the side of evil. So would he have been *traitor* to his loyal comrades, the *children* of that God whom all claimed as their Father.

So he returned to the war of the spirit. *Trouble* and toil lay before him (*v*. 16), and his *heart grew bitter*, his mind soured by the contem-plation of the facts, while there was, as it were, a mordant tooth, *gnawing* at the centre of his emotional life, like the vulture tearing Prometheus' liver (*v*. 21). Worse and worse grew the atrophy of his tortured soul, till, in utter abasement, he speaks of himself as a *very beast*, with a curious Hebrew idiom by which a plural form is used to emphasize an idea.   But at last he found himself in the *holy places* of God's heart, not merely in the outward temple, but in that inner shrine of the spirit where God and man may most surely meet (*v.* 17).   He turns to that God whose cause he has so nearly betrayed : " After all, it must be so " (again the particle of *v.* 1), the wicked, too, stand in peril, *in slippery places*, but their danger is enhanced by God's hostility.   We cannot here endorse the psalmist's attitude ; the days are long past when Jew or Christian can think of God *beguiling* men to their ruin (*v.* 18).   But these men have set themselves up against God, and must find that he *does know*, that their superiority over others is met by the fact that God will *despise* them, think no more of them than a waking man does of the figures brought before him in a *dream*, and hurl them to sudden, complete and horrible ruin (*vv.* 19 f.).

Then, once more, the emphatic pronoun at the beginning of *v.* 23 brings us back from wrath to love, from the wicked to the loyal servant of God.   Now the psalmist knows who it is that has gripped his *right hand* on the edge of the precipice, who it is that *leads* him *in the path*.   But more, he knows, too, that a vital union with God is as eternal as God himself.   He thinks, possibly, of Enoch, and, though he does not contemplate for himself an escape from physical death (cf. *v.* 26), he is certain that a material event like the dissolution of the body is powerless to break the love-forged links of the soul.   In heaven and in earth, living or dying, he has but one supreme pleasure (*v.* 25) and one passion, *nearness to God*, the only experience which he can really call *good* (*vv.* 26, 28).   Those that are false to God will perish—nay, have already been annihilated, since their real self, their very soul, has been destroyed by their sin (*v.* 27).   But the man who has once found his *refuge in the Lord*, and has known the secret of his intimate converse, has attained an experience transcending all the fortunes of the material world, and has already entered into life eternal.

Religious Teaching

In a sense, this psalm is an epitome of the book of *Job*.   While it lacks the intensity of feeling, the grandeur of conception, the dramatic character-drawing, and the intellectual depth manifested in that great poem, it deals with the same problem, follows the same line of thought, and offers one of the few Old Testament adumbrations of a genuine doctrine of immortality.   Its thought is in some ways more closely akin to that of Greece than to that of normal Israel.   The psalmist does not contemplate the resurrection of the material body, achieved by the return of the spirit that vanished at death, but rather a personality temporarily united to a physical being, which can, if it be really in touch with God, survive the disintegration of its earthly frame, and stand without veil of mortal clay in the immediate presence of the eternal Father. But the path by which this goal is reached is emphatically Hebrew, and not Greek. The Hellenic belief in immortality was based on psychology and metaphysic. That of the psalmist, like that of Job, had an ethical and religious foundation. God being what these men, in the depths of their soul, knew him to be, no other result was possible. A problem in religious thought, as in science, is created by an apparent clash between theory and fact. Either the theory must be abandoned, or further truth must be elucidated which will bring the discordant fact into the universal scheme. The theory here is the character of God, as revealed through the great prophets ; the conflicting fact is the seeming injustice and inequality of divine retribution. The psalmist resisted the temptation to abandon the basic theory, and ʻhe inevitable conclusion—the first step towards a final solution— was a recognition of another life, in which eternal values should be vindicated.

PSALM 74

PSALM 74 is called a *Maskil* (see Vol. I, p. 15), and belongs to the class of the Laments of the Community. It describes the desolation of the land, especially of the temple, and pleads for divine interposition. Its date is not easy to determine. The temple has been defiled and partially, at least, destroyed by fire. Much of its woodwork has been hewn in pieces, and the enemy has set up heathen symbols, while sacred buildings have been burnt throughout the whole country. The land is spiritually desolate, too ; though the invader has vilely insulted the God of Israel, he has made no response, and there is not even a prophet to foretell how or when the trouble will end.

There are two familiar events in the history of Israel which are commonly mentioned in connexion with this psalm : the destruction of Jerusalem by Nebuchadrezzar in 586 B.C., and the defilement of the temple by Antiochus Epiphanes in 167 B.C. Theodoret's suggestion that we have here a prediction of the burning of the temple by Titus in A.D. 70 need not be taken seriously. In favour of the earlier date we have the facts in general, though the psalmist mentions neither the destruction of the city nor the deportation of the people. Most of the details would fit the Maccabæan age—the apparent reference to the synagogues (*vv.* 4 and 8), the profanation of the temple (*v.* 7), the erection of heathen symbols (*v.* 4), while in *v.* 6 G read " doors " for " carvings " (cf. I Macc. 4³⁸), and the " dark places of the earth " in *v.* 20 have been interpreted (though wrongly, see below) as the caves

and dens in which the faithful took refuge from Syrian persecution.
Further, the failure of prophecy (*v.* 9) is held to be reflected also in
I Macc. 4⁴⁶, 9²⁷, 14⁴¹. It is pointed out, however, that the desolation
had taken place long before the psalm was written (*vv.* 1, 3, 10), that
Antiochus did not actually burn the whole temple (*v.* 7), and that the
psalm contains no reference either to the damage done in Jerusalem
itself, or to the systematic attempts made by Antiochus to stifle Judaism
by destroying the books of the Law, and by inflicting the death penalty
for certain religious observances.

Another view, championed by Buttenwieser, is that the psalm
dates from the first half of the fourth century, when certainly Judah
was involved in grave trouble with Artaxerxes Ochus (359–338 B.C.).
Our references to these events, however, are obscure and uncertain ;
it is easy to assign a work to a period of which we have so few records,
because no discordant details are known to us. In view of the licence
a poet often allows himself in describing events, and the hyperbole to
which he is sometimes given, we can hardly take psalms like this and
Ps. 79 as a basis for the reconstruction of detailed history. All we can
say is that the psalm may date from this period, and that we know of
no other which would suit it better.

A different type of explanation would make no reference to a historical situation, and see in this psalm a composite work. The first part,
vv. 1–11, may be a lament of a type familiar to us in certain Tammuz
liturgies, while the second, with its suggestions of the creation mythology, may be in some way connected with the New Year festival.
The main difficulty in this view is that *vv.* 18 ff. certainly return to the
spirit of prayer and petition, and take up again the note struck in the
first part.

Decision is difficult, certainty impossible. If the psalm arose out
of a definite historical situation, the view least open to objection may
be that of Calès, who suggests that a poem originally written about
540 B.C. was worked over and " modernized " to fit later events,
possibly the assaults of Artaxerxes Ochus or of Antiochus IV.

The metre of the psalm is 2 : 2, with 3 : 2 in *vv.* 2, 6–7, and, possibly,
20. The first part of *v.* 20 appears to have lost two significant words.

Maskil.   Asaph's

1. Wherefore, O God,
   Thine anger burns lurid
2. Remember thy congregation,
   Thou redeemedst the tribe of thy
      heritage,
3. Step with giant stride
   To the havoc once wrought

4. Thine adversaries have roared against
      thee

hast thou cast off for ever ?
against the flock thou didst feed ;
thou didst purchase of old—

Mount Zion, where thou dwellest.
to the everlasting ruins,
by the foe ° in thy sanctuary °.

in the midst of ° thy assemblies ° ;

They have raised their emblems, | emblems (5) ° we know not °.
° Like one lifting ° on high | axes in forest-thickets,
6. ° They have hewn down ° its carvings | with the axe together.
And with the hatchet they have smitten | (7) ° they have burnt ° in the fire thy
them off, | sanctuary.
They have profaned to the ground | the home of thy name.
8. And have said in their heart, | ' ° Let us smite them ° together,
° Come, and let us cause to cease ° | all God's assemblies in the land.'
9. Our emblems we see not ; | there is no more any prophet,
Nor is there with us | one that knoweth how long ?
10. How long, O God, | shall the adversary insult ?
Shall the foe despise | thy name for ever ?
11. Why drawest thou back | thy hand, ° O God ° ?
° And thy right hand withholdest ° | within thy bosom ?
12. ° But thou, O God °, | art my King for ever,
Working triumph | in the midst of the earth.

13. Thou didst defeat | the Sea by thy might,
The heads of the monsters | didst crush on the waters.
14. Thou didst shatter | the heads of Leviathan,
Gavest him as meat | ° as fodder ° to jackals.
15. Thou didst rend open | fountain and torrent ;
Thou didst dr֯ עי | perennial rivers.
16. Thine is the day ; | yea, thine the night ;
. Thou didst ordain | ° the sun for a light °.
17. Thou didst establish | all the bounds of the earth ;
Summer and winter— | thou didst form them.

18. Remember this— ° | the foe ° doth insult thee °,
And a foolish people | despiseth thy name.
19. Give not ° to the falcon ° | the soul of thy dove ;
The life of thy lowly | forget not forever.
20. Look on ° thy covenant ° |
For the dark places of the earth are | ——— ———
full | ° of pride and violence °.
21. Let them not turn back | crushed ° and ashamed ° ;
Let the lowly and poor | praise thy name.
22. Arise, O God, | plead thy cause ;
Remember thine insults | from fools all the day.
23. Forget not | the noise of thine adversaries,
The tumult of them that rise against | that cometh up continually.
thee,

Text-critical Notes

3. Read, with G, בְּקָדְשֶׁךָ for "in the sanctuary" (בְּקֹדֶשׁ). 4. Read, with many MSS, the plural מוֹעֲדֶיךָ, instead of the singular. 5. Read (cf. G, לֹא יָדְעוּ) לֹא יָדַעְנוּ for "it shall be known", and attach to v. 4. Read כְּמֵרִים for "as one bringing". 6. Read, with G, וְעַתָּ for "and now". 7. Read (cf. G), וְשָׁרְפוּ for "they sent". 8 Read, with Kittel, נָבָּם for "we will oppress them" (?). Read, following many G MSS, נָשְׁבִּיתָה. 11. Insert אֱלֹהִים (Buhl, יהוה). Read, with Bickell, תְּכַלֵּא for "destroy", and transpose to after "thy right hand". 12. Read, with Ley, וְאַתָּה אֱלֹהִים for "and God". 14. Read, with Wellhausen, לַעַם for "to a people". 16. Read, with Duhm, לִמְאוֹר שָׁמֶשׁ for "light and sun". 18. Read חֲרַף for "insulted Yahweh". 19. Read, with Perles, לְאַיָּה for "to the animal of". 20. Read, with G, לִבְרִיתְךָ for "the covenant". Read (cf. Bickell), גָּאוּת וְחָמָס for "dwellings of violence". 21. Read with Duhm, וְנִכְלָם for "ashamed".

The psalm falls into four parts of unequal length : (a) vv. 1-3, (b) vv. 4-11, (c) vv. 12-17, (d) vv. 18-23. The first of these is introductory, and puts briefly the substance of the whole. The poet feels keenly the contrast between two outstanding facts : the Love of God and the Wrath of God. Israelite tradition carried his thought back to the days of old, when Love had been manifest in the *purchase* of Israel, when God had *redeemed* his people and his city, as a wealthy man might *redeem* the lost *heritage* of an impoverished kinsman. Not only so, but all through history he has been the Good Shepherd. Israel has been his flock, not a " flock of slaughter " (cf. Zech. 11⁷), doomed to the butcher's knife, but a " flock of pasture ", to be protected, guided, and *fed*. But now it is Wrath that dominates the experience of the *tribe*. Hebrew tended to fasten on the concrete and physical evidences of emotion ; and anger suggested the distended and bloodshot nostrils of a furious animal. So fiercely does God's *anger burn*, that his breath, as it were, is *lurid* with murky smoke. To the psalmist this is unintell-igible ; he can hardly believe in his own experience, and he appeals to God to come *with giant strides*, a gait that will step high over every obstacle, and at least view the *ruins* whose restoration seems for ever impossible (*v.* 3). Surely, then, his compassion will be roused and his spirit stirred to action !

Vv. 4–11 describe, in some detail, the *havoc* in the *sanctuary* and elsewhere. The temple has been attacked, much as was the Jewish shrine in Elephantine. Its *carved* woodwork has been *hewn down with axe* and *hatchet*, perhaps to remove the gold with which it was richly overlaid, *fire* has been put to the building, and the place has been dese-crated by the erection of heathen *symbols*, probably emblems of a foreign deity. So the whole of the building has been *profaned*, from its highest pinnacle *to the ground*. Even so, the enemy has not been content, but has carried his desolation over the whole land, and, wherever he has found a place of worship, a spot where God and man may meet, he has *smitten* and dispersed the *assemblies* of worshippers ; the Hebrew *moʻed* is never used in a concrete sense. None can tell when these troubles will cease, or when God will avenge these *insults* to his *Name*. It is as if he had put out his *hand* to help, and had then changed his mind, and thrust it back into his *bosom* ; there is no longer a *prophet* through whom his purpose may be known, and men have no clue to his will except in the ruin spread about them.

The psalmist is not merely distressed, he is puzzled. For (*vv.* 12–17) there is no doubt that God *could* have saved his people had he pleased. Away back in the distant past, at the very beginning of time, he had encountered and destroyed enemies far more terrible than Israel's present oppressors. The old creation-myth, so well known to us from Babylonian and other sources, was current in Israel even in the psalmist's days, and men still told the story of how God had *defeated*, frustrated, and rendered ineffective, the mighty powers of Chaos—*the Sea, the Monsters, Leviathan*, or, in Babylonian terms, Tiamat and Kingu with all their brood. The form of the myth (for it varied in Israel, cf. *Myth and Ritual*, pp. 177 f.) adopted by the psalmist recorded the

destruction of the enemies, the *giving* of them as *meat* to the " howling
things " of the desert. These creatures will inevitably be identified
as *jackals* by any one who has heard them making the Eastern night
hideous, but they may be spirits of the wild ; the frontier between
zoology and demonology was not strictly drawn in ancient Israel.
This triumph had been only a preliminary to the construction of the
universe as man knows it, the making of *fountains*, the *day*, the *night*,
the *sun*, and the coasts which formed the *bounds of the earth*.

The psalmist believes intensely that all this is the work of the God
of Israel. Again and again, with almost aggressive repetition, he uses
the emphatic pronoun *Thou*, its significance being constantly reinforced
by the strong metrical accent it receives. Perhaps the poet had in
mind the myths of foreign peoples, and was insisting that it was *his*
God, and no other, who had won this cosmic triumph. Certainly
it gave him ground on which his renewed appeal for deliverance and
vengeance (*vv.* 18–23) might be based. A *foolish people* has *insulted*
and *despised* Israel's God, and pursues his *covenant* race as a *falcon*
hunts a *dove*. The *dark places of the earth* are sometimes interpreted
as the dens in which the pious Israelites hid from their oppressors,
but the psalmist would hardly have said that these were *full of violence*—
i.e., of crime. They are rather the spots in the land which have been
most afflicted by the adversary, where iniquity has most been rampant,
and the poet may have had in mind a thought like that of Isa. 9[1]. So,
with a moving appeal to the divine honour and compassion, the psalmist
pleads with God to vindicate at once himself and his *lowly* people.

Religious Teaching

We do not look for formal theology in a *cri du cœur* like this psalm ;
we can but note in a word the faith on which its pleading is based.
God is the victorious Creator of the universe, the righteous and
omnipotent Ruler of the world. At the same time, he has a special
interest in Israel, and a plea addressed to his loving heart will scarcely
fail of its purpose.

PSALM 75

In its present form this psalm is a community hymn of thanksgiving,
and may have had a place in some ritual of praise following on a national
victory, or may have been intended as an expression of eschatological
hopes. The opening verse is normal in this type of psalm, but would
naturally be followed by a recital of the " deeds of wonder " which are
being acknowledged. Here a pronouncement by Yahweh (*vv.* 2–3)
follows immediately, without the introductory words which we should
expect. While the doctrine of " corporate personality " would make

it possible for such a psalm to be sung by the community as a whole, its expressions would fit an individual rather better. *Vv.* 2–3, the words of Yahweh, were presumably uttered by a priest (or prophet ?), but such statements are usually the answer to an appeal by the worshipper, whether an individual or the whole community. We are thus led to suspect that we have here a part only of an original psalm of an individual, to which, after the loss or intentional omission of the opening sentences, *v.* 1 was prefixed to give the psalm a communal reference. Further, the tone of the whole (from *v.* 2 onwards) rather suggests the *formulæ* of a prayer for success than a thanksgiving for a victory already won. The normal scheme of such psalms is : (*a*) petition, (*b*) divine response, (*c*) assurance of triumph. The two latter elements are obvious in the psalm as it now stands.

The structure of the psalm is interesting, since it falls naturally into well-marked pairs of verses, and the arrangement may be genuinely strophic. Commentators are not agreed as to the extent of the divine utterance, but *vv.* 6 f., which are clearly put in the mouth of the worshipper, seem to presuppose some such language as that of *vv.* 4 f.

We have no clue to the date of the psalm ; it is probably a comparatively late adaptation of a pre-exilic hymn.

Metre : 3 : 3, with 2 : 2 : 2 in *v.* 7 and 3 : 3 : 3 in *v.* 8b. *V.* 1 is 2 : 2.

For the Precentor : To " Hurt not." Psalm. Asaph's. Song.

1 (2). We praise thee !
    ° And we call on thy name,

O God, we praise !
we recount ° thy deeds of wonder.

2 (3). ' ° I ° will choose an appointed time,

I will judge uprightly,

3 (4). The earth melteth, and all that dwell therein,

I established its pillars.' Selah.

4 (5). I say to the boasters, Boast not !
5 (6). Lift not your horn on high,

and to the wicked, Lift not your horn !
° speak not ° arrogantly ° against the Rock °.

6 (7). For not from east nor from west,

nor ° from the wilderness cometh uplifting °.

7 (8). For in Yahweh's hand is a cup

and ° foaming ° wine filleth the ° wineskin °.

8 (9). And it hath passed from one to ° another °,
    yea, its dregs ° are never drained out °,

all the wicked of the earth drink of it.

9 (10). But ° I will exult for ever °,
10 (11). And all the horns of the wicked I will hew off,

I will sing to the God of Jacob.
and the horns of the righteous shall be exalted.

Text-critical Notes

1. Read, with V (cf. G), וְהָרָאֵנוּ בְשִׁמְךָ נְסַפֵּר for "and near is thy name ; they tell of". 2. Read אֲנֹכִי for "for". 5. Insert אַל with G. Read בְּצוּר (cf. G) for "with the neck". 6. Read מִמִּדְבַּר הָרִים for "from the wilderness of mountains". 7. Read, with G, חֶמֶר for "fermented". Read מֶשֶׁךְ (cf. Köhler in *ZAW* LV. 161, and Urdu *maʿak* = goatskin bottle). 8. Insert אֶל־זֶה with G. Read, with G, לֹא יִמָּצוּ for " they drain ". 9. Read, with G, אָגִיל for " I will declare ".

Most of the phrases used in the heading to this psalm are familiar, but we have one most interesting addition, found again in Pss. 57–59. This is the phrase " Hurt not ", which apparently indicates the tune or mode to be used. It is natural to suggest that it is connected with the old vintage song beginning, " Hurt it not, for a blessing is in it ! " cited in Isa. 65^8.

The opening ascription of praise is of a familiar type. As we have seen, a plea for help may have dropped out before v. 2, and we pass at once to the divine answer. It comes with an emphatic " *I* ", if the suggested text be right. Yahweh may have delayed his action, but he has appointed a time, which he will use aright (cf. Hab. 2^3), to give his just decision. Lest there be any doubt as to his power to enforce his sentence, he cites his control over the physical universe. It seems as though there had been an ancient myth which told of an earlier stage in world history, which, owing to the weakness or the blunders of the older world-rulers, ended in confusion and chaos. Then came Yahweh and *established its pillars.*

In confidence born of this pronouncement, the psalmist turns to his enemies, *the wicked, the boasters,* who have *lifted* their *horn on high*— a familiar metaphor for arrogance. They have *spoken arrogantly against God,* and the enormity of their offence is emphasized by the choice of the divine epithet—the Rock. What folly to magnify oneself against the Immoveable and the Immutable ! Nowhere in the world, *east* or *west,* is the power to *lift high* found, except in God, and the psalmist has already had the assurance that God will act in this case. Primitive myths told of a poisoned cup which the old gods might force on a vanquished enemy, a cup which would intoxicate, if not destroy. Yahweh has such a cup, which he makes to *pass* from hand to hand. He has, too, a whole *skin,* full of the *foaming wine* of his wrath. It is inexhaustible ; *for its dregs are never drained out* (the metre shows the stress on the negative), and however many be *the wicked of the earth, all* must *drink of it.* And so the psalmist concludes on the double note of vengeance and deliverance. The *horns* that the wicked have *lifted* so high in their arrogance will be hewn off by the psalmist, through the might of Yahweh, while he himself will *exult* and *sing* praises to *the God of Jacob,* from the proud height to which he himself has been raised.

Religious Teaching

Like most psalms of this type, Ps. 75 breathes a vindictive note which is repulsive to Christian thought and feeling. But it does stress the omnipotence and the righteousness of God, and expresses the intense conviction that " right the day must win ".

PSALM 76

MOST recent commentators are of opinion that this psalm belongs to a group connected with the ritual of the New Year festival. On this theory the ceremonial included a mimic warfare in which Yahweh overcame and destroyed the forces of darkness and death, so bringing life to the world and salvation to his people. Older interpreters held that it was a song of thanksgiving commemorating the triumph of a Judæan king over his enemies. But the references at the end to the divine judgements and to the justification of the poor do not fit either of these two hypotheses, and it would seem that an original pre-exilic hymn was adapted for more than one purpose. In any case, *v.* 11 is quite out of place in the original psalm (note, *e.g.*, the use of the *tetragrammaton*), and must be regarded as the latest of the adjusting phrases. As with so many psalms, the best explanation of the present form seems to be a pre-exilic hymn thus repeatedly worked over to suit new situations.

The text is fairly well preserved, and where it is in doubt the versions generally offer some help. Possibly *vv.* 4 and 5 need a more drastic reconstruction than that adopted below, but none of the attempts (*e.g.*, that of Gunkel) commend themselves to the present writer as being more than brilliant free compositions, and there seems to be no compelling reason for supposing that they offer us what the psalmist actually wrote :

Metre : 3 : 3 ; *vv.* 4–5, 3 : 2, 3 : 2, 2 : 3 ; *v.* 11, 2 : 2, 2 : 2.

For the Precentor : To stringed instruments.   Psalm.   Asaph's.   Song.

1 (2). Famed is God in Judah, — in Israel his name is great,
2 (3). And his booth is in Salem, — and his dwelling in Zion 3 (4) ° is set °.
He hath shattered the flames of the bow, — the shield and sword and war-weapon. Selah.

4 (5). ° More terrible ° art thou, O mighty one, — ° than ravening lion °.
5 (6). Spoiled are the stout of heart, — stilled in their sleep.
Nor have the mighty men — found their power.
6 (7). At thy rebuke, O God of Jacob, — ° sank in slumber the riders on horseback °.

7 (8). Thou art terrible, — and who shall stand in thy sight ° for thy wrath ° ?

8 (9). From heaven thou utterest judgement ; — earth feareth and is still.
9 (10). ° When thou risest ° for judgement, O God, — to save all the lowly of the earth.
10 (11). For the wrath of man doth praise thee, — the remnant of wrath ° hold festival to thee °.
11 (12). Make vows and fulfil them — to Yahweh your God,
Let all about him bring — a gift ° to the terrible one °.
12 (13). ° Thou cuttest off ° the spirit of princes, — thou that art terrible to the kings of the earth.

Text-critical Notes.

3. Read יָשֻׂם (שׁוּמה =) for " there ".   4. Read, with Targ., נוֹרָא for " glorious,"
Read (cf. Gunkel), מֵאָרְיֵה טֹרֵף for " from mountains of prey ".   6. Read, with G,

נִרְדְּמוּ רִכְבֵי סוּס for "the chariot is made to slumber and the horse". 7. Read
with G, מֵאַפְּךָ for "from that time thine anger". 9. Read, with Schlögl, בְּקוּמְךָ for
"when (he) rises". 10. Read, with G, תַּחְגֹּךְ for "thou girdest thyself". 11. Read,
with G, לַנּוֹרָא? for "to fear". 12. Read תִּבְצֹר for "he cuts off".

For the title, see Vol. I, p. 11.

The note of praise is struck in the opening words of the psalm.
Yahweh (here, as elsewhere in Bks. II and III, "God" has been substituted for this name) is *famed*; he may be known; indeed, he makes
it difficult for men not to know him. *His name is great*, for he has a
reputation, and his personality and deeds (all this is involved in the
Hebrew concept of the "name") have impressed themselves both on
Judah and on *Israel*. The two terms may be an instance of synonymous parallelism, or, especially if the psalm be early, they may be
intended to include both north and south. But, wherever else he may
be *famed*, it is especially in Jerusalem that Yahweh has set up his
booth—a term strongly suggestive of the New Year ritual.

In *vv.* 4–6 the psalmist gives an outline of the deeds which have
won this *fame*. Yahweh has shown himself mighty in battle; he has
shattered the arrows that have leapt like *flames* from the *bow*, and all
other weapons, defensive and offensive. Repeatedly the word *terrible*
strikes the emotional keynote of the psalm. Yahweh is as a *ravening
lion*, and his foes, despoiled of their arms, *sink* into such helplessness
that they seem to slumber to the point of death. Even men possessed
of the unseen battle-power (and we have here a remote survival of
the *mana* conception) have lost the use of *their hands* (cf., for the
general idea, Am. 2¹⁴ ᶠ.). Mounted warriors, yet stranger than chariots
to Israel, fall into a *slumber* deeper than natural sleep at the divine
word.

Once more, in *vv.* 7–9, the Terror is presented, but this time it is
primarily in *judgement*. The former picture was that of Yahweh
returning in triumph from the conquest of his foes, and may well have
formed part of a scene from the enthronement drama. If the same
theme be continued here, Yahweh has now taken his seat *in heaven*,
presumably to pass sentence on his captured enemies. *The earth
feareth and is still*, but the thought of the psalm (possibly owing to a
later adaptation) passes from the cosmic struggle to the needs of *the
lowly* in his own land. No Hebrew could contemplate justice without
thinking of the depressed classes.

This is but a passing note, and the psalmist returns to the main
theme in *vv.* 10, 12—*v.* 11 is obviously a late adaptation; there is nothing to attract *vows* in the story of the great triumph. Many commentators see in *v.* 10 a reference to Edom and Hamath: "The wrath of
Edom doth praise thee, the remnant of Hamath doth hold festival to
thee". But, as far as our knowledge goes at present, we have no reason

to suppose that the New Year Myth involved these two countries in particular, and, though they might have indicated the southern and northern limits of Israel, the expressions would be very unusual in this sense.   On any rendering, however, we have the bold statement that even human *wrath* can be used for the *praise* of Yahweh.   Here is the supreme conquest ; a dangerous passion can be overcome, controlled, and sanctified.   The very *remnant*, the last extreme of man's anger, can be used to the glory of God.   If Yahweh can bring this about, no wonder that he can *cut off the spirit of princes*, as a grape-gatherer strips his vines, or that he is *terrible to all the kings of the earth*.

Religious Teaching

The psalm hymns the majesty and power of God, particularly in his dealings with the human world.   Here it adds something to the normal Enthronement psalms, which commonly stress the conquest of personified forces in the realm of Nature.   God's attributes are such as to make men stand in awe of him—note the conversion of human anger and the closing words.   The writer put a very high value on the personality of Yahweh, but he had not attained to the perfect love which casts out fear.

PSALM 77

PSALM 77 presents some interesting features.   It begins as a dirge, probably of the community, and ends as a hymn of praise, celebrating Yahweh's deeds in Nature and in History.   It is, then, only to be expected that some commentators have seen in it a combination of two pieces, though they differ as to whether the division should come after *v.* 9 or after *v.* 15.   There is, however, no real incongruity between the appeal of *vv.* 1–9 and the recollection of a glorious past in *vv.* 10 ff. ; a suppliant often seeks to strengthen his case with a compliment, or to comfort himself with the memory of deliverance in days gone by. There are, however, one or two facts which suggest a division after *v.* 15.

The first point is the structure of the whole.   It is worth noting that the use of *Selah* here seems to be significant.   It occurs at the end of *vv.* 3, 9, and 15.   Each of the sections 4–9 and 10–15 contain six lines, and each may be regard as a self-contained whole within the larger complex.   In other word these sections have the marks of the true " strophe ".   We may even conjecture that the opening section was once longer than it now is ; the transition from 2b to 2c is very abrupt and awkward, and the last clause lacks any real balance.   It is quite possible that some two and a half lines have been omitted, either by accident or by design. This, of course, is pure conjecture, but it is fairly clear that the metrical form changes after *v.* 15. *Vv.* 1–15 are 3 : 3 (except *v.* 2, which, as it now stands, is 3 : 3 : 3, but see above), while *vv.* 15–19 are 3 : 3 : 3 throughout. They might possibly be arranged as 3 : 3 six times, or we might suppose that (3 : 3 : 3) × 4 = (3 : 3) × 6 is a good metrical equation in Hebrew. But the latter suggestion is too uncertain, and the parallelism is very strongly in favour of the 3 : 3 : 3 arrangement. The combination of 3 : 3 : 3, as an occasional variant, with 3 : 3 is quite regular, but the two are normally interspersed, and we rarely find a solid block of the longer form linked up with the shorter.

It is, further, undeniable that with *v.* 16 we meet a new tone and style. The theme, it is true, naturally continues that of *vv.* 9–15, except that (a significant point) *v.* 15 should logically follow *v.* 19. But while *vv.* 9–15 recall the acts of God in meditative language, *vv.* 16–19 seem to break irrepressibly from a heart overflowing with joy, and move with a vigour and a swing quite foreign to the earlier portion. The contemplative mood indicated by the verbs of *v.* 12 (הגה and שׂיח) is emphatically not a likely source for the spontaneous outburst of exultation which thrills us in *vv.* 16–19.

The balance of probability, then, lies on the side of a division after *v.* 15. The combination of the two pieces, however, may well have been intentional. Neither reaches a formal conclusion, and the facts suggest that a compiler found these two fragments and put them together. It may be noted in passing that *vv.* 16–19 would form a good transition from *vv.* 1–15 to Ps. 78.

Nothing has yet been said about *v.* 20. Its metrical form is 3 : 3, which suggests an accidental mutilation, and the appearance of Aaron in the last clause looks like a late addition. We may suspect that the original poem, whose opening sentences have not survived, was much longer, and went on to illustrate the power of Yahweh as exhibited in the history of Israel. The surviving portion has some of the marks which we commonly associate with the New Year ritual, especially in the terror shewn by the vanquished " Deep ". But there is nothing in the ritual pattern which leads us to suppose that it involved a poetic history of Israel, and we may rather suggest that the poet was drawing on some form of the creation liturgy to make the introduction to his story of Yahweh's deeds in Israel.

Metre : *Vv* 1–15, 3 : 3 ; וּבַעֲלִילוֹתֶיךָ in *v.* 12 has two beats. *Vv.* 16–20, 3 : 3 : 3.

For the Precentor : On Jeduthun.   Asaph's.   A Psalm.

1 (2). My voice was Godward ! ° and I   my voice was Godward ! ° and he gave
            cried ° ;   ear °. ° °

2 (3). In the day of distress I sought the Lord,
° ____ ____ ____ °
3 (4). I must recall God, and must moan,

4 (5). ° Fixed ° are the guards of mine eyes,
5 (6). I have considered the days of old,
° I commune ° by night with my heart;
7 (8). Will the Lord cast off to eternity?
8 (9). Is his love ended for ever?
9 (10). Hath God forgotten to shew favour?

10 (11). And I said: That is my wounding—
11 (12). I will recall ° thy deeds °, O Yah,

12 (13). And I will consider all thy working,
13 (14). O God, thy way is in holiness;
14 (15). Thou—
O God, thou workest wonders,

15 (16). Thou redeemest with thine arm thy people,

16 (17). The waters saw thee, O God,
the waters saw thee and were troubled,
17 (18). The clouds streamed with water,
heaven's vault uttered its voice,
18 (19). Hark! ° the thunder of thy chariot-wheels °,
thy lightnings illumine the world,
19 (20). Thy way is in the sea ° O God °,
and thy path in great waters,
20 (21). Thou leddest thy people as a flock,
by the hand of Moses and Aaron,

my hand ° was outstretched and never grew numb.
my soul refused to be comforted.
I must meditate, and let my spirit faint away.

I am disturbed and may not speak.

years long past (6) (7). I recall.
I must meditate, and my spirit ° make search °.
will he never be pleased again?
finished ° ° to all generations?
or shut up his compassion in wrath?

that the right hand of the Most High doth change.
for ° glorious ° of old was thy wonder-work.
and on thy deeds I would meditate.
who is a great God like God?

thou shewest among peoples thy strength.
the sons of Jacob and Joseph.

yea, even the deeps kept shaking.

yea, verily, thine arrows were abroad.
the earth trembleth and quaketh.
and thy footprints may not be known.

_____   _____   _____

Text-critical Notes.

1. Read וָאֶ for "that I might cry". Read, with G, וַיַּאֲזֵן for "to give ear". Om., with Buhl, "unto me". 2. Om., with Buhl, "by night". Apparently a part of the original text has been lost. 4. Read (cf. G), אֲחַזּוֹרת for "thou hast held". 6. Read, with G, הֲגִיתִי for "my harp-playing". 8. Omit "a word" (אמר doublet of נמר; G omits both words). 11. Read, with Schlögl, מַעֲלְלֶיךָ for "deeds". Read, with Duhm, אַדִּיר for "let me remember". 18. Lit. "thy thunder in the chariot-wheel". 19. Insert אֱלֹהִים.

For the title, see Vol. I, p. 15.

As it has come down to us, this psalm falls into four parts. In the first (*vv.* 1–3) the psalmist indicates his approach to God. The second section (*vv.* 4–9) states the problem in more detail, the third (*vv.* 10–15) is directed to Yahweh (for whose name, as in all this large group, the word "God" has been substituted), and recalls his mighty deeds in the past, while the last division (*vv.* 16–20) seems to have been taken from some other source, though it serves in a way to carry further the thought of *vv.* 10–15.

Vv. 1–2 describe a common experience in familiar terms. The psalmist has already received the assurance that he needs, but he must place the facts on record. So he tells us that he *cried* to Yahweh, and *sought* him in anxiety. In the attitude of prayer his *hands* had been *outstretched*—a strange word in this connexion, for it normally means " poured out "—and the supplicant posture had been maintained, though his arms might well have *grown numb*. Then it seems as if there were a gap, and when we come to the last clause of *v.* 3, we find the psalmist already in the midst of his troubles. His " *soul* " *refused to be comforted*, and he was driven by some strong inward compulsion to *remember* God, and to come with humility and weakness even to *fainting*-point, " spent with the utter agony of prayer ".

In *vv.* 4–9 we have a fuller statement of the sufferer's plaint. His eyelids, *the guards of* his *eyes*, are *fixed* so that they cannot close in sleep. Worry has *disturbed* him, smitten him as the hammer smites on the anvil, with steadily repeated blows In his enforced silence he has turned to history, and has *considered*—counted up, as it were—the records of *years long past*. He has *communed with* his *heart*, in that muttering undertone in which the Oriental reads to himself, a sound meaningless to the hearer, but rich in possibilities of mystic experience to the reader or speaker. Is there any hope ? Can God *be pleased again* ? It is as if the psalmist thought of him as temporarily cross and peevish, and wondered when, if ever, he would be in a good humour again. It is noticeable that there is no confession of sin. If Israel had deserved all this, the punishment would have been intelligible, but, as it is, the facts are as puzzling as they are painful. It seems as if God's tender emotions—*favour* and *compassion*—had become atrophied, and would never be active again.

The third section, *vv.* 10–15, introduces an element familiar in this type of psalm, the *recalling* of the *glorious deeds* of Yahweh in the past. It is the *change* in the divine attitude which is at once the psalmist's despair and his hope, and, after a general statement of this part of the theme, he reminds Yahweh of the ancient redemption of Israel. *The sons of Jacob and Joseph* had been in Egypt, helpless as a widow or a fatherless infant. But in their destitution they had found a champion, who had taken up their cause and *redeemed* them. May this experience be repeated !

The fourth section of the poem, *vv.* 16–19, as we have seen, appears to have an independent source ; its poetic movement has a vigour and power entirely different from the plaintive beauty of the earlier sections. We note at once the stair-like parallelism of *v.* 16, and the quick change from the perfect—*the waters saw*—suggesting a single

AA

event, to the imperfect of *were troubled* and *kept shaking*. One glimpse of God in his majesty, and *the sea* is thrown into permanent writhing terror, shown in the restless heaving of its surface. *Even* (the particle is metrically emphatic, and therefore has abnormal force) the ancient *deeps* of whom the creation-myths spoke have fallen into a state of trembling. From the primæval conquest of the chaos-ocean, the psalmist's thought passes in *vv.* 17–18 to the phenomena of the sky. It is in the thunderstorm that God is most clearly seen in ancient Israel, and these verses recall the magnificent description of Ps. 29. Here we have the sudden floods *streaming* from above, the crash of the thunder in the cloudy *vault of heaven*, and the rolling which follows, suggesting some great *chariot* whose *wheels* rumble over celestial pavements. The lightnings, the fiery *arrows* of God, dart hither and thither, and, so continuously do they thread their way across the sky (note the imperfect again!), that, with bold metaphor, the psalmist can say that they are walking about in the heavens—as Yahweh walked in the Garden of old. Then back we come once more to the *sea*, and this time the *sea* as it is, and not the deep of sacred myth. God moves across it and his path is in it, but the waters leave no trace of the divine *footprints*, and the mystery of his passage is kept sealed.

All this is but preliminary. The psalmist has depicted the universality and cosmic domination of Yahweh, but he passes on the Israelite conviction—surely the most audacious claim ever made in human history—that Yahweh's primary interest is in his people. To the chaos powers he is a mighty conqueror, to Nature an omnipotent Lord, but to Israel a tender shepherd. He has led them, using Moses and Aaron as his underlings—and the rest is lost.

Religious Teaching

This psalm, as it left the hands of its final editor, strikes two notes, both familiar elsewhere. One is the old, imperfect conception of Yahweh as a God of whimsical and uncertain temper, who may and does inflict suffering with no obvious cause except his own changing mood. The other is a realization of the supremacy of Yahweh in Nature and in history. The latter view is echoed repeatedly by the prophets, but in the former the psalmist has hardly risen to the level of their spiritual insight.

PSALM 78

Like Pss. 105–107, Ps. 78 is mainly a poetical record of the story of early Israel. It defies classification, and it is difficult to think of any part or aspect of the cultus to which it was especially adapted ; probably it was never actually used in worship.   It almost certainly comes from a comparatively late period.   The Pentateuch is accepted, practically in its present form ; the treatment of history is that which we associate with Deuteronomy and the Deuteronomists, and the account of the crossing of the Red Sea (Sea of Reeds) (cf. *v.* 9) makes it practically certain that the poet was acquainted with P.   The purpose of the poem is, apparently, to show the pre-eminence of Judah, and, in particular, of the House of David.   The psalmist's method is to work through the history of the early days, contrasting Yahweh's benefits with Israel's rebelliousness and infidelity.   He seems to feel that Judah was guiltless in this respect ; it is as if he assumed that every reference to " Israel " in the old story implied the northern kingdom, which goes under that name, in contrast to Judah in the books of *Kings*. . He carries back the overthrow of Israel and the triumphant accession of David to the period in which Shiloh was destroyed.   Both Saul and the later northern monarchy are completely ignored.   Such a presentation— we may almost say distortion—of history was hardly possible till a late date.   The style and language do not suggest an early period ; there is at least one very striking Aramaism (*v.* 41).   The metre, too, presents features which do not appear commonly in Hebrew poetry until the book of *Job*.

It is possible that the present form is an expansion of a shorter original, perhaps by the insertion of fragments from one other historical poem or more.   *Vv.* 42–52, for example, go back again to the Mosaic age, already treated in *vv.* 12 ff., with more detail in certain parts. The story is interrupted from time to time by reflections on the loving bounty of Yahweh and on the sinfulness of Israel.

Metre : 3 : 3, with 3 : 3 : 3 in *vv.* 21, 31, and 55, and 2 : 2 : 2 in *vv.* 6ab, 7bc, 20, 38, and 45.   Probably 5b, 40 41, 43 44, 46–48 are 3 : 2, with 2 : 3 in *v.* 42.   Anacrusis in *vv.* 20, 21.

Maskil.   Asaph's.

1. Give ear, my people, to my instruction,   bend your ear to my words.
2. I would open my mouth in wise sayings,   pour out riddles from the past.
3. What we have heard and known,   and our fathers recounted to us.
4. We will not hide ° from our sons °,   telling to an after age.
   The praises of Yahweh and his might,   and the marvellous deeds he wrought.
5. How he raised up a testimony in Jacob,   and set the Law in Israel ;
   How he gave commands to our fathers,   to teach them to their sons.
6. That another generation might know,   sons that should be born.
   That they might rise and recount to their sons,
   And not forget   the feats of God,   7. and put their trust in God.
                                              and keep his commands,
8. And not become as their fathers,   a generation perverse and defiant,
   A generation that ordered not its heart,   whose spirit kept not faith with God
9. The sons of Ephraim ° were a false bow   that turned ° in the day of battle.
10. They kept not the convenant of God,   and refused to walk in his Law.

11. And forgot the ° feats of Yahweh °, and his marvels which he had shewn them.

12. Before their fathers he wrought marvels, in the land of Egypt, the field of Zoan.

13. He clave the sea and brought them through, and made the waters stand up as a heap.

14. And he led them in cloud by day, and all night in the radiance of fire.

15. He clave rocks in the wilderness, ° and gave them drink ° in abundance as from oceans.

16. And he brought out streams from the crag, and water down as rivers.

17. But they still sinned against him yet more, revolting against the Most High in the desert.

18. And they tempted God in their heart, asking food for which they longed.

19. ° ° And they said, ' Can God spread a table in the wilderness ?

20. Behold !
He hath smitten the rock   and waters gushed forth   and torrents in spate ;
Can he also give bread.   or provide flesh for his people ?

21. Therefore—
Yahweh heard in fell rage,
and fire blazed out in Jacob,
yea, hot anger went up in Israel.

22. For they did not believe in God, nor trusted his saving power.

23. So he commanded the skies above, and the doors of heaven he opened.

24. And he rained upon them manna, ° ° and gave heaven's bread to them.

25. Food of angels did man eat ; he sent ° ° their fill of victuals.

26. He loosed the east wind ° from heaven °, and brought the south in its strength.

27. And he rained down ° ° flesh as dust, and flying fowl as the sand of the seas.

28. ° And they fell ° in the midst of ° their camp °, about their dwellings.

29. And they ate and were utterly sated, and their desire he brought home to them.

30. They were not yet estranged from their lust, with their meat still in their mouth ;

31. When the anger of God rose high against them,
and he slew among their stout ones,
and brought low Israel's youth.

32. For all this they sinned yet more, and believed not his wonder-works.

33. And he ended their days in vanity, ° and all ° their years in dismay.

34. Had he slain them, they surely would seek him, and once more quest for God ?

35. But they forgot that God was their rock, and God Most High their champion.

36. And deceived him with their mouth, and lied to him with their tongue.

37. And their heart held not firmly with him, nor trusted in his Covenant.

38. Though he had been merciful, atoning for their iniquity, and not destroying.
And often he turned back his wrath, and stirred not up all his fury.

39. And remembered they were but flesh, a passing breath that cometh not back.

40. How oft they defied him in the wilderness, pained him in the desert !

41. And again they tempted God, and hurt the Holy of Israel.

42. They remembered not his hand, the day he redeemed them from the adversary.

43. When he appointed his signs in Egypt, and his marvels in the field of Zoan.

44. And he turned their Nile-streams into blood, that they drank not their waters.

45. He sent against them
the locust and it devoured them,
and the frog and it destroyed them.

46. And he gave their produce to grass-hoppers, and their toil to the locust.

47. He killed their vines with hail, and their sycamores with hailstones.

48. And delivered their beasts to hail, and their cattle to lightnings.

49. He loosed on them the heat of his wrath
fury and rage ° he commissioned °.

A mission of angels of evils,

He kept not their soul from death
51. And he smote all the first-born of Egypt,
52. And he moved his people as sheep,
53. And led them secure and unafraid,
54. And brought them to his holy precinct,
55. And he drove out before them nations, brought them under the lot-line as a possession,

56. And they tempted and defied God,

57. And went back and were treacherous as their fathers,
58. And they angered him with their high-places,
59. God heard in fell rage,
60. And tore down the habitations of Shiloh,
61. And he gave his strength to captivity,
62. And delivered his people to the sword,

63. Fire devoured his youths,
64. His priests fell by the sword,
65. And the Lord awoke as a sleeper,
66. And he smote his adversaries backwards,
67. And he spurned the tent of Joseph,
68. But chose the tribe of Judah,
69. And built his sanctuary ° as in the height °,
70. And he chose David his servant,
71. He brought him from following ewe-mothers,
72. And he `fed them in perfection of heart,

50. he made a smooth road for his anger.
and their life he delivered to pestilence.

first-fruits of vigour in the land of Ham.
and guided them as a flock in the wilderness.
and whelmed their foes in the sea.
the mount his right hand had won.

and made the tribes of Israel dwell in their tents.
the Most High, and his testimonies they observed not.

they turned as a deceitful bow.

and with their idols roused his jealousy.
and utterly spurned Israel.
.
the tent ° where he dwelt ° among men.
and his beauty to the power of the foe.
and against his inheritance raged in fury.

and his virgins none did praise.
and for his widows none did weep.
as a warrior shouting through wine.

age-long shame he put upon them.
and chose not the tribe of Ephraim.
the mountain of Zion which he loved.

founded it as the earth for ever.
and took him from the pens of the flock.

to pasture Jacob his people ° °.
and with the skill of his hands he led them.

Text-critical Notes

4. Read, with Cheyne, מִבְּנֵימוֹ for " from their sons ". 9. Read (cf. Duhm) קֶשֶׁת רְמִיַּה הֹפְכָה for " equipped with shooters of the bow ". 11. Read, with Baethgen (cited by Gunkel), עֲלִילוֹת יהוה for " his feats ". 15. Read, with G, וַיַּשְׁקֵם for " and he gave drink " (without objective pronoun). 19. Om., with Briggs, "and they spake against God ". 24. Om., with Briggs, " to eat ". 25. Om., with Buhl, " to them ". 26. Read, with G, מִשָּׁמַיִם for " in heaven ". 27. Om., with Baethgen, " upon them ". 28. Read, with G, וַיִּפְּלוּ for " and he caused to fall ". Read, with G, מַחֲנֵיהֶם for " his camp ". 33. Insert, with Gunkel, וְכֹל. 49. Read (cf. Graetz), צָרָה for " and distress ". 60. Read, with G, שָׁכֵן for " he caused to dwell ". 69. Read, with Hitzig, כִּמְרוֹמִים for כְּמוֹ רָמִים (probably with same meaning). 71. Om., with Baethgen, " and Israel, his inheritance".

The purpose of this psalm is to illustrate Yahweh's choice of Judah, Jerusalem, and David, in preference to northern Israel, its sanctuaries and its kings. The poet, disregarding the fact that Judah was equally implicated with the rest of the people in its early sins, runs in summary fashion through the history, down to the accession of David. The narrative is interspersed with reflections on the iniquity and faithlessness of the people.

1–11 form the introduction, and show that the aim of the poet is didactic. His own contemporaries and *generations* yet to be *born* are to keep the facts for ever in mind, that they may not *become as their fathers*, especially as the tribe of Ephraim.

In 12 the record begins with the deliverance from *Egypt*. *The field of Zoan*, a northern city (the Greek Tanis), is specified as the scene of Yahweh's deeds. The place was very ancient (cf. Num. 13²²), though it came into prominence only with the XXIst (1090–945 B.C.) dynasty. 12–16 tell briefly the story of the *marvellous* deeds of Yahweh, the crossing of the Red Sea (where the mention of *the waters standing up as a heap* betrays familiarity with the later narrative of Exod. 14), and the bringing of *water* from the *rock*. More space is given to the sins of the people, especially to the murmurs which culminated in the giving of the *manna* (17–25). The writer imports into his narrative the cosmology and mythology of his own day. The *doors* of the vast storehouse of God above the firmament are *opened*, and *food of angels* is *rained* down upon them. As in Exod. 16, the *manna* is closely connected with the quails (26–31), though the psalmist fastens rather on the other quail narrative, that of Num. 13, especially 31–35. His language is vigorous and, at times, picturesque. The Israelites ask for the *food for which they longed*, the food for which their " soul " yearns. The speed with which the pestilence followed on the quails is illustrated by the remark that the people *were not yet estranged from their lust*, their passionate desire for flesh had not yet been sated. The references in 32–37 are quite general, illustrating the loving patience of God. *Had he slain them*—the poet is, of course, not thinking of total annihilation—the survivors would have repented. The insistence on Israel's failure to remember that *God was their rock* and their *champion*, however, and their refusal to *trust in his Covenant*, suggests that the psalmist had the story of the spies in mind. In spite of repeated acts of apostasy, God had still been *merciful* (38–39). It might have been expected that so rebellious a spirit would·have roused the *fury* of God, but he would not·give free rein to his own passions, for he remembered that they were but flesh (cp. Gen. 6³, Ps. 103¹⁴).

With 40 the poet makes a fresh start, and goes back to the beginning to give a more detailed account of the plagues of Egypt, culminating in the slaughter of the *first-born* (41–51). Then he touches on the crossing of the *sea*, and the guiding of the people to the *holy precinct*, *mount Sinai*. 55–58 describe the conquest of Palestine, condemning the religious life of the nation during the age of the Judges, as being contaminated with *high places* and *idols*.

In 60 we approach the climax of the poem, with references to the destruction of *Shiloh*, and the capture of the Ark, the *strength* and the *beauty* of Yahweh, by the Philistines. The subjection of Israel is vividly described ; the marriage rites, in which *virgins* are *praised*, and funeral ceremonies, in which *widows* are mourned, alike cease, while *the priests*, Hophni and Phineas, *fall by the sword*. With a curious compression of history, which eliminates Saul altogether (perhaps because there is no mention of an Ark-shrine in his story), the disaster at Aphek marks the final rejection of the northern tribes, *Joseph* and especially *Ephraim*. David follows immediately, and the psalmist so far ignores the record as to make him, not only the shepherd who *fed his people with perfection of heart*, but the king who *built the sanctuary*, copying the model that exists *in the height* of the heavens, but establishing it *on the earth for ever*.

Religious Teaching

We cannot mistake the definite religious purpose of this psalm. But it belongs to a theology which has long passed away, and was never applicable to any but the people of Israel. It may have been a polemic against the temple on Mt. Gerizim, insisting, in the spirit of *Deuteronomy*, that in Jerusalem is the place where men ought to worship. But for the rest it simply reiterates doctrines which are woven into the whole fabric of the Old Testament, from first to last—the corruption of the human heart, God's long patience, yielding at last to the irresistible moral demand for punishment, and the truth that history itself is not the least of the channels of divine revelation. In one striking phrase, however (*v.* 38), we get a suggestion of an idea rarely expressed in the Old Testament, though it lies at the heart of the Christian Gospel. The breach between God and man, cleft by human sin, must be bridged by " atonement ". This is true of all religions, and the almost universal theory is that this atonement must be made from the human side. In his ascription of the initiative to God, the psalmist seems unconsciously to foreshadow the great truth whose full expression is that "God was in Christ reconciling the world unto himself."

PSALM 79

IN this psalm we have a cry of suffering, uttered in a time of appalling national distress. Jerusalem has been laid waste, the Temple defiled, numbers of people slaughtered, others imprisoned and condemned to death. It is true that the sanctuary has not been actually destroyed, but Israel has been brought so low as to incur the mockery and scorn of her neighbours. The psalmist pleads for deliverance and for vengeance.

His grief is none the less real, and his lament none the less sincere, because he found it difficult to express himself in language of his own. His poem is a *cento* of verses and phrases derived from various sources, as even the metrical arrangement suggests, with its sudden change from the 3 : 3 (3 : 3 : 3) to the dirge rhythm in *v.* 6. Many of the sources are recognizable. We may compare the last phrase in *v.* 1 with Mic. 3[12]. The phraseology of *v.* 2 recurs again and again; the best parallels are, perhaps, Jer. 19[7] and Ezek. 29[5]. *V.* 4 recalls Jer. 20[7 f.], and is almost identical with Ps. 44[13]. *V.* 5 differs very slightly from Ps. 89[46 (47)]. With two slight variations in the text, *vv.* 6–7 agree with Jer. 10[25]. Two rather striking phrases in *v.* 8b are closely paralleled, the one in Ps. 59[10], the other in Ps, 142[6]. *V.* 10a appears again in Ps. 115[2], and similar language is used in Ps. 42[3]. *V.* 11 is another form of Ps. 102[20], while 13a, with a necessary change in the personal pronoun, is also found in Ps. 100[3]. In the circumstances it is not unreasonable to suggest that parts of the psalm for which no extant parallel can be cited are dependent on poems which have not otherwise survived.

The structure thus suggests a late date, but no single event is known which fits all the circumstances. In 586 B.C. the temple was not merely defiled, it was destroyed, and Antiochus IV, in 167 B.C., did not make Jerusalem a ruined mound. It would be easy to refer the psalm to the obscure disaster which befell Judah in the time of Artaxerxes Ochus (359–338 B.C.), but, in view of the form of the psalm, a Persian date seems rather too early. On the other hand, the considerations urged against Maccabæan psalms in general in Vol. I, pp. 67 ff., are too strong to be overlooked, and in the present case the evidence is almost overwhelming. For *v.* 3 is cited (though not exactly) in I Macc. 7[17], where it is applied to the execution of sixty men of Jerusalem by the treacherous Bacchides (the text reads as though the offender were Alkimus, but it seems more probable that it was the Syrian general who actually perpetrated the deed).

The psalm may have been used in a special ritual on fast days, or at other times of national humiliation in the face of disaster and oppression.

Metre : *Vv.* 1–2, 3 : 3 : 3 ; *vv.* 3–5, 3 : 3 ; *vv.* 6–13, 3 : 2, with 2 : 2 in *vv.* 6–8a, 11–12a, and 2 : 3 in 13b. Anacrusis in *vv.* 1 and 5. *V.* 12c is an isolated 3 ; the writer has probably cited part of a verse from some other source.

A Psalm. Asaph's.

1. O God !
   Gentiles have come into thine inheritance,
       they have defiled thy holy temple,
           they have made Jerusalem ruin-heaps.

2. They have given the carcases of thy servants
       as food to the birds of the heavens,
           the flesh of thy saints to the beasts of
           the field.

3. They have poured out their blood like   ,round about Jerusalem, with none to
   water,   bury.

4. We have become a mockery to our
   neighbours,   a scorn and a derision to those about us.
5. How long!
   O Yahweh, wilt thou be wroth for
   ever?   will thy jealousy burn as fire?
6. Pour out thy wrath ° on ° the Gentiles,   that have not known thee.
   And on kingdoms   that have not called on thy name.
7. For ° they have devoured ° Jacob, and wasted his dwelling.
8. Remember not for us   the iniquities of the past.
   Let thy pitying love swiftly meet us,   for we languish sorely.
9. Help us, O God of our salvation,   for thy glorious name's sake,
   And deliver us, and purge away our sins,   for thy name's sake.
10. Why should the Gentiles say,   " Where is their God ? "
    Let there be known among the Gentiles   vengeance for the blood of thy
    in our sight   servants.°
11. Let there come before thee   the prisoner's plaint.
    According to the greatness of thine arm   ° deliver ° the sons of death.
12. And requite our neighbours   sevenfold into their bosom,
    For their insult wherewith they have insulted thee, O Lord.
13. But we are thy people,   and thy pastured sheep.
    We will praise thee for ever,   to all generations tell thy praise.

Text-critical Notes

6. Read, with G, עַל for " unto ". 7. Read, with G and Jer. 10²⁵, אָכְלוּ for
" has devoured ". 10. Om. " which has been poured out " (gloss). 11. Read, with
Ps. 102,²⁰ הֹתֵר for " leave over ".

A terrible disaster has befallen Israel (1–4). It has struck a blow,
not only at the political life of Jerusalem, but also at its religion. It is
true that the city has suffered, though to say that it has been *made
ruin-heaps* may be a piece of poetic hyperbole. There has been a cruel
slaughter, whose horror has been intensified by the brutal refusal of
the aggressor to give the corpses burial. Neighbouring tribes have
participated, and are pointing the finger of *scorn*. But worst of all is
the fact that *Gentiles have come into the inheritance* of Yahweh, and
defiled the Temple. Surely Yahweh must take note of this, even if he
is not moved by the piteous state of his people?

V. 5 begins a plea for deliverance, with which is interwoven a
demand for vengeance on the enemy. Like many another man of faith,
from the days of Habakkuk onwards, the psalmist is puzzled by Yahweh's
government of the world. He cannot understand why a God whose
honour, *his glorious name*, is bound up with Israel, should pour out his
wrath *on Jacob*, and not on the *Gentiles*, who *have not known him*. It
is true that Israelites of the *past* have been guilty of *iniquities*, and even
now a measure of sinfulness is admitted (9). But surely, in view of
the issues at stake, God will *atone* for all this, and sweep away the
wrong? But that is not all; Israel will not now be satisfied with
deliverance. With a bitter resentment, which is intelligible, even if
it be not defensible, the psalmist demands *vengeance for the blood of
Yahweh's servants*. This, he feels, is necessary to vindicate the offended
majesty of Yahweh against the *insults* in act and word perpetrated by
the *neighbours* of Israel. The world, too, must know of it, and the poet
naïvely betrays the depth of his own feeling when he demands that the

victims, too, shall see the tables turned. When an Oriental receives a
present, he loosens a fold in his copious robes, and places it therein;
the gift that Yahweh is asked to lay in the enemy's *bosom* is that of
seven-fold punishment. After all, Israel is the *people*, the *sheep* of God,
and, if they can see their desire on their adversaries, they will hymn
the praises of their saving God as long as man endures upon earth.

Religious Teaching

For religion, the centre of this psalm is the problem which it raises.
It makes no attempt at an answer, but is content to plead for a reversal
of the conditions. In *v.* 8 the psalmist seems to hope that God, not
man, will make the needed " atonement ". An " atonement " is that
which restores the right relationship between God and man after it
has been broken by human sin. In most religions it is made from the
human side—*e.g.*, through the use of sacrificial blood by the Jewish
priests. The psalmist, however, seems to foreshadow the specifically
Christian thought that a valid reunion between a holy God and a sinful
man can be effected only when the initiative is taken by God himself.

PSALM 80

As in Psalms 78 and 79, so here, we have a cry of distress, a national
lament. The situation, however, is not that of the two preceding
pieces. Each of them originally contemplated a single catastrophic
event, though in neither case can we be certain as to what that event
was. Ps. 80, on the other hand, reflects a condition more or less
permanent, a desolate state which has long been in existence, and
which promises no immediate change except through the direct intervention of Yahweh. It seems to refer to northern Israel, for Ephraim
and Benjamin are expressly mentioned, while *v.* 17 seems to contain
a play on the latter name. It is true that in *v.* 1 Yahweh is described
as seated on the cherubim. We know that this phrase would be quite
suitable to the Jerusalem Temple, and on this ground some commentators have been led to conclude that the psalm belongs to the south,
and not to the north. But we do not know that cherubim were absent
from all the northern sanctuaries, and it is at least probable that they
were in many places an element in the Yahweh mythology. Generally
speaking, the conditions may be those of northern Israel after 721 B.C.,
as described in II Kings 17[26]—note especially the reference to wild
beasts in *v.* 13.

The structure of the psalm is interesting. A refrain appears in
vv. 3, 7, and 19; in each of the two former cases it is preceded by
three lines of verse. An abbreviated form is found again in *v.* 14,

and it is natural to suppose that a similar line once stood after *v.* 10. The fact that *vv.* 8–13 all deal with the same subject is not a fatal objection. Complete symmetry, however, cannot be secured merely by inserting the same refrain before or after *v.* 16, since 14b–19 contain only five lines instead of six. If, then, the poem was written in fully strophic form, either a line in addition to the refrain has dropped out, or two extra lines have been inserted; the former would seem to be the more probable hypothesis, since none of the existing verses appears intrusive. The omission (if it took place) was probably after *v.* 16. It remains to add that in all extant forms of the text the latter half of *v.* 15 is nearly identical with the latter half of *v.* 17. Probably in one place or the other some words dropped out in the process of transmission, and the gap was filled from the other verse.

This psalm contains certain evidence of the substitution of Elohim for Yahweh. The phrase אֱלֹהִים צְבָאוֹת is grammatically impossible, whilst יהוה צְבָאוֹת is a common contraction for יהוה אֱלֹהֵי צְבָאוֹת. The presence of the Tetragrammaton in *vv.* 4 and 19 is to be explained on grounds of textual corruption at a comparatively late stage.

Metre   3 : 3, with 2 : 2 : 2 in *v.* 9.

For the Precentor : Of Šošannim.   'Eduth.   Asaph's.   A Psalm.

1 (2). O Shepherd of Israel, give ear,	that leddest Joseph as a flock.
Thou that sittest on the Cherubim, shine forth	
° And from slumber ° arouse thy valour,	2 (3). before Ephraim and Benjamin. and come for our salvation.
3 (4). O God ° of Hosts °, restore *us,*	and lighten thy face that we may be saved,

---

4 (5). °° O God of Hosts, how long !	Thou hast fumed at the prayer of thy people,
5 (6). ° Thou hast fed us with bread of tears,	° and has made us drink ° tears by large measure.
6 (7). Thou makest us a strife to our neighbours,	while our foes mock at us.
7 (8). O God of Hosts, restore us,	and lighten thy face that we may be saved.

---

8 (9). Thou movedst a vine from Egypt,	drivedst out nations and plantedst it.
9 (10). Thou madest level ground before it,	
	and didst firmly root it,
	and it filled the land.
10 (11). Its shadow ° covered ° mountains,	and its boscage cedars of God.
° O God of Hosts, restore us,	and lighten thy face that we may be saved.°

---

11 (12). It sent forth its boughs to the Sea,	and unto the River its tendrils.
12 (13). Why brakest thou down its fences ?	that all passing the road may pluck it.
13 (14). The boar from the forest ° may trample it °,	and wild creatures feed upon it.
14 (15). O God of Hosts ° restore us,	and lighten thy face that we may be saved °.

Look from heaven and see,	and visit this vine.
15 (16). ° And the garden ° thy right hand planted,	

16 (17). 'Tis burned with fire ° and up-
          rooted °,
          ° O God of Hosts, restore us,

at the rebuke of thy face ° it perisheth °.
and lighten thy face that we may be
saved.°

17 (18). Be thy hand on the man of thy
          right hand,
18 (19). And we will not turn back from
          thee,
19 (20). ° ° O God of Hosts, restore us,

on the man thou madest strong for
thyself.
if thou revive us we will call on thy
name.
and lighten thy face that we may be
saved.

Text-critical Notes

2. Read וּמִשֶׁנָה for " and Manasseh ".   3. Insert, with S, צְבָאוֹת, as elsewhere in the refrain.   4. Om. " Yahweh ".   5. Read, with G, הַאֲכַלְתָּנוּ   and
וַתַּשְׁקֵנוּ for " . . . them ".   10. Read, with G, כֻּסָּה for " were covered ".   Insert
refrain, with Briggs, as in *vv.* 3, 7, and 19.   13. Read יְרַמְסֶמָּה. for יַרְסֶמָה (?).
14. Read refrain, with Briggs, as in *vv.* 3, 7, and 19, for " O God of Hosts, return ".
15. Read, with Graetz, וְכַנָּה for וְכַנָּה (?).   Om. " and on the man thou madest
strong for thyself " (see introduction to the psalm).   16. Read, with G, וּכְסוּחָה,
inserting " and ".   Read תֹּאבֵד for " they perish ".

For the title, see Vol. I, pp. 16, 18.

The opening stanza of this psalm (1–3) is a simple plea for help,
starting with the familiar metaphor of the *Shepherd* God.   With
characteristic Hebrew liveliness, the picture changes, and Yahweh is
seen seated *on the cherubim*, those strange composite creatures of
ancient myth and art.   His *valour* is beyond question, but now it
slumbers; on no other ground can the poet account for Yahweh's
inaction.   The refrain, to be repeated at regular intervals by the
worshipping community, is an appeal to God to *lighten his face*.   The
metaphor of light and darkness is readily applied to the favour or
displeasure shown in a man's expression.   A cheerful, kindly look is
naturally light, while a frown is darkness.

The idea of the refrain is taken up at once with the beginning of
stanza II (4–7).   *How long !* is here, as in many other places, an ejaculation rather than a question, and the psalmist at once complains that
the *prayer* of God's *people* has been answered with the dark look, not
with the light; the divine countenance has been blackened with the
murky cloud of smoke rising from the fire of anger—a striking development of the familiar image.   *Tears* to eat, and *tears* to *drink* have been
Israel's portion, offered in great vessels such as those in which God once
measured out the dust of the earth (Isa. 40¹²).   The nation has been an
object of strife (cf. Jer. 15¹⁰), a butt for all the cruelty and *mockery* of
their quarrelsome *foes*.   So once more the listening congregation lifts
up the refrain.

With stanza III (8–10) the poet introduces yet another metaphor—
that of the vine.   Again we have a common image, for as the sheep
demanded more care than any other domestic animal, so the vine needed

more continuous attention and careful protection than any other product of the ground. The seed had been sown in *Egypt*, whence Israel had been transplanted to a land whose soil had been already *levelled* and prepared by the *driving out* of nations settled there. We note the theory of history presented by the later elements in the book of Joshua. *Planted* in its new home, the vine had flourished greatly and *covered mountains*, and even the wild *cedars*.

Stanza IV (11–14a) starts where stanza III ends, and figures the vine spreading from the Mediterranean *sea* to the *river* Euphrates. But now comes the contrast between the glorious past and the miserable present. The *fences*—" dry " walls built of stones cleared from the soil—have been torn down, and the vine is exposed to the ravages of man and beast. Curiously enough, damage done by the wild *boar* is mentioned only here in the Bible, though it must have been only too familiar to ancient Israel.

A renewed plea for deliverance naturally follows in stanza V (14b–16), based in the first instance on the ground that it is Yahweh's *right hand* that *has planted* the vine and the surrounding *garden*. This section seems to have suffered in course of transmission, but its general purpose is clear. Apparently it has been telescoped into stanza VI (17–19), where the final appeal is made. Here there is a delicate play on Benjamin, the " son of the *right hand* ", and the psalm closes with a promise of fidelity and devotion if deliverance is granted. The language of the last clause, with its condition, *if thou revive us again*, recalls the ancient liturgical formula preserved in Hosea 6[2].

Religious Teaching

As in all psalms of this type, there is little explicit presentation of doctrine. The psalmist is convinced of Yahweh's special relation to Israel, and of his care manifested in the past. He cannot believe in the final desertion of the people, and pleads that the power of Yahweh, which he does not for an instant doubt, will be once more revealed in the restoration of his chosen race. It is true that calamity has befallen the nation, that it seems as if Yahweh had answered the appeal of his people only with fresh outbursts of wrath. A problem thus arises, for the poet is not conscious of any wrong-doing which might explain the divine anger. Others, like the author of *Job*, would be tortured by the problem ; others again would admit that they might have sinned unawares. But this poet is one who feels rather than thinks ; unlike so many of the Psalmists, he does not seek for " the root of the matter " in himself, and he can simply turn back to the Shepherd of Israel with his faith unshaken, and be sure that in the end all will be well.

PSALM 81

THIS psalm, in the form in which it has come down to us, presents
several puzzling features. It opens with all the exultation of a hymn of
praise, apparently to be sung at some festival. The exact occasion is
disputed; the new moon, the full moon, and the " festival " are all
mentioned in *v.* 3, with special stress on the blowing of trumpets. The
last feature suggests New Year's Day, on which it is still used as a proper
psalm, the special term " festival ", implying a season of pilgrimage,
one of the three great occasions, Tabernacles, Passover, or Weeks. If
the psalm be pre-exilic, the former is the more probable, if post-exilic,
then the second. Kittel's note on *vv.* 1–3, which would apply to any
of these occasions, is worth quoting in full: " The community is
gathered in the forecourt, priests make ready the offering, in the halls
about the Temple and at tables in the court preparations for the
festal meal are made by the separate clans and groups of celebrants.
Through the doors of the great court streams a surging festal throng;
ever-fresh hosts of pilgrims and participants approach the altar on
which the sacred ritual must be consummated. Into this scene we are
transported by the rousing note of our psalm, which itself was intended
to contribute to the glory of the great festival. At once it supplies us
with an illuminating picture of the lyric element in such festivals;
the court re-echoes with the joy and exultation of the festal crowd (cf.
Lam. 2⁷). At intervals hymns ring out, sung by priestly choirs, often,
as we know, by appointed individuals, accompanied by zither, lute and
harp. Elsewhere cymbals control the rhythm of worshippers moving
in stately procession or pacing round the altar, and when the sacrifice
is burned, the priests make their ram's horns heard in solemn, hollow
tones, to tell even distant worshippers that the sacred rite has been
consummated."

With this vivid picture before us, we can see the function of our
psalm. Its place is near the beginning of the ritual, and its purpose is
to remind the worshippers of the ancient law, " Thou shalt worship
Yahweh thy God, and him only shalt thou serve ". So much is clear.
But suddenly, between *v.* 10 and *v.* 11, the tone changes. It is no
longer exultation; it is a condemnation of Israel for national apostasy,
and ends with a reference to the blessings the nation might have
enjoyed had it only been faithful.

It is not surprising that several modern commentators are unable to
accept the psalm as a unity without drastic alteration. There seems to
be no motive for the third clause in *v.* 10, and it looks as if parts of two
psalms had been telescoped into one another. Nor does *v.* 16 offer a
natural conclusion; 10c–16 has every appearance of being a fragment
attached to a psalm whose true conclusion has not been preserved.

There is nothing in either part which suggests a post-exilic date. The opening passage may be quite early; the rest of the first part, though now organically united with it, suggests the age of the great prophets. The language of *v.* 12 strongly suggests that the second part comes from the end of the seventh century B.C., as the word for "stubbornness" occurs elsewhere only in *Deuteronomy* (once) and *Jeremiah* (eight times). If we had to guess an occasion to which both parts were generally adapted, the best conjecture would be Josiah's great Passover celebration. Even so, we should have to remember that parts of the psalm, at any rate, have a much longer tradition behind them, and may have been used on a variety of occasions.

Metre: 3 : 3, with 3 : 3 : 3 in 5c–6 (6c–7) and 10c–11(11c–12), possibly both due to mutilation. במועצותיהם in *v.* 13 counts as two units.

For the Precentor : On Gittith.   Asaph's.

1 (2). Break out praise to God our fortress !

shout aloud to the God of Jacob !

2 (3). Lift up harp-song and play the timbrel,

sweet lyre with lute.

3 (4). Ring the new-moon blast on the horn,

at the full moon on our festal day.

4 (5). For an ordinance in Israel is it,

a decree of the God of Jacob.

5 (6). A testimony he appointed in Joseph,

when he came ° from the land of ° Egypt.

The voice of one I know not do I hear—

6 (7). " I have freed ° thy shoulder ° from the burden,
° thy hands ° have done with the basket.

7 (8). In affliction thou calledst and I delivered thee,
I answered thee in the secret home of the thunder,
I assayed thee at the waters of Meribah.

8 (9). Hear my people, and let me testify to thee,

O Israel, if thou wilt hearken to me.

9 (10). There shall be no strange god in thee,

nor shalt thou bow to a foreign god.

10 (11). I am Yahweh, thy God,

that brought thee up from the land of Egypt."

open wide thy mouth that I may fill it.

11 (12). But my people obeyed not my voice,

and Israel showed me no good will.

12 (13). ° So I let them go ° in the stubbornness of their heart,

they should walk in their own desires.

13 (14). Would my people ° were hearkening ° to me,

Israel were walking in my ways !

14 (15). Soon would I subdue their enemies,

and over their foes bring back my hand.

15 (16). °·They that hate them ° would come cringing ° to them °,

° and their terror ° would be for ever.

16 (17). ° But I would feed them ° with the cream of the wheat,

and with honey from the rock ° would I sate them °

Text-critical Notes

5. Read, with G, מֵאֶרֶץ for " upon the land of ". 6. Read, with Duhm, שְׁכְמֹו and כַּפָּיו for " his shoulder " and " his hands ". 12. Read וָאֲשַׁלְּחֵם for " so I let him go ". 13. Read, with Buhl, יִשְׁמַע for שֹׁמֵעַ. 15. Read שֹׂנְאֵיהֶם for " they that hate Yahweh ". Read לָמֹו for " him ". Read, with S, בְּעֶרְתָם for " their time ". 16. Read (cf. Houbigant) וָאַכִילֵם for " and he fed him ". Read (cf. G) אַשְׂבִּיעֵם for " would I sate thee ".

For the title, see Vol. I, p. 13.

The great assembly of worshippers stands silent in the forecourt of the Temple. A priest stands out and leads the call to exultant song and prayer. All the instruments of music (see under Ps. 150, pp. 589 ff.) ring out their notes of gladness, and the opening of the solemn festival—*new moon* or *full moon* or some other—is proclaimed. The constituent authority for the celebration is none other than *the God of Jacob*, who has long since promulgated his *ordinance* and *decree*—"*Israel*" may well be a contracted phrase for "the God of Israel".

The word passes to a prophet, who speaks in the name of Yahweh. He, too, cites his authority; it is not that of ancient prescription, but of direct personal communication. A *voice* is in his ears, and the speaker is no familiar human acquaintance, but one whom he does *not know*; it can be no other than Yahweh. The divine message begins with an appeal to the distant past, to the days when Israel's *shoulder* still bore the Egyptian *burden*, and his *hands* still carried the *basket*—one of the most familiar of the "coolie's" instruments. The well-known story is swiftly summed up in a few telling words—the *call*, the *deliverance*, the revelation amid the crashing storms of Sinai, where it seems as if the *thunder* had its *secret home*, the *assaying* of Israel (a curious inversion of the usual picture) at the waters of Meribah. Here, it seems, there is a gap—silence or words accidentally omitted—before the actual demand is made. The language and spirit are those of *Deuteronomy*, and the supreme lesson is that it is Yahweh, and Yahweh alone, who must be worshipped by Israel.

At this point (10c) the whole tone and purport of the poem change, and we feel instinctively that we are in a totally different atmosphere. Yahweh is still speaking, yet his next words, offering to *fill* the *open mouth* of his people, involve a transition too abrupt even for the Hebrew mind. If this be a part of the same piece as *vv.* 1–10b, it is surely clear that some introductory words have fallen out before 10c. For this is what Yahweh would have said to his people if they had been faithful, and the verses that follow are a divine lament over Israel's refusal to accept his gifts. This is hardly consistent with the festal note of the preceding verse, especially if the occasion be the Feast of Tabernacles or Passover. The great tragedy is that the people would not *obey* the *voice* of Yahweh, and left him no alternative but to *let them go*, dismiss them altogether from association with him. If only they had *hearkened to him*, and *walked in his ways*, they would have known victory instead of defeat, and it would have been their enemies who would have been *subdued* and *come cringing to them*, living for all time lives of *terror*. Israel, on the other hand, would have had the best of fare, *the cream of the wheat*—the Hebrew word is "fat", used in just the same metaphorical way as our "cream"—and abundance of wild honey. And there the poem breaks off—surely not its natural conclusion.

Religious Teaching

Even if this psalm be not a structural unity, it has a single lesson. Absolute and unwavering fidelity and consecration to the one living and true God is the indispensable condition of success and prosperity. While human experience belies the doctrine on the lower planes, in the highest sense it still remains, and ever must remain, profoundly true.

PSALM 82

THIS psalm, like Ps. 58, presents the reader with an interesting problem. It speaks of certain " gods ", whose function is to act as judges of men, and condemns them for their failure to use their authority aright. Who are they ? The traditional interpretation, going back to the Targum, is that they are human judges, and two or three passages, of which Exod. 21[6] is the best example, are cited in support of this view. But it is now generally recognized that in all these passages the word " God " is to be taken in its normal sense. Another theory is that they are simply the heathen gods, or, more specifically, the guardian spirits assigned by Yahweh to the various nations. Such subordinate deities are referred to in Dt. 32[8] (Septuagint), 29[26 (25)], Isa. 24[21], and a similar doctrine is found both in Ecclus. 17[17], and in connexion with the " princes of the kingdoms " in Dan. 10[13, 20, 21], where Michael is named as the " prince " of Israel. On the whole, some such explanation as this best fits the psalm. Yahweh is the supreme ruler of the universe, but deputes his authority to inferior gods. Their government is so unjust that they must be deposed, reduced to the rank of men, and suffer in the end the penalty of death.

The little psalm is regular in form, the lines falling into pairs. *V.* 5 seems to have little to do with the rest of the poem, and is best regarded as an accidental insertion due to one or more marginal notes. *V.* 8 is the exclamation of a pious reader, easily attached to the end.

There is no indication of date, but the passages quoted show that the thought is not necessarily early, having survived in some form from pre-exilic times well into the second century B.C.

Metre : 3 : 3 ; of the two intrusive verses, *v.* 5 is 2 : 2 : 2 (possibly 4 : 3), and *v.* 8 is 4 : 3.

A Psalm.   Asaph's.

1. God is set in the divine council,   in the midst of the gods he judgeth.
2. How long will ye judge unrighteously,   and lift up the face of the wicked ?
                                              Selah.

3. Judge ye ° the crushed ° and the orphan,　　see right done to the humble and needy.
4. Rescue the lowly and the poor,　　　　　　from the power of the wicked deliver
　　　　　　　　　　　　　　　　　　　　　　them.
(5. They know not, nor understand,
　　　　　　　　　in darkness they walk,
　　　　　　　　　　　all the foundations of the earth are
　　　　　　　　　　　moved).
6. I said, Ye are gods,　　　　　　　　　all of you sons of the highest.
7. But surely like men shall ye die,　　　and as one of the princes shall fall.
(8. Rise, O God, judge the earth,　　　　for thou art master in all the earth.)

Text-critical Note

3. Read, with Graetz, דָּךְ for " lowly ".

As in one or two other passages in the Old Testament (*e.g.*, I Kings
22$^{19 ff.}$; Job 1$^{13 ff.}$; 2$^{1 ff.}$), we are taken into the heavenly court. About
the central throne is gathered the celestial hierarchy, the servants of
Yahweh to whom he has entrusted the government of the world. This
is the *divine council*, and its proceedings open when Yahweh *is set* on
the throne of judgement. He speaks at once in terms of condemnation ;
as Eliphaz says (Job 4^{18}), " He putteth no trust in his servants, and
unto his holy ones he imputeth folly ". To these lower deities, or
guardian spirits of the nations, has been committed the oversight of
mankind, and it is their duty, in the psalmist's eyes, to administer the
decrees of Yahweh on earth. But everywhere injustice and oppression
are rife ; the depressed classes—the *orphan*, the *lowly*, and the *poor*—
can get no justice. If one of them comes into court, no matter how
deserving his case may be, it is the *wicked*, the man who ought to be
condemned, who emerges triumphant (2–4). At this point a copyist
seems to have inserted a couple of marginal notes, one emphasizing
the helplessness of the sufferers, who do *not understand*, and grope in
the *darkness* of ignorance, and the other comparing the moral situation
to a world-destroying earthquake. After this interruption, the divine
Judge continues. It was he who had given the subordinate deities their
rank, and *said* they were *gods* and *sons of the highest*, a phrase which
does not necessarily imply an actual relationship with Yahweh, but
only that they belonged to the highest of all classes under him. It is
true that in the Ugaritian texts found at Ras Shamra there is a genuine
pantheon, in which the gods are arranged in natural families, and a
physical kinship within each group is assumed. But, while Israel
took over much of the mythology of its neighbours, we have nowhere
any trace of a true pantheon. A goddess seems to have been
associated with Yahweh in some circles (Anat-Yahu, in the Elephantine Papyri), but we have no allusion which even suggests that
they produced a child. With 7 comes the sentence passed on the
divine criminals. Immortality is the property and gift of Yahweh
alone. Just as *man* was condemned to *die* for his primeval offence in the
garden of Eden, and just as the whole human race was thereby rendered

subject to mortality, so they must perish and share the lot of all mankind, commoners and princes alike. Finally, the psalm ends with an appeal by the worshippers (probably later than the original poem), asking Yahweh to dismiss all these lower beings, and rule the world directly himself.

Religious Teaching

The psalmist has not yet attained to a full and complete monotheism. But his position is nevertheless interesting and important. It shows a way in which the thought of Israel passed from polytheism (monolatrous though it may have been) to a real belief in the one God. The other gods are first relegated to a lower rank, in which they are subject to mortality (we may compare the old legend of the death of Pan), and then, finally, disappear altogether. It may be recalled that in the Ras Shamra texts we have the death of Baal and Aleyan. There may be also an attempt to explain the inequality of human fate, and so to give some kind of answer to the question first propounded by Habakkuk and Jeremiah, " Why lookest thou on . . . while the wicked swalloweth up the man that is more righteous than he ? " (Hab. 1¹³, cf. Jer. 12¹ᶠᶠ.). The failure of justice is due to the fact that the world has been placed in charge of fallible and unprincipled governors, and if only Yahweh would remove them and rule directly, all would be well. It is true that the psalmist has only pushed the problem one step farther back, but he and others of his time may have been relieved by this attempted solution of the greatest problem which an ethical monotheism has to face.

PSALM 83

THIS psalm is a national lament, composed for a time of peril, when a coalition of the surrounding nations was threatening the very existence of Israel. Curiously enough, it occurs in ancient Jewish rituals as one of the psalms proper for the Passover feast. No fewer than ten peoples are mentioned ; the most prominent appear to be Moab and Ammon (v. 8), but Edom, Philistia and Tyre are also mentioned, together with a number of Bedawin tribes and " Assyria ". Damascus is a significant omission. The psalmist recalls two great events in the distant past : the victory of Deborah, and the overthrow of the Midianites by Gideon. He calls down on his people's immediate foes an imprecation based on the fate of these ancient invaders, and prays that the new enemies may be utterly routed.

This is one of the psalms for which a Maccabæan date has been most confidently claimed by a series of scholars, with Theodore of Mopsuestia at their head. For reasons against this view, see Vol. I, pp. 68 ff ; in its favour is the fact that six of the ten peoples mentioned in *vv.* 6–8 were included in a coalition formed against Judas Maccabæus (I Macc. 5), together with the common use of the name "Assyria" for Syria in the later literature. On the other hand, there was a Bedawin tribe bearing the same name, mentioned in Gen. 25³ as descended from Abraham by Keturah, and therefore allied to Ishmael.

A combined attack on Jehoshaphat is recorded in II Chron. 20; there, as here, the leaders are Moab and Ammon. Nehemiah, again, was the object of concerted acts of hostility, and some commentators refer the psalm to the age of Artaxerxes Ochus. We must, however, face the possibility that *vv.* 6–8 form no part of the original psalm, since the catalogue of nations is by no means necessary for the progress of its thought. It may well have been inserted to adapt an older and more general poem to a definite situation. But in this, as in so many other cases, an attempt at exact dating can be little more than a precarious conjecture.

The structure is simple; though *Selah* appears at the end of *v.* 8, there is no sign of genuine strophic arrangement. The text is, on the whole, well preserved.

The metre is 3 : 3; *vv.* 6 and 17, 3 : 2. Anacrusis appears in *v.* 4 (5) עַל־צְפוּנֶיךָ (*v.* 3) and וּבְסוּפָתְךָ (*v.* 15) count as two units each.

A Song. A Psalm. Asaph's.

1 (2).	O God, let no rest be thine,	be not silent nor still, O God.
2 (3).	For behold, thy foes roar in tumult,	and they that hate thee lift up their head.
3 (4).	Against thy people they take crafty counsel,	and plot against thy treasured ones.
4 (5).	They say: Come, and let us destroy them that they be no people,	let Israel's name be remembered no more.
5 (6).	For they have planned in their heart together,	against thee have they made a covenant.
6 (7).	Tents of Edom and Ishmaelites,	Moab and Hagarites,
7 (8).	Gebal and Ammon and Amalek,	Philistia, with the dwellers in Tyre.
8 (9).	Yea, Assyria is confederate with them,	and hath become an arm to Lot's sons. Selah.
9 (10).	Deal with them ° ° as with Sisera,	as with Jabin at Kishon's torrent.
10 (11).	(Which) were destroyed at Endor,	dung they became for the ground.
11 (12).	° As Midian ° make their princes,	as Oreb and Zeeb ° ° their chieftains.
12 (13).	Who said, Let us take for ourselves	the ° holy ° homestead of God.
13 (14).	O my God, make them as thistle-down,	as chaff before the wind.
14 (15).	As when fire kindleth in the forest,	as when flame blazeth on the hills,
15 (16).	So pursue them with thy storm-wind,	and with thy hurricane confound them.
16 (17).	Fill their faces with contempt,	and let them seek thy name, O Yahweh.
17 (18).	Let them be ashamed and confounded for ever,	yea, let them be dismayed and perish!
18 (19).	And let them know that thou alone	art Most High over all the earth.

Text-critical Notes

9. Trs. "Midian" to the beginning of *v.* 11.   11. See on *v.* 9. Read, with G, שִׁירָתֵם; M adds "them". Om., with Buhl, "Zebah and Zalmunna".   12. Insert (cf. G), לְךָ שֵׁם.   18. Om., with Duhm, "thy name is Yahweh".

The first verse of the psalm is an appeal to Yahweh to come himself
and make his power felt. The writer pleads that he will break the
stillness, the *quiet* that surrounds him. There are enemies about (2–5),
and they, at least, are making themselves felt and heard. Can God be
silent when his *foes roar in tumult*, howling like an infuriated mob, and
lifting their head like a wild beast as it roars? Unlike the animals,
these enemies have intelligence, and are *crafty* in their *plotting* against
the nation which God has *treasured*, and kept safe in his own hiding-
place. They would *destroy Israel*, so that it should cease to be a *people*
altogether.

6–8 give a list of the hostile nations. A settled people, *Edom*,
Moab, or *Ammon*, is followed by a wilder Bedawin tribe, *Ishmael*,
Hagar, Amalek. *Gebal*, too, is almost certainly not Byblos, but a nomad
clan mentioned by Eusebius as ranging over territory in the region of
Petra. *Philistines* and *Phoenicians* are involved, perhaps, as slave-
traders who disposed of Jewish captives, and, in spite of the apparent
prominence accorded to them, the Assyrians also may be a wilderness
tribe (see above).

With 9 begins the imprecation. Both in blessing and in cursing,
a recognized method was to cite instances of supreme happiness or
misery, and pray that their fate might also be that of the object of curse
or blessing. So the psalmist goes back to two stories in the book of
Judges. The one is that of *Sisera* and *Jabin*, crushed by the Israelite
levies under Deborah and Barak. The mention of Jabin shows that
the psalmist knew the story as told in Judg. 4, though instead of Mt.
Tabor he mentions the town of Endor, situated almost at its foot. The
other event is the overthrow of the *Midianites* by Gideon, and the
slaughter of their *princes, Oreb and Zeeb*. There is no reference in the
story of *Judges* to any attempt by the Midianites to *possess* the *homestead*
(the word might mean also " pasture ") of *God*, unless we are to take
the phrase as meaning the land of Israel in general, which is improbable.
Now that the country is once more attacked from the outside, may the
new invaders share the fate of their ancient predecessors!

13–15 continue with more direct imprecation. The poet prays that
the enemy may become as *thistle-down*. This, however, is not an exact
rendering of the Hebrew word, which properly means a " rolling
thing ", and probably indicates the dried heads of a common Palestinian
weed, a wild artichoke, which " . . . throws out numerous branches of
equal size and length in all directions, forming a sort of sphere or
globe, a foot or more in diameter. When ripe and dry in the autumn,
these branches become rigid and light as a feather, the parent stem
breaks off at the ground, and the wind carries these vegetable globes
whithersoever it pleaseth " (W. M. Thomson, *The Land and the Book*,
p. 212 (1881)). Another metaphor is drawn from destruction wrought

by *fire in forest and on mountain*, or, perhaps, from the speed with which the flames are hurried along by the *storm-wind* and the *hurricane*.

The closing verses (16–18) add a note which tends to mitigate the vindictiveness of the psalm in general. The aim of the psalmist, according to them, is not the annihilation of the enemies, but their conversion. They are to feel the *contempt* to which their calamities will expose them, but only that they may *seek the name* of Yahweh; the purpose of all that happens to them is that they may *know* that the God of Israel *alone* is the *Most High over all the earth*. It is difficult to avoid the impression that this final paragraph is an afterthought, perhaps even a later addition, modifying the severity which offended the spiritual taste of the better minds in Israel.

Religious Teaching

Apart from the last verses, the psalm is almost purely vindictive imprecation. Christian and later Jewish feeling could not endorse its sentiments without a sacrifice of principle. But, if we cannot approve, we may understand; if we had been where the psalmist was, we might well have felt and spoken as he did.

PSALM 84

THE great autumn festival is at hand. The long year's toil in field and vineyard is over, the produce of the land is gathered in, and the cycle is about to begin once more with solemn ritual and stately ceremony. The ground is parched, and all the *wadis* are dry, but the summer is nearly at an end, and almost before the feast is over the autumn rains may be expected, to soften the earth and make it once more fit for husbandry. From every village in the country comes a train of pilgrims, and as they draw near to their journey's end they sing a song like this.

The psalm has a regular strophic form, each of its three stanzas containing six lines. At the close of the first two we find the word *Selah* (*vv.* 4 and 8); after the third comes an isolated line (*v.* 12). It is tempting to suggest that this is a refrain, which is intended to be sung after *vv.* 4 and 8 as well. In the first stanza the pilgrims dwell on the happiness of those who can make their permanent home in the sanctuary, in the second they contemplate the journey now nearly completed, and in the third they pray for divine help and protection, especially for the king on whose well-being their prosperity will largely depend.

The psalm almost certainly dates from pre-exilic days, and is to be connected with the group which belong to the ceremonial of the Feast

of Tabernacles (see Vol. I, pp. 49 f.), though it clearly did not form a part of the actual ceremonial. It is interesting to note that the Tetragrammaton occurs more often than is usual in psalms belonging to this section of the Psalter.

Metre : 3 : 2, with 2 : 2 in *vv.* 6b, 11, and 2 : 3 in *v.* 12.

For the Precentor : On Gittith. Of the Sons of Korah. A Psalm.

1 (2). How lovely are thy dwellings,   O Yahweh of hosts !
2 (3). My soul longeth, ° yea °, fainteth   for Yahweh's courts.
      My heart and my flesh cry aloud   (to greet) the living God.
3 (4). Yea, the sparrow hath found a
      house,   and the swallow her nest,
      Where she hath laid her brood—
      thine altars,   Yahweh of Hosts.° °
4 (5). Blessed are the dwellers in thy
      house ;   they praise thee° for ever.°   Selah.
5 (6). Blessed are men whose strength is
      in thee,   ° who love pilgrimage °.
6 (7). They pass through the Vale of   ·
      Balsams,   a fountain they make it.
      ° With pools of ° blessing   the early rain covereth it.
7˙ (8). They go from strength to strength,   ° they shall see God ° in Zion.
8 (9). Yahweh, God of Hosts,   hear my prayer !
      Give ear, O God of Jacob,   ° my king and my God °.   Selah.
9 (10). Look to our Shield, O God,   and behold the face of thine Anointed.
10 (11). For a day in thy courts is better   than a thousand ° in my own chamber °.
      To haunt the threshold of
      Yahweh's house,   than a home in wicked tents.
11 (12). For a sun and a shield   is Yahweh, our God ;
      Grace and glory   doth Yahweh give ;
      He withholdeth no good   from them that walk in perfection.
12 (13). O Yahweh of Hosts,   blessed is the man that trusteth in thee.

Text-critical Notes

2. Read, with G, בָּם for " and also ".   3. Trs. " my king and my God " to end of *v.* 8.   4. Read, with G, עֲדִי־עַד for " still ".   5. Read, with G, מְעַלּוֹת בִּלְבָבָם for " high ways in their heart ".   6. Read, (cf. Schlögl) אַגְמֵי for " also ".   7. Read (cf. G and Kittel) יֵרָאוּ־אֵל for " shall appear unto God ".   8. See on *v.* 4.   10. Read with Gunkel, בְּחֶדְרִי for " I have chosen ".

For the title, see Vol. I, p. 13.

The psalm, as has been pointed out, falls into three equal parts. 1–4 form a meditation on the beauty of the *dwellings* of *Yahweh*, and on the privileges enjoyed by those who can make the sanctuary their permanent home. The poet is stirred by intense emotion as he thinks of this *lovely* and lovable place. So deep is the *longing* of his *soul* that his heart for a moment fails ; he *fainteth*, his face grows pale, and it seems as if the tension of his spirit would strain the very cords of life. Then comes the swift revulsion ; once more the blood rushes through its accustomed channels, and his whole being, *heart and flesh*, *break*, as it were, into a sudden exultant shout of joy at the thought that he will soon enter the presence of *the living God*. The language of 3 suggests that the temple, like some modern mosques, was sanctuary for the wild things, and he envies the very *sparrows* and *swallows* which have made their *nests* about the *altar*.

Such bliss as that of the *dwellers* in Yahweh's *house* is not to be had by every man. Yet there is a profound value in pilgrimage, and the second part of the poem starts where the first ended, with *blessedness*. It may not be of such high quality as that enjoyed by the permanent resident in Yahweh's home, but, nevertheless, he who *loveth pilgrimage* (literally " hath pilgrimage in his heart "), who plans and carries out the sacred journey, does make Yahweh his *strength*, and so wins a *blessing*. Further, there is some mystic virtue attached to the pilgrim. He is not merely blessed in himself, he is a channel of blessing to others, and serves as a vehicle of divine mercy. When, for instance, he passes through a dry valley where only the *balsam* tree will grow (2 Sam. 5[22 n.] suggest that there may have been such a valley to the south-west of Jerusalem, through which some pilgrim route would almost certainly lie), doubly parched by the long summer drought, the face of the land changes. *Rain* falls, and springs rise from the ground, over whose surface the pools spread like a veil. They are *pools of blessing*, for water is one of the supreme blessings of Eastern life. In fact, the word used here, with a slight vowel modification, would mean " pool ", as, perhaps, in Judg. 1[15], while in Arabic a word from the same root is used to indicate rain. So, thinks the psalmist, the pilgrim goes, receiving and transmitting blessing, for he is bent on *seeing* his *God*. In this spirit he can offer the *prayer* with which the third part of the poem begins.

The last section proper occupies 9–11. After all, the Feast of Tabernacles, with its mimic presentation of the divine war that led to creation, and of the marriage, death and resurrection of the life-giving deity, had a practical object. Its purpose was to secure the fertility of the land for the coming year. Closely bound up with national prosperity was the welfare of the king, who was both the *Anointed* of Yahweh and the *Shield* of his people. This request once made—the time is not yet come for more extensive petition ; that is reserved for the festival itself—the psalmist reverts to the theme with which he started, and once more contemplates the bliss of being in the sanctuary. He is a pilgrim, and must make his way home again all too soon, but even if he had only a *day* instead of a week to spend in Yahweh's *courts*, he would gain something which *a thousand* days in his *own chamber* could not supply. Though, for some reason, he were unable to enter the sacred precinct itself, and passed no farther than the *threshold*, being compelled to behave like a " hanger-on " at the gate, he would still be better off than if he had an assured standing and a permanent position in a godless community. Both in what Yahweh is—a *sun* to give light and a *shield* to protect—and in what he gives—*grace, glory,* and *good*—

the man who *walks in perfection* will find abundant reason for exclaiming, in the words of 12, " *O Yahweh of Hosts, blessed is the man that trusteth in thee.*"

Religious Teaching

This hymn is a triumphant expression of the blessedness which is to be found in communion with Yahweh. Our conception of religion, its methods and its purposes, has grown during the centuries. Material prosperity is no longer the sole test of divine favour, nor do we think of the welfare of the community as summed up in the life of its individual head. But it is still true that the highest bliss known to the human spirit is the sense of communion with God, and that in the " fellowship of the Holy Spirit " we have most certainly an experience of that which is unseen and eternal.

PSALM 85

THREE divisions are clearly marked in this psalm. According to the usual interpretation, *vv.* 1–3 (2–4) refer to the return from the Babylonian Captivity ; the nation's sins, for which the Exile was the punishment, are forgiven, the divine wrath is assuaged, and the land is restored to Yahweh's favour. This section, therefore, refers to the past ; the restoration of the people has taken place. In the second division, however, *vv.* 4–7 (5–8), there is a prayer to Yahweh to restore his people, to withdraw his anger, which still rests upon them, so that they may rejoice in him, and that he may have mercy on them, and grant them salvation. This section, therefore, refers to the present ; so far from the restoration having taken place, the people stand condemned under the wrath of God. The third division, *vv.* 8–13 (9–14), tells of a divine message accorded to the psalmist ; it depicts a state of righteousness, peace, and happiness in the land ; Yahweh himself is among his people. Here again the reference is to the present, but see the exegetical notes on these verses for the force of the tenses.

It should be noted at the outset that the first section cannot possibly refer to the return from the Babylonian Captivity ; one has but to read the details of the condition of things in the land after the Return, as given in the books of *Ezra, Nehemiah, Haggai,* and *Zechariah* (see the notes under Ps. 126, pp. 515 f.) to realize that this is out of the question. The second section might conceivably refer to the evil plight of the people during the early periods after the Return. But the third section takes us into the domain of the supernatural ; the glory of Yahweh is thought of as abiding in the land, and Yahweh himself walks on earth with righteousness and uprightness, personified, before him. It is, thus, evident that the content of the psalm must be explained on other lines. To grasp its true meaning the first requisite is to recognize that in the opening verse a technical term is used which belongs to the language of the prophets. In the English Version the second half of *v.* 1 (2) is rendered: " Thou hast turned back the captivity of Jacob " (*šabtā šᵉbûth ya'ăqôb*; Jacob is a term of endearment for Israel); this phrase is used by the prophets of the bringing back of the time of primeval happiness, the " Golden Age ", a theme which plays an important part in the teaching of the prophets concerning the future. The word translated in the English Version by " captivity " should, according to its technical use by the prophets, be rendered " restoration "—namely, the restoration, or bringing back, of the happy age as at the beginning; an instructive illustration occurs in Jer. 33¹¹: " I will cause the restoration (*šᵉbûth*) of the earth to return *as at the first* (or, *as in the beginning,* כְּבָרִאשֹׁנָה *kᵉbāri'šônāh*), saith Yahweh "; in *v.* 7 of the same chapter we have, in connexion with this restoration, the phrase: " I will build them (*i.e.,* re-establish them) as at the first " (see also Jer. 32⁴⁴, 33²⁶, Ezek. 39²⁵, and elsewhere). The conception was of extra-Israelite origin, but was adopted by the prophets who interpreted it as in reference to the " Messianic Age " (see, *e.g.*, Am. 9¹⁴, Jer. 33¹⁴⁻¹⁶). The whole subject is a very large one, and cannot be further dealt with here.[1]

It is, then, this prophetical conception of the re-establishment, or restoration, of the primeval age of bliss, which is the subject of this psalm; it is, thus, an eschatological psalm.

Further, it must be pointed out that, in describing the happy time of restoration, all the verbs are in the perfect tense, as though a past event were being referred to; it is, presumably, largely owing to this (though see the note on *šᵉbûth* in *v.* 1 [2]) that the first section of the psalm has been explained in reference to the Babylonian Captivity. It must, however, be remembered that in Hebrew the perfect is used " to express facts which are undoubtedly imminent, and, therefore, in the imagination of the speaker, already accomplished (*perfectum confidentiæ*). . . . This use of the perfect occurs most frequently in prophetic language (*perfectum propheticum*). The prophet so transports himself in imagination into the future that he describes the future event as if it had been already seen or heard by him." [2] It is in this sense that the perfects in our psalm must be understood.

As sung in the Temple worship, it is probable that the first section was sung by one voice, section two by the whole congregation, while a different voice sang the last section.

The date of the psalm is impossible to determine; the depressed

[1] See Oesterley, *The Evolution of the Messianic Idea* (1908); Dietrich, שׁוּב שׁבוּת *Die endzeitliche Wiederherstellung bei den Propheten* (1925).
[2] Gesenius' *Hebrew Grammar,* Engl. transl. by Cowley, 106 *n*; pp. 312 f. (1910).

state of the people reflected in the second section is variously applicable; the language is thoroughly classical; were it not that prophetical influence is so often to be observed in post-exilic psalms, we should be inclined to postulate a pre-exilic date, especially as there is nothing in the psalm that points necessarily to post-exilic times. Its position, however, among many post-exilic psalms suggests the later period. The metre is regular, 3 : 3.

For the Precentor. Of the Sons of Qorah. A Psalm.

1 (2). Thou hast shown favour, Yahweh, to thy land, thou hast brought back ° the restoration ° of Jacob;

2 (3). Thou hast forgiven the iniquity of thy people, thou hast covered all ° their sins °; Selah.

3 (4). Thou hast withdrawn all thy wrath, ° thou hast ceased ° from the fierceness of thine anger.

4 (5). ° Turn now °, O God of our salvation, ° and take away ° thine indignation ° from us °.

5 (6). Wilt thou be angry with us for ever? wilt thou prolong thy wrath to all ages?

6 (7). ° Wilt thou not ° revive us again, that thy people may rejoice in thee?

7 (8). Show us, Yahweh, thy love, and thy salvation grant unto us.

8 (9). I would hearken to what ° Yahweh ° will say, To his people and unto his loved ones, ° will not Yahweh ° speak peace ° and to them that turn to him in confidence? °

9 (10). Of a truth, nigh to them that fear him is his salvation, that ° his glory ° may abide in our land.

10 (11). Love and Truth are met together, Righteousness and Peace ° kiss each other °;

11 (12). Truth sprouteth forth from the earth, and Righteousness looketh down from heaven.

12 (13). Yea, Yahweh giveth that which is good, and our land yieldeth her increase.

13 (14). Righteousness goeth before him, and ° Uprightness ° on the way of his steps.

Text-critical Notes

1. Read שְׁבוּת, following the K'thib, not שְׁבִית "captivity" (cp. Dietrich, *op. cit.*, pp. 11 ff. 2. Read, with the Versions, הַטֹּאתָם for חַטָּאתָם "their sin". 3. Read הִשְׁבַּתָּ for הֲשִׁבוֹתָ "thou hast caused to turn". 4. Read שׁוּב נָא for שׁוּבֵנוּ. Read, with G, וְהָסֵר for וְהָפֵר "and annul". Read מֵעִמָּנוּ for עִמָּנוּ "with us". 6. Read הֲלֹא, omitting אַתָּה "thou", emphatic, which overloads the half-line, cp. Ps. 71²⁰. 8. Add יהוה. Read הֲלֹא יהוה for הָאֵל יהוה "the God Yahweh". Read, with Gunkel, וְאַל־יָשׁוּבוּ לְכִסְלָה for וְאֵלָי שְׁבֵי־לוֹ כִּסְלָה "and let them not turn again to folly"; for כִּסְלָה in the sense of "confidence" or "hope" see Job 4⁶. 9. Read כְּבוֹדוֹ for כָּבוֹד "glory". 10. Read נָשְׁקוּ for נָשָׁקוּ "they kiss". 13. Read וְיָשֶׂם for וְיָשֵׂם "and he maketh".

1–3. The psalmist speaks of the time of perfect happiness in the land because it is blest with Yahweh's favour; the land is called his, *thy land*, a thought which occurs·in the prophetical books (" my land ", Isa. 14²⁵, Jer. 2⁷, Ezek. 36⁵, Joel 1⁶, but not in any other book). What is meant by the *favour* which *Yahweh* has *shown* is expressed in the words : *thou hast brought back the restoration of Jacob*; the significance of the phrase " to bring back the restoration " (*šûb šebûth*) has already been dealt with; the English rendering here given is confessedly *faute de mieux*, but it is not possible to reproduce the Hebrew without a paraphrase. The Hebrew word for " restoration ", or " returning ", is *šᵉbûth*; in the verse before us—and the same is true of many other passages in which it occurs—this is the written form of the text; but the marginal reading (*Qᵉrē*) has *šᵉbith*, which means " captivity " and represents what the mediæval Jewish critics held to be the right reading. Which of the two readings is the correct one is further complicated by the question of grammar—viz., there are two roots in Hebrew : *šābāh*, " to take captive ", and *šûb*, " to return " ; and the derivations from these, respectively, *šᵉbîth*, " captivity," and *šᵉbûth*, " restoration," or " returning," are attended by grammatical difficulties ; into these we cannot go here. If, therefore, in deciding whether *šᵉbûth* or *šᵉbîth* should be read, we had to depend on early Jewish criticism or on Hebrew grammatical points, the difficulty would be wellnigh insoluble. Fortunately, there are other means whereby this can be decided in most cases. Almost always, when read in the light of the context, it becomes clear whether the word should be read *šᵉbûth* or *šᵉbîth* (whether, or not, there is a marginal reading). In the case of our present psalm the seer presents us with a picture of an entire obliteration of sins among the people, with the consequent withdrawal of divine wrath ; this means that all those things which were always recognized as the signs of God's anger for sin have disappeared ; that this cannot conceivably refer to the conditions of land and people as these existed after the return from the Captivity, should be obvious to anyone who reads in the Biblical records what the actual facts were (for details see under Ps. 126). Clearly, we must, therefore, read here *šᵉbûth*, " restoration," or " returning "—*i.e.*, of the primeval age of bliss—and not *šᵉbîth*, " captivity " (cp. Ps. 53[7]). The weight of iniquity had crushed down the people, and now the burden had been taken from them ; the ghastly horror of sin had lain before them, too horrible a sight for their eyes ; now it is hidden, and they can look fearlessly before them. A mass of living wrath had spread over the land, and now it has been gathered and its last trace and remnant swept away ; in a word, the fierce heat of Yahweh's anger has been quenched.

In the first section of our psalm, therefore, this apocalyptist, as we might call him, envisages the return of the " Golden Age ". With this is contrasted, in the second section (4-7), the present actual state in which the people find themselves ; that the reference here is not a general one, but that it tells of some definite period of national calamity, probably famine or drought, see *v.* 12, may be regarded as certain, for it was just this that called forth the picture of comfort and encouragement contained in the first section ; but what the particular time of distress was cannot be determined ; it happened too often to be identified without some definite indication; and this is wanting. As sung in the Temple, this part of the psalm was probably rendered by the congregation collectively. There is, as it were, a contrasting parallelism between this and the preceding section; there we have: " thou hast brought back," or " restored " (*šabtā*); in contrast to this the second section has: " restore " (*šûb-nā'*); there the divine anger has all disappeared; here it weighs heavily and is unceasing: *Wilt thou be angry with us for ever* ? they cry, for there lies before them only a vista of the long-drawn agony *prolonged* by Yahweh's *wrath*, generation after generation *to all ages*. There the entire disappearance of Yahweh's anger has given new life; here there is this plaint: *Wilt thou not revive us again* ? This contrasting parallelism is both purposeful and effective, and emphasizes the poetical beauty of the psalm. The threefold pleading in question-form is then followed by a prayer, in direct form, that *Yahweh* would *show* his *love* (*ḥesed*), and *grant salvation* to his people. Here " salvation " has a meaning different from that in which the Hebrew word is ordinarily used (" deliverance," " rescue," " welfare," " help," according to the context), it means the permanent state of bliss when Yahweh brings back the primeval age of happiness.

8–13. The answer to the prayer is then proclaimed. This section takes the form of a divine oracle. Like the prophets of old, the psalmist listens first for Yahweh's message: *I would hearken to what Yahweh will say*; and in question-form denoting conviction of an affirmative, he asks: *Will not Yahweh speak peace to his people. . .* ? They are called *his loved ones* (*ḥăsidāyw*), an expression peculiarly characteristic of the *Psalms*, because of their trust and *confidence* in him. Then follows the divine message which has been received. Here the psalmist reverts to the opening theme of the psalm; the verbs are all in the " prophetic perfect "; so certain is he of the fulfilment of his prophecy that he envisages it as already come to pass; and he describes the final state of bliss as present: *salvation* has come, it is *nigh to them that fear him*, cp. Matt. 3², " The Kingdom of heaven hath drawn nigh " (ἤγγικεν). Now has come the time when the divine presence, *his glory*, can *abide* permanently in a *land* where all men serve Yahweh in reverential awe; with the whole verse (9) cp. Isa. 51⁴⁻⁶, 56¹, 60¹⁹, ²⁰. In words as beautiful as any in the Psalter, the psalmist then goes on to describe the result of the divine presence: *Love and truth are met together, righteousness and peace kiss each other*; very striking is the personification of these virtues (cp. Isa. 58⁸); they are, perhaps, thought of as angelic beings, much as Zoroastrianism personified certain divine characteristics as the Amesha Spentas (Archangels). Earth and heaven are, as it were, joined together; from the former *Truth sprouteth forth,* like some beautiful plant (cp. Ps. 72³), while from above the windows of heaven are opened earthwards, and *Righteousness looketh down* on an earth

transformed. All things are the gifts of Yahweh, who *giveth that which
is good*, the psalmist continues, *and our land yieldeth her increase.* To
our ears the mention of this in such an otherwise sublime connexion
sounds somewhat incongruous; but it must be remembered that
materialistic ideas often find expression in the prophetic pictures of the
final restoration (see Isa. 4², 30²³, ²⁴, Jer. 31¹², Hos. 2, ²¹, ²², Am. 9¹³);
purely spiritual conceptions had not yet developed (see the whole of
Job 31). The final words of the psalm are very striking; it is not only
the sign of Yahweh's presence, *his glory*, that will appear on earth, but
he himself will come among his people (cp. Joel 2²⁷), preceded by
Righteousness and *Uprightness*, again personified; with this conception
cp. Ps. 89¹⁴, " Love and truth go before his face," see also Isa. 58⁸.
With the thought of God coming to dwell among his people, we recall
the words of Rev. 21³: " Behold, the tabernacle of God is with men,
and he shall tabernacle with them, and they shall be his peoples, and
God himself shall be with them. . . ."

Religious Teaching

The special interest and importance of the religious teaching of this
psalm (and the same applies to Ps. 126) centre in its picture of the time
of universal restoration; for this lies behind the more fully developed
conceptions and accounts occurring in the apocalyptic literature proper;
and these again form the basis of some of the teaching of the early
Church on the Second Coming. There are some passages in the
book of *Revelation* which should be read in connexion with this psalm
(7²⁻¹⁰, 14⁶, ⁷, 21¹⁻⁵). Above all, the reign of righteousness, and the
consequent entire abolition of sin, is a conception of extreme beauty,
and recalls Rev. 21¹: " And I saw a new heaven and a new earth; for
the first heaven and the first earth are passed away; and the sea is no
more "; the " sea " here means the embodiment of all evil; it is
synonymous with *Tehom*, the primeval monster, " the dragon, the old
serpent, which is the Devil and Satan " (Rev. 20²). The world is foul
with sin, crushed by the burden of iniquity. So deeply has it sunk
into the morass of evil that nothing but the direct interference of God,
a drastic and complete reversal of existing conditions, can ensure
amendment. So far the psalmist is at one with all apocalyptic thought.
But whereas normal eschatology can envisage only the complete
destruction of the present world-order as a preliminary to the new age,
the psalmist is strong in the belief that God can heal the universe as
it is, and create a new world within the old.

PSALM 86

PSALM 86 is a cry for help against the writer's enemies. Some expositors regard it as the utterance of the community speaking as an individual, thus illustrating the familiar Israelite doctrine of corporate personality. Others, with more probability, hold it to be an expression of the religious emotion of an individual. In the latter case it might be classed among those psalms which present the legal aspect of the plea of a defendant protesting his innocence and pleading for the divine acquittal, but there are certain terms and phrases (*e.g.*, the reference to miracle in *v.* 10) which are hardly suitable in such-circumstances.

In its present form the psalm appears to be late, though it is hopeless to attempt even an approximate dating. Psalms of this kind are particularly likely to have received accretions from time to time, adapting them to the needs of successive generations of suppliants ; one or two of these seem fairly obvious. On the other hand, the reference to other gods in *v.* 8 can hardly come from the latest period in Israelite thought. Links with early psalms are not absent ; *e.g.*, *v.* 14 is very similar to Ps. 54³ ⁽⁴⁾. It is even possible that portions of two or three psalms of similar tone and purport have been combined to form a single psalm. *Vv.* 6 and 12 open with phrases of a kind commonly used at the beginning of a psalm, but they may have marked simply the start of a new verse-paragraph. If this be so, the inequality of the three parts makes the suggestion of a genuine strophic arrangement improbable, unless we are to suppose that the difference in length as between them is due to additions made during the transmission of the psalm.

The metre is mainly a combination of 2 : 2 and 3 : 2 (or 2 : 3) ; it is interesting to note that a fairly large proportion of the 2 : 2 lines are genuine " fours ", with a caesura and external parallelism. The first and last lines now contain seven stresses each, and the first member of *v.* 16 is an isolated 3 ; either there has been some interpolation or a couple of significant words have dropped out.

A Prayer. David's.

1. Incline, O Yahweh, thine ear and answer me,
for lowly and poor am I !
2. Guard my life,
for godly am I,
Save thy servant, °   ° O my God,
which trusteth in thee.
3. Shew me thy favour, Yahweh,
for to thee do I cry all the day.
4. Gladden the soul of thy servant,
for to thee °   ° do I lift up my soul.
5. For thou, O Lord,
art good and forgiving,
And plenteous in love
to all that call upon thee.

6. Give ear, O Yahweh, to my prayer,
and attend to my suppliant voice.
7. In the day of my adversity
I will call thee, for thou wilt answer me.
8. None is like thee among gods, O Yahweh,
nor are any deeds like thine.
9. Let all the nations,
whom thou hast made, come ;
And let them bow before thee, O Lord,
and let them honour thy name.

10. For great art thou,
Thou, O God,
11. Teach me, Yahweh, thy way;
May my heart ° rejoice °

and a doer of marvels;
alone ° art great °.
I will walk in thy truth.
to fear thy name !

12. Let me praise thee, O Lord, my God,
And let me honour thy name for ever,
And thou shalt deliver my life
14. O God, the arrogant
And the council of the tyrants
15. Thou, O Lord, art a God
Slow to anger,
16. Turn unto me, and shew me favour,
Give thy strength to thy servant,
17. Shew unto me
And let them that hate me fear and be
ashamed,

with all my heart,
13. for great is thy love °   °,
from nethermost Sheol.
have risen against me,
seek my life °   °.
compassionate and gracious,
and great in love and truth.

and deliver thy handmaid's son.
a token for good,
for thou, O Yahweh, hast helped and
consoled me.

Text-critical Notes

2. Om., with G, " thou ".   4. Om., with Jerome " O Lord ".   10. Add, with G, גָּדֹל.   11. Read, cp. G, S, יַחְדְּ for " shall be one ".   13. Om. " upon me ". 14. Om., with Gunkel, " and have not set thee before them "; possibly the whole verse has been inserted from Ps. 54³.

In the first part of this psalm (*vv.* 1–5) the psalmist prays in general terms for the help of Yahweh. There are two grounds, the one being his own need, and the other the character of Yahweh. Much of the language is familiar and almost conventional. Thus he asks that Yahweh will *incline* his *ear* (*v.* 1), *save* him (*v.* 2), *shew favour* (*v.* 3) and *gladden* his *soul* (*v.* 4). His is *lowly* and *poor*, and counts himself among the *godly*—*i.e.*, among the " saints " (see Vol. I, pp. 56 ff.). On the other side, too, we meet with well-worn terms; Yahweh is *good* and *plenteous in love*. But there is one epithet not found elsewhere—*forgiving*. True, the thought is one of the most familiar in the Old Testament, but the form is unique. It belongs to a class of words indicating normal occupation, trade, or profession. Yahweh is a " forgiver "—it is his " nature and property ", and the psalmist might well have endorsed Voltaire's famous " *il pardonnera, c'est son métier* ".

The second part of the psalm (*vv.* 6–11) also starts with a plea that Yahweh will *give ear*. In what follows, however, the emphasis is less on the *adversity* (*v.* 7) into which the psalmist has fallen than on the power and majesty of Yahweh. Other *gods* may exist, but none can boast the character and *deeds* of the God of Israel (*v.* 8). The writer feels dimly that the divine prestige will be enhanced by his deliverance; he would have *all nations come and bow before* Yahweh, recognizing that he *alone* is *great*. In *v.* 11 he vows that, if he be delivered, he will henceforth *walk in* the *truth* of Yahweh, ever remaining faithful to him. Some scholars would emend the text in the latter part of the verse, substituting a word meaning " desire " for that rendered above " *rejoice* " (the Septuagint reading, here adopted, assumes the same consonants as the traditional Hebrew text, though with different vowels).

But this is to misunderstand all that the Hebrew felt when he used the word *fear*. It implies an attitude which is by no means incompatible with *rejoicing*; it is not only—indeed, not usually—akin to terror, but may imply, as here, respect, fidelity, worship. It is the proper emotional tone for any person who finds himself in the presence of a superior, not only when the superior may be hostile, but also when the relationship between the two is one of loving sympathy. In some ways it is the nearest single word in Hebrew for what we call " religion ", and it may well be accompanied by a solemn exultation inspired by the presence of a morally perfect omnipotence.

Finally (*vv.* 12–17), the psalmist passes to a more exact statement of his need. This part of the psalm also opens as if it were a fresh hymn ; the writer is conscious of an inward impulse to *praise* and *honour* his *God* (*v.* 12). He expects (or, perhaps better, as Buttenwieser suggests, prays) that Yahweh will *deliver* him *from nethermost Sheol*; apparently his conception of the hereafter was so far advanced that he recognized different levels in the underworld. At last, in *v.* 14, he comes to a definite point. He is being persecuted, perhaps accused, by *the arrogant* and *the tyrants*. In this extremity he turns to that God who, from of old (cf. Ex. 34⁶), had been proclaimed as *compassionate and gracious, slow to anger, and great in love and truth* (*v.* 15). He can *give strength* to his *servant* (*v.* 16), and in his humility the Psalmist takes the lowest of all social levels. The *servant* might be a temporary slave, working out his six years of bondage. But the *handmaid's son*— the child of the female slave, the "house-born" (cf. Gen. 15³, Exod. 21⁴·⁷, Jer. 2¹⁴)—was from his birth the property of his mother's owner, and could never hope for liberation. Just because Yahweh is his absolute and permanent owner, the psalmist believes that he will even *shew* a *token*, and secure deliverance. So the psalm ends, with this note of hope and confidence, not without the natural desire for the discomfiture of the adversary.

Religious Teaching

We do not look for systematic theology in a poem of this kind. In harmony with the normal post-exilic view, the psalmist believes in the character and supremacy of Yahweh, even if he has not attained to an absolute monotheism. But Yahweh has the power and the goodness to save, and his loving nature will lead him to pardon and restore his distressed saints.

PSALM 87

THE grandeur of this short psalm is somewhat obscured by dislocations in the text. These dislocations are due to the lines having been copied out in their wrong order. This may be hypothetically explained in this way : a scribe, in copying out the psalm, inadvertently omitted some of the lines, which he subsequently added in the margin ; a later scribe, in making his copy of the psalm, naturally wished to include the lines which had been placed in the margin ; but this was no easy matter, because there was, presumably, no indication as to where they belonged in the text. The later scribe had, therefore, to do the best he could ; but he was somewhat wanting in discernment, otherwise he would not, for example, have begun the psalm with a meaningless sentence, as it is in its present form ; nor would he have been content with the illogical sequence of the lines as we now have them ; nor does he seem to have realized the great significance of the refrain : " This one was born there ".

To place the lines in their original order may not be possible—scholars differ on the subject—but it may, at any rate, be claimed that the following reconstruction brings out the universalistic note which runs through the psalm, and which makes it, from this point of view, one of the most inspiring in the Psalter.

The psalmist proclaims Zion as the most loved by Yahweh of all the centres of his worship ; this is because Zion will become the world-centre of his worship. Zion is thought of, figuratively, as the spiritual mother of all men, so that of every nation the psalmist says : " This one was born there ". Egypt, Babylon, Philistia, Tyre, and distant Kush receive special mention, but all peoples are included ; and this sublime refrain is taken up by the worshippers in Zion itself, who in their song of praise and in their sacred dance in the sanctuary enthusiastically respond : " This one was born there ". A brotherhood of man in the highest sense !

The question of date is difficult. The pronounced universalism was either due to prophetic influence—Deutero-Isaiah was its greatest exponent —or else it points to the Greek period. But the mention of Babylon as the great world-power by the side of Egypt indicates a time after the end of the Assyrian empire ; a pre-exilic date is therefore improbable. On the other hand, this mention of Babylon is against a post-exilic date ; and in post-exilic times Deutero-Isaiah's universalistic teaching was ignored, at any rate until the Greek period. We seem, therefore, to be led to the period of the Exile itself as the date of our psalm, and at the very end of this period, when the Return was

approaching. To this it can be objected that the worship in the
Temple seems to be in full operation, since "the singers and the dancers"
are spoken of. To this it can, however, be replied that the psalmist
is envisaging in his mind's eye the re-establishment of the Temple
worship, much in the same way that Deutero-Isaiah did (see, *e.g.*, Isa.
52¹¹, ¹², and note also 56¹⁻⁸).

In the present state of the text there is practically no metrical
structure; in the emended form of the text, which is confessedly
conjectural, the metre is irregular.

Of the Sons of Qorah ; A Psalm, A Song.

2. Yahweh loveth the gates of Zion above all the dwelling-places of Jacob;
1. ° Her foundation ° is upon the holy hills, 5°. he hath founded it ° for ever °.
3. Glorious things ° are told ° of thee, O city of God °: Selah °.
6. Yahweh writeth down in the peoples'
 ° register °:
 " This one was born there ";
4. ° I record ° Rahab and Babylon as those
 that know me: ° " This one was born there "; °
 Behold, Philistia and Tyre, with Kush:
5ᵃᵇ. Yea, to Zion it shall be said, ° each one °
 was born in her; ° singers and dancers " This one was born there ";
 all respond in thee °:
 ° " This one was born there." °

Text-critical Notes

For the title see Vol. i. p. 15.   1. Read יְסוּדָתֹה for רתוֹ—, " his foundation ",
as though in reference to Yahweh, which comes in the next half-line. 5c. Read
לְעוֹלָם for עֶלְיוֹן, " Most High ". Where this half-line stands in the Hebrew
text it is inappropriate, while in *v.* 1 a half-line is wanting. We follow Gunkel here.
3. Lit. " it is told ". *Selah* is included in the Hebrew metre, as sometimes elsewhere.
6. Read בִּכְתָב for בְּכְתוֹב, " when he writeth down ". 4. Lit. " I make
mention ". The refrain in this *v.* is a conjectural addition; but it is demanded both
because of " I record ", and because otherwise a half-line is wanting; moreover, the
symmetry requires it. 5a. Lit. " a man and a man ". Read, with Gressmann:
שָׁרִים כָּחֹלְלִים כָּל־מַעְיָנַי בָּךְ for שָׁרִים וְחֹלְלִים כֻּלָּם כְּלָם עֲנִי בָּךְ " and singers
like dancers all my springs are in thee ". The Hebrew text is obviously corrupt.
The refrain here is again a conjectural addition, but it is required after " all respond
in thee "; the refrain, moreover, is the obvious antiphon.

1-3. The words of the two opening verses recall Isaiah's belief
in the inviolability of the holy city; *the gates* is a synonym for the city.
Yahweh's sanctuary is often spoken of as his *dwelling-place*; the reference is, therefore, to the other sanctuaries in the land. The *glorious
things* to which the psalmist refers may well have been such utterances
of Deutero-Isaiah as are recorded in Isa. 54¹⁻⁸—*e.g.*, *v.* 3 : " For thou
shalt spread abroad on the right hand and on the left; and thy seed
shall possess the nations ". The *city of God* occurs also in Ps. 46⁴.
6-5ᵃ. These verses contain the psalmist's main theme—viz.,
Yahweh's recognition of the Gentiles as the children of the Holy City,
figuratively represented as their mother. Here again Deutero-Isaiah's
words seem to be in the psalmist's mind; in Isa. 54¹ it is said : " For

more are the children of the desolate than the children of the married wife, saith Yahweh ", and in *v.* 5 the prophet says : " For thy Maker is thine husband. Yahweh of hosts is his name." The Gentiles are thus regarded as his spiritual children, and they are recorded as belonging to his family in the heavenly *register*. This idea of Yahweh's book of life was a familiar one—see, *e.g.*, Exod. 32^{32}, Ps. 69^{28}, 139^{16}, Isa. 4^{3}. In this book, according to the psalmist's universalistic outlook, Yahweh registers against the name of each people : " *This one was born there* ". The refrain occurs in the text twice only, but in view of the displacements in the text, referred to above, we have added it in two places where it seems to be called for. Among the peoples specifically mentioned Egypt is called by the emblematical name of *Rahab* (see note on 89^{10}) ; together with *Babylon* it was the leading world-power when the psalmist wrote, though the downfall of Babylon was near at hand ; *Philistia* and *Tyre* (Phœnicia), who for centuries were the neighbouring peoples of Judah and Israel, respectively, are appropriately mentioned ; while *Kush* (Ethiopia) represents the more distant peoples who are all to be received as Zion's children. The psalmist ends by picturing to himself the worshippers in the Temple, soon to be rebuilt, joining in the refrain : " *This one was born there* ".

Religious Teaching

The psalmist who wrote this psalm was an idealist of the highest order. That he contemplated the realization of his ideal in reference to his own time, as Gunkel holds, we cannot believe. Nor can we accept the contention of some other authorities that the psalmist is thinking of the conversion of the Gentiles in the " last times ". His thought soars beyond the present ; but the future of which he conceives is not that of the end of the present world-order. The psalmist's central and foremost thought is of God, who made all men, and who will, in his own time, draw all men unto him. The All-Fatherhood of God is an eternal fact which demands the brotherhood of man. God is true to himself ; but men are not true to themselves. Nevertheless, the psalmist, with his sublime outlook, envisages a time in world-history when, irrespective of nationality, men will come to themselves, and therefore to God. It is an ideal ; but, with divine optimism, the psalmist portrays its superb realization as taking place within time-space. The when is not his concern ; he is content with framing the beautiful ideal. That he should picture Jerusalem as the home of welcome to the wanderers was a necessity, for this alone was the world's centre of the worship of God.

PSALM 88

THIS psalm is unique. It is a desperate cry of suffering, unrelieved by a single ray of comfort or of hope. In form it is the utterance of an individual, but the doctrine of corporate personality has enabled some expositors to regard it as an expression of national sorrow. Not a few readers, however, will feel that the agony is too keen to be that of sympathy, even of the deepest sympathy for the calamities of the people. It is written with the very heart's blood of the poet.

If we take the piece as a " dirge of the community ", its date will almost certainly be that of the early exile, and it will be contemporary with the earliest of the poems in the book of *Lamentations*. But there are good grounds for supposing that the author was acquainted with the book of *Job*, and may himself also have been a leper. In that case the fourth century is the earliest period to which we can assign the psalm.

The thought and language of *v*. 8 are closely paralleled in *v*. 18, and *Selah* occurs at the end of *vv*. 7 and 10—in the latter case it was not read by the Septuagint. These facts, however, hardly warrant us in finding a formal strophic arrangement ; there is no break in the subject-matter corresponding to the divisions suggested by the points just noted.

The metre is 3 : 3 throughout, with 2 : 2 : 2 in *v*. 5a. Anacrusis occurs in *vv*. 1, 13 and 14, and the word בְּעֵינָי in *v*. 16 counts as two metrical units.

A Song. A Psalm. Of the Sons of Qorah. For the Precentor :
On Maḥalath l'annoth. Maskil. Of Heman the Ezrahite.

1 (2). O Yahweh !
° My God ! I have cried ° ° by day °, cried out in the night before thee.
2 (3). May my prayer come before thee ! incline thine ear to my ringing note.
3 (4). For my soul is sated with sorrows, and my life draweth near to Sheol.
4 (5). I am numbered with them that go down to the Pit, I am become as a man strengthless.
5 (6). ° As the dead ° I am free, as the slain, that repose in the tomb.
Whom thou hast remembered no more, seeing that they have been cut off from thy hand.
6 (7). Thou settest me in the nethermost Pit, ° among them that are restrained ° in the depths.
7 (8). Upon me resteth thy wrath. all thy breakers ° thou hast brought over me °. Selah.

8 (9). Thou hast put mine acquaintance far from me, thou hast made me loathsome to them.
° I am shut up °, I cannot go forth, 9 (10). mine eye languisheth from affliction.

I called thee, O Yahweh, every day, I spread out my palms unto thee.
10 (11). Wilt thou work a wonder for the dead ? or shall shades rise to praise thee ? Selah.
11 (12). Shall thy love be told in the tomb ? ° or ° thy fidelity in Abaddon ?
12 (13). Shall thy wonders be known in the darkness ? thy triumph in the land of oblivion ?

13 (14). And I!
    Unto thee, O Yahweh, have I cried,   and in the morning my prayer was wont to greet thee.
14 (15). Wherefore?
    O Yahweh, dost thou cast off my soul?   hidest thy face from me?
15 (16). Afflicted am I, and am weary from my youth,   I suffer thy terrors, ° I grow faint °.
16 (17). Thy fury hath passed over me,   thy terrors ° have made an end of me °.
17 (18). They are about me as water all the day,   they have made their circuit against me altogether.
18 (19). Lover hast thou taken far from me,   and comrade ° and acquaintance thou hast withdrawn °.

Text-critical Notes

1. Read, with Bickell, אֱלֹהֵי שַׁוְעָתִי for " God of my salvation ". Read, with G, יוֹמָם for " day of ". 5. Read, with some Hebr. MSS and T, בַּקְּבָרִים for " among the dead ". 6. Read כְּמוֹ חֲשֵׁכִים for " in the darkness ". 8. Read, with G, אֶכָּלֵא for " shut up ". 11. Insert וְאִם (omitted by haplography). 15. Read, אָפוּנָה (cp. Ps. 77²) for אָפוּגָה " I am distracted ". 16. Read צִמְּתוּנִי for צִמְּתוּתֻנִי (same meaning). 18. Read (cf. Jerome, S) וּמְיֻדָּע חָשֵׁכְתָּ for " mine acquaintances are darkness ".

For the title, see Vol. I, p. 18.

The whole psalm is a cry from the night of suffering and doubt. We must not look too carefully for coherence and continuity of thought; the poet's mind turns swiftly from one aspect of his case to another. But he begins, in the only way a man in such straits can begin, with a direct appeal to *Yahweh*, metrically emphasized by the anacrusis, to whom he *cries* for help continuously *by day* and *in the night*. The spontaneous urgency of his plea is emphasized by the fact that it is a *ringing note*—a term normally reserved for an outburst of sudden exultation. It is as if the whole of his emotional world had been inverted by his pain, and the natural expression of the keenest joy has become a token of the most poignant grief (2). The same twist in thought appears in the next metaphor; the hungry, when at last full-fed, says he is *sated*—satisfied. But it is sorrow that has glutted the psalmist's appetite, his very *soul*. So had Yahweh himself spoken to Isaiah of the sacrifices of Israel (Isa. 1¹¹). One thing only is left for the sufferer—death which will bring him to *Sheol* (3). We cannot escape a comparison with Job's point of view (cf. Job 7⁹, ²¹, 10²¹, 14¹⁸ ᶠᶠ, 16²², 17³, etc.). So far has this experience gone that the victim is already *as one dead*. The use of the word *free* may be an audacious and bitter parody and perversion of Job's phrase in Job 3¹⁹, but even so in the psalmist's mind it probably carries a suggestion of leprosy. A closely allied word is used of the " lazar-house " in which Uzziah was confined (2 Kings 15⁵), and much of what the psalmist says is consistent with his having suffered from the most terrible disease known to ancient Israel. A characteristic feature in the treatment of leprosy was that the victim was already accounted dead, and the psalmist's

experience tells him that it is not only man, but also God, who has
ceased to think of him as still existing, has *remembered* him *no more*,
and has *cut* him *off from* the divine *hand*, that is from the nearness and
power of Yahweh (5). The thought is continued in 6, where the poet
sees himself as already *restrained in the nethermost Pit*—either in Sheol
in general or in an especially deep portion in Sheol—or in the *depths*.
The last word is one which suggests the bottom of the sea, and may
hint at a form of the creation-myth current in Israel, according to which
the primeval chaos-monster was not slain, but imprisoned beneath the
ocean, or even equated with the sea (cf., *e.g.*, Job 7^{12}). The sea-
metaphor is repeated in 7, where the psalmist thinks of himself as overwhelmed by the *wrath* of Yahweh, as by *breakers* on a rocky coast—
surely a reminiscence of Ps. 42^7.

A new aspect of the case is introduced in 8, again recalling the fate
of the leper. All the sufferer's friends have left him ; he is utterly
lonely, and absolutely bereft of human companionship. He is indeed
loathsome to others, as Job was to his *acquaintance* and even to his wife
(Job $19^{13, 14, 17}$, cf. also Isa. $53^{3, 4}$—another case of leprosy). Even
if others would see him, he cannot reach them, for he is segregated,
shut up, and *cannot go forth* (8–9a). To this thought the psalmist will
return again in the last verse of the psalm.

With swift transition the poet comes back to God. It is his relation
to Yahweh (again we find a parallel with Job) that is central ; the other
elements in his bitter experience are but peripheral. In Sheol he will
be utterly and for ever cut off from God. The divine power cannot
reach him to *work a wonder*, and he cannot lift up his voice in *praise*
to Yahweh. Yahweh has nothing to gain (cf. Job $10^{4\,ff.}$) by consigning
him to torture and destruction—the literal meaning of *Abaddon*, a
synonym for Sheol, the *darkness* and *oblivion* where the divine *wonders*
and *triumph* cannot *be known*.

So once more he comes to the great gulf between himself and God,
and recalls how he has *cried* for help, and how he has been wont to
send his *prayer* to *greet* his Lord in the early dawn (14). Hence the
great puzzle—*why*, in spite of all this, has Yahweh *cast* him *off*? Like
Job, he has done his best, and all is in vain. *Afflicted* and *weary*, almost
expiring, from the sickness that has clung to him from his early *youth*,
he feels that the only possible source for his sufferings is the divine *fury*
which has overwhelmed him with deadly *terrors* (the only other occurrence of the word is in Job 6^4). Repeated grades and type of horror
have *made their circuit against* him, following one another, as it were,
in a continuous orbit, and each in turn swooping on him as it comes
nearest to him, so stabbing his soul with an endless succession of
cumulative agonies (17). And all this he must bear alone.

Religious Teaching

In the whole Bible there is no other place where we have so forcibly presented to us the meaning and results of a refusal to believe in the life to come. As we have seen, the situation of the psalmist is much that of the poet to whom we owe the book of *Job*, but the sufferings of that noble spirit lead him in the end, after desperate battles of the soul, to the conviction that death is not the end of God's dealings with man. The psalmist seems aware of that view, but cannot accept it, and is, therefore, left in utter hopelessness. If the drama of religion (to consider no other aspect of the case) is to be played out to the very end upon the stage of this world, then there is no possibility of belief in final goodness. Many men may get some kind of compensation for their suffering—and suffering is a universal experience—during their earthly life ; there are those who do not. Their number may not be great, and only a small proportion may be capable of intense feeling, but if, in all human history, there had been but one who had had to endure what this man endured, with no hope of God in the hereafter, then a true optimism would be impossible—there is an evil power in the world before which good may be powerless. A belief in immortality is fundamental, not merely to human happiness, but to divine justification, and there can be no valid theodicy if it be excluded. If this psalm does nothing else, it puts the issue before us in clear-cut alternatives, and bids us make our choice.

PSALM 89

THERE is some justification for the belief, though opinions on the subject differ,[1] that this psalm is a combination of three originally independent psalms (cp. Pss. 19, 27, 127, each of which is a combination of two separate psalms). This is suggested by the entirely different subject-matter of each of the three component parts. The purpose of the compiler in combining these appears to have been to set in review the origin, development, and final disappearance of the kingship. The first two verses are introductory. The first psalm extols the all-powerful might of Yahweh in heaven and earth ; he is King above, and his throne is in heaven (*v.* 14) ; the earthly kingship is from him and under his protection (*vv.* 17, 18). Then the compiler illustrates, by the second psalm chosen, the glory of the kingship as exemplified by the royal Davidic house. And, finally, he adds, in what appears to be only part of another psalm, the record of the final disappearance of the

[1] See the very interesting essay by Aubrey R. Johnson, *The Rôle of the King in the Jerusalem Cultus*, in *The Labyrinth*, pp. 77 ff. (ed. S. H. Hooke [1935]).

kingship. The component parts, after the introductory verses, are :
(*a*) *vv.* 5–18 ; (*b*) *vv.* 3, 4, 19–37 ; (*c*) *vv.* 38–51 ; the last verse, 52, is a
benediction which marks the close of Book III (see Vol. I, pp. 2 ff.). For
the purpose, perhaps, of seeking to unify his material, the compiler
separated *vv.* 3, 4 from the psalm to which they belong, and placed
them (after the two introductory verses) at the beginning of the whole
amalgamation. In the following rendering these two verses are placed
in what we conceive to have been their original position.

The first of the three psalms here combined is a Hymn of Praise
glorifying the supremacy of Yahweh among the heavenly hosts. The
second commemorates Yahweh's covenant with the house of David.
The third is a pathetic plaint over the downfall of the monarchy. The
three themes are thus of a very different nature.

The difficulty and precariousness of assigning dates to the psalms
in general are fully recognized ; quite tentatively, therefore, we suggest
the following dates for these three psalms, respectively : (*a*) The
mention of Tabor and Hermon in *v.* 12 shows that this first psalm
(*vv.* 5–18) was written by one living in northern Israel ; *vv.* 15–18
make it clear that it belongs to the time of the monarchy. The psalm
must, therefore, be dated before 722/1 B.C., when the northern kingdom
fell. That it was a time of prosperity is evident from *vv.* 16, 17 ; it is,
therefore, quite possible that the psalm was written during the
prosperous reign of Jeroboam II (see II Kings 14[25]) ; his date was 788–
747 B.C.

(*b*) That the second psalm belongs to the southern kingdom is
obvious on the face of it. A time of prosperity is likewise indicated by
vv. 28, 29 ; it is therefore possible that this psalm was written during
the reign of Josiah (639–608 B.C.).

(*c*) There could be no greater contrast than that between this and
the preceding psalm. Here we have depicted nothing less than the
downfall of the Davidic monarchy (*vv.* 43, 44). The date is clearly
indicated in *v.* 45, which must refer to Jehoiachin : " Thou hast
shortened the days of his youth ", cp. 2 Kings 24[8] : "Jehoiachin was
eighteen years old when he began to reign ". The date may, therefore,
with some confidence, be given as 597 B.C. The final combination
belongs to post-exilic times.

The metre of (*a*) is almost uniformly 4 : 4 (with anacrusis, " O
Yahweh " in *v.* 8) ; the three concluding *vv.* 16–18, are 3 : 3 ; that of
(*b*) is 3 : 3 throughout ; in (*c*) it varies, *vv.* 38–45 are 3 : 3, *v.* 46 is
4 : 3, and *vv.* 47–51 are 4 : 4.

Maskil of Ethan, the Ezrahite.

1 (2). ° Of thy loving-acts,° Yahweh, will I ceaselessly sing,
        will ever make known thy faithfulness with my mouth ;
2 (3). For I said, For ever ° is thy love ° built up,
      ° like ° the heavens is thy faithfulness ° established for ever °.

(a)

5 (6). The heavens give praise for thy wondrous-acts, Yahweh,
        yea, for thy faithfulness, ° the assembly of ° holy ones ;
6 (7). For who in the skies can compare with Yahweh,
        is like Yahweh among the sons of gods ?
7 (8). God, who is fearful in the assembly of the holy ones,
        ° mighty is he ° and awe-ful among all around him !
8 (9). O Yahweh !
    God of hosts, who is like thee ?
        ° thy might and thy terror ° are round about thee.
9 (10). Thou rulest the raging of the sea,   ° the roaring ° of its waters thou stillest ;
10 (11). Thou didst crush Rahab as one pierced,
        with thy mighty arm thou didst scatter thy foes.
11 (12). Thine are the heavens, and thine is the earth ;
        the world and its fulness,—thou didst found them ;
12 (13). North and south thou didst create them ;
        Tabor and Hermon shout for joy in thy name °.
13 (14). Thine is the arm, ° and thine ° is the might,
        strong is thy hand, lifted up thy right-hand.
14 (15). Righteousness and justice are the stay of thy throne,
        love and truth enter in before thee.
15 (16). Blessed are the people who know the shout,
        in the light of thy countenance they walk, ° Yahweh °.
16 (17). In thy name they rejoice all the in thy righteousness ° they shout for
        day,   joy ° ;
17 (18). For the glory of their strength art
        thou,   in thy favour our horn ° is exalted ° ;
18 (19). For to Yahweh belongeth our
        shield,   to the Holy One of Israel our King.

(b)

3 (4). ° Thou didst make ° a covenant ° didst swear ° to David ° thy servant ° ;
        with thy chosen °,   and build up thy house eternally ".
4 (5). " For ever will I establish thy   Selah.
        seed,
19 (20). At that time thou spakest in   ° unto thy sanctified one °, and saidst :
        vision   have exalted one chosen from among
        " I have set ° the crown ° on a   the people ;
        mighty one,   with my holy oil I anointed him,
20 (21). I found my servant David,   and him mine arm doth strengthen ;
21 (22). One whom mine hand upholdeth,   no son of wickedness oppress him ;
22 (23). No enemy shall conquer him,
23 (24). I will crush his foes out of his them that hate him will I strike down ;
        sight,
24 (25). My faithfulness and love are with in my name shall his horn be exalted ;
        him,   and on the rivers his right-hand.
25 (26). I will set his hand on the sea,
26 (27). He shall call unto me, ' My Father
        art thou,   my God, and the Rock of my help ' ;
27 (28). Yea, I have made him my first-
        born,   most high among kings of the earth.
28 (29). For ever I will keep for him my   and my covenant shall stand fast with
        love,   him ;
29 (30). I will establish his seed for ever, and his throne as the days of heaven.
30 (31). If his sons forsake my law,   and walk not in mine ordinances,
31 (32). If they profane my statutes,   and keep not my commandments,
32 (33). I will punish their sin with a rod, and with scourges their iniquity.
33 (34). Yet my love will I not ° deny °
        him,   nor suffer my faithfulness to fail ;
34 (35). I will not annul my covenant,   nor change the issue from my lips.
35 (36). One thing have I sworn by my
        holiness,   —and I will not deceive David— :
36 (37). His seed shall endure for ever, and his throne as the sun before me ;
37 (38). Like the moon shall it stand for ° and as long as the sky standeth
        ever,   firm ° ". Selah.

(c)

38 (39). But thou hast spurned and rejected, hast been wrath with thine anointed;

39 (40). Hast annulled the covenant with thy servant. hast polluted his crown to the earth;

40 (41). Hast broken down all his walls, hast made his defences a ruin;

41 (42). All that pass by have plundered him, he is become the scorn of his neighbours;

42 (43). Thou hast exalted the right-hand of his foes, hast gladdened all his enemies;

43 (44). Thou hast turned his sword ° from the adversary °, hast not granted him victory in battle;

44 (45). ° Thou hast broken the sceptre from his hand °, and his throne to the ground hast thou cast;

45 (46). Thou hast shortened the days of his youth, hast covered him ° with grey-hair °. Selah.

46 (47). How long, Yahweh, wilt thou hide thyself for ever, shall thy wrath burn like fire?

47 (48). ° Remember how I come to an end for ever, hast thou created for nought all the sons of men? °

48 (49). What man doth live who shall not see death? shall his soul escape from the hand of Sheol? Selah.

49 (50). Where are thine acts-of-love, the former ones, ° Yahweh °, which, thou swarest to David in thy faithfulness?

50 (51). Remember, O Lord, the reproach of ° thy servant °, which I bear in my bosom—° the contempt of ° the peoples—

50 (51). Wherewith thine enemies reproach, Yahweh, wherewith they reproach the footsteps of thine anointed.

52 (53). Blessed be Yahweh for ever, Amen and Amen.

Text-critical Notes

For the title see Vol. I, p. 18.   1. Read, with G, חֲסָדָיו for חַסְדֵי " the loving-acts of ".   2. Read חַסְדְּךָ for חֶסֶד " love ". Add כְּ before " the heavens ".   Read, with G, תָּכִין for תָּכִין " thou wilt establish "; and for בָּהֶם " in them ", read לְדוֹר וָדוֹר as in v. 1; two words under one beat.

(a)

5. Om. בְּ " in ", the subject of " shall praise " is both " the assembly of the heavenly ones " and " the heavens ".   7. Read, with G, רַב הוּא for רַבָּה " greatly ".   8. Read חֲסִין יָהּ וֶאֱמוּנָתְךָ for חֲסִנְךָ וֶאֱמוּנָתְךָ " the might of Yah and thy faithfulness ".   9. Read, with G, בְּשׁוֹא for בְּשׂוֹא " when it riseth up ".   12. Or read, alternatively, with G, לְשִׁמְךָ " at thy name ".   13. Read, with S, וּלְךָ for עִם " with ".   15. Transpose יהוה " Yahweh " to the end of the v.   16. Read יֵרֻגְּנוּ, being a better parallel to " they rejoice ", for יָרוּמוּ " they are exalted ".   17. Read, with Q're, תָּרוּם; K'thibh has תָּרִים " thou dost exalt ".

(b)

3. Read כָּרַתִּי for כָּרַתִּי " I made "; and read לִבְחִירְךָ for לִבְחִירִי " with my chosen "; נִשְׁבַּעְתָּ for —תִּי " I swore "; עַבְדֶּךָ for עַבְדִּי " my servant ". The reason for these emendations is that when utterances are put into the mouth of God they are always preceded by some introductory words, which is not the case here.   19. Read לַחֲסִידֶךָ for לַחֲסִידֶיךָ " thy sanctified ones ". Read נֵזֶר for עֵזֶר " help ", cp. v. 39. 33.   Read אָסִיר (lit. " take away ") for אָפִיר " I will violate ".   37. Read, with Duhm, וְעֵד בַּשַּׁחַק שָׁחַק נֶאֱמָן for וּבְעֵד בַּשַּׁחַק נֶאֱמָן " and a faithful witness in the sky ".

(c)

43. Read מִצֻּר for צוּר " flint " or " edge ".   44. Read מִיָּדוֹ מִטֵּה שָׁבַרְתָּ
for הִשְׁבַּתָּ מִטְּהָרוֹ " thou hast caused to cease from his purity ".   45. Read
שֵׂיבָה for בּוּשָׁה " shame ".   47. Read, with Baethgen and Gunkel, זְכֹר מֶה־חָדֵל
זְכֹר אֲנִי מֶה־יֶחְדַל עַל־מַה־שָּׁוְא בְּרָאתָ for אֲנִי עֶלֶם הַשָּׁוְא בְּרָאתָ כָל־בְּנֵי אָדָם
כָל־בְּנֵי אָדָם " Remember, what is duration ?   On account of what vanity hast
thou created all the sons of men ? "   The corruption of the Hebrew text is manifest.
49. Read, with many MSS, יהוה " Yahweh ", for אֲדֹנָי " O Lord ".   50. Read
עֲבָדֶךָ for עֲבָדֶיךָ " thy servants ".   Read כְּלִמַּת for כָּל־רַבִּים " all many ".

(a)

1, 2.   In these introductory *vv.* the psalmist announces the theme
with which he is going to deal, viz. the *loving-acts* of *Yahweh.* This
word (*hesed*) connotes more than " mercies ", as it is usually rendered
in the English Versions ; it means " love " and all that love involves.
The note of continuity is very pronounced ;   he *will sing ceaselessly,*
lit. " for ever " ;   he will make known Yahweh's *faithfulness for ever,*
lit. " to generation and generation ", but this term is often used for
" ever " ;   and again, Yahweh's love is built up " for ever ", and *his
faithfulness established " for ever "* (on this last see crit. note).   The
thought of God's love being *built up* occurs here only, it expresses
permanence, *like* the eternal structure of the *heavens* ; for the idea of
the heavens as a building, see Gen. 7[11], Am. 9[6], Mal. 3[10].

3 and 4 are dealt with after *v.* 18.

5–10.   This opening section, which tells of the praise accorded to
Yahweh by the heavenly hosts, is of importance for the history of the
Hebrew conception of God.   We have here echoes of ancient non-
Israelite beliefs which were taken over by Israel's religious teachers,
and ultimately adapted.   The *wondrous-acts* of Yahweh are in reference
to the old Babylonian myth of the primeval combat between the god
Marduk and the monster Tiamat, who was the enemy of the gods ;
the *rôle* of Marduk was in Hebrew religion transferred to Yahweh.   The
assembly of the holy ones refers to the gathering of all the gods in council,
just as in the Babylonian myth all the gods assembled to decide how best
they might be able to meet and overcome their enemy Tiamat.

Later Jewish monotheistic teaching explained that the " gods "
were ministers of Yahweh, and wholly subordinate to him.   The
expression *sons of gods,* applied to them, attests the ancient belief, see
further Ps. 29[1, 2].   For *the assembly* (of the *holy ones*) two different
expressions are used ;   in *v.* 5 *qahal* is the ordinary word for a gathering,
but used also in the technical sense of " the congregation " of Israel ;
in later days, the word used in *v.* 7, *sōdh,* means rather the exclusive,
or secret, council of the gods ;   in this sense of a kind of " parliament "
of the gods it occurs here only.   The expression God of hosts points
to the original meaning of " Yahweh *Sebhā'ôth* ", the " hosts " referring

to the heavenly beings, and indicating that in the divine assembly Yahweh is *par excellence*, the warrior God, Captain of the superhuman armies ; in later times the name was used of Yahweh as the leader of the armies of Israel. In 9, 10 there is again a reference to the primeval combat, *the sea* being identified with Tiamat ; the corresponding Hebrew name, Tehom (Gen. 12), means " the deep ". The *raging of the sea* refers to Tiamat's wrath at Marduk's approach, *the roaring of its waves* is in reference to the shouting of the helpers who fought on Tiamat's side. Rahab, used as an emblematical name for Egypt (cp. Ps. 87⁴, Isa. 30⁷), lit. the " proud ", or " defiant ", one, was another name for Tiamat (Job 9¹³, 26¹²). The details of this primeval combat, transferred from Marduk to Yahweh, occur in the Fourth Tablet of the Babylonian Creation-myth (see further, *Myth and Ritual*, ed. S. H. Hooke, Essay III [1933]).

11-14. As the result of Yahweh's victory, *heaven and earth* became his ; and his work of creation began ; hitherto the earth had been " waste and void " (Gen. 1²), now the *world*, as a place for man to dwell in, is founded, together with all that it brings forth. *North and south—i.e.*, from end to end—the world was *created* by Yahweh. Then the psalmist naturally turns to his own land, the centre of the worship of Yahweh, and refers to the two prominent sanctuaries, *Tabor and Hermon*, in which *men shout for joy in* his *name*. In earlier days these were evidently well-known places of worship, though the syncretistic character of worship there called for the prophet's censure (for Tabor see Hos. 5¹, and cp. Baal-Hermon in Judges 3³) ; but the psalmist is thinking now only of the worship of Yahweh offered on these mountain-tops, mentioning specifically his *righteousness and justice, love and truth*.

15-18. These *vv.* tell of the trust that the people have in Yahweh, and their joy in worshipping him who is their strength and stay. The *shout* is a technical term referring to the welcome of Yahweh in the sanctuary (cp. 1 Sam. 4⁵, ⁶, 2 Chron. 15¹⁴, Ps. 47⁵), uttered by *the people* of Israel who were skilled by long experience in his worship. The *horn* is symbolic of strength (cp. Ps. 75⁵).

(b)

3, 4, 19-37. Yahweh's covenant with David, whose royal house is to endure for ever. With *vv.* 3, 4, cp. 2 Sam. 7¹⁶.

19-28. These verses deal with God's mercies to David personally, and are based on the records preserved in the books of *Samuel*. *At that time* refers to the time when the divine message was received by the prophet Nathan to announce to David (see 2 Sam. 7⁴ ᶠᶠ·) the permanency of his dynasty ; thy *sanctified one* is Nathan. *For one chosen*, cp. 2 Sam. 7⁸. *With my holy oil . . .*, David's anointing is mentioned in 1 Sam. 16¹³, and he is called " the anointed of Yahweh " in 2 Sam.

19²¹ ⁽²²⁾. With 22–25 cp. 2 Sam. 7⁹ ᶠᶠ·. *My father art thou* recalls
2 Sam. 7¹⁴: " I will be his father, and he shall be my son."

29–37. In these *vv.* it is the seed of David which is spoken of.
The psalmist contemplates the unfaithfulness of the later kings of the
Davidic line, and the punishment which followed; yet God's love
looked in mercy upon them, and his covenant with David held good.
Until the time appointed, his throne stood sure.

(c)

38–51. The great contrast between this and the preceding section
justifies the contention that we have here a composition belonging to a
different period. The nation is in a pitiable state; God seems to have
been on the side of its enemies, for his wrath against his people has been
justly aroused. The piece falls into two parts:

38–45. The covenant so firmly maintained by Yahweh through
all the history of the Judahite monarchy has now been repudiated; the
nation is as a flock of sheep, the *walls* of whose fold, as the Hebrew
word used here for *wall* implies, have been broken down; this, as the
second part of 40 shows, is a figure for the cities of Judah. The
interplay between metaphor and reality continues in 41, where the
people, now without defence, are exposed to the *plundering* and *scorn*
of every *passer-by*. We may suppose that the historical reference is
to the inroads of the *neighbours* of Judah, especially the Edomites,
during the last days of the kingdom of Judah (2 Kings 24²), and to
the Exile (cp. Ps. 137⁷, Lam. 1²¹, 4²¹, ²², Obad. 10). Against these
gloating invaders Judah is helpless; her fighting power has gone with
the shattered *sceptre* and dismantled *throne* of a king whose youth is
spent too soon, and which gives place to premature age (see the
introductory section).

46–51. The psalmist turns from description to petition, and,
putting his words into the king's mouth, pleads that the *fire* of Yahweh's
wrath may be quenched. He appeals to Yahweh's work in the creation
of man, to his power to save from death, to the historic benefits which
he has conferred on the house of David; if these are not all to be futile,
then surely Yahweh will intervene to rescue his *servant* from the
reproaches of those who are as much the enemies of God as of his
anointed.

Religious Teaching

As an act of congregational praise this psalm is one of the most
striking in the Psalter; its component parts have been skilfully and
appropriately joined together for the purpose of liturgical worship.
The teaching it conveys is of profound and permanent importance.
This can be set forth under two heads:

The use made of ancient and non-Israelite material is not to be accounted for mèrely as a matter of antiquarian interest to the psalmist ; it is, in effect, an illustration of the prophet's words : " Art thou not from everlasting Yahweh, my holy God ! " (Hab. 1¹²). The psalmist accepts the old Babylonian and pre-exilic Israelite myth as a groping in darkness after truth. Similarly, with regard to the old-world idea of the great " parliament of the gods " assembled in the heavens. Just as among the Babylonians Marduk stood out as a champion among the gods, so to the psalmist Yahweh stood supreme among the denizens of heaven. The fact that later Israelite teachers could thus adapt primitive, inadequate, and erroneous ideas, illustrates the truth that God, who is from everlasting, reveals himself to men in every age in accordance with their capacity for apprehension ; he has never left himself without witness (cp. Acts 14¹⁷).

The other great truth which the psalm teaches is that there is an intimate relationship between the destiny of the nation and the divine purpose concerning it. God, all-powerful in heaven and earth, ordained the kingship for his people as a means of social well-being among them, and chose the Davidic line. But the divine plan was thwarted by the sinful will of men, as the psalmist seems to be beginning to realize, though he did not see the final end of the monarchy which was near at hand. Thus, again under prophetic influence, the psalm teaches that God is the God of history ; and though men, being free agents by God's will, blight his purposes, yet in his mercy he overrules their folly. Ultimately the theocratic form of government made the nation better than it had ever been before. Though the psalmist did not see this signal illustration of his teaching, yet he fully recognized the truth of God's guiding hand in history.

PSALM 90

IN this poem we have one of the best-known pieces in the Psalter. It is classed by Gunkel as a hymn, but, though it begins with an ascription of praise and an expression of confidence, the more fitting title is that provided by the traditional heading, *A Prayer*. It is essentially a prayer, a *cri du cœur* which has never failed to make its appeal to the heart of its readers. It may even be regarded as a dirge over the futility of all human effort and the evanescence of all human achievement, and may be compared with the lament which Æschylus puts into the mouth of Cassandra :

> " Ah for the fate of man ! if prosperous
> 'Tis but a sketch, and if misfortune come,
> The wet sponge with its touch blots out the lines."
> (*Ag.* 1327–1329.)

But the Hebrew poet, even more than the Greek, has an intense conviction of a personal God, who, however far he may be removed from the frailty of man's brief life, is yet open to an appeal, and can, if he will, secure to his creatures a durability like his own.   It is to be noted that there is no thought of immortality, and it is only the belief in a continuity of personal existence after death that has given man the assurance for which the psalmist so passionately longs.

The poem was ascribed by tradition to Moses.   The reflective type of mind here exhibited, however, suggests a later rather than an earlier date.   The author was possibly familiar with the book of *Job*, and knew the story of Paradise much as we now have it in Gen. 3¹. He may also have been acquainted with the creation narrative as given in Gen. 1⁹, though it is possible that the reference in *v.* 2 is to an old myth on which the narrative of Paradise was ultimately based.   In the complete absence of any reference to historical events—there were many periods in Jewish history in which an individual or the whole people might endure hardship—we may assign it to the same age in spiritual development as that to which the book of *Job* belongs.

The text seems to have suffered in course of transmission, though not as badly as some commentators have supposed. This in itself suggests that the psalm was a favourite, which was frequently copied and re-copied.   Occasionally the Septuagint offers a better text, but its rendering of this psalm presents some curious features.

The metre is 3 : 3 throughout, with 3 : 3 : 3 in *v.* 2.

A Prayer.   Of Moses, the Man of God.

1. O Lord !
   A dwelling hast thou been — for us in all generations.
2. Ere the mountains were born,
      ere the earth had travailed, and the world,
          ° from everlasting ° to everlasting thou art God.
3. Thou bringest man back to destruction, — and sayest, " Return, sons of men ".
4. ° For a thousand years in thy sight — are as a passing yesterday, ° and a watch.

   ° In the night 5. thou checkest their sleep ° ; — in the morning they become as ° grass °.
6. At morn it doth blossom and burgeon, — at eve doth it droop and wither.
7. ° So ° perish we in thine anger, — and in thy wrath are we confounded.
8. Thou hast set our iniquities before thee, — our secret sins in the light of thy face.
9. For all our days have declined in thy fury, — our years ° are ended ° as a sigh.
10. The days of our years °   ° are seventy years, — or through strength eighty years ;
    Yet their pride is pain and sorrow, — for it is cut off swiftly, and we have flown.

11. Who knoweth the power of thine anger ? — ° and who feareth the stroke ° of thy fury ?
12. To number our days so ° teach us °, — ° that we may let wisdom enter our heart °.
13. Back, O Yahweh ! How long ! — and repent concerning thy servants.
14. Satisfy us at morn with thy love, — that we may exult and be glad all our days.

15. Gladden us as the days when thou
    afflictedst us,   the years when we saw evil.
16. Let thy working appear to thy servants,   and thy splendour upon their sons;
17. And let the loveliness of the Lord
    ° ° be upon us,   and the work of our hands ° establish °.

Text-critical Notes

2. Om. " and ". 4-5. Read בְּלַיְלָה זָרְמְתָּ שְׁנָתָם : אַשְׁמוּרָה for " a watch
in the night. Thou floodest them away (?) in sleep ". 5. Om. " that passeth away ".
7. Read, with Cheyne, לֹא for " for ". 9. Read, with S, כָּלוּ for " we bring
to an end ". 10. Om., with Baethgen, " in them ". 11. Read, with Gunkel,
וּמִי־יָרֵא חֵן for " and according to thy fear ". 12. Read, with Budde, הוֹדִיעֵנוּ
for " teach ". Read, with Kautsch–Bertholet, בְּלֵב חָכְמָה for " a heart of wisdom ".
17. Om., with 2 Heb. MSS, " our God ". Om. (cf. Baethgen), " upon us, yea, the
work of our hands establish thou it " (doublet).

Is life worth living ? For the individual it is one long struggle
against forces which threaten its destruction, and the wrestler, impelled
by the physical instinct of self-preservation, battles on, with the certain
knowledge that, sooner or later, the powers of decay will triumph. In
the meantime we must face the universal experience of pain—pain of
body, mind and soul—the sense of frustration and of ineptitude. For
most men there are pleasures, joys, comforts, even happiness, which in
greater or less degree serve to counterbalance the load of suffering, but
there are cases—we think inevitably of Ps. 88 and its writer—which
seem to offer no alleviation.

What is the purpose of it all ? We may answer, in altruistic mood,
that the aim of all true human striving, often unconsciously pursued,
is the preservation and betterment of the race. Our conflict and our
failure, our spent strength and limited achievement, may win a happier,
more comfortable life for those who are to follow us in ages yet to come.
But we know only too well that mankind, as a physical species, is doomed
as surely as the individual. Countless æons may still come and go
before the end is reached, but it is certain that, at long last, all life
must vanish from this planet, and our earth, with all that it bears, be
left an atom of dust in a vast whirling universe of senseless matter.
Physical life, in its human as in its other forms, is but a temporary
incident in the story of a world of death.

At first sight it would seem that the tragedy of life is but enhanced
by an instinct which, as far as we know, is not only peculiar to man,
but is confined to the higher developments of his spirit. There is a
natural demand for that which will survive, the poet's " monument
more durable than bronze ". In the last resort we can never be
satisfied with the temporary and the evanescent. Eternity is set in our
hearts, and the eternal alone can meet our needs. It is not infinity,
but finitude that is inconceivable (since every limit implies a beyond),
and the deepest, most passionate yearning of the human soul is to be
and to do something that will outlast time itself.

DD

In Ps. 90 we have the reflection of a mood in which such inevitable facts as these are faced. It opens with a brief ascription of praise (*vv.* 1–2), which is not mere theology, but the product of experience. Man has, *in all generations*, found in God a *dwelling*; he has made his home in the eternal. (Gunkel is surely right in preferring this, the reading of the Hebrew text, to the easier, but more superficial word " fortress " handed down through the tradition of the ancient Egyptian Jews.) God is older than time, older than the world, and the poet's thought goes back to the mythology dimly reflected in Gen. 1[12], according to which the earth herself was the mother of all that lives upon her breast.

But at once the thought of human evanescence rises up against that of divine eternity; the poet feels instantly the contrast between the deathless God and his perishing creatures. He *brings man back to destruction*, crushing him to powder, and bids him *return* to that dust from which he was taken (cf. Gen. 3[19]). Again God and man stand opposed. The one is above all time, for to him all time is one, and *a thousand years are as a passing yesterday*, or a single four-hour *watch*. Very different is the fate he imposes on men. Even by *night*, when rest might be sought in *sleep*, God intervenes. The psalmist uses a rare and obscure Hebrew word, whose meaning is best understood by reference to an Arabic root indicating the *checking* or stoppage of certain bodily functions or of the flow of speech. The " flow " of sleep, smooth and peaceful, is interrupted, so that when *morning* comes, man has no more strength or vitality than the *grass* (*vv.* 4–5). The metaphor thus introduced is carried further; the herb that *blossoms* in the morning and goes on to reach its full development (for which the psalmist uses a term which also suggests " passing away "), languishes and *withers* by night (*v.* 6). Thus do men pass away, and the only explanation the psalmist can find is the *anger* of God, through which men are *confounded* (*v.* 7). The ground for that *anger* is human *iniquity*—once more a contrast, this time between the purity of God and the foulness of man. We may seek to gloss over or to conceal the wrong that lies within us, but the very *face* of God is a *light*, a piercing sun, which reveals the blackest and most *secret* depths of the soul (*v.* 8).

The reason why the psalmist knows that God has taken his sins into account is that punishment has come. Death is the penalty for sin (again an implicit reference to the Paradise story of Gen. 3), and man's days *decline*, turning towards their evening, with such speed that there is time but for a single gasp, *a sigh* (*v.* 9). True, *seventy* or *eighty years*, as men count years, may be the allotted span, but the best of them, their peak and *pride*, is painful toil and empty *sorrow*, and the psalmist emphasizes the *swiftness* with which life is *cut off* by the use of two sharp, sibilant, monosyllabic verbs (*v.* 10).

Wistfully the poet turns back to God. If only men *knew the power of* God's *anger*, or *feared the stroke of* his *fury*, they might so live as to avoid at least excess of pain, even if death were still inevitable (*v.* 11). Therefore he prays for *teaching* and *wisdom* (*v.* 12), for that forgiveness which looks as if God *repented*. It is *love*, *ḥesed*, for which the spirit longs (*v.* 14). Much may yet be retrieved from the ruin of life, and the balance of suffering may be redressed, if Yahweh will but *gladden* his *servants*, and give them happiness equal in content and in duration to the misery that they have endured (*v.* 15). This will be God's true *working*, and the sign that he is active. But, above all, the psalmist pleads for something that will endure. If he and his contemporaries must pass away, at least let their *work* abide. Two millennia and more have passed since the poet wrote these words, and hitherto his closing prayer has been fulfilled. *The loveliness of the Lord* has been upon him, and the *work of his hands* has been *established*, for his prayer is still to-day among the best-known of all the outpourings of man's spirit.

Religious Teaching

We cannot but be inspired by the psalmist's clear facing of the facts of life and death, and by his refusal to abandon his faith. God is still his dwelling-place and final hope, and, even if he does not see how all his problems are to be solved, he still trusts in the Lord, who has the solution to give. He is prepared to recognize that man is, at least in part, responsible for his fate, but his belief in Yahweh includes the confidence that this eternal God can and will forgive. But once more, as so often in reading the Old Testament, we realize that the most devout and sincere thought in Israel can be satisfied only with a doctrine of spiritual immortality.

PSALM 91

THIS psalm is a polemic, in devotional form, against the means employed to counteract the assaults of demons. The belief in demons and their activity was shared by the psalmist in common with that universally held in his day; this is amply illustrated in the psalm itself, as the commentary will show. Where he differed from the bulk of his contemporaries was in the methods adopted to ward off demoniacal attacks. Not in formulas or by magic acts and enchantments, nor yet by the help of wizards and witches, was the malevolent activity of demons to be met, but only by placing oneself under the protection of Yahweh. This is the purpose and content of the psalm.

In Rabbinical literature the psalm is called " A song for evil en-counters " (Bab. Talmud, *Shebuoth* 15*b*), and its use is recommended for the purpose of averting the attacks of demons.

The date of the psalm must, on account of the developed demonology among the Jews, be late, and may be assigned to the Greek period. The metre is, with the exception of *vv.* 1, 15, uniformly 3 : 3.

1. ° Blessed is he °that abideth under the shelter of the Most High, that lodgeth under the shadow of Shaddai,

2. ° That saith ° to Yahweh : " My refuge, my fortress, my God, whom I trust ".

3. For he delivereth thee from the net, ° he preserveth thee ° from the destructive word ° ;

4. With his pinion he covereth thee, and under his wings thou findest refuge ° ;

5. Thou wilt not fear the terror at night, And the arrow that flieth by day,

6. The pestilence that roameth in darkness, or Qeteb that destroyeth at noon.

7. A thousand shall fall beside thee, To thee it shall not come nigh, and ten thousand at thy right-hand, ° a shield and buckler is his truth ° ;

8. ° (Only with thine eyes shalt thou behold, and shalt see the recompense of the wicked.) °

9. For, as for thee, Yahweh is ° thy refuge °, thou hast made the Most High ° thy stronghold ° ;

10. No evil shall befall thee, nor plague come nigh to thy tent ;

11. For his angels he will give charge over thee, to keep thee in all thy ways ;

12. Upon their hands they will bear thee, lest thou strike thy foot against a stone.

13. On lion and adder shalt thou tread. shalt trample on young-lion and dragon.

14. " For on me he hath set-his-love, so will I deliver him, I will exalt him, for he knoweth my name.

15. He calleth me, and I will answer him, Will be with him in trouble, Will deliver him and honour him ;

16. I will satisfy him with length of days, and cause him to see my salvation."

Text-critical Notes

1. Insert אַשְׁרֵי ; as the Hebrew stands the syntax causes difficulty. 2. Read אֹמַר for אֹמֵר " I will say ". 3. Read יְשָׁמְרֶךָ for יָקוּשׁ " a fowler ". Read, with GS, דֶּבֶר for דְּבֵר " pestilence ". 4. Place צִנָּה וְסֹחֵרָה אֲמִתּוֹ " a shield and buckler is his truth ", at the end of *v.* 7. 8. Om. this *v.* as being out of harmony with the context. 9. Read מַחְסִי for מַחְסֶךָ " my refuge ". Read, with G, מְעוֹנְךָ for מְעוֹנֶךָ " thy habitation ".

1. *1.4* The key-note of the psalm is struck in these opening words ; all the onslaughts of demons, referred to in the body of the psalm, will be averted if trust is placed in God. There is special significance in the use of the word *abideth*, which means, strictly speaking, " to pass the night " (see Gen. 19[2], Judges 19[13], 2 Sam. 17[16]) ; for it was especially at night-time that the demons' power was supposed to be greatest, and consequently their activity most pronounced. Hence it *1/2* is especially at night-time that *the shelter of the Most High* must be sought for protection against demons. Parallel with this is the shadow *1/2* of *Shaddai*, *ṣēl* (" shadow ") coming from the root meaning " to be dark ". It is probable that the use of the name *Shaddai* (" the Almighty ") for God here is intended to express the antithesis to *šēd*, " demon " ; this word occurs, it is true, only in Deut. 32[17] ; Ps. 106[37] ; in Jewish demonology, which was already fully developed in pre-

Christian times, one of the main categories into which demons were divided was that of the *šēdîm*, whose leader was Asmodæus, mentioned in Tob. 3[8, 17] (*circa* 200 B.C.). On the other hand, one of the most prominent figures of the Babylonian spirit-world was *šēdû*, a kind of guardian-deity, usually in the form of *Lamassu* or bull-colossus.

In 2 the psalmist puts words into the mouth of him whose trust is in Yahweh, a contrast being intended between this attitude and that of those who employed the popular methods to ward off demoniacal attacks.

In 3–7 six kinds of such attacks are mentioned : *For he delivereth thee from the net* ; emphasis is laid on *he*,—that is, Yahweh. The word for *net* (*paḥ*) is very rarely used in a literal sense, but frequently in reference to the plots and evil machinations of men ; but in these verses there is nothing to show that the evils from which Yahweh gives protection have anything to do with the works of evil-disposed men ; so that the mention of " the fowler " is out of place, and may well have been introduced by a copyist influenced by Ps. 124[7], Hos. 9[8]. In view of the quite obvious reference to demons in the rest of these verses, there is justification for holding that the *net* here refers to the entanglement caused by a demon, or, more probably, as a parallel to the second half of the verse, to a demon incarnated in a witch. The ancient Arabs held that witches were the incarnations of demons ; similarly the Babylonians taught that, like demons, witches took up their abode in forsaken sites ; when a witch " spies " her victim, it is said, she " follows him ", " entangles his feet in her net " and " drags him to the ground ". The *destructive word* (see crit. note) refers to the spell, used by witches, which forced demons to do an injury, to cause sickness, or even to encompass the death of a person. These evils, the psalmist teaches, can be counteracted only by placing oneself under the protecting care of Yahweh : *With his pinion he covereth thee, and under his wings thou findest refuge.* Possibly there is a covert contrast intended here between the protecting wings of Yahweh, and those which some kinds of demons were supposed to possess ; the demons used their wings to fly swiftly on their harmful errands ; but under Yahweh's wings the terror-stricken are safe. In the *Midrash* on the *Psalms* it is taught that " there is a harmful spirit that flies like a bird, and shoots like an arrow " ; the reference is evidently to Lilith (Isa. 34[14]), the Night-hag, who, according to traditional Jewish belief, got her name from *lāyĕlāh*, or *layîl*, " night " ; the etymology was false (she was a Babylonian demon), but that does not affect the belief that Lilith was the night-demon *par excellence.* According to Jewish tradition, too, the meteor-stone was known as " the arrow of Lilith ". It is in the light of these beliefs, taken over from the Babylonians, that *the terror at night* and *the arrow that flieth by day* must be explained.

In connexion with *the pestilence that roameth in darkness*, reference must be made to the Babylonian pest-demon Namtar; in a Babylonian text it is said : " Wicked Namtar . . . who plagues a man like the pestilence, who has no hands, no feet, who goes about at night . . . " [1]; this is strongly reminiscent of the psalmist's words. Then, with regard to *Qeteb that destroyeth at noon*, it must be remarked, first, that the word, *Qeteb*, usually translated " destruction ", occurs elsewhere only in Deut. 32^{24}, Isa. 28^2, Hos. 13^{14}; in each case there are reasons for believing that the reference is to a demon. In the verse before us the Septuagint and Aquila both expressly make mention of a demon. In Rabbinical literature the verse is understood in this sense (*e.g.*, Bab. Talm. *Pesahim* 111 *b*), and *Qeteb* is there used as the proper name of a demon. In the *Midrash* on the *Psalms* part of the comment on this verse runs, in reference to *Qeteb*: " Our Rabbis said, It is a demon (*šēd*) . . . The poisonous *Qeteb* was covered with scales and with hair, and sees out of only one eye, the other is in the middle of his heart ; and he is powerful . . . and stalks about from the fourth to the ninth hour (*i.e.*, 10 a.m. to 3 p.m.) from the 17th of Tammuz to the 9th of Ab (*i.e.*, July and August) ; and everyone who sees him falls down on his face ". These are traditional ideas, handed down for centuries.

The belief in innumerable hosts of demons goes back to a hoary antiquity ; it is reflected in the Midrashic comment on this verse : " If a thousand evil spirits assemble at thy left hand they . . . and if ten thousand assemble at thy right hand they will fall . . . " It is the angels who overcome them, cp. *v.* 11. It will be seen that the words at the end of *v.* 4, *A shield and buckler is his truth*, come more appropriately here.

8–13. Following upon *v.* 7, the words of *v.* 9 come logically : *For, as for thee, Yahweh is thy refuge* ; it is probable, therefore, that *v.* 8 is a marginal gloss which has found its way into the text. The theme of Yahweh's protection from demons is then continued. The ancient belief that before any dwelling-place is entered into, demons must be placated, occurs in the words : *Neither shall any plague come nigh thy tent.* To *angels*, acting according to the divine behest, we have already referred, cp. Ps. 34^7, Tobit 6^{1a}. On the quotation of *vv.* 11, 12 in Matt. 4^6, Lk. $4^{10, 11}$, see Intro., Vol. I, p. 95.

According to ancient Semitic belief, a relationship existed between certain animals and demons, who appeared in the wilderness in the form of wild beasts ; the closest connexion was held to be between demons and serpents ; *jinn* and *ghūl* are synonymous with " serpent " in Arabic ; hence the significance of : *On lion and adder shalt thou tread, shalt trample on young-lion and dragon.*

14–16. With words put into the mouth of Yahweh, the psalmist

---

[1] Quoted in full by O. Weber, *Dämonenbeschwörung* . . . in *Der alte Orient*, vii, p. 16 (1906).

concludes with the thought of the beginning of the psalm, namely the blessedness of him who *hath set his love on* Yahweh.

Religious Teaching

Of this it is unnecessary to say more than that trust in God avails to overcome every evil. This is illustrated in the psalm by references to various kinds of evil spirits, because belief in their activity was intensely prevalent in bygone days ; demoniacal onslaughts are rendered harmless when the protection of Yahweh is sought.

PSALM 92

THE age-long problem of the prosperity of the wicked and the adversity of the righteous is, in this psalm, solved, according to the psalmist. He tells of his own experience ; he himself is a living illustration of a godly man prospering ; it may go well with the wicked, but that is merely temporary ; as the enemies of God destruction will come upon them soon enough. The psalm may be described as a summary of Ps. 37, see also Ps. 73. To be sure, this was no real solution of the problem, for many righteous suffer, and many wicked are permanently prosperous through life ; but the psalmist gives his own experience, and that sufficed for him.

The title of the psalm designates it as one for the Sabbath, so, too, in the Septuagint, but there is nothing in it which makes it specially appropriate for this day ; it has, however, together with Ps. 93, been one of the proper Sabbath psalms in the Jewish Church from time immemorial.

The metre is 3 : 3, excepting in *v.* 9 which is 3 : 3 : 3.

A Psalm. A Song for the Sabbath-day.

1 (2). Good it is to give thanks to Yahweh, and to sing praise to thy name, O Most High,

2 (3). To tell of thy lovingkindness in the morning, and of thy faithfulness in the nights,

3 (4). With a ten-stringed ° harp, with soft playing on the lyre.

4 (5). For thou hast made me glad ° through thy doings °, I shout for joy because of the works of thy hands.

5 (6). How great are thy works, Yahweh, thy thoughts are very deep !

6 (7). A brutish man knoweth this not, and a fool doth not understand it.

7 (8). When the wicked sprout like grass, and all the workers of iniquity flourish,

8 (9). It is ° only ° that they will be destroyed for ever ; but thou art on high for evermore °.

9 (10). For, lo, thine enemies, Yahweh, for, lo, thine enemies shall perish, All the workers of iniquity shall be scattered ;

10 (11). But thou hast exalted my horn like a wild-ox, ° thou hast poured out upon me ° fresh oil.

11 (12). Mine eye gloateth over ° them that watch for me °, mine ears hear concerning them that rise up against me.

12 (13). The righteous flourisheth like a palm-tree, he groweth like a cedar in Lebanon ;

13 (14). They are planted in the house of
    Yahweh,   they flourish in the courts of our God;
14 (15). Even in old age do they bear fruit,   they are full of sap, and green,
15 16). ° Showing ° that Yahweh is   my Rock is he, in him is no unrighteous-
    righteous,   ness.

Text-critical Notes

3. Om. with G, וְעָלֵי " and upon ". **4.** Om. יהוה for the rhythm's sake.
Read, with many MSS. and S, בְּפָעֳלֶיךָ for לְךָ — " thy doing ". **8.** Add אַךְ,
for the construction see Ps. 37⁸ Prov. 11²⁴, etc. Om. יהוה for the rhythm's sake.
10. Read, with ST, בַּלֹּתִי for בַּלֹּתִי, " I am anointed ". **11.** Read, with the
Versions, בְּשׁוּרְרָי for בְּשׁוּרָי; cf. Ps. 56²⁽³⁾ 59¹⁰ ⁽¹¹⁾ . Read עָלַי קָמַי (for this
use of עָלַי see, e.g., Ps. 32⁶) for בַּקָּמִים, " against them that rise up "; and omit
מְרֵעִים, " evil-doers ", which overloads the half-line. **15.** Lit. " to declare ".

1-4. Most fittingly the psalmist begins his psalm with thanksgiving
and praise, for he has been the recipient of many blessings ; both *in
the morning* and at *nights* does he *tell of the lovingkindness* which God
has shown him. Though not actually mentioned, the reference to the
temple later in the psalm (*v.* 13), makes it certain that *in the morning*
and at *nights* implies the times of offering sacrifice, see Exod. 29³⁹, ⁴¹,
Num. 28⁴, so that in what follows we get some insight into the ritual
which accompanied the sacrificial service. That prayer was offered
during the offering of sacrifices we know ; here we learn that the song
of praise accompanied these offerings, and what the psalmist says is
full of interest. The words of praise and thanksgiving, by which, of
course, psalms are meant, were sung to the accompaniment of the *ten-
stringed harp* (Ps. 33², 144⁹), the large stringed instrument which rested
on the ground, while the smaller harp, or *lyre*, was carried in procession
(see, further, the notes on Ps. 150) ; the expression used in connexion
with the latter, which we have rendered *soft playing*, comes from the
root meaning " to moan ", " murmur ", and also " to muse " or
" meditate " ; it therefore implies subdued playing. Thus, the
accompaniment of stringed instruments to the singing of psalms varied
so as to be in harmony with the nature of the words sung. In these
opening words, then, the psalmist tells of his daily praise to God in
gratitude for the benefits which he has received. His temporal well-
being and enjoyment of life are joyfully acknowledged as due to Yahweh's
doings, and *the works of* his *hands*. 5. From this the psalmist turns to
speak of other divine *works*, the outcome of his *thoughts* that *are very deep*.
6. Of these the man with merely animal instincts, the *brutish man* (cp.
Pss. 49¹⁰, 94⁸) can know nothing ; they are not understood by *a fool*—
i.e., one who is stupid, dull of understanding. Of these *works* and
thoughts the psalmist then speaks; and he proceeds (7, 8) to set forth what
is to him the solution of the problem of the prosperity of the wicked, which
had seemed to so many to be not in accordance with divine justice. The
comparison of *the wicked* with *grass* points to the nature of his solution :

for a brief space the grass sprouts and flourishes ; but how soon it fades (cp. Isa. 40[7, 8]) ! Thus it is with the wicked ; to those who, like the psalmist, look beyond the immediate present, the prosperity of the wicked is merely the prelude to their everlasting destruction ; and then, with bated breath, as it were, the psalmist adds the tremendous contrast : *but thou art on high for evermore.* It must be recognized that here the psalmist, like the writer of the book of *Job,* was on the very verge of being forced into a fuller belief regarding the conditions of life after death ; he speaks of the everlasting destruction of the wicked ; but he says nothing about the righteous in the Hereafter, those who are faithful to Yahweh who is *on high for evermore* ; the reason of this is that our psalmist was still held down by the traditional belief that " in death there is no remembrance of thee, in Sheol who can give thanks unto thee ? " (Ps. 6[5]) ; he had not yet reached the sublime belief of the writer of Ps. 73[23–25] ; but he was not far from it. The logic of religious belief should have led him, as one faithful to God *on high for evermore,* to the conviction that death could not break that relationship ; but to that he had not yet attained. His thoughts were concentrated on this world. He goes on, therefore (9, 10) to contrast the lot of the *enemies* of Yahweh, who *shall perish* and *be scattered,* with that which he enjoys : *But thou hast exalted my horn like a wild-ox*—i.e., like the horn of a wild-ox. The picture expresses consciousness of strength ; and, *thou hast poured out upon me fresh oil,* indicating gladness (cp. Ps. 45[7]). With pardonable exultation the psalmist adds (11) *Mine eye gloateth over them that watch for me,* for he had heard the envious words of *them that* had *risen up against him*—i.e., his enemies. Then (12–15) he describes further, in poetical language, the happy lot of the man—he is doubtless thinking of himself—whose godly life has brought him happiness : *the righteous flourisheth like a palm-tree,* a symbol of prosperity, its graceful form is referred to in *Song of Songs* 7[7] ; *he groweth like a cedar of Lebanon* ; another picture of stateliness (cp. Ps. 80[10]). This enviable state of the righteous, he goes on to explain, is because *they are planted in the house of Yahweh*—i.e., from earliest days they have been constantly present in the temple ; hence, *they flourish in the courts of our God*—i.e., they rejoice in being within the temple precincts. It need hardly be said that trees did not grow within the temple area, as has sometimes been *naïvely* supposed, the words are purely figurative, as in Ps. 52[8] ; the metaphor is continued in 14, like an aged, but healthy tree, so do the righteous *even in old age bear fruit, they are full of sap* (lit. " fat "), *and green* ; a living proof *that Yahweh is righteous,* always to be relied upon like an impregnable *Rock* (cp. Ps. 31[2], 62[7], 71[3]) ; in him is no unrighteousness.

Religious Teaching

Apart from the problem of divine retribution which the psalmist believes himself to have solved, and to which we have made reference elsewhere, this psalm sets forth very beautifully the truth that temporal benefits are the gifts of God, and that gratitude for these must be expressed in praise to the Almighty. It is not too much to say that these things are but too often taken for granted, or ascribed to personal prowess and industry; of course these have their part to play, the divine gift of free-will is accorded to every man; but it must not be forgotten that all things are in the hand of God. This psalm should be read in the light of the words of the General Thanksgiving in the Prayer Book : " We bless thee for our creation, preservation, and all the blessings of this life."

PSALM 93

THIS is the first of a group of eschatological psalms (93, 96–99) sung at the ceremony of Yahweh's Enthronement (Ps. 47 also belongs to the group) ; the phrase " Yahweh is become King " makes this clear. The subject is dealt with in Vol. I, pp. 48 ff., and need not be further enlarged upon here. The psalm concentrates on only one element in the great Eschatological Drama, and that in not more than a summary manner— namely, the victory of Yahweh over his enemies. This is described pictorially by the reference to the myth of the primeval combat when Yahweh overcame the evil powers symbolized by the waters of the Great Deep. For the interpretation of the psalm in an eschatological sense, see Vol. I, pp. 51 f.

The form in which the psalm is constructed is unique ; four short lines with two beats are followed in the rest of the psalm by single lines with three beats.

On the date of the " Enthronement " psalms, see Vol. I, pp. 44 ff.

1.
Yahweh is become King,
Apparelled in majesty,
Apparelled is Yahweh,
Girded with strength.
Yea, ° he hath established ° the world, it shall not be moved ;

2.
Established is his throne from of old,
From everlasting art thou, ° Yahweh °.

3.
The floods rose up, Yahweh,
The floods raised up their roar,
The floods ° raised up ° their crashing.

4.
More (glorious) than the roar of many waters,
° More glorious than the raging of the sea °,
Is Yahweh, glorious on high.

5.
Thy testimonies are very sure,
Holiness becometh thine house,
Yahweh, for evermore.

Text-critical Notes

1. Read, with the Versions, תִּכֵּן cf. 75³⁽⁴⁾ for תִּכּוֹן " is established ". 2. Add יהיה as demanded by the rhythm. 3. Read, as in the other lines, נָשְׂאוּ, lit. " were lifted up ", for יִשְׂאוּ. " they lifted up ". 4. Read אַדִּיר מִמִּשְׁבְּרֵי־יָם for אַדִּירִים מִשְׁבְּרֵי־יָם, " glorious are the breakers of the sea ".

1. For the phrase *Yahweh is become King*, and all that it involves, see Vol. I, pp. 46 f. The ancient myth of the starry heavens being the mantle of the mighty ruler above is here adapted and spiritualized, and Yahweh is thought of as *apparelled in majesty*, and *girded with strength*. In illustration of his majesty and strength, the psalmist points to *the world* which he set up, or *established*, in such a way that it cannot *be moved* ; but the main thought lying behind the psalmist's mind is that it was established in the very far distant past ; its age, therefore, witnessing to the eternity of Yahweh. This is brought out in what follows (2) : *Established* (the same word as that used in reference to the world) *is his throne from of old* ; its foundation is mentioned in 97². That Yahweh has a throne in heaven is an idea borrowed from an extraneous source, and is connected, of course, with his Kingship ; this has been dealt with in Vol. I, pp. 44 ff. But the world and the throne are as nothing in age compared with Yahweh, for he is *from everlasting*. 3, 4. One of the themes commemorated at the celebration of Yahweh's Enthronement is then briefly referred to, *the floods rose up* . . ., in reference to the primeval combat dealt with in the Babylonian Creation Epic (see above). Awe-inspiring as was the rush and *roar of many waters* and *the raging of the sea*, infinitely greater is *Yahweh, glorious on high*.

5. In sudden contrast to the tremendous scene just depicted, the psalmist transports his thoughts into calm waters ; leaving the distant past, he thinks of the present, and of the attributes of Yahweh as now revealed : faithfulness and holiness. It can hardly be doubted that the psalmist intends here to place on record the difference between his conception of Yahweh and that presented in the ancient myth, or, rather, in its adaptation, by the prophets. If we are correct in this, it points to a decreasing importance attached to the old-world myths, and, in consequence, to a corresponding decrease in the need of commemorating them. In other words, the time was drawing near when the celebration of Yahweh's Enthronement was to be a thing of the past.

For the religious teaching of this psalm and others dealing with the same subject, see Vol. I, p. 81.

PSALM 94

To regard this psalm as originally two distinct psalms—so, *e.g.*, Hans
Schmidt—is quite unnecessary, and betrays a misunderstanding of the
psalmist's mentality. The psalm witnesses to the presence among his
people of men who are guilty not only of the most violent cruelty, but
also of blasphemy against the God of their fathers. That they were
Jews, and not aliens, to whom reference is made, is clear from their
attitude towards, and the way in which they speak of, Yahweh; heathen
oppressors would not be concerned with reviling the God of Israel
in the way here described; he would simply not come into their
consideration. These Jews were members of the higher grades of
society, since they were in a position to oppress their less fortunate
fellow-creatures; the epithet "proud", applied to them, and their
arrogance, point in the same direction. The psalmist stands forth as the
champion of the poor and oppressed, as did the prophets (cp. Isa. 1[23],
Jer. 22[3], Ezek. 22[7], Zech. 7[10], Mal. 3[5]); like them, he does so with
boldness, knowing that God is with him. The social conditions
reflected in the psalm might point to various periods; but the mention
of renegade Jews suggests that it belongs to the Greek period. Some
commentators assign it to the Maccabæan age, but quite wrongly, for
they do not sufficiently take into consideration the conditions of those
times; the ruling powers were the Maccabæan leaders, loyal and God-
fearing men, beloved of the people. Renegade Jews, to be sure, were
in evidence, but they exercised no power, and were opposed by those in
authority. Moreover, *vv.* 16–23 would be quite inappropriate at that
time.

The metre is predominantly 3 : 3; but *vv.* 9–12 have two beats to
the half-line; the change of metre, coinciding with a difference in
subject-matter, is evidently intended to express special emphasis, and
is very effective, above all when sung; for it can hardly be doubted that
at the singing of these short periods the musical accompaniment underwent change.

1. A God of vengeance is Yahweh; O God of vengeance, ° shine forth °!
2. Lift up thyself, O Judge of the earth, render to the proud their desert.
3. How long shall the wicked, Yahweh, how long shall the wicked exult?
4. They brag, they speak arrogantly, they boast themselves, all the workers of iniquity;

5. They crush down thy people, Yahweh, and thine inheritance they afflict;
6. Widow ° and orphan ° do they slay, and murder ᶜ the stranger and the down-trodden °;

7. And they said: " Yah seeth it not, the God of Jacob observeth it not."
8. Be understanding, ye brutish ones among the people, yea, ye foolish ones, when will ye exercise wisdom?
9. He that planted the ear,
    doth he not hear?
    He that formed the eye,
    doth he not see?

10. He that instructeth the peoples,
doth he not chastise ?
He that teacheth men,
° should he not have knowledge ? °
11. Yahweh knoweth
the thoughts of man,
that they are ° vain °.
12. Blessed is the man
whom thou instructest, Yah,
and teachest from thy law,
13. That he may have respite from evil days,   till the pit be digged for the wicked,
14. That Yahweh cast not off his people,   nor forsake his inheritance,
15. ° That the righteous may come to his   ° and his latter end (be) like the upright
     own °,   in heart °.
16. Who will rise up for me against the   who will stand up for me against the
     evil-doers,   workers of iniquity ?
17. Unless Yahweh had been my help,   ° my soul had dwelt in silence.
18. When I said : " My foot slippeth ",   thy love, Yahweh, upheld me.
19. When many were the anxieties within
     me,   thy comforts refreshed my soul.
20. Hath the throne of destruction ° fellow-   which frameth mischief against the
     ship with thee °,   statute ?
21. ° They lie in wait ° against the soul of
     the righteous,   and condemn innocent ° men °.
22. But Yahweh ° is ° my strong tower,   and my God is the Rock of my defence ;
23. And he hath recompensed unto them   ° and because of their wickedness ° he
     their iniquity,   doth annihilate them,
Yahweh, our God, doth annihilate them.

Text-critical Notes

1. Read הוֹפִיעָה (cf. Ps. 80³) for הוֹפִיעַ, " he hath shined forth ". 6. Read
with G, וְיָתוֹם for וְגֵּר, " and stranger ". Read, with Gunkel, following Zech. 7¹⁰,
גֵּר וְעָנִי for וִיתוֹמִים, " and orphans ". 10. Read הֲלֹא יֵדַע for דַּעַת, " knowledge ";
as it stands the half-line is defective. 11. Lit. " breath ". 15. Lit. " that his right
may return unto the righteous ", reading צַדִּיק and מִשְׁפָּטוֹ. Read וְאַחֲרִיתוֹ
כִּישְׁרֵי־לֵב for וְאַחֲרָיו כָּל־יִשְׁרֵי־לֵב, " and after him all the upright in heart ".
17. Om. כִּמְעַט, " soon ", for the rhythm's sake. 20. Read הַיִחְבְּרְךָ for הַיְחָבְרְךָ.
21. Read, with T, יָגוּדוּ (cf. Ps. 59³), for יָגוֹדוּ " they gather themselves together ".
Read וְאָדָם for וְדָם " and blood ". 22. Read וַיְהִי for וַיֱהִי, " but . . . hath
been ". 23. Read וּבְרָעָתָם for וּבְרָעָתָם, " and in their wickedness ".

1–7. The righteous wrath of the psalmist explains the abrupt
opening of the psalm ; he calls upon Yahweh to reveal himself as the
God of vengeance (cp. Deut. 32³⁵· ⁴¹· ⁴³), and to rise up as *Judge of the
earth* in order to recompense *the proud* for their ill-doings. For the
expression *shine forth*, used in reference to Yahweh as *Judge*, see
Ps. 50¹⁻⁴. The reference here is to the powerful rich among the Jews
who *exulted* in their wealthy position and gloried in their evil doings,
speaking arrogantly and *boasting themselves* ; moreover, they had abused
their power by maltreating the poor and helpless. *Thy people* and
thine inheritance are generally used in reference to the nation as a whole,
but they are also used at times in a restricted sense, as here (*e.g.*, Hos. 10¹⁴
and Deut. 10⁹), see also *v.* 7 ; *widow, orphan,* and *stranger* (cp. Isa. 10²),
i.e., proselyte ; that the oppressors are said to *slay* and *murder* their
helpless victims is doubtless somewhat of an over-statement, due to

the psalmist's indignation. With the blasphemous assertion of the godless oppressors that *Yah seeth it not, the God of Jacob observeth it not*, cp. Ps. 10⁴, ¹¹, 73¹¹; *observeth it not* should perhaps be rendered " is without understanding ", as it is the same word which is used in the next verse, where the *brutish ones among the people* are bidden to *be understanding*; the force of the epithet *brutish* is that it implies both cruelty and stupidity; as a parallel to *foolish* it occurs also in Ps. 49¹⁰, 92⁶. *When will ye exercise wisdom ?* the psalmist asks; and in words of wisdom, he gives the reply himself, 9–11. The change of metre makes an effective emphasis. In question-form he exposes the foolish ignorance of these godless men. It was, moreover, an ignorance which was wilful, a deliberate ignoring of a truth of which they were certainly cognizant, for their question in *v.* 7 shows that they believed in the existence of the Creator. In the questions which follow, with their implied affirmatives in this case, we have an illustration of the mode of instruction so often employed by the Wisdom writers, doubtless in the following of the prophets (see, *e.g.*, Isa. 10⁸⁻¹¹, 58⁵⁻⁷, Jer. 3⁴⁻⁵, Ezek. 15²⁻⁵, Am. 3³, ⁶, 6¹², and Prov. 8¹, 22²⁰, ²¹, 23²⁹, 30⁴, Ecclus. 2¹⁰, 10¹⁹, 18¹⁶, ¹⁷, 28³⁻⁵, etc.). A curious expression, which does not occur elsewhere, is used in the words, *He that planted the ear*; the idea is that of " fixing in", cp. Eccles. 12¹¹, where the words of the wise are spoken of as " nails well fastened ", lit. " planted " ; neither this nor *He that formed the eye* is meant figuratively, the belief being that every human organ was separately created. The meaning of 10 is that Yahweh, who has the power of instructing all men, has also the power of chastising them when they ignore his instruction. As compared with the *knowledge* of Yahweh, whereby he *teaches* men, their *thoughts* are mere breath, *vain*, passing away and leaving nothing behind them. In contrast to the generality of men, the psalmist now speaks of the man who heeds the instruction of Yahweh, 12–15 : *Blessed is the man whom thou instructest. Yah*, the abbreviated form of the divine name is again used. It is this true instruction and the observance of the *law* which uphold a man even in the *evil days*, for he knows that they will pass and that he will have *respite* from them ; he can take heart in the conviction that *Yahweh* has *not cast off his people*, *i.e.*, his own faithful ones ; seeing that ultimately *the righteous will come to his own* (a free rendering, see text-crit. note), and that *his latter end* will be that of *the upright in heart* (an emendation of the corrupt Hebrew text). Finally (16–23) the psalmist speaks of his own experiences. He has been through dangers and has suffered in times of mental perplexity ; but the *love* of *Yahweh* has ever *upheld* and *refreshed* him. In speaking to himself (20) he asks : *Hath the throne of destruction fellowship with thee*, an evil dominion *which frameth mischief against the statute ?* The verse is difficult, and susceptible of more than one interpretation ; but, paraphrased, it

seems to mean : Hast thou anything to do with that anti-God *régime*
which sooner or later brings destruction because it is against the divine
statute ? It is that followed by those who *lie in wait against the righteous*
and the *innocent*. Among these latter the psalmist, with every justification, counts himself, and therefore he knows that *Yahweh* is his *strong
tower*, his *Rock of defence*, and that he is safe ; but the wicked have been
recompensed for *their iniquity, Yahweh doth annihilate them* ; the repetition
of this at the end of the psalm, witnesses to what the psalmist has seen.

Religious Teaching

If this partakes largely of the nature of warning, it is none the less
important for that. Two attributes of God are set forth. The first is
expressed by the phrase, the " God of vengeance ". While this form
of expression betrays a somewhat too anthropomorphic conception of
the Almighty, it seeks to place on record something that can be all too
easily lost sight of by men ; it is necessary to insist sometimes on the
truth that there is such a thing as divine retributive justice. It will
not be denied that too frequently there is to be discerned an attitude
of mind which is inclined to regard human weaknesses—in plain
language, sin—as inevitable, and therefore excuseable. It is the counterpart of what in this psalm is recorded as obtaining in a rougher age.
God who is righteous cannot condone sin ; nevertheless, punishment
for sin is not an act of divine vengeance, but the ineluctable consequence
of departing from the path of righteousness.

The other divine attribute which finds expression in this psalm,
and very often in other psalms, is the love of God. On this man can
always rely ; whether external troubles assail, or perplexities of mind
cause worry and anxiety, he who brings them in trustful faith before
God knows that, in the beautiful words of the psalmist, His love upholds, His comforts refresh.

PSALM 95

THIS psalm consists of two clearly differentiated parts : a hymn of
praise (*vv.* 1–7ᵃ), and an historical retrospect in the nature of a warning
lest the people should follow the faithlessness of their forefathers in
the wilderness. Owing to the mention of Yahweh as King, and to a
very cursory reference to the creation of the sea and of the dry land,
this psalm has been reckoned by some commentators as belonging to
the " Yahweh-is-become-King " group. This is entirely uncalled for ;

the contention illustrates the way in which an idea will sometimes obsess the mind and upset the sense of proportion. Both the application of the title " King " to Yahweh, and references to his creative acts often occur without the slightest indication of the Enthronement theme ; so, too, with regard to processions (see Vol. I, p. 51). The same is the case here.

The psalm was sung by worshippers on the way to the temple ; they had gathered together for the purpose of celebrating the Sabbath ; this is, at any rate, suggested by later usage among the Jews (B. Talmud, *Shabbath* 119*a*), and even at the present day it is one of the special psalms for Morning Prayer on the Sabbath. This usage has been followed by the Christian Church from very early times, though not restricted to the Lord's-Day worship. " Saint Benedict (*circ.* A.D. 480–543), the founder of the Benedictine Order, directed that Ps. 95 (preceded by Ps. 3) should be said by the whole monastery together, when the monks first arose from sleep. It has been included in our English Matins from 1549 onwards." [1] The usage of the Christian Church may well have been founded on that of the Jewish Church.

To judge from the warning words of the second part of the psalm, it may well belong to the period some time after the building of the second temple ; there are passages in Hag. 2, Mal. 2, 3, Trito-Isa. 57–59, which show the spiritual state of the people to have been similar to that which called forth the rebuke in the latter portion of the psalm. The date may thus be about the middle of the fifth century B.C., or possibly a little later.

The metre is 3 : 3 excepting in *v.* 7, where we have again the purposeful and effective lines with two beats.

1. O come, let us sing to Yahweh, let us cry out for joy to the Rock of our salvation.

2. Let us come before his presence with thanksgiving, let us shout unto him with psalms.
3. For a great God is Yahweh, a ° King above all gods.
4. ° In his hand are ° the ends of ° the earth, and the peaks of the mountains are his.
5. ° The sea is his, and he made it, and the dry land,—he formed it.
6. Let us enter in, let us worship and bow down, let us kneel before ° our Maker :
7.
For he is our God,
and we are ° his people °,
° and the flock of his pasture ° ;
Would that to-day ye would hearken unto his voice :

8. " Harden not your heart as at Meribah, as on the day of Massah, in the wilderness ;
9. When your fathers tempted me, where they tried me though they had seen my work.
10. Forty years had I loathing ° against that generation °, and said :
A people erring of heart are they, and they have not known my ways ;
11. So that I swore in my wrath, ' They shall not enter into my rest '."

---

[1] Barnes, *The Psalms,* Vol. II, pp. 456 f. (1931).

Text-critical Notes

3. Om. the repetition of גָּדוֹל " great ", which overloads the line. 4. Om. אֲשֶׁר " which ", an unnecessary addition which overloads the line. Read, with G, מֶרְחַקֵּי, lit. " the distant parts ", for מֶחְקְרֵי, " the searchings ". 5. Om. אֲשֶׁר (see above). 6. Om. יהוה, which gives too many beats to the half-line. 7. Read, with S, עַמּוֹ for עָם, " people ". Read, with S, וְצֹאן מַרְעִיתוֹ for מַרְעִיתוֹ וְצֹאן יָדוֹ, " his pasture and the flock of his hand ". 10. Read, with the Versions, בַּדּוֹר הַהוּא for בְּדוֹר, " against a generation ".

1, 2. The throng of worshippers ascending the temple-mount encourage each other with the words : *O come, let us sing to Yahweh, let us cry out for joy to the Rock of our salvation* ; with this last expression, cp. Ps. 89²⁶, indicating firm reliability ; they say : *let us shout unto him with psalms* ; this noisy mode of worship, as it appears, is thoroughly characteristic of emotional Orientals. 3–5. In the light of what is said in the second part of the psalm, there is a special significance in the reminder to the people, sung perhaps by a leader, that *a great God is Yahweh, a King above all gods*; the temptation to worship other gods was one to which the people during post-exilic times were often subject ; and the reference to the hardening of their hearts in the wilderness (*v.* 8) points to a lack of faith in Yahweh. The further emphasis on the creative acts of Yahweh was doubtless due to the same cause ; the people were losing hold of their faith in him who was the Creator of all things. Perfunctory as the worship was which they offered, they nevertheless made their pilgrimage up to the temple ; but more than mere observance was required ; the outward acts of worship were to be the earnest of genuine belief : 6. *Let us enter in, let us worship and bow down, let us kneel before our Maker.* 7. And once more the leader reminds his people that Yahweh is their God, and that they belong to him : *He is our God, and we are his people.* Then comes what is at once a pleading and a warning : *Would that to-day ye would hearken unto his voice* (cp. Ps. 81⁸) ; this, together with what follows, being addressed to the processionists, will have been sung by a priest standing at the entrance to the temple ; he puts the words into the mouth of the Almighty ; there is much in the section reminiscent of Ps. 81⁷⁻¹³. For *Meribah and Massah*, see Exod. 17⁷, Num. 20⁸⁻¹³, *my work* is in reference to the smiting of the rock in Horeb, when Yahweh " stood before " Moses. But it was not only on that occasion that the Israelites *hardened* their *heart* ; during the whole of the *forty years* Yahweh *had loathing* against them ; this is the force of the Hebrew word. The abrupt ending of the psalm with the words, *so that I swore in my wrath, ' They shall not enter into my rest '*, sets in relief the stern warning directed, by implication, against those who were now standing at the entrance to the temple. By *rest*, or *resting-place*, the promised land was originally meant (cp. Deut. 12⁹), but the psalmist uses it in a more spiritual sense ;

EE

perhaps, in view of Isa. 32[18], where the word occurs, it is used here in an eschatological sense, as there.

Religious Teaching

Especially to be noticed here is the way in which the joy in worship is emphasized; this is engendered by the conviction of the divine presence. The true worship of him who is all-powerful and all-loving will of necessity inspire happiness. On the other hand, the psalm contains a warning for every age; mere external acts of worship, without sincerity of heart, become a mockery. The true rest of God can be the lot of those only who worship him " in spirit and in truth ".

PSALM 96

THE phrase " Yahweh is become King ", occurring towards the end of the psalm (v. 10), marks it as one of those which were sung during the ceremony of Yahweh's Enthronement. Praise to Yahweh is, therefore, the main content of the psalm. But it contains incidental references to other themes belonging to the New Year Festival psalms, thus showing that the Enthronement ceremony was one belonging to the New Year celebration, and not a self-contained festival. While the whole psalm bears, mostly by implication, an eschatological character, it is only in the concluding verses that this becomes definite in expression.

Curiously enough, in the long psalm of thanksgiving in 1 Chron. 16[8-36], purporting to have been sung " before the ark of Yahweh ", in the time of David, our psalm is embodied almost entire; borrowings from Pss. 105, 106 also appear. The fact, however explained, must warn us against being too dogmatic about the use of these " Enthronement " psalms.

The date is post-exilic, but much of the material is, of course, much earlier; see further, Vol. I, pp. 45 ff.

The metre is somewhat irregular, varying between 3 : 3 and 4 : 3; the irregularity may be due to the fact that the psalmist borrows so much, e.g., with vv. 7–9 cp. Ps. 29[1ff].

1. Sing to Yahweh a new song,   sing to Yahweh, all the land,
2. Sing to Yahweh, bless his name,   show forth his salvation from day to day;
3. Declare among the nations his glory,   among all the peoples his wondrous works.
4. For great is Yahweh, and highly to be praised,   terrible is he beyond all gods;
5. For all the gods of the peoples are things of nought,   but Yahweh made the heavens;
6. Honour and majesty are before him,   strength and beauty are in his sanctuary.
7. Render to Yahweh, ye kindreds of the peoples,   render to Yahweh glory and strength,

8. Render to Yahweh the glory of his name,
9. Worship Yahweh in holy array,
10. Declare among the nations : Yahweh is become King,
11. Let the heavens be glad, let the earth rejoice,
12. Let the field exult, and all that is in it,

13. Before Yahweh, for he cometh,
He judgeth the world in righteousness,

bring gifts and enter his courts.
° entreat his favour °, all the earth.
° he hath established ° the world, it shall not be moved.°

let the sea roar, and the fulness thereof.
°yea °, let all the trees of the forest shout for joy
for he cometh to judge the earth;
and the peoples in his faithfulness.

Text-critical Notes

9. Read חֲלוּ פָנָיו (cf. Zech. 7² and Ps. 119 ⁵⁸) for חֵילוּ מִפָּנָיו, " tremble before him ". 10. Read, with the Versions, תִּכֵּן (see Ps. 93¹) for אַף־תִּכּוֹן, " Yea . . . is established ". Om., see 1 Chron. 16³¹, יָדִין עַמִּים בְּמֵישָׁרִים, " he shall judge the peoples with equity ". 12. Read אָף for אָז, " then ".

1-3. The threefold repetition : *Sing to Yahweh*, giving a jubilant tone to the psalm at the outset, indicates its nature and purpose—viz., praise to Yahweh. It is *a new song* (cp. Ps. 33³, 98¹), which the psalmist has composed for the occasion, others having, of course, been long in use. *All the land* is bidden to take part in this hymn of praise ; by the *land* is meant the land of Israel, which is to *declare among the nations his glory, among all the peoples his wondrous works* ; the works of Creation are meant : but, above all, *Yahweh made the heavens*. 4-6. In speaking of *all the gods of the peoples* as *things of nought*, the psalmist has doubtless such passages as Isa. 40¹⁹ ⁿ·, 41²³, ²⁴, 46⁵⁻⁷, and especially 44⁹ ⁿ·, in mind ; in spite of this, however, he believes in the existence of such gods ; Yahweh is *terrible beyond all gods* ; but in comparison with Yahweh they are *things of nought*. In contrast to these gods the psalmist thinks of the beautiful ministers that wait upon Yahweh ; as often in the psalms, abstract things are personified, so he says : *Honour and majesty are before him, strength and beauty are in his sanctuary.* 7-13. The knowledge of Yahweh having been brought to the nations by Israel, according to the envisaging of the future by the psalmist, they are now called upon to worship him. Very interesting to note here is what we might call the order of service at the ceremony of the Enthronement of Yahweh : first, the act of homage : *Render to Yahweh glory and strength*—i.e., acknowledge those external qualities which belong to Yahweh as supreme ; then an act of praise : *Render to Yahweh the glory of his name*—i.e., acknowledge the glorious power of his name (cp. Ps. 29²) ; utterance is followed by action, and the next rite in the service was to *bring gifts and enter his courts* ; the offerings were brought into the temple courts and received by the Levites, who prepared them for the altar, and presented them to the priests who then offered them on the altar. Those who brought their offerings are bidden to *worship Yahweh in holy array*—i.e., to be clothed in garments appropriate to the occasion (cp. Ps. 29²); of what kind these were it is not possible to say, but it is conceivable that the reference is to a wide mantle (*p^ethîgîl*) ¹ mentioned in Isa. 3²⁴. And finally, there is the act of prayer: *entreat his favour.* Thus, homage, praise, offerings, prayer, may well have been the order of service during this particular ceremony; further rites are not mentioned here; but that these took place is indicated in other psalms of this type. One thing that one cannot well help noticing is the incidental and secondary way in which the phrase "Yahweh is become King", is mentioned in our psalm. It tends to bear out what we have already more than once insisted on, that the Enthronement ceremony was not a self-contained festival, but that it was celebrated during the New Year Festival observed at the Feast of Tabernacles. It is here that the eschatological character of the psalm becomes particularly evident; the psalmist envisages the future consummation when Yahweh's rule will become world-wide. *Declare among the nations: Yahweh is become King*, he has *established the world.* But the Kingship of Yahweh is too stupendous a thing for man alone to herald with joy; *the heavens* above are called upon *to be glad,* and *the earth* to *rejoice, the sea* to *roar* in delight, *the field* to *exult,* and *all the trees of the forest* to *shout for joy,* in the presence of *Yahweh*; for he is about to come as Judge, and his judgements will be *in righteousness* and *faithfulness.*

For the religious teaching of this psalm, and others of the same type, see Vol. I, pp. 40 ff.

PSALM 97

THE opening phrase of this psalm, "Yahweh is become King", followed by some apocalyptic pictures, clearly indicates its eschatological character; but the present is also largely dealt with. The apocalyptic elements are echoes of early traditional ideas applied to eschatological expectations.

There is to some extent a lack of logical thought-sequence, and the impression is gained that familiar phrases have been gathered together rather than that the psalmist has composed an original poem; but in one respect this psalm stands out as of prime importance; for the psalmist shows a striking independence of thought by the way in which he sets forth and reiterates the conception of Yahweh's ethical righteousness. In this respect the psalm surpasses all others of eschatological content.

The date of these "Enthronement" psalms is dealt with in Vol. I, pp. 46 ff.

¹ Nowack, *Hebräische Archäologie*, Vol. I, p. 125 (1894).

The metre is for the most part 3 : 3 ; but *vv.* 1, 2 are respectively
4 : 3 and 3 : 4, and *vv.* 8 and 10 are respectively 3 : 3 : 3 and 4 : 3 : 3.

1. Yahweh is become King, let the earth
   rejoice,   let the multitude of the isles be glad.
2. Clouds and darkness are round about   righteousness and justice are the
   him,   foundation of his throne ;
3. Fire goeth before him,   and burneth his adversaries round about.
4. His lightnings lighten the world,   the earth seeth it, and trembleth,
5. The mountains melt like wax °,   before the Lord of all the earth.
6. The heavens declare his righteousness, and all the peoples behold his glory.
7. All that serve graven images shall be that boast themselves in things of
   ashamed,   nought,
                    ° Worship him, all ye gods °.
8. Zion heareth, and is glad,   the daughters of Judah rejoice,
                 Because of thy judgements, Yahweh ;
9. For thou °art the Most High over all   thou art exalted far above all gods.
   the earth,
10. Yahweh ° loveth them that hate ° evil, he keepeth the souls of his godly ones
    He delivereth them from the hand of the wicked.
11. Light ° ariseth ° ° upon ° the righteous, and joy to the upright of heart.
12. Rejoice in Yahweh, O ye righteous,   and give thanks to his holy ° name °

Text-critical Notes

5. Om., a gloss which overloads the half-line, מִלִּפְנֵי יהוה, " from before the
presence of Yahweh ". 9. Om. the repetition of יהוה. 10. Read אָהֵב, making
Yahweh the subject ; and, with some MSS and S, read שֹׂנְאֵי for שֹׂנֵא. 11. Read,
with one MS and the Versions, זָרַח for זָרֻעַ, " is sown ". Read עַל for לְ,
" to ". 12. Lit. " memorial ", see exeg. note.

1-6. The eschatological character of the psalm is indicated by the
opening words that as *Yahweh is become King*, therefore *let the earth
rejoice* (cp. Ps. 96¹¹), and *let the multitude of the isles be glad* (cp. Isa. 51⁵,
60⁹), meaning, of course, their inhabitants. Such a thought envisages
the future divine dominion over the whole world, a central theme in
the Eschatological Drama. The psalmist then depicts how Yahweh
will appear, terrible and glorious, when he comes to possess the world :
enveloped in *clouds and darkness* (cp. Ps. 18¹¹), with an all-devouring
fire before him (cp. Ps. 50³), *his lightnings*, bursting forth from the dark
clouds (cp. Ps. 77¹⁸), shoot through the world, terrifying all men, *the
earth seeth it, and trembleth* (cp. Ps. 96⁹), the *mountains melt like wax* (cp.
Judg. 5⁵) before him who is *Lord of all the earth* (cp. Mic. 4¹³, Zech. 4¹⁴,
6⁵). The picture is a terrifying one ; the more striking is it that there
should be introduced into the middle of it what appears, at first sight,
to be a somewhat incongruous thought : *righteousness and justice are
the foundation of his throne* ; but it is just this disregard for congruity
which witnesses to the presence in the psalmist's mind of his dominating
thought, the ethical righteousness of Yahweh. The same is true of the
words in 6 which are likewise out of harmony with their context : *the
heavens declare his righteousness* ; the context speaks of the melting
mountains, on the one side, and of *all the peoples* who *behold his glory*,

on the other; so that here again what is foremost in the psalmist's mind comes to the fore. 7–12. A sudden change of subject then occurs; the denunciation of *all that serve graven images*, and *that boast themselves in things of nought*, was doubtless inspired by Isa. 44⁹ ᵃ. and similar passages; and the apparent contradiction between the *things of nought* and the words, *worship him, all ye gods*, has its parallel in Ps. 96⁴, ⁵. Then, in 8, we have another change of subject, reverting to the psalmist's dominating thought; the *judgements* of *Yahweh*, the outcome of his righteousness, make *Zion glad* and *the daughters of Judah rejoice*; the words are taken from Ps. 48¹¹; by *the daughters of Judah* are meant the daughter-cities of Zion, conceived of, metaphorically, as the mother of the whole people (cp. Ps. 87). Once more, in 10–12, the psalmist speaks of the righteousness of Yahweh in the words : *Yahweh loveth them that hate evil, he keepeth the souls of his godly ones*; " souls " has here, as often elsewhere, the sense of individuality; on " godly ones " see Vol. I, pp. 56 ff.; similarly, in saying that *Light ariseth upon the righteous, and joy to the upright of heart*, it is meant that the light and the joy come from him who is the Author of all righteousness. And finally, when *the righteous* are bidden *to rejoice in Yahweh*, and *give thanks to his holy name*, it is because he is the source of their righteousness, and that his name embodies the revealed character of Yahweh as righteous (see, *e.g.*, Isa. 57¹⁵).

For the religious teaching of the psalms of this type see further Vol. I, pp. 44 ff.

PSALM 98

THAT this psalm should be reckoned among those belonging to the " Enthronement of Yahweh " group is justified by the reference to the " King " in verse 6; its purely eschatological content also marks it as one of this type. As always in psalms of an eschatological character, the belief expressed in the future consummation of the present world-order is so firmly held that it is envisaged, after the prophetical style, as having already come to pass; hence the use of the verbs in the perfect tense in *vv.* 1–3; and it is no incongruity when in *vv.* 7, 8 the present tense occurs, and in *v.* 9 the future; the changes simply reflect the writer's variation of envisagement.

The points of contact between this psalm and Ps. 96 will be noticed in comparing them.

On the date, see Vol. I, pp. 44 ff.

The metre in *vv.* 1–3 is 3 : 2, an extra two-beat line occurs in *v.* 2; but in the remainder of the psalm it is 3 : 3.

A Psalm.

1. Sing to Yahweh a new song,
His right-hand hath holpen him,
2. Yahweh hath made known his salvation,

3. He remembered his love and his
faithfulness,
All the ends of the earth have seen
4. Make a joyful noise unto Yahweh, all
the earth ;
5. Sing praise to Yahweh with the harp,
6. With trumpets and the blast of the
ram's-horn,
7. Let the sea roar, and the fulness thereof,
8. Let the streams clap their hands,
9. Before Yahweh, for he cometh,
He judgeth the world in righteousness,

for he hath done marvellous things ;
and his holy arm.
before the eyes of the nations hath he
revealed his righteousness.

to the house of Israel ;
the salvation of our God.
break forth, shout for joy, and sing
praise ;
with the harp and the sound of praise ;

make a joyful noise before the King ° ;

the world and the dwellers therein ;
let the mountains shout for joy together.
° for he cometh ° to judge the earth ;
and the peoples with equity.

Text-critical Notes

6. Om. יהוה, which overloads the half-line. 9. Add, as in Ps. 96¹³, בָּ יִ רָק.
" for he cometh ".

1–3. Like Pss. 96 and 98, this is another *new song* composed for the celebration of the " Enthronement " ceremony ; since it was an annual celebration, it was but fitting that new psalms should be composed for the occasion. The special reason for singing praise to Yahweh here given is that *he hath done marvellous things* (cp. 96³). The originally anthropomorphic expressions, *his right-hand and his holy arm,* are here used in a purely spiritual sense of Yahweh's will and power. The *marvellous things* to which the psalmist refers are embraced in the word *salvation* (cp. Ps. 96²) ; this includes both deliverance from external evils as well as spiritual blessings ; these, which have been vouchsafed to *the house of Israel,* have been *made known before the eyes of the nations* (cp. Ps. 96²³), to whom has also been *revealed* Yahweh's *righteousness,* frequently used as a parallel to *salvation (e.g.,* Isa. 51⁶). *Love* and *faithfulness* are the things that belong to *salvation,* the remembrance of them, *i.e.,* the lavishing of them upon *the house of Israel,* is the act of *righteousness.* This has been seen by *all the ends of the earth.* Here we have, then, a very interesting illustration of the combination of the particularistic conception of Israel as the people of God, and the universalistic conception of all peoples being brought to the knowledge of Yahweh. There is no sort of doubt that this beautiful thought originated, under God, with Deutero–Isaiah.

In the second part of the psalm (4–8), therefore, *all the earth* is called upon to rejoice that the knowledge of God, *the salvation of* Israel's *God,* has been vouchsafed unto them, and to join with the people of Yahweh in worshipping him : *Make a joyful noise unto Yahweh, all the earth ; break forth, shout for joy, and sing praise.* That the psalm is to be understood in an eschatological sense comes out here clearly, for the joining together

of all the earth in worship with Israel could be possible only with the
final advent of Yahweh as King of all the earth ; and thus, the Enthronement ceremony, which is now referred to, was what we may call a
prophetic representation of Yahweh's ultimate entering upon his world-
dominion : *With trumpets and the blast of the ram's-horn, make a joyful
noise before the King.* Other eschatological conceptions follow : *Let
the sea roar, and the fulness thereof* (cp. Ps. 96[11]), *i.e.,* all that is in it ;
streams are to *clap their hands,* an action of exultation, *mountains* to
shout for joy ; in a word, the whole Creation is bidden to rejoice in the
advent of the King : *for he cometh, for he cometh, to judge the earth, in
righteousness* and *equity* (cp. Ps. 96[13]) ; the reign of universal peace,
justice, and happiness has begun in the psalmist's prophetic vision.

PSALM 99

ONCE more an " Enthronement " psalm, the last of the group, opening
with : " Yahweh is become King ". It differs, however, from other
psalms of the type in the attitude adopted towards the Gentiles ; they
are not bidden to rejoice over Yahweh's dominion, but to tremble ;
and there is in general a sterner note. Then, again, the eschatological
traits are less prominent than in the related psalms ; but this is not to
deny its eschatological character, which is clear from the mention of
Yahweh's exaltation over all peoples, and the call to them to praise his
name ; and the phrase " let the earth shake " is thoroughly eschatological. As in Ps. 97, emphasis is laid on the righteousness of Yahweh,
though not to the same extent as there. The psalm consists of two parts,
vv. 1-5 and 6-9, each concluding with a refrain. The text of *vv.* 3, 4
has suffered some disorder ; for the emendations see the text-critical
notes.

The metre is irregular.

For the date, see Vol. I, pp. 44 ff.

1. Yahweh is become King, let the peoples tremble, ° he sitteth upon ° the cherubim, let the earth shake.
2. Yahweh is great in Zion, and exalted is he above all the peoples ;
3. Let them praise ° his name °, great and terrible,
   " ° Thou hast established equity ° in Jacob °, holy is he, 4. ° and a mighty King ° ; justice and righteousness ° hast thou ordained."
5. Exalt Yahweh our God, and worship at the stool of his feet,
   ° For holy is Yahweh our God °.
6. Moses and Aaron among his priests, and Samuel among those that called upon his name,
   They called unto Yahweh, and he answered them ;
7. In the pillar of cloud spake he unto them, ° they heard ° his testimonies and the statute he gave them ;

8. " Yahweh, our God, thou didst answer   a forgiving God hast thou been to
them,   them,
           Yet an avenger of ° all ° their doings."
9. Exalt Yahweh, our God,   and worship at his holy hill,
           For holy is Yahweh our God.

Text-critical Notes.

1. Read יֹשֵׁב עַל for יֹשֵׁב, " sitting ". 3. Read שְׁמוֹ for שְׁמֶךָ, " thy name ".
4. Read, with Gunkel, וְיִמְלֹךְ עָז for וְעֹז מֶלֶךְ " and the strength of a king ".
Om., with Gunkel, מִשְׁפָּט אָהֵב "justice he loveth". Add בְּיַעֲקֹב. Om.
בְּיַעֲקֹב. 5. Read as in v. 9 כִּי־קָדוֹשׁ יְהוָה אֱלֹהֵינוּ, 7. Read שָׁמְעוּ for
שָׁמְרוּ, " they kept ". 8. Add, with G, כָּל־.

1. *Yahweh is become King* is, instead of, as in Ps. 97¹, a cause for
rejoicing among the peoples, an event inspiring fear among them :
let the peoples tremble. Again, in place of the majestic picture of Yahweh's
throne given in Ps. 97², it is here said that *he sitteth upon the cherubim*
(cp. Ps. 80¹). The mention of these mythical beings is an illustration
of the utilization of very ancient material of which this group of psalms
is full. Mediated doubtless through Ezek. 1, the idea of the cherubim
is of Accadian origin, and went through various stages of development ;
originally they were guardians who stood at the entry of temples ; their
guardianship of the Ark (Exod. 25¹⁹, ²⁰) points, however, to Egyptian influence. In the *v.* before us the implication probably is that the cherubim
were the guardians of Yahweh's throne. To discuss their further
functions would take us too far afield (see Gen. 3²⁴, 1 Kgs. 6²³ᵐ·, Ps. 18¹⁰,
Ezek. 10¹ ᵃ·, 41¹⁸, ¹⁹). When it is said further in our psalm, *let the
earth shake*, the thought in the mind of the psalmist may conceivably
be that of the mighty throne-chariot of Ezek. 1, the rumbling of which
makes the earth to shake. But however this may be (2), the centre of
Yahweh's dominion is Zion : *Yahweh is great in Zion* ; to say that
" here is the tone of Jewish exclusiveness " is simply to misunderstand
the whole purport of the psalm ; Yahweh is here enthroned, *exalted
above all the peoples* as Israel's God, no doubt, but also as the God of
all the peoples ; the tone is not one of exclusiveness, but of universalism.
It may well be that those commentators are right who explain Zion here
as the heavenly Zion ; Yahweh, enthroned in heaven, rules over all the
world. Therefore it is said, in reference to *all the peoples : Let them
praise his name* (cp. Ps. 111⁹), which is *great and terrible* (cp. Deut. 10¹⁷) ;
and of Yahweh himself : *holy is he* (cp. Isa. 6³) *and a mighty King* ;
the phrase occurs in Isa. 19⁴, but not in reference to Yahweh. Further
attributes of Yahweh are that he has *established equity in Jacob*, implying
that he will do so in all the world ; similarly with *justice and righteousness*,
which he has *ordained*. This ethical righteousness of Yahweh is also
emphasized in Ps. 97¹⁰, ¹¹, ²⁶. 5. The first part of the psalm closes with
the refrain : *Exalt Yahweh our God, and worship at the stool of his feet, for*

holy is Yahweh (cp. Isa. 66¹, " the earth is my footstool "). 6–9. This second part of the psalm, though of a very different character from the first, is, nevertheless, directly connected with it, because it tells of the great figures who in the past had been Yahweh's ministers and had *called upon his name*; it is in the following of such that all the peoples were bidden, in the first part (*v*. 3), to " praise his name ". *Moses* as well as *Aaron* are reckoned *among his priests*; Moses is not elsewhere spoken of as a priest, but he performs priestly functions in Exod. 24⁶⁻⁸, 40²²⁻²⁷, Lev. 8¹⁰ ᵃ· (cp. Gray, *Sacrifice in the Old Testament*, pp. 194 ff. [1925]); he is mentioned, together with *Samuel*, in Jer. 15¹ as those who " stood before me ". The inclusion of Samuel in connexion with *the pillar of cloud* must be due to some legendary tradition. There is a little difficulty about the meaning of 8; we take it to mean that *Yahweh did answer them, i.e.*, Moses, Aaron, and Samuel, when they pleaded to him for their people, and that he had been a *forgiving God* to them, *i.e.*, the people; nevertheless, when the people persisted in evil-doing, Yahweh was *an avenger of all their doings*. The psalm concludes with a somewhat similar repetition of the refrain in *v*. 5.

For the religious teaching of the psalm, see Vol. I, pp. 74 ff.

PSALM 100

As the psalm itself indicates, it was sung by a procession of worshippers as they drew near to the gates of the temple to sacrifice the thank-offering. It is thus purely liturgical in character. Its brevity points to its being introductory to the sacrificial service. It is reminiscent of Ps. 95. The contention that the psalm belongs to the Enthronement group is quite beside the mark; there is nothing in it that suggests this.

The date is certainly post-exilic.

The metre is three beats to short lines, with the exception of the last verse, which, as in many other psalms, differs from the rest.

A Psalm. For the Todah.

1.	Shout for joy to Yahweh, all the land,
2.	Serve Yahweh with gladness,
	Enter into his presence with a ringing cry.
3.	Know that Yahweh he is God,
	He made us, and we are ° his °,
	His people, and the sheep of his pasture.
4.	Enter his gates with thanksgiving,
	His courts with praise,
	Give thanks unto him, bless his name.
5.	For Yahweh is good,
	His love is eternal,
	And his faithfulness is for all generations.

3. Read, with the *Q'rê* and many MSS, וְלֹו for וְלֹא, " and not " (so *K'thíbh* GS). " According to the Masora, לֹא is found fifteen times for לֹו", GK 103*g*.

The title indicates that the psalm was for the *Todah*, " thank-offering "; this does not necessarily mean that it was sung during the sacrifice; the psalm suggests that it was introductory to the ceremony.

1. As in Ps. 95[1, 2] we have here the loud lifting-up of the voices in worship (see also *v.* 2); by *all the land* is to be understood the land as a whole, represented by the assembled worshippers, who, as in Ps. 95, formed a procession ascending the temple mount. Emphasis is again laid on joy in worship, *shout for joy*; and (2) *serve Yahweh with gladness*; the Hebrew word for *serve* is used technically of serving God in worship (cp. Exod. 3[12], Isa. 19[21, 23]). *Enter into his presence* is similarly a technical liturgical term (cp. Exod. 28[30], it occurs also in Ps. 95[6], 96[8]). *V.* 3 is similar in thought to 95[5-7]. In 4 *thanksgiving* is used in a general sense, but indicates the service for which the worshippers are to *enter his gates* and *his courts*. For the exhortation to *bless his name* cp. 96[2]. Very beautifully does the psalm conclude with the recognition of the *goodness* and *love* and *faithfulness* of Yahweh.

The religious teaching of this psalm is similar to that of Ps. 95, excepting for the absence of the warning note there sounded.

PSALM 101

THE content of this psalm shows that it is the utterance of one who has been made a ruler, and who, on assuming his position of authority, makes a declaration in which he expresses the principles whereby he will be guided in the exercise of his new duties. Whether the ruler in question was a king or a provincial governor is uncertain, but the latter is more likely, for the despotic Oriental king would not have thought it necessary to ingratiate himself among his subjects by making a declaration of this kind. The last verse sounds, it is true, more like the utterance of a king; but the words are not meant to be taken literally, they are in the nature of hyperbole, a form of expression not infrequently used by the psalmists.

The possibility must, however, be recognized that we have here a composition in which a psalmist has set forth an idealistic conception of rulership, putting the utterances in the mouth of an imaginary potentate. This seems to us, upon the whole, to be the true interpretation of the psalm.

But whichever interpretation be the correct one, the two opening verses constitute a difficulty; for they imply that the psalm was to be sung in praise of Yahweh's mercy and justice, whereas in the psalm itself there is no word of this, and the name of Yahweh does not occur again. This difficulty may be explained on the supposition that the edifying contents of the psalm induced some later psalmist to adapt it to liturgical use by altering the opening words to an appropriate form for worship. Hence the emendations adopted in our rendering of these verses.

In seeking to assign a date to the psalm, much depends upon how it is interpreted. If it refers to a king, the date is obviously pre-exilic; but if a provincial governor is in question, a post-exilic date is more likely—he might well have been a Jew, cp. Gedaliah (2 Kgs. 25[22]); the idealistic conception set forth suggests the later date.

The metre is 3 : 2.

David's. A Psalm.

1. ° I will exercise ° mercy and justice,   ° I will take heed unto Yahweh °;
2. I will act wisely in an upright manner
   of life,   ° truth shall abide with me °;
   I will walk in integrity of heart   within my house,
3. I will not set before mine eyes   a base thing;
   ° An act of apostasy ° I hate,   it shall not cleave to me;
4. A perverted heart shall depart from me,   I will not know evil.
5. He that secretly ° slandereth ° his
   neighbour,   him will I destroy;
   He that hath an high look, and an
   arrogant heart,   I will not suffer.
6. Mine eyes shall be upon the faithful
   in the land,   that they may dwell with me,
   He that walketh in a perfect way,   he shall minister unto me.
7. Not in my house shall he dwell   that acteth deceitfully,
   He that speaketh lies shall not be
   established   before mine eyes.
8. Every morning will I destroy   all the wicked of the land;
   To cut off from the city of Yahweh   all the workers of iniquity.

Text-critical Notes

1. Read, with Gunkel and Hans Schmidt, אֶעֱשֶׂה (cp. 1 Sam. 20[14], 2 Sam.10[2]) for אָשִׁירָה, "I will sing"; and לְךָ יְהוָה אֲזַמֵּרָה for לַיהוָה אֲשַׁמְּרָה, "to thee Yahweh will I sing praise" (see further, the intr. section). 2. Read, with several commentators, אֶמֶת תָּבוֹא-לִי for מָתַי תָּבוֹא אֵלַי, "when wilt thou come unto me?" 3. Lit. "to do swervings" in reference to swerving from allegiance to Yahweh. 5. Read מְלָשְׁנִי for the form מְלָושְׁנִי.

The whole psalm consists, as we surmise, of the words of a ruler, ideally conceived of by the psalmist. 1. He *will exercise mercy and justice*, and in doing so he will be observing the precepts of Yahweh. 2–4. In these *vv.* the ruler concentrates upon the guiding principles whereby he will be actuated : wisdom in thought and act constitute the foundation principles in the ruler who is determined to live *in an upright manner of life* (lit. " perfect way "). For this, *truth* is, of course, a prime requisite (for the emendation see text-crit. note); it is personified, as virtues often are by the psalmists, and it is spoken as abiding with him.

In the privacy of his *house* he *will walk in integrity of heart*; he will, that is to say, entertain thoughts which are good and noble, and will not even contemplate *a base thing*, lit. "a thing of Belial", by which is meant anything and everything suggestive of evil; the word means lit. "worthlessness", but it has also the sense of "wickedness" (see Prov. 6¹²); in later times it became a proper name synonymous with Satan (often in the apocalyptic literature, and cp. 2 Cor. 6¹⁵, also in Rabbinical literature). The worst type of such an evil thing is disloyalty to Yahweh, *an act of apostasy I hate*; that he will not entertain, *it shall not cleave to me*; in post-exilic times, when the Jews lived under Gentile suzerainty, the temptation to apostasy was especially rife among the ruling classes owing to their necessary contact with the officials of the suzerain power; so that the words in the psalm are very significant. Apostasy was the mark of *a perverted heart* (cp. Prov. 11²⁰), or "crooked" thoughts; that *shall depart from* the godly ruler; he refuses to have anything to do with such an *evil*. In the verses which follow, 5–7, the ruler speaks alternatively of those whom he abominates, and those whom he will favour. Of the former is the *slanderer*, through whose wickedness the innocent so often suffered; and the proud (lit. "high of eyes", cp. Prov. 21⁴), who oppressed the helpless. But he will look favourably on those who are *faithful in the land*, *i.e.*, those upon whom he can rely for their loyalty to him; they shall *dwell* with him because they walk aright, and can be trusted to serve him. On the other hand, he *that acteth deceitfully* shall *not dwell* in the ruler's *house*, nor can *he that speaketh lies* look for favour from him. 8. The zeal for righteousness by which the ruler is actuated is drastically expressed; but the words are not to be taken literally.

Religious Teaching

From the nature of the psalm the religious element is not prominent; but the insistence on the ruler's loyalty and faithfulness to Yahweh is very fine, and a notable way-mark for all in authority.

PSALM 102

THAT this psalm is not a unity becomes evident as soon as one compares *vv.* 12–22 with the rest of the psalm; for these verses break the continuity of, and have nothing in common with, *vv.* 1–11, 23–28. The insertion may perhaps be accounted for by the desire of a compiler to place in contrast the shortness of human life (*v.* 11) with the eternity of Yahweh (*v.* 12), a point of contact being thus established with the latter part of

the psalm (*vv.* 26, 27); but otherwise the insertion presents conditions
which differ entirely from the rest of the psalm. In its original form
our psalm is the outpouring of one who is the victim of sickness and
enmity; the inserted portion speaks of the desolation of Zion, but
expresses the hope of better times, and may thus possibly be part of a
psalm belonging to early post-exilic times, but see further exeg. notes.
The date of the main portion cannot be determined with any degree of
certainty; all that can be said is that the thought-connexions with
other psalms which are post-exilic would point to this period, though
later than the inserted portion. The metre is 3 : 3 with some variations;
this applies to the whole psalm as it stands.

1. *A Prayer of an afflicted one when down-cast and he poureth out his trouble*
before Yahweh.

1 (2). Yahweh, hear my prayer,   and let my cry come unto thee.
2 (3). Hide not thy face from me   in the day of my distress, ° Yahweh °;
       Incline thine ear unto me,   when I call, haste to answer me;
3 (4). For my ° inward parts ° waste   and my bones glow like a hearth.
       away ° like smoke °,
4 (5). Smitten like grass ° is my heart,   for I forget to eat my food.
5 (6). ° I am weary ° with the sound of
       my groaning,   ° my flesh cleaveth to my bones °;
6 (7). I am like a pelican in the wilder-
       ness,   I am like an owl in ruined places;
7 (8). I watch ° and I groan °,   like a solitary bird on the house-top.
8 (9). All the day mine enemies reproach   they that boast themselves against me
       me,   take an oath with me °.
9 (10). For I eat ashes like bread,   and I mingle ° my drink ° with weeping,
10 (11). Because of thine indignation and   for thou didst take me up, and didst cast
        thy wrath,   me away.
11 (12). My days ° decline ° like a shadow,   and I am withered like grass.

12 (13). But thou, Yahweh, abidest for   and thy memorial from generation to
        ever,   generation;
13 (14). Thou wilt arise and have mercy   ° for the time is come to be gracious
        on Zion,   unto her °,
14 (15). For thy servants have a delight in
        her stones,   and look graciously upon her dust,
15 (16). Then shall the nations fear ° thy
        name °,   and all the kings of the earth thy glory.
16 (17). For Yahweh doth build up Zion,   ° and shall appear ° in his glory ° in the
                                                  midst of her °.
17 (18). He hath regard unto the prayer of
        the destitute,   and despiseth not ° their supplication °:
18 (19). Let this be written down for the   and a people that shall be created shall
        generation to come,   praise Yah,
19 (20). For he looked down from his holy
        height,   from heaven ° he beheld the earth,
20 (21). To hear the sighing of the
        prisoner,   to release ° those condemned to death °,
21 (22). That the name of Yahweh may be
        proclaimed in Zion,   and his praise in Jerusalem,
22 (23). When the peoples are gathered
        together,   and the kingdoms, to serve Yahweh.

23 (24). ° My strength too soon is ex-   ° a cutting-off of my days is decreed for
        hausted °,   me °;
24 (25). ° Snatch me not away ° in the   thy years are throughout all ° genera-
        ° midst ° of my days,   tions °.
25 (26). Of old thou didst found the earth,   and the heavens are the work of thine
                                                  hands;

26 (27). They shall perish, but thou
　　　° endurest °,
　　Like a vesture dost thou change
　　　them, and they are changed ;
29. The children of thy servants shall
　　　° continue °,

yea, they all shall wear out like a
garment,

28. but thou,—thy years have no end.
and their seed shall be established
before thee.

Text-critical Notes

2. Add יהוה for the rhythm's sake. 3. Read מֵעָי, as a better parallel, for יָמַי, " my days ". Read, with many MSS and the Versions, כְּעָשָׁן for בְּ, " in smoke ". 4. Om., as overloading the half-line, וַיִּבַשׁ, " and withered ", probably an explanatory gloss on חוּקָּה, an unusual form. 5. Add, with some commentators, יָגַעְתִּי (cp. Ps. 6⁶), for the rhythm's sake; a verb has obviously fallen out. Read דָּבְקָה עַצְמִי לִבְשָׂרִי " my bones cleave to my flesh ", cp. Lam. iv. 8. For דָּבַק לְעַצְמִי בְשָׂרִי in a collective עַצְמִי For .8 .iv Lam. cp. ",flesh sense, with the predicate in fem. sing., see GK 122s 145k. 7. Read, for the rhythm's sake, and to complete the half-line, וָאֶהְמְיָה with two beats, for וָאֶהְיֶה, " and I am become ". 8. See exeg. note. 9. Read שִׁקֻּוַי. 11. Read כְּמֵי, making יָמַי the subject, for נְטוּי. 13. Read כִּי־בָא עֵת לְחֶנְנָהּ, omitting כִּי and מוֹעֵד, which overloads the half-line. 15. Read, with GS, שֵׁם for אֶת־שֵׁם יהוה, " the name of Yahweh ", which overloads the half-line. 16. Read, with Duhm, וְכִרְאֹה (so G) and add בְּקֵרְבָּהּ. 17. Read, cp. G, תְהִנָּתָם, to avoid the repetition of the same word. 19. Om. יהוה for the rhythm's sake. 20. Lit. " the sons of death ". 23. It is difficult to make sense of this v. as it stands ; read עִנָּה בַדֶּרֶךְ כֹּחִי, lit. " my strength is humbled (cp. Lev. 23²⁹) in the way ", i.e., in the midst of life. Read, cp. GS, לְצָר יְמֵי מַאֲמַר־לִי ; for this use of אמר see 1 Kgs. 11¹⁸, 2 Chron. 29²⁴. 24. Lit. " lift me not up ", cp. 2 Kgs. 2¹. Lit. " half ". Read, with S, לְדוֹר for בְּדוֹר. 26. Lit. " standest ", for this use of עמד cp. Isa. 66²², Jer. 32¹⁴. 29. Lit. " dwell ", for this sense of שָׁכַן see Judg. 5¹⁷.

For the title, see Vol. I, p. 19.

Unlike most of the titles of psalms, which purport to indicate authorship or to give musical directions, this title describes the character of the psalm.

1–11. The plaint poured forth in these verses is one of the most poignant of the many which find expression in the Psalter. In his *distress* the psalmist cries, *Yahweh, hear my prayer,* but his trouble is such that his thoughts become concentrated on his state of suffering. The somewhat exaggerated utterances used witness to the intensity of that suffering, which is both physical and mental. 3. A burning fever makes him compare his whole body to a consuming fire, his *inward parts* and his *bones glow like a hearth* heated by the flames. Then he turns to his mental sufferings ; 4. the *heart* is the seat of the emotions, and the simile, *smitten like grass,* in reference to the effect of the scorching sun, expresses a despairing mental state in which ordinary wants are forgotten : *I forget to eat my food* ; 5. so much so, and here he speaks again of physical suffering, that his *flesh* seems to *cleave* to his *bones.* Then (6), turning once more to his mental suffering, he feels so utterly forsaken that he compares himself with *a pelican in the wilderness,* or *an owl in ruined places* ; the word rendered " pelican "

is of uncertain meaning; it is a water-bird, and therefore hardly likely
to dwell in the wilderness; owls habitually took up their abode in ruins
(cp. Isa. 34[11]). 8. His suffering is aggravated by his boastful enemies,
who use his name in *an oath*, whereby they could bring a curse upon
him, as was believed; *with me*, means with my name. In 9–11 the
psalmist, by implication, reveals the reason why he has been stricken;
he has sinned, and has brought down upon himself God's *indignation*
and *wrath*; but he is repentant, sitting in *ashes*, and *weeping*, expressed
hyperbolically in the words: *I eat ashes like bread, and I mingle my drink
with weeping, i.e.*, with tears. From here we go to *v.* 23 (*vv.* 12–22 will
be dealt with below). In his sickness and despair, the psalmist feels
that his end is near: *My strength too soon is exhausted* is a free rendering (see text-crit. note), it expresses the conviction that his days are
numbered, *a cutting-off, i.e.*, shortening, *of my days is decreed for me*.
24. Nevertheless, he prays that he may yet live, and not be suddenly
snatched away, a very forcible expression, meaning lit. " lifted up "
from the earth. This leads him to speak of the endless years of the
Almighty, 25–28; far back in time, immeasurable in length, God
already lived, when he created *the earth* and *the heavens*; but even
they will pass away in the far-distant future; *but thou—thy years have
no end*. This thought of God's eternity induces a feeling of comfort:
though his days may be numbered, the descendants of the *servants* of
God *shall continue*, and *their seed be established before* him. Some
commentators hold that *v.* 29 does not belong to the original psalm;
and it is true that *v.* 28 makes a more logical and impressive close; but
it must be remembered that the Oriental is not always strictly logical in
his thought-sequence.

Turning now to the inserted portion, 12–22; its beginning, *But
thou, Yahweh, abidest for ever*, implies some preceding verses, so that it
would seem to be an extract from some other psalm. The picture
presented is that of Zion in ruins, but the conviction is expressed that
Yahweh will have *mercy* on her, and *build* her *up*; when that time comes
the nations will *fear* the *name* of Yahweh, for he will *appear in his glory
in the midst of her*; we have here an eschatological *trait* due to prophetic
influence. The difficulty is to ascertain to what period the ruined state
of Zion, here depicted, is to be assigned; that of the Exile, or soon
after, naturally suggests itself, especially as there are various thought-
contacts with Deutero–Isaiah. On the other hand, the psalmist's
indebtedness to other psalms, of later post-exilic date, forbids this date.
A Maccabæan date has been suggested, but the description of Zion
given in 1 Macc. 1[33] and elsewhere, compared with what is said in *v.* 14
of our psalm, shows the untenability of the suggestion. The probability
is that, as in the case of some other psalms, the reference here is to the
inroads of the Persian army under Artaxerxes III Ochus (see further

Vol. I, p. 72). However this may be, the faith of the psalmist in Yahweh is indestructible : *He hath regard unto the prayer of the destitute, and despiseth not their supplication*; so firm is the psalmist's certitude that the prayer will be answered that he wishes it to be written down in order that in later days men may know of it, and *praise Yah*. 19–22. The subject of the prayer is then recorded in a form which takes for granted that it is answered, although actually it is in the future that this will be done.

Religious Teaching

What the psalm teaches in this respect is the same as that which occurs in many others, and which is dealt with in the relevant sections. It will suffice, therefore, briefly to mention three points. First, there is the earnest appeal to God when in trouble ; in this case, as so often elsewhere, the trouble is occasioned by sickness and by the cruel behaviour of enemies; it will be noticed that here, unlike so many other psalmists, no divine punishment is called down upon the enemies. A further cause of the psalmist's trouble is a spiritual one, the bitterness of a contrite heart. The second point, though occurring in other psalms, is especially marked here—namely, the opening out of the heart to God, telling him, as to a dear and intimate friend, all his innermost feelings ; this is the most touching and appealing element in the religious teaching of the psalm. And, finally, there is that beautiful *trait*, so characteristic of the godly Israelite, of the certainty that prayer will be answered ; of this we have illustrations in many other psalms.

PSALM 103

In words as beautiful as any in the Psalter, the psalmist tells of the love of God towards those who fear him. This love is shown forth, above all, by the divine longsuffering and forbearance towards sinful humanity. That the psalmist speaks as an individual, and not as representing the community, needs no insisting on ; the first five verses should make this clear enough. The contrary is maintained by some commentators because of the mention of " our sins ", " our iniquities ", " our transgressions " ; but this does not make the psalm any the less personal ; just as when one prays " Our Father ", the prayer is that of an individual on behalf of himself, even though " us " and " we " occur in it. It is a striking *trait* in the psalmist that he feels his gratitude for the love of God to be so inadequate, however earnest, that he calls upon the heavenly host to bless Yahweh, so that spiritual beings may join with him in blessing God. The conception of sin, and the influence of some of the later books, mark the date of the psalm as post-exilic. The occurrence of several Aramaisms points in the same direction. The metre is almost wholly 3 : 3.

David's.

1. Bless Yahweh, O my soul,   yea, ° all within me °, his holy name.
2. Bless Yahweh, O my soul,   and forget not all his benefits :
3. Who forgiveth all thine iniquities,   who healeth all thy diseases,
4. Who redeemeth thy life from the Pit,   who crowneth thee with lovingkindness
                                                 and tender mercies,

5. Who satisfieth (thee) with good ° as
   long as thou livest °,   so that thy youth is renewed like the eagle.
6. Yahweh executeth righteous acts,   and justice for all that are oppressed.
7. He made known his ways unto Moses,   his doings unto the children of Israel.
8. Merciful and gracious is Yahweh,   long-suffering, and plenteous in loving-
                                                 kindness ;

9. ° For ° he chideth not for ever,   nor is he resentful everlastingly.
10. He doth not deal with us according to   nor doth he recompense us according to
    our sins °,   our iniquities °.
11. For as high as the heavens above the   so ° high ° is his love over them that
    earth,   fear him ;
12. As far as the east from the west,   so far hath he put our transgressions
                                                 from us ;

13. As a father hath compassion on his   so hath Yahweh compassion on them
    children,   that fear him ;
14. For he knoweth our frame,   he remembereth that we are but dust.
15. As for man, his days are like grass, ·   as a flower of the field, so doth he
                                                 flourish,
16. For the wind passeth over it, and it is   and the place thereof knoweth it no
    not,   more.
17. But the love of Yahweh is ° on them that   and his righteousness is to children's
    fear him,   children,
18. To them that keep his covenant ° and   to them that remember his statutes, to
    his commandments °,   do them.
19. Yahweh in the heavens hath established
    his throne,   and his kingdom ruleth over all.
20. Bless Yahweh, ye angels of his,   ye, mighty in strength, that fulfil his
                                                 command ° ;

21. Bless Yahweh, all ye ° his host °,   ye servants of his that do his will.
22. Bless Yahweh, all ye his works,   in all places of his dominion.
                    Bless Yahweh, O my soul.

Text-critical Notes

1. Read פְּל־קִרְבִּי for פְּל־קִרְבֵי as חֶרֶב is never used in the plur. 5. Read, cp. Ps. 104³³, 146², עוֹדֵך for עֶדְיֵך, " thine ornament ". 9. Add, with S, כִּי for the rhythm's sake. 10. Om. לָנוּ, " to µs ", for the rhythm's sake. Om. עָלֵינוּ, " upon us ", for the same reason. 11. Read גָבַהּ for גָבַר, " is mighty ". 17. Om. מֵעוֹלָם וְעַד־עוֹלָם, " from everlasting to everlasting ", which overloads the half-line. 18. Add וּמִצְוֹתָיו, see Deut. 7⁹ ; the half-line is too short as it stands. 20. Om. with S, בְּרוֹ לִשְׁמֹעַ בְּקוֹל דְּבָרוֹ, " to hearken unto the voice of his word ", a marg. gloss. 21. Read צְבָאוֹ for צְבָאָיו ; the plur. of צָבָא is צְבָאוֹת (so the Kᵉthibh), cp. Ps. 148².

1-5. As in the opening words of Ps. 104, the psalmist exhorts his own *soul* to *bless Yahweh*. The further calling upon his whole inner being to bless his *holy name* illustrates the Hebrew conception of man's being ; it is not only the heart (*lēb*), which is the seat of the emotions and thoughts, for *all within me* comprises also the " kidneys ", or

" reins " (*k'lâiôth*), parallel with the heart, *e.g.*, Jer. 11²⁰, 17¹⁰; the "liver" (*kâbēd*), in Lam. 2¹¹ it is said to be " poured out ", *i.e.*, in sorrow; and the " bowels ", (*mē'im*), which is also parallel to "heart" *e.g.*, Jer. 4¹⁹, as a seat of the emotions; included also are the " bones " ('*âzāmôth*), cp. Ps. 6², 35¹⁰, where they are parallel with the " soul " (*nephesh*). Another, though rare, expression, which would seem to be parallel to *all within me*, is *tûhôth*, " inward parts ", lit. the things " covered over ", which occurs in Ps. 51⁸ and in Job 38³⁶. It will thus be seen how full of meaning the psalmist's expression was to him. His further exhortation to himself, *forget not all his benefits*, is again very significant, first, because of his frank implication of his liability to forget, and also because of the nature of these benefits, which he then proceeds to describe. They are both spiritual, *who forgiveth all thine iniquities*, and temporal, *and healeth all thy diseases*, the word is always used in the literal sense of sickness (cp. 2 Chron. 21¹⁹, Jer. 14¹⁸, 16⁴); both kinds of benefits are further enumerated in *vv.* 4, 5. The divine lovingkindnesses are then more fully described (6–13) in words of sublime beauty. All is summed up in : *Yahweh executeth righteous acts*. From the days of *Moses*, to whom he revealed himself, he showed forth *his doings*, *i.e.*, his righteous acts; to *the children of Israel*, too, *he made known his ways*. All centres in the blessed truth that *merciful and gracious is Yahweh*. The verses which follow require no exegetical notes; their exquisite beauty seems to forbid comment, they are so self-expressive; all that we would add is that they, as it were, forestall the apostolic words : " God is love ". And this is only enhanced by what follows, 14–16, where the infinitude of the love of God is shown forth by the almost contemptible littleness of them upon whom it is expended—*dust, grass*; what a grand insight was vouchsafed to the psalmist in recognizing how pitiably insignificant man must be in the sight of God, but for his love. 17, 18. Nevertheless, in spite of this, *the love of Yahweh is on them that fear him*; self-evident though it may be that Yahweh's love can find expression only on them that fear him, the psalmist feels impelled to remind men of it; their part of the *covenant* made with them, solely out of divine love, must be kept, and *his statutes* observed. Let them remember, too, the psalmist seems to say, that they are the subjects of a Heavenly King : *Yahweh in the heavens hath established his throne, and his Kingdom ruleth over all.* Then (20–22), in holy exaltation of spirit, he calls upon the glorious angelic host to *Bless Yahweh*; and wheresoever in the illimitable space of his dominion his works are manifest, let all and everything *Bless Yahweh*; and in soul-felt gratitude and adoration he repeats once more : *Bless Yahweh, O my soul.*

The religious teaching of this psalm, with its beautiful witness to the love of God, is so fully expressed all through that a further section

on this could add nothing. Let the psalm be re-read, which will more
than suffice.

PSALM 104

THE central theme of this psalm is the glorification of Yahweh for his
creative work, and the continued existence of the earth, and all that is
in it, by his will. Of particular interest is the psalmist's utilization of
extraneous material; here we have echoes of the ancient Iranian
conception of the Deity being clothed in light; of the Babylonian myth
of the wings of the south wind (mentioned in the *Adapa*-myth); of
the *Tehom*-myth; and of some others. And, above all, there appears
to be some actual borrowing from the ancient Egyptian hymn of praise
to the sun-god; this was composed by the Pharaoh Amenophis IV
(Ikhnaton), who reigned 1375–1358 B.C.[1]; *vv.* 1–5, 10–26 of our psalm
contain many parallels with this. The psalmist's knowledge of all these
things is very remarkable; other psalms contain references to one or
other of them, but this psalm is unique for the wealth of such references
which it contains. There are certain points of contact between this
psalm and Ps. 103, but it will be noted that while in the latter Yahweh
is praised as the God of History, here it is as the God of Nature that
he is magnified.

Very fine as this psalm is, one cannot get away from the fact that the
psalmist gives expression to some *naïve* ideas of his own; this is
altogether in the nature of things; but the fact must be recognized.

The exceedingly old-world ring of the psalm suggests a pre-exilic
date; the general considerations regarding the dates of the psalms, so
instructively set forth by Gunkel–Begrich in their *Einleitung*, § 12, leads
to the same conclusion. Buttenwieser, too (*op. cit.*, pp. 161 ff.), argues
for a pre-exilic date; though his arguments are sometimes weak, he
makes out a good case on the whole.

The metre is, with but few exceptions, 3 : 3.

1. Bless Yahweh, O my soul;   ° my God, thou art very great;
   Thou art clothed with majesty and   2. ° thou coverest thyself ° with light as
     honour,   with a garment;
   Who spreadeth out the heavens like a 3. who layeth the beams of the upper
     canopy,   chambers in water,
   Who maketh clouds his chariot,   who goeth forth on the wings of the
                                             wind,
4. Who maketh winds his messengers,   fire ° and flame ° his ministers.
5. ° Who founded ° the earth upon its
     pillars,   it moveth not for evermore.

---

[1] Quoted below, p. 444.

6. Tehom ° covered it ° like a garment, upon the mountains did the waters stand;
7. At thy rebuke they fled, at the sound of thy thunder they hurried away,
8. ° They went up to ° the mountains, they went down to the valleys,
To the place which thou hadst founded for them;
9. A bound thou didst set which they should not pass over, nor cover the earth again.
10. He sent forth springs in the valleys, they run among the mountains;
11. They give to drink to all the beasts of the field, the zebras ° quench ° their thirst;
12. Beside them the birds of the ° air ° abide, from among the branches they give forth ° their song °.
13. He watereth the mountains from his upper chambers, ° from the moisture of thy heavens ° the earth is sated.
14. He causeth the grass to grow for the cattle, and herb ° for the service of ° man;
He causeth ° moisture ° to come forth from the earth, 15. and wine that rejoiceth the heart of man,
To make his face to shine through oil, and bread to strengthen man's heart.
16. The trees of Yahweh are sated, the cedars of Lebanon which he planted,
17. Where the birds make their nests, (and) the stork, the fir-trees are ° its dwelling-place °.
18. The mightiest mountains are for the wild goats, the rocks a refuge for the badger.
19. ° He made ° the moon for (indicating) seasons, ° he made the sun to know ° its going down;
20. Thou makest darkness that it may be night, when all the beasts of the forest creep forth;
21. The young lions roaring after their prey, to seek their meat from God;
22. ° Thou causest the sun to rise °, they get them away, and they lay them down in their dens.
23. Man goeth forth unto his work, and to his labour until the evening.
24. How manifold are thy works, Yahweh, ° the earth is full of ° thy creatures °:
25. There is the sea, great and wide, wherein are things creeping innumerable,

Beasts small and great, in wisdom hast thou made them all;
26. There go ° the sea-monsters °, Leviathan, whom thou madest to sport therein.
27. These all wait upon thee, that thou mayest give them their food in due season;
28. Thou givest it to them, they gather it up, thou openest thine hand, they are satisfied with good.
29. Thou hidest thy face, they are dismayed, thou withdrawest their breath, they die,
And unto their dust they return;
30. Thou sendest forth thy breath, they are created, and thou renewest the face of the earth.
31. May the glory of Yahweh endure for ever, may Yahweh rejoice in his works;
32. Who looketh on the earth, and it trembleth, he toucheth the mountains and they smoke.
33. I will sing to Yahweh while I live, I will sing praise to my God while I have my being.
34. May my meditation be pleasing unto him, I will rejoice in Yahweh.
35. May sinners be consumed from the earth, may the wicked be no more.
Bless Yahweh, O my soul.
Hallelujah.

Text-critical Notes

1. Om. the repetition of יהוה for the rhythm's sake. 2. Read תִּעְטֶה for עֹטֶה, " covering ", *i.e.*, that coverest. 4. Read וְלָהַט for לֹהֵט, " flaming " 6. Read כִּסִּתָה (both תְּהוֹם and אֶרֶץ are fem.). 8. Read, with Gunkel, עָלוּ for יַעֲלוּ, the subject is " the waters ", as לָהֶם shows. 11. Lit. " break ". 12. Lit. " heavens ". Read קוֹלָם for קוֹל " song ", lit. " voice ". 13. Read, with Budde and Hans Schmidt, מִפְּרִי מַעֲשֶׂיךָ for מְרִי שָׁמֶיךָ " from the fruit of thy works " (see, further, exeg. note). 14. Read לַעֲבֹדַת (cp. Gen. 26¹⁴, Job 1²) for לְעֲבֹדַת " for the labour ". Read לָח for לֶחֶם, " bread ". 17. Lit. " its house ". 19. Point again as partic. עֹשֶׂה. Read, cp. G, יָדַע for יָדַע " he knoweth ". 22. Read תִּזְרַח הַשֶּׁמֶשׁ for . . , תִּזְרַח " the sun ariseth ". 24. As this *v.* has a half-line too much, and one is wanting in the next *v.*, place, with Gunkel, כֻּלָּם בְּחָכְמָה עָשִׂיתָ at the end of *v.* 25. Read, with many MSS קִנְיָנֶךָ for קִנְיָנֶךָ, " thy creature ". 26. Read הַתַּנִּינִים for the quite inappropriate אֳנִיּוֹת, " ships ".

The verse-numbering at the opening of the psalm does not tally with the rhythmic balance of the verse-divisions ; *v.* 1 and the first half-line of *v.* 2 belong together, and form the introductory address to Yahweh ; with the second half-line of *v.* 2, of which the first half-line of *v.* 3 forms the second member, the main subject-matter of the psalm begins. This is indicated in our rendering by the change from " Thou " to " Who ".

1. With his mind full of thoughts concerning the stupendous might of Yahweh, which he is about to describe, the psalmist's first utterance proclaims the greatness of his God : *my God, thou art very great.* 2. His conception of the Almighty *as clothed with majesty and honour* (cp. Ps. 96⁶) through the brilliance of *light* with which he envelops himself, was taken from ancient Iranian belief ; according to this, the Good Spirit, *i.e.*, Mazda, " chose the Divine Righteousness ; yea, he so chose, who clotheth upon himself the firm stones of heaven as his robe," [1] *i.e.*, the stars which are full of light. But in the very next sentence the psalmist gives utterance to a different idea, adapted from Babylonian cosmology : *who spreadeth out the heavens like a canopy*, a poetical way of describing the firmament (lit. something " beaten out "), as in Isa. 40²², Job 9⁸. 3. Of Babylonian origin, too, is the conception of the heavenly dwelling-place, the pillars of which rest in the waters beneath ; [2] similarly, according to Egyptian belief, four pillars support the heavens.[3] *Who maketh clouds his chariot . . .* ; in one of the Ras Shamra texts the god is spoken of as " he that rideth upon the clouds " ; for the Babylonian conception see the introductory section. 4-9. These verses contain also echoes of Babylonian beliefs occurring in the Creation Epic ; [4] the victory of the god over his enemies,

[1] The Gathas ; Yasna xxx. 5 (*The Zend-Avesta*, Part III, transl. by L. H. Mills, in " The Sacred Books of the East ", Vol. 31 [1887]).
[2] Meissner, *Babylonien und Assyrien*, Vol. II, p. 108 (1920).
[3] Erman, *Die Religion der Ägypter*, p. 16 (1934).
[4] See, *e.g.*, Gressmann, *Altorientalische Texte zum alten Testament*, pp. 108 ff. (1926).

i.e., the Deep, is mentioned also in a Ras Shamra text. That all these ideas from extraneous sources had long been current in Israel is, of course, the fact; and it is of the deepest interest to see how they were adapted to Israelite belief. In what follows the psalmist speaks of the divine solicitude for all that lives on earth. 10–18. It will be noticed how emphasis is laid on the presence of water; in a country like Palestine this was looked upon as one of the greatest of God's gifts. Water for *beasts* and *birds*; water to make *the grass to grow for the cattle*, and *herb* for the various animals who do *service* for *man*, such as oxen, donkeys, and camels; water (*moisture*, as we must emend) to nourish the vine and the olive for man's benefit; water for the sustenance of the mighty trees, so necessary for the feathered flocks. From the creative act which gives water to man and beast and flying things the psalmist turns to speak of the moon and the sun, also indispensable for man and beast. 19–23. First to be spoken of is *the moon*; that this should be mentioned before the sun is significant as showing its greater importance. Among the Semites in the nomadic stage flocks and herds were led to fresh pasturage at night on account of the heat by day; it was natural enough, therefore, that the moon was at one time their chief deity.[1] The old belief in the moon and the sun as deities, though now, of course, subservient to Yahweh, is re-echoed here; the moon is thought of as having been *made* to mark off the divisions of time; the word is, however, used specifically in reference to sacred seasons, *i.e.*, the times of the great feasts (cp. Gen. 1^{14}, Lev. 23^{2-8}, Ecclus. $43^{7, 8}$). Of less importance was *the sun*, of which it is merely said that Yahweh had taught it when *to go down*. It is interesting to contrast this with the importance and glorification of the sun in Ikhnaton's hymn (see below). 20. *Darkness* is spoken of as a separate created thing; it does not supervene because the moon or the sun cease to shine; both light and darkness were thus conceived of as entities separately created (cp. Gen. 1^{3-5}). With this verse and 21–23 cp. Ikhnaton's hymn, quoted below. 24–26. Having spoken of the earth and all that lives thereon, the psalmist pictures *the sea great and wide* with all the *beasts small and great* moving about in it. 27–30 form a new section; the psalmist, thinking of all that lives on earth or in the sea, says that *These all wait upon thee, that thou mayest give them their food in due season*, and he goes on to declare that life and death are in the hands of God : *Thou sendest forth thy breath, they are created ; thou withdrawest their breath, they die.* 31–35. The psalm concludes with a short hymn of praise; in view of all the glorious acts of Yahweh and his benefits conferred on everything living, the psalmist deplores the fact that there should be any who do not *rejoice in Yahweh*, as he does ; they are not fit to share in the mercies so freely lavished : *May sinners be consumed from the earth, may the*

---

[1] Nielsen, *Die altarabische Mondreligion*, pp. 33 f. (1904).

wicked be no more. But his final thought reverts to God, and he ends as he began : *Bless Yahweh, O my soul.*

The parallelism of thought, sometimes verbal, between *vv.* 1–5, 10–26 of our psalm with Ikhnaton's hymn of praise to the Sun-god is so striking that it will be worth while quoting some part of it ; the conclusion is difficult to resist that our psalmist was familiar with it. The following extract is translated from the German versions of Ranke, in Gressmann, *op. cit.,* pp. 15 ff., and of Erman, *op. cit.,* pp. 111 ff.

> " Thou appearest in beauty on the horizon of heaven,
> Thou living sun, the first to live.
> Thou risest on the eastern horizon,
> Suffusing all lands with thy beauty.
> Glorious art thou, and mighty,
> Shining on high o'er the lands.
> Thy rays encircle the countries
> To the farthest limit of all thy creation ;
> Thou art Re (*i.e.,* the Sun-god) reaching out to their uttermost border,
> Subduing them for thy beloved son (*i.e.,* the Pharaoh).
> Far off art thou, yet thy beams touch the earth ;
> Thou art seen of men, but thy pathway they know not.
>
> Thou settest in the western horizon,
> And the earth becometh dark as death.
> Men rest in their chambers,
> With head enveloped, no eye sees aught ;
> Should their goods be taken that lie under their heads,
> They would fail to perceive it.
> The lion comes forth from his lair,
> And the serpents bite.
> Darkness rules, and the earth is still,
> For he that made all resteth in the horizon.
>
> When the earth becometh light, thou risest on the horizon,
> And, as the Sun, dost illumine the day ;
> The darkness fleeth when thy rays thou dost spread ;
> The two lands (*i.e.,* Upper and Lower Egypt) rejoice ;
> They (*i.e.* the inhabitants) awake, stand up on their feet,
> When thou hast raised them up ;
> They cleanse their bodies and clothe themselves,
> Their arms give praise (*i.e.,* by uplifting them), for thou hast appeared ;
> The whole earth goeth forth to labour,
> The cattle are satisfied with grass ;
> The trees and the herbs grow green,
> The birds from their nests fly forth,
> With their wings they offer thee praise.
> The beasts spring up on their feet,
> The birds and every flying thing
> Live, when thou art risen."

Religious Teaching.

Apart from the teaching of the creative acts of Yahweh, and that he is the God of Nature, and of his solicitude for all his created beings, there is in this psalm a further element in its religious teaching which provokes thought. The psalmist utilizes and adapts the conceptions and beliefs of peoples who do not acknowledge Yahweh as their God ; and yet he obviously discerns elements of truth in these old-world ideas ; otherwise he, as a loyal and devout believer in the God of gods, would not have employed them. The principle here accepted by the psalmist, unconscious as he doubtless was of its implications, is far-reaching in its application. Could there ever have been a time since the creation of man in which the Almighty did not evince an interest in the highest of all created things, man ? Was there ever a time in which God, in his love for men, ceased from his self-revelation to men, according to their capacity for apprehension ? We think of the grand words : " Jesus Christ, the same to-day, and yesterday, and for ever " (Hebr. 13[8]), and must realize that from the very beginnings of human history ultimate truth was vouchsafed in " divers portions and in divers manners " (Hebr. 1[1]). Thus, in all the crude beliefs of other peoples, Egyptian, Babylonian, Iranian, echoed by the psalmist, there are to be discerned germs of truth, held by men struggling through light and darkness—divine light and human darkness—to attain, no matter how slow the process, to the fulness of truth. " Art not thou from everlasting, Yahweh, my God, mine Holy One ! " (Hab. 1[12]).

One other element must be briefly mentioned. It is impossible to read this glorious psalm without feeling the triumphant joy that pulsates throughout. It reflects, as undoubtedly the psalmist intended that it should, the solemn happiness of the Creator in the beneficent work he has wrought ; in his loving forethought in providing all living beings with what they need, he has brought satisfaction, gratitude, joy to all. Should not that happiness granted by a loving Creator to all his creatures give happiness to him too ? It could not be otherwise. We must, therefore, discern in this psalm the thought, unexpressed but not the less present and real, of the happiness of God—a thought as beautiful as it is true.

PSALM 105

OF the type of Ps. 78, this psalm is primarily a thanksgiving, called forth by Yahweh's wondrous acts in the past. The detailed account of the Exodus and the subsequent events during the wanderings in the wilderness (as in Ps. 78) illustrate the great importance attached to them ; and with reason, since they record the constitution of Israel as a nation, and the institution of the Mosaic religion, making Yahweh the God of the nation. Four other topics receive special attention : the promises to Abraham, the story of the patriarchs, the covenant of Yahweh, and Canaan as the people's inheritance. The early part of the psalm, vv. 1–15, is largely identical with 1 Chron. 16[8-36]. A number of indications make it certain that the psalm is of late post-exilic date.

The metre, with the exception of *vv.* 1, 11, 15, is 3 : 3.

1. Give thanks to Yahweh,
Call upon his name,
Make known among the peoples his doings.

2. Sing unto ° Yahweh °, sing praises unto him,
be speaking of all his wondrous acts.

3. Glorify yourselves in his holy name,
let the heart rejoice of them that seek Yahweh.

4. Enquire of Yahweh and his strength,
seek his face continually,

5. Remember his marvellous works which he hath done,
his wonders, and the judgements of his mouth,

6. O ye seed of Abraham, his servant,
ye sons of Jacob ° his chosen °.

7. He, Yahweh, is our God,
his judgements are in all the world.

8. He remembereth his covenant for ever,
—the word which he commanded to a thousand generations,—

9. Which he made with Abraham,
and his oath to Isaac ;

10. And he confirmed it to Jacob for a statute,
to Israel for an everlasting covenant :

11. " ° To you ° will I give
the land of Canaan,
the lot of your inheritance."

12. When they were but few men in number,
yea, very few, and strangers therein,

13. Then went they about from nation to nation,
from one kingdom to another people ;

14. He permitted not a man to harm them,
and rebuked kings for their sakes :

15. " Touch not mine anointed ones,
And do my prophets no harm."

16. When he called for a famine on the land,
and broke every staff of bread,

17. Then sent he a man before them,
Joseph was sold as a slave ;

18. They hurt his feet with fetters,
his neck entered into the iron,

19. Until the time that his word came to pass ;
the saying of Yahweh proved true ;

20. The king sent and loosed him,
a ruler of peoples, and set him free ;

21. He made him lord of his house,
and ruler of all his substance,

22. ° To teach ° his princes ° according to ° his will,
and ° all ° his elders he instructed.

23. And Israel came into Egypt,
and Jacob sojourned in the land of Ham.

24. And he made his people very fruitful,
and made them stronger than their adversaries.

25. He turned their heart to hate his people,
to deal subtilly with his servants.

26. He sent Moses his servant,
and Aaron whom he had chosen ;

27. ° He brought about among them his signs by their word °,
and wondrous things in the land of Ham :

28. He sent darkness and made it dark,
but ° they observed ° not his words ;

29. He turned their waters into blood,
and slew ° all ° their fish ;

30. Their land swarmed with frogs,
° and they entered ° into the chambers of ° the king ° ;

31. He commanded, and there came swarms of flies,
and gnats in all their region ;

32. He gave them hail for rain,
and flaming fire in their land ;

33. He smote their vines and fig-trees,
and brake the trees in their border ;

34. He commanded, and the locust came,
and the cankerworm, yea, without number,

35. And ate up every herb in their land,
° and consumed ° the fruit of their ground ;

36. And he smote all the firstborn in their land,
the best of all their strength.

37. And he brought them forth with silver and gold,
there was not one that stumbled among their tribes.

38. Egypt was glad when they went forth,
for the fear of them had fallen upon them.

39. He spread a cloud for a covering,
and fire to give light at night.

40. ° They asked, and there came ° ° quails °,
and he satisfied them with bread from heaven.

41. He opened the rock, and waters gushed out,
42. For he remembered his holy word
43. And he brought forth his people with joy,
44. And he gave them the lands of the nations,
45. That they might keep his statutes,

they ran in dry places, a river.
with Abraham, his servant.

and his chosen ones with shouting;
and they took the labours of the peoples in possession ;
and observe his laws.

Hallelujah.

Text-critical Notes

2. Read יהוה for לוֹ, " to him ", both for the rhythm's sake, and on account of the following לוֹ. 6. Read, with some MSS בְּחִירוֹ for יו ,. . . " his chosen ones ". 11. Read לָכֶם, cp. I Chron. 16¹⁸, for לְךָ, " to thee ". 22. Read, with GS, לִיַסֵּר for לֶאְסֹר, " to bind ". Read, with GS, כְּ for בְּ " with ". Add כֹּל for the rhythm's sake. 27. Read אֹתוֹתָיו בְּדְבָרִים שָׁם־בָּם for שָׂמוֹ and דְּבְרֵי. 28. Read שָׁמְרוּ for מָרוּ, " they rebelled ". 29. Add כָּל־ for the rhythm's sake. 30. Add וַיָּבֹאוּ for the rhythm's sake. Read הַמֶּלֶךְ, for מַלְכֵיהֶם, " their kings ". 35. Read, with Duhm, וַיֹּכַל to avoid the repetition of וַיֹּאכַל, " and ate up ". 40. Read, with GS, שָׁאֲלוּ וַיָּבֵא, for שָׁאַל וַיָּבֵא, " he asked and brought ". Read, with Gunkel, שְׂלָוִי for שְׂלָו.

1-6. These verses form an introductory exhortation to the psalm, calling upon the people, spoken of as the *seed of Abraham*, and the *sons of Jacob*, to *give thanks to Yahweh* ; the Hebrew word connotes both thanksgiving and giving praise. Instructive is the way in which the psalmist indicates how this is to be shown forth ; viz., by calling upon Yahweh's name, making known his acts among all peoples, singing to him, rejoicing in him, seeking his face, remembering his works ; it is a beautiful conception of worship which the psalmist thus places on record. 7-11. The central thought here is the *covenant with Abraham*, as well as with Isaac and Israel (Jacob), see Exod. 2²⁴, *i.e.*, the promise to give them, in their posterity, *the land of Canaan*. The fulfilment of this is then developed in detail. 12-15. First a brief outline of the story of the patriarchs. It will not be necessary, excepting in a few cases, to give references to the earlier books ; as a rule, the events which the psalmist has in mind are sufficiently familiar ; he makes use of the Pentateuch in its present form, *i.e.*, including the latest document (P) embodied. In this section the only verse demanding a comment is 15 ; only here and in 1 Chron. 16²² are the patriarchs spoken of as *mine anointed ones*, indeed, the plur. occurs nowhere else. Again, *my prophets*, in reference to the patriarchs, is found here only ; once Abraham is called a prophet (Gen. 20⁷). 16-23. Here we have a brief reference to the Joseph narrative, somewhat involved, it is true. *The famine on* (so the Hebrew) *the land* is ascribed to Yahweh's direct action ; the curious phrase, " *staff* " *of bread* (cp. Lev. 26²⁶, Ezek. 4¹⁶, 5¹⁶, 14¹³, Ecclus. 8²), owes its existence to the custom of pressing newly baked pieces of bread on small pointed wooden sticks for temporary storing ; the " staff " supported the bread, if it was broken the bread might

easily come to grief from one cause or another. Another phrase which
reads strangely is that in 18, *his neck* (lit. " his soul ") *entered into the
iron*; this sense of " neck " for *nepheš* (" soul ") occurs in Ps. 69[1] :
" the waters have come unto my neck "; in the verse before us the
reference is to the iron collar round the neck of a slave; this is not
mentioned in Gen. 39[20]. In 19, *his word* means the " purpose " of
Yahweh. In the next section, 24–38, there is but little that calls for
comment; the plagues of Egypt form a theme dealt with elsewhere
(*e.g.*, Ps. 78[43–51]). A few textual corruptions have crept in; they are
briefly dealt with in the text-critical notes. In contrast to the detailed
enumeration of the plagues, the wanderings in the wilderness, 39–41,
are very summarily dealt with; the wondrous acts of Yahweh are the
psalmist's main preoccupation, as in the preceding section. One
somewhat surprising thing is that, unlike in other psalms of this type,
no reference is made to the sins of the people (see 78[8ff., 17ff.], 106[13 ff., 32ff.]).
In the concluding *vv.* 42–45, the psalmist reverts to the covenant, *the
holy word*, with Abraham; all that has intervened has been the outcome of this; and it culminates in Israel's possession of *the lands of
the nations*, which Yahweh *gave them*. Stress is laid in the final words
on Israel's part of the covenant, viz., *that they might keep his statutes,
and observe his laws.*

Religious Teaching

One matter of deep importance has already been referred to, but a
few further words on the subject are called for; we mean the elements
of worship which the psalmist sets forth. There can be no doubt that
his words reflect what was said and felt by the devout in the Temple-
worship, as also in the later Synagogue-worship, on which that of the
Church was originally based. Notable is the stress laid on joy in
worship; the feeling of happiness in offering praise and thanksgiving
is one the cultivation of which cannot be too strongly insisted on; and
the way in which, in this psalm, this element in worship is brought out
must be thankfully recognized.

Another thing to be noted is the divine guidance in history; with
this we have, however, dealt in discussing the religious teaching of
various other psalms, see especially Ps. 44; we shall not, therefore, say
more about it here.

And, once more, the psalmist calls upon his people to remember,
and to be grateful for, the divine mercies accorded in the past; another
lesson greatly needed in all ages, whether in regard to nations or
individuals. The preoccupations of the present are but too apt to
absorb all thought and attention; so that the numberless blessings of
days gone by are forgotten. A psalm like this, therefore, reminds men
of a duty too often lost sight of.

PSALM 106

THIS psalm is the third of those which contain a retrospect of early Israelite history. But while being of the general type of Pss. 78 and 105, it comes closer to the former of these in one important particular—namely, in the stress laid on the sinfulness of the people during those early days. In this respect it partakes, like Ps. 78, of the nature of a national confession uttered by one representing the nation; but unlike Ps. 78, the confession is not only in respect of past generations, it is uttered also on behalf of the present one : " We have sinned with our fathers, we have committed iniquity, and we have done wickedly " (v. 6); that is a striking addition.

The psalm was written by one living in the Dispersion : " Gather us from among the nations " (v. 47); its inclusion in the Psalter affords an interesting indication of the contact between the Jews of the Dispersion with their brethren in the home-land.

The late post-exilic date of the psalm is shown by its copious use of other post-exilic psalms.

The metre is, with few exceptions, 3 : 3.

1. Hallelujah !
   O give thanks to Yahweh, for he is good, / for his lovingkindness (endureth) for ever.
2. Who can utter the mighty acts of Yahweh, / or make all his praise to be heard ?
3. Blessed are they that observe justice, / ° that do ° righteousness at all times.
4. ° Remember us °, Yahweh, in the favour towards thy people, / ° visit us ° with thy help,
5.   That we may see the prosperity of thy chosen ones,
              That we may rejoice in the joy of thy nation,
              That we may glory with thine inheritance.
6. We have sinned with our fathers, / we have committed iniquity, ° and ° we have done wickedly.

7. Our fathers in Egypt
   They remembered not the abundance of thy lovingkindnesses, / understood not thy wondrous acts; / they rebelled ° against the Most High ° at the sea of reeds;
8. But he helped them for his name's sake, / that he might make his power to be known.
9. He rebuked the sea of reeds that it dried up, / and he led them through depths as through pasture-land;
10. And he delivered them from the hand of the hater, / and redeemed them ° from the clutch ° of the enemy.
11. And the waters covered their adversaries, / not one of them was left.
12. Then believed they his words, / ° whereupon ° they sang his praise.
13. ° They soon forgot ° his works, / ° and ° waited not for his counsel;
14. But ° they lusted exceedingly ° in the wilderness, / and tempted God in the desert;
15. And he gave them their request, / and sent ° food ° ° according ° to their desire.
16. And they envied Moses in the camp, / and Aaron, the holy one of Yahweh.
17. The earth opened, and swallowed up Dathan, / and covered the company of Abiram;
18. And fire was kindled in their company, / the flame burned up the wicked.
19. They made a calf in Horeb, / and worshipped a molten image,
20. And they changed their glory / for the likeness of an ox that eateth grass;
21. They forgot God their saviour, / who did great things in Egypt,
22. Wondrous things in the land of Ham, / terrible things at the sea of reeds,

23. And he said ° that he would destroy them °,
He stood in the breach before him,
but for Moses, his chosen,
to turn away his wrath from destroying them.

24. And they despised the pleasant land,
25. And they murmured in their tents,
° and ° trusted not in his word.
° and ° hearkened not unto the voice of Yahweh;

26. Therefore he lifted up his hand against them,
27. And ° to disperse ° their seed among the nations,
to overthrow them in the wilderness,
and to scatter them in the lands.

28. And they joined themselves to Baalpeor,
29. And they provoked ° him ° to anger by their deeds,
and ate the sacrifices of the dead.
and the plague brake in among them;

30. But Phinehas stood up and mediated,
31. And it was reckoned unto him for righteousness
and the plague was stayed,
to generations and generations for ever.

32. And they angered him at the waters of Meribah,
33. For ° they had embittered ° his spirit,
and it went ill with Moses for their sakes;
so that he spake unadvisedly with his lips.

34. They did not destroy the peoples,
35. But mingled themselves among the nations,
as Yahweh had commanded them,
and learned their works;

36. And they served their idols,
37. And they sacrificed their sons
38. And they poured out innocent blood °,
39. They became unclean by their deeds,
40. Then was the wrath of Yahweh kindled against his people,
and they became a snare unto them;
and their daughters to demons,
and the land was polluted with blood.
and went a-whoring in their doings.
and he abhorred his inheritance.

41. And he gave them into the hand of the nations,
42. Their enemies also oppressed them,
and they that hated them ruled over them.
and they were bowed down under their hand.

43. Many times did he deliver them,
44. Nevertheless he regarded their distress
45. And he remembered for them his covenant,
but they rebelled ° against his purpose °.
when he heard their cry;
and repented according to the abundance of his lovingkindness;

46. And he gave them for (objects of) mercy
47. Save us, Yahweh our God,
That we may give thanks to thy holy name,
among all who had taken them captive.
and gather us from among the nations,
and triumph in thy praise.

48. Blessed be Yahweh,
the God of Israel,
from henceforth
and for evermore;
And let all the people say: " Amen."
Hallelujah.

Text-critical Notes

3. Read, with some MSS. and the Versions, עֹשֵׂי for עֹשֵׂה, "he that doeth". 4. Read, with some MSS. and the Versions, זָכְרֵנוּ for זָכְרֵנִי, "remember me". Read, with some MSS. and G, פָּקְדֵנוּ for פָּקְדֵנִי "visit me". 6. Add, with many MSS. וְ, "and". 7. Read עֶלְיוֹן for עָלְיָם, "at the sea", and עַל for בְּ, "in". 10. Read מִכַּף, lit. "palm" of the hand (see Ps. 71[4]) for מִיַּד, "from the hand", the repetition of which in the same v. is unusual. 12. Add אָז for the rhythm's sake. 13. Lit. "they hasted, they forgat". Add, with some MSS. and S, וְ. 14. Lit. "they lusted a lust". 15. Read, with Briggs, מָזוֹן. Read לְ for בְּ, "into". 23. For the construction see GK 114fo. 24. Add, with GS, וְ. 25. Add, with some MSS. and S, וְ. 27. Read, with S, לְהָפִיץ, parallel with " scatter". 29. Add, with GS, הוּ—. 33. Read הִמְרוּ for הִמְרוּ, "they were rebellious", which is used of rebellion against God, see vv. 7, 43. 38. Om., as a later gloss, כְּנַעַן . . . דְּב־, "the blood of their sons and their daughters whom they sacrificed to the idols of Canaan". 43. Read בַּעֲצָתוֹ for —תָם "their purpose". Om. וַיִּמֹּכּוּ בַּעֲוֹנָם, "and they were brought low in their iniquity", a marg. note which disturbs the rhythm.

As in the case of Ps. 105, the character of this psalm, being merely
a repetition of the details of early Israelite history, does not call for
many exegetical notes.

1–6. The introductory words of praise (1, 2) are followed (3) by an
expression of the blessedness of those *that observe justice* and *do righteousness*. The prayer (4, 5) and confession (6) are said in the name of the
people, as clearly indicated in *v.* 6; we should, therefore, read:
Remember us, visit us, with the Versions and some MSS., not " me ",
as in the English Versions. The error arose, no doubt, because of the
words, *in the favour towards thy people*, which seemed to differentiate
between the psalmist and the people, but " towards *us* thy people "
was self-understood, though this was not recognized by the Masoretes,
hence " remember me ", " visit me ", in the present Hebrew text.
A similar error occurs in the second half of *v.* 3, where *that do*, not
" he that doeth ", should be read. *Thy nation* (5), the Hebrew *gôy*,
when used in reference to Israel or Judah, denotes them as a sinful
nation (*e.g.*, Deut. 32[28], Judg. 2[20], Isa. 1[4], 10[6]) because *gôy* is ordinarily
used of the Gentiles; that it refers here to Israel is, therefore, very
exceptional. 7–12. The historical events begin here with a brief
account of the passage of the Red Sea, as usually designated; the
Hebrew is *Yām-Sûph* " Reed sea ", or sea of reeds, or weeds; it is the
long narrow arm of the Red Sea, the Aelanitic Gulf, or the Gulf of
Akaba. A textual difficulty occurs in 7; the Hebrew, as it stands,
has: " they rebelled upon, or at, a sea, in the *Yām-Sûph* "; the
repetition of " sea " (*Yām*) can hardly be original as it is a clumsy mode
of expression; the letters are very similar to *'Elyôn*, " Most High ",
and as the phrase " they rebelled against the Most High " occurs twice
in Ps. 78[17, 56], it is justifiable to read this here. 13–15. Then we have
an abridged account of the episode of the quails, see Num. 11[4, 13, 31–33];
the text of 15 offers another difficulty; the word rendered " food " is
an emendation; for the word in the Hebrew text is *rāzôn*, meaning
" leanness " (cp. Isa. 10[16]); that is inappropriate, seeing that the
reference is to the quails which had been sent; we have, therefore,
adopted the very similar word, suggested by Briggs, *māzôn*, meaning
" food ". 16–18. Cp. Num. 16[1–35]. 19–23. The narrative of the
worship of the golden calf is contained in Exod. 32[1–6, 11–14]; in *v.* 20
their glory means " their God " as in Ps. 3[3]. 24–27. The reference
here is to Num. 14[1–3]; but in 27 the psalmist has the Exile in mind.
For 28–31 see Num. 25[1–9, 10–13]; in Num. 25[2], cp. Exod. 34[15], it is
said that the sacrifices were offered to gods; when, in the verse before us,
it is said that *they ate the sacrifices of the dead, i.e.*, offered to the dead,
it is possible that the gods, being lifeless things, were thought of as
dead (cp. Isa. 44[9–20], Ps. 135[15–17]); but it is more probable that the
words are to be understood in a literal sense; offerings to the departed

were widespread in antiquity, and doubtless also among the Israelites.
32, 33. See Num. 20$^{2-13}$. The psalmist then (34–46) describes the
disloyalty of the Israelites to their God after the settlement in Canaan,
and the divine mercy accorded to them in spite of it. This section is
all perfectly straightforward, and does not call for further notes. The
psalm ends (47, 48) with prayer and praise.

For the religious teaching of the psalm reference may be made to
the relevant section of Ps. 105, though not all that is said there applies
to this psalm.

PSALM 107

APART from *vv.* 1–3, which are introductory, and *vv.* 33–43, which is
an independent piece, added later, this skilfully constructed psalm of
thanksgiving (see *v.* 22) consists of four self-contained strophes, having,
however, a point of attachment in the refrain which is repeated in each.
Each of the four strophes tells of those who had been in dire straits,
but who had been delivered by the mercy of God, and are called upon
to express their gratitude to him.   Thus, the first strophe (*vv.* 4–9)
tells of wanderers in the wilderness, who have been brought safely
to their destination ; the second (*vv.* 10–16) describes the plight of
captives who had been released from prison ; the third (*vv.* 17–22)
speaks of the sick who had recovered from their sickness ; and the
fourth (*vv.* 23–32) gives an account of the perils experienced by seafarers, from which they have been rescued.   All these are gathered
in the Temple to give thanks to God for the mercies vouchsafed to
them.   The occasion was doubtless one of the great festivals, probably
the Feast of Tabernacles.   The psalm of thanksgiving was sung after
the sacrifice of thanksgiving had been offered, if we may judge from
Ps. 50^{14}, 66$^{1-3}$, 116$^{17, 18}$, Jon. 2^{9}, see also *v.* 22 of our psalm, where
the offering of the sacrifices of thanksgiving are mentioned before the
singing.

As to the outward form of these strophes, there is not absolute
uniformity ; the normal form would seem to be : two 3 : 3 lines,
followed by the first half of the refrain ; then a single 3 : 3 line, followed
by the second half of the refrain, after which another 3 : 3 line concludes
the strophe ; this is the form of the first and third strophes, and, but for
an additional line, the form of the second ; but the fourth strophe is
considerably extended.   Hence some commentators believe *v.* 11 in
the second strophe, and a large part of the fourth strophe, to be later
additions.   With this we find it difficult to agree ; *v.* 11 is quite
appropriate, and even if it breaks the external symmetry of the strophe,

there is no reason to suppose that the ancient Hebrew poets were tied
to a rigid uniformity ; and as to the fourth strophe, there was ample
reason why this should have been somewhat developed ; the sea and
the sea-faring life had been unfamiliar in the past ; the perils of the
sea and its mysterious changes were awe-inspiring ; what more natural
than that, in speaking of it, the psalmist should feel prompted to dwell
somewhat fully on its dangers ? It must also be recognized that the
fourth strophe reaches a climax ; it tells of the most signal marks of
God's mercy, and of his power in stilling the elements. Some little
development of treatment is, therefore, fully comprehensible.

As to the final section (*vv.* 33-43), it may be noted, first, that it
contains no word of thanksgiving ; if it were the concluding portion
of the psalm of thanksgiving some expression of this would assuredly
have found a place. Further, the absence of the refrain, present in
each of the other sections, cuts it off from the body of the psalm.
Its content, moreover, differs from the psalm itself ; it describes, on
the one hand, the punishment inflicted on men for their wickedness
by the Almighty, and, on the other, his merciful treatment of the needy
and the upright ; this, together with the contrasts presented, is different
from the whole course of the preceding psalm. And, finally, there is
the difference of outward form between the two. For these reasons the
impression is gained that *vv.* 33-43 are not an original part of the psalm,
but were added later.

The date of the psalm is indicated in *v.* 3, where the people are
spoken of as being gathered out of the lands ; this points clearly to the
Dispersion. The psalm was probably not written much earlier
than about 300 B.C., or even later. The reference to the Jews as
seafarers emphasizes this.

The text has come down to us with but few corruptions.

The metre is 3 : 3 ; where 2 : 2 : 2 occurs (*vv.* 3, 25, 26, 37) the
change comes in effectively. The psalm is one of the so-called
" orphan " psalms, as having no title.

1.   ° HALLELUJAH.°

O give thanks to Yahweh, for he is
good,   for his mercy endureth for ever.
2. Let those saved by Yahweh utter   whom he saved from the hand of
thanks,   distress ;
3.   From the lands he gathered them,
                          from east and from west,
                          from north and from ° south.°
4. ° They that wandered ° in desert and
waste,   the way to dwelt city they found not,
5. Hungry, yea, and thirsty,   their soul within them fainted.
6. *They cried to Yahweh in their need,* *out of their distresses h° delivered them ;*
7. He led them upon the right way,   to go to the city of habitation ;
8. *Let them thank Yahweh for his love,* *for his wonder-works to the children of*
                                         men !
9. For he satisfied the parched soul,   and the hungry he filled with good.

                                                        GG

10. Such as dwelt in darkness, and deep gloom,
11. For they had rebelled against the words of God,
12. But he humbled their heart with hard labour,
13. *They cried to Yahweh in their need,*
14. He brought them out of darkness and deep gloom,
15. *Let them thank Yahweh for his love,*

16. For he shattered the gates of bronze,

17. Fools, for their way of transgression
18. All food their soul doth abhor,

19. *They cried to Yahweh in their need,*
20. He sent forth his word to heal them,

21. *Let them thank Yahweh for his love,*

22. Let them offer sacrifices of thanksgiving,

23. They that went down to the sea in ships,
24. They saw the works of Yahweh,
25. He spake °, and stirred up ° the wind of the tempest, and lifted up the waves thereof,
26. they mounted heavenwards, went down to the depths, their soul melted;° °
27. They reeled and staggered like one drunken,
28. *They cried to Yahweh in their need,*
29. ° He stilled ° the storm to calmness,
30. Then were they glad, that they were hushed;
31. *Let them thank Yahweh for his love,*

32. Let them exalt him in the assembly of the people,

33. He turneth rivers into a wilderness,
34. A fruitful ground to salt-land,

35. He turneth the wilderness into a pool,
36. There caused he the hungry to abide,
37. They sow fields, they plant vineyards, that bring forth fruits of increase;
38. He blesseth them and they yield abundantly,
40. He poureth contempt on princes,

° 39. (And they are minished and bowed down,
41. But he lifteth up the poor from his affliction,
42. Let the righteous see it and rejoice,
43. Who is wise? Let him heed these things,

being bound in affliction and iron— and contemned the counsel of the Most High,—
they stumbled, and there was none to help;
out of their distresses he delivered them;

and their binding cords he snapped;
for his wonder-works to the children of men;
and the bars of iron he hewed asunder.

and for their iniquities are afflicted;
they have drawn nigh the gates of death;
out of their distresses he delivered them;
° to deliver them ° ° from their destroyer °;
for his wonder-works to the children of men;
and declare his works with a shout of joy.

trading in mighty waters,
yea, his wonder-works in the deep:

and all their skill was confounded;
out of their distresses he delivered them;
° the waves of the sea ° were silent;
he brought them to their desired haven;
for his wonder-works to the children of men;
where the elders sit let them praise him.

and watersprings into a thirsty land,
for the wickedness of the dwellers therein;
and parched land into water-springs;
and they founded a city to dwell in;

and suffereth not their cattle to decrease.
and maketh them wander in a pathless waste,
through oppression, trouble, and sorrow;)°

and maketh him families like a flock.
and all iniquity close its mouth.
° let him consider the lovingkindnesses of Yahweh.

Text-critical Notes

1. This has been erroneously placed at the conclusion of the preceding psalm; it is not a title, but the opening of the psalm itself.

3. Read מִיָּמִין for מִים "from the sea". 4. Read תָּעוּ for תָּעוּ as in *vv.* 10, 23. 20. Read וַיְמַלְּטֵם for וַיְמַלְּטֵם "he delivered"; and מִמַּמְחֻתָם for מִשְּׁחִיתוֹתָם "from their destructions". Some commentators read מִשְּׁחַת חַיָּתָם "their life from the pit", see Hag 1¹⁴ (cp. Ps. 103⁴). 25. Read, with Hans Schmidt, וַיֵּעַר for וַיַּעֲמֵד "he caused to stand". 26. Delete בְרָעָה "with trouble". 29. Read גַּלֵּי הַיָם for גַּלֵּיהֶם (their waves). 39. This *v.* is possibly an insertion by a later copyist. 43. Read יִתְבּוֹנֵן for יִתְבּוֹנְנוּ "let them give heed".

1–3. A comprehensive reference to all those spoken of in the body of the psalm, who are called upon to give thanks to God for the signal marks of His love bestowed on them. The words *from the lands he gathered them* indicate that the Dispersion of Jews had already taken place. By the Dispersion is meant not the forcible settling of Israelites and Judahites in other lands, which took place in 722 B.C. and 597 B.C., respectively, as well as in 351 B.C., but the voluntary settlements formed for the purpose of trading and the like, which took place, mainly, during the Greek period·(*circa* 300 B.C. onwards); it is graphically described in the *Sibylline Oracles* 271 : " Every sea and every land is full of thee " (belonging to the second century B.C.). The dispersed Jews experienced a sense of national unity in regarding Jerusalem as the nation's centre ; thither they went on one or more of the great annual feasts, of which that of Tabernacles, in the autumn, was the most important ; it is probable that this psalm was sung on this occasion, though in the later Synagogue service it was one of the proper psalms for the Passover feast.

4–9. The first of whom the psalmist speaks are travellers from the east or the south, who had lost their way in the wilderness, *the way . . . they found not*; their extremely precarious position is tersely, but graphically, described : *Hungry, yea, and thirsty, their soul within them fainted.* Their cry to God is heard, who leads them to the *right way*, not " straight ", as the R.V. renders ; it might be ever so winding provided it was the right way. *Soul* (*nephesh*) is used in a very wide sense in Hebrew ; as a man's personality, as the seat of the emotions and physical appetites, as here ; but also in other senses. We have rendered the Hebrew *ḥesed* " love " ; it is usually translated " mercy ", or " lovingkindness ", but the word connotes more than this.

10–16. In speaking next of captives who had *sat in darkness*, and had been *bound in affliction and iron*, the psalmist attributes their sufferings to their having *rebelled against the words of God*, that is, his commandments (cp. Exod. 34²⁸) ; the reference here is evidently to imprisonment for theft, or other cause, of which some of the Jews had been guilty in the country of their adoption. It is implied that they are brought to repentance, and forgiven ; as a result God brings about their deliverance. One sees here the many-sidedness of *ḥesed*.

17–22. In this section those who had been stricken with sickness are spoken of ; as always, in ancient Hebrew belief, sickness is regarded as a mark of divine disfavour for sin ; the sick are spoken of as *fools for their way of transgression*. Their appeal to God is not in vain : *He sent forth his word to heal them* ; for this expression see Ps. 147^{15} Isa. 55^{11}. In recognition of this they are called upon to *offer sacrifices of thanksgiving* ; the technical term for this type of sacrifice, *todah*, is the same as that for the thanksgiving itself.

23–32. Finally, the psalmist speaks of the seafarers ; that these are more fully dealt with is natural enough, for trading on the seas was a comparatively new calling for the Jews. The perils of the sea are graphically described ; the sailors on board the storm-tossed ship *reel and stagger*, their seamanship is of no avail, *all their skill* is *confounded*. But at the divine will the storm subsides. *Then they were glad that they* (*i.e.*, the waves of the sea) *were hushed*. How the last verse of the section (32) is to be understood is uncertain. One expects the reference to be to the temple ; but *the assembly* (*qahal*) is used both of the congregation at worship, and in a quite general sense. As to *the seat of the elders*, there is no evidence that they occupied any special place at the temple-worship. The verse may, therefore, mean that the rescued sailors were to express their gratitude to God both among any gathering of the people in general, as well as in the more august assembly of the elders, wherever this may have been held.

33–43. On this section see the introduction to the psalm.

Religious Teaching

Probably in no other psalm is the belief in the divine intervention in the ordinary affairs of men expressed in more detail than here. The intense conviction that, when in need or stress, men seek help from God, that help is forthcoming, is also a striking characteristic of the psalm. This faith in the divine response to prayer which this and other psalms teach has impressed itself in a touching way on the prayers of the Jewish Liturgy ; here again and again a prayer is concluded with a blessing on the Almighty for granting the petition prayed for ; thus, for example, at the end of a prayer for God's help for those in affliction come the words : " Blessed art thou, O Lord, who answerest in time of trouble ".

The psalm is also remarkable for the picture it gives of congregational worship.

PSALM 108

THIS psalm consists of two extracts : *vv.* 1–5 are taken from Ps. 57$^{7-11}$, and *vv.* 6–13 from Ps. 60$^{5-12}$. There are five slight variations, four of which are negligible ; one is, however, of interest : in *v.* 3 the divine

name Yahweh is used in place of *Adonai* in 57[9], indicating the fact that
our psalm belonged to a group in which the name of Yahweh was used
in speaking of the Deity; nevertheless, everywhere else in the psalm,
when God is mentioned, *Elohim* is used, following herein the two
other psalms, both of which belong to the Elohistic group. The point
is of interest as showing that our psalm utilized Pss. 57 and 60, not
vice versa.

For the commentary and other details see under Pss. 57 and 60.
The metre of *vv.* 1–5 is 3 : 2 ; that of *vv.* 6–13 is mainly 3 : 3.

A Song.   A Psalm.   David's.

1 (2). My heart is fixed, O God, I will sing and make melody ° to thee °,	° my heart is fixed °, ° thou art ° my glory.
2 (3). Awake, harp and lyre,	I will awake the dawn.
3 (4). I will give thanks to thee among the peoples, Yahweh,	I will make melody to thee among the nations.
4 (5). For great is thy love,° unto ° the heavens,	and unto the skies thy truth,
5 (6). Be thou exalted, O God, above the heavens,	and above all the earth thy glory.
6 (7). In order that my beloved may be delivered,	save with thy right hand, and answer me.
7 (8). God hath spoken in his holiness,	I will exult, I will divide Shechem,
And mete out the valley of Sukkoth :	
8 (9). Gilead is mine,	
Manasseh is mine	
Ephraim is the defence of my head,	
Judah is my staff,	
9 (10). Moab is my washpot,	over Edom will I cast my shoe,
Over Philistia will I shout.	
10 (11). Who will lead me to the fenced city ?	who ° will bring ° me unto Edom ?
11 (12). Hast thou not, O God, cast us off ?	thou goest not forth, O God, with our hosts.
12 (13). Give us help against the adversary,	for vain is the help of man,
13 (14). With God we shall do valiantly,	yea, he will tread down our adversaries.

Text-critical Notes

1. Add נָכוֹן לִבִּי as in 57[7]. Add, with G, לָךְ. Read, with Duhm, אַתָּה,
for אַף, " even ". 4. Read, as in 57[10], עַ. 10. Read, with G, יַנְחֵנִי for נְחֵנִי,
" hath led me ".

PSALM 109

THIS psalm belongs to magical texts rather than to religious literature.
There are imprecatory elements in some other psalms, but in none is
there the exaggerated vindictiveness characteristic of this one. The
contention of some commentators that the imprecations are the
quotations of his enemies, and not those of the psalmist himself, is due
to a misunderstanding of the nature of the psalm. The only extenuation
that can be pleaded for the terrible sentiments expressed by the psalmist

against his adversaries, and against one in particular, is the fact that the enemies of the righteous—and righteous the psalmist feels himself to be (*vv.* 1, 4, 5, 21, 26, 30)—were regarded also as the enemies of God. The personal note, however, greatly predominates, and that its vindictive spirit made it unfitting for public worship was early recognized by the Jewish Church; the most ancient Jewish liturgical records never mention it as used in worship; it is certain that from before the beginning of the Christian era it never figured in the Jewish Liturgy.

In the early mediæval *Sepher Shimmush Tehillim*, " The Book of the use of the Psalms ", the recitation of this psalm is recommended as a sovereign remedy against the machinations of an enemy.

The date is late post-exilic.

The metre is 3 : 3, with the exception of *vv.* 28, 30.

For the Precentor.   David's.   A Psalm.

1. O God of my praise, be not silent,

  They speak against me with a lying tongue,
  And they fight against me without cause ;
5. And ° they return ° evil for good,
6. Set thou over him a wicked man,

7. When he is judged let him come forth guilty,
8. Let his days be ° few °,
9. Let his children be fatherless,
10. Let his sons be vagabonds, and beg,

11. Let the extortioner ensnare all that he hath,
12. Let him not have one that extendeth him kindness,
13. Let his posterity be cut off,

14. Let the iniquity of ° his father ° be remembered,
15. Let them be before Yahweh continually,

16. Because he remembered not to show mercy,
  And he persecuted the afflicted and poor,
17. He loved cursing—let it overtake him,
18. Yea, he put on cursing like his garment,
  Let it come like water to his inner part,
19. Let it be to him like raiment wherewith he clotheth himself,
20. This is the recompense of mine accusers °,
21. But thou, Yahweh, ° look upon me °,
  ° According to the goodness ° of thy love deliver me,
22. For afflicted and needy am I,
23. Like a shadow when it lengthens I go hence,
24. My knees totter through fasting,
25. ° I am become a reproach to them,
26. Help me, Yahweh, my God,

2. for the mouth of ° wickedness ° ° is opened ° against me,

3. and words of hatred encompass me,
4. ° in place of ° my love they accuse me,
and hatred ° in place of ° my love.
and let an accuser stand at his right-hand ;

and ° his sentence ° let it be for sin.
and his wealth let another take ;
and ° let ° his wife ° be ° a widow.
° and let them be driven forth from their company °.

and let strangers plunder his gains.

nor one that hath pity on his orphans ;
in ° one ° generation let ° his name ° be blotted out.
and the sin of his mother let it not be blotted out;
that he may cut off ° his memory ° from the earth.

°   .   .   .   .   °

and the broken of heart ° to death °.
he desired not blessing—let it be far ° ;
°   .   .   .   .   °
and like oil into his bones ;
and like a girdle wherewith he always girdeth himself.
and of them that speak evil against my soul.
deal with me for thy name's sake,

.   .   .   .   .   .
and my heart is pierced within me ;
° I am swept away ° like a locust, ° and am no more °.
and my flesh is lean, without fatness.
they look at me, they shake their head.
save me in thy ° great ° mercy,

27. That they may know that this is thy hand,
28. Let them curse, but bless thou,

thou, Yahweh, hast done it.
° and let them that rise up against me be ashamed °, but let thy servant rejoice;

29. Let mine accusers be clothed with dishonour,
30. I will greatly give thanks to Yahweh with my mouth,
31. For he standeth at the right-hand of the needy,

and let them clothe themselves with their shame like a mantle.
and in the midst of many will I praise him.
to save him ° from them that persecute ° his soul.

Text-critical Notes

2. Read רָשָׁע for וְרֶשַׁע " the wicked (man) "; cp. שִׂנְאָה, " hatred," in v. 3. Om. וּפִי־מִרְמָה, " and the mouth of deceit," which overloads the text. Read with G, פָּתוּחַ for פָּתְחוּ, " they opened ". 4. Lit. " instead of ". Om. וַאֲנִי תְפִלָּתִי, " and I, my prayer," which overloads the text. 5. Read, with S, וַיְשׂוּבוּ for וַיָּשִׂימוּ, " and they laid ". Delete עָלַי, " upon me ". Lit. " instead of ". 7. Read, with Briggs, פְּלִילָיְתוֹ, as in Isa. 28⁷, for תְּפִלָּתוֹ, " his prayer ". 8. This plur. form is late Hebrew, cp. Eccles. 1⁶, Pirqe Aboth 1¹⁸. 9. Add תְּהִי for metre's sake. 10. Read, with G, יְגֹרְשׁוּ מֵחָרְבֹתָם, cp. Job 30⁵, 34⁸—i.e., from their associates, for וְדָרְשׁוּ מֵחָרְבוֹתֵיהֶם, " and let them seek out their desolate places ". 13. Read, with G, אֶחָד for אַחֵר, " after ". Read, with many MSS and G, שְׁמָם for שְׁמוֹ, " their name ". 14. Read אָבִיו for אֲבוֹתָיו, " his fathers ". Om., with S, אֶלֿ־יְהוָֹה, " unto Yahweh ". 15. Read, with G, זִכְרוֹ for זִכְרָם, " their memory ". 16. A half-line seems to have fallen out here. Read, with S, לְמָוֶת for לְמוֹתֵת, " to slay ". 17. Om. מִמֶּנּוּ, " from him ", which overloads the text. 18. A half-line seems to have fallen out here. 20. Om. מֵאֵת יְהוָֹה, " from Yahweh ", which overloads the text. 21. Read, with Gunkel, רָאֵנִי for אֲדֹנָי, " my Lord ". Read כָּטוֹב for כִּי־טוֹב, " for good is . . . " A half-line seems to have fallen out here. 23. Read, with Gunkel, נִסְעָרְתִי for נִגְעַרְתִּי, " I am poured out ", which, in reference to a locust, is inappropriate. Add וְאִיכַנִי for the metre's sake. 25. Om. the pronoun, וַאֲנִי, which overloads the text. 26. Add, with G, בָּרֹב for the metre's sake. 28. Read וְקָמֵי יֵבֹשׁוּ for חָמוּ וַיֵּבֹשׁוּ, " they rise up and are ashamed ". 31. Read, with G, מֵרֹדְפִים for מִשֹּׁפְטֵי, " from them that judge ".

1–5. The psalmist begins by bringing his complaint before God; he is the victim of slander, *they speak against me with a lying tongue*; his enemies have shown him hatred in return for his love. 6–15. Against one enemy in particular the psalmist entertains the bitterest feelings. He pictures a court scene, where the judge is a *wicked man*; at the *right-hand* of the enemy stands his accuser, the Hebrew word for which is *sātān*, often used of an adversary in the ordinary sense (e.g., 1 Kgs. 5⁴ ⁽¹⁸⁾, 11¹⁴, ²³, ²⁵, and elsewhere); in reference to a superhuman being the term occurs in 1 Chron. 21¹; Job 1⁶ ff. 2¹ ff.; Zech. 3¹, ²; it is never used as a proper name in the Old Testament. The enemy is to be judged as *guilty*, and the sentence is to be in accordance with his *sin*. The supreme desire, a long life, is not to be his lot: *let his days be few*; and *his office let another take*; the term used for this, *pequdāh*, refers to a civil post, not to the priestly office, as some commentators erroneously suppose; its use in a number of passages

makes this clear. The words do not refer to the loss of his office, from
which he is to be displaced in favour of someone else, but to its vacancy
owing to his death. Similarly the words : *Let his children be fatherless,
and let his wife be a widow* are in reference to his death, not to ill-will
on the part of the psalmist towards them. The suffering of his children,
through the loss of what might have been their inheritance, is dealt
with in 10, 11 ; on 10 see critical note ; and here again it is not against
the children that there is any feeling ; what was in the psalmist's mind
was what is said about " visiting the iniquity of the fathers upon the
children, and upon the third and upon the fourth generation of them
that hate me " (Deut. 5⁹) ; but in his case the psalmist says : *In one
generation let his name be blotted out*; *i.e.*, he is to have no posterity.
And once more, in referring to the sins of the enemy's father and
mother, the reason why these sins should be *before Yahweh continually*,
is that their penalty should rest on him, *that he may cut off his memory
from the earth.* The words in 8, *And his office let another take*, are
quoted in Acts 1²⁰ in reference to Judas ; hence this psalm became known
as *Psalmus Ischarioticus* in the Christian Church. 16–20. The retribution upon the enemy is to be that the very sin of which he has
been guilty is to react upon him : *He loved cursing, let it overtake
him.* . . . In 20 the psalmist reverts to his enemies in general, as in
2–5 ; a similar change from many enemies to one, and *vice versa*, occurs
elsewhere, *e.g.*, Ps. 35⁴ ff. and 8, 55¹³, ¹⁴. 21–31. The psalmist now
leaves the subject of his enemy, and speaks of himself, pouring out his
complaint to God. He is suffering from sickness, believed to be in
consequence of sin : *I am become a reproach unto them, they look at me,
they shake their head*; this is not in reference to his enemies, but to the
belief held generally among his fellows. The psalmist himself recognizes
this, and prays for divine help. The enemies are once more referred to
in 28, 29. The psalm closes with a note of thankfulness to God for
answering the prayer of his servant.

Religious Teaching

The subject-matter of this psalm accounts for the fact that it offers
but little of an edifying character. That the psalmist should believe
that by appealing to God the curses which he calls down upon the head
of his enemy will assume a kind of magical force, reveals an element of
religious superstition common enough in those days, but which is
far removed from the true religious spirit so predominant in the psalms
generally. There is something to be said for the contention of some
commentators that in its original form the psalm was an exorcism
directed against a sorcerer, and that this accounts for the expressions
of hatred ; and that it was subsequently worked over and adapted to
different conditions.

That this psalmist is not, however, lacking in the religious sense comes out clearly enough in the latter part of the psalm, where he expresses his better feelings. There is one point in these final verses which should, in fairness to the psalmist, be noted : he is suffering grievously in body, and there is some excuse for one in such a case if peevishness and irritability should temporarily master him, and induce a state of mind alien to his normal self. True, it would have been better had he not written his psalm under such conditions ; nevertheless, let it be recognized that this frank laying bare of the weaker side of human nature may be instructive ; even the faults of others have their uses—*injuriarum remedium est oblivio.*

PSALM 110

FEW of the psalms have been subjected to more diverse interpretation than this one ; yet, in spite of the difficulty of some passages, owing to textual corruption, the general meaning seems clear enough. The words of the psalm are addressed to the king. The psalmist, in the prophetic mode, utters a divine oracle, in which the king is assured of victory over his enemies. Thereupon the psalmist, on his own behalf, addresses the king. He recognizes the divine kingship, and exhorts the king to act in accordance with the divine oracle. He declares that the king has from his birth been sanctified to the kingship ; and, in thoroughly Oriental style, prophesies for him lasting youth. Then he utters the well-recognized truth regarding the priestly office of the king, and recalls, what is likely to have been the traditional belief, that this office of priest-king was derived from Melkizedek. The psalmist closes with the assurance that Yahweh will fight the battles of his anointed.

The psalm thus belongs to the time of the monarchy ; a comparatively early date being further suggested by the style of its composition, which is that of the pre-exilic literary period.

Which king it was to whom the psalm was addressed is quite uncertain. The contention held by some that the psalm belongs to the Maccabæan age because the letters composing the name of Simon, the Maccabæan leader, are the initial ones of the first four lines, can only be described as fantastic ; for the fact is that these letters are not the initial ones of the lines in question, and can be made so only by arbitrary manipulation. Moreover, Simon was not a king ; the first of the Hasmonæan rulers to assume the royal title was John Hyrcanus (134/3–104/3 B.C.).

On the Messianic interpretation of this psalm, and its use in the
New Testament, see Vol. I, pp. 97 f.

As will be seen in the critical notes, the text of the psalm is corrupt
in parts; textual emendation is in some cases difficult and uncertain,
and there is considerable difference of opinion among scholars on many
points.

The metre is mostly 3 : 2.

David's.   A Psalm.

1. Oracle of Yahweh to my lord :
   ° Until ° I make thine enemies
2. Thy mighty sceptre ° stretch forth °,
   Rule thou in the midst of thy foes,
   ° In the day of thy birth thou wast
   honoured,
   From the dawn cometh forth
4. Yahweh hath sworn,
   Thou art a priest for ever,
5. ° Yahweh ° doth shatter in the day of
   his wrath ;
   ° With corpses he filleth the valleys °,
   ° He watereth the brooks with their
   blood ° ;

' Sit at my right-hand
a stool for thy feet.'
O God, from Zion °,
3 ° thine are the princes °.

sanctified from the womb ;
the dew of thy youth °.
he will not repent,
° of the order ° of Melkizedek.

6. kings doth he judge ;
° maketh red the hills ° ;

Therefore he lifteth up ° thy head

Text-critical Notes

1. Read, for the metre's sake, עַד אֲשֶׁר for עַד. 2. Read שְׁלַח for יִשְׁלַח,
"he will stretch forth". 3. Read עַמְּךָ נְדִיבִים (cp. Ps. 107⁴⁰) for עַמְּךָ נְדָבֹת,
"thy people are freewill offerings". For the rest of this *v.* we have adopted Gunkel's
emendation :

קָדוֹשׁ מֵרֶחֶם   בְּיוֹם חוֹלֶלְךָ הָדַרְתָּ
טַל יַלְדֻתֶךָ   מִשַּׁחַר יֶלֶד

The present Hebrew text is largely corrupt. 4. Read with some MSS., עַל־דִּבְרַת for
עַל־דִּבְרָתִי. 5. Read, with many MSS., יהוה, "Yahweh", for אֲדֹנָי, "my
lord "; and om. עַל־יְמִינְךָ, "on thy right hand ", which overloads the half-line ;
it ends with אַפּוֹ "his wrath". 6. The verse begins with מְלָכִים, "kings".
Read בְּגֻיּוֹת מָלֵא גֵאָיוֹת for בַּגּוֹיִם מָלֵא גְוִיּוֹת, "among the nations he hath
filled corpses ". Read הָמַץ רָאשִׁים for מָחַץ רֹאשׁ, "he shattereth a head ".
Om. עַל־אֶרֶץ רַבָּה, "over a broad land ", which overloads the half-line. 7.
Read מִנַּחַל בַּדֶּרֶךְ יִשְׁתֶּה for נְחָלִים בַּדָּם יִשְׁקֶה, "from the brook in the
way he drinketh ". Read רֹאשׁוֹ for רֹאשׁ "a head ".

1-6. The psalm opens with an *Oracle* which the psalmist has
received from God in reference to his lord, the king. How far the
contents of the " oracle " extend is a point on which opinions differ ;
but to us it seems most probable that it is restricted to *v.* 1, and that
in *vv.* 2-5 the exhortation to the king to use the powers conferred on
him is uttered. Apart from 36² this is the only instance of the term
" oracle " being used in the *Psalms*; it is the technical expression of a
divine communication to a prophet, and connotes the idea of whispering
in the ear rather than " utterance ". In the communication itself two
thoughts are prominent. The first is the treatment which God accords
to the king. He is placed at God's *right-hand*, the place of honour, cp.

Ps. 45⁹, 80¹⁷. The picture is a poetical way of expressing the truth that he is under divine protection, as well as being honoured. But, further, he is to *sit*, an attitude which throughout the East, ancient and modern, implies inactivity. The king is to do nothing himself; he is to be, as it were, a spectator of the work of God. For it is the divine power that makes the king's enemies a *stool* for his *feet*, a gesture of triumph with which we may compare Josh. 10²⁴, where Israel's victorious chiefs " put their feet upon the necks " of the defeated kings. So far the Oracle; then the psalmist speaks in his own name; in *vv.* 2–6 he sets forth the conception of those times that the king is God's representative among his people, and therefore, in a certain sense, to be identified with God. He begins by bidding the king arise and exercise the authority bestowed upon him as God's representative, and to *stretch forth* his *sceptre*; this is to indicate that he is lord of the enemies lying prostrate under his feet. The king is even addressed directly as *God*, for though the Hebrew text has " Yahweh ", the context shows that the king is meant. So in Ps. 45⁶ the king is directly addressed as God (on the divine kingship, see Vol. I, pp. 49 f.). It is probable that " Yahweh " was put in place of " God " in later days, when the belief in the divine kingship was no longer held.

The sceptre is a token of universal dominion; the king is to *rule in the midst of* his *foes*, and the world's *princes* are to be his slaves. For he has been destined for sovereignty from the first, set apart, made " holy ", *sanctified*; from birth the divine kingship has been recognized as inherent in him. We may recall how Jeremiah was designated *from birth* to the prophetic office (Jer. 1⁵, 49¹). On the king had fallen, according to an old-world conception, the heavenly *dew* which comes at *dawn* and confers eternal youth upon whomsoever it falls (cp. Isa. 26¹⁹, and see Gunkel, *Psalmen*, p. 482, Frazer, *The Golden Bough : Adonis, Attis, Osiris*, 1²⁴⁶ ff. [1927]). Lest there should be uncertainty of any kind, *Yahweh hath sworn* an oath to the king. To us this antique idea is distasteful; but it occurs, too, in the prophetical books, Am. 4², 6⁸, Isa. 14²⁴, Jer. 22⁵, and elsewhere, cp. also Ps. 89³⁵. It may be explained as being a prophetical mode of expressing the binding character of divine communications, for it is inconceivable that God should *repent*, *i.e.*, go back upon what he has ordained. The promise confirmed by the oath, is that the king shall be a priest *for ever of the order* of *Melkizedek*, a phrase whose meaning has already been discussed in Vol. I, p. 97. To fulfil the oath Yahweh is prepared to put forth all his strength upon the king's enemies, and the whole passage portrays the ancient conception of Yahweh as one mighty in battle (cp., *e.g.*, Ps. 24⁸), raging irresistibly in the day of his wrath (cp. Isa. 13⁹, ¹³), dominating *kings*, *filling the valleys with corpses*, and *making red the hills*, *i.e.*, with blood. Here the psalmist uses a verb which plays on the similar Hebrew word for " shatter " or " smite ", in the previous verse (cp. Isa. 34³, ⁶, ⁷) ; and the *hills* are lit. " heads ", as iṅ Ezek. 6¹³ and elsewhere. They are the protruding tops of the giant pillars on which, according to another old-world conception, the earth rests. Down in the valleys, too, the *brooks* run *with blood*. All this lurid description has a single purpose, the exaltation of the king, whose *head* is to be *lifted up*. For the achievement of this aim God will shrink from nothing, and the express statement of his purpose gives a fitting conclusion to the passage ; it ends where it began, with the anointed king sitting in lofty triumph : *He lifteth up thy head.*

Religious Teaching

In spite of the old-world ideas occurring in this psalm, it would be a mistake not to recognize in it some underlying beliefs of a distinctly religious character. The belief in ancient Israel that the kingship was a divine institution contains a living truth. However quaint the human origin of the thought, and however much in practice the ideal was perverted—the history of the kings of Israel and Judah furnishes a melancholy illustration of this—there is something about this belief which must demand respect wherever the religious instinct is allowed play. In the head of the State authority is centred ; that was the case in the monarchical period of ancient Israel, and in the post-exilic period when authority was centred in the High-priesthood ; similarly in still later times St. Paul teaches that " there is no power but of God, and the powers that be are ordained of God " (Rom. 13¹). The authority of rulership, that is to say, when rightly exercised, is of divine ordering.

Again, however crudely expressed, there is the germ of truth contained in our psalm in the belief that there is a divine over-ruling in history. This is one of the outstanding elements in the prophetical doctrine of God. The psalmist puts into the mouth of God the words : " Until I make thine enemies a stool for thy feet ", implying that battle is won by divine intervention ; that is a crude way of expressing the belief that history, with the making of which battles have had so much to do, is directed by God. Allowing for the undeveloped mental outlook of the writer, we may discern here too an element of truth. While we are, of course, convinced that the issues of battles are not directed by the divine will, we are justified in believing in *the over-ruling guidance of divine providence in history*. In recognizing this, however crudely, the psalmist expresses a religious truth.

And, once more, one cannot fail to observe the absolute trust in God which the psalmist exhibits. The divine action described betrays, it is true, a very undeveloped conception of God ; but in so far as there is a living trust in him, we must again recognize an element of true religion in the psalm.

We cannot read this psalm without thinking of our Lord's words in reference to it, recorded in the three synoptic Gospels. He evidently applied it to himself, recognizing that the writer adumbrated some eternal truths. Christ is a King : " My kingdom is not of this world " ; he identified himself with God : " I and the Father are One " ; he was sanctified from the womb : " His name shall be called Jesus " ; he was a priest : " I lay down my life for the sheep ", as well as the victim offered.

PSALM 111

THIS is an acrostic psalm in which each line begins with a letter of the Hebrew alphabet, in order. It is doubtless due to this that the psalm is somewhat lacking in logical sequence. A matter of interest concerning Hebrew metrical structure arises in connexion with the form of this psalm. As is well known, in Hebrew poetry a line consists normally of two halves divided by a hiatus, each half-line having its regular beats ; but this psalm is an illustration, of which there are quite a number, showing that this rule was not necessarily rigidly adhered to. In this case it is the exigencies of the acrostic which make what would ordinarily be a half-line into a self-contained entity ; it is not always so in the psalm, in *vv.* 1, 2, 6, 7, 8 the two halves belong together, but in the other verses the half-line is self-contained. In order to indicate the alphabetical order of the half-lines, they are printed separately in the following rendering.

The psalm belongs to the late post-exilic period, though thoughts belonging to pre-exilic times find expression. Its text has come down to us in almost perfect condition.

The half-lines have mostly three beats, but in *vv.* 6 and 10 there are four beats, while in *v.* 7 the metre is 2 : 2 : 3.

Hallelujah.

1.	א	I will give thanks to Yahweh with all my heart,
	ב	In the assembly of the upright, yea, in the congregation.
2.	ג	Great are the works of Yahweh,
	ד	Sought out of all who delight in them.
3.	ה	Glorious and majestic is his action,
	ו	And his righteousness standeth-fast for ever.
4.	ז	He ordained a memorial of his wondrous-works ;
	ח	Gracious and merciful is Yahweh.
5.	ט	He gave food to them that fear him,
	י	He remembereth his covenant for ever.
6.	כ	The power of his works he made known to his people,
	ל	In giving to them the heritage of the nations ;
7.	מ	The works of his hands are truth and justice,
	נ	Trustworthy are all his precepts;
8.	ס	Standing-firm for ever and ever,
	ע	Wrought in truth and ° uprightness °.

9. פ   He sent release to his people,
    צ   He commanded his covenant for ever.
    ק   Holy and awe-ful is his name.
10. ר   The zenith of wisdom is the fear of Yahweh.
    ש   (It is) Insight, profitable to all ° who cultivate it °;
    ת   The praise of it endureth for ever.

Text-critical Notes

For the title see under Ps. 105. 8. Read, with G, וְיָשָׁר for וְיִשָּׁר, "and an upright one ". 10. Read, with G, עֹשֶׂיהָ, in reference to wisdom, for עֹשֵׂיהֶם, " that cultivate them ".

1. The opening words suggest that this psalm was sung as a solo in the presence of the Temple *congregation*, described as the *assembly of the upright*. To *give thanks* is equivalent to " praise ".

2-6. In these verses the psalmist refers to some of the *great works of Yahweh* in the past; though somewhat cryptic, the references were clear enough to his hearers, for, as those *who delight in them*, these *great and majestic works of Yahweh* were constantly recalled and thought about, *sought out*, by them. These works are as follows : the *memorial* which God *ordained* was the institution of the Passover : " And ye shall observe this thing for an ordinance to thee and to thy sons for ever " (Exod. 12²⁴); the words *Gracious and merciful is Yahweh* are in reference to the release from the Egyptian bondage (Exod. 12²⁹⁻³⁶, ⁴²). The psalmist then refers to the giving of the manna (Exod. 16¹¹⁻¹⁴); the word used for *food* means lit. " prey " (*tereph*), chosen, no doubt, because its opening letter was required for the acrostic; it is, however, used for ordinary food in Job 24⁵ and Prov. 31¹⁵, also in post-Biblical Jewish literature. *He remembereth his covenant for ever* is evidently in reference to the Sabbath, spoken of immediately after the manna episode (Exod. 16²⁸⁻³⁰). And, finally, the conquest of Canaan is referred to : *In giving to them the heritage of the nations* (cp. Num. 34).

7-10. The final verses are of a somewhat miscellaneous character ; the release from the Babylonian Exile is referred to in the words *He sent release to his people*; and a favourite saying from the Wisdom literature is quoted in 10 : *The zenith of Wisdom is the fear of Yahweh* (cp. Prov. 1⁷, 9¹⁰, Ecclus. 1¹⁴); we have rendered the Hebrew *r'ešith* " zenith ", in place of the more familiar " the beginning ", since *the fear of Yahweh* is the consummation, the highest form, of wisdom; it gives understanding, *insight*, and is *profitable to all who cultivate it*.

Religious Teaching

This psalm offers an excellent illustration of what is a beautiful characteristic of Judaism—viz.. gratitude for past mercies. This religious element, while not wanting in Christian liturgies, is not so prominently expressed as in the Old Testament, as well as in the Jewish liturgies both ancient and modern.

PSALM 112

LIKE the preceding psalm, this is an acrostic psalm of the same character ; its opening words echo the conclusion of the former, so that probably enough both are from the same author ; some identities of expression point in the same direction ; moreover, the wisdom element of the preceding psalm is developed in this one. The subject-matter throughout is the blessedness and reward of him who fears Yahweh ; only in the concluding verse is the contrast of the lot of the wicked alluded to.

The text is again admirably preserved. The metre, as in the preceding psalm, is almost uniformly three beats to the half-line, four beats occur in *vv.* 2, 4, 6, 7.

Hallelujah.

1.	א ב	Blessed-the-man that feareth Yahweh, That greatly delighteth in his commandments ;
2.	ג ד	Mighty in the land shall be his seed, The generation of the righteous shall be blessed.
3.	ה ו	Wealth and riches are in his house, And his righteousness standeth-fast for ever.
4.	ז ח	To the upright there ariseth light in the darkness, Gracious and merciful ° is the righteous °.
5.	ט י	Happy-the-man who is gracious and lendeth, And maintaineth ° his ways ° with justice ;—
6.	כ ל	For he shall never be moved, An enduring memorial shall the righteous have.
7.	מ נ	He will fear no evil report, His heart is fixed, ° trusting ° in Yahweh,
8.	ס ע	His heart is firm, he will not fear, While he gloateth over his enemies ;
9.	פ צ	He disperseth, he giveth to the poor ; His righteousness standeth-fast for ever,
10.	ק ר ש ת	His horn shall be exalted with honour. The wicked shall see it, and be vexed, He shall gnash with his teeth, and faint, The desire of the wicked shall perish.

Text-critical Notes

For the title see under Ps. 105. 4. Read צַדִּיק for וְצַדִּיק, " and righteous ". 5. Read דְּבָרָיו for דְּבָרָיו, " his words ", cp. Ecclus. 49⁹. 7. Read, with G. בָּטֵחַ for בָּטֻחַ, " trusted ".

1. A characteristic thought from the Wisdom literature introduces the main theme of the psalm : *Blessed-the-man* (a compound word in the Hebrew with only one beat) *that feareth Yahweh.* The blessedness includes material prosperity as well as spiritual happiness, cp. Prov. 3⁹, ¹⁰, 22⁴.

2, 3. One of the signal marks of God's favour to the righteous was for him to see his prosperous state enjoyed by his sons : *Mighty in the land shall be his seed*; the word *mighty* (*gibbôr*) is not altogether appropriate in this connexion, for it is used mostly in a warlike sense ; it may have been chosen on account of its initial letter, the third one of

the alphabet. Some commentators would read *gebîr*, " lord "; but
this is not to be commended, as it is an extremely rare word, occurring
elsewhere only in Gen. 27$^{29,\ 37}$.

4–7. These verses describe the conduct and happy lot of him who
lives in the fear of Yahweh ; the words *To the upright there ariseth light
in the darkness* are to be understood in the same sense as in Ps. 97^{11},
Isa. 58^{10} *i.e.*, the light of prosperity which disperses the darkness of
poverty, see also Prov. 4$^{18,\ 19}$; this induces him to be *gracious and
merciful*. In what follows there is not a strictly logical sequence, owing,
no doubt, to the exigencies of the acrostic form of the psalm. This is
also the case in *vv.* 8–10, where the stability of the upright man, his
generosity to the poor, and his prosperous state, interchange with
references to the wicked ; in these latter the psalmist's thoughts are of
an unbeautiful nature ; but he wishes to place in contrast the merited
lot of the righteous with the deserts of the wicked.

Religious Teaching

What is striking here is the psalmist's optimism; unlike many
others, he does not contemplate the other side of the picture, which
shows how often the godly suffer adversity. Nevertheless, the happy
frame of mind of him who, with soul-felt trust in God, looks on the
bright side of things, is well worth cultivating.

PSALM 113

THIS is the first of a group of psalms known as the *Hallel* (" Praise ") in
Rabbinical writings—namely, Pss. 113–118. The group is often spoken
of as the " Egyptian Hallel " (in reference to 114^1, " When Israel went
forth from Egypt "), to distinguish it from what is called the " Great
Hallel ", Ps. 136, and from the group 146–148, which, on account of the
frequently expressed note of praise in them, was also called *Hallel*.
But it is the group 113–118 which is usually spoken of as *the Hallel*;
and these psalms were, from long before the beginning of the Christian
era, the special ones for the great festivals of Passover (*Pesaḥ*),
Tabernacles (*Sukkôth*), and Weeks (*Shabu'ôth*) ; and when the feast
of Dedication (*Ḥanukkah*) was instituted in 164 B.C. (1 Macc. 4$^{52-59}$),
they became likewise the special psalms sung during this feast.

This, like the other psalms of the group, belongs to a comparatively
late period; this is suggested by the utilization of thoughts and
expressions occurring in earlier psalms.

The metre is irregular.

Hallelujah.

1.	Praise, ye servants of Yahweh,	praise the name of Yahweh,
2.	Blessed be the name of Yahweh,	from henceforth, even for ever;
3.	From the rising of the sun to the going-down thereof,	the name of Yahweh is praised.
4.	Exalted over all nations is Yahweh,	his glory is above the heavens.
5ª.	° Who is like Yahweh our God	6ᵇ. in heaven and earth,
5ᵇ.	That dwelleth on high	6ª. that looketh down below ° ?
7.	He raiseth the poor from the dust,	from the ash-heap he lifteth the needy,
8.	° Making him to sit ° with princes,	with the princes of his people ;
9.	Causing the barren to dwell in a house,	a joyful mother of children.°

Text-critical Notes

5. 6. The half-lines of these *vv.* have got misplaced, as the sense shows. 8. Read, with GS, לְהוֹשִׁיבוֹ for לְהוֹשִׁיבִי, "to make to sit"; for the *ḥireq compaginis* in the participial forms in *vv.* 6 ff. see *GK* 90 *m.* 9. "Hallelujah", with G, is the title of the next psalm.

1–3. The worshippers of Yahweh, His *servants*, are called upon to *praise the name of Yahweh*, cp. Ps. 135[1]; the name is the manifestation of the Person of Yahweh. The phrase *from henceforth and for ever* is a frequent one in the psalms of the later period (115[18], 121[8], 125[2], 131[3]). The ideal of praise being offered to God the live-long day is beautifully expressed in the words *From the rising of the sun . . .*

4–6. The universalistic note, *Exalted over all nations is Yahweh*, marks the psalmist as belonging to that enlightened section of the people whose outlook is illustrated in the book of *Jonah*. The Hebrew construction of *vv.* 5ᵇ : *That dwelleth on high*, and 6ª : *That looketh down below*, is difficult ; literally rendered they run : " That maketh high to dwell ", and " That maketh low to see ", and their meaning is clear from Ps. 11[4], cp. also Ps. 138[6].

7–9. These verses are taken from 1 Sam. 2[8 and 5], in part verbally.

Religious Teaching

It is impossible to read a psalm such as this, in which the threefold mention of the *name* of God occurs so impressively, without recalling the words of the Lord's Prayer : " Hallowed be thy name ". We have here a striking illustration of the fact that Christ accepted Jewish conceptions, even though in their origin the germ of truth contained in them was intermixed with superstitious elements. The identification of a name with the personality of the bearer of it goes back to very early times ; but we are here concerned with the " Name " of God, and the central point of importance is that, according to ancient Hebrew belief, it was God himself who revealed his " Name " (Exod. 3[14]).

We need further to realize that in communicating his " Name " to certain men, he laid on them the responsibility of presenting him to the world as a whole. If their standards of religious life and thought are too low, they may profane his holy " Name ", cp. Am. 2[7], and defile him in the eyes of men. On the other hand, if they rightly appreciate his character and demands, and present him to mankind as he would be understood, they will hallow his " Name ".

PSALM 114

THE often referred-to story of the flight from Egypt was so familiar that the psalmist merely mentions the great event without giving details, as in Ps. 105²³⁻³⁸. Similarly in dealing with the entry into Canaan, which is merely a summary. But it is a remarkable example of concise, yet vivid, description, reminiscent of some of the prophetical discourses. In his enthusiasm and excited imagination, the psalmist permits himself to indulge in poetical exaggeration, and he pictures the very mountains and hills as moved to wonder and awe by the mighty acts of God ; and the whole earth is called upon to tremble at his presence (cp. Ps. 96⁹). As belonging to the " Hallel ", this psalm was, of course, sung at all the great festivals ; but, besides this, it was, as might be expected, one of the proper psalms for the Passover festival (see further, Vol. I, pp. 100 f.).

The psalm may possibly belong to exilic times, but a post-exilic date is more probable ; see, further, the notes on this.

The text has come down in perfect condition. With the exception of *v.* 7, which has 4 : 3, the metre is 3 : 3.

1. When Israel came forth from Egypt, the house of Jacob from a people of strange-tongue,
2. Judah became his sanctuary, Israel his dominion.
3. The sea saw it, and fled, Jordan turned backwards ;
4. The mountains skipped like rams, the hills like the young of the flock.
5. What hast thou, O sea, that thou fleest, O Jordan, that thou turnest backwards ?
6. Ye mountains, that ye skip like rams, ye hills like the young of the flock ?
7. Tremble, O earth, at the presence of the Lord, at the presence of the God of Jacob,
8. Who turned the rock to a pool, the flint to a spring of water !

1, 2. The psalmist compresses centuries of history in these two opening verses, and indicates that at the Exodus Israel was constituted a nation. *Israel* is often used in post-exilic times as including both the northern and southern kingdoms. *The house of Jacob* as a parallel to *Israel* is doubtless in reference to the fact that it was the family of Jacob that went down into Egypt (Gen. 46²⁻⁷). The Egyptians are spoken of as *a people of strange-tongue*, meaning probably, as in Isa. 33¹⁹, a stammering tongue, as it would seem to the Israelites who did not understand the Egyptian language. Hebrew was the divine language, in comparison with which every other was barbaric. In much later days it was taught that prayers must be offered in Hebrew, otherwise the angels would be unable to present them before the Almighty.

An indication of the date of the psalm is contained in the words :
Judah became his sanctuary, Israel his dominion ; Judah being mentioned
first, and designated God's *sanctuary*, points to a time when Jerusalem
was the centre of worship. In contrast to this presentation of Judah,
the description of *Israel* as God's *dominion* is not without significance.
The words reflect the thought of a time when the temple-worship had
reached its full development ; and this can hardly have been the case until
well after the time of Ezra, so that the date of the psalm is likely to have
been the early Greek period, some time during the third century B.C.

3-6. In these verses Nature itself is represented as cowed and wonder-
struck at what is taking place ; in reference to Exod. 14²¹, ²² it is said :
The sea saw it and fled ; then, as a parallel to this, the psalmist recalls
the episode, though happening long after, of the crossing of the Jordan,
recounted in Josh. 3¹²⁻¹⁷, *Jordan turneth backwards*. The picture of
the *mountains* that *skip like rams*, and *the hills like the young of the flock*,
i.e., the lambs, was doubtless suggested by Judg. 5⁵, Ps. 68⁸, not by
Exod. 19¹⁸, where we must read, with the Septuagint and a number of
Hebrew manuscripts, " all the people trembled greatly " (not " the
whole mount quaked greatly "), for the Hebrew verb for " tremble "
(*ḥarad*) is used almost always in reference to persons (Isa. 41⁵, of the
earth, and Ezek. 26¹⁸ are the only exceptions). In *vv.* 5, 6 the psalmist
transports himself in imagination back into the times of which he is
thinking ; the verbs in these rhetorical questions are in the present.

7, 8. The whole earth is called upon to tremble at the presence of
the Lord ('*Adon* is written without the article here only) ; why the earth
is to tremble (the verb is not *harad*, but *ḥûl*, lit. to " writhe ") is because
of the wondrous acts of the Lord ; the *God of Jacob turned the rock to a
pool, and the flint to a spring of water* (cp. Exod. 15²⁵, 17⁶, Num. 22⁸⁻¹¹,
Deut. 8¹⁵) ; the psalmist allows himself some embellishment of the
records. The concluding reference to this giving of water in the
wilderness, which, compared with the other wonder-works spoken of,
was of greatly less importance, must strike one, at first sight, as somewhat incongruous. As a matter of fact, it is highly significant. The
Passover feast, of which, as we have seen, this was one of the proper
psalms, was celebrated in the month Nisan (March–April), when the
latter rains were ceasing and the period of drought was beginning ; the
psalmist, therefore, recalls the divine power of giving water, so that,
although there is going to be a period of dryness, the God of Jacob
will again show forth his power in due time, and turn the dry land
into springs of water.

Religious Teaching

In this psalm, which commemorates the stupendous event when
Israel became a nation, and when the knowledge of Yahweh was accorded

to them, we have an element to which reference has already been made—namely, the recognition of, and gratitude for, past mercies. Then there is also the oft-expressed belief in Yahweh as the God of Nature; somewhat *naïve* as the expression of this belief may be, there is the underlying conviction that Nature is subject to the will of the divine Creator.

PSALM 115

THE construction of this psalm points clearly to its liturgical use; which parts were sung by the priests, the temple choir, and the congregation, respectively, cannot well be decided with certainty; the opinions of commentators differ on the subject. The divisions of the psalm are, however, fairly obvious, and help to indicate by whom the different parts were sung. Thus, *vv.* 1–8, by their content and by the use of the plural, " not unto us," " our God is in the heavens," suggest that they were sung by the temple choir and the congregation. *Vv.* 9–11, with the threefold refrain, were undoubtedly sung antiphonally, perhaps by a priest and the congregation, the latter taking up the refrain. *Vv.* 12–15, as the contents indicate, were sung by the priests; and the final verses, 16–18, by priests, temple choir, and congregation.

The contents of the psalm will be more appropriately dealt with in the section on *Religious Teaching*.

The form of composition points with certainty to a late post-exilic date for the psalm; similarly the expression " house of Aaron ", the ruling aristocracy; and " Israel " applied to the Jewish nation as a whole. The text is almost wholly intact.

The metre is, with one or two possible exceptions, 3 : 3.

1. Not unto us, Yahweh, not unto us,   but to thy name give glory;
    °   .   .   .   . °   because of thy love and thy truth.
2. Wherefore should the nations say :   " Where, then, is their God ? "
3. But our God is in the heavens,   whatsoever he pleased hath he done.
4. Their idols are silver and gold,   the work of the hands of man.
5. A mouth is theirs, but they speak not;   eyes have they, but see not;
6. Ears they have, but hear not;   a nose they have, but smell not;
7.   Their hands,—but they feel not,
       Their feet,—but they walk not,
       They speak not through their throat.
8. Like them shall be their makers,   all they that trust in them.
9. O Israel, trust in Yahweh,   their help and shield is he;
10. House of Aaron, trust in Yahweh,   their help and shield is he;
11. Ye that fear Yahweh, trust in Yahweh,   their help and shield is he.
12.   May Yahweh ° remember us ° and bless us,
       May he bless the house of Israel,
       May he bless the house of Aaron,
13. May he bless them that fear Yahweh,   the small ones with the great;
14. May Yahweh give you increase,   to you and to your children.
15. Blessed are ye of Yahweh,   the maker of heaven and earth.

16. The heavens are Yahweh's heavens,   but the earth he gave to man.
17. The dead praise not Yahweh,   nor ail that go down into silence ;
18. But we will bless Yah,   from henceforth for evermore.
                 Hallelujah.

Text-critical Notes

1. It is more likely that a half-line has fallen out here than that the last half-line is a later insertion. 12. Read יִזְכְּרֵנוּ for זְכָרֵנוּ, " hath remembered us ".

1–8. The real point of the words with which this psalm abruptly begins, *Not unto us, Yahweh, not unto us, but to thy name give glory*, comes out in the second verse: *Wherefore should the nations say, " Where, then, is their God ? "* From this it is evident that the Jews had suffered a defeat, or were being oppressed by some Gentile foe, who had scoffed at the idea that God could help his people. The psalmist implicitly expresses the belief that God *will* save his people from their enemy, but, in his deep trust and reverence, he repudiates the idea that the coming deliverance will be due to the efforts of his people ; not to them, but to God, in spite of the enemy's scoffing, shall *glory* be given. It seems to us probable, therefore, that in the second part of the first verse some words have fallen out, such as, " For thy name's sake grant us deliverance " (cp. Ps. 54[1]), or something to this effect. The psalmist continues : so far from God being unable to help his people, he is *in the heavens*, whence he guides all things on earth, and dispenses his lovingkindness, cp. Ps. 36[5]. The adversity of his people is for good, being according to his will : *Whatsoever he pleased hath he done.* The scathing mockery which is uttered against the idols of the Gentiles may well have been inspired by such passages as Isa. 41[21-24], 44[9-20] ; the makers of such useless things are no better than the things themselves : *Like them shall be their makers, all they that trust in them.*

9–11, 12–15. In contrast to the reliance placed by the Gentiles on their idols, there follows the very effective exhortation, sung antiphonally, calling upon all grades of the people to *trust in Yahweh, their help and shield* : first the whole nation of *Israel*, then their spiritual rulers, the *house of Aaron*, and then those that *fear Yahweh*. There is some uncertainty as to who are meant by these last ; many commentators hold that proselytes are meant ; the objection to this is that in the next three verses, which are a responsive repetition of the preceding, they *that fear Yahweh* must refer to Israel as a whole, for the words, *The small ones with the great ; May Yahweh give you increase, to you and to your children*, cannot refer only to proselytes ; it seems more probable that they *that fear Yahweh* is a comprehensive summing-up of priests and people.

16–18. In the final outburst of praise which concludes the psalm, mention is made of the heavens above, God's dwelling-place, the earth beneath, man's sphere, and the underworld, the abode of the departed ;

this is done to emphasize the fact that God in heaven is worshipped by those living on earth ; they in the underworld cannot do so ; therefore the final words : *But we will bless Yah, from henceforth for evermore.* On the abbreviated form of the divine name see Ps. 68[18], " for evermore " is to be understood in the sense of a length of time, as in such passages as Pss. 21[6], 22[26], 61[7].

Religious Teaching

This is one of three psalms, and they are the only ones, in which a pure and perfect monotheism is expressly taught; the others are 86[9, 10], 135[15, 17]. In spite of the teaching of Deutero–Isaiah, it is found again and again in the psalms that the existence of other gods is either definitely stated, or implied (*e.g.*, 81[9], 86[8], 89[6], 95[3], 96[4, 5]) ; naturally, Yahweh was believed in as infinitely above other gods, as of an utterly different nature, and as incomparably mightier ; but a pure monotheistic belief does not recognize the possibility of any gods, however inferior, other than the One God.

One thing in this psalm which betrays an inadequate conception of God is contained in the words : *The dead praise not Yahweh, nor all that go down into silence* ; this traditional Sheol doctrine restricts God's relationship to man to this world ; and thus fails to apprehend the divine nature (see further on Ps. 73).

On the other hand, in the expression " trust in Yahweh ", and in the absolute conviction of his protecting help, this psalm stands as one of the most impressive in the Psalter.

PSALM 116

As indicated in the psalm itself (*vv.* 17–19), it was sung either immediately before, or during, the sacrifice of the *Tôdah*, or "thank-offering ". On Egyptian and Assyrian pictorial inscriptions it is seen that the offering of sacrifices was accompanied by instrumental music, and doubtless by song too. From Am. 5[22, 23], we may gather that similarly in Israel both instrumental music and singing took place during the offering of sacrifices ; see also Isa. 30[29], 38[20], 2 Chron. 5[13]. Our psalm is thus a thanksgiving to God, sung during the temple-worship, in recognition of deliverance from some dire peril, see *v.* 3 ; and it was sung by an individual, as indicated again and again, the first person being used throughout ; and this, not collectively of the people, but of an individual, see especially *vv.* 8, 14, 18.

The question as to whether the psalm is to be regarded as forming a unity or not is a difficult one. The Septuagint makes two psalms of it, *vv.* 1–9 and 10–19. There can be no doubt that *vv.* 1–9 are self-contained, and that *v.* 9 makes a fitting conclusion. Further, the text of the beginning of the second part (*vv.* 10, 11) is manifestly out of order, and this might conceivably have been due to the adoption of a portion of some other psalm which was joined on to the first part. There are also some repetitions in *vv.* 10–19 of words in *vv.* 1–9, owing to which it could be argued that the two parts were originally distinct, as such repetitions are unlikely to recur in one and the same psalm. In spite of these considerations, however, the unity of the psalm is not necessarily to be denied when its nature is realized ; for we have here the heart's outpouring of one who has come safely through some grave danger, and whose whole being is overflowing with gratitude to God ; when such an one records his innermost thoughts and feelings he is not concerned with the niceties proper to a carefully constructed composition. The sequence of his uttered thoughts may be expressed somewhat as follows : His first impulse, when recalling the peril through which he has safely passed, is to recognize the Author of his deliverance, and to offer him thanks ; the turmoil of his heart is assuaged, and he can live in quietude of mind among his friends again. But then it suddenly comes into his mind that though in the midst of the peril his trust was in God, nevertheless doubts did arise ; this he recalls in humble regret. But he is safe now, so that his thoughts naturally revert to God, and he is anxious to show forth by deed as well as by word the sincerity of his gratitude. That he should, in these circumstances, repeat some of the words he had already uttered is a very human and natural proceeding. Most commentators delete the words of repetition ; they may be right, but it may, at any rate, be claimed that the considerations adduced offer some justification for regarding the psalm as a unity.

The late post-exilic date of the psalm is indicated by the occurrence of Aramaisms in *vv.* 7, 12, 16, and also by the use of the term *Hasidim*, " godly ones " (*v.* 15), in reference to the particular group among the people.

The text has, in *vv.* 1–9, on the whole, been well preserved ; but in *vv.* 10–19 there is some dislocation. The metre is somewhat irregular ; 3 : 2 predominates, but 3 : 3 is frequent ; 2 : 2 comes in here and there effectively.

1. I love ° Yahweh °, for he heareth ° the cry of ° my supplication ;
2. For he inclined his ear unto me ° in the day ° I cried.
3. The cords of death encompassed me, ° and the horrors of ° Sheol ° confronted² me ;

Trouble and distress I experienced ;
4. Then I called on the name of Yahweh :
" Ah, Yahweh.
Deliver my soul."

5. Gracious is Yahweh, and righteous,   yea, our God is merciful;
6. Yahweh preserveth the helpless,   I languish, and he helpeth me.
7. Return, O my soul, to thy rest,   for Yahweh hath dealt bountifully with thee.
8.   ° He delivered ° my soul from death,
    ° Mine eyes ° from tears,
    ° My feet ° from stumbling.
9. I will walk before Yahweh   ° in the lánd ° of the living.
10. I trusted ° in Yahweh, and spake ° :   " I am greatly ° humbled ° " ;
11. ° For ° I said in my alarm :   ° " all trust is in vain." °
12. How shall I make return to Yahweh   ° for all ° his benefits to me ?
13. The cup of deliverance will I raise,   and call on the name of Yahweh.
14. My vows to Yahweh will I pay   ° in the presence ° of all his people.
15. Precious in the eyes of Yahweh   is ° the death ° of his saints.
16.   " Ah, Yahweh,
    ° I ° am thy servant ;
    I am thy servant,
    A son of ° thy people °,
    Thou hast loosed my bonds.'
17. I will offer ° the sacrifice of thanks-
    giving,   and call on the name of Yahweh ;
18. My vows to Yahweh will I pay   ° in the presence ° of all his people,
19. In the courts of the house of Yahweh,   in the midst of thee, O Jerusalem.
    Hallelujah.

Text-critical Notes

1. The Hebrew text has no object to " I love ", so that this must be obtained by a slight aiteration in the order of the words. Read קוֹלִי for קוֹלִ֫י, " my voice ", or " cry ". 2. Read, with S, בְּיוֹם for בְּיָמַי, " in my days ". 3. In late Hebrew the word means " a rope ", and perhaps we should render " ropes " instead of " horrors ".; it gives a better parallelism. "Confronted me " is lit. " found me ". 8. Read חָלַּץ for חִלַּצְתָּ, " thou didst deliver " ; Yahweh is not being addressed. Read עֵינַי for עֵינִי, " mine eye ", and רַגְלִי for רַגְלִי, " my foot ". 9. Read בָּאֶרֶץ for בְּאַרְצוֹת, " in the lands of ". 10. Read בִּיהוֹה וָאֲדַבֵּר for כִּי אֲדַבֵּר, " when I shall speak ". Read עֲנִיתִי for עָנִיתִי. 11. Add כִּי, " for ". Read כָּל־אָמָן כֹּזֵב (cp. Deut. 32²⁰) for כָּל־הָאָדָם כֹּזֵב, " every man is a liar ". 12. Read כְּכֹל for כָּל־, " all ". 14. Read, also in *v*. 18, נֶגֶד for נֶגְדָה־נָּא, a form not occurring elsewhere in the O.T. 15. Read תְּמוּתַה for הַמָּוְתָה / הַמָּוְתָה, a form otherwise unknown. 16. Read אֲנִי for כִּי־אֲנִי, " for I (am) ". Read, with Wutz, אֲפַתֶךָ (cp. Gen. 25¹⁶, Num. 25¹⁵, Ps. 117¹, but always in the plur.), for אֲמָתֶךָ, " thine handmaid ".

1-9. The psalmist expresses his *love* for Yahweh, called forth by the answer to his prayer when in .grievous danger. The verb used expresses human affection, and with Yahweh as its object occurs in the *Psalms* elsewhere only in 31²³, 97¹⁰, 145²⁰ ; on the other hand, its use is frequent when the object is the law, the commandments, and the name of Yahweh. His feelings are the deeper in that his life had been in jeopardy : *the cords of death encompassed me*, cp. Ps. 18⁴ ; death is figuratively represented as a cruel personality who entangles men with cords and ropes, and drags them down to the underworld, *Sheól*. In his straits the psalmist *called on the name of Yahweh* ; and because Yahweh is *gracious*, *righteous*, and *merciful*, *he preserveth the helpless* ; the word for *helpless* is literally " simple-minded " ; used here, therefore, of one who has unquestioning faith ; there is probably a special significance in the use of this word in view of the psalmist's confession in 10, 11. His mind is now at *rest* since *Yahweh hath dealt bountifully with him*; he has escaped death, and therefore he can *walk before Yahweh in the land of the living.*

10–11. In what follows we have a passage of great difficulty, which has always caused commentators much trouble. That there should be differences of opinion as to its meaning, and a variety of suggested emendations of the text, is in the nature of things; for as the text stands it is impossible to make sense of it. We have already indicated in the introduction to this psalm what we believe to be the meaning of the passage—namely, that in spite of his trust in Yahweh, so great was the psalmist's alarm at the danger in which he found himself, that he had a momentary doubt as to whether Yahweh could help him; he recalls this : *I trusted in Yahweh*; and then he said to himself, *I am greatly humbled*, for in his fear he had given up hope : *All trust is in vain*, lit. " a deceptive thing ". The emendation involved is somewhat drastic, it is granted (see crit. note); but it must be allowed that the mention of men, "All men are liars ", lit. " are lying ", is extremely inappropriate. The first half of this *v.* (11) is taken from Ps. 31²², and the possibility cannot be altogether excluded that the very apt second half also stood in our psalm at one time, viz. " I am cut off from before thine eyes ". But that is, of course, pure surmise; and, as things stand, we must make the best emendation we can. It may, at any rate, be claimed that the suggested emendation fits in with the context, and gives good sense.

In the *vv.* which follow (12–19) the psalmist reverts to what is foremost in his mind—viz., how to show his gratitude for what God had done for him : *How shall I make return to Yahweh for all his benefits to me ?* The illogical sequence of the verses here, and the wrong order in which the ritual acts are mentioned, make it highly probable that there is some dislocation of the text. It will be noticed that 14, 18 are identical; one or the other must, therefore, be deleted. Judging from Lev. 23³⁷, Deut. 32³⁸, Ezek. 20²⁸, the order of the ritual acts should be : the offering of the sacrifice, the drink-offering, the vows. Tentatively, therefore, we suggest that the verses ran originally in this order, omitting *v.* 14 altogether :

12. *How shall I make return to Yahweh*	*for all his benefits to me ?*
17. *I will offer the sacrifice of thanksgiving,*	*and call on the name of Yahweh ;*
13. *The cup of deliverance will I raise,*	*and call on the name of Yahweh ;*
18. *My vows to Yahweh will I pay*	*in the presence of all his people,*
19. *In the courts of the house of Yahweh,*	*in the midst of thee, O Jerusalem.*

Vv. 15, 16 then make a fitting conclusion; by fulfilling his religious duties the psalmist has shown himself to be Yahweh's *servant*; the triumphant words, *Thou hast loosed my bonds*, i.e., the bonds of death, so that life is now before him, form an effective conclusion.

By the *cup of deliverance* is meant the drink-offering (*nesek*) poured out before the altar in recognition of the deliverance granted by Yahweh ; with the ritual act of *raising* may be compared the similar action in connexion with the " waving " of the firstfruits before the altar, technically called the *Tenuphah* (Lev. 23[10 ff.] and 18[11]). The words, *Precious in the eyes of Yahweh is the death of his saints* are a little difficult ; one would rather expect the life of the saints to be precious, for which reason the life of the psalmist has been preserved ; but the words are probably to be understood in the sense that the death of the saints is too precious a thing in God's sight to be often permitted. The repetition of *I am thy servant* marks not merely the stress laid on the psalmist's self-dedication to the service of God, but in joining the repeated words to *the son of thy people*—i.e., the chosen people—it is intended to express the permanence of his being a servant.

Religious Teaching

Apart from the recognition of God's mercy in delivering from peril, and the gratitude for this, expressed in so many psalms, there are two special points of great religious significance which must be emphasized. The first is that the thanksgiving is proclaimed in the midst of the congregation ; the grateful heart must bear witness before others of what God has done, thereby glorifying the name of God and strengthening the faith of others in him. There is also, doubtless, the desire that others should share in the joy felt by one who had nearly lost his life, but had now, by God's mercy, recovered it. Spontaneously there arises in the mind the teaching of the Gospel : " And when she hath found it, she calleth together her friends and neighbours, saying, Rejoice with me, for I have found the piece which I had lost . . ." (Luke 15[8-10]).

The second point is the ardent impulse to show forth gratitude to God both by word and act ; it is not only the offering of sacrifice with appropriate words of praise which, according to the conceptions of the times, was acceptable to God ; even more significant is the affirmation : " I am thy servant " ; there lay the true and enduring expression of gratitude ; the definite self-dedication to carry out the will of the Master.

PSALM 117

THIS cannot be regarded as more than a fragment which has become detached from its context, presumably through the carelessness of a copyist. Whether it formed part of the preceding or of the following psalm, as in some manuscripts, or whether the psalm to which it originally belonged has been lost, must remain uncertain, though the latter is far more likely, for in neither of the psalms in question would it be appropriate. To justify its brevity, thereby postulating it as an entity, by comparing it with the Song of Miriam (Exod. 15²¹), as some commentators have done, is hardly to the point, for that song was not intended for liturgical worship. The psalmist, in his enthusiastic gratitude for God's favour shown to his people, calls upon the Gentiles to praise him for his mercy toward Israel (cp. Ps. 47¹, ²); the thought seems hardly logical as it stands, though in such a psalm, for example, as the 100th, it would be appropriate. The content, therefore, supports the view that it is a fragment from some other psalm.

The metre is 3 : 3.

1. Praise Yahweh, all ye nations,   laud him, all ye peoples,
2. For his love over us is great,   and the faithfulness of Yahweh is ever-
                                           lasting.
                     Hallelujah.

The first verse is quoted in Rom. 15¹¹ to show that Jew and Gentile are to be united in one Church. With the words, *For his love over us is great*, cp. Ps. 103¹¹, ¹⁷, and with the concluding words cp. Ps. 100⁵. The universalistic note points to the goal of the conversion of the Gentiles.

PSALM 118

THE insight into the liturgical ritual and worship of the temple during post-exilic times which this psalm gives, makes it, from this point of view, one of the most important in the Psalter. It is the last psalm composing the *Hallel* (see p. 99), sung at all the feasts ; but it occupied a special position at the Feast of Tabernacles, since it was one of the proper psalms for this feast.

The construction of the psalm shows that it was sung antiphonally, but opinions differ as to details. While it is impossible to state with any degree of certainty to whom the different verses are to be assigned, there is some justification for assuming the following arrangement :

Vv. 1–4 clearly form an introduction ; the first half of each verse here would seem to have been sung as a solo, presumably by one of the priests, while the second half, in the nature of a refrain, was taken up by the whole of the Levitical choir. As will be seen, the sequel suggests that this was sung in the outer court of the temple, near the entrance, but within the temple precincts ; it was here that priests

and choir awaited the procession of worshippers coming up the hill of
Zion to the sanctuary.   *Vv.* 5–21 are all in the first person, and were,
therefore, sung by an individual, in reference to himself, not in the
name of the people; *vv.* 8, 9 should make this clear.   It is, however,
possible that *vv.* 10–12, 15, 16, 19, 20 were later insertions; we make
the suggestion merely as a possibility (see the exegetical notes on
these verses).   This individual, we may assume, was among those
who formed the procession ascending the hill of Zion.   It is true
no direct mention is here made of such a procession, but it is implied
in *vv.* 19, 20, and in the final section of the psalm it is directly referred
to.   In addition, the procession at this festival is described in the
Mishnah (see further, the exegetical notes), which echoes traditional
usage.   *Vv.* 22–29 were sung antiphonally by the worshippers forming the festal procession, and the Levitical choir.   The whole psalm
thus presents us with a vivid picture of the temple-worship during
the Feast of Tabernacles.

The occasion on which this psalm was sung in public worship,
however—an opinion held by most, but not all, modern commentators—presents a difficulty which must be dealt with, for it is one
which is met with in some other psalms.   The difficulty is this: if
the main body of the psalm was the utterance of an *individual*, or even,
as Hans Schmidt holds, of three different individuals, how can the
psalm as a whole have been used by *the whole body of worshippers*
during what was probably the most important festal celebration of the
year?   The answer is to be sought, we believe, in recognizing that
the psalm has a history behind it.   This psalm, like certain others,
is one of thanksgiving for deliverance from peril, and in its original
form consisted of the central part only, *vv.* 5–21, with the possible
exception of 10–12, 15, 16, 19, 20.   Psalms like this, because they
expressed so fully the thoughts and emotions of any who had passed
through similar experiences, were adopted for general use in worship.
This being so, additions were made to the original kernel of a psalm
in order to adapt it to congregational use.   In the present case this
was done by prefacing it with the opening *vv.* 1–4.   Thus, in the
second stage of its history the psalm ended with *v.* 21, and its original
individual character came to be understood of the people collectively.
The final stage in the history of the psalm was when it became
specifically used as a festal psalm, at the Feast of Tabernacles; when
this took place there are no means of ascertaining, any more than it is
known when the " Hallel ", as such, originated; we know only that
it was so used.   But the reason why it was chosen as the special psalm
for the Feast of Tabernacles may well have been as follows: on each
day of this feast a procession took place, the worshippers all carrying
palm-branches (*lulab*); on the seventh day this was performed seven

times (Mishnah, *Sukkôth* iv. 4); during the procession the people shouted *Hoshi'ah-na'* (Hosanna = " Save now ") from *v.* 25 of this psalm. From this the seventh day of the feast was known as *Yôm Hoshi'ah-na'* (" Hosanna day "), and the palm-branch came to be called *Hoshi'ah-na.* This word was, therefore, a kind of catch-word in connexion with the ritual of the Feast of Tabernacles. Now in our psalm we have in *vv.* 14, 21 the words: " He is (or thou art) become to me for deliverance, or *saving, Lîshu'ah,* which is from the same root, and contains the same thought, as *Hoshi'ah-na'.* Knowing, as we do, the fondness of the Hebrews for catch-words, it is quite possible that we have here what was considered an appropriate link with the hallowed expression belonging specifically to the Feast of Tabernacles; hence its choice for the psalm of the festival. Added to this there were the opening verses (1–4) which had been attached to the psalm, making it appropriate for festal use; and the contents of the body of the psalm, being now understood in a collective sense, emphasized this. The point of attachment between the psalm as it now stood with the final addition was skilfully made by beginning this latter with the words: " The stone which the builders rejected is become the head of the corner . . .", on the meaning of which, see the exegetical notes. *Vv.* 19, 20, and possibly also 10–12, 15, 16, were added at the same time.

The date of the psalm, owing to the developed form of worship implied, must, at any rate in its present form, be late post-exilic. The text has been well preserved; there are but few corruptions. The metre is a difficulty; opinions differ; some hold that it is almost uniformly 3 : 3 with 3 : 2 here and there, while others maintain that it is 3 : 2 throughout. We hold the former view, recognizing that there is something to be said for the latter.

1. Give thanks to Yahweh, for he is good,   For his love is eternal;
2. Let ° the house of ° Israel say: For his love is eternal;
3. Let the house of Aaron ° say °:   For his love is eternal;
4. Let them that fear Yahweh ° say °:   For his love is eternal.
5. In distress I called on Yah,   ° he brought me forth into freedom °.
6. Yahweh is mine, I fear not   what men may do unto me;
7. Yahweh is mine, ° he helpeth me °,   and I look in triumph on foes.
8. 'Tis better to trust in Yahweh   than confide in man;
9. 'Tis better to trust in Yahweh   than confide in princes.
10. All the nations surrounded me,   in the name of Yahweh ° I trod them down °;
11. They surrounded me, yea, they surrounded me;   in the name of Yahweh ° I trod them down °;
12. They surrounded me like bees ° the honeycomb °,   ° in the name of Yahweh ° I trod them down °.
13. ° I was sorely thrust at ° that I might fall,   but Yahweh helped me.
14. My strength and ° my song ° is Yah,   and he is become my deliverer.
15. Hark, a cry of joy and victory   in the tents of the righteous;
    The right-hand of Yahweh doeth mightily,   16. The right-hand of Yahweh is exalted;

17. I shall not die, but live,   and recount ° the works ° of Yahweh.
18. Yahweh did chasten me sorely,   but to death he did not deliver me.
19. Open me the gates of righteousness,   I will enter them and praise Yah ;
20. This is the gate of Yahweh,   the righteous shall enter therein.
21. I will thank thee because thou hast
    answered me,   and art become my deliverer.
22. The stone which the builders rejected,   is become the head of the corner ;
23. From Yahweh hath this come to pass,   it is ° a wonder-work ° in our eyes
24. This is the day Yahweh hath ordained,   let us rejoice and be glad in it.
25. Ah, Yahweh, save now,   Ah, Yahweh, grant prosperity.
26. Blessed is he that cometh in the name
    of Yahweh,   we bless you from the house of Yahweh ;
27.   Yahweh is God,
               ° May he give us light.°
        ° Marshal the procession with leafy-branches,°
                 Unto the horns of the altar.
28. My God art thou, I will thank thee,   My God, I will extol thee.
29. Give thanks to Yahweh, for he is good,   for his love is eternal.

Text-critical Notes

2. Add, with G, בֵּית. 3. 4. Read יֹאמַר, as in v. 2, for the plur. יֹאמְרוּ.
5. Read (see 2 Sam. 22¹⁰) עָנָנִי בַמֶּרְחָב יָהּ for וַיִּאָ לַמֶּרְחָב אֹתִי.
" Yah answered me in a wide place ". 7. On the form בְּעֹזְרָי see GK 119*i* 124*k*,
10. Read, with Kittel, אֲמַלֵּם (מלל) for אֲמִילַם (so, too, in vv. 11, 12), "I will cut
them off " ; for the form of the suffix see GK 6o*d*, and for the force of the impf. see
GK 107*b* ; for the use of the preceding כִּי here see GK 159*ee*. 12. Add
with G, דֹּלְקָב, this word does not, however, occur in this sense elsewhere ; but
cp. Deut. 1⁴⁴. Om. דֹּעֲכוּ כְּאֵשׁ קוֹצִים, "they are quenched as the fire of thorns ",
which gives a half-line too much. 13. Read, with G, דָּחֹה נִדְחֵיתִי for דָּחֹה דְחִיתַנִי,
" thou didst thrust sore at me ". Yahweh is not directly addressed elsewhere in
these vv. 14. Read זִמְרָתִי for זִמְרָת, but see GK 8o*g*. In Exod. 15², from which
the passage seems to have been taken (but cp. Isa. 12²), G has " my hiding-place ",
or " refuge " (=סִתְרִי) ; this may originally have stood here. 16. Om., with many
G MSS, the repetition of v. 15ᶜ. 17. Many MSS have מַעֲשֵׂה, " work of ", instead
of the plural. 23. Read נִפְלֵאת for נִפְלָאת. 27. Read יָאֵר for וַיָּאֶר " and he
gave light ". The rendering : *Marshal the procession* . . . is based, in part, on that
of G : συστήσασθε ἑορτὴν ἐν τοῖς πυκάζουσιν, " Set in order the festival with leafy
(branches) ". For this sense of אסר see 1 Kgs. 20¹⁴, 2 Chron. 13³ ; for the
justification of " procession " as the rendering of חג here, see Job 26¹⁰ : " He hath
worked out a circle (חָג) upon the face of the waters " ; the festal procession
encircled the altar ; and for the rendering "leafy-branches" for עֲבֹתִים see Lev.
23⁴⁰ : "And ye shall take you . . . and boughs of thick trees (וַעֲנַף עֵץ־עָבֹת) . . .";
this is in reference to the Feast of Tabernacles.

1-4. This introduction to the psalm of thanksgiving follows the
pattern of Ps. 115⁹⁻¹¹ (see the notes there), while the refrain, *For his
love is eternal,* is taken from that of Ps. 136. We hold that the *For* is
accented in the Hebrew, though this is exceptional. The two parts
of each verse were sung antiphonally, as already pointed out.
This obviously *congregational* act of worship introducing a psalm of
purely personal character supports the view that the two parts did not
originally belong together, but that this introduction was put in its
present place when the psalm was adapted to public worship.

5. In all that follows the original personal note is now understood
collectively of the people as a whole, as in a number of other psalms.

That in some of the verses a collective sense is inappropriate cannot be denied; but it could not be otherwise when an " individual " psalm was thus adapted. This verse is a case in point; the psalmist *called on God in distress.* It may well be that by *distress* the reference is to imprisonment (see Hans Schmidt *in loc.*), from which, as the second half of the verse shows, the psalmist had been liberated: *He brought me forth into freedom* (lit. " a wide place "); these words, taken from 2 Sam. 22²⁰, are substituted for the somewhat doubtful Hebrew text. On the abbreviated form of the divine name, *Yah*, see on Ps. 68¹⁸. In the verses which follow (6–9) the expressions of trust in God are very impressive; where this trust is a firm conviction the threat of men counts for nothing: *Yahweh is mine, I fear not what men may do unto me*, words which seem to be borrowed from Ps. 56⁴, ¹¹; but more, with his help, as the psalmist says: *I look in triumph on foes* (cp. Ps. 59¹⁰). Far better, therefore, is it *to trust in Yahweh* than *in man* or *princes*. With the " individual " character of the psalm it is a little difficult to reconcile 10–12: *All the nations surrounded me. In the name of Yahweh I trod them down* . . .; this would be appropriate enough in reference to the nation collectively which had overcome its enemies, and now offered thanks to *Yahweh* in whose *name* they had fought—the *all* may be put down to poetical hyperbole—but in reference to an individual these words sound incongruous. The possibility must therefore be recognized of 10–12 having been added when the psalm was adapted to congregational worship. In this connexion it is worth noting that the very unusual simile contained in the words, *they surrounded me like bees the honeycomb*, occurs elsewhere only in Deut. 1⁴⁴ (Isa. 7¹⁸ is not a parallel), which may well have been in the mind of the psalmist, and that in that passage the reference is to a nation, the Amorites, surrounding the Israelites. 13, *I was sorely thrust at that I might fall* . . ., which is again thoroughly individualistic, comes very appropriately after 9; this further emphasizes the possibility that 9–11 may have been added later. The psalmist again affirms his trust in God in the words of 14, *My strength and my song is Yah*, quoted from Exod. 15², or Isa. 12²; " strength " and " song " are not good parallels, but they occur also in the Isaiah passage, where the Septuagint has " praise " (= " song "); but in the Exod. passage the Septuagint has the better parallel, " refuge " in place of " song "; conceivably " refuge " stood in our verse originally. *My deliverer* is lit. " deliverance ", or " saving, to me ". The individualistic note recedes again in 15, 16, *Hark, a cry of joy and victory in the tents of the righteous* . . ., for this reads like the triumphal shout of an army, *righteous* because they ascribe their victory to Yahweh. So that, once more, we must recognize the possibility of these verses having been inserted when the psalm was adapted to public worship; and again, the words in 17, *I shall not die but live* . . ., come more appropriately after 14. In a number of manuscripts the text reads: *the work of Yahweh*, in place of the plural, *the works*; if the former is original the reference will be to the special act of divine deliverance to the individual; the plural may be a later correction, and will then refer to many occasions on which divine help had been accorded to the nation. The former accords well with the bitter experience of the individual psalmist (18): *Yahweh did chasten me sorely, but to death he did not deliver me*; therefore he cries (21) *I will thank thee because thou hast answered me, and art become my deliverer* (cp. 14). And now, once more, we have to suggest the possibility of another later insertion, made again for the purpose of adapting the psalm to congregational worship. We have already, in the introductory section to this psalm, mentioned that in 19, 20 the well-known festal procession, which took place during the Feast of Tabernacles, is referred to; these *vv.* run: *Open me the gates of righteousness, I will enter them and praise Yah ; this is the gate of Yahweh, the righteous shall enter therein*. The picture here presented is that of the festal procession which has reached the temple gates, and now seeks admission; one of their number comes forth and calls to the Levites within: *Open me the gates of righteousness*, i.e., the gates of the place where righteousness dwells, and through which only the righteous may enter: *I will enter them and praise Yah*; thereupon the response comes from the company within the gates (cp. 1–4: *This is the gate of Yahweh, the righteous shall enter therein*). If, now, these two verses were sung or intoned as the procession neared the gate, they belong to congregational worship; and it is for this reason that we suggest their having been inserted when the psalm was adapted to this purpose. It is true, they would come better after 21 which follows 18 very appropriately; and probably this was originally the case.

It is fully realized that these suggestions as to various verses having been inserted later may be distasteful to many readers; but it must be allowed that the procedure is a very natural one, and, indeed, a very edifying one, when the religious instinct feels that the beautiful outpouring of an individual should be adapted to wider use. It explains also why in one and the same psalm both individual and congregational elements appear.

We come now to the last section. This originally began, as suggested, with 19, 20. Then follow the very well-known words: *The stone which the builders rejected is become the head of the corner*. This constitutes the point of attachment with the psalm as originally written; it refers, in the first instance, to him who had been in grievous peril, and had been saved by God's mercy; but it is now adapted and applied to the nation as a whole. The picture is a striking one: just as builders cast aside a stone which to their mind is of indifferent value, but which is ultimately found to be the most beautiful, so the enemies of the psalmist, " the builders ", scorned and maltreated him (see 13), but, as one who was righteous in the sight of God, he was raised to a position of high honour; and so, too, the nation, which had been overcome and despised by the Gentiles, but had been delivered by God, and was now honoured in their sight. In each case, *From Yahweh hath this come to pass, it is a wonder-work in our eyes.* The words have thus a kind of proverbial sense : the despised of many is become the honoured one. On the Messianic interpretation of this passage see Vol. I, p. 100 f.

In the Mishnah (*Sukkôth* iii. iv) much is said about the special importance of the first day of the feast when this fell on a Sabbath, which was, in any case, a day of rejoicing; there may, thus, well be a special significance in the words of 24 : *This is the day Yahweh hath ordained* (cp., e.g., Exod. 16²⁹), *let us be glad and rejoice in it.* Very impressive must have been the great shout raised by the whole body of the processionists : *Ah, Yahweh, save now (Hoshi'ah-na'),* on which see further above, *Ah Yahweh, grant prosperity*; in the Hebrew the interjection *Ah* is written *'Anna'* with each vowel accented. When the shout of the multitude outside the temple gates had died down, a voice from within welcomed the worshippers in the words : *Blessed is he that cometh in the name of Yahweh, we bless you from the house of Yahweh,* uttered by one of the Levitical choir. Thereupon the worshippers respond : *Yahweh is God, may he give us light* (cp. Num. 6²⁵ : " Yahweh make his face to shine upon thee, and be gracious unto thee "). The worshippers now enter the temple, and the leader of the Levitical choir gives the command : *Marshal the procession with leafy-branches* (see text-critical note), *let it proceed unto the horns of the altar.* The rendering of the English version : " Bind the sacrifice with cords, even unto the horns of the altar ", is due to a misunderstanding of the Hebrew; to have done this would have been contrary to the ritual; and, in any case, it would hardly have been possible to bind the sacrificial victim to the " horns " of the altar, for these were quite small protuberances. The reference in this verse is to the solemn procession within the temple, described in the Mishnah (*Sukkôth* iv. 5-7), during which all the worshippers carried palm-branches (cp. Lev. 23⁴⁰); whenever the shout of *Hoshi'ah-na'* was raised the palm-branches were waved to and fro. The mention of the altar is in reference to the ritual act of the worshippers who beat their palm-branches on the ground on each side of the altar (*Sukkôth* iv. 6).

The command for the procession to begin having been given, each of the worshippers utters the words : *My God art thou, I will thank thee, my God, I will extol thee,* which he is now about to do, and then all present repeat the opening words of the psalm.

Religious Teaching

The primary point of religious teaching offered by this psalm, apart from the detailed essence of religion running through the whole body of the superb composition, is the stress laid on the need of congregational worship. However devout, and earnest, and sincere the true believer may be in his silent and private intercourse with God, there is something lacking if the individual member does not realize that he is indissolubly joined to the body (cp. 1 Cor. 12^{12-27}); and this, in the religious sense, cannot be fully experienced apart from joint-worship. This is the implication which the psalm, in the form in which we now have it, insists upon. To the Christian the inspiring sense of "altogetherness" in the sight of God is an assurance of the active fulfilling of the two great commandments (Mark 12^{29-31}). The whole conception of the content of worship portrayed in this psalm is extraordinarily fine: praise, thanksgiving, supplication, acknowledgement of God's mercies, the expression of trust in him.

PSALM 119

THIS is an acrostic psalm which differs from all others of the kind (viz., 9 and 10 as one, 25, 34, 37, 111, 112, 145) in that the opening letter of each of the eight lines of each section, respectively, is the same; in this way the whole Hebrew alphabet is worked through. It is largely due to this artificial construction that the composition abounds in repetitions which makes the reading of it somewhat monotonous. That the composer is greatly indebted to the writers of other psalms, as well as to the Wisdom writers, soon becomes evident.

The main purpose of the psalmist is the glorification of the Law, which is described in various ways: testimonies, statutes, precepts, commandments, judgements, word; this last is sometimes used in the sense of "promise"; two nouns occur for this, *dābār* and *'imrāh*, but they are often parallel to one another in this psalm, and are used of the divine utterance in the Law. The conception of the Law as here set forth is very striking, and demands a brief description. Its divine origin is, of course, fundamental; it is the embodiment of truth, is full of wonder-works, illumines the pathway of life, is the means of divine grace, gives peace, keeps from sin, gives life, counsel, and comfort, is the most beautiful of all possessions, more precious than gold, and lasts to eternity. The psalmist never tires of expressing his delight in, and love for, the Law; in it he recognizes the will of God which he discerns at work everywhere.

While the expression of this deep and sincere devotion to the Law was the primary purpose for which the psalmist wrote, there is reason to believe that he had a subsidiary object in view in his glorification of it. There are a number of passages which witness to the existence of a difference of religious outlook; the forceful language which is sometimes used may be the echo of the bitterness of controversy with those of differing views, who, in the eyes of the psalmist, were sinners and enemies of the Law because they did not observe it in the strict way which he held to be right. In other words, the psalm seems to reflect the clash of views within Judaism. There is nothing to suggest that the writer had Gentiles in mind when speaking of his adversaries; indeed, the whole way in which their enmity and hatred are spoken of precludes this; they are Jews like the psalmist; and this psalm reflects the opposition between two religious attitudes among the Jews which in later days issued in the formation of parties. The beginnings date back to the time of the return from the Babylonian Exile; it was then that the stricter and more orthodox form of exilic Judaism, held by those who returned, was opposed to the laxer religious outlook and practice of those living in the homeland. Through the centuries the antagonisms, then formed, continued, and ultimately there arose the definitely constituted and opposed parties of the Sadducees and Pharisees. Our psalm reflects these conditions as they existed during about the middle of the third century B.C.; to this date we feel impelled to assign it, as against those who, on the one hand, favour the late Persian period, about a century earlier, and, on the other, those who bring the date down to Maccabæan times. As against the former, full time must be allowed for the great development of the Law as presented in our psalm; and, as against the latter, there is no indication in the psalm of the existence, as yet, of a definitely formed party, such as the *Hasidim*, the spiritual ancestors of the Pharisees, mentioned in 1 Macc. 2^{42}, 7^{13}, 2 Macc. 14^6. Our psalmist glories in the Law in devout simplicity; he does not discuss its meanings and implications, after the manner of the Pharisees; the study of the Law had not yet reached that well-meaning, though often hair-splitting, method of interpretation which was characteristic of Pharisaism.

The metre is almost wholly 3 : 2, in only a few instances is there a change to other metres; this, however, was probably not due to the original writer.

א

1. Blessed are the blameless in the way,   who walk in the law of Yahweh.
2. Blessed are they that keep his testimonies,   that seek him with all their heart,

3. Who verily do no wrong, who walk in his ways.
4. Thou hast commanded thy precepts, to observe them diligently.
5. O that my ways were stedfast in keeping thy statutes;
6. Then should I not be ashamed in contemplating all thy commandments.
7. I will thank thee in uprightness of heart when I learn thy righteous judgements;
8. I will keep thy statutes ° to the full °, forsake me not.

Text-critical Notes

8. Place עַד־מְאֹד here instead of at the end of the verse, as demanded both by the sense and the metre.

1–3. The psalm opens in the style of the Wisdom writers, insisting on the happiness of those who walk in innocency of life, who *are blameless in the way* (cp. Prov. 11[20], 13[6]), as it is expressed, for this is to *walk in the law of Yahweh* (cp. Prov. 29[18]). A somewhat similar use of *way* occurs in Acts 9[2]. The Hebr. of 4 is difficult to translate without paraphrasing, viz.: " *Thou hast commanded that thy precepts should be observed diligently.*" In spite of every intention to do right, the psalmist recognizes his shortcomings, and bursts forth, *O that my ways were stedfast in keeping thy statutes*; had that been the case he would have been spared the shame felt in *contemplating* God's *commandments* which he had so often neglected. Nevertheless, he trusts that, with God's help, he will *learn* his *righteous judgements*, and *thank* him in *uprightness of heart, i.e.*, in heartfelt sincerity. Very touching is the resolution, *I will keep thy statutes to the full*, uttered with the sense of self-distrust and therefore accompanied by the prayer: *Forsake me not.*

ב

9. Whereby shall a young man ° By taking heed ° ° to thy word °. keep pure his way ?
10. With all my heart have I sought thee, let me not stray from thy commandments.
11. In my heart have I laid up thy word, that I might not sin against thee.
12. Blessed art thou, Yahweh, O teach me thy statutes.
13. With my lips do I tell forth, all the judgements of thy mouth.
14. In the way of thy testimonies do I rejoice, ° more than over ° all wealth.
15. On thy precepts will I meditate, and will contemplate thy ways;
16. ° In thy law ° will I delight myself, I will not forget thy word.

Text-critical Notes

9. For the construction see GK 114o. Read, with GS, דְּבָרֶךָ, omitting כְּ, " according to ". 14. Read, with S, מֵעַל for כְּעַל, " as over ". 16. Read בְּתוֹרָתֶךָ for בְּחֻקֹּתֶיךָ, " in thy statutes ", a form which does not occur in this psalm.

9. Fully in accordance with the Wisdom writers is both the form of question and answer, and the warning against the sin of impurity among young men (Prov. 7[7] ff., Eccles. 11[9, 10,] and cp. 2 Tim. 2[22]); the only safeguard is to take *heed* to the *word*, or command, of God. That the psalmist is innocent of sin here is because he has *sought* God, *with all* his *heart*, and *laid up* God's *word* in his *heart*. For this he

blesses *Yahweh*, and protests his determination to be faithful to all the divine precepts, in which he rejoices more than in *all wealth*.

ג

17. Deal bountifully with thy servant that
    I may live,
    and I will observe thy word;
18. Unclose mine eyes that I may see
    the wonder-works of thy law.
19. A stranger am I on earth,
    hide not from me ° thy word °.
20. My soul is overborne with longing
    for thy judgements at all times.
21. Thou rebukest the proud; accursed
    are they that wander from thy commandments.
22. ° Take away ° from me reproach °,
    for ° thy testimonies ° have I kept,—
23. Even princes sat, talking together
    against me,
    thy servant doth meditate in thy statutes,—
24. Yea, thy testimonies are my delight,
    ° thy statutes ° are my counsel.

Text-critical Notes

19. Read אִמְרָתֶֽךָ for מִצְוֹתֶיךָ, " thy commandments ", which occurs in *v.* 21; in *v.* 17 a different noun for " word " is used.   22. Read, with G, גֹּל for גַּל, " he hath taken away ".   Om. with S, · וָבוּז, " and contempt ", which overloads the half-line.   Read, either here or in *v.* 24, where the same word occurs, פִּקּוּדֶיךָ, " thy precepts ".   24. Read חֻקֶּיךָ for אַנְשֵׁי, " men of ", which, applied to spiritual things, is inappropriate; the verse is a continuation of *v.* 22.

The ardent yearning to live in accordance with the divine ordinances in these verses is very edifying; the prayer is for divine grace that God's *word* may be observed, that the understanding may be quickened, so that the ethical beauty, the *wonder-works*, of his Law may be apprehended.   Man's days on earth are but few; he is, as it were, merely a sojourner, a stranger, there; of all things that the psalmist desires, the revelation of God's word is foremost: *Hide not from me thy word*, which includes both command and promise.   A strong expression is used to portray the intense yearning for the things of God, " my soul is overborne ", lit. " crushed ", with the weight of the longing. The arrogant, or proud, are rightly rebuked by God; in his horror for those who *wander* from the divine commandments, the psalmist pronounces them *accursed*.   He is the victim of reproach on the part of *princes*, *i.e.*, the highly-placed among his people; but God will answer his prayer and *take away from* him the undeserved insult, for, as God's *servant*, his thoughts are ever directed towards his *statutes*.

ד

25. My soul cleaveth to the dust,
    quicken me according to thy word.
26. My ways I recounted, and thou didst
    answer me,
    teach me thy statutes.
27. Make me to understand the way of
    thy precepts,
    and I will meditate on thy wonder-works.
28. My soul weepeth for grief,
    raise me up ° by ° thy word.
29. The way of lying put away from me,
    and be gracious unto me with thy law.
30. The way of faithfulness have I chosen,
    thy judgements ° do I desire °.
31. I cleave unto thy testimonies,
    Yahweh, put me not to shame.
32. In the way of thy commandment I run,
    for thou enlargest my heart.

Text-critical Notes

28. Read, with G, בְּ for כְּ, " according to ".   30. Read אִוִּיתִי for שִׁוִּיתִי, " I have set ".

As elsewhere in this psalm, *soul* is used of the personal self. The psalmist recalls how in self-abasement he has lain prone on the ground in worship (cp. Job 16¹⁵⁻¹⁷): *My soul cleaveth to the dust*, but he knows that God will *quicken* him, *i.e.*, inspire him with new life. He pours out to God the trials he has gone through, and prays for guidance by means of the divine *statutes*. He has wept for *grief, my soul weepeth*, lit. " melteth ", because of his shortcomings, and he prays that God will *raise* him *up* by his *word*. He has not always been truthful, but prays that God will be *gracious* to him by imparting to him strength to fulfil his *law*. His whole bent is to be faithful to God, *the way of faithfulness have I chosen* ; therefore *Yahweh* will not *put* him to *shame*. He runs in the *way* of God's *commandments*, because God has opened wide his heart to receive them : *for thou enlargest my heart*.

ה

33. Teach me ° the way of thy statutes,	and I will keep it in gratitude ;
34. Give me understanding that I may keep thy law,	yea, I will observe it with all my heart.
35. Lead me in the path of thy commandments,	for therein do I delight.
36. Incline my heart unto thy testimonies,	and not to covetousness ;
37. Turn mine eyes from beholding vanity,	quicken me ° according to thy word °.
38. Confirm thy word unto thy servant,	which is ° for them that fear thee °.
39. Turn away my reproach which I dread,	for thy judgements are good.
40. Behold, I long for thy precepts,	quicken me in thy righteousness.

Text-critical Notes

33. Om. יהוה, " Yahweh ", for the metre's sake. 37. Read כִּדְבָרֶךָ, as in *v.* 25, for בִּדְרָכֶךָ, " in thy way ". 38. Read לְיִרְאָתֶךָ for לְיִרְאָ֫תֶךָ.

In this section, which consists of a number of petitions, there are only a few points which call for comment. The opening *v.* 33 is a little difficult on account of the word rendered *gratitude* ('*ēqeb*) ; it is a noun which is often used adverbially, " because of ", " in consequence of ", *e.g.*, Ps. 40¹⁵, 70³ ; but here, as in Ps. 19¹¹, Prov. 22⁴, it means lit. " gain ", or " reward " ; but it is uncertain whether the " reward " is intended to apply to God or to the psalmist ; thus, paraphrased, the *v.* may be rendered : *Teach me the way of thy statutes, and I will keep it*, *i.e.*, the way, in recognition of the answer to my prayer, *i.e.*, his *gratitude* is something given to God in return. On the other hand, it may mean that the keeping of the way of God's statutes is a reward, or gain, to the psalmist. It is the former which we have adopted here, as the Godward thought is what is the more prominent throughout this psalm. 34 is, in some sense, a parallel to 33. In 36 the mention of covetousness on the part of the psalmist is unexpected ; that the sin was prevalent is evident from Pss. 49⁶, 62¹⁰ ; that he confesses to it is all to his credit. 37 is presumably intended to be parallel to 36.

ו

41. May thy lovingkindnesses come unto me, Yahweh, thy salvation, according to thy word;
42. That I may answer my slanderer by word, for I trust in thy word.
43. Withdraw not from my mouth the word of truth °, for I hope for thy judgements;
44. And I will observe thy law continually, for ever and ever;
45. Yea, I will walk in freedom, for thy precepts have I sought;
46. Yea, I will speak of thy testimonies in the presence of kings, without fear;
47. And I will delight myself in thy commandments which I love,
48. And I will lift up my hands ° unto thee °, and will meditate in thy statutes.

Text-critical Notes

43. Om. עַד־מְאֹד, " utterly ", which is inappropriate here, and overloads the half-line. 48. Read אֵלֶיךָ for אֶל־מִצְוֹתֶיךָ, " unto thy commandments ", and om. אֲשֶׁר אָהַבְתִּי, " which I have loved ", repeated from the previous verse.

The chief import of this section concerns the resolutions made by the psalmist to walk in the ways of godliness. 43. *Withdraw not* is lit. " snatch not away ", a somewhat unusual use of the word.   Difficult to reproduce in English is 45, *Yea, I will walk in freedom*, the idea is the wide scope in which God's precepts will be observed, they will be the psalmist's guide in all circumstances (cp. Prov. 4¹²).   In 46 *without fear* is lit. " and I shall not be ashamed."

ז

49. Remember ° thy word ° to thy servant, for ° I wait ° for it.
50. This is my comfort in mine affliction, that thy word hath quickened me.
51. The arrogant have me greatly in derision, from thy law I swerve not.
52. I remember thy judgements of old, Yahweh, and take comfort.
53. Burning-wrath taketh hold of me because of the wicked, who forsake thy law.
54. Songs of praise have thy statutes been to me in the house of my sojourning.
55. In the night-time I remember thy name °, and observe thy law.
56. This did I have, ° Yahweh °, for I keep thy precepts.

Text-critical Notes

49. Read, with G, דְּבָרְךָ for דָּבָר, " a word ".   Read יִחַלְתִּי for יִחַלְתָּנִי, " thou hast made me to hope ". 55. Om. יהוה, " Yahweh ". 56. Add יהוה.

It will be noted how, again, stress is laid on the *word*, which embodies so much; here the thought is probably that of " promise ", trust in which is *comfort in affliction*.   However much the *arrogant* may deride the devout believer in God, the psalmist will *not swerve from* observing *the law* (cp. Ps. 44¹⁸).   *Songs of praise have thy statutes been unto me*, (54), is to be taken in a literal sense; *the house of my sojourning* means, as in 19, the transient abode on earth (cp. Ps. 39¹²).   *In the night-time I remember* . . ., (55), cp. Ps. 42⁸, 88¹.

ה

57. My portion is Yahweh; I said,	I will keep ° thy word °;
58. I sought thy favour with all my heart,	be gracious unto me, according to thy word.
59. I thought on ° thy ways °, and turned	my feet unto thy testimonies.
60. I made haste, and I did not delay,	to keep thy commandments.
61. The cords of the wicked entangled me,	thy law I did not forget.
62. At midnight I rise to praise thee,	because of thy righteous judgements.
63. A companion am I to all that fear thee,	and to them that keep thy precepts.
64. The earth is full of thy love,°	teach me thy statutes.

Text-critical Notes

57. Read דְּבָרֶיךָ for דְּבָרְיךָ, " thy words ". 59. Read דְּרָכֶיךָ for דְּרָכַי, " my ways ". 64. Om. יְהוָה, " Yahweh ", for the metre's sake.

With *My portion is Yahweh*, (57), cp. Ps. 16⁵, 73²⁶, 42⁵. The phrase *I sought thy favour* (59) is lit. " *I entreated thy face* ", cp. Ps. 45¹². The libellous behaviour of the wicked is metaphorically compared with a trap, *The cords of the wicked entangled me* (61); the only retort which the psalmist makes is that he observes the *law*, cp. 51.

ט

65. Well hast thou dealt with thy servant,	Yahweh, according to thy word.
66. Teach me ° discretion and knowledge,	for I trust in thy commandments.
67. Before I was afflicted I was going astray,	but now thy word I observe.
68. Good art thou, and doest good,	teach me thy statutes.
69. The arrogant have besmeared me with lies,	I keep thy precepts.°
70. Gross is their heart like fat,	I delight in thy law.
71. Good for me that I was afflicted,	that I might learn thy statutes.
72. Better for me is the law of thy mouth	than thousands of gold and silver.

Text-critical Notes

66. Om. טוֹב, " good ", which is repeated from the previous verse, and overloads the half-line. 69. Om. בְּכָל־לֵב, " with all (my) heart ", which overloads the half-line.

Most of this section repeats what has already been said.. A curious, but expressive, metaphor is used in 69, *The arrogant have besmeared me with lies*; the thought is that falsehood has been imputed to him, lit. they have so plastered him with lies, that he is unrecognizable. His attitude, in face of this, is simply to *keep* the divine *precepts*. Another pointed metaphor is contained in 70, *Gross is their heart like fat*; the heart was regarded as the seat of understanding, and just as a " fatty degeneration " of the heart is fatal, so the beclouded understanding of man condemns him as useless. In face of this the psalmist has but one recourse, *I delight in thy law*. Twice in this section does the psalmist emphasize the remedial property of affliction ; evidently he speaks from personal experience ; and the spirit in which it is accepted is notable ; his affection for all that appertains to God outweighs everything that the world can offer : *Better for me is the law of thy mouth than thousands* (of pieces) *of gold and silver*, 72 (cp. Ps. 19¹⁰, Prov. 8¹⁰).

73. Thy hands have made me and established me,
give me understanding that I may learn thy commandments.

74. They that fear thee shall see me and be glad,
for I have hoped in thy word.

75. I know ° that thy judgements are righteous,
and in faithfulness thou didst afflict me.

76. Let, now, thy love be my comfort,
according to thy word to thy servant ;

77. Let thy mercies come unto me that I may live,
for thy law is my delight.

78. Let the arrogant be ashamed, for they wrongfully oppress me,
I meditate in thy precepts.

79. Let those that fear thee turn unto me,
° and those that know ° thy testimonies.

80. Let my heart be perfect in thy statutes,
that I be not ashamed.

Text-critical Notes

75. Om. יהוה, " Yahweh ", for the metre's sake. 79. Read, with the *Qᵉrê*, וְיֵדְעֵי for the *Kᵉthibh* וְיֵדְעוּ, " that they may know ".

The psalmist emphasizes the truth that God has not only created him, but has also endowed him with the faculty to do what is right ; he is *established*, lit. " prepared " for his walk in life ; the psalmist, therefore, prays that he may use this faculty, *give me understanding that I may learn*, and thus fulfil, *thy commandments* (73). The result will be that those who *fear* God will *be glad* ; the force of *word* here is " promise " (74) ; so, too, in 76. In 79 the psalmist prays that both those who *fear* God, and those who know his *testimonies*, may *turn unto him*, i.e., seek his companionship.

ב

81. My soul pineth for thy salvation,
for thy word do I hope.

82. Mine eyes pine for thy word °,
when wilt thou comfort me ?

83. For I am like a wine-skin in smoke,
I do not forget thy statutes ;

84. How many are the days of thy servant ?
when wilt thou execute judgement on my persecutors ?

85. The arrogant have dug pits for me,
they are not according to thy law ;

86. All thy commandments are truth,
they persecute me without cause, help me ;

87. Well-nigh had they swept me ° from the earth °,
but I forsook not thy precepts.

88. According to thy love quicken me that I may observe
the testimony of thy mouth.

Text-critical Notes

82. Om., with S, לֵאמֹר, " saying ". 87. Read מֵאֶרֶץ for בָּאָרֶץ, " in the earth ".

The psalmist has more than once spoken of enemies by whom he is beset, but in this section they are more fully dealt with. The psalmist begins by expressing his deep yearning for divine help. He uses a strong word for describing his feelings, *my soul pineth*, lit. " is come to an end ", or " done for " ; *salvation* here means " help ", and

word has again the force of " promise " (81), while in 82 it is a different
word, meaning rather " utterance ". At first, the words, *mine eyes
pine for thy word*, sound strange; but that is only because of the
pregnant mode of expression in the Hebrew; what they mean is that
the psalmist is utterly weary in looking for the visible fulfilment of the
divine *dictum* regarding the punishment of the wicked; *v.* 82 must be
read in connexion with 84 : *when wilt thou execute judgement on my
persecutors ?* A somewhat quaint, but very pointed, simile occurs in
the words : *I am like a wine-skin in smoke* (83) ; what happens to a wine-
skin in such a case is that it becomes shrivelled up if left too long;
it was customary to hang wine-skins over the smoke of the fire in order
to modify the strength of the wine. The psalmist finds himself in this
plight owing to the evil machinations of his enemies, *who have dug
pits for him*, a figurative expression for deceptive dealing, cp. Ps. 57⁶;
they who act thus do what is against the law, *they are not according to
thy law* (85) ; their doings *had well-nigh swept me*, lit. " consumed ", their
victim *from the earth* (87).

ל

89. Thy word, Yahweh, is for ever,   it standeth firm ° like the heavens °,
90. Thy faithfulness is to generation and   thou hast established the earth, and it
      generation,   standeth;
91. According to thine ordinances they   for all ° serve thee °.
      stand ° unto ° this day,   I should have perished in mine affliction.
92. Unless thy law had been my delight,   for with them thou quickenest me.
93. I will never forget thy precepts,   for thy precepts have I sought.
94. I am thine, O save me,   I give heed to thy testimonies.
95. The wicked wait for me to destroy me,   thy commandment is exceeding broad.
96. ° To all things ° an end I see °,

Text-critical Notes

89. Read בַּשָּׁמַיִם for בַּשָּׁ֫, " in the heavens ". 91. Add עַד, " unto ". Read,
with V, עֲבָדוּד for עֲבָדֶיךָ, " thy servants ". 96. Read לְכֹל for לְכָל. Om.
קֵץ, " end ", a marginal explanatory note on the rare word תִּכְלָה " end ".

89–91 belong together in reference to the divine creative work;
but otherwise the section is mainly a repetition of what has already
been said. A new thought is contained in 96, where the transitoriness
of all visible things is contrasted with the all-spreading power of the
divine commandment.

מ

97. How I love thy law !   all day it is my meditation.
98. ° Thy commandment ° maketh me   for it is mine for ever.
      wiser than mine enemies,
99. I have more understanding than all   for thy testimonies are my meditation.
      my teachers,
100. I have more discernment than the   for I have kept ° thy statutes °.
      aged,
101. I keep back my feet from every evil   that I may observe thy word.
      path,
102. From thy judgements I do not swerve,   for thou teachest me.
103. How sweet to my palate are ° thy
      words °,   more than honey to my mouth ;
104. Through thy precepts I get under-
      standing, therefore   I hate every false way.

Text-critical Notes

98. Read מִצְוֹתֶךָ for מִצְוֹתֶךָ (defectively written), " thy commandments ".
100. Read פִּקּוּדֶיךָ for פִּקּוּדֶיךָ, " thy precepts ". 103. אִמְרָתֶךָ for אִמְרָתֶךָ,
" thy word ".

The main point to be noticed in this section is the claim to superior
wisdom on the part of the psalmist; this is especially significant in the
words, *I have more discernment than the aged,* for this points to the rise
of a somewhat altered conception of wisdom than that of an earlier
generation. A comparison between the earlier and later books of the
Wisdom literature shows that in the latter the religious element is distinctly more pronounced than in the former. In this section, therefore,
we have a clear indication of the trend of the Wisdom writers towards
a deeper religious insight in setting forth their ideas on Wisdom;
indeed, the whole psalm bears witness to this.

נ

105. A lamp ° to my feet ° is thy word, and a light to my path.
106. I have sworn, ° and I will keep it °,
to observe thy righteous judgements.
107. I am greatly afflicted, Yahweh, quicken me, according to thy word.
108. The offerings of my mouth accept,
Yahweh, and teach me ° thy commandments °.
109. My life is continually in my hand, but thy law I forget not.
110. The wicked have laid for me a snare, but I strayed not from thy precepts.
111. ° Mine inheritance ° are thy testi-
monies for ever, for the joy of my heart are ° they °.
112. I have inclined my heart to fulfil thy
statutes, for ever and ever.

Text-critical Notes

105. Read, with GS, לְרַגְלִי for לְרַגְלִי, " my foot ". 106. Read וָאֲקַיֵּמָה
for וָאֲ " and I have kept ". 108. Read מִצְוֹתֶיךָ for מִשְׁפָּטֶיךָ " thy judgements ". 111. Read, with V, נָחַלְתִּי for נָחַלְתִּי " I have inherited ". Read
הֵנָּה for הֵמָּה " they " (masc.).

There is but little that calls for notice in this section. In 109,
My life is continually in my hand, we have an expression which may well
have been taken from such passages as Judg. 12[3], 1 Sam. 19[5], 28[21],
Job 13[14]; in all these it means to take a grave risk, and thus to endanger
one's life. The psalmist does not explain in what way, and why, he is
placed in this position; and the general context in which the statement
stands gives the impression that it may be rhetorical, as in 87, 95.

ס

113. I hate the double-minded, but thy law do I love.
114. My hiding-place and my shield art
thou, I hope in thy word.
115. Depart from me, ye evil-doers, that I may keep the commandments of
my God.

116. Uphold me according to thy word,   and let me not be disappointed of my
         that I may live,   hope.
117. Hold me up that I may be safe ° and
         delight myself °   in thy statutes continually.
118. Thou despisest all that err from thy
         statutes,   for false is ° their intention °.
119. Dross ° dost thou account ° all the
         wicked on earth,   therefore I love thy testimonies.
120. My flesh trembleth for fear of thee,   and I am afraid of thy judgements.

Text-critical Notes

117. Read, with GS, וְאֶשְׁתַּעֲשֵׁע for וְאֶשְׁעָה, "and I shall have respect".
118. Read, with the Versions, תַּרְעִיתָם for תַּרְמִיתָם, "their deceit". 119.
Read הִשְׁבַּתָּ, cp. v. 59, for הִשְׁבַּתָּ, "thou causest to cease".

The mention of *the double-minded* (113), here only in this sense, is
in reference to Hellenistic Jews; the word is possibly connected with
that for " branch ", cp. Isa. 27[10], which is broken off from the tree;
and thus, here, those upon whom the precepts of the Law sat lightly,
and who were broken off from the body of the orthodox. They are
again spoken of in 118, *false is their intention*, or perhaps better " their
outlook "; the word is Aramaic, and gives better sense than that in
the Hebrew text, " their deceit ", which is obviously *false*.

ע

121. I practise justice and righteousness,   leave me not to mine oppressors.
122. Go surety for thy servant for good,   let not the arrogant oppress me.
123. Mine eyes pine for thy salvation,   and for thy righteous word.
124. Deal with thy servant according to
         thy love,   and teach me thy statutes.
125. Thy servant am I, give me under-
         standing,   that I may know thy testimonies.
126. It is time for Yahweh to act,   they have broken thy Law.
127. ° Above all ° do I love thy command-
         ments,   more than gold and pure-gold.
128. Therefore ° in thy precepts I walk
         rightly °,   Every false way I hate.

Text-critical Notes

127. Read עַל־כֹּל for עַל־כֵּן, "therefore". 128. Read יִשָּׁרְתִּי לְפִקּוּדֶיךָ
for כָּל־פִּקּוּדֵי כֹל יִשָּׁרְתִּי, "all thy precepts of all I esteem right".

In 121 to *practise*, lit. " do ", is the technical term for carrying
out the ordinances of the Law, in post-exilic Judaism, cp. Isa. 56[1].
The Hellenistic Jews are again referred to, so much so that the intervention of God is called for: *It is time for Yahweh to act, they have
broken thy law* (126).

פ

129. Wonderful are thy testimonies, there-
         fore   my soul doth keep them.
130. The revealing of thy words giveth
         light,   instructing the simple.
131. My mouth do I open, and pant,   for I long for thy commandments.
132. Turn unto me, and be gracious unto
         me,   as is due to them that love thy name.
133. Make firm my footsteps in thy word,   and let no iniquity master me.

134. Redeem me from the oppression of man,

135. Make thy face to shine upon thy servant,

136. Mine eyes run down with streams of water,

that I may observe thy precepts.

and teach me thy statutes.

because they keep not thy law.

In 130, the Hebrew word for *revealing* is lit. an " opening ", or " door "; the verse means that when the import of the divine words is apprehended the spirit is illuminated; even the *simple, i.e.*, the unlearned, can receive instruction thereby, cp. Ps. 19[7, 8]. For the justification of the rendering *As is due to them that love thy name* (132), see, *e.g.*, Deut. 18[3] : " And this shall be the priests' due from the people."

צ

137. Righteous art thou, Yahweh,
138. Thou hast commanded thy testimonies in righteousness,
139. My zeal hath o'erwhelmed me,

140. Purified to the full is thy word,
141. Insignificant am I and despised,
142. Thy righteousness is rightness for ever,
143. Trouble and anguish have come upon me,
144. Righteous are thy testimonies for ever,

° and upright ° are thy judgements.

and in very faithfulness.

because mine adversaries forget thy words.
and thy servant loveth it.
I forget not thy precepts.

and thy law is truth.

thy commandments are my delight.

give me understanding that I may live.

Text-critical Note

137. Read וִישָׁרִם for the sing. וְיָשָׁר.

As in some other passages, the rendering is offered with the purpose of giving the thought of the original rather than a literal translation, which might obscure what is really meant; thus, *my zeal hath o'erwhelmed me*, is lit. " my zeal hath made an end of me " (139); again, in 140, *purified to the full* is lit. " purified much "; and in 143, *trouble and anguish have come upon me*, is lit. " have found me ".

ק

145. I call with all my heart, answer me,°
146. I call upon thee, ° Yahweh °, save me,
147. I forestall early-dawn, ° and ° cry,
148. Mine eyes forestall the night-watches,
149. Hear my voice according to thy love,

150. They draw nigh ° that persecute me ° wickedly,
151. Nigh art thou, Yahweh,
152. Of old have I known from thy testimonies

thy statutes do I observe.
that I may keep ° thy precepts °.
and hope for ° thy word °.
that I may meditate on thy word.
Yahweh, quicken me, according to thy justice.

they are far from thy law.
and all thy commandments are truth.

that thou hast founded them for ever.

Text-critical Notes

145. Om. יהוה " Yahweh ". 146. Add יהוה. Read פִּקּוּדֶיךָ for עֵדְוֹתֶיךָ, " thy testimonies ". 147. Read וָ for וְ. Read, with SV, דְּבָרֶךָ for דְּבָרֶיךָ, " thy words ". 150. Read, with G, רֹדְפַי for רֹדְפֵי.

There is nothing in this section that calls for particular comment.

ר

153. Look upon mine affliction, and
     deliver me,
154. Plead my cause, and redeem me,
155. Far is help from the wicked,
156. Great is thy mercy, Yahweh,

157. Many are my persecutors and mine
     adversaries,
158. I beheld the treacherous-dealers, and
     felt loathing,
159. See, how I love thy precepts,

160. The sum of thy word is truth,

for I forget not thy law.
quicken me according to thy word.
for they seek not thy statutes.
quicken me according to thy judge-
    ments.
from thy testimonies have I not
    swerved.
men who keep not ° thy command-
    ments °.
Yahweh, quicken me according to thy
    love.
and all thy righteous judgements are
    eternal.

Text-critical Note

158. Read, with G, מִצְוֹתֶיךָ for אִמְרָתֶךָ, " thy word ".

In the final verse of this section, *The sum of thy word is truth* (160),
there is a little uncertainty as to the precise force of the sentence;
the Hebrew word rendered *sum* (*rô'š* lit. " head ") has various meanings;
here it can mean either that the chief, or most important, part of the
word of God is its truth (this is the force of the word in Ps. 137⁶),
or else that everything contained in the word of God is summed up in
the word " truth " (for this sense see Ps. 139¹⁷); it is the latter which
is probably intended here, as the parallel to " sum " in the other half-
line, *all thy righteous judgements*, suggests.

ש

161. Princes persecuted me without a
     cause ;
162. I rejoice because of thy word,
163. Lying do I hate and abhor,
164. Seven times in the day do I praise
     thee,
165. Great peace have they that love thy
     law,
166. I hope for thy salvation, Yahweh,
167. My soul observeth thy testimonies,
168. I observe thy precepts and thy
     testimonies,

my heart standeth-in-awe of thy words.
as one that findeth great spoil.
thy law do I love.

because of thy righteous judgements.

and they have no occasion-of-stumbling.
and thy commandments do I fulfil.
yea, I love them greatly.

for all my ways are before thee.

A somewhat inappropriate comparison, unusual in the psalmist,
occurs in 162, *I rejoice because of thy word, as one that findeth great spoil*,
the nature of spiritual joy being so different from satisfaction of material
gain in war; but a similar comparison occurs in Isa. 9². Some commentators, with justification, emend *as one that findeth* so as to read
as one that bringeth forth, *i.e.*, from the battle; it must be granted that
spoil is not the kind of thing one " finds ". It is doubtful whether
Seven times in the day do I praise thee (164) is to be taken literally
here; seven was often used as an indefinite number of times (cp.
Ps. 12⁶, Job 5¹⁹, Matth. 12⁴⁵, 18²²); Ps. 55¹⁷ suggests rather three times
a day as the hours of prayer.

ת

169. Let my cry come near before thee °,   according to thy word give me under-
                                                standing.
170. Let my supplication come before
     thee,   according to thy word deliver me.
171. Let my lips pour forth praise,   because thou teachest me thy statutes.
172. Let my tongue sing of thy word,   for all thy commandments are righteous-
                                                ness.
173. Let thy hand be for helping me,   for I have chosen thy precepts.
174. I long for thy help, Yahweh,   and thy law is my delight.
175. Let my soul live, and it shall praise
     thee,   and let thy judgements help me.
176. I have strayed °, seek thy servant,   for I do not forget thy commandments.

Text-critical Notes

169. Om. יהוה "Yahweh", for the metre's sake.   176. Om. פְּשֹׂה אֹבֵד,
"like a lost sheep", probably a marginal note which has been inserted in the text.

There is nothing in this section which calls for special comment.

Religious Teaching.

The weariness, one might almost say the boredom, experienced
in reading through this psalm is apt to cause the reader to overlook
the intensely religious feeling which runs all through it.   It is perfectly
true that the main purpose of the psalmist is the glorification of the Law,
and the setting forth of the joy that he, as a truly godly man, experiences
in observing its precepts ; but, as he constantly emphasizes, the Law
is the expression of the divine will ; it is not the Law, *per se*, that he
loves, a well-meaning element often prominent in later Judaism ;
he loves the Law because it tells of God's will ; and he loves it because
he loves God first.   Unless this fact is recognized all through, we shall
neither do justice to the writer, nor apprehend the deeply religious
character of the whole psalm.   It is well, therefore, that we should
draw out the psalmist's conception of his relationship to God ; and
if his words often echo those of other psalmists, that is not a question
of mere imitation, but the appropriation of expressions of truth which
tell of his own personal convictions and feelings.   *With all* my heart
have I sought thee, 10 ; *my portion is Yahweh*, 57 ; *I am thine, O save
me*, 94 ; *Hear my voice according to thy love*, 149 ; and so again and
again, words which tell of a close walk with God.   Then, again, it
must be noted how often he protests that, as already pointed out, his
love for the Law is always the outcome of his love for God : *I will delight
myself in thy commandments, which I love, and I will lift up my hands
unto thee*, 47, 48 ; *Well hast thou dealt with thy servant, Yahweh,
according to thy word*, 65 ; *They that fear thee shall see me and be glad,
for I have hoped in thy word*, 74 ; *Let thy mercies come unto me that I
may live, for thy law is my delight*, 77 ; *See how I love thy precepts,
Yahweh, quicken me according to thy love*, 159 ; *Seven times in the day
do I praise thee, because of thy righteous judgements*, 164.   And many

other passages could be quoted showing this intimate connexion
between the love of God and therefore the love of his Law.   In spite,
therefore, of the artificial character of the psalm in its external form,
it pulsates with religious feeling from beginning to end.

PSALM 120

THIS is the first of the group of fifteen psalms (120–134) which have
the title *Shîr ha-ma'ălôth*, " Song of Ascents ".   Four are ascribed
to David (only two in the Septuagint), and one to Solomon ; but these
ascriptions are not to be taken seriously.   Considerable differences
of opinion are expressed as to the meaning of the title " Song of
Ascents ".   We may dismiss that which understands it to be in reference to the " step-like " repetition of certain words taken up in
one verse from a preceding verse (*anadiplosis*)—*e.g.*, " dwell " in 120[5, 6],
" slumber " in 121[3, 4], " in vain " in 127[1, 2], and others ; for the same
occurs in other psalms outside this group ; moreover, it is doubtful
whether such *anadiplosis* occurs in 126, 130–133.   Equally unacceptable
is the idea that the " Ascents " refer to the fifteen steps leading from the
court of the women to that of the Israelites on which the Levites stood
when singing ;   this is based on a passage in the Mishnah tractate
Middôth 2[5] :   " Fifteen steps led from it (*i.e.*, the court of the women,
mentioned previously) to the court of the men (*i.e.*, the Israelites) ;
they corresponded to the fifteen ' step-songs ' in the *Psalms* ; on these
the Levites sang their song ".   But this does not necessarily refer to
the psalms under consideration ;   that the respective numbers corresponded was quite sufficient for the fact to be mentioned ;   but the
" Levites' song " does not by any means necessarily refer to these
psalms ;   indeed, in his commentary on the *Psalms*, Kimchi, who
mentions this theory, was himself in doubt as to its validity, for he goes
on to say that the " Ascent refers perhaps to the ascending of the
captives from Babylon " !   The most probable explanation of the title
is that it refers to the ascent of pilgrims up the hill of Zion, during which
these psalms were sung, at the great festivals ; this is borne out by some
passages in the psalms themselves (*e.g.*, 121[1], 122[1-4], 125[1, 2], 132[13, 14]).
On the other hand, it must be confessed that some of the psalms in
the group are not in the nature of pilgrim-psalms (120, 124, 125, 130,
131).   This may perhaps be accounted for on the supposition that
they were incorporated, for one reason or another, in course of time,
in a collection of rolls which contained originally only pilgrim-psalms.

   As to the dates of the psalms in this group as we now have it, the

probability is that they are all post-exilic, though within this period the
dates vary.   At the same time, it may well be that some of them are
in origin pre-exilic ; for the command to make pilgrimages to Jerusalem
occurs in Exod. 23[10, 17] (E), and 34[23] (J) ; they are also referred to in
such passages as Isa. 2[3], possibly, and 30[29].

In the psalm with which we are now concerned (120) there is nothing
to indicate its date.   The metre is 3 : 2 with the exception of *v.* 5, which
is 3 : 3.

A Song of Ascents.

1. To Yahweh, when I am in trouble,   I call °, and he answereth me ° ;
2. Yahweh, deliver my soul   from the lip of falsehood °.
3. ° What shall be given to thee °, ° yea,
     what added °,   O false tongue ?
4. Arrows of a warrior, sharpened,   with red-hot broom-wood.
   Woe is me !   5. That I sojourn in
   Meshech,   that I dwell among the tents of Kedar ;
6. Too long hath my soul dwelt   with them ° that hate ° peace ;
7. I am for peace, but when I speak (of it), they are for war.

Text-critical Notes

1. Read וְיַעֲנֵנִי for וַיַּ֫, " and he answered me ".   2. Om. מלשון רמיה,
which breaks the rhythm ; erroneously copied from the next verse.   3. Read, with G,
מַה־יִתֶּן לְךָ וּמַה־יִתֶּן לְךָ for לְךָ, " what shall he give to thee ? " ; " thee " being
in reference to " tongue ", should be fem.   Read, with G, וּמַה יֹסִף, omitting
לְךָ (*lāk*), for וּמַה־יֹסִיף לְךָ, " yea, what shall he add unto thee ? "   6. Read, with
GS, שׂוֹנְאַי for שׂוֹנֵא *sōnē'*, " him that hateth " ; cp. next verse.

1, 2.   With his deep trust in *Yahweh*, the psalmist begins his plaint
by recalling past experiences—viz., whenever he has found *trouble*
at hand, he has called upon *Yahweh*, and the answer has come.   This,
therefore, he does now, and he prays that *Yahweh* will *deliver* his *soul
from the lip of falsehood*.   He is, thus, the victim of calumny.

3, 4.   Just as he has suffered from the cruel libel of a *false tongue*,
so, in like manner, he protests, shall retribution, sharp and burning,
overtake his calumniator ; according as he has done, so may it be done
to him, cp. Ps. 7[16], 28[4], Jer. 50[15 29].   This is put in the rhetorical form
of question and answer (cp. Hos. 9[14]) : *What shall be given to thee ?*—
i.e., by Yahweh ; the words : *yea, what added?* are a curse or an oath
formula (cp. 1 Sam. 3[17], 1 Kgs. 2[23], " God do so to me and more also ",
lit. " and thus may he add " ; and often elsewhere).   The answer is :
Arrows of a warrior, sharpened (cp. Ps. 7[13]), meaning, not merely arrows
as are used—*e.g.*, by a hunter—but such as a mighty man shoots in
battle ; *and red-hot broom-wood* (lit. " *with coals of* broom-plants ") ;
the point here is that the wood of the broom (*genista*), being very
hard, retains the glow, when kindled, longer than any other kind of
wood ; Burckhardt found the Bedouin of Sinai burning the roots of
this bush into coal, and says that " they make the best charcoal, and

KK

throw out the most intense heat " (Thomson, *The Land and the Book*, Vol. I, p. 345 [1881]). When this, therefore, is flung into a tent, or dwelling-place, it will soon set it ablaze. The words of this verse are to be understood figuratively, and this applies also to those which follow. 5, 6. Here the psalmist pictures his present abode as though in the midst of wild hordes of nomads, so inimical are his neighbours ; *Woe is me*, he says, *that I sojourn in Meshech, That I dwell among the tents of Kedar.* A difficulty arises in connexion with the name of Meshech (the classical *Mosci*, the Accadian *Moshki*) ; it occurs elsewhere always together with Tubal (Gen. 10², 1 Chron. 1⁵, Ezek. 27¹³, 32²⁶, 38², ³, 39¹), whereas in Gen. 25¹³, ¹⁴, 1 Chron. 1²⁹ Kedar and Massa are mentioned together ; the sons of Kedar dwelt in the Syrian desert (Jer. 49²⁸), and Massa was the name of a North Arabian tribe ; whereas Meshech was a district between the Black Sea and the Caspian Sea. The contention of some commentators, therefore, that Massa should be read for *Meshech* has much in its favour. In Isa. 21¹⁷ the sons of Kedar are spoken of as " archers and mighty men ". 6, 7. Like these war-like dwellers of the desert, then, are those among whom the psalmist has *dwelt too long*, for they *hate peace* ; lover of peace as he himself is, no sooner does he begin to speak than they declare themselves for *war.* Actual war used figuratively of the war of words occurs elsewhere in the psalms (*e.g.*, 109², ³).

Religious Teaching.

Of this there is but little to be said. The spirit of *lex talionis* which pervades the psalm is not edifying ; and the implied expectation that the injured one will receive divine support in taking vengeance on his enemy witnesses to an undeveloped conception of God. The psalm must be regarded as a lapse from the teaching of the Law—see, *e.g.*, Lev. 19¹⁸. But even such a psalm as this has its uses, if only as showing how the spirit of revenge perverts true religion.

PSALM 121

THIS beautiful little psalm is antiphonal in form ; but it is by no means easy to decide which verses are to be assigned to the respective speakers or singers. The difficulty is increased by the fact that a copyist seems to have altered the pronouns in *vv.* 2, 3, having himself been uncertain as to how the verses were to be assigned. That there should be differences of opinion is natural enough. A further difficulty arises regarding the question as to who the speakers were. Three possi-bilities suggest themselves, each of which has much in its favour. It is held that the psalm represents a kind of dialogue between a layman and a priest; and a certain didactic tone in the psalm supports this view. But if, as the title of the psalm indicates, and the opening words confirm : " I lift mine eyes to the hills ",—if this was a pilgrim song, sung by a band of pilgrims ascending the hill of Zion, then some doubt is cast upon this view, because the priest would be in the temple, and not accompanying the band of pilgrims. A second view is that the psalmist is communing with himself, quickening his religious sense by asking himself questions and giving his own answers ; that also is a beautiful idea, but it is open to the same objection as the foregoing. Holding, as we do, that this is a pilgrim psalm, it seems more natural to suppose that the psalm presents us with the picture of a body of pilgrims, one of whose number acted as leader ; he began with *v.* 1, to which his fellow-pilgrims responded with *v.* 2 ; then, in *v.* 3, he uttered a wish, and in chorus the pilgrims reassured him, *v.* 4. The remainder of the psalm, *vv.* 5–8, is then again taken up by the whole band of pilgrims in chorus. That many of the psalms, especially such a short one as this, were known by heart through constant repetition, may be confidently assumed.

Like the other psalms in this group, this one is, no doubt, of post-exilic date, though no actual indication is given in the psalm itself.

The metre varies ; in *vv.* 1, 2 it is 3 : 3, *vv.* 4, 5 are 2 : 2 : 2, and the remaining verses 3 : 2.

A Song of Ascents.

1. I lift up mine eyes to the hills !   From whence cometh my help ?
2. " ° Thy help ° is from Yahweh,   Maker of heaven and earth ! "
3. May he not suffer ° my foot ° to slip,   may ° my Guardian ° not slumber !
4.   " Behold, he slumbereth not,
                        He sleepeth not,
                        The Guardian of Israel ! "
5.   " Yahweh is thy Guardian,
                        Yahweh is thy defence,
                        At thy right-hand ;
6. That the sun may not smite thee by day,   nor the moon by night,
7. Yahweh doth shield thee from all harm,   he guardeth thy soul ;
8. Yahweh doth guard thy going-out and
   coming-in,   from now until evermore.

Text-critical Notes

Title. Read הַמַּעֲלוֹת for "לַמ". 2. Read עֶזְרְךָ for עֶזְרִי, " my help ". 3. Read רַגְלְךָ for רַגְלִי, " thy foot "; and שֹׁמְרִי for שֹׁמְרֶךָ, " thy Guardian ".

1–2. One among the band of pilgrims ascending Mount Zion looks upwards and around *to the hills*, or mountains, round about Jerusalem, and triumphantly asks his fellow-pilgrims : *From whence cometh my help ?* In his mind there is doubtless the thought expressed in Ps. 125[2]: " Jerusalem,—mountains are around her, and Yahweh is round about his people ". Therefore the whole band of pilgrims make reply: *Thy help is from Yahweh* ; adding the oft-repeated article of belief :

Maker of heaven and earth, cp. Ps. 115¹⁵, 124⁸, 134³, 146⁶. Then the
first pilgrim again raises his voice in words which, in their Hebrew
form, express conviction : *May he not suffer my foot to slip* (cp. Ps. 66⁹),
may my Guardian not slumber (3) ; we have here the echo of an old-world
idea of an anthropomorphic character, cp. 1 Kgs. 18²⁷ ; but that it is
only an echo, and not to be intended to be taken in a literal sense, is
clear from what follows (4, 5), in which the band of pilgrims respond ;
Yahweh is not like the Baals, who might be thought of as slumbering.
Certain as it is that his care is for his individual faithful ones who trust
in him, yet more, he is *the Guardian of Israel* (cp. Deut. 32⁹). He is
the Guardian of both nation and individual ; so the singers continue :
Yahweh is thy Guardian and *defence*, lit. " shade ", or " shadow ",
cp. Ps. 91¹. The nearness of Yahweh, often emphasized by the
prophets (*e.g.*, Isa. 50⁸, 55⁶), is graphically expressed : *at thy right hand*,
lit. " upon the hand of thy right hand " (cp. Pss. 16⁸, 109³¹). Yahweh's
protection is further described in 6, for, as the God of Nature, he will
see to it that *the sun may not smite by day*, *i.e.*, him who is under his care
(cp. Ps. 91⁶, Isa. 49¹⁰), *nor the moon by night* ; the belief in the harmfulness of the moon's rays was widespread in ancient times (cp. Matth. 4⁴,
σεληνιαζομένους, 17¹⁵). Indeed, *Yahweh doth guard* from every
kind of ill, whithersoever his faithful one may go ; for the expression
thy going-out and coming-in, cp. Deut. 28⁶, 31², 1 Sam. 29⁶.

Religious Teaching

The expression, simple yet deep, of trust in God's guidance through
every walk in life is the keynote of this psalm ; and it could hardly be
set forth in greater beauty. The Creatorship of God, and His power
over Nature—*i.e.*, his illimitable greatness, are truths which might well
induce the feeling that the individual, so utterly insignificant in the sight
of God, is unworthy of his notice ; it was one which many had experienced, and was pointedly rebuked by Ben-Sira : " Say not, I am
hidden from God, and in the height who will remember me ? . . .
They that lack understanding think these things ; and a man of folly
thinketh thus " (Ecclus. 16¹⁷⁻²³). In the same way, the psalmist, so
far from thinking that he is beneath God's notice, emphasizes the
guardianship and defence which he bestows on the individual,—" from
now until evermore ".

PSALM 122

IN this psalm the psalmist recalls his visit to Jerusalem on the occasion
of one of the festivals. In the opening verse he tells of his delight on

hearing of the intention of a number of his fellow-citizens (the locality is not indicated) to make the pilgrimage. It was necessary for a number to join together for this purpose because the journey would be hazardous if undertaken by a single individual ; the danger of robbers was ever present (cp. Luke 20³⁰). Then, in the next verse, the psalmist pictures to himself how they had all stood together on entering the Holy City. The remainder of the psalm is a song of praise glorifying Jerusalem.

The date to be assigned to this psalm depends, to some extent, on the interpretation of *v*. 3, on which the notes must be consulted. That it belongs to a time after the Deuteronomic legislation is suggested by *v*. 4, which points to the centralization of worship in Jerusalem (" Thither the tribes go up ") ; this of itself would not necessarily indicate a post-exilic date ; but *v*. 5, which looks back to the time when justice was administered by the king, points to a post-monarchical date.

The metre varies ; but opinions differ here ; we estimate it as follows : *vv*. 1, 8, 9 are 3 : 3 ; *vv*. 2, 3, 4, 6, 7 are 3 : 2 ; and *v*. 5 is 2 : 2 : 2.

A Song of Ascents. ° David's °.

1. I was glad ° when they said unto me ° : "We are going to the house of Yahweh ! "
2. Our feet stood within thy gates, O Jerusalem.
3. Jerusalem,—built like a city ° that uniteth us ° together ;
4. ° Thither ° the tribes go up, the tribes of Yah,
   A law for Israel, to give thanks to the name of Yahweh.
5. For ° there ° were set up
   The seats of justice °
   Of the house of David.
6. O pray for the peace of Jerusalem, may they prosper that love thee ;
7. May peace be within thy ramparts, quietude within thy palaces.
8. For my brethren and companions' sake, I will say : " Peace be within thee."
9. For the sake of Yahweh's-house, our God, I will pray for thy welfare.

Text-critical Notes

Title : om., with some G and V MSS, לדוד. 1. Read בְּאָמְרָם for בְּאָמְרִים. 3. Read, with Budde, cp. G, שֶׁחֻבְּרָה־לָּהּ for שֶׁחֻבְּרָה־לָּה יַחְדָּו, " that is compacted with herself together ". 4. Read שָׁמָּה for שָׁם. 5. Read שָׁם for שָׁמָּה. Om. כִּסְאוֹת, " seats ", lit. " thrones ".

1. As already pointed out, the psalmist recalls to mind how his friends had *said* to him that they were *going to the house of Yahweh*, to keep the feast. He *was glad* at this, because otherwise he would have been unable to go, on account of the perils to which he would be exposed in undertaking such a journey by himself. Incidentally, the verse shows that it was not always possible for men to observe the injunction of the Law : " Three times in the year shall all thy males appear before Yahweh thy God in the place which he shall choose ; in the feast of unleavened bread (*Mazzôth*), and in the feast of weeks (*Shabu'ôth*), and in the feast of tabernacles (*Sukkôth*) ; and they shall not appear

before Yahweh empty . . ." (Deut. 16$^{16, 17}$, cp. Exod. 23^{17}, 34^{23}).
The Passover feast coincided with that of Unleavened bread.   This law
seems to be referred to in *v.* 4, and the mention of *giving thanks to the*
name of Yahweh may indicate which of the feasts was here in question ;
the feast of Tabernacles was specifically that of *giving thanks* for the
whole produce of the year, and at the same time its observance was in
the nature of a guarantee of a fruitful production of the soil in the
coming year.   If this surmise is correct, the prayer for peace and
welfare in the concluding verses of the psalm gains in significance ; for,
apart from war, peace and prosperity depended, above all else, on a good
harvest in an agricultural community.

2. It was for our psalmist a very precious reminiscence as he pictured
to himself how he and his fellow-pilgrims had on earlier occasions
stood within the *gates* of the holy city, *Jerusalem*.   This centre of worship, where, according to the belief of the times, the presence of the
Deity was pervasive in a special way, was held in reverence and affection
by every God-fearing Jew ; no wonder that our psalmist now sings in
praise of the hallowed site, 3–5.   He begins with the thought of the
unity of Jerusalem ; but here a difficulty arises as to the kind of unity
that was in the writer's mind.   At first sight, the most obvious reference
would appear to be to the literal building of the city ; for the word used
(*bānāh*) very rarely occurs in the Old Testament in any other than a
literal sense ; but in a few passages it has a figurative meaning when
used in connexion with a house (*e.g.*, Prov. 14^1, 24^3, Ruth 4^{11}) ; those
passages in which it is connected with men (Job 22^{23}, Jer. 12^{16}, Mal. 3^{15})
do not come into consideration here.   It may be added that in post-
Biblical usage the word is sometimes used figuratively.   The majority of
commentators take it in a literal sense, and refer it to the rebuilding of
the city walls by Nehemiah (Neh. 2$^{12\,ff.}$) ; and consequently the psalm
is dated soon after the time of Nehemiah.   This literal interpretation,
however, is not borne out by the context.   First, we have in the words
that uniteth us together a root (*ḥabar*, it is the same whichever reading be
accepted) which is never used in reference to a building being joined
together or compacted, but almost invariably of men uniting together.
That this is the sense in which it is used here is suggested by the words
which follow : *Thither the tribes go up*, the thought being that of the
fellowship among all the tribes which centred in worship ; hence they
are called the *tribes of Yah* instead of the ordinary phrase " the tribes of
Israel ".   The going-up together was the visible sign of unity.   And the
tribes went up in accordance with the *law*, lit. " testimony " ; the
purpose of going up was *to give thanks to the name of Yahweh* ; here,
though the Hebrew verb means also " to praise ", its primary meaning
is " to give thanks " ; the significance of this in the present connexion
has already been dealt with.   The mention of the *law for Israel*—i.e.,

of the divine ordinances—reminds the psalmist also of the judgements
put forth by the divine representative on earth, the king, in days gone
by; here in Jerusalem *there were set up*, lit. " abode ", *the seats*, lit.
" the thrones ", *of justice*, tribunals presided over by the king, to whom
disputes and the like were brought to be adjudicated upon (cp. 1 Kgs.
3^{16–28}). 6–8. Finally, the psalmist exhorts men to *pray for the peace of
Jerusalem*, expressing the wish that all they who *love* her may *prosper*;
we have in the Hebrew of these words one of the most striking illustrations of alliteration in the Old Testament: *šă'ălu šalôm Jerûšalâim,
yišlāyu 'ohăbāik*, " O pray for the peace of Jerusalem, may they
prosper that love thee ". A beautiful expression of affection for the
city of God. And then, in his concluding words, he addresses Jerusalem, as though personified; for her own sake, as well as for the sake
of his own *brethren and companions*—another note of unity—his heart's
desire is that there may be *Peace within thee*. The welfare of the city
is desired, above all things, on account of the presence within it of the
house of Yahweh, our God; a contented people will, he feels sure,
ascribe their welfare to the true source of it, and will therefore worship
in the temple, the *house of Yahweh*, in the spirit of gratitude and love.

Religious Teaching

The joy expressed in contemplating the assembling together for
common worship sets forth an ideal which may not always be experienced in actual life; but that is because what is involved is not
always adequately appreciated. And yet this is so fully and beautifully
expressed in the *Te Deum*: the glorious company of the Apostles, the
goodly fellowship of the Prophets, the noble army of Martyrs, praise
God; so that joint-worship is a literal anticipation of what belongs to
our life hereafter; it is an illustration of the truth that " the kingdom
of Heaven is within you ", whether we interpret this as of the kingdom
of Heaven being in the midst of us, or, in our hearts. To be sure,
this fullness of truth is not what the psalmist meant; but to us, to whom
the complete revelation has been vouchsafed, joint worship is not to be
thought of as restricted to the visible assembly of worshippers; and
therefore the joy in Christian worship is prompted by the knowledge
that those in the bliss of the fullness of life are joining in praise and
prayer with us.

PSALM 123

THE psalmist speaks here in the name of his people. It may be surmised that the band of pilgrims had come from some city of the Dis-

persion, where they were living amid Gentile surroundings, and were often victimized by the contemptuous attitude taken up towards them. That the Jews were often treated in this way by those among whom they had settled does not admit of doubt. A vivid illustration of this occurs in a treatise of Apollonius Molon, quoted by Josephus (*Contra Ap.* II, 148) ; though of later date than the time at which our psalm was composed (he lived about 100 B.C.), his words may well echo what had obtained in earlier days. Josephus, in reference to him, says that "he sometimes reviles us as atheists, and man-haters ; sometimes he reproaches us with cowardice ; at other times, on the contrary, he accuses us of temerity, and as being devoid of sense (ἀπονοίαν). He says also that we are the most untalented (ἀφυεστάτους) among the barbarians, for which reason we are the only people who have contributed no improvement to human life (μηδὲν εἰς τὸν βίον εὕρημα)." That something of this kind prompted the utterance of this psalmist is likely enough ; so that his plaint, and appeal to God, are readily understood. The extreme brevity of the psalm does not detract from its poignancy.

The date is suggested by the subject-matter ; the psalm belongs to a fairly late period of post-exilic times, when numbers of the Jews had settled down in different centres of the Dispersion.

The metre is uniformly 3 : 2 (2 : 2 in *v.* 2b).

A Song of Ascents.

1. Unto thee do I lift up mine eyes,   O thou that dwellest in the heavens ;
2. Behold, as the eyes of slaves   toward the hand of their lord,
   As the eyes of a maid   toward the hand of her mistress,
   So are our eyes toward Yahweh, our
       God,   until he have mercy on us.
3. Have mercy on us, Yahweh, have mercy
       on us,   for ° we are sated with contempt ;
4. Greatly sated is our soul   with the mockery ° of the proud.

Text-critical Notes

3. Om. רַב "exceedingly", it overloads the half-line. 4. Om. הַשַּׁאֲנַנִּים הַבּוּז, "they that are at ease, the contempt", probably a marg. gloss, it overloads the half-line ; the Hebr. text as it stands is ungrammatical. Read, following the Kᵉthibh, לַגֵּאיוֹנִים for לִגְאֵיוֹנִים = לִגְאֵי יוֹנִים, "of the proud ones among the oppressors".

1. In words expressive of the deepest feelings of comfort and reliance does the psalmist, oppressed by the contemptuous treatment to which he and his fellow-pilgrims have been subjected, *lift up* his *eyes* (cp. Ps. 121¹) as he ascends Mount Zion, and addresses himself to him who *dwells in the heavens* (cp. Ps. 2⁴, 115³). We may here picture to ourselves a band of pilgrims who have undertaken a long journey from some uncongenial surroundings in order to join in a festal celebration at the religious centre of the nation. 2. As the eyes of their leader soar upwards to the sphere where he conceives that the Almighty dwells,

the thought arises in his mind that just as he is doing to his God, on behalf of those who are following him, so are *the eyes of slaves* riveted on *the hand of their lord*, and *the eyes of a maid* on that of *her mistress*. The Hebrew idiom permits of the omission of the verb " look ", or the like, for which reason we have not thought it necessary to insert it in the translation given above. The mention of the *hand* is not without significance ; as the instrument whereby a gift is conveyed, it is on the *hand* that the slaves gaze in the hope of receiving something. The comparison is the psalmist's way of expressing his sense of unworthiness in the sight of God. Slaves were regarded as inferior beings, and among the Gentiles, from whose midst the pilgrim-psalmist had come, there did not exist the consideration to which they were entitled by the Jewish legislation (cp., *e.g.*, Exod. 21$^{26-32}$, Deut. 21$^{10-14}$, and especially Lev. 25$^{35-46}$). 3, 4. Thus, speaking on behalf of his fellow-pilgrims, he looks with appealing eyes towards *Yahweh*, their *God*, until his *mercy* is accorded. How this is to be manifested in these particular circumstances the psalmist does not presume to indicate ; that will be as God wills. The reiterated words *Have mercy on us* express the measure of their need ; for they are shocked, filled with repugnance, *sated*, with the treatment to which they had been subjected by the mocking behaviour of the overbearing tyrants among whom their lot was cast.

Religious Teaching

Extremely short as this psalm is, it suggests two matters touching practical religion which are of weighty import ; though not expressed in words, they are none the less impressive. The first is the wholly beautiful spirit which seeks refuge from the aggravation caused by contact with disagreeable fellow-creatures in an appeal to the Almighty, with whom lies the power to effect a change of heart in the most obstinate. And the second is the entire absence of any sign of retaliation for the injury done ; this is in striking contrast to the bitterly revengeful spirit so often evinced in other psalms (*e.g.*, 109$^{6\,n}$, 120$^{3,\,4}$). The psalm witnesses to what was best in the Jewish religion. But, further, it may be said that this psalm illustrates the effect that social humiliation and oppression may have on the way of envisaging the relation to God, and the conception of God. Those people who feel that they are slaves prefer to think themselves as the slaves of God, and the feeling of their absolute dependence on his favour is deepened by the hopelessness of their present situation. Religion plays an important *rôle* here in preserving the spirit of men from falling into servile attitudes to those who have a present advantage over them. One can humble oneself before God without losing one's self-respect ; but one cannot do so before human pride and power.

PSALM 124

THIS is not a pilgrim-psalm, in spite of the title. The words in the opening verse, " Let Israel say ", point to its being a liturgical psalm sung by the body of the worshippers in the temple. A priest, it may be surmised, sang the words : ".' If Yahweh had not been for us " (Let Israel say), and they were then taken up by the whole congregation as the key-note of the psalm which followed. The psalm is an expression of grateful recognition of divine help at a time of critical peril. That some definite occurrence is referred to, rather than that it records a general thanksgiving for past deliverances, as, *e.g.*, in Ps. 129, seems certain by the vivid and circumstantial way in which the danger is described. But the psalm gives no indication as to what particular event is referred to.

There are several linguistic usages which mark the psalm as of late post-exilic date.

The metre is somewhat irregular. Many commentators suggest a few textual emendations ; but we fail to see the need of these.

A Song of Ascents.   ° *David's* °.

1. " If Yahweh had not been for us,"   Let Israel say :
2. If Yahweh had not been for us,   when men rose up against us,
3. Then had they swallowed us alive   when their wrath was kindled against us ;
4. Then had the waters swept us away,   the torrent had gone over our soul ;
5. Then had it gone over our soul,—   the raging waters.
6.   Blessed be Yahweh,
                          Who hath not delivered us
                          As a prey to their teeth,
7. Our soul did escape like a bird   from the snare of the fowlers,
                          The snare is broken,
                          And we have escaped.
8. Our help is in the name of Yahweh,   Maker of heaven and earth.

Text-critical Note

Apart from the title, where לדויד, " David's ", is omitted by some MSS and by GV, no textual notes are necessary.

1, 2. The repetition of the words in these two verses has already been accounted for. *If Yahweh had not been for us—i.e.*, on our side, rendered lit. is : " If it had not been Yahweh who was for us " ; our rendering is offered in order to retain the metre of the Hebrew. This recognition of divine help in the case of enemy onslaughts finds frequent utterance (*e.g.*, Ps. 56[9], 118[10-12]) ; similarly, when the enemy had been victorious, it was ascribed to the withholding of divine help (*e.g.*, Ps. 44[9-14], 74[10, 11], 108[11-13]). This echoes the prophetic teaching on Yahweh as the God of History. The indefinite reference here, *when men rose up against us*, makes it impossible to form any idea of what occurrence was in the mind of the psalmist ; but it is clear that it was both critical and recent. The metaphors used in describing the enemy witness to one who was cruel, powerful, and crafty. He is compared with a cruel monster which *swallows up* his victim *alive* when his *wrath* is *kindled* by resistance (3). Then, further (in 4–6), he is compared with the torrent, the *waters* of which sweep away everything before it ; *the raging waters*, they are called because the noise and foaming overflow recall the insensate rage of men. Here, again, as so often, the word *soul* is used of the individual person. At this point the psalmist is constrained to express his gratitude to God who had *delivered* his people from becoming a *prey to their teeth* ; he reverts to his first comparison of the enemy being like a ravenous monster. We must guard ourselves here against being hypercritical. The psalmist speaks of the monster's *teeth* ; previously he had said that it would have *swallowed us alive* ; trivial incompatibilities of this kind must not be pressed, for the ancient Hebrew writers were not tied to logical niceties such as modern usage demands. A third comparison is that which speaks of the enemy as *fowlers* (7) ; the thought seems to have been taken from Ps. 91[3], cp. also Prov. 6[5], Hos. 7[12], Am. 3[5]. When it is said that the *snare is broken* the reference is to the woodwork to which the net was fastened. A final acknowledgement of the divine help, which made escape from the enemy possible, appropriately closes the psalm (8). The contention that this is a later addition seems uncalled for ; an expression of thankfulness or praise occurs very often in the concluding verse of a psalm, *e.g.*, 35[28], 45[17], 46[11], 57[11], and elsewhere. *Our help is in the name of Yahweh* means that help is accorded by calling upon the name of Yahweh ; as *Maker of heaven and earth* (cp. Ps. 115[15], 121[2]), his power is illimitable.

Religious Teaching

The central point here, whole-hearted recognition of the true source of help in trouble, has already been emphasized in the preceding notes.

PSALM 125

THE purpose of this psalm is to contrast the indestructible security of those who trust in Yahweh with those who are unfaithful to him. Difficulties arise in seeking to ascertain to whom " the sceptre of the wicked " refers, and who are meant by those " who turn aside on their crooked ways ". There are, however, good grounds for believing that we have here an allusion to the conditions as these existed during the first visit of Nehemiah to Jerusalem ; this took place in 444 B.C.,

and lasted till 432 B.C. (Neh. 13⁶), when he returned to the Persian
Court.   Palestine was at this time under Persian suzerainty; it is to
this that the psalmist refers in speaking of " the sceptre of the wicked ",
and it is possible that he was thinking more particularly of Sanballat
and his friends.   The antagonism between the orthodox Jews who
had returned from the Exile, and " the people of the land ",
supported by the Samaritans, is well known from the books of Ezra
and Nehemiah.   The orthodox are, of course, those spoken of by the
psalmist as " the righteous ", while their opponents are, appropriately
enough, described as " they who turn aside on their crooked ways ";
for they professed to worship Yahweh (cp. Ezra 4²), but consorted
with the Gentiles, and perhaps joined in their worship; in any case,
they were not loyal to the Law (cp., e.g., Neh. 5⁹).   Therefore, as the
psalmist says, Yahweh will abandon them with " the workers of
iniquity "—i.e., the Samaritans.

Our psalm cannot, then, be regarded as a pilgrim-psalm; the
reason of its inclusion in the group may well have been the reference
to mount Zion in the opening verse.

The metre is again somewhat irregular.

A Song of Ascents.

1.   They that trust in Yahweh are like mount Zion,
          It shall not be moved, it abideth for ever.
2. Jerusalem ! the hills are around her,   and Yahweh is around his people.°
3.   For the sceptre of ° the wicked °
          shall not rest
          on the lot of the righteous,
That the righteous put not forth   their hand to iniquity.
4. Do good, Yahweh, to the good   and to the upright in heart ;
5. But them who turn aside on their   ° he ° ° will abandon ° with the workers
   crooked ways   of iniquity °.

Text-critical Notes

2. Om. מֵעַתָּה וְעַד־עוֹלָם, " from henceforth and for evermore ", a later addition
which interferes with the rhythm.   3. Read, with GS, הָרֶשַׁע for הַרֶשַׁע,
" wickedness ".   5. Om. יהוה, " Yahweh ", which overloads the half-line.   Read
יוֹלִיךְ for יוֹלִיכֵם, " he will abandon them ", lit. " he will cause them to go ".
Om. שָׁלוֹם עַל־יִשְׂרָאֵל, " peace upon Israel ", a later addition.

1. The striking picture that *they that trust in Yahweh are like
mount Zion*, for they are upheld unshakeably by him, is probably
based on the last clauses of Isa. 28¹⁶, " he that believeth shall not be
moved " (reading *yāmuš* for the meaningless *yāhiš* " shall not make
haste ").   The comparison is further developed in the next verse (2),
where *the hills around Jerusalem* are compared with Yahweh's care
which surrounds his people ; this picture is the more pointed in that
the hills around Jerusalem are higher than that on which the city
stands, so that they appear as a protecting bulwark.   It is because of

the care which Yahweh has for his people that the psalmist is convinced that the present usurpation of the enemy will not last. The
sceptre, often used metaphorically for " rule " (*e.g.*, Gen.
49[10]), refers to Persian overlordship; but *the wicked* (it is in the singular, "the
wicked one ") must refer to an individual. We have adopted the
reading of the Versions, " the sceptre of the wicked one ", in preference to that of the Hebrew, " the sceptre of wickedness ", because
this latter is an otherwise unknown expression. We have given
grounds, in the introductory section, for believing that the psalm
reflects the conditions of the time of Nehemiah; if this is correct,
the mention of " the wicked one " is significant; it cannot refer to
Artaxerxes I, who was very friendly disposed to the Jews, and showed
much kindness to Nehemiah; but it may well refer to Sanballat, the
governor of Samaria, who showed himself the enemy of Nehemiah,
and sought to lord it over the southern province; he was " grieved
exceedingly " on hearing that " there was come a man (*i.e.*, Nehemiah)
to seek the welfare of the children of Israel " (Neh. 2[10]); his enmity
against Nehemiah, and general attitude towards the followers of
Nehemiah, may well have marked him out as " the wicked one "
par excellence (cp. Neh. 4[8], 6[2, 14]). When, further, the psalmist says
that the sceptre of this wicked one *shall not rest on the lot of the righteous*,
we recall the words of Nehemiah to Sanballat and his followers : " Ye
have no portion, nor right, nor memorial, in Jerusalem " (2[20]). During
Nehemiah's governorship, again, there was the constant danger of his
own people, through their contact with the Samaritans and " the
people of the land," being seduced into evil ways; Nehemiah says
to them, *e.g.*, in Neh. 5[9] : " The thing that ye do is not good; ought
ye not to walk in the fear of our God, because of the reproach of the
heathen our enemies ? " In the light of this there is much significance
in the psalmist's words : *In order that the righteous, i.e.*, the orthodox
Jews, *put not forth their hand to iniquity.* It is on behalf of the righteous,
the faithful followers of Nehemiah, that the psalmist prays : *Do good,
Yahweh, to the good*, the rendering represents the Hebrew literally,
and to the upright in heart (cp. Ps. 7[10]). 5. In contrast to these are
those *who turn aside on their crooked ways*; the form of the adjective
is intensive, it is used in Judg. 5[6] of byways which turn off from the
main road; in its figurative sense here, it refers to the turning away
from the straight path of the Law of Yahweh into byways of heathen
observances. The reference is evidently to those who had at one
time walked in the straight path, and who had, therefore, been able
to look for Yahweh's care and protection; and this would apply to
" the people of the land "—*i.e.*, those who had been left in the land
of Judah in 586 B.C., and their descendants. Through their contact
with *the workers of iniquity*—*i.e.*, the Samaritans and the Gentiles—

they had become unfaithful to Yahweh, who therefore *abandons* them
to go their own way.

Religious Teaching

Two points call for brief notice here. The first, which appears in
most of the psalms, is the indestructible faith in Yahweh in the face
of adverse conditions. Belief and trust in God when things go well
offer no difficulties; it is when the believer in an omnipotent, all-
good God, suffers misfortune, or has become the victim of the evil-
disposed, that problems arise, and faith is tried. Our psalmist found
the solution in the conviction that the adverse conditions would pass,
and that the evil-disposed would get their deserts. So far as it goes
this may offer some consolation; but it is no real solution of the
problem, which, as is well-known, exercised the minds of many devout
Jewish thinkers. The solution lies elsewhere; but obviously this
cannot be dealt with here; this is not a treatise on Apologetics. It
must suffice to say that the whole question turns on the fact that the
gift of human free-will has been granted to men by God; the way
of exercising his free-will is man's business.

The second point is the danger of consorting with the wicked; in
regard to this it will be enough to say: " They that touch pitch will
be defiled."

PSALM 126

THIS psalm is usually interpreted as in reference to the Return from
the Babylonian Exile; but if so interpreted, we are faced with
two difficulties. The first is that the psalm directly contradicts the
actual facts. It describes the time after the Return as one of un-
alloyed gladness and delight; laughter and shouts of joy are universal;
so great is the happiness of all that it seems like a dream to the returned
exiles. When we turn, however, to the Biblical historical records, it
is seen that the conditions were very different; what are the facts?
Bad harvests; want of food, drink, and clothing; no payment for
work; drought, blasting, mildew, and hail; corn, wine, oil, all are
wanting; and the cattle are perishing (Hag. 1[6, 11, 16, 17, 19]); in consequence, general discontent (Zech. 7[11–14]); so that it took nearly
twenty years before the people could be persuaded to finish the re-
building of the temple; even in the year 520 B.C. " it was not yet
completed " (Ezra 5[16]), the Return having taken place in 537 B.C.;
this lack of interest in the requirements for worship is ominously
significant; religion was at a low ebb. Then came the difficult times
during the governorship of Nehemiah: Jerusalem still lying waste

(Neh. 2[17]); external troubles (Neh. 2[19], 4[1-3, 7, 8], 3[33-35], 4[1, 2]); further discontent among the people (Neh. 5[1ᵃ]); non-observance of the Law (Neh. 13[15-18], Ezra 10[10, 11]). It is thus inconceivable that the psalmist can have been thinking of the time after the Return from the Exile.

The second difficulty is this: if *vv.* 1-3 refer to the happy state of the people on their return from the Exile, they are directly contradicted by what is said in *vv.* 4-6, which represent the people as in a sorrowful condition, but as encouraged by the prophecy of a happy time to come.

The fact is that this psalm must be interpreted in precisely the same way as Ps. 85. Evil times have fallen upon the people, but the psalmist seeks to raise their spirits by prophesying the near approach of the restoration of all things, the return of the " Golden Age ", so often foretold by the prophets (see further, Vol. I, p. 92).

As to the date of the psalm, the same applies as to what has been said in reference to that of Ps. 85.

The metre is mostly 2:2:2, while 3:2 occurs in *vv.* 4, 6, and 2:2 in *v.* 5.

A Song of Ascents.

1. When Yahweh bringeth back the ° restoration ° of Zion
   we shall be as those who dream;
2. Then shall be filled our mouth with laughter, and our tongue with shouting;
   Then will they say °: " Yahweh hath done great things for them."
3. Yahweh hath done great things for us, we are joyful.

4. Bring back, Yahweh, ° our restoration ° as streams in the Negeb.
5. They that sow with tears shall reap with shouting;
6. He that goeth weeping, bearing his seed-sack,
   Shall surely come with shouting, bearing his sheaves.

Text-critical Notes

1. Read שְׁבוּת (*šebûth*) for שִׁיבַת (*šîbath*, an error for שְׁבִית *šebîth*, " captivity "). 2. Om. בַּגּוֹיִם (*baggôîm*, " among the nations "), a marginal gloss which breaks the rhythm. 4. Read שְׁבוּתֵנוּ (*šebûthēnû*) for שְׁבִיתֵנוּ (*šebîthēnû*, " our captivity ").

1-3. We have here the thought of the bringing back of the " Golden Age ", which, as already pointed out, was a frequent theme of the prophets. For the expression *restoration*, or " Bringing back ", see the notes on Ps. 85. The conditions brought about by the return of the happy time as at the beginning of all things are envisaged as so blissful that they will seem like a dream; if, however, the psalmist is here influenced by the prophet Joel—or both may be indebted to some earlier source—then we must understand *dream*, not as in its ordinary sense, but in that as used in Joel 2[28, 29] (3[1, 2]), where it stands as a parallel to the outpouring of the divine spirit—*i.e.*, spiritual discernment; the whole context there deals with the " restoration ". In describing the joyful experiences in that happy time, the psalmist uses expressions which sound a little incongruous to our ears, the mouth being *filled with laughter, and the tongue with shouting* (cp. Job 8[21]); but it must be remembered that the Western ideal of seemly self-control in all circumstances is not shared by Orientals, who surrender themselves to unrestrained and boisterous manifestations of delight which to them seem fitting. It was an element in the prophetic vision of the coming age of bliss that the Gentiles would be brought to acknowledge Yahweh (see, *e.g.*, Isa. 11[9, 10], 60[1–3, 14], Jer. 16[19]); to this the psalmist refers in making the Gentiles say: *Yahweh hath done great things for them*—*i.e.*, for Israel; the Hebrew text has: *Then will the Gentiles say*, but there is no need to express the word " Gentiles ", because this is self-understood, and its insertion interferes with the rhythmic beats. The *great things* refer to the prosperity enjoyed by the Jewish people and their supremacy among the nations, which were among the characteristics of the happy time to come. To emphasize this, the words of the Gentiles are put into the mouth of the people of Yahweh, and thus repeated; these great things, with every reason, cause the people to be *joyful*.

The first part of the psalm was written for the purpose of giving comfort and hope to the people living in adverse circumstances. In the second part, 4–6, the present condition of the people is indirectly indicated, but it is overborne by words of triumphant trust; this spirit of optimistic assurance is one of the most admirable *traits* among the many beautiful expressions of faith which abound in the Psalter. The psalmist begins with a petition, couched in the form of prophetic terminology, that *Yahweh* may *bring back* the time of primeval happiness, *our restoration*, as we have, though inadequately, expressed it; *as the streams in the Negeb* is a comparison the force of which it is at first not easy to grasp. The *Negeb*, a proper name, meant the whole district in the south of Palestine which led into the desert proper; this was called the *Negeb* (from the root meaning " to be dry ") because, but for a few spots here and there, it was arid land. The stream-beds were, therefore, for the most part dry; but in the rainy season the streams bubbled forth with overflowing water. The poetical psalmist, then, compares the present untoward condition of the people with the period of the arid, waterless *Negeb* during the summer months, and offers the prayer that this condition may be changed and give place to happy times, just as the dried-up watercourses in due time become running streams. Then, almost in the style of the *hakam* (" wise-man "), he utters a proverb of comforting import: *They that sow with tears shall reap with shouting* (cp. Jer. 31[9]); the picture, continued in the next verse, is that of the sower laboriously trudging over the uneven ground with his leather seed-sack (for this meaning of the Hebrew word see Köhler, in *ZAW* for 1937, pp. 161 f.); but it is certain that in due season he will *come with shouting, bearing his sheaves*, the rich product of the insignificant seeds.

Religious Teaching

See under Ps. 85.

PSALM 127

THIS psalm consists of two independent fragments (*vv.* 1, 2 and 3–5) belonging to the Wisdom literature ; it contains several points of contact with *Proverbs*. Hence the ascription to Solomon in the title, added later. The psalm is in no sense a pilgrim-psalm ; the reason why it was included in the group was doubtless owing to the opening words, which were taken to refer to Yahweh's house—*i.e.*, the temple.

The two fragments are, however, appropriately placed together, since they deal, respectively, with building in a literal and in a metaphorical sense : the building of a house, and the building-up of a family. In each case, the sage insists, the safety and prosperity of the building can be ascribed only to Yahweh, and to him alone ; he is the Masterbuilder.

The final clause of the first fragment presents us with a point of exegesis of great difficulty ; owing to the unsatisfying way in which it is dealt with in the commentaries, we have permitted ourselves a somewhat drastic emendation of the text (see the exegetical notes on *v.* 2).

The fragments belong to the time when the teaching of Wisdom had developed, among the Hebrews, into a literature in the strict sense —*i.e.*, they are post-exilic ; but their content is otherwise too indefinite to permit assigning to them a more definite date.

The metre in the first fragment is almost uniformly 3 : 3 ; in the second fragment almost uniformly 3 : 2.

A Song of Ascents. ° *Solomon's* °.

1. If Yahweh doth not build the house,   they labour in vain that build it.
   If Yahweh doth not guard the city,   the watchman watcheth in vain.
2. ° If Yahweh doth not grant prosperity,°   in vain do ye rise up early,
   Taking rest so late,   eating the bread of toil. ˙

3. Behold, sons are the heritage of Yahweh.   ° his gift.° is the fruit of the womb ;
4. Like arrows in the hand of a warrior,   so are the sons of youth ;
5. Happy ° is he ° that filleth   his quiver with them,
   ° He shall not be ashamed ° when ° he
   speaketh °   with his enemies in the gate.

Text-critical Notes

Title : omitted in G, see further p. 500. 2. Read אִם יְהוָֹה לֹא־יִתֵּן יֵשַׁע for כֵּן יִתֵּן לִידִידוֹ שֵׁנָא " so he giveth his beloved sleep ", transposing the clause to the beginning of the verse 3. Read שֹׂכְרוֹ for שָׂכָר, " gift ", lit. " reward ". 5. Om. הַגֶּבֶר, " the man ". Read, with G, יֵבֹשׁ for יֵבֹשׁוּ " they shall (not) be ashamed ". Read יְדַבֵּר for יְדַבְּרוּ, " they will speak ".

1. In contrast to the belief of the times (it applies also to modern times, see Doughty, *Arabia Deserta*, p. 136 [1888]), that unless the *daimon (jinn)* of the land was propitiated whenever a house was built, or even a tent erected, evil results would ensue, the Sage here teaches that unless it is in accordance with Yahweh's will and with his help that the house is built, the *labour* of those who *build* it is *in vain*; meaning either that the builders will be unable to complete their work, or that the building will collapse when built. It is, of course, implied, on the other hand, that if the work is undertaken with Yahweh's permission and blessing, no harm can come to the building or the builders—*i.e.*, no resentful *daimon* will be able to molest them (cp. Ps. 91[9, 10]). In the same way, unless it is Yahweh's protection against external foes that is sought, the city will fall, *the watchman watcheth in vain* (cp. Prov. 21[31]).

2. As the Hebrew of this verse stands, it is exceedingly difficult to make adequate sense of it; all kinds of ingenious explanations are offered in the commentaries; it is explained, for example, as meaning that God gives his chosen beloved one as much food in his sleep as those who have toiled hard for it; or that " sleep " is to be taken in a figurative sense of not worrying about food and drink, which God will supply, and Matth. 6[24 ff.] is referred to; or that we have here the echo of the fairy-tale, according to which a man goes to sleep hungry, and dreams of eating; then he wakes up and finds the food by his side; or else the text is emended so as to read, " and so there is given restless sleep ", *i.e.*,—those who worry about earning their livelihood have bad nights. Explanations of this kind strike us as unsatisfactory. We suggest, therefore, that the word for " sleep ", *šena'*, is an error for *yēša'*, lit. " salvation ", but not infrequently used in the sense of " welfare " or " prosperity " (see, *e.g.*, Ps. 24[5], 25[5], 65[5]); with this emended form of the text, cp. Prov. 10[22]. Further, we suggest that, as in the case of some other psalms, there has been a slight dislocation of the text, and that the last half-line of *v.* 2 should be the first one of the verse; this, with " Yahweh " inserted, gives a threefold consecutive insistence on " If Yahweh doth not " in the first half of each line, with the threefold " in vain " in the second half; a symmetry is thus gained, which is paralleled elsewhere (see Ps. 22[4, 5], and 87). Moreover, by this not all too-drastic emendation, we get a logical sequence and edifying teaching.

The second fragment, 3–5, has, as already remarked, a point of attachment with the preceding in that it, too, speaks of a " building " though in a metaphorical sense—*i.e.*, in the " building-up " of a family (*e.g.*, Deut. 25[9], Ruth 4[11], 1 Sam. 2[35], 1 Kgs. 9[38]), and this is ascribed to the will of Yahweh (şee, *e.g.*, Gen. 14[2], 30[3], Exod. 1[21]), hence the words of 3 : *Behold, sons are the heritage of Yahweh*; the capability of bearing children was the *gift*, lit. " reward ", of Yahweh : *his gift is the fruit of the womb*. There was no greater joy to the ancient Israelite than that of becoming the father of a numerous progeny (cp. Ps. 128[3, 4]), sons rather than daughters, for, according to antique thought, the male was the more important because he alone was thought to be competent to worship (*kultfähig*, as it is succinctly expressed in German); the duties of sons to their deceased father were considered of paramount importance. The Hebrews married young, so that while a man was still in his prime he might have several sons who had reached manhood; the Sage compares them with *arrows in the hand of a warrior*, or " mighty man " ; they are called *sons of youth* because their father was in the vigour of youth when they were born (cp. Prov. 5[18]) ; surrounded by them he can look *his enemies in the gate* boldly in the face (5).

Religious Teaching.

The special point of interest is the stress laid on the divine interest and intervention in the ordinary affairs of every-day life. The conviction that all human activities are under divine oversight is beautifully expressed in Deut. 28[6], where it is said of the godly man : " Blessed shalt thou be when thou comest in, and blessed shalt thou be when thou goest out " ; similarly in Ps. 121[8]. This is a truth only too often lost sight of, but it is one often taught by our Lord : " Your heavenly Father knoweth that ye have need of all these things " (Matth. 6[32]) ; " The very hairs of your head are all numbered " (Luke 12[7]).

PSALM 128

COMMENTATORS differ in their opinions as to whether this psalm is to be regarded as containing a statement of facts, or whether it expresses a series of wishes. It embodies both. Written in the style of the Wisdom-writers, it opens with a statement of fact, following upon which other statements of fact are pronounced; and it concludes, in the last two verses, with the expression of wishes. Not that the Sage is addressing a particular individual, as some commentators hold ; he pictures in his mind's eye the God-fearing man in general—in this case a man of the peasant class—and apostrophizes him as though present. This is in the style of the Wisdom-writers (see, *e.g.*, Prov. 19[18-20], 25[16, 17, 21, 22], and often elsewhere).

The psalm illustrates the truth of the outstanding theme of the Wisdom-literature : the fear of Yahweh is the beginning (better, " zenith ") of wisdom. That the Sage is not advocating a purely utilitarian view of religion, such as is expressed, *e.g.*, in Gen. 28[20, 21], is seen from the words : " And mayest thou see the welfare of Jerusalem all the days of thy life " (v. 5) ; as Jerusalem was the centre of worship, the wish implies that the God-fearing man may cultivate worship for itself, not merely for what may be gained by it.   To contend, as some commentators do, that vv. 4–6, or any portion of them, are not part of the original psalm, but due to a glossator, is to do an injustice to the author.

That the psalm is not a pilgrim-psalm is clear from its contents ; its inclusion in the group may have been due to the opening words (v. 1).   The date is the same as that of the preceding psalm. The metre is uniformly 3 : 2.

A Song of Ascents.

1. Happy is every one that feareth Yahweh,   that walketh in his ways :
2. The labour of thy hands ° thou dost eat,   happy art thou, and well it is with thee ;
3. Thy wife is like a fruitful vine,   within thy house ;
   Thy sons are like shoots of olive-trees   about thy table.
4. Behold, thus ° is the man blest   that feareth Yahweh.
5. May Yahweh bless thee from Zion   ° . . . . . °
   And mayest thou see the welfare of Jerusalem   all the days of thy life ;
6. And mayest thou see thy sons' sons ;   Peace upon Israel.

Text-critical Notes

2. Om., with G, יָ, ־׳ for ״.   4. Om., with some Hebr. MSS and the Versions, יָ.   5. A half-line seems to have fallen out.

1. The inculcation of the *fear* of *Yahweh* belongs predominantly to the Ḥakamim, " Wise-men ", in their writings (Ps. 111¹⁰, Prov. 9¹⁰, 14²⁶, ²⁷, 15¹⁶, 19²³ and elsewhere) ; the word connotes reverential awe, which induces a man to *walk in his ways* ; everyone who does so is *happy*, which expresses the original better than " blessed " (see 1 Kgs. 10⁸, Prov. 3¹³, 8³⁴, 14²¹, and vv. 2, 3, of our psalm) ; for the sense in which we understand " blessed " another word is used in Hebrew, see v. 5 of our psalm.   The Sage then goes on to indicate wherein this happiness consists.   2, 3. The figure pictured by the Sage is that of a prosperous Palestinian peasant, prosperous because he is God-fearing. One would suppose that for the small peasant proprietor to be able to partake of the food produced by his own labour would represent what was normal and obvious ; so that when the Sage speaks of the man as *happy* and fortunate—*well it is with thee*—because *he eats the labour of his hands*, it indicates that there must have been frequent periods during which very different conditions held sway ; and, indeed, the history of Israel in both early and late times shows this to have been the case. The small land-owners and peasants were only too often the victims of oppression and maltreatment, whether owing to wars and foreign domination (Jer. 21⁷), or to powerful tyrants among their own people

(Am. 5¹¹, Mic. 6¹⁰⁻¹²), not to speak of times of drought and famine, (Hag. 1¹¹), locust pests, and the like (Joel 1⁴). However, at the time when this psalm was written conditions were, at any rate temporarily, propitious. The Sage contemplates a homely scene, a picture of ideal family life. The peasant's wife he compares with *a fruitful vine* (cp. Ezek. 19¹⁰); just as the clusters hang upon the vine-stock, so do her children cling to her *within the house*; the word used refers to that part of the house set apart for the wife, lit. " the innermost parts." The sons, sitting round the table, are compared with the young *shoots of olive-trees* (cp. Ps. 52⁸); the word used (*zaîth*) refers only to the cultivated tree, not to the wild olive; it is an ever-green, and the prophet extols its beauty (Hos. 14⁶); the comparison is, therefore, a very pretty one. On the great desire to have sons, see above, p. 519. A happy home, a good wife, numerous offspring, and sufficiency of food—these things are the possession of him who fears Yahweh, and they are the signs of his being *blest* by him. 5. This blessing is sent forth from Zion, where the divine presence was sought; thus the Sage expresses the wish, *May Yahweh bless thee from Zion*; and he adds words of much significance; for the further wish that the recipient of the divine blessing *may see the welfare of Jerusalem all the days of his life* expresses, in effect, the long-cherished conception of the solidarity of the people; the welfare of the individual is conditioned by that of the community; and this can be assured only by loyalty in the worship of Yahweh, the centre of whose worship was Jerusalem. The addition in 6 of the wish, *and mayst thou see thy sons' sons* (cp. Prov. 17⁶), in this connexion, implies something more than that the happy father may live to be a grandfather, though doubtless this is present too, since long life was one of the greatest blessings; but the close connexion of this with the mention of *the welfare of Jerusalem all the days of thy life* makes it not fanciful to perceive here also the implied wish that the welfare of Jerusalem may be prolonged. Jerusalem, as the " mother " of the people (*e.g.*, Isa. 50¹, 54¹), was ever in the minds of the true worshippers of Yahweh, and the psalmists were among the most outstanding of those who conceived of Jerusalem as the place where his glory dwelt (Ps. 26⁸). With the concluding words, *Peace be upon Israel*, cp. Ps. 125⁵, 131³, 134³.

Religious Teaching.

This has been sufficiently indicated in the exegetical notes.

PSALM 129

THE psalmist casts a glance back on the past history of his people, with
its long tale of enemy invasions and cruel oppression ; but he reflects
that all attempts to subjugate the people had been in vain, because
Yahweh had frustrated the intentions of the enemy. The contemplation of this convinces the psalmist that no attempt against Zion (synonymous with Jerusalem, *e.g.*, Ps. 51[18]) will succeed, cp. Isa. 40[9, 10].

It must be recognized that if this psalm was written in post-exilic
times, it is difficult to understand how the psalmist, in looking back
over the past history of his people, could say—putting the words into
the mouth of the nation—that their enemies had not prevailed against
them. After the Exile Palestine was under Persian suzerainty until
the end of the fourth century ; then it came under Ptolemaic rule until
early in the second century ; after that it was incorporated in the
Syrian Empire, and soon after the accession of Antiochus IV, in 175 B.C.,
Jerusalem was attacked, " and all the house of Jacob was clothed with
shame ", and "the sanctuary was laid waste like a wilderness"
(1 Macc. 1[20 ff., 39]).   In 166/5, it is true, the victory of Judas Maccabæus,
and after him the heroism of his brothers and their followers, ultimately
succeeded in throwing off the Syrian yoke (142 B.C.), and for about
three-quarters of a century the Jewish nation was independent ; in
63 B.C. the land was incorporated in the Roman Empire. When, therefore during the whole of the post-exilic period, could the words " yet
they prevailed not against me " apply ? And how could the psalmist
possibly say : " put to shame and turned backward are all that hate
Zion " when recalling past history ? The answer given is, of course,
that the reference is to the victory of Judas Maccabæus, and the re-
dedication of the temple on mount Zion. There are, however, one
or two considerations which raise doubts as to the correctness of this
conclusion. The state of affairs, in spite of the victory of Judas
Maccabæus, could not have prompted the words, " Yet they prevailed not against us " ; for the Jews were still a subject nation, and
significant are the words in 1 Macc. 5[1, 2] which follow immediately
after the account of the re-dedication of the temple : " And it came to
pass, when the Gentiles round about heard that the altar was built,
and the sanctuary dedicated as aforetime, they were exceeding wroth.
And they took counsel to destroy the race of Jacob that was in the midst
of them, and they began to slay and destroy among the people."   Further,
the context in which, in our psalm, the words " put to shame and
turned backwards are all that hate Zion " stand, makes it clear that non-
Israelite enemies are referred to. Now, apart from the fact that these
words would be quite inappropriate if they referred to the victory

of Judas Maccabæus, as the quotation from 1 Macc. 5[1, 2] shows,
the attack on the temple and the desecration of the altar on Mount
Zion were largely due to the co-operation of renegade hellenistic Jews
(see 1 Macc. 1[34], " and they (*i.e.*, the Syrians) put there a sinful nation,
transgressors of the law ", and cp. 1[11 *f.*]) ; if the psalmist had been
referring to this event, some reference to the unfaithful among his own
people might well have been expected.   The fact is that in the case of
all those psalms which some commentators assign to the Maccabæan
period, the details recorded in the very reliable book of *1 Maccabees*
do not seem to have been sufficiently considered.   We have, moreover,
seen that there is some reason to believe that the psalms as we now have
them were already in existence by about 200 B.C. ; definite proof of this
is not claimed, but the possibility must be granted (see Vol. I, pp. 67 ff.) ;
and if there is any justification for the belief, the contention that certain
psalms were written during the Maccabæan period cannot be sustained.

With regard to this psalm there are certainly, so far as the language
is concerned, one or two indications of late date ; but these may well
be due to the working-over of scribes in subsequent times ; a process
to which many of the psalms have been subjected.

We come, then, to consider the question as to whether our psalm
may not have been written, originally, in reference to some other event.
Let us note, first, that the words " Put to shame and turned backwards,
are all that hate Zion " imply belief in the inviolability of Jerusalem.
This was a conception held by the prophet Isaiah (Isa. 31[5]), and was
first prompted by the quite astounding withdrawal, as it appeared to
the people, of the Assyrian army which was besieging Jerusalem,
701 B.C., in the reign of Hezekiah (2 Kgs. 19[32–36]).   Assuming, for the
sake of argument, that our psalm was written in reference to this event,
vv. 1, 2 record historical truth ; over and over again the land had
been attacked ; but Judah had hitherto always remained an independent kingdom.   The words of *v.* 3 become very significant if
read in the light of Isa. 10[28–32], where the prophet describes the route
of the ravaging Assyrian army, through the country towards Jerusalem.
In 2 Kgs. 19[26], Sennacherib's army is compared with " the grass on
the house-tops ", the identical expression used in *v.* 6 of our psalm,
so, too, in Isa. 37[27].   We contend, therefore, that there is something
to be said in favour of a pre-exilic date for our psalm.

The metre is 3 : 2 ; the final line of *v.* 8, which has three beats,
is held by some commentators to be a later liturgical addition ; but a
final benediction occurs in other psalms (*e.g.*, 84, 89, 128).

A Song of Ascents.

1. Greatly have they afflicted me from my
     youth up,   well may Israel say,
2. Greatly have they afflicted me from
     my youth up,   yet they prevailed not against me ;

3. On my back the ploughers ploughed,   made long ° their furrows .
4. Yahweh—he is righteous, may he cut
   asunder   the cord of the wicked.
5. Let them be put to shame, and turned
   backward,   all that hate Zion;
6. Let them be like the grass on housetops, ° which the east-wind blighteth °.
7. Wherewith the reaper filleth not his
   hand,   nor the binder his bosom.
8. And they that pass by do not say :   " Yahweh's blessing ° on you °,
                                            We bless you in the name of Yahweh ".

Text-critical Notes

3. Read, with *Kethîbh* לְמַעֲנוֹתָם for the *Qerê* יתָם— " their furrow "; for
the use of לְ here see GK 143e.   6. Read, with some commentators, שָׁקְדִים
תִּשְׁדֹּף for the present text, " which before one draweth it forth drieth up "; see
further, exeg. note.   8. Read עֲלֵיכֶם for אֲלֵיכֶם, " unto you ".

1–2. The past history of *Israel*, used here collectively of the northern
and southern kingdoms, furnished ample grounds for the words
which the psalmist represents as spoken by the nation personified;
enemy onslaughts had continued intermittently for centuries, first
the Canaanites (Josh. 9[1. 2], Judg. 4, 5), then the Philistines (1 Sam. 4
31, 2 Sam. 5[19–25], cp. Isa. 9[12]), later the Aramæans (Syrians, 1 Kgs. 20,
2 Kgs. 6), followed by the Assyrians (2 Kgs. 18[9 ff.]; 19); from the
beginning of the history of Israel as a nation this had gone on, from
its *youth* onwards—*i.e.*, from " the day when she came up out of the
land of Egypt ", " the days of her youth " (Hos. 2[15 (17)], cp. Deut.
26[5–7], Jer. 2[2]).   Yet in spite of all these invasions of the land, even in
spite of defeats, the nation continued to be independent; so that it
could truly be said that the enemies *prevailed* not against Israel.

3. The metaphor which the psalmist uses is twofold: first, Israel
identifies herself with the land upon which the *ploughers made long their
furrows*, cp. Isa. 51[23], " Bow down that we may go over; and thou
hast laid thy back as the ground, and as the street, to them that go·
over "; and we are reminded of the ravages of the Assyrian army
passing over the land (see Isa. 10[28–32]).   4. Then Israel is compared
with the oxen attached to the plough by a rope, or *cord* (cp. Isa. 5[18],
where the same word is used); but this rope *Yahweh cuts* asunder,
so that *the wicked*—*i.e.*, Israel's enemies—can no longer continue
ploughing; in other words, the attack of the enemy is frustrated by
Yahweh (cp. 2 Kgs. 19[35], " And it came to pass that night, that the
angel of Yahweh went forth, and smote the camp of the Assyrians . . .").
5. Thus, all the enemies who attempted to seize Zion (identified with
Jerusalem as in Isa. 4[3], 64[10], Mic. 3[10, 12]), *all that hate Zion, are put
to shame and turned backward*; 6. they are compared, so complete
is their discomfiture, with the *grass* that grows on *housetops* (cp. 2 Kgs.
19[26], Isa. 37[27]), where there is very little soil, and the grass cannot take
firm root, so as soon as the east wind blows it is *blighted* (cp. Ps. 48[7],

78²⁶ and Gen. 41²³, ²⁷) ; as the present Hebrew text stands, it can hardly
be correct : " which drieth up before one draweth it forth " ; the simile
is inappropriate, and the Hebrew word for " draweth forth " is used
only of drawing a sword, and drawing on a sandal; hence our
emendation. 7, 8. *Grass*, especially grass like this, so insignificant
and transient, is not worth gathering ; it is not like the ripened, golden
corn, no *reaper* (the word is used ironically) *filleth his hand, nor bindeth
in his bosom*, it is such a contemptible weed ; let alone the idea of
giving such a " reaper " the usual greeting of those *that pass by* :
Yahweh's blessing on you, we bless you in the name of Yahweh.

Religious Teaching.

It is only in *vv.* 4, 5 that any religious teaching appears in this
psalm ; and here the prophetical doctrine of Yahweh as the God of
History emerges. Because Yahweh is righteous, he has not permitted the enemies to prevail against Israel, and their designs upon
the sanctuary of Zion have been frustrated. The enemies of Israel
are the enemies of Yahweh; they are described as the wicked ones
because they do not acknowledge him. The righteousness of Yahweh
is thus vindicated. But it must be recognized that in one respect
this psalm lacks an element which the prophets constantly emphasized,
and which is prominent elsewhere in the *Psalms*. In recalling the
past sufferings of his people, this psalmist has no word to say as to why
they had been subjected to these sufferings. When it is remembered
how often the prophets insisted on the fact that all the calamities which
the nation suffered were the consequences of sin ; when it is noted,
further, that often in the psalms when, as here, the historical past is
recalled, it is confessed that sin has been the cause of national sufferings
(*e.g.*, Ps. 78²¹, ²², ⁵⁶⁻⁶⁴, 79⁸, ⁹, 106⁶ ⁱ.), then it must be recognized that the
absence of all mention of sin where it is rightly to be expected betrays
a lack of the sense of sin on the part of the writer of this psalm. The
somewhat uncharitable wish expressed in *v.* 6 may, in part, be due to
this want of the sense of sin. Attention is drawn to this solely because
it is well to recognize the negative side, as well as the far more abundant
positive contributions to religious teaching, found among the psalmists.

PSALM 130

THAT this psalm should be reckoned as one of the " Songs of Ascents "
shows in what a haphazard way this title has been used. The psalm
is in striking contrast to that which precedes it, in that it expresses a
sense of sin as sincere and deep as can be found anywhere in the Old

Testament. The subject of its contents will be more appropriately
dealt with in the exegetical notes, where the religious teaching is set
forth.

That the Hebrew text of *vv.* 5–7 is in some disorder is held by most
commentators to be the case. Probably they are right. Nevertheless,
the suggested emendations are somewhat drastic; we have, therefore,
sought to keep as near as possible to the text as it stands; for it is
possible that its uneven form may be due to the nature of the psalm
as the outpouring of a penitent's over-full heart.

The metre seems to be a combination of 3 : 2 and 2 : 2; though if
emended on the lines of most modern commentators, it is 3 : 2
throughout.

The developed sense of sin marks the psalm as of late date.

A Song of Ascents.

1. Out of the depths do I cry unto thee,
       Yahweh,   2. ° hear my voice;
   Let thine ears give heed   to the cry of my supplication.
3. If thou retainest iniquities, ° Yahweh °,   ° who shall stand ?
4. But with thee is forgiveness,   that thou mayest be feared.
5.   I wait for Yahweh,
              My soul doth wait,
              I hope for ° his word.
6.   My soul ° for Yahweh ! °
              More than watchers for the morn,
              Than watchers for the morn.
7.   O Israel, wait for Yahweh,
              For with Yahweh is love,
              And, plenteous redemption with him;
8. And he redeemeth Israel   from all his sins.

Text-critical Notes

2. Om. אֲדֹנָי for the rhythm's sake. **3.** Read יהוה for יָהּ. Om. אֲדֹנָי for
the rhythm's sake. **5.** Om. וֹ, " and ". **6.** Read לַיהוה for לַאדֹנָי, " for the Lord ".

1, 2. Through a misunderstanding of the use of Hebrew tenses,
the English Versions represent the psalmist as referring to the past,
whereas he is dealing solely with the present. There is a peculiar
significance in the expression *out of the depths*, used in this connexion
of a penitent sinner pleading for forgiveness; by *the depths* are meant
the depths of the sea, and, as will be seen from Isa. 51[10], the sea is
identical with *Tehom Rabbah*, " the great deep ", which is the Hebrew
form of the Babylonian Tiamat, the primeval monster, who was *the
embodiment of evil*. By the expression *out of the depths*, therefore,
the psalmist means that, as one steeped in sin, he cries to Yahweh.
The contention of some commentators that the psalmist speaks as one
suffering from sickness, inflicted because of his sins, has nothing to
support it; not physical suffering, but the agony of a penitent heart,
is what is here presented. In fitting humility the psalmist feels that
he is far from God, and therefore uses the word for I *cry* which means

to "cry aloud" (cp., *e.g.*, Judg. 9⁷), pleading that Yahweh will *give heed to the cry* (lit. " voice ") of his *supplication*; this word is a plural abstract, and should not be used as a word in the plural number (cp. Ps. 128², ⁶, 31²³, 86⁶, 140⁶). Fully in accord with his sense of unworthiness is the striking way in which the psalmist refrains from pleading directly for that which he most earnestly desires; nowhere does he pray, in so many words, for forgiveness, but he implies that this is his deepest yearning, see *v.* 4. 3. If there is no forgiveness, if Yahweh still retains in his memory the acts of rebellion against him, who can abide it ? *If thou retainest iniquities, Yahweh, who shall stand?* Possibly the last word is used as in Job. 30²⁰ : " I stand (in prayer), and thou lookest not at me." 4. But with Yahweh, as the psalmist knows, there is *forgiveness* (cp. Ps. 86⁵). The words which follow : *that thou mayest be feared*, mean that divine forgiveness, whereby sin is obliterated, quickens in the heart of the forgiven sinner reverential awe and love for Yahweh. Hence the soul-felt gratitude engendered by the conviction that he is forgiven, and expressed by the firm resolution of amendment of life : *I wait for Yahweh.* 5, 6. The words of, as it were, breathless devotion are poured forth in spontaneous utterance, careless of literary *convenances.* 7, 8. And, like every true and faithful servant of God, his thought is for others as well as for himself; his happiness must be shared ; and he calls upon his people to *wait for Yahweh*, with whom is *love* and *redemption* from sin.

One cannot fail to be struck by the fact that in this psalm, with its deep sense of sin and yearning for forgiveness, there is not a word about atoning sacrifices. Another mark of the intense spirituality of the writer.

Religious Teaching

This has been sufficiently dealt with in the foregoing notes.

PSALM 131

THIS beautiful little psalm, unique in the Psalter, is in part a confession, and in part a revelation of deep religious experiences. The writer, in repudiating the spirit of presumptuous knowledge, implies that at one time this had been his attitude of mind ; but now he has come to his better self, and has quieted the restless turbulence of his thoughts. In sweet humility he compares his trustful rest in the Lord with that of a little child lying in blissful repose on its mother's breast. Like other psalmists, what he has gained he wishes others to share, and his yearning is that they should experience the happy calm which he enjoys ;

so he ends with an exhortation to his people to "wait for Yahweh from henceforth and for ever".

The psalm is difficult to render worthily in translation; the Hebrew words imply so much that they can be expressed adequately only by paraphrase.

There is no indication of date; but that is immaterial in a psalm like this. The metre is 3 : 2.

A Song of Ascents. ° *David's* °.

1. Yahweh, my heart is not presumptuous,   not arrogant mine eyes;
   Not do I ponder things too great,   too wonderful, for me;
2. Truly I have stilled, have quieted my
   soul,   like a weaned-child on its mother.°
3. O Israel, wait for Yahweh   from henceforth and for ever.

Text-critical Notes

Title : לדוד should probably be omitted, as in G. 2. Om. כְּגָמֻל עָלַי נַפְשִׁי, "like the weaned-child upon me is my soul" as it gives a half-line too much.

1. The opening words of the psalm, *my heart is not presumptuous*, are susceptible of more than one meaning; the Hebrew word rendered *presumptuous*, is lit. "to be high", or "exalted", and can have the sense of "lifted up"—*i.e.*, drawn upwards, in the ways of Yahweh (2 Chron. 17[6]); this is not likely to be the meaning here, though it might conceivably imply spiritual pride; again, in the light of the context, it may mean pretentiousness in claiming to possess great knowledge. Probably, however, whatever else it may include, it means here the attitude of self-sufficient, presumptuous pride (as in Ezek. 19[11], 31[5, 10, 14]), which, according to the context, is more specifically defined. The psalmist is thinking of the time when, in self-esteem, he thought he knew more than others, and considered himself superior, when in arrogance he looked down upon his fellow-men (cp. Ps. 18[27], 101[5]). But he has cast all this aside now; he does not *ponder*, lit. "walk in", *things too great*, and *too wonderful* for him—*i.e.*, deep matters which are beyond his comprehension. What it was which produced the profound change in the psalmist's mental and spiritual condition, he does not say; but that he went through severe struggles is evident from his words: 2. *I have stilled, have quieted my soul*; the former of these expressions means lit. "to be smooth", and is used of levelling unevennesses on the ground (Isa. 28[25]), while in Isa. 38[13], it refers to the quieting of mental disturbance; the other expression means lit. "to be silent", so that the words might be paraphrased: I have calmed the disturbing arguments, and silenced the disconcerting questionings that worried me. The comparison of his reposeful state of sublime self-abandonment to God with a child's unspoken trust in its mother's love and care, is as touching as it is beautiful. And the mention of a *weaned-child* (it is only one word in Hebrew) is not

without significance: the psalmist might well have said, " suckling ",
but the point is that the children were weaned comparatively late
(see 1 Sam. 1²²⁻²⁴), and the weaned child knew not only instinctively,
but by experience, what a mother's love and care were; similarly,
the psalmist's childlike trust in Yahweh rests on the experience of his
love, " I know him whom I have believed " (2 Tim. 1¹²). The final
words of the psalm (3) are thought by some to be a later addition;
this may be doubted; they express the hallowed wish, found in other
psalms too, and characteristic of every truly pious Israelite, that others
might partake of the spiritual peace which he himself enjoys (cp. Ps.
128⁶, 130⁸).

Religious Teaching

In spite of the extreme brevity of this psalm, its religious teaching
is of inestimable value. The first thing to note is that *self-knowledge*
leads to *confession*, which implies *repentance*. Whatever form the
psalmist's presumptuous arrogance may have assumed in the past,
whether spiritual pride which despised others, like a certain type of
Pharisees " who trusted in themselves that they were righteous, and set
all others at nought " (Luke 18⁹), or whether a claim to superior knowledge, " this multitude which knoweth not the law are accursed "
(John 7⁴⁹)—both seem to be implied—he has been brought to know
himself; he has acquired self-knowledge, a thing which can be attained
only by those who are truly honest with themselves. To such, as the
psalmist implies, self-esteem is impossible; and his comparison with
a little child witnesses to his conception of the blessedness of genuine
humility (" Whosoever therefore shall humble himself as this little child
shall be great in the kingdom of heaven ", Matth. 18⁴). And, lastly,
the psalmist tells of the restful peace engendered by a childlike trust in
God. Very appositely does Herkenne quote St. Augustine's words:
" Our heart is restless till it rests in Thee, O God " (*Conf.* 1¹).

PSALM 132.

SOME verses in this psalm (7–9, 13–16) fully account for its having been
incorporated in the collection of " pilgrim songs ". Its liturgical
character is evident: a solo voice sang *vv.* 1, 2, another singer took
up *vv.* 3–5, whereupon the temple choir sang *vv.* 6–10. It may be
surmised that *vv.* 11, 12 were sung by a soloist, after which another
solo voice sang the remainder of the psalm. Like others of the " royal "
psalms, this one was composed by a court official in the name of the
king. To interpret the psalm in a Messianic sense is to miss its mean-

ing; it recalls the past, but deals with the present. That it was so interpreted in later times, when the Davidic dynasty was no more in existence, is easily understood; but there is nothing in the psalm itself to show that the writer intended his words to be understood in a Messianic sense. It has been contended that the psalm was written in Maccabæan times; but that it cannot refer to a Maccabæan ruler should be obvious, for the Hasmonæans did not belong to the house of David (see 1 Macc. 2¹, and cp. 1 Chron. 9¹⁰); other indications in the psalm show the weakness of this contention. The psalm is of pre-exilic date, and belongs to the later period of the monarchy.

In one or two particulars there are variations from the accounts contained in the historical books; this may be due to the psalmist permitting himself some poetical licence, or to legendary material which has not come down to us, or they may be due to the hand of some later scribe.

The metre is uniformly 3 : 3.

A Song of Ascents.

1. Remember, Yahweh, David, ° thy servant °, and all his affliction,
2. How he sware to Yahweh, vowed to the Mighty One of Jacob :
3. " I will not enter the habitation of my house nor ascend the couch of my resting place,
4. I will not give sleep to mine eyes, to mine eyelids slumber,
5. Till I find a place for Yahweh, a dwelling for the Mighty One of Jacob."

6. Lo, we heard of it in Ephratah, we found it in the fields of Ja'ar ;
7. Let us go unto his dwelling-place, let us worship at the stool of his feet.
8. Arise, Yahweh, to thy resting-place, thou and thy mighty Ark.
9. Let thy priests be rightly clothed, and thy saints ° let them shout for joy °.
10. For the sake of David thy servant, turn not away the face of thine anointed.
11. Yahweh did sware to David, of a truth, he will not turn from it :
    ° [I will set up thy seed after thee, and I will establish the throne of thy kingdom] °

12. " If thy sons keep my covenant ° and my testimonies ° which I teach them,
    Their sons also for ever shall sit upon thy throne."
13. For Yahweh hath chosen Zion, hath desired it for his habitation :
14. " This is my resting-place for ever, here will I abide, for I have desired it.
15. Her provision will I greatly bless, her poor will I satisfy with food ;
16. Her priests will I clothe with prosperity, and her saints shall shout for joy.
17. There will I cause to flourish the horn of David, I have prepared a lamp for mine anointed ;
18. His enemies will I clothe with shame, but on him shall his crown glisten."

Text-critical Notes

1. Add לְעַבְדְּךָ as the rhythm requires another word. 9. Read, as in v. 16, רַנֵּן יְרַנֵּנוּ. 11. Something has fallen out of the text here; for the expression " the fruit of thy body " in the present text cp. Mic. 6⁷. We have, quite tentatively, adapted the words which occur in 2 Sam. 7¹⁴ˑ¹²: אָקִים אֶת־זַרְעֲךָ אַחֲרֶיךָ וְכֹנַנְתִּי אֶת־כִּסֵּא מַמְלַכְתֶּךָ : 12. Read, with G, וְעֵדֹתִי for ־תִי— " and my testimony ".

1. The word of prayer with which the psalm opens, *Remember, Yahweh, David thy servant*, is reiterated in 10, and is prompted by the oath of Yahweh, recalled in 10. The reference to David's *affliction*, lit.

" his being afflicted ", causes some little difficulty ; the context shows
that the meaning here cannot be as in Ps. 119[71], Isa. 53[4], where the
affliction is from God ; it is therefore probable that it is used in the
technical sense, as in Lev. 23[29], of afflicting oneself with fasting or
castigation (1 Chron. 22[14] has a different form of the word) ; but if so,
there is nothing in the historical books to suggest that David underwent
such self-infliction as a preparation for gathering the money required
for the building of the temple ; either, therefore, we have here some
poetical exaggeration on the part of the psalmist, or else the echo
of some legendary account of the life of David which has not been
otherwise preserved. 2. David's oath to Yahweh is then spoken
of. There are several references to David's intention of building a
house for Yahweh (1 Chron. 22[7], 28[3], 1 Kgs. 8[17], and elsewhere),
but it is not said that he *sware to Yahweh* to do this ; nor is there any
mention of *the Mighty One of Jacob* in this connexion ; this title of
Yahweh occurs elsewhere only in Gen. 49[24], Isa. 49[26], 60[16] (in Isa. 1[24]
it is " the Mighty One of Israel ") ; it is very ancient, and originally
was probably *'ăbbîr ya'ăqôb*, " the bull of Jacob " (cp. the parallel
" the Stone of Israel " in Gen. 49[24]), and was altered to *'ābîr ya'aqôb*
later to avoid its being associated with the bull-worship of northern
Israel (cp. 1 Kgs. 12[28, 29], " calf " = a young bull). Here again,
then, the psalmist seems to be echoing the words of some source which
has not come down to us. And this applies with especial force to what
follows in 3-5, which seem to be something more than a poetical exaggeration of 2 Sam. 7[2, 3], 1 Kgs. 8[17, 18].

In 6-10, which were probably taken up by the temple choir, the
psalmist places himself in the past and purports to quote the words oi
David and of those who, with him, brought up the Ark from Kirjath-
jearim to Jerusalem (1 Sam. 7[1, 2], 2 Sam. 6[2-12], 1 Chron. 13[1-14]). It
was when David was living in *Ephratah*—i.e., Bethlehem (see·Ruth 4[11],
Mic. 5[2], cp. 1 Sam. 17[12])—that he first heard of the existence of the
Ark ; thereupon he went to seek it, and *found it in the fields* (better
" pasture-land ") of *Ja'ar*, an abbreviated form of Kirjath-jearim.
There is some difference of opinion as to what is to be understood by
the " it " in *we heard of it*, and *we found it* ; the Hebrew has " her "
(*'ărôn*, " Ark ", is fem. in 1 Sam. 4[17], 2 Chron. 8[11]) ; but the Vulgate
renders it in the masc., " him ", in reference to Yahweh ; this rendering
is followed by Gunkel. Then, again, as in Hebrew, the fem. gender
is often used as neuter, Kittel takes it in a neutral sense, " we heard
about it "—i.e., the whereabouts of the presence of the Ark ; but this
cannot possibly apply to " we found it ". A similar objection must be
urged against Yahweh being the object, unless it be conceded that
Yahweh was identified with the Ark, in which case there is no need to
alter the text to " him ". Now it is evident that the close association

of Yahweh with the Ark occasioned its identification with him to be
held in early times; Num. 10³³⁻³⁶ (J) illustrates this; our psalm, of
later date, presents a fluctuating frame of mind, which at one time
identifies, at another clearly differentiates, between the Ark and Yahweh;
thus, while it cannot be meant that Yahweh was first *heard of in
Ephratah*, nor that he was *found in the fields of Ja'ar*, yet something
approaching the idea of identification is at least adumbrated in the
parallelism: *Arise, Yahweh, to thy resting-place, thou and thy mighty
Ark*, lit. " the Ark of thy strength ". On the other hand, there is a
clear differentiation in the words : *Let us go unto his dwelling-place—
i.e.*, Zion—*let us worship at the stool of his feet*; the Ark is spoken of
as " the footstool of our God " in 1 Chron. 28² (though in this passage
the " building of an house " is used for the Ark); this differentiation
reflects a later stage in the conception of Yahweh. The mention of
the Ark as playing a *rôle* in the temple cult is another proof of the
pre-exilic date of the psalm, though, as there are various Deuteronomic
references to the Ark (Deut. 31²⁵, ²⁶, cp. Josh. 8³³, 1 Kgs. 3¹⁵, 4¹⁹,
8⁹, ²¹), the psalm must belong to late pre-exilic times; for the final
disappearance of the Ark is referred to in Jer. 3¹⁶; in Ezra 1⁷⁻¹¹ no
mention is made of it in the list of sacred vessels. In 9, 10 the psalmist,
while still thinking of the past, in fact envisages the present; at the
bringing in of the Ark to the sanctuary the priests must be clothed in
fitting—*i.e.*, festal—garments ; for this force of *ṣedeq*, in the sense of
" normal " or " right ", cp. Deut. 31¹⁹, Ps. 4⁵, 51¹⁹; and the *saints*
(*Ḥāsîdîm*)—*i.e.*, the true worshippers of Yahweh—and therefore *thy
saints*, are called upon to *shout for joy*. And, finally, a prayer is offered
that Yahweh will look favourably upon the king; *turn not away the
face of thine anointed*, and this, *for the sake of David, thy servant*. For
the thought of reaping the reward of the righteousness of the forefathers cp. Gen. 26²⁴. For 9, 10, cp. 2 Chron. 6⁴¹, ⁴².

Just as in the opening words of the psalm David's oath to Yahweh
is recalled, so now (11, 12) Yahweh's oath to David is spoken of, an
oath which, *of a truth he will not turn from*, cp. Ps. 89³, ³⁵, ⁴⁹, 110⁴.
But the condition is that David's successors will *keep* the *covenant*,
and observe the *testimonies* which Yahweh teaches them.

After the words of promise, put into the mouth of Yahweh, regarding the permanence of the monarchy in the Davidic line, there follows
a further utterance of Yahweh (14-16) regarding the permanence of the
sanctuary : *This is my resting-place for ever*. Yahweh's abiding in
Zion assures that the indispensable need of sustenance will always
be forthcoming ; the *poor*, so often the victims of insufficiency of *food*,
will be satisfied. The mention of the *priests*, whom Yahweh will
clothe with prosperity, is not without significance ; that due provision
should be made for them was naturally a matter of importance, see,

e.g., Deut. 18¹⁻⁸; *prosperity (yĕša')*, often translated " salvation ", means here welfare in a material sense. The priests, being well provided for, are ardent in the fulfilment of their duties in public worship, and therefore the *saints*, the true worshippers, *shout for joy*, a liturgical term (Ps. 51¹⁴, 71²³, 84², 145⁷).

Finally (17, 18), the psalmist reverts to the Davidic dynasty, the prosperity of which must depend on Yahweh, who *causeth to flourish the horn of David*, an expression denoting the strength (cp. Deut. 33¹⁷) of the Davidic dynasty ; what is meant by the psalmist in saying that Yahweh has *prepared a lamp* for his *anointed*, is not easy to decide, and various opinions are held. In 2 Sam. 21¹⁷ David is spoken of as the " lamp " of Israel, an appropriate expression in reference to the king who judges and guides his people (1 Sam. 8²⁰, Prov. 20⁸, 25², ³, 29⁴, cp. 16¹³, ¹⁵) ; similarly, the successor of David on the throne is called a " lamp " (1 Kgs. 11³⁶, 15⁴, 2 Chron. 21⁷) ; in the verse before us, then, taking " mine anointed " as parallel to " David " in the first half of the verse, the meaning will be that Yahweh continues to prosper the dynasty of David, in accordance with which he has again *prepared*, or provided, a successor—a " lamp "—to his anointed, David, who was the anointed of Yahweh *par excellence*. In contrast to the *shame* wherewith Yahweh will *clothe*, or " cover " his enemies, the *crown* of this successor to the Davidic throne, will *glisten* ; the reference is to the gold of which it is constructed (cp. the " plate of pure gold " on Aaron's mitre, Exod. 28³⁶⁻³⁸).

Religious Teaching

It must be recognized, first, that the doctrine of God, as portrayed in this psalm, illustrates the persistence of old-world ideas : viz. those of God taking an oath, his desire for a dwelling-place on earth, and the quaint belief in his connexion with the Ark. These all witness to materialistic conceptions of the Deity which belong to a comparatively early religious stage. It required the experience of the Exile, and the teaching of a Deutero-Isaiah, to generate more spiritual conceptions. But there is, in spite of this, one element in the psalm which is of special interest, since it witnesses to the innate religious instinct of ancient Israel in every sphere ; we mean the principle of the union which should subsist between religion and the State. The basic purpose of the psalm is to glorify the Sanctuary together with the kingship, which are inextricably bound together. The subject has been already referred to (see under Ps. 110), and there is no need to deal further with it here ; but the principle involved is of profound and far-reaching importance, and the way in which it is set forth in this psalm demands grateful recognition.

MM

PSALM 133

It may sometimes happen that a technical term, owing to its familiarity among the Hebrews, had, for them, a significance which may not, at first sight, be appreciated nowadays. An illustration of this is presented in the psalm before us. In Deut. 25[5, 6] reference is made to a marriage-custom in ancient Israel which we know as the Levirate marriage (from the Latin *levir*, "brother-in-law"); according to this custom, when a man dies and has no sons, his brother must marry the widow. In Hebrew there is a verb meaning "to do the duty of a brother-in-law" (*yabam*); as Driver remarks: "The fact of Hebrew possessing a special word to indicate this particular relation is evidence that it must have been a prominent factor in ancient Hebrew society, and that the rights and duties connected with it must have been important ones".[1] The purpose of the custom, according to Deut. 2[6], was that the name of the brother who had died should "not be blotted out of Israel"—*i.e.*, that his name and family should be perpetuated among his people, and no doubt also that the family property should remain intact. The family tie in the earliest periods of Israel's social history was more closely maintained than in later days; the paternal authority was in those early times more absolute than in subsequent periods. In those early days sons continued to live under their father's roof, and to be subject to his authority even after they were married and had sons; in this way the unity of the family was secured, and continued to be more effectively preserved than if the sons, when they married, set up a household on their own account, and lived, it might be, in some far-off spot. And it was the custom of the Levirate marriage which further cemented family union. Now, when, in Deut. 25[5], the subject of the Levirate marriage is mentioned, it is introduced by the words: "When (not "If") brethren dwell together"—*i.e.*, it is the technical phrase used in reference to the ancient custom of brothers, even when married, all living together under the paternal roof; implying, further, that by means of the Levirate marriage-custom the perpetuation of the family was assured. Bearing this in mind, therefore, the significance of the opening verse of our psalm will be appreciated; and this significance is accentuated by the fact that, in course of time, the old Levirate marriage-custom had given place to that in which a son, on marrying, became emancipated from paternal authority, left his father's house, and set up an establishment of his own, whereby the family unity was broken, and its perpetuation, at

---

[1] *A Crit. and Exeg. Com. on Deuteronomy*, p. 283 (1902).

any rate, endangered. Thus, the psalmist, like Jeremiah (6¹⁶), extols the " old paths ".¹

The objection to this interpretation of the psalm, that a song of so highly inspired a nature is not likely to have been prompted by an isolated family affair of this kind ("*eine derartige einzelne Familien-angelegenheit* "),² fails to realize the great importance of family social life in ancient Israel ; nor does it take into account the significance attaching to a legal technical term of hoary authority.

The date of the psalm is difficult to determine, as definite indications are wanting ; but it may well belong to early post-exilic times, when the return of the exiles to the homeland brought to mind in a pointed manner the family social life of long ago.

The metre is 3 : 2, with the exception of the opening verse, which is 3 : 3.·

A Song of Ascents.   ° David's °.

1. Behold, how goodly and how beautiful,   the dwelling together of brethren :
2. Like precious oil (it is) upon the head,   ° which runneth down ° upon the beard,

—The beard of Aaron,—which runneth down   upon the collar of his garments ;
3. Like the dew of Hermon, which runneth down   upon the hills of ° 'Iyyôn ° ;
For there Yahweh commanded   life for evermore.

Text-critical Notes

Title : some Hebr. and G omit לְדָוִד, " David's ". 2. Read שֶׁיֵּרֵד for יֵרֵד.
3. Read עִיּוֹן for צִיּוֹן, see exegetical note. Om. אֶת־הַבְּרָכָה, " the blessing ", which overloads the half-line.

1. As pointed out in the introductory section, the *dwelling together of brethren* (there is nothing about " in unity " in the Hebrew) is a technical phrase used in reference to the earliest family custom in ancient Israel, in which brothers continued to live, even as married men with their own sons, in the dwelling-place of their father. This is *goodly* and *beautiful*, not because the brothers are living in unity— that is taken for granted—but because it was the means of perpetuating the family and its name in Israel. The metre of this line, differing from that of the rest of the psalm, seems to be purposeful ; the opening words are a kind of text. 2, 3. The psalmist uses two pictures to illustrate the ideas of family continuity and family union which the ancient custom achieved. The comparisons may sound a little strange to modern Western ears, but to the Oriental mind they were sufficiently appropriate. From the father, the first founder and head of the family, the descendants issue, running down through the ages ; with this the psalmist compares the *precious oil—i.e.*, the " holy anointing oil "

¹ This interpretation of the psalm was first brought to our attention by a pamphlet published by S. Rauh : *Hebräisches Familienrecht in vorprophetischer Zeit*, pp. 35 ff. (1907)
² Hélxenne, *Das Buch der Psalmen*, p. 420 (1936).

(see Exod. 30$^{23-30}$, 37^{29}), *running down upon the beard*; the reason for the mention of Aaron is that when the holy anointing oil is spoken of it is in connexion with the high-priest (Num. 35^{25}), *Aaron* is specifically named in Exod. 29$^{4-7}$, 30^{30}. If the oil ran down to *the beard of Aaron*, as was likely enough, it would necessarily flow on to *the collar of his garments*; the word for *collar* (*pîy*, lit. " mouth ", or " opening ") is used in the description of " the robe of the ephod ", where it is said, " and there shall be an opening for his head in the midst thereof " (Exod. 28^{32}); the opening round the neck is obviously what we understand by a collar.   Then the psalmist uses for comparison the *dew of Hermon which*, likewise, *runneth down upon the hills of 'Iyyôn*; but here there is also the idea of diffuseness, compared with the spreading family under the old conditions.   The Hebrew text has " the hills of Zion "; but the dew of Hermon, far away to the north, could not possibly run all the way through Palestine to get to Zion; as Barnes remarks, it is " geographically a grotesque conception "; but his rendering : " Plenteous as the dew of Hermon is that which descendeth upon the mountains of Zion ", does not represent the Hebrew.   Jirku, followed by Gunkel, is surely right in reading *'Iyyôn* for *Zion*; it is mentioned in 1 Kgs. 15^{20}, 2 Kgs. 15^{29}, 2 Chron. 16^{4}, and refers to the hilly country which lay on the south-west foot of mount Hermon.   The two words in Hebrew are almost exactly alike (עִיּוֹן and צִיּוֹן); nothing could be easier than for a copyist to have misread what was before him.   It is also worth noting that the Hebrew reads " hills "; the " hill of Zion " occurs very frequently, but the " hills of Zion " never.

In the concluding line the psalmist, as might logically be expected, reverts to the thought of the opening verse : *For there*—i.e., in the family as composed, and united as a religious unit, under the ancient *régime*—*Yahweh commanded*, or ordained, what results : *life for evermore*, in reference to the perpetuation of the family ; " for evermore " is not to be taken in a literal sense; the expression is often used in Hebrew in the sense of long enduring—*e.g.*, Ps. 21^{6}, 26^{26}, 61^{7}, Am. 1^{11}, Isa. 26^{4}, 47^{7}.

Religious Teaching

Although the psalm deals specifically with the subject of social conditions in ancient Israel, it contains an element of a pronouncedly religious character.   The conviction, which is implied all through, and definitely stated at its conclusion, of God's interest in the affairs of family life, witnesses to one of the most beautiful *traits* in Hebrew religion of all ages.   In ancient Israel the family was, in the first instance, kept together by community of worship ; whatever other purposes the Levirate law may have served, the religious motive lay at its base.   This is clearly emphasized in our psalm, and constitutes its abiding value.

PSALM 134

THIS is the last of the so-called Pilgrim-songs. The reason for its inclusion in the collection is clear. It is an introductory exhortation to the priests, sung by the High-priest, before the beginning of the service; the last verse is the response, sung by the priestly choir. It is a vigil service, held, as was usual, on the eve of one of the great festivals; this would obviously have been attended by the crowds of pilgrims, who had gathered from far and near to keep the festival. Hence the presence of the psalm in this collection. The metre is irregular.

A Song of Ascents.

1. ° Bless Yahweh,   all ye servants of Yahweh,
   That stand in the house-of-Yahweh   '° at nights °;
2. Lift up your hands in the sanctuary,   yea, bless Yahweh.
3. May Yahweh bless thee from Zion,   Maker of heaven and earth.

Text-critical Notes

1. Om. הִנֵּה, " Behold ", as inappropriate in this connexion; it may have been added from the opening word of the preceding psalm by mistake. בַּלֵּילוֹת two beats.

That the words of 1, 2 were chanted by the High-priest is probable, as Josephus specially mentions his presence in the temple at the festivals (*Bell. Jud.* v²³⁰). The words were addressed to the priests, *Bless Yahweh*, for it was only the priests who uttered blessings (cp. Deut. 10⁸, 21⁵); the *servants of Yahweh*, though often used in a wider sense, refer in this connexion specifically to the priests, not to the worshippers in general, for the reason given. The priests are those who *stand in the house-of-Yahweh*, the word " stand " is used here in the technical sense of minister (cp. Deut. 10⁸, Judg. 20²⁸, Ezek. 44¹⁵, 2 Chron. 29¹¹). Their doing so *at nights* tells us the occasions on which this psalm, if it can be so called, was sung. The most important of the Jewish feasts was *Sukkôth* (" Tabernacles "), known as " the " feast ; its outstanding character in post-exilic times comes out clearly in Zech. 14¹⁶⁻¹⁹, where it is said that in the Messianic times the nations " shall go up from year to year to worship the King, Yahweh of hosts, and to keep the feast of Tabernacles. . . ." It was on the eve of each of the seven (later nine) days, as is to be gathered from the Mishnah (*Sukkôth* ii. 4, 9), that a service was held at *nights*, hence the plural. That it is unlikely to have been the Passover feast may be gathered from the fact that the night preceding the first day of this feast (14. Nisan, = April) was the time for the searching of leaven in the houses, and removing it, a ceremony known as *Bĕdîqath ḥāmeṣ* (" Removal of leaven "); for details see Mishnah, *Pesachim* i. 1. If night services were held during this feast, the first night, the eve of the feast, would assuredly have been observed; but there is no mention of this as there is in the case of the feast of Tabernacles. The *lifting up of the hands* was the attitude in blessing (Lev. 9²² in reference to Aaron, Ecclus. 50²⁰ in reference to the High-priest Simon I). The priests are called upon to *bless Yahweh*, in response to which they reply: *May Yahweh bless thee from Zion*; the mention of Zion is to recall the solemn truth that it was here that the divine presence rested (cp. Ps. 9¹¹, 76²). Yahweh, though conceived of as dwelling in Zion, is nevertheless *Maker of heaven and earth* (cp. Ps. 115¹⁵), immanent everywhere, but specifically in his sanctuary.

Religious Teaching

We have here a very instructive indication of the preparation for divine service on the part of God's ordained ministers. They upon whom devolved the high privilege of blessing the worshippers, utter a preparatory mutual blessing upon each other, and are thus endowed with spiritual power. Strengthened by the knowledge of this power having been conferred on them, they can undertake their sacred duties in the sanctuary in the conviction that they are acting under divine guidance, and imparting to others the blessing of which they themselves have been recipients.

PSALM 135

ALTHOUGH the writer of this psalm makes considerable use of other psalms, and borrows from some other Biblical books, he has constructed it all into a logically arranged scheme of thought; the contention that " it has many glosses " is, we maintain, mistaken. The psalmist deliberately unites himself with those who had gone before him, by quoting their words, or by reiterating their thoughts; but he has composed a well-ordered and logical hymn of praise. Thus: it opens with an ascription of praise to Yahweh (1-4); this is appropriately followed by two outstanding reasons why praise should be offered to him—viz. he is the God of Nature (5-7), and he is the God of History (8-14); in contrast to this, the utter unreality of the gods of the nations, by whom the Jews were surrounded, is proclaimed (15-18); therefore a final exhortation to bless Yahweh fittingly closes the psalm. It will thus be seen that the psalm forms a well-thought-out unity.

That it was composed for use in the worship of the temple is obvious; and that it was sung antiphonally is also clear; but to assign the different parts to the respective singers is a somewhat precarious proceeding, especially as it is impossible to say for certain which verses were sung by a solo voice, and which by the temple choir, and whether the whole congregation took any part in it. The question is, however, not of great importance.

With one exception (v. 17) the text has been well preserved; only a few slight emendations are called for.

The date of the psalm would seem to be late post-exilic; this is suggested by the indebtedness to other psalms, especially Ps. 115, which is clearly late post-exilic; and also by the form of the relative.

The question of metre offers some difficulty; where it is 3 : 3 there will be general agreement; but in vv. 5-7, 15-17 we have marked the metre as two beats to a line; most authorities would not allow two beats only to a line, but would take four of these as forming a 4 : 4 metre; it will, however, be seen that in neither of these two sections do we get the requisite parallelism. The two-beat line is very effective when a change of subject is introduced, as in this psalm. An occasional three-beat line is, in any case, often found, whether the metre is otherwise 4 : 4 or not.

Hallelujah.

1. Praise the name of Yahweh,   praise, ye servants of Yahweh,
2. Who stand in the house of Yahweh,   in the courts of the house of our God.
3. Praise ° Yahweh °, for he is good,°   sing-praise to his name, for it is beautiful;
4. For Jacob hath Yah chosen for himself,   Israel for his peculiar-treasure.
5.   For I do know
        that greater is Yahweh,
        our Lord, than all gods.
6.   All that he willed
        hath Yahweh done,
        in heaven and earth,
        in the seas ° and in all ° deeps;
7.   He bringeth up mists
        from the ends of the earth,
   He maketh lightnings for the rain,   ° he bringeth forth ° wind from his treasuries.

8. He smote the firstborn of Egypt,   from man ° even unto ° beasts;
9. He sent signs and wonders °   against Pharaoh and all his servants;
10. He smote great nations,   and slew mighty kings:
11. Sihon, king of the Amorites,   and Og, the king of Bashan,
       And all the kingdoms of Canaan;
12. And he gave their land for an heritage,   an heritage for Israel, his people.
13. "Yahweh, thy name is everlasting,   Yahweh, thy remembrance is unending."
14. For Yahweh vindicateth his people,   and hath compassion on his servants,

15.   The idols of the nations
        are silver and gold,
        the work of the hands of men;
16.   mouths have they, but speak not,
        eyes have they, but see not,
17.   ears have they, but hear not,
        noses ° have they, but smell not °.
18. Like them are they that make them,   ° and all ° that trust in them.

19. House of Israel, bless Yahweh;   house of Aaron, bless Yahweh;
20. House of Levi, bless Yahweh;   fearers of Yahweh, bless Yahweh.
21. Blessed be Yahweh ° in Zion'°,   that dwelleth in Jerusalem °.

Text-critical Notes

3. Read יהוה "Yahweh" for יה "Yah", and delete, with S, יהוה at the end of the first half-line, for the sake of the rhythm. 6. Read וּבְכָל־ for וְכָל־, "and all". 7. Read מוֹצִיא for מוֹצֵא, but see GK 530. 8. Read, with some MSS, וְעַד for עַד, "unto". 9. Om. בְּתוֹכְכִי מִצְרָיִם, "in thy midst, Egypt"; an unnecessary insertion which breaks the rhythm. 17. Read, as in Ps. 115⁶, לָהֶם וְלֹא יְרִיחוּ, in place of the present Hebrew text: "neither is there any breath in their mouths"; the mouths have already been mentioned in the preceding verse. 18. Read וְכֹל for כֹּל, following some MSS. 21. Read בְּצִיּוֹן for מִצִּיּוֹן "from Zion". Om., with G, הַלְלוּ־יָהּ; it is the title of the following psalm.

1–4. Following, almost verbally, Ps. 113¹, our psalm opens with an exhortation, sung probably by the High-priest, to priests and people, to *praise Yahweh*; they are collectively designated *servants of Yahweh*; but the two bodies are differentiated : they who *stand in the house of Yahweh* are the ministering priests (see Ps. 134¹, and the note on that verse), while they who are gathered *in the courts of the house of our God*, are the body of the worshippers (cp. Ps. 92¹³, ¹⁴, 100³, ⁴ 116¹⁸, ¹⁹). *Praise* is due to him, for *he is good* (cp. Ps. 136¹), and *his name is beautiful* (cp. Ps. 52⁹, 54⁶), and also because he *hath chosen Jacob for himself, Israel for his peculiar treasure* (cp. Deut. 7⁶, ⁷, 14², 26¹⁸) ; the expression *peculiar treasure*, means lit. a "possession" (cp. Mal. 3¹⁷) ; in 1 Chron. 29³ it is used of a "treasure" of gold or silver. 5–7. As this section begins with the use of the first person, it may have been sung by one of the priests, but it is equally possible that it was sung by the temple choir, the " I " referring to each individual singer (and cp. " our Lord "), or even by the whole body of worshippers. That, however, is a minor matter ; of far greater importance is the recognition of Yahweh as the God of Nature. The belief among other nations in the creative power of their gods, and of their being lords of nature, is here repudiated ; *Yahweh is greater than all gods* ; all that happens in the world of Nature is according to his will (cp. Ps. 115³), whether in the skies above, *heaven*, or on the *earth*, or beneath the earth (cp. Ps. 77¹⁷⁻¹⁹). Though *mists*, brought up *from the ends of the earth*, as it seemed when rising in the distance, were soon dispersed in Palestine with the rising sun, they were believed to portend rain on account of their coolness ; moreover, according to an old-world belief, mists, dew, and rain were all connected with each other ; in the *Book of Enoch* we read that the clouds of rain and the clouds of dew " and the clouds of the mist are connected, and the one gives to the other " (60²⁰, cp. 41⁴). In Palestine rain is often accompanied by storm : *he maketh lightnings for the rain*. Finally, the *wind* which *he bringeth forth from his treasuries*; here again we are reminded of the *Book of Enoch* 18¹, where " the treasuries of all the winds " are spoken of. With the verse before us, 7, cp. also Prov. 25¹⁴, Jer. 10¹³, 51¹⁶.

8-14. After having sung the praise of Yahweh as the God of Nature, wherein his power has been shown forth, the psalmist turns to the more restricted area of divine activity, and records how the history of Israel, in its most significant period—the formation of the nation and its settlement in Canaan—was effected by Yahweh as the God of History. With the details of this section it is not necessary to deal ; it is largely based on Ps. 78[43, 51, 55], and more especially on Ps. 136[17-22], with which there are verbal similarities. 13 is quoted from Exod. 3[15], and 14 from Deut. 32[36], cp. Ps. 90[13]. In 15-18 the psalmist reverts in fuller detail to what he has said about the gods of the nations in 5 ; this comes in appropriately here, for he wishes to contrast with the omnipotence of Yahweh the empty uselessness of all so-called gods. This denunciation against idols may well have had a greater significance than appears at first in view of the fact that Hellenism had a great fascination for many Jews ; the words of Hecatæus of Abdera, who lived at the end of the fourth century B.C. are of ominous import : " Under the later rule of the Persians, and of the Macedonians, who overthrew the empire of the former, many of the traditional customs of the Jews were altered owing to their intercourse with aliens ".[1]   This section is almost verbally the same as Ps. 115[4-6, 8].

The final verses, 19-21, are based on Ps. 115[9-11] (see the notes there). The last verse (cp. Ps. 128[5], 132[13, 14]) is held by some commentators to be a later addition, with insufficient reason. The " Hallelujah " at the end is, as the Septuagint shows, the title of the following psalm.

Religious Teaching

The prophetical teaching concerning Yahweh as the God of Nature, and as the God of History, which is so marked an element in this psalm, has been referred to in the exegetical notes. Another matter concerning the doctrine of God is the monotheistic belief implied. The words : " Greater is Yahweh our Lord than all gods ", would seem to imply a belief in other gods, however inferior to the one God ; but these words must be read in the light of what is said in vv. 15-18 ; for the idols there spoken of are identical with gods, and they are described as non-existent. It may therefore be said that monotheistic belief, if not directly stated, is implied. Such pure monotheism is very rare in the psalms. It occurs in Ps. 115[3-7], on which our psalm is based, and in Ps. 86[9, 10] ; but elsewhere the existence of other gods is taken for granted. While, of course, Yahweh is conceived of as of a wholly different nature from any other god, yet, as a rule, the gods of the nations are not thought of as non-existent, as in this psalm.

[1] Quoted by Reinach, *Textes d'auteurs Grecs et Romains relatifs au Judaisme*, p. 20 (1895).

PSALM 136

As already pointed out (see p. 100), this psalm is known as the " Great Hallel " (*Hallel hā-Gadôl*) in the Talmud and other Rabbinical writings, reflecting, doubtless, earlier usage. Like Ps. 135, it contains many quotations from other psalms. Its form is unique in the Psalter; the first half of each verse was sung either by one of the priests, or perhaps by the Levitical choir; while the second half, taken from 2 Chron. $7^{3,6}$, was sung by the whole body of the worshippers. It will be noticed that in reading the first half of the verses alone we have a self-contained and independent psalm, the even flow of which is often interrupted by the refrain; this suggests that the refrain was not an original part of the psalm, especially as it occurs sometimes in a most inappropriate context (*vv.* 10, 15, 17–20). It was added for liturgical purposes.

The first three verses are an exhortation to give thanks to Yahweh, the reasons for which are then enumerated : for his creative works, for his having delivered his people from their Egyptian oppressors, for the settlement of the people in Canaan, for deliverance from other oppressors ; and, finally, for the gift of food ; this last seems to come in somewhat strangely after what has preceded it ; but it is probably of great significance, for there is reason for believing that this psalm was sung at the New Year festival.

The psalm in its present form is doubtless late post-exilic in date, but it is possible that in its origin it belongs to far earlier times. It cannot be denied that the historic sections (*vv.* 10–15, 16–22, 23 and 24) are not altogether appropriate after the commemoration of the creative acts of Yahweh (*vv.* 1–9) ; we suggest, therefore, the possibility that the whole of the historical reminiscences were added later to the psalm.

That both the sun and the moon were regarded as fertility deities, and were worshipped in ancient Israel, is plainly intimated in the Old Testament ; in later days their functions were ascribed to Yahweh, thanks to the teaching of the prophets. If, now, it be granted, for the sake of argument, that the historical sections of our psalm were later additions, *vv.* 25, 26 would come immediately after the mention of the creative acts of Yahweh : ". . . who made great lights, The sun to rule by day, The moon to rule by night ; he giveth food to all flesh, Give thanks to the God of Heaven ". In this case the appropriateness of the mention of food becomes evident, and the incongruity disappears. We suggest, therefore, that this psalm was one of those sung at the New Year festival. It has, according to ancient custom, always been, in the Jewish Church, one of the proper psalms for the feast of Passover, the spring festival ; we should have expected it to have been one of the special psalms for the feast of Tabernacles (*Sukkôth*), in the autumn, when the New Year began ; but with the Exile, the Jews, following Babylonian usage, celebrated the New Year Festival both in the spring and in the autumn. With the reason of this double celebration we are not concerned here ; see Hooke, in *Myth and Ritual*, pp. 46 f., and the same writer's *The Origins of Early Semitic Ritual* (Schweich Lectures), pp. 51 ff. (1935).

The metre is 3 : 2, with the exception *vv.* 12, 15.

Hallelujah.

1. Give thanks to Yahweh, for he is good, — for his mercy endureth for ever,
2. Give thanks to the God of gods, — for his mercy endureth for ever,
3. Give thanks to the Lord of lords, — for his mercy endureth for ever,
4. Who alone doeth ° wonder-works, — for his mercy endureth for ever,
5. Who made the heavens with wisdom, — for his mercy endureth for ever,
6. Who spread forth the earth on the waters, — for his mercy endureth for ever,
7. Who made great lights, — for his mercy endureth for ever,
8. The sun to rule by day, — for his mercy endureth for ever,
9. The moon ° to rule ° by night, — for his mercy endureth for ever,
10. Who smote Egypt in their firstborn, — for his mercy endureth for ever,
11. And brought out Israel from their midst, — for his mercy endureth for ever,
12. With mighty hand and outstretched arm, — for his mercy endureth for ever,
13. Who cut Yam-sûph in twain, — for his mercy endureth for ever,
14. And made Israel to pass through the midst of it, — for his mercy endureth for ever,
15. And cast Pharaoh and his host into Yam-sûph, — for his mercy endureth for ever,
16. Who led his people into the wilderness, — for his mercy endureth for ever,
17. Who smote great ° nations °, — for his mercy endureth for ever,
18. And slew famous kings, — for his mercy endureth for ever,
19. Sihon, king of the Amorites, — for his mercy endureth for ever,
20. And Og, the king of Bashan, — for his mercy endureth for ever,
21. And gave their land for an heritage, — for his mercy endureth for ever,
22. An heritage to Israel, his servant ; — for his mercy endureth for ever,
23. Who in our abasement remembered us, — for his mercy endureth for ever,
24. And rescued us from our oppressors, — for his mercy endureth for ever
25. He giveth food to all flesh. — for his mercy endureth for ever,
26. Give thanks to the God of heaven, — for his mercy endureth for ever.

Text-critical Notes

Title: add הַלְלוּ־יָהּ, "Hallelujah", from the end of the preceding psalm. 4. Om. גְּדֹלוֹת "great", cp. Ps. 72¹⁸. 9. Om. וְכוֹכָבִים for the rhythm's sake ; and read, following the Versions, לְמֶמְשָׁלָה for לְמֶמְשְׁלוֹת, plur. 17. Read, with Gressmann and Gunkel, לְאֻמִּים for מְלָכִים, "kings", which comes in the following verse.

1–3. The opening word of each of these verses, *Hôdū* ("Give thanks"), is the same as in Pss. 105–107, 118, hence they are called "*Hôdū*-psalms" in Rabbinical writings. We have rendered the refrain in its familiar English form, but in its Hebrew form there is no verb, it is simply : "for his mercy (is) for ever" ; and *ḥesed* ("mercy"), as we have remarked elsewhere, connotes more than mercy : it means

" love " in its varied forms.   For the expressions *God of gods, Lord of lords*, cp. Deut. 10¹⁷.

4–9. Thé first of the reasons for which praise is to be given to Yahweh is because of the *wonder-works* of creation ; *he made the heavens with wisdom*, lit. " understanding " or " discernment " (cp. Jer. 10¹²), presumably in reference to the divine forethought that man would need *the sun* and *the moon* (cp. Gen. 1¹⁴⁻¹⁷).   Another quaint idea is expressed in the words *who spread forth the earth on the waters* ; this is a somewhat different conception of the creation of the earth from that of Gen. 1⁹, but is in accordance with Babylonian stories of Creation.[1] 10–15. The psalmist then gives a further reason for thankfulness to Yahweh by recalling the circumstances connected with the deliverance from Egypt ; the smiting of the *firstborn in Egypt* (cp. Ps. 78⁵¹, 135⁸) was what actually induced the Pharaoh to release the Israelites (Exod. 12²⁹⁻³³), and was ascribed directly to Yahweh with his *mighty hand and outstretched arm* ; the phrase is taken from Deut. 4³⁴, Jer. 32²¹. In speaking of the dividing of the *Yam-sûph*, " the sea of reeds " (usually, but erroneously, rendered the Red Sea, it was the eastern arm of the Red Sea, now known as the Aelanitic gulf), the psalmist uses a curious, but expressive, term never elsewhere used in this connexion ; it is lit. " he cut into cuttings ", or " portions " ; in Gen. 15¹⁷ the noun is used of the two halves of a sacrificed animal between which the two parties of a covenant passed. This covenant-rite, of great antiquity, must have been in the mind of the psalmist.   In 16–22, with which cp. Ps. 78⁵²⁻⁵⁵, 135¹⁰⁻²¹, yet further causes for thankfulness are enumerated ; the first is that Yahweh led his people into the wilderness ; this was not always thought of as something to be thankful for (cp. Deut. 32¹⁰, Jer. 2⁶, Hos. 13⁵) ; then the overthrow of Canaanite kings ; and, thirdly, the giving of the *land* of Canaan for *an heritage to Israel* (cp. Am. 2¹⁰).   Once more, in 23, 24 the psalmist recalls periods of oppression through which his people had passed, thinking of the Philistines, Aramæans, Assyrians, and perhaps chiefly of the Exile, out of all of which Yahweh had delivered them ; for all these mercies gratitude to Yahweh is called for.   And, lastly, in 25, 26, the psalmist mentions as a cause for thankfulness the fact that Yahweh *giveth food to all flesh* (cp. Ps. 104²⁷, ²⁸, 145¹⁵, ¹⁶) therefore : *Give thanks to the God of Heaven* ; see further on this the introductory section.   The expression " the God of Heaven " does not occur in the older literature ; it is used several times in the book of *Ezra* and also in that of *Daniel* ; its origin is possibly Persian, and if so, it is in itself ancient.

---

[1] See Gunkel's translation in *Schöpfung und Chaos* . . ., p. 420 (1895).

Religious Teaching

This centres in two aspects of the doctrine of God : his creative acts, and his guidance of the early history of Israel to the time of their becoming a nation. Of particular importance is the stress laid on the due recognition of divine mercies uttered in the refrain " for his mercy endureth for ever " ; the expression of national gratitude for divine mercies in the past, which have led to those of the present, is an element in various other psalms too. This has always been characteristic of Jewish worship. Thus, while the personal relationship to God is never lost sight of, the divine solicitude for the nation as a whole is also duly recognized. That is an element in worship which is of profound significance.

PSALM 137

THIS psalm is, in character, unique in the Psalter. Short as it is, it presents some points of difficulty concerning which there are, not without reason, differences of opinion among commentators. The difficulties will be dealt with in the exegetical notes. Here it will suffice to express the belief that the psalm was written by one of the exiles who returned from Babylon in 538 B.C., and that he records one of his experiences while in exile. As Jerusalem was the most obvious objective for the returned exiles, it would be in this city that the psalmist wrote his psalm, though some commentators think that vv. 5, 6 imply that the writer was not in Jerusalem ; the words against Edom suggest the psalmist's presence at any rate in Palestine, where he would be more forcibly reminded of the hated people, rather than somewhere in the Dispersion.

As an ancient folk-song this psalm was in later days incorporated in the great national collection ; but that it was ever used liturgically in the worship of the temple may well be doubted. It is not used in the worship of the Synagogue. On the metre cp. what has been said regarding that of Ps. 135.

1.   By the waters of Babylon,
           There we sat and wept,
           When we remembered Zion.
2.   On the willows in the midst thereof
           We hanged up our harps,
3.   For there our captors asked of us
           Words of song, ʼ
           ° And our plunderers °, mirth :
           " Sing to us
           ° Of the songs ° of Zion."
4. How should we sing Yahweh-songs   in a foreign land ?
5. If I forget thee, Jerusalem,   may my right-hand ° fail ° (me) ;

6. May my tongue cleave to my palate,   if I remember thee not,
   If I exalt not Jerusalem   above my greatest joy.
7.   Remember, Yahweh,
                     the sons of Edom—
                     the day of Jerusalem !
      Who said : " Rase ° it, rase it to its very foundation."
8. O   daughter   of   Babylon,   ° thou
      devastater °,   blessed he that requiteth thee,°
9. Blessed he that seizeth, and dasheth   thy little ones against the rock !

Text-critical Notes

Title : G has " David's ". 3. Read, cp. GS and especially the Targum, וְשׁוֹלְלֵינוּ
for וְתוֹלָלֵינוּ, lit. " and that cause us to howl ". Read, GV, מְשִׁירֵי for מָשִׁיר,
sing. 5. Read, with Cheyne and Gunkel, תִּבְחַשׁ (cp. Job 3¹⁷, Hos. 9²,
Hab. 3¹⁷) for תִּשְׁכַּח, " may . . . forget ". 7. For the imperat. form עָרוּ see GK
75cc. 8. Read הַשְּׁדוּדָה for הַשְּׁדוּדָה, " the devastated, see exeg. note. Om.
אֶת־גְּמוּלֵךְ שֶׁגָּמַלְתְּ לָנוּ, " thy dealing which thou didst deal to us ".

1. The psalmist begins abruptly by placing the *mise en scène* before
his readers without any words of introduction. He has, according to
our interpretation of the psalm, just returned with his fellow-exiles
from Babylon to Jerusalem. In the decree of Cyrus permitting the
return of the Jews, as recorded in Ezra 1²⁻⁴, it is said : ". . . Whosoever there is among you of all his people, his God be with him, and let
him go up to Jerusalem, which is in Judah, and build the house of
Yahweh, the God of Israel ; he is God, which is in Jerusalem. . . ."
The fourfold mention of Jerusalem in the short *résumé* of the decree
(see also 2¹) shows that Palestine, and primarily Jerusalem, was what the
exiles yearned for. Thither, therefore, our psalmist came, and
described to his compatriots who had not been in exile something of his
experiences in Babylon. On one occasion he had, with some of his
fellow-exiles, been resting *by the waters of Babylon* ; and as they thought
of their far-away home, and of *Zion*, the national centre of worship,
which it had never yet been their lot to behold, they were filled with
grief, *and wept*. In his description of Babylon, Herodotus tells us,
among other things, that there was " a moat, deep, wide, and full of
water, which runs entirely round it. . . . And the city consists of two
divisions, for a river, called the Euphrates, separates it in the middle ;
this river is broad, deep, and rapid. The wall on either bank has an
elbow carried down to the river." He tells us, further, that all the
streets lead to the river, and that at the end of each street " a little gate
is formed in the wall along the river-side . . . they are all made of
brass, and lead down to the edge of the river ". He also speaks of a
landing-place and seats to rest on, on which those who go there sit down
and rest themselves (1¹⁷⁸⁻¹⁸¹). These few details fully explain the
allusion to *the waters of Babylon* in our psalm.

2, 3. Along the banks of the river running through Babylon willows
grew (see the interesting illustration of this in Meissner's *Babylonien und*

Assyrien i. No. 108 [1924]; cp. also Isa. 44⁴, " willows by the water-courses "); to these the psalmist alludes; he and a few of his fellow-exiles had, it would seem, been singing some of the sacred songs their fathers in exile had taught them, with the accompaniment of those harps which the first exiles had brought with them. But while they were singing they saw some of their *captors* approaching; at once they ceased their singing, and hung their harps on the willows to show that they had no intention of singing in the presence of their hated enemies. There-upon these Babylonians, perhaps out of mere curiosity, asked them to sing *words of song* (for the expression see the title of Ps. 18); it never entered their minds that the exiles had been singing sacred songs; the harps (the *kinnor*) were the small kind, distinct from the larger *nebel* (cp. Ps. 33², 144⁹), and were used for accompanying secular, as well as sacred, songs (cp. Isa. 5¹²); so these *plunderers* (in reference to the plundering of Jerusalem by the Babylonian army, 2 Kgs. 25⁸⁻¹⁰) thought that the exiles had been singing songs of *mirth*, and asked the exiles to continue their singing: *Sing to us (some) of the songs of Zion*; they little realized what those *songs of Zion* really were. 4, 6. The indignation of our psalmist can be readily understood; as though the sacred songs sung in honour of Yahweh could be sung before Gentiles *in a foreign land*! To do this would be to forget the sanctity of Jeru-salem, the dwelling-place of Yahweh; and the psalmist threatens him-self with a curse: *If I forget thee, Jerusalem, may my right-hand fail (me)*; this emendation of the text (" fail " for " forget ", the words are very similar in Hebrew, see critical note) is justified, for the Hebrew verb for " forget " is never used in such an incongruous connexion, whereas the " failing " of the hand to do its part in using the harp, which accompanied the sacred song, would be to mark the worshipper as incapable of fulfilling his proper part in worship—*i.e.*, as failing in his duty to God; it was as bad, for it involved the same incapacity for true worship—as if his *tongue* were to *cleave to his palate* so that he could not utter words of praise and thanksgiving. Such a curse the psalmist calls down upon himself if he should *remember not* the city of his God, if he should not *exalt Jerusalem above his greatest joy*. 7, 9. The language is exaggerative, and reveals the passionate character of the psalmist; he was intensely human; and this is further brought out by the frank and unabashed way in which, immediately after his expression of religious fervour, the spirit of bitter revenge asserts itself. The one excuse is that he regards the enemies of his people as being also the enemies of his God. The sudden turn of thought from the surround-ings he was envisaging to that of the enemy nearer home (Edom) can be explained only by remembering that he was now for the first time in Palestine, in Jerusalem. He had been taught how, when Jerusalem had been surrounded by the Babylonian army, Edom, the near neighbours of his people, their " brother " (Am. 1¹¹) had sided with the enemies of Judah ; " in that day when thou wast present (lit. when thou didst stand in front), in the day that strangers carried away his substance, and foreigners entered his gates, and cast lots upon Jerusalem, even thou wast as one of them " ; thus does the prophet Obadiah (*v.* 11) speak of the action of the Edomites at that time. And the psalmist, in bitter wrath, cries : *Remember, Yahweh, the sons of Edom—the day of Jerusalem*—*i.e.*, the day of visitation, cp. Isa. 9⁴, Jer. 50²⁷⁻³¹, *who said, Rase it, rase it, to its very foundation.* Then he reverts to his main subject ; *O daughter of Babylon*, he says, lit. " O daughter Babylon ", addressing the city as a young woman (similarly in Isa. 47¹ and the " daughter Zion " in Isa. 1⁸), *the devastater* ; the emendation is needed, for the corrupt Hebrew text, " the devastated ", would imply that Babylon had already fallen ; whereas the verbs are all in the future tense ; and, in any case, Babylon was not devastated when conquered by Cyrus ; both the " Nabonidus Chronicle " and the " Cyrus Cylinder " show that he treated the city with great consideration. When the psalmist describes Babylon as *thou devastater*, he is referring to the devastation of Jerusalem in 586 B.C. He speaks of him *that requiteth thee* as *blessed* ; the word, which is used in the sense of " happy " or " fortunate ", has here, doubtless, as often elsewhere, a religious meaning, " blessed " of Yahweh ; that the term should be used in reference to one who would take vengeance on the enemy of God's people, and therefore of God himself, is comprehensible ; but that it should be applied also to one who would *seize* the *little children* and *dash* them *against the rock*, is unpardonable ; true, such cruelty was common enough (2 Kgs. 8¹², Isa. 13¹⁶, Hos. 13¹⁶ (14¹), Nah. 3¹⁰) in those days ; but the perpetrators are never called " blessed ". The psalmist here gives way to human passion, which is to be deplored ; that is all that can be said.

Religious Teaching

The clash of emotions expressed in this psalm reveal human nature at its best and at its worst. Sorrow at the thought of being hindered from singing the praises of God in the sanctuary where his presence rested was the outcome of deep devotion to him, and reveals a heart imbued with all that is best. In contrast to this there is the outrage on religion which calls down a blessing on the atrocious wretch who should dash innocent little children against the rock because they happened to be born in Babylon. While then, on the one hand, the religious teaching in the psalm sets forth a spirit of true devotion, this is marred, on the other hand, by approval of action which is a disgrace to human nature. Let it, however, be remembered that though the *lex talionis* was a

recognized law, it was never intended to be carried out to the extent
exhibited in this psalm. The writer was a man of passionate feelings,
and among even the best of those with a temperament like that, evil
will at times preponderate. The dominant note, however, of the psalm
is a truly religious one, and witnesses to the loyalty of those who, in the
land of their captivity, were surrounded by subtle temptations, but who
withstood them in the strength of that loyalty.

PSALM 138

OUR interpretation of this psalm differs from that of other commentators, but we hope that the exegetical notes will show that there is
some justification for the view here presented. That there should be
nearly a dozen points of contact, either of thought or word, between
this short psalm and the writings of Deutero-Isaiah (Isa. 40–55), in
which the conditions of the times depicted would seem to be identical, is
an argument in favour of the view here advocated that the psalmist
wrote during the last months of the Exile. The ascription of the psalm
to Zechariah in the title of two important Septuagint texts may reflect a
tradition which is not so far from the truth as is often supposed ; and
its close proximity to such a psalm as the preceding may have some
significance. Not that we mean to imply that the prophet Zechariah
was the author of the psalm ; but the tradition which connects his name
with it presupposes a date near that to which we assign it.

There is some uncertainty about the metre, but for the most part it is
3 : 3.

David's.

1. ° Yahweh °, I give thanks to thee with
   all my heart,   before the gods do I sing praise to thee.
2. I worship toward thy holy temple,   and give thanks to thy name for thy
                                               love,°
              For thou hast magnified ° thy name over all °.
3. In the day that I called thou didst
   answer me,   ° didst increase ° strength in my soul.
4. All the kings of the earth, may they   for they have heard the words of thy
   confess to thee,   mouth,
5. ° May they meditate ° upon the ways of
   Yahweh,   for great is the glory of Yahweh ;
6.   Exalted is Yahweh,
             yet he considereth the lowly,
             But the haughty he knoweth from afar.
     7.   Thou stretchest forth thine hand,
           thy right-hand doth save me.
Though I walk in the midst of trouble,   thou preservest me against the wrath of
                                             mine enemies,
8.   Yahweh will accomplish it for me,
             Yahweh, thy love is everlasting,
             Forsake not ° the work of ° thine hands.

NN

PSALM 138

Text-critical Notes

Title : G (Cod. A) adds ζακαριου. 1. Add, with some Hebr. MSS and the Versions, יְהוָֹה "Yahweh". 2. Om. עַל־אֲמָתֶךָ "and for thy word", for the rhythm's sake. Read שְׁמֶךָ עַל־כָּל for עַל־כָּל־שִׁמְךָ "over all thy name", and om. אִמְרָתֶךָ. 3. Read וַתַּרְבֵּה for תַּרְהִבֵנִי, " thou didst make me wide". 5. Read (*Oxf. Hebr. Lex.*) יָשִׁירוּ for יָשִׁירוּ, " may they sing ", cp. Ps. 105². Read, with many Hebr. MSS מַעֲשֵׂה for מַעֲשֵׂי " the works of ".

1. In the depths of his gratitude the psalmist not only *gives thanks to Yahweh with all* his *heart,* but he feels that he must also *praise* him in the presence of other *gods.* We have here, thus, the frank recognition of the existence of other gods ; and the psalmist, in order to show his belief in the superiority of Yahweh, praises him *before them.* This raises the questions as to what gods the psalmist was referring, and as to how he came to be in their presence, so that he might, as it were, mock them by praising Yahweh before them. Preliminary to these questions there is, however, another : what was this dire trouble from which the psalmist thanks God that he has been delivered, and can yet say : *Though I walk in the midst of trouble, thou preservest me against the wrath of mine enemies ?* How can he give thanks for deliverance while still surrounded by danger ? These questions, together with one or two others which arise on reading through the psalm, are, we maintain, easily answered when once it is realized when and where the psalm was written.

The psalmist was living in the year 538 B.C., in Babylon, among the Jewish exiles there ; for some of these exiles life was, no doubt, bearable ; but not for the mass ; our psalmist was among those of whom the great prophet of the Exile spoke : " They are all of them snared in holes, and they are hid in prison houses ; they are for a prey, and none delivereth ; for a spoil, and none saith, Restore " (Isa. 42²²). What must have been the feelings of these unhappy captives when they heard from the mouth of that self-same prophet the words spoken in the name of Yahweh, their God : " I have raised up one from the north, and he is come ; from the rising of the sun one that calleth upon my name ; and he shall come upon the rulers as upon mortar, and as the potter treadeth clay " ? But more ; of Cyrus, this conqueror of their oppressors, the prophet, speaking again in the name of Yahweh, says : " He is my shepherd, and shall perform all my pleasure ; even saying of Jerusalem, She shall be built ; and of the temple, Thy foundation shall be laid " (Isa. 44²⁸). Then, very soon after, came the conqueror's decree concerning the Jewish captives : " All the kingdoms of the earth hath Yahweh, the God of Heaven, given me ; and he hath charged me to build him an house in Jerusalem, which is in Judah. Whosoever there is among you of all his people, Yahweh his God be

with him, and let him go up to Jerusalem, which is in Judah, and build
the house of Yahweh, the God of Israel; he is God, which is in
Jerusalem " (2 Chron. 36²², ²³, Ezra 1², ³). Truly there was every
reason for the inspired psalmist among the captive exiles to *give thanks
to Yahweh with all his heart.* He had been living among the Babylonians
and seen them worshipping their gods; many among his fellow-exiles
worshipped them too (Isa. 42¹⁷); but he was not one of them; nevertheless, he believed that they really existed—naturally enough, when he
saw the powerful and cultured Babylonians offering them their worship.
So, to give vent to his feelings of gratitude to Yahweh for deliverance
now assured, he goes into one of the temples, and *before the gods* there
gives praise to Yahweh, witnessing to his belief that his God was far
superior to them.

2. Then the psalmist speaks of his accustomed worship; this, in
accordance with the custom of the devout Jew when distant from his
own land, is offered while looking in the direction of the temple,[1]
toward thy holy temple (cp. 1 Kgs. 8⁴⁸, Dan. 6⁹, Tob. 3¹¹, ¹², Jer. Talm.
Berakhoth iv. 5, has " towards the holy land "); *he giveth thanks* for
the *love* which Yahweh has shown forth to his people, by *magnifying* his
name, i.e., showing his supreme power, *over all* (cp. the words in the
decree of Cyrus : " All the kingdoms of the earth hath Yahweh, the
God of heaven, given me ").

3. That the exiles had constantly offered up prayers for deliverance
from their captivity needs no insisting on (cp. Isa. 49⁸); many of them
must have been like our psalmist who prayed in faith, and whose faith,
in answer to prayer was strengthened : *In the day that I called thou didst
answer me, didst increase strength in my soul*; we are reminded of Isa.
40²⁹ : " He giveth power to the faint; and to him that hath no might he
increaseth strength ", words which, as Duhm rightly insists, are to be
understood in a spiritual sense (*Das Buch Jesaia,* in loc).

4, 5. From thoughts of the past the psalmist returns to the present;
deliverance has come because Yahweh of his mercy had raised up Cyrus,
his anointed, to subdue nations and loose the loins of kings—*i.e.,* their
cincture to which their weapons were attached (Isa. 45¹); in his deep
gratitude to Yahweh he expresses the devout wish that *all* these *kings
of the earth may confess to him,* to his honour and glory. In saying that
they have heard the words of thy mouth, he is referring to the words in
the Cyrus decree, where it is said that Yahweh " hath charged me to
build an house in Jerusalem " (2 Chron. 36²³). It will, of course, be
understood that this form of the decree is to some extent modified in
accordance with Jewish ideas. *May they meditate upon the ways of*

[1] For the proof that the temple, though in a dilapidated condition, was used for
worship during the whole of the exilic period, see Oesterley and Robinson, *A History
of Israel,* ii. 91–94 (1934).

Yahweh, continues the psalmist, thinking perhaps of the prophet's words, speaking in the name of Yahweh, " For my thoughts are not your thoughts, neither are your ways my ways, saith Yahweh. For as the heavens are higher than the earth, so are my ways higher than your ways, and my thoughts than your thoughts " (Isa. 55[8, 9]). In envisaging the conversion of the Gentile kings to belief in Yahweh, the psalmist may well have been influenced by the prophet's words : " Kings shall see and arise ; princes, and they shall worship ; because of Yahweh that is faithful, even the Holy One of Israel, who hath chosen thee " (Isa. 49[7]). *Exalted* as *Yahweh is*, he takes due note of *the lowly* ; as this is said in close connexion with the *kings of the earth*, it is not fanciful to see again an allusion to the great exilic prophet, who spoke of the lowliness of kings in ministering to and honouring the people of Yahweh : " And kings shall be thy nursing fathers, and their queens thy nursing mothers ; they shall bow down to thee with their faces to the earth, and lick the dust of thy feet " (Isa. 49[23]). 7, 8. As already pointed out, we hold that this psalm was written by one of the exiles after the decree of Cyrus had gone forth ; the prospect of going to Jerusalem was what called forth the psalmist's thanksgiving. But for the moment the people were still captives. The bitterness of the defeated Babylonians can easily be conceived ; that they should vent their wrath on the despised Jewish captives was natural enough ; from what the prophet says in words addressed to Babylon it is clear that the Jews had often been maltreated : " Thou didst show them no mercy ; upon the aged hast thou very heavily laid thy yoke " (Isa. 47[6]). And now the captives were to go free, while the Babylonians were the slaves of their Persian conqueror ; human nature being what it is, it cannot cause surprise that the Babylonians seized their last opportunity of showing their contempt for the Jews in drastic ways. And the psalmist was one of the victims of their rancour ; but he knows that God will protect him : *though I walk in the midst of trouble, thou preservest me against the wrath of mine enemies . . .* ; he knows that Yahweh's purpose will be *accomplished* both for himself and for his fellow-exiles, for *Yahweh's love (hesed) is everlasting*, he will *not forsake*, leave undone, the great *work* of release from captivity to which he has put *his hands*. Once more we see how our psalmist was influenced both in thought and word by his great contemporary : " Thus saith Yahweh, the Holy One of Israel, and his Maker : Ask of me the things that are to come ; concerning my sons, and concerning the work of my hands, command ye me . . . I have raised him up (*i.e.*, Cyrus) in righteousness, and I will make straight all his ways ; he shall build my city, and he shall let my exiles go free, not for price nor reward, saith Yahweh of hosts " (Isa. 45[11–13]). This was *the work of thine hands* ; we can understand why many of the MSS. have " works " !

The religious teaching of this psalm has been sufficiently indicated in the exegetical notes.

PSALM 139

FOR the conceptions regarding the Divine Nature, the omniscience, and the omnipresence of God, this psalm stands out as the greatest gem in the Psalter. Parallels to it have been thought to exist in Babylonian and other sacred writings of the past; but in the religious literature of the ancient world it is unique. To point to the Vedic hymn (Atharvaveda iv. 16) as a parallel is beside the mark (see Hommel in *ZAW* 1929, pp. 112 f., Barnes, *The Psalms*, ii. 635 [1931]); the translation of Max Müller, which is followed by these scholars, makes the parallelisms appear much closer than is really the case, as may be seen by reading the more literal version of Geldner (see Bertholet's *Religionsgeschichtliches Lesebuch*, pp. 109 f. [1908]).

As the subject-matter of the psalm and the mode of its treatment from beginning to end would lead one to suppose, it is a *unity*; it presents truths, long pondered over, which a man of deep religious instincts had come to recognize as indubitable. The psalm is free from dogmatism and the use of theological technical terms, but the writer, with his profound religious insight, is so convinced of the truth of his statements, that he treats them as axiomatic. Doubts as to unity of authorship may be disregarded.

There are few psalms which present so many exegetical difficulties, and we frankly confess our doubts as to whether, in some cases, these have been satisfactorily solved. The difficulties arise partly from textual uncertainties, and partly from linguistic problems, for rare words and Aramaisms abound, the precise meaning of which admits of more than one opinion. Differences of interpretation are, therefore, inevitable. But as to the general sense of the psalm there can be no two opinions.

Both the teaching of the psalm and its linguistic form mark it as of late date; it must belong to the Greek period.

Owing to the state of the text, the rhythmic measure is by no means always certain; upon the whole, however, it would seem to be 3 : 3.

For the Precentor: David's. A Psalm.

1.   Yahweh, thou searchest me out, and knowest me;
2. ° Thou ° knowest my downsitting and   thou discernest ° my thoughts ° from
   mine uprising,   afar;
3. My going and my resting thou dost
   sift,   art familiar with all my ways;
4. For no word is there on my tongue,   lo, Yahweh, thou knowest it altogether;

5. Behind and before thou dost encircle me,
6. Too wonderful for me is °that° knowledge,
7. Whither should I go from thy spirit,
8. If I ascended to heaven—thou art there,
9. If I took the wings of the dawn,
10. Even there would thy hand ° rest upon me °,
11. If I said °, " Surely darkness ° will cover me °,
12. But darkness would not darken from thee,
13. For thou didst form my reins,

14. I thank thee, for ° thou art awe-ful,°

and layest thine hand upon me.
too high, I cannot (attain) unto it.
whither should I flee from thy presence ?
if I ° descended ° to Sheol, lo, thou art there,
or abode in the farthest sea,
and thy right-hand take hold of me ;
and night be ° a veil ° about me ",
and night like day would give light ! °
didst knit me together in my mother's womb ;
° thou art wonderful °,—wonderful are thy works ;

And my soul knoweth it right well.

15. Not hidden was my frame from thee skilfully-wrought in the depths of the earth,
16. ° My doings ° did thine eyes behold, ° All my days were numbered °,
17. How inscrutable to me are thy thoughts,
18. Would I count them, they would out-number the sand,
19. O God, that thou wouldest slay the wicked,
20. That speak of thee in wickedness,
21. Do I not hate them that hate thee °,
22. With utter hatred do I hate them,
23.

at the time I was fashioned in secret ;
in thy book ° my ways ° are inscribed :
° and not one was overlooked.°

O God, how great is their number ;
° did I finish °, ° I should still be counting °.
that the bloodthirsty men ° might depart °,
° they take ° ° thy name ° in vain ;
and loathe them ° that loathe thee ? °
as enemies are they to me.

Search me, O God,
And know my heart,
Try me, and know my thoughts,

24. And see if ° a grievous ° word ° be in me,

and lead me in the way of ° peace °.

Text-critical Notes

2. Om. אַתָּה, emphatic " thou ". Read לְרֵעִי for לְרֵעִי, " my thought ", cp. *v.* 17. 6. Read with S, הַדָּעַת for דַּעַת. 8. Read, GS, וְאַצִּיעָה for יָא. 10. Read תַּנְחֵנִי for תַּנְחֵנִי " would lead me ", as a better parallel to " take hold of ". 11. Read וָאֹמַר for וָאֹמַר. Read, with most modern commentators, יְשׂוּפֵנִי(=)יְסַכֵּנִי from (סכך for יְשׁוּפֵנִי " will crush me ". Read, with Wutz, אֵיד for אוֹר, " light ". 12. Om. כַּחֲשֵׁיכָה כָּאוֹרָה, " like darkness like light ", which overloads the line, and is probably a marginal comment (Aramaic) which has got into the text. 14. Read נוֹרָאֹת for נוֹרָאֹות, " fearful things ". Read נִפְלֵית for נִפְלֵיתִי, " I am wonderful ". 16. Read, with Gunkel, גְּמֻלִי for גָּלְמִי " mine embryo ". Read, with Wutz, כֻּלְמִי for כֻּלָּם, " all of them ". Read, with Wutz, יֻרְצוּ (aram. רצה) for כְּלֵימֵי for יֻצָּרוּ יָמִים " days will be formed ". Read, With Wutz, אֶחָד לֹהֶם וְלֹא for בָּהֶם אֶחָד וְלֹא, " and not one among them ". 18. Read, with Gunkel, הֲקִצֹּותִי for הֱקִיצֹתִי " I awake ". Read, with Wutz, עֹוְדִי שֶׁכֶם -שֶׁכֶם Neo-Hebr.) for עִמָּךְ וְעֹודִי, " I should still be with thee ". 19. Read יָסוּרוּ for סוּרוּ. 20. Read, GS, נָשְׂאוּ for נָשָׂא. Read שְׁמֶךָ for עָרֶיךָ, " thy cities ". 21. Om. יהוה for rhythm's sake. Read, with Gunkel, וּבְמִתְקֹומְמֶיךָ for וּבִמְקֹומֶיךָ. 24. Read, with Gunkel, דְּבַר־עָצָב (cp. Prov. xv. i) for דֶּרֶךְ־עֹצֶב, " a way of toil ". Read שָׁלֹום for עֹולָם, everlasting ".

1-6. What the psalmist here says of the omniscience of God in respect of himself personally would, of course, apply to all men, as he, doubtless, would have been the first to recognize ; but it is *personal* apprehension and experience which must first find expression. That he was far in advance of most of his contemporaries in his conception of God goes without saying, for we have here the conviction of a contemplative mind which had attained to a knowledge of God beyond anything that had heretofore existed in Israel. When we ask whence this new insight into the divine nature was derived, the answer is two-fold: it came partly through the development of the teaching of such a prophet as Deutero-Isaiah (see, e.g., such passages as Isa. 40$^{13, 14, 28}$, 43$^{1-3, 13}$, 44$^{1, 2, 24}$, 46$^{3, 4}$, 48$^{12, 13}$, 49^{15}), but still more through the direct communion between the Divine Spirit and the mind of one who, in holy self-abandonment, had waited expectantly for inspiration. Such a one realizes that God has sounded the depths of his being; he knows that he is known: *thou dost search me out, and thou knowest me.* Even the most ordinary concerns of life are noted; every purpose and intention, even such trifles as physical fatigue which demands rest, or the effort of rising to carry out the duties of the daily round, *downsitting* and *uprising*, all is known to God who discerns the thoughts which prompt every action, though *from afar*, as it seems to man's bounded mental horizon. It is an expressive term which the psalmist uses in describing the divine weighing of motives, *thou dost sift my going and my resting*; just as the farmer winnows his corn, dividing the wheat from the chaff, so does God estimate what is of value and what is worthless, for He is *familiar with all* the *ways* of man; not a *word* on the *tongue*, but he knows its purport. Truly touching is the psalmist's certitude of God's nearness to him in his walk through life; protection *behind*, a guide *before*; like a rampart round a city *thou dost encircle me*; that is the force of the expression used (cp. Isa. 29^3); and, lest harm should come, *thou layest thine hand upon me.* Overwhelmed by the all-knowledge of God concerning his every thought and movement, the psalmist cries in ecstasy: *Too wonderful is that knowledge for me*; it is beyond his apprehension, *too high*, he *cannot attain unto it*!

7-12. So far the psalmist has spoken of God's knowledge of all his thoughts, words, and acts—and he is but one among the countless multitudes to whom the same applies. The thought of this divine omniscience leads him to the contemplation of what necessarily follows: God's omnipresence. And again it is, naturally, his individual relationship with God of which he speaks, though implying its universal application. There is no spot in heaven, or on earth, or under the earth, in which God is not present. The stress which the psalmist lays on the Personality of God shows that he is far from holding any pantheistic conception, after the manner of Greek speculation; to him (to use modern expressions) divine transcendence and divine immanence centre in Divine Personality. In question-form he asks: *Whither should I go from thy spirit, whither should I flee from thy presence?* Not

that he could ever wish to; it is his impressive way of presenting the
fact of the ubiquity of the Divine Spirit. The psalmist then sets forth
four suppositions, none of which, however, does he conceive to be
possible of accomplishment in his earthly existence; they are intended
to express the truth that God is everywhere. The two most widely
separated places possible to imagine are *Heaven* and *Sheol*; yet, could
he, conceivably, penetrate to either, God would be there: *If I ascended
to heaven—thou art there, if I descended to Sheol, lo, thou art there*,
cp. Am. 9². The thought of God's presence in *Sheol* is of profound
significance; the normal belief is expressed several times in the *Psalms*,
according to which God is unconcerned with those who go down to
Sheol; he does not remember them, they are cut off from his hand
(88⁵, ¹⁰⁻¹², cp. 30⁹); this clearly implies that there is no relationship
between God and those who are in *Sheol—i.e.*, the departed. But the
thought of his presence there, presented by our psalmist, necessarily
postulates a developed conception regarding the Hereafter. The
importance of the psalm from this point of view must be recognized.
There are but few psalms in which this fuller belief in life hereafter is
expressed (cp. Ps. 73); and it is the developed conception of the Divine
Personality which inspires and necessitates that belief.

    After his thought of the divine presence in the two most widely
separated places beyond the compass of the earth, the psalmist refers
to what he conceives to be the farthest limits of the earth itself: *If I took
the wings of the dawn*; here he uses a picture taken from Greek mythology; Eōs, the Greek goddess of the dawn, had white wings, and flew
from the Eastern Ocean, illuminating the sky with red glory. *The
farthest sea* is the extreme west. If he took the wings of the dawn,
and flew from one end of the earth to the other, here, too, would God
be present, his *hand would rest upon* his servant, his *right-hand* would
take hold of him (cp. Job 38¹², ¹³, ¹⁶⁻²⁰, and for the *dawn* cp. also
Job 41¹⁸ ⁽¹⁰⁾). Finally, the psalmist pictures himself as enveloped in
darkness—surely that must, from its impenetrability, hide from God's
presence; but with God there is no such thing as darkness, *it would
not darken from him*.

    13–18. There are good grounds for the contention (Gunkel) that the
first two half-lines of *v.* 14 originally preceded 13; we should only like
to add that 14ᶜ should be included. The whole verse, 14, forms an
introduction to what follows (13, 15ᵃᵇ, and 15ᶜ 16). There is here a
distinct difficulty in deciding how these verses should be divided;
and we recognize the differences of opinion on the subject. The new
subject begins with an expression of thanksgiving for the marvels of
God's works: *I thank thee, for thou art awe-ful*; we use this expression
for the want of a better one; the word means " fearsome, awe-inspiring "; and it is because God is *wonderful* that the psalmist is

struck with reverential wonder in contemplating his works, and is filled with thankfulness that God is such as He is; the Hebrew word is used both of giving thanks and of giving praise. In saying, *and my soul knoweth it right well*, the psalmist shows that he has thought deeply on these wonders; and then he proceeds to mention two of them which touch him most closely. First, the gradual formation of his body in the womb, which he conceives of as divinely directed : the *reins*—*i.e.*, the kidneys—believed to be the seat of the emotions and affections (cp. Ps. 16[7], 73[21]), and then the *knitting together* of his bodily frame; the same thought occurs in Job 10[11] : " Thou hast clothed me with skin and flesh, and knit me together with bones and sinews ". So that his *frame was not hidden from* God *at the time* he *was fashioned in secret.* And then the psalmist gives expression to an old-world and widespread belief that, prior to its entry into the womb, the human body has been *skilfully wrought in the depths of the earth.* This belief in the pre-existence of the body may have come to the Jews from Zoroastrianism (see, *e.g., Bund.* i. 8); though very different from the belief in the pre-existence of the soul, this latter is but a refined form of the other. But the whole subject is too large a one to enter into here. It is another ancient belief to which the psalmist refers when he speaks of God's *book* in which all his *ways are inscribed,* " ways " meaning manner of life ; not only so, but *all* his *days* of life are *numbered, not one* has been *overlooked* by God. This is, in effect, a belief in predestination. All these things the psalmist mentions in order to place on record his realization of the fact that the thoughts of God are as unfathomable as they are numerous : *How inscrutable to me are thy thoughts, O God, how great is their number.*

19–22. In view of the sublime conceptions regarding the nature of the Divine Personality which the psalmist has expressed, the wrathful words which he now utters need not cause surprise. That there should be men who deliberately set themselves by act and word against God who is so immeasurably great, so inconceivably exalted beyond the capacity of human apprehension, fills the psalmist with righteous indignation. Such men, who even dare to *speak* of God in *wickedness,* and *take* His *name in vain* are not fit to live : *O God, that thou wouldest slay the wicked, that the bloodthirsty men might depart.* The psalmist cannot do other than *hate them,* for they *hate* God ; as the *enemies* of God, they are his *enemies* too. 23, 24. After this justifiable outburst, the psalmist, in humble piety, prays that God, who *knows* his *heart,* will root out all that is wrong, and thus lead him in the *way of peace* (for this phrase cp. Isa. 59[8]).

The religious teaching of the psalm has been sufficiently indicated in what has been said in the exegetical notes. See further the *Religious Teaching* section under Ps. 73.

PSALM 140

THERE are expressions in this psalm which support the contention
that it reflects the bitterness of party strife among the Jews. Unfair,
dishonourable, even violent, methods have but too frequently characterized the waging of feuds within a community. There is nothing
to show that the psalmist's antagonists were Gentiles ; had that been
the case, some indication of the fact would have found expression.
The outstanding instances of feud among the Jews, or those closely
connected with them racially in post-exilic times, were (1) the Samaritan
schism, and (2) the divisions which ultimately issued in the formation
of the Sadducæan and Pharisaic parties ; though in this latter case
neither appears as a distinct party—so far as the available evidence
goes—until after the middle of the second century B.C., the differences
which led to this date back in their origin to early post-exilic times,
and probably even earlier (see Vol. I, pp. 62 ff.) ; clear indications
appear in the books of *Ezra, Nehemiah,* and *Malachi.* To decide as
to which of these two is the subject of our psalm is hardly possible,
owing to the want of more definite allusions.

While it must be confessed that this is one of the least edifying of
the psalms, allowance must be made for the strong feelings engendered
by party strife, especially if, as seems probable, religious differences
were in question.

The text of the psalm, especially in the latter part, has undergone
considerable corruption ; some uncertainty as to the correctness of
emendations must be recognized ; the opinions of commentators differ
in some cases.

The rhythm appears, for the most part, to be 4 : 3 ; but here again,
owing to corruptions in the text, there is uncertainty in some of the
verses.

The date may well be some time during the fourth or third
century B.C.

For the Precentor :   A Psalm.   David's.

1 (2). Deliver me, Yahweh, from evil
men,
                                          preserve me from violent men ;
2 (3). They who harbour evil-things in
their heart,
                                          daily ° do they stir up ° quarrels ;
3. (4). They sharpen their tongue like a
serpent,
                                          viper's venom is under their lips.
                                          Selah.
4 (5). Keep me, Yahweh, from the hands
of the wicked,
                                          from the violent men preserve me ;
They who purpose to trip up my
feet,
                                          5ᶜ (6ᶜ) by the wayside have they set
for me gins ;
5 (6). The proud have hidden a snare
for me,
                                          ° and the spoilers ° have laid a net.
                                          Selah.
6 (7). And I said to Yahweh : " My
God art thou,
                                          ° hearken ° to the voice of my
supplication ;
7 (8). Yahweh, my Lord, my strong
help,
                                          thou dost cover my head in the day of
strife ;

8 (9). Grant not, Yahweh, the desires of
    the wicked,
9 (10). ° May they who surround me not
    lift up their head °,
10 (11). May ° coals of fire ° be shaken
    upon them,
11 (12). May the speaker of evil not be set
    up in the land,
12 (13). I know that Yahweh will maintain

13 (14). Of a truth, the righteous shall give
    thanks to thy name,

° that which they plan ° prosper not ".
    Selah.
may the mischief of their lips over-
    whelm them ; Selah.
° may they fall ° into pits, and not rise
    up ;

may calamity pursue the violent man.°
the cause of the oppressed, the right of
    the needy.

the upright shall abide in thy presence.

Text-critical Notes

2. Read יָגֻרוּ for יָגוּרוּ, " they do sojourn ". 5. Read וּמֵחֹבְלִים (cp. Cant. 2¹⁶) for וַחֲבָלִים, " and cords ". 6. Om. יְהֹוָה " Yahweh ". 8. Read אֲשֶׁר זָמְמוּ for רָשָׁע זְמָמוֹ, " the wicked his device ". 9. Read אַל־יָרִימוּ רֹאשׁ מְסִבַּי for רֹאשׁ מְסִבָּי : יָרוּמוּ סֶלָה, " they are exalted Selah. The head of them that surround me ". 10. Read, GV, גֶּחָלֵי אֵשׁ for בָּאֵשׁ גֶּחָלִים, " coals with fire ". Read, S, יַפִּילוּ for יַפְּלֵם, " may he cause them to fall ". 11. Om. לְמַדְחֵפֹת, " into deep pits ", which overloads the half-line, and is probably an accidental doublet of בְּמַהֲמֹרוֹת in the preceding verse.

1–5. In view of the many dangers which beset him through the action of evil-disposed men, the psalmist's first impulse is to seek for help from God : *Deliver me, Yahweh, from evil men* ; " man " in the Hebrew is used collectively, as the plural verbs show. That the dangers were twofold, consisting both of malicious and libellous speech, as well as of actual physical violence, is evident ; but it is not always possible to decide in each case whether the expressions used are to be understood in a literal or a metaphorical sense ; thus *violent*, whether as a noun, verb, or adjective, is often used in reference to injurious language or the like (*e.g.*, Ps. 27¹², 35¹¹, Job 21²⁷, Prov. 16²⁹), and often elsewhere of physical violence (*e.g.*, Ps. 18⁴⁸, 72¹⁴). On the other hand, the *harbouring* of *evil things in the heart*, with which *quarrels*, lit. " wars ", is paralleled, clearly refer to violence of thought and speech. How bitter and dangerous these were is seen by their being compared with the *tongue* of a *serpent* and *viper's venom*. Equally clearly, on the other hand, is physical violence meant when the psalmist prays that Yahweh may *keep* him *from the hands of the wicked*. But the expressions *trip up, set gins, hide snares, lay a net*, are all used figuratively as well as literally in different passages. Some of the expressions used suggest the use of the magic art.[1]

6–8. Against all these dangers the psalmist again prays that Yahweh will protect him ; and he is confident that his prayer will be answered ; for he protests that *Yahweh is his God*, his *strong help*, and that he will cover his *head in the day of strife*, a phrase which again suggests actual violence ; he may, therefore, be confident that *Yahweh will not grant*

[1] See Mowinckel, *Psalmenstudien* V., *Segen und Fluch in Israels Kult und Psalm-dichtung*, p. 93 (1924).

the desires of the wicked, nor *prosper* their *plan*. 9–11. But the psalmist is not content with the conviction that God will protect him ; he pronounces a series of curses upon his enemies which graphically expose the bitterness of his feelings. First, he expresses the wish that they who beset him, *surround me*, may *not lift up their head*, a phrase meaning to be victorious (Ps. 3³, 27⁶, 110⁷), and that the *mischief* which the malicious utterances *of their lips* was intended to inflict, may fall upon them, and *overwhelm them*. Then, in figurative language, he wishes that *coals of fire may be shaken upon them* ; the phrase occurs in Ps. 120⁴, cp. Prov. 26²¹, and a somewhat similar one, expressing the falling of divine wrath upon the sinner, occurs also in Ps. 11⁶ ; in a very different sense it is used in Prov. 25²². Further, they are to *fall into pits, and not rise up* ; here again the language is figurative ; the word does not occur elsewhere in the canonical books, but it is used in a figurative sense in Ecclus. 12¹⁶ of treacherous thoughts ; the meaning here will then be as in the preceding verse : may the harm intended for others be their own lot. And, finally, the psalmist wishes that the evil speaker *may not be set up in the land*—*i.e.*, established in a secure position in the land of Judæa (the Hebrew *'ereṣ* can be translated " earth " only in special connexions) ; this may well contain a hint of the nature of the strife with which the psalmist is concerned ; for the reference here is to those who are in an influential position, and this can only mean the ruling classes, in this case the priestly aristocracy, represented in later days by the Sadducæan party. It points therefore to the religious strife of which mention has been made in the introductory section. 12, 13. This is further borne out by the psalmist's words about the *oppressed* and *the needy*. The words of Josephus, though referring to later times, may well reflect long-standing conditions ; in speaking of the Sadducees and Pharisees in the time of John Hyrcanus (134–104 B.C.), he says that " great disputes and differences have arisen among them, while the Sadducees are able to persuade none but the rich, and have not the populace obsequious to them, the Pharisees have the multitude on their side " (*Antiq.* xiii. 298). The latter included the *oppressed* and the *needy* whose *cause* and *right* the psalmist *knows that Yahweh will maintain*. These are the *righteous* and the *upright* who *give thanks* to the *name* of *Yahweh*, and abide in his *presence*—*i.e.*, are continually present at the temple worship.

Religious Teaching

It would be unreasonable to expect to find in the *Psalms* the Christian ideal of a man's attitude towards his enemies : " Love your enemies, and pray for them that persecute you " (Matth. 5⁴⁴) ; but in this psalm we have the next best thing to it ; for there is no hint of the desire of any personal retaliation against the vindictive enemies of the psalmist; all is left in the hands of God. That there should be some words of bitterness is natural enough; but the passive attitude of the victim of oppression himself reveals a spirit of true godliness. The result of the curses uttered, even though the magic art, as some commentators hold, enters in, is brought about, in the mind of such a deeply religious man as this psalmist, by the will of God.

PSALM 141

ALTHOUGH this psalm is not reckoned among the seven penitential psalms, it is in its essence, as the exegetical notes will show, a striking illustration of the penitent's *rôle*. It is one of the "individual" psalms, being uttered by the psalmist in his own name. A matter of much interest in regard to it is that we may discern in *v.* 2 an intermediate step between the offering of sacrifices and that of purely spiritual worship. It does not go so far as certain passages in Psalms 40, 50, 51, 69, where the absence of sacrifices is envisaged, but, as the verse referred to shows, there is a distinct tendency in this direction.

The text of the psalm has suffered considerable corruption, and some part of it does not appear to have belonged to it in its original form (see the exegetical notes, *vv.* 5–7).

Even as originally written, it must belong to a late post-exilic period. The metre would seem to be 4 : 3 for the most part; but the state of some parts of the text makes this uncertain.

A Psalm. David's.

1. Yahweh, I cry unto thee, haste thee unto me,
give ear to my voice when I call to thee;
2. Let my prayer be set forth as incense before thee,
the lifting-up of my hands as an evening-oblation:
3. Set, Yahweh, ° a watch ° o'er my mouth,
° a guard ° on the ° door ° of my lips;
4. Do not thou incline my heart to aught that is evil,
° I will not sit with them ° that do iniquity,
to act shamelessly ° like the doings of the wicked.°
5. Let the righteous smite me, let ° the godly chastise me °,
nor will I partake of their dainties.
(but) the oil of the ° wicked ° let it not ° adorn ° my head.
[For yet, and my prayer (shall be) against their wickednesses.
6. Their judges are cast down by the sides of a rock,
and they shall hear my words, for they are pleasant.
7. Like one who cleaveth and rendeth the earth,
our bones are scattered at the mouth of Sheol.]
8. ° And as for me °, toward thee, Yahweh,° are mine eyes,
in thee do I trust, pour not out my soul;
9. Keep me from the snare they have laid for me,
° and from the gins ° of the workers of iniquity.
10. May the wicked fall ° in their own nets °,
° while I altogether escape °.

Text-critical Notes

3. Read, with G, שָׁמְרָה for שָׁמְרָה‎, a noun which does not occur elsewhere. Read נִצְּרָה for imperat. נִצְּרָה‎. Read דֶּלֶת for דָּל‎. 4. Read פֹּעֲלֹות רֶשַׁע for אֶת־אִישִׁים‎ for אֶת־אִישִׁים‎, " deeds of wickedness ". Read בַּל־אֶשְׁב עִם־ for "with men". 5. Read הָסִיד for חֶסֶד‎, " kindness ", and יֹוכִיחֵנִי for וְיֹוכִיחֵנִי‎. Read רֶשַׁע for רֹאשׁ‎, " head ", and יָנִיא (with some MSS) for יְנִי‎, " refuse ". The rest of v. 5 with 6, 7 do not seem to be part of the original psalm, the text is very corrupt, and does not give adequate sense. 8. Read וְאָנֹכִי for כִּי‎, " for ". Read יְהֹוָה for יְהֹוָה אֲדֹנָי‎, " O God my Lord ", for the rhythm's sake. 9. Read, with G, וּמִמֹּקְשֹׁות for וּמֹקְשֹׁות‎, " and gins ". 10. Read, with S, בְּמַכְמְרֵיהֶם for מִבְמְרֵיהֶם‎, " his nets ". Read יַחַד אָנֹכִי אֶעֱבֹור for יַחַד אָנֹכִי עַד־אֹ‎, " together I escape for ever ".

1. The psalm opens with the cry of one who realizes his own shortcomings, hence the preliminary prayer that *Yahweh* would *haste* to hear him when he *calls* (cp. Ps. 70⁵). 2. The thought of *prayer* being *as incense*, and the *lifting-up of* his *hands*, synonymous with prayer (Ps. 28²), as *an evening-oblation*, foreshadows what in later days was to become actual fact; for in the Synagogue the forms of prayer for daily worship corresponded to the original daily sacrifices; we are also reminded of the prophet's words : " We shall render as bullocks (the offering of) our lips " (Hos. 14²). The *incense* and the *evening-oblation* (lit. " meal-offering " = *minhah*) are mentioned together in accordance with the traditional use : " When anyone bringeth near the gift of a minhah to Yahweh, his gift shall be of fine flour ; and he shall pour oil upon it and put frankincense thereon " (Lev. 2¹, see also 6⁷, ⁸ ⁽¹⁴, ¹⁵⁾). That prayer was offered during the ceremony is evident from 1 Kgs. 18³⁶. Our psalm was doubtless sung at the offering of the evening *minhah* ; this sacrifice was offered both morning and evening (Exod. 29³⁹⁻⁴¹, Num. 28⁴⁻⁸). With the thought of prayer as incense cp. Rev. 8³. There follows (3, 4) the central prayer, in which the penitent singer points, by implication, to his besetting sin : *Set, Yahweh, a watch o'er my mouth, a guard on the door of my lips* (cp. Ps. 34¹³) ; the prevalence of opprobrious language, lying, libel, cursing, and the like, appears from various psalms to have been common (cp., too, *Pss. of Solomon* 12⁵ : " In flaming fire perish the slanderous tongue ", and Sir. 5¹⁴, 28¹³⁻²⁶) ; and because evil-speaking is the outcome of evil thoughts, the prayer continues that his *heart may not incline to aught that is evil* (cp. Matth. 15¹⁹, " For out of the heart come forth evil thoughts . . . false witness, railings "), which result in *acting shamelessly*. The right-minded man, therefore, makes the resolution not to consort *with them that do iniquity*, nor to *partake of their dainties*, and thus keep out of temptation's way ; the reference seems to be to social intercourse, hence the emendation, *I will not sit*—i.e., at feasts—as parallel to *partaking of their dainties*. 5. Far better to suffer in wise humiliation the *smiting* of the *righteous* than

to be flattered by *the wicked* who anoint his head with oil at their feasts (cp. Eccles. 9[7, 8], Luke 7[46]). As pointed out in the text-critical notes, the contents of the rest of *vv.* 5 and 6, 7 make it extremely improbable that they belong to the psalm as originally written ; even the desperate emendations suggested by some commentators do not bring them satisfactorily into logical connexion with the context ; and the variety of these emendations shows their uncertain character ; the text has suffered grievous corruption. We have, therefore, been constrained to omit these verses.

8-10. Firm in his resolution to have nothing to do with the wicked, the penitent then proclaims his trust in *Yahweh*, towards whom his *eyes* are directed ; and in trustful reliance he prays that *Yahweh* will not *pour out* his *soul*; a figurative expression meaning to take away his life (cp. Isa. 53[12]). In a final petition he prays that he may be kept from the *snares* and *gins laid for him by the workers of iniquity*, in reference, doubtless, to what is said in the latter half of *v.* 4. As so often elsewhere in many of the psalms, the wish is expressed that the wicked may fall *in their own nets* which they had prepared for others (cp. Ps. 7[15, 16], 9[15], and elsewhere), *while* he may *altogether escape.*

Religious Teaching

The psalm sets forth the steps in the penitent's return to God. First, the approach to God, that he will give heed to the prayer addressed to him. Then the confession of sin, followed by the prayer for divine help. This is followed by the resolution of amendment of life, and of keeping out of temptation's way. Here there is the frame of mind, the earnest sincerity, which will gladly undergo the humiliation of rebuke from those in a position to give it. And, finally, there is the protestation of trust in God, and the conviction that he will keep his servant from further temptation.

This psalm must, thus, be pronounced a beautiful and helpful way-mark for guidance in the religious life.

PSALM 142

THE title to this psalm (cp. that of Ps. 57), which occurs also in the Septuagint, was doubtless suggested by what is said in the last verse of the psalm ; this recalled 1 Sam. 22[1] (David in the cave of Adullam), though the cases are far from parallel ; the thought of David would constantly have been in the mind of the redactors.

We have in this psalm one of the most pathetic appeals in the

Psalter ; it is uttered by an individual who is the victim of insidious foes ; they have brought a slanderous accusation against him, and have caused him to be imprisoned. Though no indication is given of the cause and nature of the action taken against him, we may surmise that it was the outcome of party strife. An instructive illustration of this, though belonging to later times, is given by Josephus (*Antiq.* xii. 288–296). That he should feel himself utterly forsaken is natural enough, being kept in close confinement. In his forlorn state his one hope is in Yahweh, upon whom he casts himself wholeheartedly. Notable is the fact that in spite of his sufferings, the psalmist utters no vindictive cry for vengeance, an attitude not infrequently found in other psalms.

The psalm is not a liturgical one ; it has never been used in any of the synagogal rites.

The date to be assigned is late post-exilic. The metre is mainly 3 : 3, where two beats to a line occur, the change is effective (*v.* 6). The last line of a psalm, as here, often has a different metre.

Maskil. David's, when he was in the cave. A Prayer.

1 (2). With my voice to Yahweh do I cry,   with my voice to Yahweh do I make my supplication ;

2 (3). I pour out before him my complaint,   my trouble before him I recount :

3 (4). When my spirit within me languished,   thou didst know my fate ;
In the way wherein I walked,   they hid a snare for me ;

4 (5). Look to my right-hand, and see,   there is none that payeth heed to me ;
Escape hath vanished from me,   there is none that careth for me.

5 (6). I cry unto thee, Yahweh,   I say : Thou art my refuge,
My portion in the land of the living.

6 (7).   Give heed to my cry,
For I am brought very low ;
Save me from my persecutors,
For they are too strong for me.

7 (8). Bring my soul out of prison,   that I may praise thy name ;
° Thy righteousness ° shall encompass me,
When thou shalt have prospered me.

Text-critical Note

7. Read כִּי for בִּי, a particle of entreaty, and צִדְקָתְךָ for צַדִּיקִים " righteous ones ".

1, 2. In these opening verses the psalmist indicates the outward form and expression in which his supplication is made : *with my voice*, meaning that he utters his words aloud ; similarly in Ps. 64[1] the petitioner cries : " Hear my voice, O God, in my complaint ", and so often elsewhere. That this was the customary manner of offering prayer is pointedly illustrated by what is said in 1 Sam. 1[13], where Hannah " spake in her heart ; only her lips moved, but her voice was not heard ", in consequence of which ".Eli thought she had been drunken ". The term *to pour out a complaint* (cp. Ps. 42[4], 62[8], and the title of 102) is very expressive ; it is mostly used of pouring out water, or the like, so that in reference to prayer it describes the gushing forth of words from an overfull heart. As though to an intimate friend to whom one can without stint detail one's worries, so does this poor stricken one *recount* his *trouble* before Yahweh. Then follows (3, 4) his *complaint*, addressed directly to Yahweh. Particularly to be noted here is the conviction expressed that already at the very beginning of his trouble, when his *spirit within* him *languished*, God knew the outcome of it all : *thou didst know my fate*, lit., " path ", what was to come—*i.e.*, the course in which his life would run ; for this sense of the word cp. Ps. 119[105], Isa. 42[16], Lam. 3[9] ; this was when his foes *hid a snare* for him, in reference to some nefarious means of getting him into trouble. In his despairing state of mind he goes so far as to implore Yahweh to *look* on his *right-hand* side— *none payeth heed to me*—implying that his help has been wanting ; at the *right-hand* was where Yahweh was wont to stand as helper, see Ps. 63[8], 73[23], 121[5] ; it is the same forlorn mental condition as prompted another psalmist to cry : " Hath God forgotten to be gracious ? " (Ps. 77[9]) ; he feels that there is no chance of *escape*, for *there is none that careth for me*. But his better self soon gains the upper hand, and his faith in Yahweh revives (5) : *I cry unto thee Yahweh, I say* : *Thou art my refuge*. Then he utters his prayer in the knowledge that Yahweh is his *portion in the land of the living* (cp. Ps. 27[13]) ; asking that *he will give heed to his cry* (6) for he is *brought very low* because of his *persecutors* who have been *too strong for him* (7), and that he will *bring* him *out of prison* in order that he *may praise* his *name*. Being free once more and *prospered* by Yahweh, he will consort with the righteous, who *shall encompass* him, encircling him as a crown encircles the head ; this is the root-meaning of the word.

Religious Teaching

The uttering of private prayer aloud, as here taught, is something worth thinking about. The idea probably does not appeal to most ; yet we have the example of our Lord (Matth. 24[39, 42, 44]) ; and the fact cannot be denied that the sound of one's own voice in prayer tends to realism and sincerity. It helps to envisage the nearness of God, the apprehension of which must be the yearning of every true believer. This is not the place to discourse further upon the subject, but it is one which it would be well to ponder over.

One other thing which this beautiful little psalm teaches is the blessedness and comfort of telling out one's troubles to God ; a fearless, intimate intercourse with God is a means of union with him, which sanctifies life and all life's activities.

PSALM 143

THE very grave peril, even unto death, in which the writer of this
psalm stands, fully accounts for its dithyrambic character; the sentences
are thrown out in almost breathless haste; in his urgent need, the
psalmist, as it were, gasps forth his petitions and plaints. What has
occasioned the precarious condition in which the writer finds himself
is not indicated; but that his own conscience is not clear is evident
from his confession in *v.* 2, and by the implied resolution of amendment of life in *v.* 8; the entire absence of protestations of innocence,
so often found in the psalms, is significant, and points in the same
direction. Very appropriately, therefore, is this psalm included
among the penitential ones. It is intensely pathetic and appealing:
one who has done wrong is suffering for his sin; but he is repentant,
and throws himself on God's mercy. The edifying character of the
psalm is somewhat marred by the bitter spirit evinced in the concluding verse; the cruel treatment he is suffering from his enemies (see
v. 3) must be pleaded in extenuation.

The date is late post-exilic; this is indicated by the frequent points
of contact with other psalms, but especially by the comparatively
developed sense of sin.

The rhythm is irregular; this may well be purposeful in order to
reflect the worry of the writer's mind and his alternating thoughts.

A Psalm of David.

1. ° Hear my prayer
    Give ear to ° my supplication °,
    ° Answer me in thy righteousness.
2. ° Bring not ° thy servant into judge-
    ment,   for none living is righteous in thy sight.
3. But the enemy persecuteth my soul,
    He crusheth my life to the ground,
    He causeth me to dwell in dark places.°
4. And my spirit fainteth within me,   my heart in the midst of me is desolate.
5. I recall the days of old,
    I meditate on all thy doing,
    I muse on the work of thine hands.
6. I spread forth mine hands unto thee, my soul is toward thee as a thirsty-
                                          land. Selah.
7. Speedily answer me °,
    My spirit faileth;
    Hide not thy face from me,   lest I be like them that descend to the
                                          Pit.
8. Let me hear of thy lovingkindness at
    morn,   for in thee do I trust;
    Show me the way wherein I should
    walk,   for to thee I lift up my soul;
9. Deliver me from my foes °,
    Unto thee ° do I flee °.
10. Teach me to do thy will,   for thou art my God;
    May thy good spirit lead me   ° in the path ° of uprightness;
11. For thy name's sake ° preserve me,
    In thy righteousness bring forth
    My soul from trouble.

12. And of thy mercy annihilate mine
　　　enemies,　　　　　　　　　　and destroy all that trouble my soul ;
　　　　　　　　　　　For I am thy servant.

Text-critical Notes

1. Om. יהוה ; in each of the four instances of its occurrence it seems to interfere with the rhythm, and may well have been a later insertion by a copyist. Read תַּחֲנוּנַי for נִי . . ., " my supplications ". Om. בֶּאֱמֻנָתְךָ, " in thy faithfulness ", as it disturbs the rhythm; it is an explanatory gloss. 2. Read, with S, אַל־תָּבֵא for וְאַל־תָּבוֹא, " and enter not ". 3. Om. עוֹלָם כְּמֵתֵי, " as those that have been long dead ", quoted from Lam. 3⁶, as it disturbs the rhythm. 7. Om. יהוה. 9. Om. יהוה. Read, with G, נָכַתִּי for כִּסִּיתִי, " I have hidden ". 10. Read, with some MSS, בָּאָרֶץ for בְּאֶרֶץ, " in the land ". 11. Om. יהוה.

1. The threefold appeal, *Hear, Give ear, Answer*, expresses the intensity of the psalmist's need. The first two clauses are taken almost verbally from Ps. 39¹². The righteousness of God has here the sense of " faithfulness ", as the explanatory gloss shows ; the word is used as parallel to " love " (*ḥesed*) in Ps. 36¹⁰, 103¹⁷, and it often has the force of " deliverance " in Deutero-Isaiah. 2. The consciousness of guilt is implied in the form of the prayer now offered, that God may *not bring* the sufferer into condemnation, *judgement*, for he seems to recognize that it is by the divine will that punishment has come upon him ; and he utters the implied confession that he is not guiltless : *for none living is righteous in thy sight* ; with the thought cp. Ps. 103³, and it may well have been in the Apostle's mind in Rom. 3²⁰. And then (3) as though the punishment he is suffering were greater than he deserved, the psalmist goes on to describe the terrible severity of the treatment to which he is subjected. This is expressed in a threefold manner again : *the enemy persecuteth, crusheth, causeth to dwell in dark places*. We may note here the three steps in the procedure : first, the fact of persecution ; then, its mode, and finally, its intended result ; persecuted, lit. " chased after ", crushed, lit. " trodden down ", made to dwell in dark places—*i.e.*, in Sheol— the whole picture is clearly taken from Ps. 7⁵ ; and for the expression " dark places ", cp. Ps. 88⁶. In such case, small wonder that (4) his spirit *fainteth within* him, and his *heart is desolate*—*i.e.*, he is plunged in despair. Here again familiar words from other psalms were in the mind of the forlorn sufferer (cp. Ps. 61², 77³, 142³). Some comfort he finds, it is true, in recalling the many proofs of God's love and power in the past history of his people ; and here, once more, there is a threefold expression of thought : *I remember, meditate, muse* ; the remembrance of the *days* of old, of God's *doing* in the past, and of *the work* of his *hands*, had been the comfort of others in trouble too ; the whole verse is taken from Ps. 77⁵, ¹¹, ¹², cp. also Ps. 44¹, 78³ ; and with living trust that that lovingkindness will again be manifested, he spreads forth his hands in prayer to God (cp. Ps. 28², 68³¹), likening

himself in his yearning to a parched land in sore need of moisture; the simile is taken from Ps. 63[1]. The intensity of his need prompts the impatient utterance (7): *Speedily answer me* (cp. Ps. 40[13, 17], 102[3]), for he feels that his *spirit* is failing (cp. Ps. 84[2]), and he is in danger of death if God does not turn to him; *Hide not thy face from me*, he cries, as another psalmist had said, Ps. 27[9], *lest I become like them that descend to the Pit*, a synonym for *Sheol*; the words are taken from Ps. 28[1], cp. 88[6].

In a calmer frame of mind the psalmist then continues his prayer; the hours of darkness, wherein the spirit is prone to fearfulness, are past, and with the morning fresh hopes arise (8): *Let me hear of thy lovingkindness at morn, for in thee do I trust* (cp. Ps. 90[14], 25[2]); and there is the longing to walk in the way that God wills (cp. Ps. 25[4], 32[8]), for his soul is *lifted up* to God (cp. Ps. 25[1], 86[4]); he has thrown himself upon God, and prays in certitude of being heard (9): *Deliver me from my foes* (cp. Ps. 31[15], 59[2], 142[6]), *unto thee do I flee* (cp. Ps. 59[16]). Then (10, 11) once more the prayer to do God's *will* is uttered; *Teach me to do thy will* (cp. Ps. 25[4], 27[11]), followed by the protestation: *Thou art my God*; the expression *thy good spirit* does not occur elsewhere; but we have " thy holy spirit " in Ps. 51[11]. The plea that deliverance may come *for thy name's sake* occurs also in Ps. 31[3] and cp. 25[11]. As already remarked, the psalm would be the better for the omission of the last verse (12), with the exception of the final words: *I am thy servant*, cp. Ps. 116[16].

It will have been noticed how greatly our psalmist is indebted to the writers of other psalms; the point is interesting as illustrating familiarity with the Psalter as a whole. Doubtless the same is to be said of other psalmists, but there is certainly no other psalm which so fully illustrates this characteristic.

Religious Teaching

So far as the earnest appeal to God for help in time of trouble is concerned, the religious teaching of this psalm is to be paralleled by that of many others; but in one respect it differs from most of these in that the teaching is implicit, or only hinted at, rather than explicitly stated. This centres, first, in the sense of sinfulness; for though expressed in general terms, " none living is righteous in thy sight ", the psalmist, in effect, confesses his sin by the prayer that God will not bring him into judgement. And this recognition of sin calls forth repentance; and repentance is shown forth by amendment of life; hence the conviction of forgiveness. It is a spiritual process of universal application; and this it is which makes the psalm of such inestimable value when its spirit is entered into, and acted upon.

PSALM 144

AN initial difficulty presents itself in studying this psalm, namely, whether it is to be regarded as a unity or not. Opinions, not unnaturally, differ on the subject. Of one thing, however, there can be no doubt: there has been some serious dislocation of the text; this may possibly be due to the attempt of some scribe to construct a unity out of two originally independent psalms. In other words, we contend that the psalm is not a unity, though we fully recognize the difficulty of indicating exactly where the division between the two is to be sought. It is evident that two very different sets of conditions must be postulated when it is said, on the one hand: " Rescue me and deliver me from the hand of strangers " (v. 11), and, on the other, when a time of peaceful prosperity is described in such words as: " Our sheep are thousands, ten thousands, in our fields " (v. 13). It is recognized by most commentators that the psalm contains several glosses—e.g., vv. 3, 4 break the connexion between vv. 2 and 5; and that there is much borrowing from other psalms, especially from Ps. 18, in the earlier part. In the rendering given below we have put in square brackets what we regard as glosses. The main dislocation of the text occurs in vv. 8 and 11, the repetitions show clearly that some displacement has taken place. How this should be reconstructed is again subject to differences of opinion; we have endeavoured to give a logical sequence, while recognizing the element of uncertainty as to the correctness of our reconstruction.. Subjectivity can hardly fail to assert itself in such cases.

As to date, there are again a variety of opinions, a few of which may be mentioned. Briggs assigns it to " the troublous times at the beginning of the work of Nehemiah, when the people were called to arms against their treacherous neighbours ". Kittel interprets the psalm eschatologically, and regards it as one among the latest. Gunkel, followed by Hans Schmidt, assigns it to the period of the monarchy. Similarly Herkenne, who argues with much force that the speaker is king Hezekiah. Barnes quotes Westcott to the effect that " the later psalms are a softened echo of the strains of David, and not new songs ". For ourselves, we cannot doubt that, in view of v. 10, " who giveth victory to kings, who rescueth David his servant ", the psalm, in its original form, belongs to the monarchical period; we hesitate to give a more exact date, though we feel that Herkenne's contention that Hezekiah is the king in question is attractive.

For reasons already indicated the question of the rhythm is difficult ; all that can be said is that it is very irregular.

David's.°

1.   Blessed be Yahweh, my Rock,
Who teacheth my hands to war,   ° my fingers ° to the battle,
2. ° Yahweh °, ° my Rock °, and my
    fortress,   my refuge and my deliverer,
My shield, and in him do I trust,   who subdueth ° the peoples ° under me.
[3. Yahweh, what is man, that thou takest   or the son of man, that thou considerest
    knowledge of him ?   him ?
4. Man is like unto a breath,   his days are as a shadow passing away.]
5. Yahweh, bow-thy-heavens and descend,   touch the mountains and they shall
                       smoke,
6. Flash forth ° lightnings °, and scatter   shoot out thine arrows, and confound
    them,   them.
7. Put forth ° thine hand ° from above,   ° draw me ° out of many waters,°
   ° Deliver me ° from the hand of
    strangers,   8. whose mouth speaketh vanity,
        And their right-hand is a lying right-hand.
9.   ° A new song
        will I sing to thee,
        With a ten-stringed harp
        will I make melody to thee,
10. Who giveth victory to ° his king °,   who rescueth David his servant.
[11. Deliver me from the hand of strangers,   whose mouth speaketh vanity,
      And their right-hand is a lying right-hand.]
12.   ° Our sons are like plants
       Well-grown in their borders ° ;
       Our daughters like corner-stones
       Of sculptured pattern ; °
13.   Our garners ° supplying
       ° Of every kind ° ;
       ° Our sheep ° are thousands,
       Ten-thousands in our fields,
14.   ° Our oxen ° well-laden ; °
       No tumult in our broad-places.
15.   Happy the people
       In such a case,
       Happy the people
       Whose God is Yahweh.

Text-critical Notes

Title : G adds προς τον Γολιαδ, a late scribe's surmise. 1. אֶצְבְּעוֹתַי two beats.
2. Add יהוה for the sake of the rhythm. Read סַלְעִי with Ps. 18² for חַסְדִּי,
" my mercy ". Read עַמִּים with some MSS SV, cp. Ps. 18⁴⁷, for עַמִּי " my
people ". 5. Om. *vv.* 3, 4 as a later insertion. 6. Read בְּרָקִים with Ps. 18¹⁴ for
בָּרָק, " lightning ". 7. Read, with several MSS and G יָדְךָ for יָדֶיךָ, " thy
hands ". Read, following Ps. 18¹⁶ הַמְשֵׁנִי for פְּצֵנִי, " rescue me ", and place
הַצִּילֵנִי before מִיַּד, " from the hand of . . . " 9. Om. אֱלֹהִים (cp. *v.* 1) for the sake of the
metre. 10. Read כַלְפוּ for מְלָכִים, " kings ". Om., for the sake of the metre,
מֵחֶרֶב רָעָה, " from the evil sword ", added. For *v.* 11, which is a doublet, see *vv.* 7,
8. 12. Om. אֲשֶׁר, " who ". Read, with Duhm, בְּעֲרוּגוֹתָם, cp. Cant. 5¹³, 6², for
בִּנְעוּרֵיהֶם, " in their youth ". Om. הֵיכָל, " temple ". 13. Om. מְלָאִים, " full ".
For מִזַּן אֶל־זַן, cp. Ecclus. 37²⁸, Gunkel suggests מָזוֹן עַל־מָזוֹן, " sustenance on
sustenance ". Read צֹאנֵנוּ for צֹאוֹנֵנוּ. 14. Read with some MSS אֱלֹפֵינוּ for אַלוּפֵינוּ.
Om., as a marginal gloss, אֵין־פֶּרֶץ וְאֵין יוֹצֵאת, " no outburst and no going forth ",
the reference seems to be to untimely birth among the cattle ; see Gen. 38²⁹,
2 Sam. 6⁸, 1 Chron. 13¹¹, and Exod. 21¹².

1, 2. The opening ascription of praise is taken almost entirely from Ps. 18; it does not present a very edifying conception of Yahweh, but is in accordance with the ancient Semitic belief that the deities played a leading part in wars; the belief occurs even in quite late times (cp. Zech. 9$^{13, 14}$, 10^4). This belief comes out in the thought that Yahweh *teacheth* a man's *hands to war* (cp. Ps. 18^{34}, 2 Sam. 22^{35}), and his *fingers to the battle—i.e.*, how to handle spear and bow; Yahweh himself is spoken of as "mighty in battle" (Ps. 24^8), and we recall the expression "to consecrate", or sanctify, "war" (Mic. 3^5, Jer. 6^4, Joel 3 (4)^9), showing that war was, therefore, conceived of as a holy act. For the significance of the title *Rock* applied to Yahweh see the comment on Ps. 18^{46}; the two words used (in *vv.* 1, 2) are different in Hebrew, taken, respectively, from Ps. 18$^{46 \text{ and } 2}$. *Who subdueth the peoples beneath me* refers to the surrounding peoples, hence the emendation from Ps. 18^{47} and various MSS; the singular would imply that the king in question had subdued his own people! As pointed out in the text-critical notes, *vv.* 3, 4 come in here inappropriately and break the connexion; they are a marginal comment by a later scribe, and have been inserted in the text. 5–8 are an extract from the description of the theophany (Ps. 18$^{9, 14, 16, 44, 45}$, cp. also 104^{32}, 69^{14}, 106^{26}); see the notes on these psalms. In gratitude for the victory that has been gained (cp. *vv.* 1, 2), in spite of perilous episodes (7) the king, or some courtier in his name, utters a short offering of praise and thanksgiving, which concludes this part of the psalm (9, 10). A *new song*, sung to the accompaniment of *a ten-stringed harp*, recalls Ps. 33$^{2, 3}$ (cp. Ps. 40^3, 149^1). After the very marked use of older songs which, presumably, has so far characterized our psalm, the words strike one as significant, and we cannot but feel sympathy with those commentators who see in what follows, the "new song" itself. Unfortunately, this will not do; the condition of peaceful prosperity depicted in the later portion of our psalm is not such as can be expected to ensue immediately after a successful war; the bringing-about of such conditions takes time; and those described must belong to some subsequent period. It may well be that the "new song" of which the singer speaks may have figured in the original form of our psalm, but that in the vicissitudes of transmission it has been lost. At any rate, what follows can hardly have been its purport. Here the thanksgiving centres in *victory* to *his king, who rescueth David his servant.* That *David* is meant is highly improbable. The reference is either to the general idea of victory, naturally associated with the name of David, who was often victorious, or else "David" is used symbolically, and applied to one of his seed.

The abrupt way in which the last portion (12–15) begins suggests that it is a fragment from some other psalm which a compiler thought an appropriate conclusion to the one before him; a similar proceeding occurs elsewhere in the Psalter (*e.g.*, Pss. 19, 27). We have, first, a charming picture of the healthy well-being of the younger members of the community, the *sons like plants in their borders* (lit. "beds", see Cant. 5¹³, 6²); "along the brook", as Thomson tells us, "are tall daisies, flaming gladiolus, crimson iris, variegated lilies, gay oleanders, wild roses . . ." (*The Land and the Book*, i. 137 [1881]); something of this kind may well have been in the mind of the poet. Then, *our daughters like corner-stones of sculptured pattern*; the mention of the temple in such a connexion seems out of place; the picture is drawn from the tall, stately corner of any conspicuous building. Then follows an account of the prosperous state of the country, the stress being naturally laid on the abundance of cattle—somewhat over-drawn, no doubt, but permissible enough to poetical imagination. In times of such prosperity contentment reigns, and there is *no tumult in our broad places*, the open spaces near the gates, not "streets", which were always very narrow. A religious note is sounded at the close, where it is implied that all this prosperity is due to the fact that *Yahweh is the God of the people*. But otherwise it must be confessed that the religious tone of the psalm is not such as appeals to us. A special section on the religious teaching is, therefore, not called for in the case of this psalm.

PSALM 145

THIS triumphant hymn of praise, calling upon all men to glorify the greatness and majesty of God, is one of the most inspiring in the Psalter. Though largely composed of sayings from other psalms, these are so harmoniously woven together that the psalm gives the impression of an original composition. In spite of its being an acrostic psalm (it is the last of these), there is no sign of mechanical construction, such as strikes one in the case, *e.g.*, of Ps. 119. A special feature is the earnestly expressed wish that the knowledge of Yahweh may become world-wide; this universalistic outlook was by no means always prominent among the Jews in post-exilic times, as witness the polemic in the book of *Jonah*. In this connexion the mention of the kingdom of Yahweh is of special importance; it connotes God's rule from and to all time, in Heaven as on earth; there is nothing of an eschatological nature in its use here; it has been in use in the Liturgy of the Synagogue from very early times, but has never been one of the special psalms for New Year's Day.

The psalm is one of the latest in the Psalter; this is shown by the numerous points of affinity with psalms of early and late date, and also by the Aramaisms which occur here and there.

The metre is 3 : 3 ; in the earlier part of the psalm 2 : 2 : 2.

A Song of Praise. David's

1. א I will exalt thee, my God, the King,   I will bless thy name for ever.°
2. ב   Every day will I bless thee,
                             And will praise thy name
                             For ever and ever.
3. ג   Great is Yahweh,
                             And highly to be praised,
                             His greatness is unsearchable.
4. ד   ° Generation to generation
                             Let them praise thy works,
                             And declare thy mighty acts.°
5. ה   Of the majesty of thy glory,
                             Of thy splendour ° let them tell °;
                             Of thy wonder-works ° let them sing °;
6. ו Of the might of thy terrible-deeds   ° of thy great acts ° ° let them dis-
      let them speak,   course °;
(7.) ז The memorial of thy ° great °-   and let them shout-for-joy because of
      goodness let them pour forth,   ° thy righteousness °.
8. ח Gracious and merciful is Yahweh,   longsuffering and of great loving-
                                            kindness ;
9. ט Good is Yahweh to all,   and his mercies are over all his works.
10. י Let all thy works, Yahweh, give
      thee thanks,   and let thy godly ones bless thee ;
11. כ The glory of thy kingdom let them
      declare,   and discourse of thy power,
12. ל To make known ° to men ° ° thy   and the glorious majesty ° of thy
      power °,   kingdom °;
13. מ ° His kingdom ° is a kingdom of all
      ages,   and his rule throughout all generations.
    נ ° [Faithful is Yahweh in all his
      words,   and loving in all his works] °.
14. ס Yahweh upholdeth all that fall,   and raiseth up all that are bowed down ;
15. ע The eyes of all wait upon thee,   thou givest their food in its time ;
16. פ Thou ° thyself ° openest thine hand, satisfying all living with favour.
17. צ Righteous is Yahweh in all his ways, and merciful in all his works,
18. ק Nigh is Yahweh to all that call upon
      him,   to all that call upon him in truth ;
19. ר The desire of them that fear him he
      fulfilleth,   their cry he heareth, and helpeth them.
20. ש Yahweh preserveth all that love
      him,   but all the wicked he destroyeth,
21. ת The praise of Yahweh shall my
      mouth utter,   and let all flesh bless his holy name.°

Text-critical Notes

1. Om. וְעֶד, which overloads the half-line. 4. The rhythmic measure in the Hebrew is difficult to reproduce in English ; literally rendered the text runs : " Let (one) generation praise thy works to (another) generation, and let (all of) them declare thy mighty acts ". 5. Read, following GS, יְדַבְּרוּ for וְדִבְרֵי, " and the words of ". Read, following S, אָשִׁיחָה for יְשִׂיחוּ, " let me sing ". 6. Read גְּדוּלֹתֶיךָ for גְּדוּלָתֶיךָ. Read, with T, יְסַפְּרוּן for יֹסְפֵּרוּן, אֲסַפְּרֶנָּה for יְסַפְּרוּנָה, " let me discourse ". 7. Read רַב for רַב־. Two beats to צִדְקָתֶךָ. 12. Read לְאָדָם for לִבְנֵי הָאָדָם, " for the sons of man ", for the sake of the rhythm. Read, following GS, גְּבוּרָתֶךָ for גְּבוּרֹתָיו, " his mighty powers ". Read, following GS, מַלְכוּתֶךָ for —תּוֹ. 13. Read מַלְכוּתוֹ for מַלְכוּתֶךָ " thy kingdom ", in view of what follows in the verse (נ) which has fallen out of the text. 13ᵈ. This half-verse has been preserved in GSV, and can be rendered : נֶאֱמָן יְהוָה בְּכָל־דְּבָרָיו וְחָסִיד בְּכָל־מַעֲשָׂיו. 15. Om. לָהֶם, " to them ", for the sake of the rhythm. 16. Read, with G, אֶת for אֵת. 21. Om. לְעוֹלָם וָעֶד, " for ever and ever ", which is a later addition. Some MSS add : וַאֲנַחְנוּ נְבָרֵךְ יָהּ מֵעַתָּה וְעַד עוֹלָם הַלְלוּיָהּ, " and we will bless Yah from henceforth and for ever. Hallelujah ".

1. This opening verse, which serves as a kind of text, expresses the general content of what is to follow. *I will exalt thee* (cp. Pss. 99$^{5, 9}$, 107^{32}) gives the key-note, denoting in the mind of the writer the infinite distance of the Divine Personality above men. To speak of God as *King* expresses the utmost endeavour of men in those days to describe a unique superiority over mankind in general; but it is also significant, in view of what follows, as indicating the world-wide rulership of Yahweh. *For ever*, here, has the sense of " continually ". 2, 3. *Every day* is probably to be taken in a literal sense, for it may well be in accordance with traditional usage that this psalm was recited thrice daily in the synagogue by many pious Jews; the mention of this is from a third-century Rabbi (Elbogen, *Der jüdische Gottesdienst* . . ., p. 80 [1913]). To praise the *name* of Yahweh (cp., *e.g.*, Ps. 103^1), as pointed out elsewhere, reminds us that the name was synonymous with the Person. The *greatness* of Yahweh, for which praise is due to him, is also a frequent theme of the psalmists (48^1, 96^4), and its *unsearchableness*, like all that appertains to the Divine Nature—*i.e.*, the inability of man to apprehend it—is especially emphasized in the book of *Job* (5^9, 9^{10}, 11^7, 34^{24}, 36^{26}). 4–7. Very beautiful is the way in which the psalmist earnestly expresses the desire that others should bear witness to the power and majesty of Yahweh; the hope is expressed that every *generation* should hand on the knowledge of this, one to the other (cp. Ps. 78^4) telling of his *mighty-acts* (one word in Hebrew), of his *glory* and *splendour*, his *wonder-works* (one word in Hebrew), and terror-inspiring action (cp. the theophanic description); they are all the outcome of his *great-goodness* (one word in Hebrew) and righteousness. The psalmist has done his utmost to set forth the inexpressible power and might of Yahweh; and now (8–13) he extols his God from a different aspect, and speaks of his *graciousness, mercy, longsuffering* and *lovingkindness* to all (cp. Ps. 86$^{5, 15}$, 100^5, 103^8); *his mercies are over all his works* is in reference to his highest work of creation, man, as the words which follow show : *Let all thy works, Yahweh, give thee thanks* (cp. Ps. 103^{22}), *and let all thy loved ones bless thee* (cp. Ps. 132^{16}); and again all men are called upon to *declare* the *glory* of his *kingdom*, which is *a kingdom of all ages*. By kingdom is to be understood, of course, a *rule*, or dominion, and thus not connoting any thought of a land or area, the ordinary Jewish conception of the time. From the wide purview over the unlimited expanse of Yahweh's rule the psalmist directs his thoughts more particularly to his own people or the present time. 14–19. His care is for all who *fall* (cp. Ps. 37^{24}), and *are bowed down* (cp. Ps. 146^8)—*i.e.*, who are in want—but they that *wait upon* him (cp. Ps. 104^{27}) receive *their food in its time* lavishly from his open hand (cp. Ps. 104^{28}), for he is *righteous* and *merciful*, and *nigh unto all that call upon him in truth* and that *fear him*. In fine, those who love Yahweh

he *preserveth* (cp. Ps. 97[10]), but *all the wicked he destroyeth* : and the psalmist himself will ever persist in *the praise of Yahweh, and let all flesh bless his holy name* (cp. Ps. 150[6]).

Religious Teaching

As a hymn of praise to God this psalm stands out as one of the most beautiful in the Psalter. What must particularly demand our sympathetic attention is the earnest attempt to depict the glory of God. The psalmist's thoughts were prompted by such soul-exalting sights as the gorgeous gold of the rising sun, and the superbly sky-decked tints of the sun at its setting, the flashes of silver-blue lightning when the thunder's roar made him think that it must be the very voice of Yahweh, and the lurid glare of volcanic eruptions sent up from the bowels of th earth—we know, it is true, that these are but the twinkling stars i. a world which is no more than a dusty speck of one universe of many ; but let us in humble gratitude acknowledge that the psalmist did his best ; and beautiful it is, even though we are convinced that the glories of the creative power of the inapprehensible majesty of God transcend the most daring flights of human imagination ! Could we do better ? It is, in any case, fitting that we should honour the spirit which seeks to set forth the divine glory and laud the Name of him, by whom, in loving condescension, praise is accepted, though offered by his humblest worshippers. The religious teaching of this psalm centres in offering praise to God, no matter how inadequate.

PSALM 146

THIS is the first of the so-called " Hallelujah psalms ", the others being 147–150, because they begin and conclude with this expression of praise. As the offering of praise it is very fitting that it has from early times, together with the other four, been sung daily at the morning synagogal service ; the use may well have been handed down from earlier days. The psalm does not, either in outward form or in its fullness of thought, reach the inspired height of the previous one. Its reference to princes suggests the possibility that it may have been prompted by some inadvisable action on the part of the Jewish rulers in their dealings with some foreign power. At any rate, the uselessness of trusting in princes seems to be the text, as it were, of the psalmist's warning and exhortation.

Other psalms have again been much drawn upon ; but, as in Ps. 145, the psalmist utilizes his material in his own way ; quite his own, in especial, is the impressive sixfold repetition of the name of Yahweh at the beginning of the sentence, to emphasize his many-sided help, as against the feeble and unreliable efforts of man.

The date of the psalm is late, as shown both by the use of other psalms, of which some are themselves of late date, and also by the occurrence of Aramaisms.

The metre is, with the exception of *v.* 4, where the change of subject makes the change of metre distinctly effective, almost uniformly 3 : 3 (in *v.* 3 it is 2 : 2 : 2).

Hallelujah.°

1.   Praise Yahweh, my soul !
2. I will praise Yahweh while I live,   will sing praise to my God while I have
                                                                    my being.
3.   Trust not in princes,
                         in the offspring of man ;
                         in him is no help,
4.   His spirit goeth forth,
                         he returneth to his earth,
                         in that selfsame day
                         his purposes perish.
5. Blessed is he ° whose help ° is the God
        of Jacob,   whose hope is in Yahweh his God,
6. Maker of heaven and earth,   the sea and all that in them is,
     ° Who keepeth ° truth for ever,   7. who upholdeth justice for the
                                                                    oppressed,
    Who giveth food to the hungry,   Yahweh setteth free the prisoners.
8. Yahweh giveth sight to the blind,   Yahweh raiseth up those bowed down,
9. Yahweh preserveth strangers,   Orphan and widow he sustaineth ;
8c ° Yahweh loveth the righteous °,   9c but the way of the wicked he
                                                                    perverteth.
10. Yahweh reigneth for ever,   thy God, O Zion, to all generations.
                                    Hallelujah.

Text-critical Notes

1. G adds Αγγαιου και Ζαχαριου. 5. בְּעֶזְרוֹ for בְּעֶזְרוֹ, " in his help ". 6. Read שֹׁמֵר for הַשֹּׁמֵר, omitting the art. as in the other participles. 8c. This half-line has clearly become misplaced ; in the Hebrew text it comes after, " . . . those bowed down "; as it stands the logical sequence is disturbed.

1. With an utterance of self-encouragement, found elsewhere in the psalms (*e.g.*, 103¹, 104¹), *Praise Yahweh, my soul*, the worshipper begins by protesting that this is his intention as long as he lives, *while I have my being*, a very rare mode of expression in Hebrew (cp. Ps. 104³³). 2. The warning not to trust in princes (cp. Ps. 118⁹), coming in the forefront of the psalm, shows its emphasis, and must, in all probability, refer to some specific action on the part of the Jewish rulers in relation to their suzerain, or his representative. It is, of course, impossible to indicate the occasion alluded to ; but the detailed way in which this is deprecated suggests that it was an occurrence of some moment ; *help* from such a source, prince though he might be, was doomed to failure, for as soon as he ceases breathing—the flight of a vapour—*he returneth to his earth* (Gen. 3¹⁹, Ps. 104²⁹) ; the same thought, possibly with this verse in mind, was expressed by Mattathias, the father of the Maccabæan leaders, in reference to Antiochus Epiphanes (1 Macc. 2⁶³). The

words, *his purposes* (or plans) *perish*, point again to some political occasion.

5–9. In inexpressible contrast to any power that man, however highly placed, may possess, and thereby give help, is that which is accorded by *the God of Jacob*. It may be pointed out that the use of the name of Jacob as applied to Judah is restricted almost without exception to post-exilic passages (*e.g.*, Isa. 65^9, Obad. 10, Mal. 2^{12}); in the psalms the expression " the God of Jacob " occurs elsewhere in 114^7 (not 24^6); otherwise " Jacob " refers to the northern kingdom (*e.g.*, Am. 7$^{2, 5}$, Hos. 12^{13}, etc.). At any rate, as the psalmist says, *he whose hope* is set on *Yahweh his God* lives in the conviction that his help will be forthcoming when the need arises; and the stress laid on *his God* expresses the contrast between the faith of the true Jew with that of the princes who believed in many gods. Then he particularizes : This hope is founded on and embedded in the age-long faith in Yahweh as the *Maker of heaven and earth*; the separate mention of the *sea*, as though distinct from the earth, echoes the ancient belief reflected in Gen. 1$^{9, 10}$. But the creative power of Yahweh, as the psalmist goes on to show, necessarily implies care for that highest act of creation, man, and more especially for those among men who acknowledge him as their Creator and are his worshippers. While truth and justice stand foremost in all his actions, his mercy and lovingkindness take thought of all. The short sentences which follow, each beginning with *Yahweh*, in order to lay stress on *his* loving care, are, as we have said, unique in the *Psalms*, though the thoughts expressed necessarily echo those of other thinkers : *Who giveth food to the hungry* (Ps. 107^9, 145^{15}); behind that lies, of course, the thought of the creative power which enables the soil to yield its fruits (Gen. 1$^{11, 12}$, Hos. 2^8). *Setteth free the prisoners* (68^6, 107^{14}, cp. Isa. 42^7). *Giveth sight to the blind*; this thought does not occur elsewhere in the *Psalms*, but see Isa. 42^7, cp. also 29^{18}, 35^5. *Raiseth up those bowed down*—*i.e.*, those weighted down by adversity; the expression is a rare one, used in a figurative sense in the *Psalms* (57^6, 145^{14}), though in Isa. 58^5, Mic. 6^6, it is used literally of bowing down in worship. *Preserveth strangers* (on the dislocation of the text here see exegetical note); the care of strangers sojourning among the people is very often insisted upon (*e.g.*, Lev. 19^{10}, Deut. 10$^{18, 19}$, etc.); in the *Psalms* they are mentioned only in 94^6; in 39^{12}, 119^{19}, the word is used in a somewhat different sense; the care of the orphan, or fatherless, and widow is also again and again enjoined (*e.g.*, Exod. 22^{22}, Deut. 10^{18}), and in the *Psalms* 68^5, cp. 10^{14}, 94^6; all these are in the care of Yahweh. Finally, the psalmist adds the oft-expressed thought of Yahweh's love for the righteous man (see, *e.g.*, 5^{12} and often elsewhere in the *Psalms*), *but the way of the wicked he perverteth*, a word used only here in this sense.

The psalm closes (10) with the triumphant cry : *Yahweh reigneth for ever!* A universalistic note often sounded in the *Psalms* (10^{16}, $47^{2, 3, 6-8}$, $93^{1, 2}$, 96^{10}, 97^1), though there is added here—*thy God, O Zion*—that Palestine will be the centre of the divine rule ($29^{10, 11}$, $99^{1, 2}$). In the present case, at any rate, there is no thought of the Messianic kingdom ; the psalmist is proclaiming the truth of the divine rule, and as the Jews were the one people who acknowledged and worshipped Yahweh, it was natural to present him as reigning from Zion.

Religious Teaching

This has been sufficiently brought out in the exegetical notes.

PSALM 147

THE first word of this psalm, which repeats the title, indicates its entire content : praise to Yahweh for his manifold works. These, it must be allowed, are not arranged in orderly fashion, and there is but little logical sequence in the enumeration of the different and many-sided kinds of works of power and love for which Yahweh is praised. But the outpouring of a heart so full of gratitude for the marks of divine solicitude manifest in all around, must endear this psalm to all who, like this psalmist, look beneath the surface of things which happen in the world, whether in Nature or among men, and discern in them workings, infinitesimal as they may appear individually, of a divine plan of action. If in some cases things are expressed in an anthropomorphic manner not wholly to our taste, it must be remembered that modes of expression have a good deal to do with this, though it is not, of course, denied that at times somewhat *naïve* and, as yet, undeveloped conceptions of God are held.

As to the question of unity, there are in *vv.* 7 and 12 words which read like the beginning of a new psalm, and according to the Septuagint and the Vulgate, the psalm is really composed of two psalms, consisting of *vv.* 1-11 and 12-20. It is, of course, possible that we have here the joining together of more than one psalm ; the unevenness and variegated subject-matter of our psalm justify the belief that it may well be from more than one hand.

Here again, as in the two preceding psalms, there is considerable borrowing from other psalms, and also from the later portions of the book of *Isaiah*.

The date must be pronounced as late post-exilic.

The metre is uniformly 3 : 3.

Hallelujah.

1. ° Praise Yahweh °, for well it is ° to laud him °,
our God, for praise is fitting °.

2. Yahweh buildeth up Jerusalem,
the dispersed of Israel he gathereth.

3. He healeth the broken in heart,
and bindeth up their wounds.

4. He telleth the number of the stars,
he calleth them all by names.

5. Great is our Lord, and mighty of strength,
of his understanding there is no ° searching-out °.

6. Yahweh upholdeth the afflicted,
he bringeth down the wicked to the ground.

7. Sing to Yahweh with thanksgiving,
sing praise to our God with harp.

8. He covereth the heavens with clouds, He causeth grass to grow on the mountains,
and prepareth rain for the earth;

° [and herb for the service of man] °;

9. ° He giveth ° to the beast its food,
(even) to the young ravens who cry out for it.

10. He delighteth not in the strength of the horse,
nor taketh pleasure in the legs of a man.

11. Yahweh showeth favour to them that fear him,
to them that hope for his love.

12. Praise Yahweh, O Jerusalem,
praise thy God, O Zion,

13. For he strengthened the bars of thy gates,
he blessed thy sons within thee;

14. He maketh thy borders peaceful,
he satisfieth thee with full-ripe wheat;

15. He sendeth forth his commandment upon earth,
right swiftly runneth his word.

16. He giveth snow like wool,
he scattereth the hoar-frost like ashes;

17. He casteth forth his ice like morsels,
at his cold the waters ° stand still °.

18. He sendeth out his word and melteth them,
maketh his wind to blow,—waters flow.

19. He declareth his word to Jacob,
his statutes and judgements to Israel;

20. Not thus hath he dealt with any nation,
° nor made known to them ° ° his judgements °.

Hallelujah.

Text-critical Notes

G again has the title Αγγαιου και Ζαχαριου. **1.** Add הַלְלוּיָהּ, as a psalm cannot well begin with כִּי, "for". Read, with Duhm, זַמְּרוּ for זִמְּרָה, "to sing praise", or following G, זִמְרָה, "praise". Om., with G, נָאוָה, "comely". **5.** Read חֵקֶר for מִסְפָּר, "number", from the preceding verse. **8.** This half-line is added, following Duhm, from Ps. 104[14], and it occurs also in G, וְעֵשֶׂב לַעֲבֹדַת הָאָדָם. **9.** Read הַנֹּתֵן with the art. following the other participles. **17.** Read, following Gunkel and others, מִי יַעֲמֹד for יַעֲמֹד, "who standeth?" **20.** Read, with GST, בְּל-יְדָעוּם for בַּל-יְדָעוּם, "they did not know them". Read, with the Versions, מִשְׁפָּטָיו for מִשְׁפָּטִים, "judgements".

1–6. The text of *v.* 1 is a little uncertain, but *Praise* applies both to *our God* in the second half of the verse, as well as to *Yahweh*; the object of a verb occurs not infrequently in both halves of a verse in Hebrew poetry. The exhortation to praise God occurs in this form also in Ps. 33[1], where it is coupled with the thought of rejoicing, and this emotion is felt pulsating throughout our psalm. The mention of the building up of *Jerusalem* (2) recalls the time soon after the Return from the Exile (Neh. 6[1, 15], 7[1, 2]), and for the thought cp. Ps. 51[18], 102[16]; so, too, the reference to *the dispersed of Israel* (cp. Isa. 56[8]); but it is not to be inferred from this that our psalm belongs to so early a period; it is merely the recalling of events in the past history of the people for which praise to God is due. In further reference, perhaps, to those who in distant lands had sojourned with sorrowful hearts, it is said that God *healeth the broken in heart* (cp. Ps. 34¹⁸, though in a different connexion), *and bindeth up their wounds*, meant metaphorically ; the two halves of the verse are combined from Isa. 61¹, cp. also Ezek. 34¹⁶. Then an entirely different subject is dealt with, based doubtless on Isa. 40²⁶ ; it is said that God *telleth the number of the stars*, and *calleth them all by names*, meaning that they obey his voice when called, not that he gave them their names, the point being that, though regarded as deities by the Gentile nations, they were subject to Yahweh, who created them (cp. Gen. 1¹⁶⁻¹⁸, Job 9⁹, 38⁷, ³¹, ³², Am. 5⁸, and Ps. 19¹⁻⁶) ; the names were given to the stars by their worshippers (cp. Deut. 4¹⁹). The stars are mentioned in order to lay stress on God's creative power, and therefore as a further reason for offering him praise. Quite unconnected with the foregoing, but as though to contrast great things with small, the psalmist turns from contemplating the vault of heaven to men on earth : *Yahweh upholdeth the afflicted*, a word often used by those oppressed by the wicked (*e.g.*, Ps. 76⁹), but humbles the *wicked* by bringing them *to the ground* (cp. Ps. 146⁹).

With 7 a new section begins, in which the same variety of subject-matter recurs. It is again introduced by an exhortation to give thanks (cp. Pss. 95¹, ², 119¹⁷²) and praise to Yahweh, special mention being made of doing so with the *harp* (on this see further on Ps. 150). Yahweh is then proclaimed as the God of Nature (8), who *covereth the heavens with clouds and prepareth rain for the earth* (cp. Job 5¹⁰), so essential for a country like Palestine, and which *causeth the grass to grow on the mountains* (cp. Ps. 104¹⁴, Job 38²⁷), thus (9) affording *food* for the animal world (cp. Ps. 104¹⁴, ²⁷, ²⁸, 145¹⁵) ; even the young ravens are not forgotten (cp. Ps. 104³¹, Job 41¹). But it is not physical strength (10) whether in beast (cp. Ps. 33¹⁷) or in man (cp. Ps. 33¹⁶, see also Am. 2¹⁵), gained by benefitting from the products of the soil, that is pleasing to Yahweh (11)—his *favour* is towards *them that fear him*, and who *hope*— *i.e.*, put their trust—in *his love* (cp. Ps. 33¹⁸).

With 12 a new beginning is made ; the Septuagint begins a new psalm here, again assigning its authorship to Haggai and Zechariah, as in the title of Ps. 146. *Jerusalem* is now called upon to *praise Yahweh*, and further reasons are given why praise is due to him. It is somewhat striking that while hitherto all the sentences have been participial, here (13) we have suddenly verbs in the perfect : *for he strengthened the bars of thy gates, he kept safe thy sons within thee*, followed again by participles, making *peaceful thy borders* . . . with a present sense. This reads as though reference were being made to some recent attack on Jerusalem, which had been withstood. In consequence of this, peace and well-being reign in the land (14) : *He maketh thy borders*

peaceful, he satisfieth thee with full-ripe wheat, lit. " fat of wheat "
(cp. Ps. 81[16]).   The words which follow (15), *He sendeth forth his commandment upon earth . . .*, may refer either to what has preceded, or to
what follows ; they would be appropriate to either.   At any rate, there
is once more a sudden change of subject, and in 16–18 Yahweh is again
lauded as the God of Nature, who sends *snow* (cp. Job 37[6]), *hoar-frost*,
and *ice* (cp. Job 38[29, 30]) when he sends his *cold* ; they all melt at his
word when the warm *wind* blows.

Just as the command of Yahweh in the world of Nature receives
immediate obedience, so must it be also in the higher creation—namely,
among his own people (19, 20), to whom *he declareth his word, his statutes
and judgements* ; Israel alone had been privileged to be instructed in
these divine precepts.

Religious Teaching

In this psalm, again, the nature of its contents demanded so much
reference to its religious teaching in the exegetical notes, that a special
section on this does not seem called for.

PSALM 148

IN striking contrast to the preceding psalm, the subject-matter of
this Hymn of Praise is notable for the ordered lines of thought it
contains.   The whole is an exhortation to praise Yahweh : first, the
highest order of heavenly beings ; then, sun, moon, and stars, and
the lesser heavens (on these see the notes), and, lastly, the waters
beneath the heavens, though in the upper regions.   All these are of
eternal duration.   That concludes the first division of the psalm.
The second deals with the earth ; but here, unlike the enumeration
in the former half, the psalmist begins with the lower creation, all
parts of which are bidden to praise Yahweh.   In the personification
of the waters ancient myths find their echoes, while in that of fire and
hail, etc., must be discerned the remnants of animistic conceptions.
To the singer, however, these are all probably nothing more than
poetical pictures.

There can be little doubt that *The Song of the Three Holy Children*,
28–68, in the Apocrypha, was inspired by this psalm.

The date of the psalm is late post-exilic ; there are several indications which point to this ; they will be referred to in the notes.

The rhythm is, with the exception of *v.* 8, uniformly 3 : 3.

Hallelujah.

1. Praise Yahweh from the heavens :   praise him in the heights ;
2. Praise him, all ye his angels,   praise him, all ye his host.

3. Praise him, sun and moon,   praise him, all ye stars of light.
4. Praise him, ye heavens of heavens,   and ye waters ° above the heavens.
5. Let them praise the name of Yahweh,   for he commanded, and they were
                                              created ;
6. And he hath established them for ever   a statute he ordained, ° and they shall
   and ever,   not transgress it °.
7. Praise Yahweh from the earth,   ye dragons and all deeps ;
8.   Fire and hail,
                           Snow and vapour,
                           Stormy wind
                           Fulfilling his word ;
9. The mountains and all hills,   fruitful trees and all cedars,
10. Beasts and all cattle,   creeping things and winged birds.
11. Kings of the earth and all peoples,   princes and all judges of the earth ;
12. Young men, yea also maidens,   Old men together with youths.
13. Let them praise the name of Yahweh,   for his name alone is exalted,
    His glory is above earth and heaven ;   14. and he hath lifted up the horn of his
                                              people ;
    A praise for all his loved ones,   for the children of Israel, ° his friends °.
                           Hallelujah.

Text-critical Notes

Title, G again ascribes this psalm to Haggai and Zechariah. 4. Om. אֲשֶׁר, "which ", for the sake of the rhythm. 6. Read וְלֹא יַעֲבֹור for וְלֹא יַעֲבָרוּ, " and he shall not transgress ". 14. Read עַם־קְרֹבָיו, " the people of those that are near him ", for עַם־קְרֹבוֹ, " the people of his nearness ".

1. In the exhortation to *praise Yahweh from the heavens,* the thought is that in the (implied) innermost heavens Yahweh alone is present. He is to be praised *from the heavens*—*i.e.,* the outer heavens, which, though *in the heights,* are outside the unapproachable dwelling-place of Yahweh himself. This points to a developed doctrine of the divine transcendence, which indicates a comparatively late date for our psalm ; the subject will be further dealt with under *v.* 4.

First (2) the *angels,* or Yahweh's *host* of attendant " messengers " (cp. Ps. 103²⁰, ²¹), are called upon to *praise* him ; then (3) the *sun and moon,* and *all ye stars of light*—*i.e.,* shining stars ; these are all conceived of as personalities (cp. Ps. 104⁴). The *heavens of heavens* (4) is an expression which bears out what has just been said about the belief regarding the differences of the heavenly spheres. According to the teaching of the Rabbis, which is the development of earlier traditional ideas, the heavens consist of seven divisions (*Mechiza,* cp. 2 Cor. 12², ⁴), arranged in seven concentric circles ; the innermost of these is the abode of the Almighty, who sits there in unapproachable majesty on " the throne of glory ". This seventh heaven is screened from the other heavens by a curtain of clouds (*Pargôd*) ; outside of this is where the angels dwell ; they may hear the voice of the Almighty, but are not permitted to look upon him. Ideas more or less similar to these were doubtless in vogue by the time our psalmist wrote. Then, in the mention of the *waters above the heavens,* we have the echo of the Babylonian Creation-myth reflected in Gen. 1⁷ ; they, too, are thought of as personified beings. The words (5) *for he commanded and they were created*, are important as emphasizing that all these heavenly beings were subordinate to Yahweh; our psalmist was obviously well acquainted with the fact that among the Gentiles the constellations were worshipped as gods and goddesses. The thought of their being but creatures of the Most High is further emphasized by the statement that (6) *he hath established them for ever and ever*, as those, namely, who always obeyed his behests and carried out his will; this was a *statute* which *he ordained* from their creation, which *they* could not transgress. 7–10. After having thus called upon all the heavenly beings to praise Yahweh *from the heavens*, the psalmist utters a similar exhortation to all below to praise him *from the earth*. That he begins with the (to us) inanimate creation is not without significance; for to him the various elements enumerated were all personified, and vastly more powerful than men. He naturally, therefore, begins with them. Of special interest is the mention of *ye dragons and all deeps*. Likely enough as it may be that our psalmist was unaware of the ultimate origin and meaning of the myth which he, like others, here re-echoed (cp. Ps. 74¹³, Isa. 27¹, Rev. 20²)—namely, the Babylonian Tiamat-myth, yet he would certainly have known by traditional teaching that the *dragons and all deeps* signified the embodiment of the principle of all evil; so that in calling upon these to praise Yahweh—*i.e.*, to acknowledge him and his supremacy—he is, in effect, envisaging the conditions indicated, *e.g.*, by such a passage as Rev. 21¹, where, by the words " and the sea is no more ", the Seer implies that the element of evil is eliminated! That this is no mere flight of the imagination is shown by what follows (8–13) in which the entire earth-creation is thought of as praising the name of Yahweh. For his details the psalmist is largely indebted to earlier singers, but this does not detract from the beauty of and edifying way in which he constructs his poem. For *fire and hail* cp. Ps. 18¹², 105³²; they give out heat and cold; for *snow and vapour* cp. Ps. 147¹⁶, Gen. 19²⁸, which give out cold and heat; the antithesis is evidently not accidental; for *stormy wind* cp. 107²⁵.; these all, like the angels, *fulfil his word*, or, as it is expressed in Ps. 103²⁰, " hearken unto the voice of his word "; for *mountains and trees* cp. Isa. 44²³; as to *beasts and all cattle*, by which are meant wild and domestic animals, and *creeping things and winged birds*, the psalmist evidently has Gen. 1²⁰, ²⁴, ²⁵ in mind. 11–13. Finally, the psalmist addresses his exhortation to man, beginning with those in high estate : *kings* and their *peoples, princes and all judges*; and then he calls upon humanity in general, young and old, to *praise the name of Yahweh* (cp. v. 5), whose *glory is above earth and heaven* (cp. Ps. 113⁴).

There is some little difficulty about 14; Gunkel contends that the psalm proper ends with 14ᵃ, and that the remainder of that verse is a kind of footnote added by the psalmist to indicate the nature of his psalm. Against this, Herkenne makes 14[b] the end of the psalm, and regards all the rest of this verse as belonging to 147[20], whence it has been misplaced to its present position. While objections may be raised against both of these opinions, each has something to justify it, for the psalm certainly ends somewhat awkwardly.

His friends, lit. " the people of his near ones "—*i.e.*, the nation which, by acknowledging and worshipping Yahweh as their God, had been brought close to him (cp. Deut. 4[7]).

Religious Teaching

There are two subjects contained in the religious teaching of this psalm which demand brief notice. The first is this : however much there may be in it which, in view of the advanced knowledge of later ages, cannot be accepted, such as the idea of the inanimate world and of animals praising God, we can appreciate the psalmist's conception, even though erroneous, of the instinct of worship as innate in the whole of created matter. The second is more important and far-reaching—namely, the fact of mortal men joining with the heavenly hosts—traditionally called " angels "—in the worship of God. That it is wholly impossible for us, as finite mortals, to conceive either of the nature of heavenly beings or of the way in which they praise and worship God, need not detract from our belief in their existence, nor in the fact of their offering worship. In the former case we have, at any rate, the belief and teaching of our Lord about the existence and activity of beings of a higher order than mortal man (*e.g.*, Mark 12[35], 13[32], Luke 15[10]). It may be urged, further, that, given even the most rudimentary belief in a spiritual world, belief in the existence of spiritual beings is inevitable. We need not accept in its details the developed angelology of the Apocalyptic Literature, which has here and there unduly impressed itself on some of our liturgical formulas (*e.g.*, the mention of Cherubim and Seraphim), but to doubt the reality of the existence of spiritual beings, who, even like ourselves, are impelled to worship God, is, in effect, to deny the spiritual part of man's nature.

In this, then, we may feel wholly at one with the religious teaching of our psalmist—namely, in the conviction that in our worship we are joined by spiritual beings in other spheres, and—may we not add ?—by many a dear and familiar friend.

PSALM 149

ONE cannot but be struck, on reading this psalm, by the contrast between the call to worship in the first half, and the bellicose tone of the second. The somewhat unedifying spirit of the latter is, how-ever, comprehensible if, as we hold, this psalm was written by some poet on learning of the success of the Jewish army (see *v.* 4), and that he composed it in celebration of the victory, with the intention that it should be sung as a thanksgiving to God in the temple on the return of the victorious warriors ; they had fought, as the reiterated expression of " the godly ones "—*i.e.*, God's loved ones—shows, in the conviction that they were fighting the wars of the Lord. The psalm was written, that is to say, for a special occasion, and was not intended for general liturgical use. This would explain the otherwise incon-gruous combination of men singing praises to God with their mouth while holding in their hands a two-edged sword (*v.* 6).

A song of praise, sung while a dance-step was being performed in honour of the Deity, accompanied by the clashing of arms, was frequent among all peoples of antiquity (see the notes). To modern ideas such a mode of thanksgiving does not appeal ; but in those days things were different, and, in any case, the intention was well meant.

Our interpretation of the psalm, it is granted, differs from that of some other commentators. Gunkel, Kittel, and Herkenne, for example, take it to be eschatological, and there are certainly some indications which support this view; but we doubt, on the one hand, whether the realistic presentation in the psalm justifies such an interpretation ; and, in the second place, it must be insisted, eschatology usually ex-presses itself in a more definite and detailed manner than is offered in this late psalm. A very different view is that held by Hans Schmidt, who thinks that it was sung on the festival of Yahweh's ascent upon his throne, and regards the psalm as very ancient (*uralt*). With this, it must be confessed, we disagree entirely; the psalms sung at this festival were of a very different character (see, *e.g.*, 93–99) ; and the only passage (apart from *v.* 2, which is quite general in meaning) in our present psalm at all appropriate to that occasion is obtained by a very daring emendation (" Let the pious exult in the King of glory, let the perfect draw nigh to his dwelling-place with shouting ", *v.* 5). With *v.* 6 cp. 2 Macc. 15²⁷.

This psalm is assigned by many scholars to Maccabæan times, and there is undoubtedly considerable justification for this contention : the feeling of victory gained by Yahweh's favour (*v.* 4, see 1 Macc. 4³⁰⁻³³), the desire of vengeance on their enemies (*vv.* 7, 8, see 1 Macc. 7⁴⁶⁻⁴⁹), and the parallelism of thought between *v.* 6 and 2 Macc. 15²⁷ : " And so, fighting with their hands while praying to God in their hearts, they slew no less than thirty-five thousand men ". There is, more-over, the phrase " the assembly of the pious " (*Hasidim*) occurring also in 1 Macc. 2⁴². But see Vol. I, pp. 69 f. It is quite possible that the psalm may have been written in reference to a victory gained over some neighbouring people, the account of which has not come down to us; the records of Jewish history during most of the period from 400 B.C. onwards leave much to be desired.

The date of the psalm is, without doubt, late post-exilic; linguistic expressions support this (*e.g.*, in *v.* 7).

The metre, with the exception of the first verse, is 3 : 3.

Hallelujah.

1.
Sing to Yahweh
A new song,
His praise in the assembly of the pious.

2. Let Israel rejoice in ° his Maker °,   let the sons-of-Zion be glad in their King;
3. Let them praise his name in dance,   with drum and harp let them sing to him.
4. For Yahweh ° doth favour ° his people,   he adorneth the meek with victory.
5. Let the pious exult ° triumphantly °,   let them shout ° in endless joy °,
6. High praises of God in their mouth,   and a two-edged sword in their hand,
7. To take vengeance upon the nations,   and reprisals against the peoples;
8. To bind their kings with chains,   and their princes with fetters of iron;
9. To fulfil the written decree,   glory 'tis to all his pious ones.
Hallelujah.

Text-critical Notes

2. Read, with GS, בְּעֹשׂוֹ for בְּעֹשָׂיו, " his Makers ", which may, however, be a plural of " majesty ". 4. Some commentators would read the perf. רָצָה, " he hath shown favour ". 5. Lit. " in glory " בְּכָבוֹד. Read, following Isa. 35¹⁰, 51¹¹, 61⁷, בְּשִׂמְחַת עוֹלָם for עַל־מִשְׁכְּבוֹתָם, " on their beds ". 9. Om. פָּהֶם, " among them ", for the sake of the rhythm, and the general sense.

1. The exhortation to praise *Yahweh* is addressed specifically to *the pious*, or godly ones, the *Ḥasidim*, who are often mentioned in some of the later psalms. In general, the term is applied to those who in manner of living and steadfastness in worship sought to serve Yahweh faithfully; but in later days, as we learn, *e.g.*, in 1 Macc. 2⁴²ᵃ·, it was used in a narrower sense in reference to'those who had formed a party, the members of which adhered with fanatical strictness·to what they conceived to be the demands of the Law. Whether, in this psalm, the term is used in this party sense or not is a disputed point; but the threefold mention of them (*vv.* 1, 5, 9), and especially their war-like character (*vv.* 6–8 and see 2 Macc. 14⁶), suggests the latter. On the whole subject see Vol. I, pp. 67 ff. That it was a *new song* (cp. Ps. 33³, 40³, 96¹, 98¹) may be significant, for it was of a type which was new—viz., a song of triumphant thanksgiving sung by warriors in their armour on their return from battle. There would, on the other hand, be nothing new in a song which dealt with the subjects of eschatology or the divine kingship. 2, 3. These victorious *Ḥasidim* are naturally spoken of as representatives of the nation, *Israel*, and *sons-of-Zion*, for they had fought on behalf of their people in a holy war as champions of Yahweh, by whose help they had been

victorious. They are called upon, therefore, to *rejoice* in their *Maker*, and to *be glad in their King*; with the former of these two titles as applied to Yahweh cp. Isa. 44², 51¹³; the latter occurs often in the psalms and elsewhere; but it is by no means necessarily in an eschatological context, nor yet in connexion with the festival of Yahweh's ascent upon his throne. For the sacred *dance* in celebration of victory cp. Exod. 15²⁰, ²¹, Judith 15¹², ¹³, and for its wide prevalence both among the Israelites and other nations of antiquity see Oesterley, *The Sacred Dance*, pp. 159 ff. (1923). The song of praise was sung during the sacred dance, to the accompaniment of *drum* and *harp* (on these see the notes of Ps. 150).

In the verses which follow, 4–6, due acknowledgement is made to Yahweh as the Author of victory; he has shown *favour* to his *people* (cp. Ps. 147¹¹); the mention of *the meek*, or oppressed, indicates that the people had gone through a period of ill-treatment, an inappropriate expression if the reference were to Maccabæan times (what is said in 1 Macc. 1²⁹⁻⁴⁰ does not refer to the meek). The expression *adorneth with victory* means that the warriors are glorified, and therefore honoured by their people for their achievement. The incongruous combination of praising God while the weapons of war are still being carried has been referred to above. Equally distasteful to our ears is the spirit displayed in *vv.* 7, 8, where, in accordance with the usage of the times, even the most highly-placed were subjected to humiliating ill-treatment. 9. That, in justification of this, appeal is made to the *written decree*—whether we are to understand by this a reference to such passages as Isa. 45¹⁴, 49⁷, ²³, and others, or whether this is what the psalmist conceives of as the ordained divine judgement—only emphasizes the feeling of relief that a psalm of this nature is very exceptional. It does not figure in the Liturgy of the Jewish Church.

The religious teaching of the psalm centres in the call to praise God; this has been already dealt with in the section on religious teaching of a number of other psalms.

PSALM 150

THE appropriateness of this psalm, with its tenfold exhortation to praise, as the conclusion to the Psalter, needs no insisting on. Its place and composition may well have been the work of the final redactor of the various collections of psalms which had accumulated through the centuries.

The heavenly hosts are first called upon to praise God, as in Ps. 148¹, ²; then all the worshippers, to the accompaniment of wind- and string-instruments, as well as with instruments of percussion. Judging from the concluding words of the psalm, it was sung by the whole body of worshippers, though probably "everything that hath breath" included the animal-creation, as in Ps. 148[10]. It is to be noted that eight musical instruments are mentioned as used in worship, including two kinds of cymbals (see exegetical notes); elsewhere in the *Psalms* two others are mentioned, the *hasôṣᵉrah*, "trumpet" (98[6]), and the *ḥalîl*, "pipe" (87[7], the verb only); and in other books three others occur as used for religious purposes—namely, *meṣiltaîm*, "cymbals" (often in *Chronicles*), *mᵉna'anᵉ'îm*, "rattle" (mentioned only in 2 Sam. 6[5]), and *qeren*, "horn" (Lev. 25[9], Josh. 6[5], 1 Chron. 25[5]). These, like some of those occurring in our psalm, were used for secular as well as for religious purposes; there is but one instrument of a purely secular character, mentioned in the Old Testament, the *šalîšîm*, probably some form of the tambourine (only in 1 Sam. 18[6]). The only others are found in the book of *Daniel*, and do not concern us; but they are worth enumerating for completeness' sake (they all occur in chap. 3[5], etc.); two of them are clearly of Semitic origin, the *qarna* "cornet", lit. "horn"; the *mašroqitha*, "flute". lit. "whistle"; three are of Greek origin, the *qithrôs* or *qithras* (κίθαρις), "harp"; *sabbᵉka* (σαμβύκη), a triangular instrument with four strings; the *pesanterin* (ψαλτήριον), also a stringed instrument with a sounding-board beneath the strings, probably six in number; and finally, the *sumphonia* (συμφωνία), an instrument corresponding to "bag-pipe"; whether this was of Semitic or Greek origin is uncertain.

That none of these is mentioned in our psalm makes it extremely likely that its date of composition was, at any rate, prior to that of the book of *Daniel* (166-5 B.C.).

Of all the other instruments, including those mentioned in our psalm, some account will be given in the exegetical notes. Our knowledge of ancient musical instruments among the Semites has been much increased by the recent publication of Dr. Galpin's work, *The Music of the Sumerians, Babylonians, and Assyrians* (1937).

The metre is 3 : 3, with the exception of the last verse, which, as so often, has a different metre; it ends with a line of four beats. The final "Hallelujah" is not included in the metre.

Hallelujah.

1. Praise God in his sanctuary,   praise him in his mighty firmament.
2. Praise him for his acts of power,   praise him according to the abundance of his greatness.
3. Praise him with the blast of the ram's-horn,   praise him with harp and lyre.
4. Praise him with drum and dance,   praise him with strings and flute.
5. Praise him with resounding cymbals,   praise him with clanging cymbals.
6.   Let everything that hath breath praise Yah.
                    Hallelujah.

1, 2. Though not specified, as in Ps. 148[1, 2], the heavenly
hosts are here clearly exhorted to offer their praise to *God*; *his sanctuary*, as in Ps. 102[19], refers to the heavenly temple (cp. Ps. 11[4], 20[7]),
and his mighty firmament (lit. " the firmament of his strength ") means the
heavens, as in Gen. 1[8], " And God called the firmament heaven ", the
creation of which was one of his mighty acts (see Ps. 19[1]), " the firmament
showeth his handywork ", while the many other acts of creation above
and below showed forth *the abundance of his* greatness.

In the rest of the psalm the musical instruments used in the temple
worship are enumerated.   Excepting for a few incidental references in
other psalms and elsewhere, this detailed list is unique in the Old
Testament; it will, therefore, be not inappropriate if we devote some
special attention to these different kinds of instruments.

The offering of praise to deities in song accompanied by musical
instruments is, as ever-increasing evidence shows, of great antiquity.
On the analogy of what is known of the usage among other Semitic
peoples, we are justified in concluding that among the earliest Hebrews
similar forms of worship were in vogue.   Just as with the songs of praise
as we now have them, so with the musical instruments mentioned, both
represent the final stage of a long preceding history.   But in the case of
the musical instruments the evidence tends to show that the process of
development was much slower; in other words, the musical instruments
mentioned in our psalm did not, in most cases, differ from what had been
in use for many centuries.   Archæological research has given us a great
deal of information both as to the forms and uses of these instruments.

Coming now to our psalm; it is impossible to discern any underlying purpose in the order in which the various instruments are mentioned, whether as to their antiquity, importance, or type; they seem to be
enumerated quite at random.   First we have the *ram's-horn* (*šôphār*).
To connect this with the Egyptian *thupar* is now shown to be erroneous,
for there is no such word as this latter.   It is more probably the
equivalent of the Assyrian *šapparu*, the wild mountain-goat; so that
" ram," must not be understood in the strictly modern sense.   There is,
however, no doubt that in already early times *šôphār* was adapted and
used in the sense of " horn ", or " clarion ".   As a rule, in the Old
Testament, the word occurs alone; but its fuller form is *šôphār
ha-yôbel*, lit. " the horn of the ram " (Josh. 6[4]); and sometimes *yôbēl*
stands alone in the sense of " horn " (Exod. 19[13], Lev. 25[13], 27[18], Num.
36[4]), but the word means lit. "he that leads "—viz., the flock.   In the Old
Testament it is not often used in connexion with the temple worship;
it is more often a signal of alarm, as, *e.g.*, in Judg. 3[27], 1 Sam. 13[3], or it is
sounded to call warriors together, Isa. 18[3], or as a signal for attack,
Job 39[24, 25]; in Am. 3[6], Hos. 5[8], Jer. 6[1], Ezek. 33[3], its blast gives
warning of approaching danger.   According to 2 Sam. 15[10] and else-

where we read of its being sounded in order to announce the reign of a
new king. This is of special importance in view of Ps. 81³ : " Sound
the šôphār at the new moon ", for there can be little doubt that this is in
reference to the New-Year festival, when the kingship of Yahweh was
proclaimed, just as at the Babylonian New-Year's Day festival the first
appearance of the crescent moon was hailed by trumpet-blasts. See
also Ps. 47⁵, 98⁶. That the šôphār was one of the most ancient of
musical instruments is shown by Galpin, *op. cit.*, pp. 21 ff. It is worth
noting that in our psalm no mention is made of the *hasôs'rāh*, " trumpet ", which occurs in Ps. 98⁶ together with the *šôphār*, and was, therefore, a different kind of wind-instrument (cp. Hos. 5⁸) ; although not
occurring elsewhere in the *Psalms*, it is frequently mentioned in
Chronicles as a sacred instrument. No doubt it was of much later date,
since it was made of metal, brass, or silver. Josephus (*Antiq.* iii, 291)
says that " in length it was little less than a cubit ; it was composed of a
narrow tube, somewhat thicker than a flute, but with so much breadth as
was sufficient for admission of the breath of a man's mouth ; it ended in
the form of a bell, like common trumpets ". This is probably the trumpet represented on the Arch of Titus. Passing mention must also be
made of the *qeren*, " horn " ; its occurrence in the sense of a wind-
instrument is extremely rare, and it is never used in the *Psalms*; but
from 1 Chron. 25⁵ it is to be gathered that it had a religious use ; otherwise it is mentioned only in Josh. 6⁵, where it is sounded in connexion with
the falling down of the walls of Jericho. Possibly it may be equivalent
to the Akkadian *karanu*, mentioned by Galpin (*op. cit.*, pp. 23 f.),
which was evidently a trumpet used for warlike purposes, for " the
name survives in the Persian *karana* . . . the name is also found in
Sanskrit records ".

The next two instruments mentioned in our psalm are stringed
instruments, the *harp* (*nebel*) and the *lyre* (*kinnôr*). Ancient as these are,
it need hardly be said that the use of stringed instruments points to a
much higher stage of culture. The word *nebel* means also " wine-
skin " (*e.g.*, 1 Sam. 1²⁴, 10³ and elsewhere) ; the musical instrument was
no doubt so called on account of its gourd, or bottle-like, sound-chest.
Excavations at Ur show that two types of harp were used for religious
purposes : a large one which rested on the ground, and a smaller one
which could be carried and played in processions. The Sumerian
names of these two are, respectively, *zag-sal* and *mirîtu*, the latter being
the more primitive one. Both are mentioned, together with the seven-
stringed lyre, in a poem in praise of the temple of Enki at Eridu (*circa*
2200 B.C.). According to Galpin, it is the *mirîtu* which is " evidently
related to the Hebrew *nebel* " (*op. cit*, p. 29). It is often mentioned in
the *Psalms* in connexion with worship (33², 57⁸, 71²², 81², 92³, 108², and
in *Chronicles*). A still smaller one was that mentioned in 1 Sam. 18⁶,

the šālîš, its name being given in reference to its "three" strings; a similar instrument was in use among the Assyrians, and was called the šalaštu. Mention must be made also of another kind of harp, the nebel ʿāsôr, "ten(-stringed) harp", which occurs in Ps. 33², 144⁹, cp. 92³; similarly in Mesopotamia, as Galpin points out (op. cit., p. 30), there was an instrument of the harp-kind called eširtu, "ten-strings".

As to the kinnôr, "lyre", it must be noted, to quote Galpin again, that it "differs entirely from the harp in having the strings stretched over, or attached to, a bridge placed on the sound-board, instead of passing into the sound-chest itself" (op. cit., p. 31). The kinnôr was the most popular musical instrument among the Semites generally, and, as the Old Testament shows, it was used in ordinary life (e.g., Isa. 5¹², 24⁸), as well as for religious purposes, as indicated by its frequent mention in the Psalms. Very interesting is the representation in one of the tombs (circa 1950 B.C.) at Beni-Hassan of a Semite playing an elaborately shaped lyre, called by the Egyptians the kennarn-t, clearly equivalent to the kinnôr. Among the Sumerians the lyre was called al-gar, of which there were several shapes and sizes; in the temple ritual it had an important place; in a hymn to Ishtar, for example, it is said: "I will speak to thee with the al-gar, whose sound is sweet"; and in Enki's temple at Eridu we are told that "the holy al-gar sings in reverence". The Assyrian equivalent was šebitu, meaning "seven-stringed", and corresponding to the Hebrew šivaʿ or šebaʿ, Arabic sabaʿ, "seven"; in certain dialects of Aramaic it appears as šebᵉkaʾ, the sabbᵉkaʾ mentioned in Dan. 3⁵, 7¹⁰. It is described, to quote Galpin again, "as being of triangular outline, and like a boat with a ladder joined to it. The boat-shaped lyre discovered at Ur answers in a peculiar manner to this description, and makes it clear why a military siege-engine, the sambuca, was named after it" (op. cit., p. 34).

The many representations of harps and lyres given on ancient monuments, Egyptian, Sumerian, and Assyrian, as well as on Jewish coins, show that they differed greatly in size and shape, as well as in the number of strings they had; the ancient Hebrew instruments doubtless partook of this variety, if not to the same extent. They were held in the left hand when carried, and played with the fingers of the right hand, though a plectrum, of wood or other substance, was also used.

The next instrument to be mentioned in our psalm (4) is one of percussion, the tôph, "drum". This, too, was used for secular purposes (e.g., Gen. 31²⁷, Isa. 5¹²), as well as in worship (2 Sam. 6⁵, Ps. 81², 149³, cp. 68²⁵). The Sumerian name for "drum" was ub, with the determinative prefix for "skin" or "leather", su. "The hollow log of wood or the empty gourd has been developed into an instrument not only rhythmic, but tonal, by the addition of a stretched skin. For, whereas to the ordinary ear the sound of the drum is accounted as mere noise, to the delicate appreciation of the Oriental the 'note' of the instrument is not only a source of pleasure, but distinctly tuneable " (Galpin, *op. cit.*, p. 2). Drums were of various sizes, the large ones stationary, the smaller carried in procession. The *ub* was a small drum ; but another type, called in Sumerian *balag*, Assyrian *balaggu*, was of a large, as well as of a small, kind. Its use in worship is often mentioned on the inscriptions. That drums were used by the Israelites of all periods cannot admit of doubt ; the question arises, however, whether the *tôph* was a drum as generally understood, and not rather a " timbrel " or " tambourine " ; we have rendered it " drum " because *tôph* is the only word in the Old Testament which occurs for either " drum " or " timbrel " ; and we know from the usage among other Semites that the drum, in the ordinary sense, played an important part in worship. Galpin mentions, it is true, another Sumerian name for drum, the *dub*, and compares it with the Arabic *dabdab*, which might suggest a connexion with *tôph* from an onomatopæic point of view ; but he compares the Hebrew *tôph* rather with the Sumerian word for " timbrel ", *adâp*, which gave its name to the *duff*, or square-shaped timbrel, credited by Arabic tradition to Jubal, the coppersmith, as its inventor (*op. cit.*, p. 9), because the determinative *urudu*, " copper ", sometimes precedes the word ; see Gen. 4[22]. Inscriptions show it to have been used in temple worship.

In the verse before us (4), the sacred *dance* is mentioned in close connexion with the *drum*, or timbrel ; while the playing of this instrument during the dance was, no doubt, primarily for rhythmic purposes, it may well have had the effect of arousing excitement in the performers ; the word used, *māhôl*, comes from the root meaning to " whirl ", which suggests a wild kind of dance. In the same verse which we are considering (4), mention is made of *strings* (*minnim*), and *flute* ('*ûgâb*) (cp. Gen. 4[21], Job 21[12], 30[31]) ; the combination reads strangely, especially as the stringed instruments have just been referred to in the preceding verse. The only other occurrence of *minnim* is in Ps. 45[8], where the text is certainly corrupt. Now, the common name for " flute " in Mesopotamia is *ti-gi*, which, as Galpin points out, is identical with the '*ûgâb* of the Hebrews ; but the *ti-gi* is also called the *imin-e*, " the seven-note " ; is it possible that we have in *minnim* some form of a loan-word from Mesopotamia ? " Praise him with the seven-note flute " would give a more logical sense than " strings and flute ". However this may be, the flute, *ti-gi*, the simple reed-tube, held vertically, and sounded by blowing across one of the open ends, was highly esteemed in the temple ritual in Mesopotamia (Galpin, *op. cit.*, p. 13). In the next verse (5) two types of cymbals are mentioned, called respectively *resounding cymbals* and *clanging cymbals*, lit. " cymbals of hearing ", *i.e.*, which can be well heard—and " cymbals of a blast ". They are mentioned elsewhere only in 2 Sam. 6⁵. It is probable that the reference here is to a very early type of cymbals which was retained in the temple ritual, and a highly developed type. Galpin tells us that at Kish and Ur " certain curiously curved blades of thin copper have been found, generally in pairs ; at first they were considered to have been weapons of war, but they are now recognized as ' dancing sticks ', the metal blade having been fixed to a wooden handle. In one instance, at Ur—they were discovered in connexion with the remains of a lyre, and on a gold cylinder-seal also found at Ur, as well as in mother-of-pearl inlay at Kish—their real use is shown : on the seal, which dates from about the year 2700 B.C., a dancer to the strains of the lyre is depicted and, on either side, attendants clapping the curved sticks together in measured cadence " (*op. cit.*, p. 1). Here we have, then, the earliest form of cymbals ; to these would correspond the first-mentioned cymbals in our psalm, used presumably as an accompaniment to the sacred dance, like the *tôph*. It is, however, somewhat strange that the word for cymbals, *ṣelṣˀlim*, should be used twice over in the same verse, when the more common word *mˀṣiltaîm* (from the same root) was available ; it occurs frequently in *Chronicles*, and is used only in connexion with worship ; and, being dual in form, it obviously corresponds to the two " dancing-sticks " mentioned above, which represent the earliest form of cymbals. The later form, *clanging cymbals*, are no doubt the same as those described by Josephus, who says that they consisted of "two large metal plates, which were struck together " (*Antiq.*, vii, 306).

It will thus be seen that, thanks to the labours of archæologists, our knowledge of the subject of ancient musical instruments has been much increased.

Our main interest, however, in the present connexion, is the evidence offered by this psalm of the use of so many musical instruments in the temple worship. The triumphant strains resounding in this Hallelujah finale make a noble and fitting conclusion to the *Psalms*, the grandest symphony of praise to God ever composed on earth.

INDEX